THE PEOPLE'S POET EMERGING PERSPECTIVES ON NIYI OSUNDARE

THE PEOPLE'S POET
EMERGING PERSPECTIVES
ON NIYI OSUNDARE

Edited by
Abdul-Rasheed Na'Allah

Africa World Press, Inc.

P.O. Box 1892   P.O. Box 48

Trenton, NJ 08607   Asmara, ERITREA

Africa World Press, Inc.

P.O. Box 1892
Trenton, NJ 08607

P.O. Box 48
Asmara, ERITREA

Cover Design: Roger Dormann

Library of Congress Cataloging-in-Publication Data

The people's poet : emerging perspectives on Niyi Osundare / edited by Abdul-Rasheed Na'Allah.
    p. cm.
Includes bibliographical references and index.
 ISBN 0-86543-849-8 -- ISBN 0-86543-850-1 (pbk.)
 1. Osundare, Niyi, 1947---Criticism and interpretation. 2. Yoruba (African people) in literature. 3. Oral tradition--Nigeria. 4. Nigeria--In literature. I. Na'allah, Abdul Rasheed II. Osundare, Niyi, 1947-
 PR9387.9.O866 Z55 2002
 821'.914--dc21

                2002006199

For:

My dearest Father
Ahmad Alabi Na'Allah (d. April 1999);
Scholar (Mualimu), teacher of people's poetry.

and

My loving Elder & Brother
Abubakar Usman Yusuf Eleyinla (d. June 2002);
Ilorin Poet and Teacher

Fiwon s'alijanna, ya Allah
(Amin o, Olohun-Oba!)

Poetry
is
man
meaning
to
man

Osundare,
Songs of the Marketplace, p. 4

Kole bawa logigi ma o
Kole bawa logigi ma o
Aroye ni'se awa kee suwa
Kole bawa logigi ma o.
Kotie le bawa logigi, orin ni ise wa
Aà kuku s'ise mii kun, orin ni ise
                    wa!

Jaigbade Alao
Dadakuada Singer (Ilorin)

Kengbe oyin re o!
Oyin adun ree o
Eyin omo samonri emaa bo wa
                s'odo mi
Ke waa la!

Omoekee Amao
Dadakuada Singer (Ilorin)

CONTENTS

POETRY AND COMMITMENT

MEANING, TRANSLATION AND THE POET'S LITERARY ASPIRATIONS

POETRY AND PEDAGOGY

ACKNOWLEDGMENTS

There are many people to thank for the success of this project. First, I would like to thank all the contributors from around the globe—Africa, America, Asia, Europe—I would especially like to thank Professor Eldred Durosinmi Jones, who, despite the civil war in Sierra Leone and the threat to his life, made time to write his article. Next, Abiola Irele, Editor, *Research in African Literatures* and Professor of African and Comparative Studies at Ohio State University, and Biodun Jeyifo, Professor of English at Cornell University, for the Preface and Afterword respectively. Also, to Milan Dimic, George Lang, and Stephen Slemon of the University of Alberta, they have remained great friends and advisors. Sanjit Fernandes-Bakshi, for typesetting the manuscript. My family, Rahmat, Saara and Haleemah, thanks. Fran Hainline, AAS Department Secretary, Erica Potterbaum, my student and research assistant, and all other friends, student workers, colleagues, too numerous to name, my gratitude. This book has been a project so pleasurable, so pleasing, and to Allah is uncountable 'thank you.'

Abdul-Rasheed Na'Allah
Macomb, Illinois
October 2001.

PREFACE:
NIYI OSUNDARE
BETWEEN SELF AND
COMMITMENT

Beginning with his *Songs of the Marketplace*, Niyi Osundare has now published some ten volumes of poetry, and has won numerous prizes, including the Commonwealth Poetry Prize for 1986 and the Noma Award in 1991. His creativity has been manifested in a continued flow of work over more than two decades, and has been marked by a steady development of his idiom, which can now be recognized as distinctive. Osundare has established himself as one of the most significant poets writing today, with a singular sense of his mission as the voice of the underprivileged in his country Nigeria, and as prophet of hope for the African continent. It is his achievement as a poet deeply imbued with a social vision that this collection of essays in his honour seeks to celebrate.

Yet, what distinguishes Osundare's work is the tension between the two impulses that command his inspiration: on one hand, the response to immediate issues of communal life in the context of situation that his work seeks to address; on the other hand, the aesthetic imperative that he is aware places upon him the obligation to give artistic form to his mode of response. As we examine his work, it becomes apparent that Osundare has been at pains to strike a balance between these two impulses. The results of his effort have been variable, and it not until the publication of *Waiting Laughters,* that, it seems to me, Osundare achieved the unity of theme and style that marks this volume as a high point in his career. For in *Waiting Laughters*, Osundare has sought to underwrite his social vision through an aesthetic project that reconciles the need for personal statement with a mature poetic expression. But in order to fully grasp the significance of this volume, it is instructive to consider the poems collected in *Moonsongs*, the volume that immediately precedes it, for the light it throws on an aspect of Osundare's work that is not sufficiently remarked, namely, its introspective quality.

The publisher's note that accompanies *Moonsongs* explains the circumstances under which it was composed: a near fatal attack by a robber from which, going by its contents, we can surmise that the poet suffered more than a head wound—in fact, a deep psychological trauma. This explains his departure from the socially engaged tone and public attitudes of his earlier work to the exploration of self, the inward direction of the poems that compose the volume. The moon serves as an appropriate image for its prevailing atmosphere and its reflective tone, developed in a series of reflections on the passing of time, especially in the first two sections entitled "Phases I-XIV" and "Further Phases XV-XXIV.") These reflections are integrated into observations, on a more mundane though constantly sober register, of the everyday life to which the poet constantly relates. The image of the moon is also employed to figure what is termed "a complex of masks," by which is meant presumably the variety of situations as much in the universe itself (the moon being part of this larger cosmic scheme) as in human life, and the play of contrasts which this variety implies.

This summary of the volume suggests an expansion of Osundare's range in terms both of theme and of expressive means. We feel, with this expansion, a freeing of the poet's imagination and language from the restricted channels of his earlier volumes. The idea of a meditation upon a theme as abstract as the passage of time, considered as an essential aspect of human experience and awareness rather than in its immediate relation to social conditions and the conflicts they engender, must be considered something of an advance for our poet, especially considering the firm ideological perspective within which Osundare has placed his evocations of the natural world in his previous work, especially in the volume *The Eye of the Earth*. This is a development that is immediately felt as a fuller exploration of the possibilities of poetic utterance than Osundare had previously allowed himself.

There is as a consequence a noticeable gain in expression on the part of the poet, who is himself conscious of the weight of his theme and the need for a refinement of his poetic language to match the enlargement of his vision. The following lines make abundantly clear the expanded vision and the new poetics that have presided at the composition of *Moonsongs*:

From seasons which pass but never part
I borrow moonbeams to shape the wind.

The echo of Soyinka in the second line seems to indicate an influence, one which runs, albeit brokenly and intermittently, through the volume and is manifested in the unusual density of imagery in many of the poems, as in this example:

The moon the moon is the fable of stone,
the epic of iron, the syllable of wood;
the moon is the sparkling song on the lips
of retreating darkness.

Occasionally, the new resoluteness of language lends a powerful impulse to the social consciousness that has provided the inspiration for Osundare's poetry; the poem numbered XXII in the sequence "Phases" offers a striking instance of this observation. It presents two contrasting tableaux centered on the different meanings the moon seems to acquire as it shines over Ikoyi, the residential area of the rich and privileged in Lagos, and over Ajegunle, the section of the city where the poor are huddled together in their squalid condition. The sense of social conflict that opposes these two areas of contemporary life in Nigeria is given graphic and arresting representation in terms of the differentiated aspects of the moon as it reflects the atmosphere and prevailing mood of life in each of the areas over which it shines. Where the poet's evocation of the nocturnal landscape of Ikoyi associates the physical setting with a moral judgement upon the calm indifference of its residents ("The moon here / is a laundered lawn / its grass the softness of infant fluff"), the image he presents of Ajegunle is that of a collective resentment stoked by raging social frustrations and seeking an outlet in an act of collective affirmation:

here the moon
is a jungle
sad like a forgotten beard
with tensioned climbers
and undergrowths of cancerous fury
cobras of anger spit in every brook
and nights are one long prowl
of swindled leopards

The correspondence of the moon to the natural imagery employed in this evocation of repressed human energies gives to the poem an exceptional resonance in the volume. It is to my mind the most successful piece in the whole volume, in the way it succeeds in focusing its directing image on the poet's habitual preoccupations.

The incident that occasioned *Moonsongs* seems, then, to have led Osundare to a meditation upon self in relation to the larger universe of existence, a meditation that helped to deepen his conception of the poetic function. It clarified at the same time his desire to address the themes arising from his predominantly social concerns in an idiom accessible to a large audience, while satisfying the conditions of genuine poetic expression. The effort entailed by the necessity to reconcile his populist orientation with his poetic calling certainly gives a large measure of interest to his expression. In particular, his forging of an idiom derived from the Yoruba oral tradition results in a poetic style that often produces original and striking effects. It is this dimension of Osundare's poetry that is most in evidence in *Waiting Laughters*.

It is against the background provided by *Moonsongs* that, it seems to me, the achievement of *Waiting Laughters* needs to be measured. For with the later volume, Osundare has taken a major step towards resolving the difficulty that, despite its undoubted appeal from volume to volume, his poetry has so acutely raised, that is, of communicating a social vision that is not compromised either by the simplifications of a naïve commitment, or by a misguided refusal to engage the complexities of poetic language. It is significant in this respect to note that the volume is in fact made up of a sequence of poems that offer metaphors of language in its immediate relation to the actualities of contemporary African life – in other words, the volume presents itself as a long reflection on the place of language in the collective existence, represents in its own way a poetics of engagement. *Moonsongs* already provides an intimation of the direction of this reflection in lines such as these:

> From the vowel of the river
> From the consonant of the striving valleys
> We name the moon, we name the sun
> We pledge a fluent chatter to the stammering sea

Waiting Laughters is an extended development of this image, indicating the enlargement of the poet's awareness on this question of language. For it is a conscious involvement with language as a mediator of consciousness that provides the fundamental keynote of the entire volume, one from which the explicit social themes proceed, enabling Osundare to give new depth to his expression.

As far as its theme goes, the volume can of course be read as a restatement of Osundare's usual social concerns, centered on the situation in Nigeria—and by extension, Africa—and on questions of politics and social justice which that situation presents. The general problems of social change and the traumas of modernization form a comprehensive background to these questions as they are raised and explored in the volume.

There is however a new dimension and I daresay major tone given to Osundare's handling of this theme in *Waiting Laughters*. For one thing, it is a forceful statement of hope amid the dejection and pessimism that have been so much in evidence on the continent in the past few years. For while much of the evocation is pathetic—a detailing of the problems of existence at every level in contemporary Nigeria and in Africa in general—the volume is an affirmation of confidence in the ultimate possibility of triumph over the stresses of the present moment. The confident hope for the future announced in the title thus proceeds from a full grasp of reality, from an uncompromising awareness of the dilemmas we confront in Africa at this stage of our historical development. For despite the relentless movement of events tending to confound our senses, Osundare discerns the human possibility that promises to give a positive meaning to the harsh progression of African historical experience. The "waiting laughters" of the title thus reflects an affirmative rather than a tentative stance; it denotes a residual strength that will manifest itself in social revolution and thus bring an end to the continent's protracted agonies. The comment suggests the sort of pieties of all committed literature which Osundare's work has in the past been prone to, but here, there is a passion that gives force to the poet's utterance, as in these graphic and menacing lines:

> Let the cockroach beware
> Of the dance of the hen.

It is however not only in this kind of direct statement that Osundare's volume is interesting, but in the general rhetorical flow of his verse. Elsewhere he writes, for example:

> My song is space
> beyond wails, beyond walls
> beyond insular hieroglyphs
> which crave the crest
> of printed waves.

Here the point of course is that his poetry will be committed to an ethics of liberation and open in its idiom, but the phrasing itself gives a fine rhetorical lift to the thought. Moreover, it is guided along by what is obviously a deep consideration of the requirements of his expression. It is of course here that what I've called his poetics of commitment comes fully into play. The volume begins with the following statement:

> I pluck these words from the lips of the wind
> Ripe like a pendulous pledge...

This statement sets the tone for the interweaving of the theme with the idea of poetry as a structure of words, signifying an external world and in so doing participating in its reality, therefore elaborating more than a system of metaphors, for words are felt here by the poet as constitutive of experience. Hence his interrogation of history as a factor of alienation is expressed in terms of this conception of the operative power of the word:

> History's stammerer
> When will your memory master
> the vowels of your father's name?

These lines announce the recuperation of the inner self necessary for the effort of reconstruction that Africa now has to undertake. Osundare has sought to provide testimony in his poetry, most especially in *Waiting Laughters,* of the deep resources upon which that effort has to draw for its successful prosecution. Coming after *Moonsongs* with its elaboration of a cosmic vision, the poems of *Waiting Laughters* re-affirm the truth that human capacities reside in self-understanding of one's place in history and ultimately in the world.

F. Abiola Irele
October 2001

INTRODUCTION
THE PEOPLE'S POET

To say another English language poet is more widely read than Shakespeare is an unusual claim, yet "farmer-born, peasant bred" Niyi Osundare has broken the mysticism of the previous poetic aura in Nigeria, exemplified by the first generation of Nigerian poets, Wole Soyinka and Christopher Okigbo.[1] Niyi Osundare writes for the people and has Nigerians reading English poetry. This book is about a poet who naturally sings of his people's aspirations and frustrations in a manner that attracts Africans to poetry written in English.

Until now, English poetry was a scary subject for most Nigerians. Writing in a foreign tongue was hard enough, but writings in esoteric English were a tough nut to crush. The first generation of Nigerian poets was presented as prophet-poets, without spirited followers. Their work was so elevated that they became alienated from their people. Their "tongue-twisting English" was beyond reach. Alas, this alienation was not viewed as a blemish for the first generation. Rather, it was a source of pride that some Nigerians were so talented that their literary English could compete with Wordsworth's.

Osundare gave African poems back to Africa, baking sociopolitical breads with a heavy synthesis of indigenous African ingredients. Along with poets like Tanure Ojaide and Kofi Anyidoho, Osundare enriched the African tradition of total theater. These poets ensured people's teeth and tongues were not crushed while eating a feast of honey: to ensure an African may participate in a modern African literary circle—without a degree in English, French, Portuguese, or Italian, or a certificate in the Western theater arts—is one duty this generation has given to itself. Yet Osundare and members of his group often acknowledge their indebtedness to earlier writers and critics for launching African writing in European languages, for championing a cause of African culture through foreign languages, for breaking the barriers abroad, and for creating favorable impressions of African literature internationally. The contemporary poets, led by Osundare, however, are winning the battle at home as well as abroad. Osundare won the Association of Nigerian Authors poetry prize, the ANA/Cadbury poetry prize, the Commonwealth Poetry prize, and the Noma Award.

Osundare was, and still is, obsessed with applying every available method of bringing his poetry to his people. Perhaps he is consumed with this goal because of his peasant ancestry, where poetry is acclaimed as the people's property. From local newspapers to international journals, from radio houses to television stations, Osundare has become a household name among Nigerians. He has an increasing number of fans in other parts of Africa and around the world.

In a radio discussion I had with Osundare and Zulu Sofola in 1992, Osundare reemphasized his philosophy of a people oriented artistic platform:

> There is this symbiotic relationship between the artist and his society. I have never seen an artist in this world who produces works of art just solely for himself or herself. Every time we sit down to write, to compose, every time we are acting, we believe that there is a sense of the other, and that other is extremely important. Society itself is an abridgement of these others. How come the decay in our society, the depravity, is still very much there, despite the positive contributions of the writer? I will say that in terms of the pragmatic power of art, art stands at a disadvantage because a work of art can never function like a decree. A politician has a way of altering the destiny of human kind within an hour. Unfortunately an artist can only work through a process of persuasion.[2]

Osundare's multifaceted scholarship has been exemplary to young African scholars. Now, everyone wants to take after Niyi Osundare, Ojaide and Anyidoho. The number of published poets in Nigeria increases daily, and this inspiration is also spreading to other aspects of creative writing. The impact of Osundare and his generation must be researched and recorded.

Three important characteristics of Osundare's poetry can be identified. First, beyond the achievements of Nigritude and Tigritude's poetry, Osundare's creative art has a heavily theoretical platform. Osundare uses his poems to postulate and debate the basis of vision. Modern African poems now complement critical papers; alternately, Osundare's scholarly articles are read as though possessed by the poetic muse. The second characteristic of Osundare's poetry is his commitment to social issues of his country, his continent, and his world. Osundare's concept of morality is stemmed in the push for a balanced world, an equalized earth, and an uncensored goodness towards humanity. Osundare draws his personality into his art, as Jane Bryce shows in "'Courier with a live Coal in his Running Palm' ('Midlife'): Niyi Osundare as Witness to the Human in Nigerian Public Life." Answering to the call of Yoruba *Iwa-Lewa* meta-ethics, Osundare demonstrates that poets and their work must be thoroughly personable.3 *Ewa* means beauty in Yoruba poetics. According to the moral, cultural, and sociopolitical virtues, *Iwa* includes attitudes, behaviors, or patterns of a well-cultured life. To observe society's perfection seems almost un-poetic for poets because these virtues mean no smoking, no drinking, no feasible human flaws. Saying he follows Yoruba *Iwa-Lewa* meta-ethics is far from saying Osundare is an angel, yet contributors from all parts of the world suggest, "The man is his poetry." The third characteristic of his poetry is Osundare's connection with his people, often through his history as a peasant and his skill in oral performance. Osundare connects with his people with simple language, familiar rhythm, creative marketplace, common aspirations, and the spark of poetic excellence.

I could imagine people at a Yoruba festival in Ibadan Dugbe market or at the Ikere-Ekiti community square hailing in an intensely marrow-induced thrill, *Eepoooo!* 'Oh, please, bring palm oil! A sacrifice to the powering voice of the populist poet!' Stewart Brown could not have been wrong when he said that Osundare celebrates the threshold in the Yorubaness of his poetry ("Thresholds" 63). Osundare again describes his artistic philosophy in a 1998 unpublished piece, "Confessions of a Scholar-Poet." Osundare writes,

> My philosophy of art is essentially holistic: form enhances content, while content in turn enriches form; aesthetic elegance has to be balanced with social relevance. Like a typical Yoruba artist, I am constantly seeking the meeting point of the beautiful and useful. Humanity comes first, hand in hand with a clear visionary thrust: for the poem or story that has no "eye" can only stumble into sterility and darkness ... (p. 4)

Osundare supplants his work with 'eyes,' as well as voices and ears.

Osundare is regularly active in African literary theory. Like Soyinka, Achebe and his contemporary, Tanure Ojaide, Osundare gives, directs, describes, and postulates theoretical frameworks for understanding African literature:

> There is a lot in my cultural and social background that
> necessitates and sustains this personal philosophy. As an
> African writer and academic, I am constantly aware of the
> pressures and demands of my multiple roles, the fluidity
> of professional frontiers, and the need to balance abstract
> theorizing with the pragmatics of social and cultural
> practice.

Osundare analyzed traditional oral forms in "Poems For Sale: Stylistic Features of Yoruba Ipolowo Poetry." He discusses other African writers in "Words of Iron, Sentences of Thunder: Soyinka's Prose style " and "Native, Serve Your River God: The Poetry of Tanure Ojaide." Osundare deals with his theoretical currents in "Style and Literary Communication in African Prose Fiction," "African Literature Now, Standards, Texts and Canons," and "How Post-Colonial is African Literature?" Osundare lives up to his name as a stylist-, scholar poet.

His popular criticism of postmodern and postcolonial critics of African literature is cast below in charming rhetoric:

> Let me begin by confessing to a nagging unease about the
> "post-ness" tagged on to contemporary theorizing in general:
> poststructural, postmodern, post-colonial, post-Marxist, post-
> industrial, etc. There is also talk about the "posthumanist" era,
> though we hope in all earnestness that the post-human" soci-
> ety will never arrive!

Osundare directs the two-page poem "Text Worship" to postmodernists, specifically New Critics, who prefer not to deal with author intent. The New Critics have replaced the human being with the text, as a computerized voice replaces a human voice on the phone. In a rather mocking tone, the poet rants,

> Author is dead, in unmarked grave dumped
> The Reader to power with crown has rumped
> The Text writes itself with a magic hand
> In the curious way its priests can stand

Osundare was also preoccupied with the abnormality in theory still unabated in imperial and colonial bondage. "Post-colonial" suggests an aftermath to the colonial presence. Western theorists' appropriation of African ideology alarms Osundare. He is disturbed by "the ease and complacency with which Western theories take over the global literary and intellectual arena, [and] the way they inscribe themselves as though the other parts of the world were a tabula rasa" (p. 206). Niyi Osundare insists that theorizing about any part of the world is better left to people who live and experience it.

Osundare rejects the universal connotations of some Western theories, such as assuming the prefix "post-" must be affixed to colonial discourse to conform to the Western "post-ness" frameworks. Osundare insists that the term "post-colonial" is grossly inadequate in denotation. He asks,

> What are the semantic and socio-semiotic designations of this
> compounded word: beyond-colonial; past-colonial; after-colo-
> nial; free-from-colonial; anti-colonial, or simply not-colonial?
> In other words, is "post-colonial" a qualitative tag or a mere
> temporal phase marker? (p. 206–7)

Ashcroft, Griffiths, and Tiffin discuss the use of post-colonial to represent "all the culture affected by the imperial process from the moment of colonization to the present day" ("How Post-Colonial" 207). Osundare castigates post-colonialism as an "aberrant, one-catch-all metonymy in which the part is too small for the whole" (p. 207). Osundare insists that the village voice must not be subsumed under the town or city's voice, just as he also fights for the city, the country, and the world's rivers to flow into one another as a global family. Through Osundare's pen, the world is a global village where smaller villages and hamlets retain their own voices.

In a 1992 article, "Niyi Osundare's *Waiting Laughers*," Augus Calder compares Osundare's poetry to the writings of Aime Césaire and Pablo Neruda. Calder explains,

> [I]f I compare Niyi Osundare's *Waiting Laughters* not only with
> Césaire but with Neruda, I am making a very large claim for
> the book indeed. I am not saying that Osundare, born in 1947
> so still 'promising', will not write even better books— I am
> pointing to qualities he already shares with two enormous
> writers.

Speaking to me in Asmara, Kofi Anyidoho retold stories about the Noma award panel's excitement in discovering poetry as richly superb as *Waiting Laughters*[4]. Calder rightly describes Osundare as a "writer not only intellectually committed to the political transformation of Nigeria, but prepared to put himself and his talent directly in the frontline" (p. 27). Calder quotes Osundare's thesis about his generation's reason for breaking new ground for modern African poetry: "Written poetry has remained, for many years, an alienated and alienating enterprise in Nigeria— a painful irony in a country where every significant event is celebrated in song, drum and dance, where living still has a fluid rhythm and the proverb is one huge tome of uncountable wisdom" (p. 27). Osundare describes his newspaper column, *Songs of the Season*, as "aimed at 'wooing and winning' an audience for written poetry, at showing, through the mass medium of the newspaper, that poetry can indeed be read for pleasure and profit" (Calder, 1992: 27).

Still describing Osundare' *Waiting Laughters*, Calder compares Osundare in different ways, to both Okigbo and Okot p'Bitek:

> Osundare matches both the sophistication of Okigbo and the directness of Okot within the same covers. It is an ambitious sequence, 'musically' structured, playing variations on themes of waiting and laughter, posing images of sterility against evocations of fertility, moving between political satire and the cycles of the seasons. From its base in Osundare's own Yoruba homeland, it ranges across the world, so that African tyrants are conflated with Japanese shoguns and one especially powerful passage reads as if inspired by the Draculist regime of the Ceausescus, still intact when the poem was composed. (p. 28)

I have not seen anyone writing on Osundare who has not shown an obsession with the beauty of his words and the meaning these words carry for society.

The articles in this book represent the excellent, critical traditions upheld by African literature for years—traditions that have created Sedar Senghor, Chinua Achebe, Ngugi wa Thiong'O, Nawal El Saadawi, Bessie Head, and Ama Ata Aidoo. Contributors to the success of African literary scholarship have been world wide, and the story of Niyi Osundare is told by writers across the globe, from Japan to Canada, from Botswana to the United States, from Nigeria to Italy. Osundare attracts deep-rooted perspectives from world-renowned literary critics. I have preserved the multicultural outlook of this book by allowing the authors to retain their own cultural flavor. From British English and American English to Nigerian English, the essays here show (just like Osundare) that the English language need not impede on representing a native culture in a foreign medium. While British and American spelling and word choice are preserved, the diversity of essays in this collection can be further seen by the differences in length, focus, and strength. Diversity is also portrayed through the inclusion of many formats, such as essay, interview, bibliography, and poetry.

In Section Two, Eldred Durosinmi Jones defines Osundare as a wit and wisdom writer. Jones relays that Osundare is "[e]ssentially a serious poet, deeply engaged with important social issues, his wit and humor sometimes give his poem a surface lightness overlaying the deeper significance." Jones discusses some influences on Osundare's writing, vocabulary, political concerns, environment, and the world. Discussing *Midlife*, Jones calls Osundare the persona of the poem, prodding, "What does he stand for? Who are his allies, his foes? His enemies are tyrants and their tyrannical laws, their unbending attitudes and those who pander them."

Tenure Ojaide is another leading scholar and critic, a leading voice in African poetry. Ojaide's "Niyi Osundare's Poetic Choices," discusses how Osundare's poetic choices impact his work. Ojaide writes, "Like every artist in one way or the other, Osundare makes such choices that he feels will meet the demands of his fulfilling his poetic role and expectations." Ojaide explains how Osundare's developmental years at the University of Ibadan were different from earlier students' years in the same department, like Soyinka, J.P. Clark-Bekederemo, and Christopher Okigbo, who did not study African works as part of their literature program. As Ojaide identifies, Okigbo, J.P. Clark-Bekederemo, Yoruba oral forms, and "world politics of the Cold War era and the diverse implications for Africa, [the] non-alignment, and Marxism" were all influences in Osundare's poetry

Femi Oyebode, in "Green Oranges and Anthill Castle: An Alienated Literature?" examines how Osundare deals with writing in English rather than in his mother tongue. Oyebode asserts that Osundare "captured the speech patterns, [and] the verbal mannerisms of Nigerian English. He also displayed for all to see the rhetorical devices of Yoruba formal speech, the techniques of repetition and parallelism common to Yoruba poetry." Oyebode says Osundare pitches his tent with ordinary people. He insists that Osundare "twists and turns" the English language "to accommodate the vastness, the colors, the lushness and imposing audacity of the material and organic world" of his Ekiti home and compares Osundare to Spanish American poets like Valleji. While challenging Osundare's occasional abstractions, Oyebode declares that Osundare has colonized the English language and showed it "how to describe new experiences, how to speak in strange accents and tempo, [and] how to adapt to previously uncharted phenomena." Oyebode asks for poetry in African languages, and hopes that contemporary Africa writing in European languages is a "transitory phase."

Ezenwa-Ohaeto traces Osundare's development as an important poetic voice in Nigeria, again crediting his generation with removing "poetry from a stifling strait-jacket of obscure diction and represent it in a form that has attracted justifiable popular reactions." He adds that the most significant aspect of Osundare's poetry is "manifested clearly in *Songs* and *Village Voices* through his conscious attempt to weave the poems with a subject matter that captures the aspirations and human concerns of the ordinary people in the society." Ezenwa-Ohaeto declares that Osundare's achievements are "the collective poetic high point of his generation of poets."

Harry Garuba's "Explorations in Animist Materialism and a Reading of the Poetry of Niyi Osundare" argues for an understanding of Osundare's poetry through an African mythological precept he calls "Animist Materialism." The paper responds to Patrick Chabal's "something is going on in Africa" by codifying Osundare's poetry and explaining what it means in contemporary paradigms. Responding to the concept of African colonization of Western technology, ideologies, and mediums (one of Oyedepo's assertions), Garuba insists that the colonization is "a manifestation of an Animist Unconsciousness" rather than a conscious, nationalistic appropriation or a "consequence of the dialectic of 'residuality' and 'emergence' by the Africans." Garuba's thesis promotes reading contemporary African texts from "the socio-cultural arena from which they are generated."

Section three starts with Stewart Brown's "Still Daring the Beasts." The British poet, Brown, is one of Osundare's most acknowledged critics. Brown traces the history of contemporary literary commitment in Nigeria. Brown writes, "One never feels that Osundare is preaching, nor that— as reader — one is being harangued, yet the effect of much of his poetry is both to teach and to inspire a critical rage against the global inanities that are the targets of much of his own wit and anger. " His title echoes Olu Oguibe, who once declared that Osundare still "dares" the Nigerian political beasts, and yet he escapes being devoured in the wild forest.

Jane Bryce shows how Osundare continues to relate to his culture and home. Bryce examines the Nigerian public life and concludes that Osundare has emerged as a poet who, like the legendary Fela Anikulapo-Kuti, has "refused to shut his mouth." Her thesis traces Osundare as a "human witness" to Osundare's Yoruba oral tradition. Tayo Olafioye's "Osundare, the Consummate Poet of Time" asserts that Osundare couldn't have emerged at a better time. In the papers of Aderemi Raji-Oyelade and Akin Adesokan, personal experiences of Osundare's students explain the poet's public engagement.

Section Four is called "Language, Meaning and Translation" and opens with Adeyeye Samson Dare's thorough paper called "Morphology and Meaning in Niyi Osundare's Poetry." Dare opens Osundare's stylistic and linguistic operations. This paper confirms that Osundare creates his own word and experiments with his own linguistic strategies. Dare calls him an "adventurous morphological innovator." Christiane Fioupou's "Beyond 'the rope of a single idiom': Translating African Poetry," is a rich work of analysis of Soyinka's and Osundare's French translator. From her direct experiences, Fioupou looks at contentions in translating African poetry and considers the uniqueness of Osundare's work in French translation.

Section Five starts with a very fine analysis of aesthetic transfer in Osundare's *Village Voices,* by a seasoned critic, Charles Bodunde. This paper strongly continues with the perspectives of African oral traditions and "connects the [African] artist with the aesthetic forms available in his culture and provides the ground for establishing literary relations among African writers, including those in the Diaspora." Bodunde says Osundare's exploration of oral forms has a "more demanding purpose" of creating "new ideas and visions." Bodunde concludes that work just as Osundare's proves that oral forms "are not static or fossilized materials" and are "constantly being reconstructed to assume new roles."

Kofi Mensah and S. Louisa Wei present Osundare as a Nature poet and discuss his preoccupation with the environment. Mensah calls Osundare's *The Eye of the Earth* "a sustained meditation on the theme of nature." Using the German theorist's, Friedrich von Schiller, second notion of the sentimental nature poet, Mensah says that Osundare's peasant birth and the contemporary socioeconomic condition of his community informs his poetic sentimentalism. According to Mensah, Osundare brings scolarship and nature into his poetry, often through "witty and erudite language."

On the other hand, Wei claims that Osundare's poetry reconstructs and champions forgotten history, vigorously showing a "deep concern for people and [a] tireless meditation on Nature." She says Osundare's poetry enchants modern readers, regardless of nationality. Wei insists that Osundare's emphasis on lyricism makes him closer to the African tradition than Soyinka and Okigbo. She identifies a question and answer sequence and parallelism as two important features in Osundare's poetry. Wei writes,

> History is versus Nature in the sense that Nature is an eternally unchanged reminder of the latter, while History has to fight for its true existence to maintain the well being of Nature. Therefore, when Nature is forgotten due to industrialization and other causes, part of our History is also forgotten.

She insists Osundare would never forget Nature and History in his poetry because these two often forgotten phenomena are central to Osundare's ideological stance.

Section Six brings important comparative perspectives to Osundare's poetry. Kamal Abdel-Malek's very rich paper, "The Poetics of the 'Alter-Native' Tradition: The Case of Nigeria's Niyi Osundare and Egypt's Ahmad Fuad Ngim," compares two popular African poets of English and Arabic expression. Both poets have deep commitments to the ordinary people despite different languages, cultural backgrounds, and sharply different literacy attainments, for Nigm has no formal education. Abdel-Malek argues that both poets "charge their indigenous tradition with dynamic rhetoric of their revolutionary stands on issues relating to the rights of the poor and the oppressed, Third World liberation movements and the preservation of the earth's natural resources." Abdel-Malek adds that Osundare and Ngim artfully infuse modern works with native lore.

Kamau Kemayo's paper, "Long Lost Kin: Niyi Osundare Through an African American Lens" is a brother-to-brother connection. The poet Kemayo interrogates his connection to his African brother in the Diaspora. He compares Osundare's thematic focus to Madhubuti's. Through a number of Osundare's collections, and especially a review of *Horses of Memory*, Kemayo establishes inherent cultural and spiritual roots among Africans across the Atlantic, championing writers of African ancestry to trek the bridge across to ancestral brotherhood. Irene Sywenky's fine article compares Osundare's *Waiting Laughter* with Andrukhovych's carnival poetry in "Post-Colonial Context, Post-Modernist Perspectives." Olufemi Dunmade examines Value and Evaluation in Osundare's "Benin Mask" and Jack Mapanje's "Kabula Curio-Shop."

Section Seven contains sets of interviews with Osundare. Hearing a writer tell his life stories and elucidate his literary visions is always an opportunity no critic wants to miss. Stephen Arnold, Cythia Hogue, Nancy Easterlin, Frank Birbalsingh, Pietro Deandrea, Sola Olorunyomi and Raji-Oyelade have occasions in different parts of the world, and through different mediums, to put Osundare on the spot, and Osundare writes himself all over again. For Frank Birbalsingh, it was a second coming, having had one of the pioneering Osundare interviews in *Presence Africaine* in 1988.

Section Eight is about Osundare's plays. Only a few people know that he is also the playwright. Wumi Raji explains the vision and style in Osundare's plays. Sola Olorunyomi reviews the premier performance of one of Osundare's plays at Ibadan.

Section Nine, "Osundare, Bio-Bibliography", contains three very interesting articles. In "The Ambiguity of Autobiography: Anatomy of Niyi Osundare's Mid-Life," Omoniyi Afolabi discusses Osundare's life as presented in his poetry collection, *Midlife*. Afolabi hopes to uncover the mythological and philosophical dimensions of the book. Afolabi attempts to insert what he calls "a polybiographical context" into his reading of *Midlife*. Mobolaji Aluko's article, "Osundare: A Man for All Seasons" recounts Osundare's college days as told by his college brother. The short paper, which is as humorous as it is educational, relays the important background to Osundare's successes. Bernth Lindfors's paper discusses works written by and on Osundare from 1976 to 1996. This section will be very useful to anyone researching Osundare's work and is invaluable to scholars of African literature and postcolonial studies.

I have included a few poems written by some of Osundare's students and colleagues, who are eager to put their appreciation of Osundare's works into a creative structure. Scholars contributed enthusiastically to Osundare's book, and showed responses unrivaled in contemporary projects. Many people sent letters extolling Osundare's personality and poetry. Eldred Durosimi Jones demonstrated an unparalleled commitment to scholarship and to Osundare's writings, despite the brutal war that almost took his life in Sierra Leone. Jones completed his essay and sent several letters to ensure that I received his contribution. In telephone conversations, Jones told me stories of how he and his wife were hidden underground, writing and rewriting the Osundare paper, determined to finish it at all costs—all the while, news was circulating in Europe and America that Professor Jones had been killed. The uncommon will of critics like Durosinmi Jones and the dogged determination of African writers of Osundare's stance indicate that although the twentieth century ended leaving Africa with internal wars and external corporate destruction, the twenty-first century brings great hopes for a collective renaissance. The central thesis in this collection is that modern African poetry engages, resonating in literary beauty and cultural regeneration.

This first major collection on Osundare's work has surfaced at the right time. The twenty-first century sky is clearly Osundare's sky. African literature, writers and critics of African writings have shown uncommon commitment to retaining a global place for African stars. This book provides emerging perspectives on Osundare from writers of different cultural and linguistic backgrounds, and most are writing in English. This book introduces the global community to the new African commitment to culture.

Abdul-Rasheed Na'Allah
Macomb, Illinois

NOTES

1 Others in this generation include Okara and Awonoor, writing in Ghana. Without question, they are not counted among Soyinka and Okigbo when it comes to difficulty in language. Okara has a unique language experimentation in his novel, *The Voice*, and Awonoor's writing is greatly charming and simple. Tanure Ojaide spoke about a three generation framework in which the first generation were those he called the pioneers, the second, the Soyinkas, and the third, Osundare, Tanure, and others (Na'Allah 1999: 63). However, I still prefer to retain the classification recognizing Soyinka and his group as first generation.

2 Radio Conversation with Zulu Sofola and Niyi Osundare, Radio Kwara 'Focal Point,' Ilorin, Nigeria, 1992.

3 For more on writer's personality, see Abdul-Rasheed Na'Allah "Elaloro: An African Indigenous Theory for Critical Discourse." Presented at the XVIth Congress of the International Comparative Literature Association, Pretoria, August 2000.

4 I believe that Kofi Anyidoho was a member of selecting panel for the 1991 Noma.

REFERENCES

Calder, Angus. "Niyi Osundare's Waiting Laughters." *Cencratus*. 44 (1992): 27–9.

Jeyifo, Biodun. "Niyi Osundare." Ed. Yemi Ogunbiyi. *Perspectives on Nigerian Literature: 1700 to the Present*. Lagos: Guardian Books, Nigeria Limited, 1988.

Na'Allah, Abdul-Rasheed. "Elaloro: An African Indigenous Theory for Critical Discourse" Paper presented at the XVIth Congress of the International Comparative Literature Association, Pretoria, August 2000.

Na'Allah, Abdul-Rasheed and Michelin Rice-Maximin. "Thresholds: Anglophone African Literatures Conference in Toulouse, February 4–6, 1999" *ALA Bulletin*. 25.3 (1999): 61–73.

Ojaide, Tenure. *Poetic imagination in Black Africa: Essays on African Poetry*. Durham, N.C.: Carolina Academic Press. 1996.

Osundare, Niyi. "How Post-Colonial is African Literature?" *Matatu* 12 (1994): 203–16.

——. "Confessions of a Scholar-Poet" (Unpublished paper).

THEORY AND POETICS

THE WIT AND WISDOM OF NIYI OSUNDARE

Eldred Durosimi Jones

In Niyi Osundare's poem, "For John Donne," the transformation of Donne's image—a pair of compasses' twin legs—symbolizes the unchanging relationship between the speaker and his lover into a complex metaphor, and it characterizes the conversion of that earlier monarch of wit from promiscuous lover into pious priest. This transformation is both a tribute to Osundare's English predecessor as well as a demonstration of the centrality of wit to the Nigerians' own poetry. His unifying, poetic intelligence, like that of the English metaphysical poets before him, is capable of yoking seemingly contrary ideas to produce a new insight into a familiar subject. The "legs" of a pair of compasses become Donne's own legs, which at first bare his licensed hands and no doubt rove over the contours of his mistress, then soberly and "now trousered" enable the reformed man to pursue his priestly functions. The wit lies in capturing all of these suggestions in a single image:

> Then
> your compass legs (now trousered)
> completed the circle (SP, 16).

Osundare's poem acknowledges a kindred poetic spirit, but this "parodic" style demonstrates his own poetic independence. Generally, his source of poetic inspiration, as well as his store of images, is clearly Yoruba even though in this particular poem he uses Donne's vocabulary to hoist this earlier poet with his own ropes. In his poetry, Osundare's use of the Yoruba language, the translations of Yoruba oral material, and his own coinages based on the tradition amply illustrate both his literary derivation and his own creative abilities. Whether he is paying tribute to Olof Palme or his fellow Yoruba Chief Awolowo, the influence of the Yoruba ijala chant[i] is nonetheless evident.

> Let the sky eat up its roving eye
> Let the sea pour out its desert of salt
> Tell the chattering road to rein in
> Its speedy tongue;
> Ah! the elephant has fallen
> A gigantic emptiness has gripped
> The kernel of our striving forests (SS, 88).

Essentially a serious poet deeply engaged with important social issues, Osundare possesses a wit and humor that sometimes give his poems a surface lightness that overlay a deeper significance. He is concerned with the fate of a people, particularly with the fate of ordinary folk—to me, Osundare is also concerned with the fate of the land itself, its forests (threatened with denudation in the interest, of progress), its rivers, its agriculture, and its other natural resources. Even though he is always conscious of the impending threat to their integrity, Osundare's poetry rejoices in the lushness of the green forests, in the productivity of the land, and in the potential for the creation of human happiness.

> The rains have kept their time this year (Earth has (finally)
> won the love of the sky)
> Trees bob with barkward sap
> and leaves grab deepening green
> from the scanty sun.
>
> Bouncing boughs interlock overhead
> like wristwrestlers straining muscularly
> On a canvas of leaves wounded
> by the fists of time (SP, 31)

> Here where yam wore the crown
> in the reign of swollen roots
> amid a retinue of vines and royal leaves,
> between insistent sky and yielding earth,
> the sun mellowed planting pageants
> into harvest march,
> a fiery pestle in his ripening hand (SP, 38).

This passage illustrates a strong anthropomorphic quality arising from the poet's own devotion to and his people's involvement with the environment. The bouncing "wristwrestlers" are the most obvious example of the human associations, but other examples of anthropomorphism, such as "Earth has (finally) won the love of the sky," "trees bob," and "leaves grab," are equally significant. Sometimes, the effect is distinctly erotic. In "Harvest call" for example,

> coy cobs rocked lustily
> in the loin of swaying stalks.
> And when June had finally grabbed the year
> by her narrow waist
> corn cobs flashed their milky teeth
> in disrobing kitchens (*SP*, 39)

These erotic suggestions are also clear in the passages from "Farmer-born," where the speaker is the poet himself:

> I have frolicked from furrow to furrow
> sounded kicking tubers in the womb
> of quickening earth
> and fondled the melon breasts
> of succulent ridges (——47).

The poet is physically and emotionally involved with the environment; he speaks from within it, converses with it and derives his authority from it. Babalola also mentions that a similar anthropomorphic feature is common of ijala chants: "The ascription of human' characteristics, thoughts and emotions, [are attributed] to animals and birds" (Babalola 69–70).

The tensions produced by the competing claims of the preservation for the land and the exploitation of the land constantly recur with the hopeful suggestion that rational balance is not beyond the wit of man. The dilemma is evident

in Olusunta's dialogue with a rock in the poem, "The Rock's Rose to Meet Me."
By now, the hill had lost much of its earlier spiritual significance, but its physical resources remain to be exploited for the good of the people. "How was this
to be done?...How dig the gold/without breaking the rock?" (*SP*, 34).

> The gold let us dig,
> not for the gilded craniums
> of hollow chieftains
> (time's undying sword awaits their necks
> who deem this earth their sprawling throne.)
> With the gold let us turn hovels into havens
> paupers into people (not princes)
> so hamlets may hear
> the tidings or towns
> so the world may sprout a hand
> of equal fingers (SP, 34).

The strong belief that a humane democracy is the solution to his country's
problem is based on an equally strong faith about the potential of the common
man who—though seemingly controllable and exploitable—has a potential for
self-assertion, which will be the ultimate salvation of society. Thus, the poetry
maintains an intelligent optimism:

> Unfellable
> like a tree with a million roots I will shake the earth with giant
> fruits lading the four winds
> with seeds of change (SP, 25)

The essential seriousness of Osundare's poetry appears even in the seemingly lighthearted tribute to Donne cited earlier. Half mocking in its tone, the
poem does cleverly suggest doubts about the genuineness of the conversion and
hints at the possible serious consequences of Donne's earlier promiscuity. Is
not the glide from roue to priest too easy?

> Jack to John, Donne to Dean
> Don Juan to John Donne (SP, 16).

The poem bristles with the possible consequences of the young libertine's
"hopping from bed to bed" and the lines become suggestively pregnant with
meaning:

> Loving, your love songs
> penetrating like a barbed baton
> conceived new found landes and Americas solemnized mar-
> riages in bug bellies (SP, 16).

In the previous lines, almost every word becomes a moral minefield.

A similar combination of surface lightness and deeper suggestion is illustrated in "Monday Morning," where the "staccato syntax/of metalled heels" links
the contrasting locales of university campus and Crisbo Gardens (SP, 76). The
heavy, potential consequence of life in one place for life in another is unmistakable in the suggestions of "resurrection," "golgotha," "gethsemane," and "dire
Fridays" (M, 53). Osundare can be both light and serious simultaneously with
an almost "metaphysical" art. But even here it must be noted that the metaphysical style is coincidental and derives, as his style does, from characteristics,
which are part of the Yoruba ijala tradition. His fondness for wordplay—puns
and other forms of ambiguity, alliteration and coinages—can all be related to
counterparts in the Yoruba poetic tradition. His exhilaration and sheer joy in
wordplay is not borrowed from an alien tradition; this wordplay is a product of
a combination between the Yoruba tradition of verbal wit and the poet's gifts of
constructive double vision. "Collage" indulges, or over-indulges, in an almost
irreverent, verbal mask-dancing:

> From praying ground to preying ground
> from democracy to democrazy
> from conscience to con-science
> Allies or all lies
> adultery or adult tree
> message or mess age

In spite of this playfulness, the poem's intention is essentially serious.

This ability to see both sides of the question is realized in both large and small
structures in the verse. In more than one poem, two contrasting aspects of a
point may be made, hence dividing the poem into a two-part structure. In "Like
the Bee," the first two stanzas present the negative, while the third stanza turns
the thought around by stating the positive: "Not like the spider/...But like the
bee" (SP,8). The two parts can, however, be fused into a single pun as in "The
Poet." In this poem, the definition of a poet arises from a series of negative statements about what the poet is not into a series of more positive statements. The
poem ends with a deft pun in which the active and passive meanings of "smell"
sting the poet into self-awareness. In all his feathered finery, the poet must not

7

avert his nose because he himself (never mind the environment) might also smell:

> how can the poet
> strut clean in feathered sandals
> and pretend to the world he never smells? (SP,,4)

"Farmer-born peasant bred" is similarly turned on its head by the change of a single letter: "bred" changes to "bled."

The poet's constructive double vision, endowing his poetry with its thematic structures as well as its wisdom and far-sightedness, enables him to see the hope of the future while mired in the present and to see the downfall of the tyrant while still in the grip of his power. "Song of the Tyrant," whose facile gallop, rhyme scheme, and ballad form may mask the gravity of its content, puts the tyrant against the content of history and exposes the evanescent vanity of his present power. He may be:

> High on the mare, high on the horse
> He tortures the turf without remorse (SS, 28)
> But our world is a book of yester-scenes
> Scourge of tyrants and their wormy sins
> Hitler hit the pall in a rayless tomb
> Zia came to earth in a nameless bomb (SS, 29).

Yester-scenes, implying as it does in history and through the passing of time, introduce a recurring theme that is played out through various images in the corpus. In the quotation immediately above, time was going to bring the tyrant to the book and make him only another example of fallen tyranny in history. The sufferers under tyranny can hope for relief with the passing of time:

> For time it may take
> Time it may take.
> The stammerer will one day call his
> Fa-fa-fa-ther's na-na-na-me! (WL, 74)

This waiting is the central theme in *Waiting Laughters*. The structure of the poem reflects the theme of unfulfilled promise. The poet, as in the beginning, is still striving for inspiration at the end of the poem. The patterns and formulas recur. At the beginning:

> I pluck these murmurs
> From the laughter of the wind
> The shrub's tangled tale
> Plaited tree tops
> And palms which drop their nuts (WL, 2).

And similarly at the end:

> I pluck these words from the laughter of the wind
> The liquid breath of the Monsoon's millenial riddle (WL, 96).

In between are several states of waiting. Childhood, for example, is preparation, not fulfillment. In the passage on waiting in the unwelcoming and forbidding atmosphere of a visa office, presumably by one wishing to extend the scope of his preparation—if we pardon the awe-ful (my word) pun on office—"awe-fice" is very successful. The people wait patiently under a succession of oppressors, rulers sated with excess:

> Croesus heaves a glittering crown on his head,
> his neck shortening like a senile cricket's
> Beyond Reason, beyond necessity
> In the orgy of crimson claws
> which darken the rainbow of striving ribs
> in the belly of the goblet where murdered grapes
> sip their scarlet wails...(WL, 20-1).

But through images of the Bastille, reminiscent of the French Revolution, the downfall of such rulers is predicted. Before the fulfillment of the prediction, however, is the period of patient waiting.

> Teach us the patience of the sand
> which rocks the cradle of the river
>
> Teach us the patience of the branch
> which counts the seasons in dappled cropping
> Teach us the patience of the rain
> which eats at the rock in toothless silence (WL, 7).

Since the country's plight is no better, this patience is just as necessary at the end as it is at the beginning of the poem. It is still waiting.

Waiting
still waiting

Grant us

the fortitude of the lamb which lames a lion—
without inheriting its claws (WL, 95)

Osundare once again emerges as the committed poet with a strong sense of
the sufferings of his people and consciously takes on the mantle of seer and
spokesman with humility. He approaches his task conscious of its enormity:

And laughing winds
So fugitive in
Our harried seasons
Who can tie
Them down with
the rope
of a single idiom Who dare?

Blame not, then,
The rapid eloquence of the running vowel
When words turn willing courier
In the courtyard of dodging ears
Can the syllable stall its tale
In impertinences of half-way fancies? (WL, 4–5)

He is also the artist who delights as he sings—who delights
because he sings.

In a poem with so much imagery and symbolism, not all the symbols yield
their meanings as easily. The horse which appears early in the poem and returns
half-way through is clearly significant for the poet, and it is so artistically presented. But what does this image represent—another image of passing time?
Adufe's transformation into a mermaid – equally and beautifully done – is also
puzzling.

In *Midlife*, Osundare most directly demonstrates the consciousness of his
poetic role. It is indeed a poetic manifesto—an affirmation of the poet's role and
his responsibility to himself, to his community, and to the world at large. The
poet's personality and his inspiration derive from his natural environment: the

rivers, the mountains, and the flora and fauna from which also his imagery springs. Through out the poem, Osundare re-affirms this position.

> I am child of the river, child of the rock.
> Child, of rocky hills holding hands
> Above the tallest roofs (M, 11).

The poem is redolent with references to Ikiri and its dominant river.

The persona of the poem is the poet himself. He has now reached "midlife," "midstream," "midway," "midnight," or "midthrob," as he constantly reiterates with appropriate images: "I am the caller at noon." From this significant vantage point, he reviews his origins, his life, and his poetic equipment as well as his country, his continent, and the world. He faces the realities both of himself and of the world with patent honesty. He speaks with such authority at times that some parts of the poem may sound arrogant, but he counters any such suggestion by admitting his limitations.

> I am light
> I am shadow I am the luminous covenant
> Of short and tall spaces (M, 3).

Contrast, for example, the previous quotation with the following:

> I am the mason who hews stones
> and pines in a muddy shack
>
> I am a cockroach trapped in the brimming sewage
> of opulent cities (M,3).

What does he stand for? Who are his allies and his foes? His enemies are tyrants and their tyrannical laws, their unbending attitudes and those who pander to them:

> I am the spirit of the making mind
> at war with brittle facts
> at war with wills which say yes
> to the blood-stained accent of unmanning edicts
>
> at war with hectoring jab, with canons

which whip the world into a hard invariate mould
(M, 40).

The figure's condemned range from Bokassa through Pinochet to The Iron Lady with five testicles, like a Juba squirrel and their victims, are represented by Africa's imprisoned writers (M, 49).

> And Brutus's ballad, and the Apartheid dragon
> And Soyinka's shuttle in the General's crypt
> And Ngugi's travails on the Devil's cross
> And Mapanje's chameleons and Band-it gods (M ,68).

In a better world, the walls of the prisons, which he so eloquently describes in the "Breaking Walls," have to be pulled down to bring about the dreams of freedom and democracy. His concerns are universal, and he is as conscious at the deterioration of the global environment as he is of the degradation of his own native river. Since "[t]he sky is [his] robe," he is personally touched when the environment, in any part of the world, is threatened or destroyed (M, 36).

> Where is the vandal who punched a hole
> in the garment. of our sky?
> Now every rain is a storm
> the sun is ready fire above our broiling heads...(M, 50)

The "garment" (the ozone layer) is as personal to him as the Osun River. These are not images stuck on as ornaments; they are organic to the very ideas. The poet's rhythmic touch is sure, and he almost sings his message. To the listening ear, every re-hearing is like a new experience, as is its suggestiveness and essential coherence. The poet, indeed, pictures himself as a singer to his surrounding people who require a message from him.

> Sing to us about rivers, rivers tumbling
> Down to the mountain's with a concert
> of chorusing fishes (M, 44).

This extraordinary poem is his response. As an honest poet he cannot sing just happy songs; his picture is much more balanced, and he sings not only of the night but also of the approaching dawn. The picture of Africa, however, is bleak:

a continent so ancient and so infant, crawling, grey, in the
scarlet dust of twilight horsemen, ravished by the gun, crim-
soned by ample-robed natives and their swaggering fangs; our
sun so black with crying hopes, wounded by the boundless
appetite of hyena rulers (MM, 99–100).

But life's elegy is also an anthem of hope.

Poetry is not just ideas and inner consciousness. It has to be expressed
through words and syntactical devices:

Syllables sweat in the forge of the larynx lines sprawl out their
frames like basking pythons adjectives find their nouns, verbs
their active shadows every stanza is a night waiting for a breaking day (M, 55).

He prays for the gift of expression, and if this poem is anything to go by, he
is granted that gift in abundance. This is a great personal poetic statement, not
as long as Wordsworth's "Prelude" (which should have been several hundred
lines shorter anyway), but it should do as much for African poetry as the best
of the "Prelude" did for the English tradition.

Over-arching the whole corpus is the concept of time in its various manifestations. Time is represented by the timeless rocks and rivers and the process by
which, ring after ring, the giant trees of the forest reach maturity and the more
seasonal yams, pawpaw, and pumpkin provide the harvests that sustain the
community. Time, which weathers the rock and whose eternal dimensions are
the acts of tyrants, is put into perspective.

For example, the moon, whose phases mark one of the more obvious measures of time, provides the central image in *Moonsongs*. The moon changes its
role, its character, and even its sex, just as the physical moon goes through his
phases of waxing and waning. The moon sometimes appears as an all wise deity
looking down on the activities of the world but then also frequently becomes an
actor in the drama exercising an influence that is sometimes benign and sometimes malign. Thus in Phase XIX, the moon is a tyrant who plunders the wealth
of his country and seeks to maintain his power by force of crushing arms:

The moon plundered the gold
drained the diamonds
and bartered its silvery ore

> to the merchants of night
> whose claws are cold
> whose teeth are crowded tusks
> of the ivory of our dreams (MS, 37).

When challenged, the tyrant menacingly bears his claws:

> and when skysages challenge
> the dimness of the deeds
> the moon pleads its sword,
> pleads the bayonet tongue
> of its eager guns (MS, 37).

But this very moon could also be the source of life and refreshment as the images of life-giving milk suggest in the following passage.

> Oh moon oh moon where is your udder, where, your pitcher
> Who mothered the milk that bathes your limbs (MS, 39).

In other pictures, the moon is the distant deity looking down on the iniquities of the world: racial persecution, power politics, and the misery and poverty that these may bring. Thus, from the rusty roofs with their suggestion of local decay, the eye of the moon encompasses South Africa, Grenada, Managua and the deep south of America. Here, in line with its continual changefulness, the moon has changed its sex:

> She needs no spectacles to see our roofs
> rust-tongued, fear-furrowed, squeaking now
>
> like a baffled hen panting
> after the hasty exit of the hawkish sun.
>
> In Grenada where Sunset nurtures freedom with bayonets
> and cackling cannon
>
> In Managua where reddening flares
> brave the breath of Twilight storms
>
> In the sorrows of our South deep, so deep like scars of millennial lesions

The moon is a mask dancing (MS, 40).

The most frequently recurring theme is that of change. The moon is never still, just as history is never still. Through the eye of the changing moon, all life is surveyed. The actions of kings, of tyrants, of university students, of suffering poets—all of these come under the gaze of the all-seeing moon.

"Farmer born peasant bred" Osundare may be, but he has also been "classroom bled." In spite of the suggestion of regret—almost resentment in "bled" as a consequence of which his peasant stomach now aches for "Carolina rice"—he combines in his poetry the traditions of the Yoruba ijala chant with those of European poetry to produce a remarkable corpus through which he expresses his vision of a better world. From his explorations of the universal world of ideas, he returns a wanderer to the rocks, rivers, and fields of his peasant environment. He is now undergoing change from a new industrialized, commercialized, and politically tyrannizing regime and is consciously adopting the role of poet and seer. He denounces the evils of tyranny, corruption, exploitation, and "marginalization" of the common man while looking forward through the potential of this very common man to a more democratic future, where human and physical resources would be used with a respect for the natural environment "to turn hovels into havens/paupers into people (not princes)/...so the world may sprout a hand of equal fingers" (SP, 34).

NOTES

1 S. A. Babalola, *The Content and Form of Yoruba Ijala*. London: OUP, 1966: 56–84.

REFERENCES

Babalola, S. A. *The Content and Form of Yoruba Ijala*. London: OUP, 1966.

Osundare, Niyi. *Moonsongs*. Ibadan: Spectrum Books, 1988. (MS in text).

———. *Songs of the Season*. Ibadan: Heinemann, 1990. (SS in text).

———. *Waiting Laughters*. Ikeja: Malthouse Press, 1992. (WL in text).

———. *Selected Poems*. Oxford: Heinemann, 1992. (SP in text).

———. *Midlife*. Ibadan: Heinemann, 1993. (M in text).

NIYI OSUNDARE AND HIS POETIC CHOICES

Tanure Ojaide

Niyi Osundare has published a body of poems, which deserves serious study, over the past two decades that have acquired a pattern of what he does and does not do. The poet's Yoruba background, his university education, and the Zeitgeist and Volkgist of the late 1960s through the 1970s in particular, combine with other factors to shape the direction of his poetic explorations. It is in light of these factors that I intend to examine his poetic choices and how these choices impact on his work. To the poet, many poetic choices are made available, depending on one's interests and objectives. Some of these aims affect thematic and aesthetic considerations. Like an explorer, the poet's interests determine the choices of what to experience. With Osundare, some choices appear forced upon him by conditions of the time, as others arise from personal options and considerations. Thus he is influenced at certain times to "imitate" and at other times to react against. Admiring or disliking somebody or something elicits various responses, which can be seen as aspects of influence. For example, if admiring the later poetry of Christopher Okigbo makes Osundare musical, and if disliking Wole Soyinka's obscure and difficult poetry in *Idanre* makes him write what he considers to be accessible to the generality of poetry readers, there is a strong influence of both writers. Like every artist in one way or the other, Osundare makes such choices that he feels will meet the demands of fulfilling his poetic role and expectations.

A prime molder of Osundare as a poet is the education he received at the University of Ibadan from 1969 to 1972. It is not that the other universities he attended much later for graduate studies, such as Leeds and York, did not influence him, but his formative years as a poet were spent at Ibadan. Having the personal experience at the University of Ibadan at about the same time as him and knowing Osundare as a fellow student in the same English department, I know that the university curriculum and student activities of the time have had a lasting impact on him. In the English department, we had started to read African literature primarily side by side with British literature. There were courses in African literature, such as modern African poetry taught by Dan Izevbaye, modern African drama taught by Oyin Ogunba, and modern African fiction taught by Theo Vincent. These modern African literature courses were taught along with modernist poets, like T. S. Eliot, Ezra Pound, and W. B. Yeats, courses on Shakespeare, metaphysical poets, and other areas and periods of English literature.

There was a strong interest in modern African poetry that was written by J.P. Clark Bekederemo, Christopher Okigbo, and Wole Soyinka, among others who did not have the advantage we enjoyed of reading African literature. I can recollect in lecture halls, tutorials, and the creative writing club that there were heated discussions about these three Nigerian poets. Most of us seem to have chosen models from among them. Okigbo's untimely death in the war gave a great boost to the popularity of his poetry among young students of English. Soyinka's detention during the war also made him very popular among us. Niyi Osundare, no doubt, was part of this group who was fascinated by the poetic persona cut by Okigbo, the musicality, and word play of his poetry. One can adduce Osundare's interest in poetic musicality, in the forms of chant-like rhythms and the use of figures of sound—especially alliterations, to this Okigboesque disposition of most of us "budding" undergraduate poets at the University of Ibadan in the late 1960s and early 1970s. Okigbo's last poems, "Path of Thunder: Poems prophesying War" and the experiments, such as his elegiac homage to W. B. Yeats, were familiar reading materials among undergraduates of English then. What could be a stronger echo of Okigbo's "The General is up . . . the General is up . . . commandments . . . / the General is up the General is up the General is up —" than Osundare's "The general is up, up, up / The general is up . . ." in *Moonsongs*? (*Okigbo*, 69 and *Selected Poems*, 68).

The use of incantation rhythms, alliterative sounds, and word play has become part of Osundare's poetic signature. The "Eye of the Earth" best illustrates this aspect of Osundare's poetic choice. Here is "Earth":

Temporary basement
and lasting roof

first clayey coyness
and last alluvial joy

breadbasket
and compost bed

rocks and rivers
muds and mountains

silence of the twilight sea
echoes of the noonsome tide

milk of mellowing moon
fire of tropical hearth

spouse of the roving sky
virgin of a thousand offsprings

Ogeere amokoyeri (p. 1).

In using incantation rhythms, Osundare balances one line against another as each couplet further reinforces the previous one. He also uses oriki rhythms in *Moonsongs*. While later I will talk of Osundare choosing simplicity over difficulty and obscurity, as in Soyinka's *Idanre*, this use of Yoruba poetic models has been attempted earlier by Wole Soyinka in poems like "Koko Oloro" in *Idanre* and "Muhammad Ali at the Ringside, 1985" in *Mandela's Earth*. Here, both poets share experiences of poetic forms of their native culture.

Closely related to the poetic infatuation with Okigbo's musicality and play on words is a certain resistance to obscurity and difficulty of African poetry as in Soyinka's *Idanre* phase. Many young Nigerian poets of the early 1970s might agree with some of the points made by Chinweizu in *Towards the Decolonization of African Literature* about the euromodernist excesses of modern African poetry even though criticisms were made. In the English department of the University of Ibadan, during the period of Osundare's undergraduate program, lecturers and students had wondered what Soyinka meant in many of the poems—especially the title poem. Most of us left the classroom to the creative writing club and carried with us, from one place to the other, arguments as to what poetry should be. As much as we respected Wole Soyinka to the point of reverence, many of us did not want to write poetry in his manner. As I said earlier, the model was usually Okigbo and sometimes J. P. Clark-Bekederemo. A "budding" dramatist like Shadrack Agbagbarha might have had a better inclination to Soyinka's drama, but plays like *A Dance of the Forests* and *The Road* might not have endeared to some of us because of their perceived difficulty.

The obvious reaction to the euro-modernist aspects of modern African poetry, as in Soyinka's worst cases in *Idanre*, no doubt geared Osundare and many other undergraduate poets to write more comprehensible poetry, as in J.P Clark Bekederemo's "A Reed in the Tide." One way Osundare has shown this aspect in his writing is the conscious choice of simplicity in collections, such as *Village Voices*, *Songs of the Marketplace*, and *The Eye of the Earth*. To Osundare, "[T]he simple word / is the shortest distance / between two minds" (*Selected Poems*, 3). In fact, his "Poetry is" can be seen as a poetic manifesto of the younger generation of Nigerian poets of the early 1970s and as an indirect jibe at Soyinka's type of poetry. Among my coevals at Ibadan, including Osundare, the deep respect that extends to reverence for Soyinka did not endear many of us too much with his *Idanre* phase of poetry. Osundare's poetic choice at the beginning of his poetic career was for poetry that communicates directly. To him,

> "Poetry is
> not the esoteric whisper
> of an excluding tongue
> not a claptrap
> for a wondering audience
> not a learned quiz
> entombed in Grecoroman lore
>
> Poetry is
> a lifespring
> which gathers timbre
> the more throats it plucks
> harbinger of action
> the more minds it stirs
>
> Poetry is
> the hawker's ditty
> the eloquence of the gong

the lyric of the marketplace
the luminous ray
on the grass's morning dew

Poetry is
what the soft wind
musics to the dancing leaf
what the sole tells the dusty path
what the bee hums to the alluring nectar
what rainfall croons to the lowering eaves

Poetry is
no oracle's kernel
for a sole philosopher's stone

Poetry
is
man
meaning
to
man (Songs of the Marketplace, 4).

World politics of the Cold War era, diverse implications for Africa, non align-ment, and Marxism also helped to shape Osundare's poetic direction. Osundare's days at Ibadan involved radicalized student union politics. There were frequent demonstrations against policies of European or North American governments that ran contrary to African interests. Students were bussed to Lagos to demonstrate when Portuguese mercenaries invaded Guinea Bissau. Most students seem to have aligned on the part of revolution, no matter how well they understood its implications. This infatuation with revolution was man-ifested in student union politics in 1970 when Osinowo ran for the secretarial position, which he won by distributing posters emblazoned with "Osinowo, Revolution." I believe most of us voted for him because he stood for revolution. The death of Kunle Adepoju in a student demonstration in 1971 was perhaps the apogee of this student radicalism against their administrators and anti-African interests.

Osundare imbibed many Marxist ideas, and in fact, he declared himself a Marxist in the 1970s and early 1980s. Although he declared himself a Marxist, Osundare was not an ideologue for all its implications like Biodun Jeyifo, Tunde

Fatoba, and Festus Iyayi. In any case, his proletarian ideas form part of the bedrock of *Village Voices, Songs of the Marketplace,* and *Moonsongs.* Most of the poems in these collections are people/masses-oriented. "I Sing of Change" is illustrative of a classless society:

> I sing
> of the beauty of Athens
> without its slaves
>
> Of a world free
> of kings and queens
> and other remnants
> of an arbitrary past
>
> Of earth
> with no
> sharp north
> or deep south
> without blind curtains
> or iron walls
> . . . .
> I sing of a world reshaped (Songs of the Marketplace, 90).

Unlike the earlier generation, with poets like Clark-Bekederemo, Okigbo, and Soyinka, the major conflict now had nothing to do with African and Western influences but with class. This class conflict stared Osundare in the eye in two areas of Lagos:

> Ikoyi
> The moon here
> is a laundered lawn
> its grass the softness of infant fluff;
> silence grazes like a joyous lamb,
> doors romp on lazy hinges
> the ceiling is a sky
> weighted down by chandeliers
> Ajegunle
> here the moon
> is a jungle
> sad like a forgotten beard

with tensioned climbers
and undergrowths of cancerous fury
cobras of anger spit in every brook
and nights are one long prowl
of swindled leopards (p. 73).

The contradictions of society, as expressed in Marxism, became more glaring after the energy crisis of the early 1970s and after the political corruption worsened the economic plight of the common people.

Osundare adopts a communal voice, rather than an individual voice, in many of his poems in *Village Voices* and *Songs of the Marketplace*. Osundare's poetry does not appear to be personal. It is rare for him to write about a personal experience or for him to be confessional. There are no poems about his relationships—no love poems, for instance. He distances himself from the personal, but he, nonetheless, still expresses himself. One would expect personal poems in *Midlife*, but there are none. It is not that every poet must write about his or her relationships, but I have not seen an Osundare love poem. Love poetry could oftentimes show much of the sensibility, passion, and humanity of a poet. Poets like Pablo Neruda and Odysseus Elytis in recent times have been involved and distanced in their poems. The choice should not be so much between being involved and being distanced, as in a relationship, but should involve being completely human. Thus, is the paradox that while he attempts to be a literary pop artist by using the communal voice and simple language, Osundare disengages from the personal, which coalesces into pop art, and shows much of one's humanity.

Consequent upon his Marxist infatuation and a materialist approach to life, Osundare rejects the primacy of myths and the kabiyesi syndrome of Yoruba dramatists like Soyinka and Femi Osofisan. He is very selective of his use of Yoruba folklore. Unlike Soyinka, associated with Ogun and Osofisan with Eshu, Osundare has so far avoided being tagged with any party of the Yoruba pantheon. So how Yoruba a poet is he as we can say of Yoruba being the essence of Wole Soyinka and to a large extent of Osofisan? These two are more dramatists than poets, but still there is overwhelming presence of Yoruba divinity in their works. Osundare avoids the company of gods in his poetry.

But I am not saying Osundare is not a Yoruba writer. His choices are informed by ideological and political considerations, as he wants to be seen as ranging on the side of the people—as down-to-earth. Here and there are elements of Yoruba folklore, but not the myths that form the backcloth of Soyinka's and Osofisan's writings. In *The Eye of the Earth*, for instance, Osundare talks of "the one that shaves his head with the hoe." In *Moonsongs*, he no doubt employs the image of the moon of his youth as revealed in Yoruba mythology: "The moon pounds her yam / in the apron of the night" (*Moonsongs*, 1988: 29). There appears to be a growing use of materials from Yoruba folklore but not from the pantheon. *Waiting Laughters*'s strength comes from the use of Yoruba axioms, proverbs, and myths:

> I have not told a bulbous tale
> in the presence of asopa
>
> I have not shouted "Nine!"
> In the backyard of the one with a missing finger (p. 70).

"Asopa" is one with swollen scrotum.

And yet Osundare models some of his poems on oriki rhythms as "Earth," in *The Eye of the Earth*, quoted in full earlier and other poems in *Moonsongs*. His musicality is a blending of alliterative sounds and Yoruba rhythmic patterns— ijala and oriki.

Osundare's choice of certain figures of speech and sound is also very significant on the nature of his poetic style. The copious use of metaphors, personifications, epithets, and alliterations give a certain robust sing-song identity to his poetry. In *Moonsongs*, "The moon this night is an infinity of smiles" (p. 43). Furthermore, he addresses the moon:

> Oh moon, matron, master, eternal maiden
> The bounce of your bosm
> The miracle of your cheeks
> Your smile which ripens the forests
> Your frown which wrinkles the dusk
> The youth of your age
> The age of your youth. . . (Selected Poems, 55).

Metaphors and personifications make poetry not only exude sensuous delight but also concreteness. Here, Osundare sidetracks the weaker similes for stronger metaphors and personifications that give vitality to the poet's style.

Osundare has many poetic choices regarding style. In "Forest Echoes,"

> Palm-bound, scalpel-toothed,
> the squirrel pierces the tasty iris
> of stubborn nuts;
> adzeman of the forest,

> those who marvel the canine fire
> in your mouth,
> let them seek refuge in the fluffy grace
> of your restless tail (Eye of the Earth, 8).

In many other poems, epithets appear in alliterative clusters, such as "A bevy of birds" and "A barrack of beasts." Here, Osundare appears to have been influenced by the popular trio of J. P. Clark-Bekederemo, Christopher Okigbo, and Wole Soyinka, whose poetry relished metaphors, epithets, assonances, alliterations, and hyphenated words.

One of the controversial aspects of the "new African poetry" is the accusation that it pays too much attention to content at the expense of form. The critic, Ken Goodwin, has written about this particular aspect. With too many African writers, the didactic side seems to have been more emphasized at the expense of the craft. While it favors meaning, the African oral tradition does not neglect craft. This modern African literature of engagement was carried to its limits in the 1970s and 1980s during the Marxist phase. At the same time, there was a writer, like the francophone Labou Tansi who reacted in the opposite direction. For Tansi, according to Jonathan Ngarte, "[T]he emphasis now had to be put not on writing only in order to say something but rather on writing as a mode of invention, as a way of writing oneself into being with words that are so many pieces of one's own flesh; for him there can be no other aesthetic or thematic approach in a world in which mankind seems determined to kill life" (p. 132). Thus, there appears to be a binary attitude, as if African literature has to emphasize either themes or aesthetics.

It is here that Osundare stands out as bridging this unnecessary gap between "saying something" and "writing as a mode of invention." He says a lot in his work in a very artistic way. What could be more thematically engaging than "The Eyes of the Earth?" And yet the poem is aesthetically fulfilling. Osundare's choice, therefore, is to synthesize aspects of themes and form.

So far in his poetic career, Niyi Osundare has made many poetic choices that have given a certain character and identity to his poetry. There is no doubt that his being a Yoruba, the socio-political atmosphere of his years of adulthood, and his training in the English department at the University of Ibadan influenced him to take models and reject some artistic directions. His simple, people-oriented poetry, his musicality, his rejection of Yoruba pantheon for a Marxist materialist stance, his conscious attention to craft, and his lack of very personal, confessional poetry are results of his poetic choices. These choices have not just assigned him an identity, but these choices have also given poetic strength to his poetic opus.

REFERENCES

Clark-Bekederemo, John Pepper. *A Reed in the Tide*. London: Longman, 1965.
————. *Casualties*. London: Longman, 1970.
Ngate, Jonathan. *Francophone African Fiction: Reading a Literary Tradition*. Trenton, NJ: Africa World Press, 1988.
Okigbo, Christopher. *Labyrinths*. London: Heinemann, 1971.
Ojaide, Tanure. *Poetic Imagination in Black Africa: Essays on African Poetry*. Durham, NC: Carolina Academic Press, 1996.
Osofisan, Femi. *The Oriki of a Grasshopper and Other Plays*. Washington, DC: Howard UP, 1995.
Osundare, Niyi. *Songs of the Marketplace*. Ibadan: New Horn, 1983.
————. *Village Voices*. Ibadan: Evans, 1984.
————. *The Eye of the Earth*. Ibadan: Heinemann, 1986.
————. *Moonsongs*. Ibadan: Spectrum, 1988.
————. *Waiting Laughters*. Lagos: Malthouse, 1990.
————. *Selected Poems*. Oxford: Heinemann, 1992.
————. *Midlife*. Ibadan: Heinemann, 1993.
Soyinka, Wole. *Idanre and other Poems*. London: Methuen, 1967.

NIYI OSUNDARE AND THE POETIC STATEMENT OF A GENERATION

Ezenwa-Ohaeto

The role of the poet in any developing society is not enviable because he often functions against the antagonistic attitudes generated by the indifference of those in positions of authority. Moreover, the spectacular fortunes of that ruling class impede the effects of the poet's literary contributions due to the conscious encouragement of the desire in the generality of the people to appreciate wealth and material possessions rather than literary talents and literature. Thus, the poet functioning in the midst of such unfavorable circumstances is faced with the twin problem of convincing the readers that poetry ought to be read and also that poetry should be relevant. Recognition of this problem was the reason for the decision of a generation of Nigerian poets to withdraw poetry from a stifling straitjacket of obscure diction and re-present it in a form that has attracted justifiable popular reactions.

The members of this generation of Nigerian poets were born between 1942 and 1952 and many of them came into literary prominence in the late 1970s and early 1980s in Nigeria and other parts of Africa. Among these poets from Nigeria we can comfortably include Obiora Udechukwu, Tanure Ojaide, Odia Ofeimun, Chinweizu, Onwuchekwa Jemie, Catherine Acholonu, Ifi Amadiume, Niyi Osundare, Chimalum Nwankwo and Ossie Enekwe. This is by no means a comprehensive list but these poets mentioned are certainly among the most interesting in their practice of craft of poetry. However, it must be pointed out that in as much as these poets could be seen as a generation in terms of perceiving their accomplishments as a distinct feature, their works also possess common characteristics with members of my generation of poets born between 1958 and 1968. Nevertheless, among this generation of poets Niyi Osundare is a poet whose work indicate, illustrate and project the accomplishments of contemporary Nigerian poetry in English.

The prolific nature of Niyi Osundare could be assessed from the fact that he is the author of the collections of poetry: *Songs of the Marketplace, Village Voices, The Eye of the Earth, Songs of the Season, A Nib in the Pond, Moon Songs, Waiting Laughters, Selected Poetry, Midlife, Horses of Memory,A Word is an Egg* as well as a collection of poetry for children. These collections illustrate the development of Osundare as a poet as well as portraying how he has managed to pull himself up by the straps of his poetic boots. His first collection of poems was produced as cyclostyled copies and some of those who read them were quick to spot the talent there. One of those impressed readers was Gerald Moore who selected some of the poems for a new edition of his *Modern Poetry of Africa* which he edited with Ulli Beier. The second work was produced after the appearance of *Songs of the Marketplace* and *Village Voices* as *A Nib in the Pond* which was again produced as cyclostyled copies through the efforts of Biodun Jeyifo and his group at the University of Ife in Nigeria. These tentative literary steps taken by Osundare have now become giant strides through his creative diligence and perseverance.

In a way the significant contributions of Niyi Osundare to the development of contemporary African Poetry could be seen from the time that *Songs of the Marketplace* and *Village Voices* appeared on the literary scene in Nigeria. The two collections indicate both his poetic manifesto and his poetic attitude. In a much-quoted poem he says:

> Poetry is
> No oracle's kernel
> For a sloe philosopher's stone
> Poetry
> is
> man
> meaning
> to
> man (*Songs*, 4).

The indication in that extract is that poetry is not abstract but a form of creativity which aids man in the understanding of his fellow man. In effect what Osundare set out to exhibit is that poetry could be relevant, interesting and sufficiently capable of presenting several layers of meaning to the reader. This was a primary focus of the poetry of his generation as well as a much welcome development in African poetry.

The relevance of Osundare's poetry is manifested clearly in *Songs* and *Village Voices* through his conscious attempts to weave the poems with a subject matter that captures the aspirations and human concerns of the ordinary people in the society. In the poem "Excursions", he writes:

> We see village boys' Kwashiorkor bellies
> Hairless heads impaled on pin necks
> And ribs baring the benevolence
> Of the body politic *(Songs, 7)*.

The swollen "bellies" of the boys through the protein deficiency disease known as kwashiorkor became prominent during the Nigerian civil war and its appearance in a supposedly peace time portrays that the society is in difficulties since all the citizens cannot be guaranteed basic food. This poem also indicates anger for social injustice through a subsumed comparison between the deprived boys and the affluent members of the society. In effect Osundare uses these images of poverty induced by injustice to comment on the need for social, political and economic reconstruction of the society. The pictorial technique adopted in this poem is enhanced by the use of a persona who travels through the society observing those signs of dehumanization by poverty; and it is both a symbolic and physical travel.

In addition the poet attributes some of these features of injustice to a lack of cultural knowledge, intellectual ignorance, political ineptitude and confused orientation. This statement encapsulates a major aspect of the poetic focus of the generation of poets that flourished with Niyi Osundare. However, Osundare gives that focus prominence through the utilization of a blend of ironic humor and effective aphorisms. In the poem entitled "Ignorance", this blend is captured thus:

> The cow is dying
> For a trip to London
> Let it go
> It will come back
> as corned beef *(Songs, 33)*.

The image of the cow desiring for what will destroy it codifies a society uncon-sciously pursuing its own economic and social destruction. The humor blend-ed in that image of imported canned beef which the cow will unwittingly vol-unteer itself for its production succinctly suggests a neo-colonial implication where a confused society ignorantly collaborates in its own exploitation.

All the same the poet does not only perceive the instances of social abnor-malities as ironic as he describes a character known as Madaru who is a mate-rialization of this warpedness in the society. Madaru is presented as a manifes-tation of that abnormality in political terms:

> Madaru buys a crown
> and becomes King
> And you ask:
> how could sheep all agree
> to give their crown to a wolf? (*Songs*, 34).

It is significant that Madaru buys this crown and the implication of that act is that materialism has obfuscated the ability of a large number of people to dis-cern ennobling qualities in the aspiring leaders. That inability obviously accounts for the lack of opposition to such leaders. Osundare in that instance, like members of his generation of poets, is functioning as a poet who does not shirk the responsibilities of making persuasive to the reader all those images that symbolize degeneration in the socio-political culture. This is clearly social poetry but then Osundare proceeds beyond the stage of mere chronicles of real-ity. Elizabeth Drew feels that "Social poetry has a deliberate moral purpose. In it the poet speaks directly to his society and holds up its short-comings for gen-eral recognition" (Drew, 1959: 149). The illumination of these short-comings is a part of the statement of this generation of poets who are writing in a devel-oping society and Osundare undoubtedly conceives himself as performing this essential task.

In the collection of poems *Village Voices* this same concern with social injus-tice is extended into other directions. This time it is the inability to channel the abundant wealth of natural resources usefully. In a satiric poem "The eunuch's Child", the poet observes:

> Oh! If only yam would grow in Europe
> We would buy a million barns
> With our billions
> And import white princesses
> To pound for our Kings. (*Village Voices*, 53–54).

The ridicule in the above extract is obviously directed at the people's psyche which has been obfuscated by the quest for materialism. Thus Osundare condemns the confusion of values that leads to the importation of what the country can comfortably produce because the political leaders lack economic vision. The consequence is that a majority of the people suffers from poverty.

In many of the poems in *Village Voices* the thematic concerns of Osundare signify an engagement between his utopian vision and the problems of a hostile environment. In addition he also succeeds in achieving what Donatus Nwaga interestingly characterizes as the engineering of a "reaction appropriate to the pattern set by the event. This is beyond the mere act of metaphorization- a structure is set up parallel to that which the wise can interpret" (Nwoga, 1979: 51). This technique enables Osundare to use sundry characters like prisoners and farmers to comment on the reality that he perceives in his society. The presentation of these characters, even in their ordinary acts like the farmers who sees the skyscraper built with the profits from the cocoa farming activity in which he participates but which has not been particularly beneficial to him, engineers the reaction that an injustice has been perpetrated. In effect the poet uses abundant suggestions to direct the reader's attention towards the object of his censure and criticism.

Nevertheless, Osundare and his generation of poets are not permanently disillusioned because they see themselves as functioning as inspirers through the arousal of appropriate positive ideas in the readers. A statement that codifies this optimism is discernible in the following extract:

> Put my words in your left hand
> So they do not land in the stomach
> With the unwilling morsel
> Then plant them like a yam seedling
> Which multiplies the original breed (*Village Voices*, 71).

The implied injunction here is that the words of the poet must not be ignored because they are words that have been carefully selected and used to present useful ideas. These words are also capable of multiplying like yam seedlings, which means that these is a positive chain reaction because one beneficial idea leads to another

Furthermore, Osundare interestingly illustrates both the possibilities and practice of using natural phenomena in fashioning poetry relevant to the concerns of his society and generation. In the collection *The Eye of the Earth*, the forest, rocks and rain are employed as metaphors for the exploration of life and the activities associated with farming. It is this commitment to the earth and its relationship to the farmer-peasant that has singled out Osundare as a poet of nature and a poet devoted to the survival of the earth as well as the attendant environmental issues. In several of the poems in this collection we find a celebration of the earth and the poem "Forest Echoes" is illustrative of this feature especially where the persona describes the forest as containing "a thousand wonders" which charms the nose with a "universe of budding herbs and ripening roots". This ode to the bounteous earth suggests an environment that provides for all the living inhabitants:

> This is Oke Ubo Abusoro
> the distant forest which shames the lazy leg,
> where the oro tree hawks lofty fruit
> for the blue children of a hungry sky
> where pampered yams break heaps bounds
> and the plantain leans earthwards
> with the joy of heavy harvest (p.5).

The "blue children of a hungry sky" are the birds that are fed in addition to the human beings from the "heavy harvest" of the fertile Oke Ubo Abusoro. In effect many of the poems in *The Eye of the Earth* emphasize this idea of an earth that is fertile as well as an earth that should not be destroyed by disasters unwittingly induced by man or unfortunate occurrences arising from even some aspects of the natural phenomena. In the poem "Let Earth's Pain Be Soothed", the poet's concern for survival of the earth makes him yearn for the rejuvenation of rain fall on the scorched earth:

> Our earth has never lingered so dry
> in the season of falling showers
> Clouds journey over trees and over hills
> miserly with their liquid treasure (p. 27).

This lack of rain means that the earth could be scorched and that the farmers cultivating parts of it could experience poor harvests that will ultimately result in famine. The poet/persona, therefore, cautions against the degeneration of the earth which can even be perceived as a metaphor for all kinds of ecological devastations. This caution against the tendency to devastate the environment and nature arises from the poet's altruistic love of the earth because he informs us autobiographically:

Farmer-born peasant-bred
I have lived on the aroma
of fresh-felled forests (p. 43).

It is this appreciation and value of the earth that informs the injunction and hope in the poem entitled "Our Earth Will Not Die":

Our earth will see again
Eyes washed by a new rain
The westering sun will rise again
Resplendent like a new coin
The wind, unwound, will play its tune
Trees twittering, grasses dancing
Hillsides will rock wit blooming harvests (p. 51).

This last poem in this collection aptly reinforces the poetic commitment of Niyi Osundare as he makes a generational statement concerning a change of attitude to the environment and its inhabitants

The same concern for the environment and nature is discernible in the collection of poems entitled *Moonsongs*. The moon here also functions as a metaphor like the earth. However, Osundare uses it in two ways: as an indication that technology has almost overshadowed such natural phenomena as the moon and as a metaphor for creative inspiration. It is through this twin objective that Osundare widens his poetic statement that encompasses the vision of his generation of poets. The moon as a metaphor functions as an object of illumination as well as an object encapsulating the right kind of vision desired by the poet for he writes:

Spread the sky like a generous mat
Tell dozing rivers to stir their tongues
Unhinge the ills
Unwind the winds
The moon and I will sing tonight

Oh moon, matron, master, eternal maiden
The bounce of your busom
The miracle of your cheeks
You smile which ripens the forests
Your frown which wrinkles the dusk (*Selected Poems*, 54).

The characterization of the moon as varied and capable of playing several roles and also as capable of exhibiting multiple appearances stress the poet's vision of it as ennobling, soothing, and attractively beneficial. This metahporization and personification of the moon in *Moonsongs* and the earth in *The Eye of the Earth* clearly illustrate the fact that nature should not be mussed. In addition the nuanced image of the moon in these poems reminds the reader of the Igbo aphorism popularized by Chinua Achebe, which says that the world is a mask dancing (See Ezenwa-Ohaeto, *Chinua Achebe: A Biography* p. 269), and Osundare uses that aphorism to illustrate that the "moon is a mask dancing" (p.58). The poet obviously means that the mask of the moon or rather the splendor of the shining moon covers with its rays the positive and negative activities in the society; it is also a metaphor for different appearances and that there is something substantial beneath the veneer of the silvery rays of the moon. This interpretation also accounts for the poet's borrow of the phrase popularized by the African American writer Maya Angelou who declares that she knows "why does the caged bird sing?". Osundare writes:

> I know why the caged bird sings
> When the moon is a knot of strings.

This knowledge is derived from the unpleasant experience which the poet describes thus:

> A kwi-ed boot traps a star
> in a regimented shimmer
> the sky bird flips and flaps
> as a cagey night now turns
> a galaxy of sweating feathers (p. 67).

The poet is saying that the caged bird sings because the "moon is a knot of strings," which implies that there are hidden acts (obviously strings of oppression since knots are tied to secure or to restrict) and these acts are generated by the "kiwi-ed boot" – a symbol of the military that is, perhaps, dictatorial and brutal. The moon also marks the passage of time for as the night turns into dawn it disappears as its power to shine diminishes. Tn the poem "Shadows of Time", this idea of the passage of time is interwoven with the idea of a perambulating moon in a succinct manner:

> I heard moonsteps in the corridors of seasons
> The sky is aflame with dusts of hurrying dials (p. 79).

The poet personifies this passage of the moon and the passage of "Time" to illustrate the passage of humanity; in terms of the fears, the hopes and the aspirations of the people. The poet, therefor, encapsulates the vision of his generation of poets through the use of the moon and the earth as symbols and metaphors.

In *Songs of the Season*, Osundare indicates another basic concern of his generation of poets who insist on accessible and relevant poetry. This trend in creating accessible and relevant poetry can also be perceived in the poetry works of Chinweizu, Obiora Udechukwu and Tanure Ojaide. Interestingly this accessibility does not affect the craft of the poems because Osundare is conscious of this danger even as he deliberately takes his poetry to the public sphere through the publication of the poems in a weekly poetry column in the Nigerian *Sunday Tribune* newspaper in the eighties. The poems where running commentaries on events in his society at that time but he made the works interesting through his lyrical and metaphorical control. In the poem "Song of a Nigerian Driver" for instance he writes: "the car in your hand is an aeroplane/which only flies by prod and push" (p.25), while in the poem "May Day Song" he pays tribute to the worker thus:

> I salute the hands
>> which make and mould
> the hand
>> which think and act
> I salute the hands
>> which vow
>> that those who sow
>> must also reap (p. 59).

This poem not only portrays a tinge of that lyricism in Osundare's poetry but also the relevance of his works because it exhibits his poetic concern for the elimination of injustice. It is, therefore, not suprising that this poet equally makes efforts to illustrate that injustice through a depiction of the language that is often used by many of the oppressed people in his society. In the poem entitled "Buka Banter," Osundare uses pidgin to emphasize some of the unpleasant aspects of poverty and financial deprivation in his society. In the Buka (portrayed in his poem), which is a cheap eating place, several people are indicating the type of food they can afford to buy and the question, "wetin you go chop" – what do you want to eat? – elicits the answers: "three wraps of semovita / with obedient okro soup", "one thick saki (tripe)" and "one square yard of ponmon (cow skin eated as meat)". But when the waiter asks about normal tasty meat the people respond "my pocket don loos teeth" (p. 47). This is a pidgin expression that literally means that "the pocket has lost its teeth" and it suggest the fact that the pocket is empty of money. In another poem entitled "For Fela Anikulakpo-Kuti", there is a blend of pidgin and formal English as Osundare uses a popular song by the Late Afro-Beat musician Fela which says: "no agreement today / no agreement tomarrow / Make my broda hungry /.. / Ino go gree" (p.94), to reinforce the criticism that the poverty of the people is as a result of social injustice.

These pidgin expressions clearly illustrate the willingness of Osundare to widen his poetic canvas and it is this willingness that distinguishes his generation of poets. In the collection of poems *Waiting Laughters* the horizon of the poems widens to include the criticism of social and political injustices in other parts of the world, especially the injustice perpetrated by tyrants and oppressive leaders who are bound to be ultimately punished, as the poet suggests through the phrase that the tyrant waits "for his noose," (p.14); and the type of situation their tyrants have created which makes him lament:

A king there is
in this purple epoch of my unhappy land;
his first name is hunger
his proud father is Death
which guards the bones at every door (p. 45).

The personification of hunger as the father of death and also the King shows the effects of unjust social structures; a fact that arouses the strong resentment of Osundare and his generation of poets. Thus Osundare in another poem requests for a grant of "the fortitude of the lamb which lames the lion- / without inheriting its claws" (p.95).That fortitude is part of the feelings that the poet hopes that his poetry will arouse in the reader, the cultivation of inner strength and the ability to resist oppression and its on of the major objectives of many Nigerian poets whose works are relevant to their society. The collection *Midlife* expands this objective in the use of poetry to arouse appropriate feelings through the use of the poems to interrogate both personal and public issues. This blend of the private and the universal has been described as the exhibiting the use of experience as a pattern or myth and tendency by several "West African Poets" to "design and arrange their collections to reflect the patterns of their lives. They make poetry out of their lives and autobiography out of their poems" (Knipp:41). The observation applies to Osundare's *Midlife* to an extent for he informs Stephen Arnold that the collection of poems was inspired by a desire to mark the milestone of attaining the age of forty in 1987: "so the poetry came as a great source of inspiration. One great advantage is that you can hide behind it and make yourself inconspicuous in many areas" (Arnold: 15). All the same what Osundare succeeds in achieving is to extend this autobiographical approach to encompass both his vision of his society and the concept of appropriate leadership for his society. Thus when the poet describes his persona he is also describing his society:

> Child of the rock, child of the river
> Child of the river which plies
> The world with hidden legs (p. 17).

The image of the hidden legs of the river suggests an appendage that enables the river in its flow to traverse several other societies. The River Niger for instance, which flows in the Atlantic Ocean through the Niger Delta in Nigeria started its journey from the Futa Jallon Mountians in Guinea. In effect the river is linked to many societies and it equally generates different feelings in those societies, which means that the persona who sees himself as a child of this river is saying that he is a child of even those other societies associated with the river. This kind of identification also implies an identification with the hopes and fears of the people involved. Furthermore the persona in the poem perceives himself as part of the natural fauna for he insists:

> I am the speck of dust in the evening air
> bubbling butterfly in the estate of the flower,
> kite in a mellow sky,
> foe of the storm, friend of the wind (p. 34).

Although this identification emphasizes the selfhood of the poet and his private concerns it is also extended to reinforce the social concerns in the society. This observation is clearly responsible for the following statement:

> I long for open spaces
> from edicts which thicken like medieval jungles
> and streets which stumble their days
> on night of adamantine orders (p. 85).

The "edicts" and "adamantine orders" connote the political tergiversations that obstruct the development of the society. This criticism that is suggested here is directed at the political leadership and the implication is that it should construct a vision that will enable the society develop and progress economically. The question which the persona asks: "But tell me Africa; / Tell me more about this eternal childhood" (p.93), signifies this criticism and illustrates the desire of the poet for a society that is just in its distribution of social and material resources. It is not surprising that a poet who has extended his autobiography as a creative strategy beyond the limits of the works of his predecessors like Christopher Okigbo should lead Arnold to conclude that "To read Osundare is to regain prelapsian respect for history. For him, the individual is necessary aspect of the body politic, and this is what I think accounts for his populate" (Arnold, 1996 :165).

The poetry of Niyi Osundare certainly lends itself to "plurisignbation" and this is acceptable because he is creatively adaptable and he also possesses a poetic purpose that is human oriented. In an earlier study it has been stressed that he "clearly demonstrates the wide range of available patterns of orality that has rejuvenated contemporary Nigerian poetry" (Ezenwa-Ohaeto, 1997: 168). However, it is his creative capability and the innovative presentation of his works that accounts for the success of his poetry. He is clearly a writer whose works exhibit not only his achievements but also the collective poetic highpoints of his generation of poets. The interesting use of language, the employment of appropriate poetic devices, the harnessing of traditional and cosmopolitan ideas and features and relevant thematic preoccupations combine to make his poetry the encapsulation of a succint statement by a generation of Nigerian Poets.

REFERENCES

Arnold Stephen H. "A Peopled Persona: Autobiography, Post-Modernism and ⸱he Poetry of Niyi Osundare." Eds. Janos Riesz and Ulla Shild. *Genres Autobiographinques en Afrique / Autobiographical Genres in Africa*. Berlin: Dietrich Verlag, 1996: 141–163.

Drew, Elizabeth. *Poetry: A Modern Guide to its Understanding and Enjoyment*. New York: Dell Publishing Company, 1959.

Ezenwa-Ohaeto. *Chinua Achebe: A Biography*. Oxford: James Currey and Indiana University Press, 1997; Ibadan: Heinemann Nig. 1999.

———. "Patterns of Orality: Niyi Osundare." *Contemporary Nigerian Poetry and the Poetics of Orality*. Bayreuth, Germany: University of Bayreuth African Studies, 1998.

Knipp, Thomas. "Poetry as Autobiography: Society and Self in Three Modern West African Poets." Eds. Eileen Julien *et al*. *African Literatures in it's Social and Political Dimensions*. Washington, D.C.: Three Continents Press, 1986. 41–50.

Nwoga, D.I. "Modern African Poetry: The Domestication of a Tradition."

African Literature Today: No 10 Retrospect and Prospect. London: Heinemann, 1979.

Osundare, Niyi. *A Nib in the Pond*. Ife Monograph Series, 1986.

———. *Songs of the Marketplace*. Ibandan: New Horn Press, 1983.

———. *Village Voices*. Ibadan: Evans Brothers, 1984.

———. *The Eye of the Earth*. Ibandan: Heinemann, 1986.

———. *Moonsongs*. Ibadan: Spectrum Books, 1988.

———. *Songs of the Season*. Ibadan: Heinemann, 1990.

———. *Waiting Laughters*. Lagos: Malthouse Press, 1990.

———. *Selected Poems*. London: Heinemann, 1992.

———. *Midlife*. Ibandan: Heinemann, 1993.

———. *Horses of Memory*. Ibadan: Heinemann, 1998.

EXPLORATIONS IN ANIMIST MATERIALISM AND A READING OF THE POETRY OF NIYI OSUNDARE

Harry Garuba

In front of the buildings which serve as headquarters of the National Electric Power Authority of Nigeria is a larger-than-life statute of Sango, the Yoruba god of Lightning, clad in his traditional outfit, presiding, as it were, over the offices of the major power generation and distribution corporation of the country. Sango, a sixteenth-century ruler of Oyo, is an anthropomorphic deity who in his lifetime was reputed to have had the ability to "call down" lightning to destroy his enemies and burn their houses and homesteads. The Sango myth, carefully preserved and nurtured by his worshipers and devotees, is so well known in Yorubaland that till this day Sango priests are still believed to possess the power of obtaining retribution through the agency of lightning. *Oba Koso*, an excellent traditional operatic drama which focuses on the life of Sango, was hugely popular with audiences both in Nigeria and abroad in the nineteen sixties and seventies. The acclaim which greeted the production of the play at that time may partly have been due to the theatrical skills of Duro Ladipo whose dramatic evocation of this historical/mythical figure has since become one of the great moments of Nigerian theatre and performance. However, in those heady days of post-independence cultural nationalism, the Sango myth may also have pro-

vided an avenue through which the new elite could reconnect with its historical and cultural heritage. Sango was not only a figure from the historical past,
he was more importantly a symbol of the meeting point between tradition and
modernity; a mythological figure whose incipient "scientific" consciousness was
demonstrated in his ability to harness the electrical charges of lightning to serve
his own purposes, whatever they may have been.

   Apart from this attribute, Sango's life was not exactly a tale of nobility and
selflessness. On the contrary, he was the usual tyrant of history and mythology
whose pettiness leads him to overplay his hand in the end. Employing characteristic divide-and-rule tactics, he sets two of his powerful warriors against each
other in the hope that they will be so weakened by war that neither of them will
be able to pose a threat to his power. In the ensuing battle, Gbonka, one of the
warriors, defeats Timi, the other, but spares him. Not satisfied with this outcome, Sango contrives another scheme that leads to another battle, which
Gbonka once again wins. This time, however, Gbonka recognises Sango's
duplicity and invades Oyo. Deserted by his supporters, Sango suffers defeat,
withdraws from the capital and hangs himself in humiliation. His followers
gang together and deify him: the king did not hang (*Oba koso*), they claim, he
simply metamorphosed into a god. For his present day devotees and followers,
the details of his life story are subordinated to the one major event of his power
to "call down" lightning, a power supposedly bequeathed to his priests. But to
others for whom Sango possesses only a symbolic significance, these details
become irrelevant when set beside the primary event of his *discovery* of electricity, a "discovery" extrapolated from the myths of his dexterity in the manipulation of lightning. It is this association with electricity that has made Sango
the patron god of electricians and the deity who presides over Nigeria's power
corporation.

   I have chosen to begin with this account of the life of Sango, its appropriation by a traditional elite, and its symbolic deployment by a modern elite, to
underscore a form of socio-cultural practice which has become quite pervasive
in contemporary Nigeria, if not in all of Africa. Commenting on the Sango phenomenon in the essay "From A Common Back Cloth", Wole Soyinka says: "The
deistic approach of the Yoruba is to absorb every new experience, departmen-
talize it and carry on with life. Thus Sango (Dispenser of Lightning) now chair-
mans the Electricity Corporation, Ogun (God of Iron) is the primal motor-
mechanic" (p. 9). And later in a more affirmative philosophical mood in *Myth,
Literature and the African World*, Soyinka elaborates upon the sources of this
"deistic approach":

European scholars have always betrayed a tendency to accept the myth, the lore, the social techniques of imparting knowledge or of stabilising society as evidence of orthodox rigidity. Yet the opposite, an attitude of philosophical accommodation, is constantly demonstrated in the attributes accorded most African deities, attributes which deny the existence of impurities or "foreign" matter, in the god's digestive system. Experience which, until the event, lie outside the tribe's cognition are absorbed through the god's agency, are converted into yet another piece of social armoury in its struggle for existence, and enter into the lore of the tribe. This principle creates for society a non-doctrinaire mould of constant awareness, one which stays outside the monopolistic orbit of the priesthood, outside any claims to agnostic secrets by special cults. (pp. 53–54)

Soyinka claims that European scholars miss this point because "they bypass the code on which this world-view is based, the continuing evolution of tribal wisdom through an acceptance of the elastic nature of knowledge as its only reality, as signifying no more than reflections of the original coming-into-being of a manifestly complex reality"(p. 53). It is thus not only a question of "the deistic approach of the Yoruba" but also, and at a more profoundly significant level, "the code on which this world-view is based".

Social scientists who comment on the state and society in post-independence Africa have observed various aspects of this cultural practice of assimilating the various instruments and dimensions of modernity, such as science and technology, the modern state and its political machinery, into the matrix of traditional ritual and culture. This practice which has been broadly referred to as the "re-traditionalisation of Africa" can be observed in various aspects of life on the continent from the introduction of praise singers into the protocols for the inauguration of Presidents Mandela and Mbeki in South Africa to the induction of "ancestor worship" into some African churches.[1] These fairly innocuous examples are merely indices of a more widespread cultural condition that has ramifications in politics, economics and society. Cyprian Fisiy and Peter Gescheiere (1996: 194), for instance, observe in relation to Cameroun, "the impressive capacity of local discourses on witchcraft and sorcery for incorporating the images and objects of the modern world." They document not only the "ostentatious use of books on 'Eastern Magic' and Christian symbols" but also the fact that the *nganga* or 'witchdoctors' now "follow bureaucratic procedures"(p. 194) and have even penetrated the legal judicial system. Karin Barber (1991), Margaret Drewal (1992), Sekoni Ropo (1997), and Ato Quayson (1999: 84–102), among others, have examined the utilisation of traditional cultural forms such as the Yoruba *oriki,* ritual performances and other folktale motifs in the context of modern social and political life. As Andrew Apter (1992) states the case, "the genius of paganism" lies at heart in its logic which "confronts and appropriates the outside world to control it from within its kingdoms and cults" (p. 166).

In "The African Crisis: Context and Interpretation", Patrick Chabal provides an explanation of his use of the expression "the 're-traditionalisation' of Africa" and comments on its deployment as an explanatory tool in accounts and analyses of African society and politics.

I refer here to the accounts given recently of the ways in which Africans appear to outside observers to have 'gone back' to some of their 'age-old traditions' and the consequences of such 'regression' for African politics. Although much nonsense has been published in the media about Africa's 'backward' civilisation, it will be unwise to dismiss all the accounts of what I call 're-traditionalisation' simply because of these crass and gross simplifications. *There is undoubtedly something going on in Africa but, here again, we (outsiders) are uncertain what it is and, especially, what it means.* (p. 32, italics added)

Chabal's recognition of "something going on in Africa" which is yet to be adequately explained may be said to be the primary motivation for this paper which seeks to provide a model for accounting for this virtually all pervasive phenomenon of modern African society. In this paper, I make the point that the conventional accounts provided for this 're-emergence' of traditional cultural beliefs and practices in Africa, valid as they may be, do not go deep enough. I argue that the "colonisation", so to speak, of technology and the instruments and ideologies of the modern world by traditional culture is not wholly the result of a conscious nationalistic appropriation nor is entirely a consequence of the dialectic of "residuality" and "emergence" (in the manner in which Raymond Williams discusses it in *Marxism and Literature*), but a manifestation of an Animist Unconscious which operates through a process which involves what I chose to describe as a continual re-enchantment of the world.

In the rest of this paper therefore I will concentrate first on these operations of the Animist Unconscious within Nigerian, specifically, Yoruba culture and society. Thereafter, I will explore the literary and artistic strategies of representation that have arisen from this and finally locate Niyi Osundare's poetry within the context of this cultural practice. The over riding objective is to provide a theoretical and analytical framework for reading the scripts which our societies – and our artists – enact and to locate these texts within the socio-cultural arena from which they are generated.

II

It is tempting to proceed without providing – for the purpose of this essay – working definitions of the terms I have thus far so liberally employed. But the imprecision of the term 'animism' itself calls for caution and bids us pause, if only for a moment, to examine it and the concepts which I have tried to construct around it. I am aware of the amount of conceptual baggage which these terms carry. However, I have chosen to describe the practice of continually "re-enchanting" the world as a manifestation of the Animist Unconscious to move the argument away from the charge of essentialism which is likely to arise if this were seen as the natural, immutable, collective instinct of a people and to avoid the cultural binarisms which investigations of this sort often unwittingly impose. Indeed, the two terms – "Animist Materialism" and "Animist Unconscious" – have been deliberately deployed to facilitate easier accessibility by their echoes of Raymond Williams's concept of "cultural materialism" on the one hand and Frederic Jameson's "political unconscious" on the other. When Raymond Williams and Frederick Jameson coined these terms to theorize the philosophical orientations of their critical practice, they were depending upon a fairly well known discursive pedigree ranging from Karl Marx and other materialist philosophers to Freud, Jung, Lacan and other post-Freudian psychoanalytical thinkers. The expression "re-enchantment of the world" recalls Max Weber, who in his accounts of the changes in attitudes and practices occasioned by the increasingly secular rationalisation of the world brought about by modernity and the rise of capitalism, often resorted to Frederich Schiller's phrase the "disenchantment of the world". According to H.H. Gerth and C. Wright Mills, "[t]he principle of rationalization is the most general element in Weber's philosophy of history" and, for Max Weber, *"[t]he extent and the direction of 'rationalization' is thus measured negatively in terms of the degree to which magical elements of thought are displaced,* or positively by the extent to which ideas gain in systematic coherence and naturalistic consistency" (p. 51: italics added). By employing the expression "re-enchantment of the world" I wish to draw attention to the obverse of the process which Weber describes, a process whereby "magical elements of thought" are not displaced but, on the contrary, continually assimilate new developments in science, technology and the organisation of the world within a basically 'magical' world view. Rather than 'disenchantment' a persistent re-enchantment thus occurs and the rational and scientific are appropriated and transformed into the mystical and magical.

But, first, we should begin with animism. Unlike Christianity and Islam, say, which refer to particular religions, animism does not name any specific religion. Rather it is the umbrella designation for a mode of religious consciousness that is often as elastic as the user is willing to stretch it. *The HarperCollins Dictionary of Religion* defines animism as "an obsolete term employed to describe belief systems of traditional peoples that appear to hold that natural phenomena have spirits and souls"(p. 51). The tentativeness of the phrase "appear to hold" is worth noting here because it provides an opening to the general imprecision in the use of the term which was noted earlier. The dictionary then makes an attempt to trace the origins of the concept and adds a word of caution about its use. "Introduced in 1871 by the British anthropologist E.B. Tyler (1832–1917), it should be used with caution as a cross cultural term of comparison or as designating a stage in the evolution of religion"(p. 51). *The Imperial Dictionary of the English Language,* however, traces the origin of the concept further back in history, first to "[t]he hypothesis of Pythagoras and Plato of a force (*Anima mundi,* or a soul of the world) immaterial but inseparable from matter, and giving matter its form and movements." A second genealogy is said to be "[t]he system of medicine, propounded by Stahl, in which the rational soul is regarded as the principle of life…[h]ence it is inferred that the source of disease must be looked for in the soul, and medical treatment should be confined to an attempt to remove the obstacles which have arisen to the free and full working of the soul." And, finally, with the evolutionary logic so common to these definitions and which the former dictionary cautions against, animism is given a generalised definition and attributed to the infancy of humankind and of religion.

The general doctrine of souls and other spiritual beings. A philosophy explaining all phenomena in nature not due to obvious natural causes by attributing them to spiritual agency, seems to have been developed everywhere among the communities of mankind in the earliest stages of their existence. (p. 108)

A definition such as this cannot be of much analytical use. And this definition makes it possible to describe every kind of religious and pseudo-religious practice as animistic. Indeed, E. Royston Pike in *Encyclopaedia of Religion and Religions* argues that animism lies as the root of beliefs as diverse as the transmigration of souls, of "the whole structure of fetishism", of devil possession, witchcraft, sorcery and magic (p. 19).

Without meaning to take issue with the evolutionary paradigm deployed in these definitions, it needs to be stated that animist consciousness is not some kind of evolutionary tail that is shed as religious consciousness develops. Rather, it appears – to clumsily compound the metaphor – more like the digestive system which adapts itself to process previously unknown foods discovered with the progression of history. But, to return to the imprecision of definition already noted, it is perhaps more practical and useful to isolate and cobble together some elements of these various definitions to arrive at an operational description for the purposes of this paper. This becomes more imperative in the context of the fact that the term itself is considered obsolete in serious analysis of religions and religious practices (See *The HarperCollins Dictionary* 51). Deploying it within the terrain of culture and society then appears to me to be one way of rehabilitating it for purposes of social and cultural analysis. To do this, it is necessary first to identify the "logic" behind animism and then examine the working of this "logic" within the context of a particular culture and a specific society. Approached in this manner, the concept will lose its ability to name a religion but will retain its designation as originally a form of religious consciousness.

Perhaps the single, most important characteristic of animist thought is its almost total refusal to countenance unlocalized, un-embodied, un-physicalized gods and spirits. Animism is often simply seen as belief in objects such as stones or trees or rivers for this simple reason that animist gods and spirits are *located* and *embodied* in objects: the objects are the physical and material manifestations of the gods and spirits. Instead of erecting graven images to symbolize the spiritual being, animist thought spiritualizes the object world thereby giving the spirit a local habitation. Within the phenomenal world therefore, nature and its objects are endowed with a spiritual life both simultaneous and co-terminus with their natural properties. The objects thus acquire a social meaning within the culture far in excess of their natural properties and their use value. Rivers, for example, become not only natural sources of water but are prized for various other reasons. (In this regard, it may be stimulating to refer to the introductory essay in Arjun Appadurai's interesting book *The Social Life of Things* in which he describes how exchange value is created for goods through their "social life"). The animist urge to reification may have been religious in origin but the social and cultural meanings which become attached to the objects often break off from the purely religious and acquire an existence of their own as part of the general process of signification in the society. The "locking" of spirit within matter or the merger of the material and the metaphorical which animist logic entails then appears to be reproduced in the cultural practices of the society.

This may be said to be the first sense in which I use the term "Animist Materialism" in this essay. But to allay any fears of covert idealism, it may be better, as earlier mooted in the paper, to align the concept with Williams Raymond's cultural materialism. It is easier to understand animism as a "fugitive" materialist practice (*pace Williams*) when we see it as a socio-cultural phenomenon produced and reproduced by particular institutions, employing specific institutional procedures which carry the imprint of power and authority. To briefly refer to the Sango story again, there can be little doubt that here we have an "industry" controlled by a cult of priests involved in the "production and distribution of commodities" (the cause and prevention of lightning, the dictation of the means and prices of sacrifice, appeasement and atonement, etc.). Being so solidly situated within the social world of material practice controlled and regulated by powerful participants, Foucault's ideas about the production and circulation of discourse should help us better appreciate how material practices of this sort begin to frame other forms of signification in society. Even when discourses are based on mystification, they still possess real effects and, through the power of normalization, exert an influence on subjects and an impact upon culture. We need to bear in mind, in making the connections I draw here, that what distinguishes cultural materialism from other forms of materialism is its insistence on the materiality of cultural production because it is in the same vein that I argue the materiality of animist cultural production.

The Ogun cults in several parts of Nigeria which are more directly related to economic production may provide an easier-to-grasp example of this dimension of animist materialism. Ogun, "God of Iron and metallurgy, Explorer, Artisan, Hunter, God of war, Guardian of the Road, the Creative Essence", as Soyinka describes and eulogizes him in the epic poem "Idanre", is the god of iron smiths, motor mechanics, drivers, and all those whose trade has to do with iron. Artisans and workers of various hues including soldiers and traffic wardens often seek Ogun's protection in the form of consultations with the priests and sacrifices of appeasement to save them from the hazards of their jobs and/or to keep them in employment. It is common knowledge, at least in the south western part of Nigeria, that Ogun priests provide a form of traditional "insurance policy" to which many taxi drivers, policemen, soldiers, and even robbers subscribe. In *Black Critics and Kings,* Andrew Apter describes, by way of photographs, an occasion in metropolitan Lagos in which a hotel manager, whose old car had been stolen, sacrifices a dog to Ogun to protect his new Peugeot 504. This ritual appeasement is performed without self-conscious embarrassment in front of a Lagos hotel. The mystification and reification or worship of tools of work that the Ogun phenomenon exemplifies is neither unique nor confined to Nigeria. Studies by subaltern historians, anthropologists and sociologists have shown similar practices in India and Latin America, to name only two instances.

And these instances have led some to call for a rethinking of the linear Weberian narrative of modernity and its "counterpart", the orthodox Marxist secular narrative of history. In *Rethinking Working Class History*, Dipesh Chakrabarty calls for a historiography that recognizes "difference" and moves away from "the continuist conception of time in historicism to times which may well be out of joint with one another" (p. 20). The presence of the pre-modern within the sphere of modern capitalist modes of production is, however, not the focus of this paper. Rather, it is the manner in which an animistic mode of thought is embedded within the processes of material, economic activities and then reproduces itself within the sphere of culture and social life. Being so structurally embedded, it is no longer just an epiphenomenon or simply an effect but becomes a producer of effects and therefore acts as a driving force in the formation of collective subjectivity. And from this emerges what I have described as the Animist Unconscious.

The literature on subjectivity and the construction of the subject is quite vast and hardly needs any rehearsing except to note the process of subliminal identification and subjective conformation it entails.

III

Situating individual cultural practices within the continuum of animist production of meaning is a task beyond the scope of this essay. It is easier, however, to provide a broad picture of the horizons it opens up and the possibilities of signification it facilitates. Many of these have been identified in studies in literature, culture and society in Africa, India and Latin America, even when they have gone by different names and have not been directly related to the idea of an Animist Unconscious. Some accounts of the operations of this phenomenon in culture and social life in Nigeria may be found in Margaret Drewal (1992), Karin Barber (1991, 1997), Andrew Apter (1992) and so on. Ato Quayson (1997, 2000) has been concerned with demonstrating the manner in which the traditional resource base of the Yoruba has been put to service in literary texts and has recovered the lineaments of a Yoruba historiography in Samuel Johnson's *The History of the Yorubas*. In these excellent works of cultural analysis, representational strategies and narrative techniques which are demonstrably superstructural effects of an animist conception of reality and the world are often attributed to the indigenous resource base or more broadly to "orality". I will return to these strategies later in this paper but for the moment it is necessary to underscore the broad picture of possibilities.

A recurrent theme in accounts of the meeting between traditional ways of life and modernity is the clash of cultures and the agony of the wo/man caught in the throes of opposing conceptions of the world and of social life. In these narratives a binary structure is usually erected and within this world the agonistic struggle of the protagonist is drawn. The animistic trajectory of accommodation sketched here appears to belie the rigid binarisms of this narrative and undermine the agonistic relationship often drawn by an elite in search of sites of agency and identity. What may be much closer to the reality is that animist logic destabilizes the hierarchy of science and magic by reabsorbing historical time into the matrices of myth and magic. For the mass of ordinary people, animism cushions the movement into modernity by providing cultural certainties which create the "illusion" of a continuum rather than a chasm, thus giving an imposed subjective order to the chaos of history. Whether this is seen as evidence of a "conflicted modernity" or of difference within modernity or of the disruption of linear time, what is clear is that it subverts the authority of the West/Science by reinscribing the authority of magic within the interstices of the rational/secular/modern. Animist culture thus opens up a whole new world of poaching possibilities, pre-possessing the future, as it were, by laying claim to what in the present is yet to be invented. It is on account of this ability to pre-possess the future that continual re-enchantment becomes possible.

This also opens up a different time outside the usual linear, positivist time encoded with notions of progress and increasing secularization. Discussing the works of Gabriel Garcia Marquez and Salman Rushdie in her essay "The Politics of the Possible", Kumkum Sangari speaks of this conception of time as "poised in a liminal space, which, having broken out of the binary opposition between circular and linear, gives a third space and a different time the chance to emerge" (235). And as she cautions earlier in the same piece this "absence of a single linear time need not be read as the absence of a historical consciousness but rather as the operation of a different kind of historical consciousness" (p. 231). This different kind of historical consciousness, I would argue, provides the warrant for what she describes as "[t]he talismanic notion of technology as a type of 'magic' art" (p. 232) and for which I have adopted the reworked Schiller/Weber expression – the re-enchantment of the world.

Writers from Africa, Latin America, India constitute the most visible group which has taken advantage of the possibilities of narrative representation inherent in the animist conception of the world. There can be little or no doubt that the animist world view presents writers such as Ben Okri, Garcia Marquez and Salman Rushdie with the techniques and strategies to construct a narrative universe in which transpositions and transgressions of boundaries and identities predominate. Perhaps the simplest and most effective statement of the core idea of animist belief appears in Gabriel Garcia Marquez's *One Hundred Years of Solitude*. In the novel, the gypsy artist Melquiades arrives in Macondo with two "magnetized ingots" with which he performs "magical" feats.

He went from house to house dragging two metal ingots and everybody was amazed to see pot, pans, tongs and braziers tumble down from their places and beams creak from the desperation of nails and screws trying to emerge, and even objects that had been lost for a long time appeared from where they had been searched for most and went dragging along in turbulent confusion behind Melquiades' magical irons. *'Things have a life of their own,'* the gypsy proclaimed with a harsh accent. *'It's simply a matter of waking up their souls.'* (p. 9: italics added)

Melquiades' explanation meant to assuage the curiosity and amazement of the first Jose Arcado Buenda sums up the basic creed of animist belief and the magnets were simply "freeing the breath that makes metals live" (p. 36). This creed is made up of two basic tenets – one, that things possess a life of their own and two, that by waking up their souls the breath is freed and may migrate into other objects. According to Brenda Cooper, "African writers very often adhere to this animism, incorporate spirits, ancestors and talking animals, in stories, both adapted folktales and newly invented yarns, in order to express their passions, their aesthetics and their politics" (p. 40). The major strategy adopted by these writers is to ascribe a material aspect or existence to what are perhaps only really ideas or states of mind in the manner in which animism imputes a spiritual dimension to material objects. This, in a sense, is an ancient literary practice and to women, long familiar with the metaphorization of their bodies, this is really not as new as it may at first appear. However, when this approach to reality frames the entire narrative then it begs a new name. Of the various terms that have been used to name this representation practice, "magical realism" is definitely the most widely used. And this derives, of course, from the runaway success of the Latin American magical realist novelists.

In a paper already bristling with so many new concepts and terminologies, it seems patently unfair to introduce another at this stage. But having come this far in my explication of the "deep structure" of animism and the various *paroles* it generates, I cannot help but note that "magical realism" is too narrow a concept to describe the multiplicity of representational practices which animism authorizes. A few illustrative examples will do to show this inadequacy. Wole Soyinka's first novel *The Interpreters* begins with a sentence which for a while critics struggled to interpret: "Metal on concrete jars my drink lobes." Reading this sentence for the first time, I was immediately reminded of an expression that baffled me the first time when, as a child, I heard my grandmother use it. Speaking to a drunken relative, she had prayed that whoever planted the calabash that eternally demanded to be filled with wine in his stomach should never prosper. The idea of an imploring calabash in somebody's stomach intrigued me for a long while until I came to understand that this *materialization* of ideas, this habit of giving a concrete dimension to abstract ideas was a normal practice within the culture. My unproblematic access to Sagoe's "drink lobes" on first encounter, I believe, was facilitated by my familiarity with this linguistic, cultural practice. And I also believe that African critics who had difficulty with it would have solved the problem if they only tried translating the expression into their own languages. And several years later when I was confronted with the riddle of the tobacco tin of secrets lodged in Paul D's heart in Toni Morrison's *Beloved*, I knew I was within familiar territory. Soyinka's *The Interpreters* cannot really be called a magical realist text by the usual criteria with which texts are classified as such, yet here in it first line is a sentence in the representational mode of animism.

The point, I seek to make, is that the representational and linguistic practices underwritten by an animist conception of the world are much larger in scope and dimension than the concept of magical realism could possibly describe; they may appear as individual instances within certain texts as in the examples above and at other times may become the organizing principle of the entire narrative. It is in the latter instance that the term magical realism has often been employed. However, magical realism as developed by the Latin American writers and theorized by its foremost critics possesses an urban, cosmopolitan aspect (from the perspective of the writers) and an ionizing attitude which are not necessarily elements of the animistic narrative or its writers. It is in recognition of this limitation that I have elsewhere employed the term 'animist realism' to describe this predominant cultural practice of according a physical, material aspect to an abstract idea. Animist realism, I believe, is a much more encompassing concept of which magical realism may be said to be a subgenre with its own connecting characteristics and its formal difference. By repetition and difference, magical realism at once signals its dependence on the enabling code of animist discourse and its representational 'realism' and also marks its difference. To state it somewhat more precisely by repetition, animist materialism subspeciates into the representational technique of animist realism which may once again further subspeciate into the genre of magical realism.

Two further examples from Wole Soyinka's *The Road* and *A Dance of the Forest* may help to clarify the distinction I am trying to draw. In the play *The Road*, Soyinka presents a mute character, Murano, who is knocked down by a vehicle while engaged in the *agemo* ritual, a rite of transition between life and death among the Ijebu people of South Western Nigeria. The accident results in his being 'frozen' in time between life and death, and this liminal, indeterminate state is *written* physically on his body in the unequal length of his legs. Since metaphorically, he has one leg in this world and the other in the afterworld, this state of being is literally reproduced. This is an instance of a well worn, culturally recognizable representational strategy. But in the earlier play, *A Dance of the Forest,* the strategies of animist representation take over the entire play – the unborn, the ancestors, spirits and gods, all physically embodied, act out a drama of historical self-examination and communal soul searching. These plays are so far from employing the techniques of magical realism as outlined by the theorists that they point is hardly worth making; these are instances of animist aesthetics boldly inscribed. Their coupling of the realistic and the fantastic are clearly effects of animist materialism rather than magical realism. Their strategies of representation are what I describe with the broader, more appropriate term animist realism. To reiterate the point made earlier many of the literary techniques of the artists who have been labeled magical realist writers derive their warrant from traditional animist cultures.

IV

Niyi Osundare's poetry presents an interesting textual resource for the consolidation of these explorations of animist materialism. Locating his poetry within the continuum of animist signification presents an interesting challenge for several reasons, not least of all because Niyi Osundare is a Marxist socialist poet and animism is often regarded a reactionary, metaphysical mystification opposed to the spirit of historical materialism and scientific socialism. But before we proceed any further, it is imperative to recall Soyinka's description of animist spirituality as "a non-doctrinaire mould of constant awareness" which I hasten to add is imprinted with an irreducible sociality and historicity. Its spirit of constant awareness functions on a logic of inclusion rather than exclusion; its assimilative reach admits of no binarisms and therefore no contradictions in our usual sense of the words. As Chinua Achebe glosses it from the ethnophilosophy of the Igbo in *Morning Yet On Creation Day*

> Wherever Something stands, Something else will stand beside it. Nothing is absolute. *I am the truth, the way, and the life* would be called blasphemous or simply absurd, for it is well

known that a man may worship Ogwugwu to perfection and
yet be killed by Udo. (p. 161)

Thus a wo/man may worship Ogwugwu, Udo and as many other gods s/he
chooses, gods which may be as different as the passionate, wine-loving Ogun
and the serene, wine-abhorring Obatala of the Yoruba, without any sense of contradiction. This point needs no belaboring since the syncretism of African and
African-descended religions in the New World is so well documented. In similar vein, even though animism may conflict with the ideological vocabulary of
Marxism the expansiveness of animist thought elides those 'contradictions'.

Rather than see a contradiction between the secular vision of Marxism and
the metaphysical nature of the animist inheritance, Niyi Osundare's poetry provides an example of how both can be creatively deployed. In his poetry we
encounter again and again, the lyrical evocation of nature and the poetic self
dramatization that we associate with the Romantic tradition: a nature suffused
with mystical presences and healing essences; a Whitmanesque self so ex₁ an-
sive that it encompasses the rocks and the rivers, the birds and stars of the
galaxy, and every light and shadow that falls between. And these are all
anchored, in the manner of Pablo Neruda, to a socialist commitment to change
in an African postcolony. It is necessary to provide this comparative dimension
to signify the breadth of analogies that his poetry invites before returning to the
narrower concerns of this paper.

Osundare's first collection of poems, *Songs of the Marketplace,* begins with a
poem that has since come to be regarded as his poetic manifesto. In this early
poem, Osundare spells out his intentions and outlines the goals of his poetry.
The poem, "Poetry is", defines the nature of the poet's calling and enterprise by
using a simple set of binary oppositions to set forth what poetry should be
against what it should not be. This poem deserves quoting in full here because
it has become a sort of Archemedean fulcrum in the interpretation of his poetry and also became a source of controversy in the light of his later poetic practice.[2]

Poetry is
not the esoteric whisper
of an excluding tongue
not a clap trap
for the wondering audience
not a learned quiz
entombed in Grecoroman lore

54

Poetry is
a lifespring
which gathers timbre
the more throats it plucks
harbinger of action
the more minds it stirs

Poetry is
the hawker's ditty
the eloquence of the gong
the lyric of the marketplace
the luminous ray
on the grass's morning dew

Poetry is
what the soft wind
musics to the dancing leaf
what the sole tells the dusty path
what the bee hums to the alluring nectar
what the rainfall croons to the lowering eaves

Poetry is
no oracle's kernel
for a sole philosopher's stone

Poetry is
man
meaning
to
man. (pp. 3–4).

This poem, written in response to the perceived eurocentricism of an earlier generation of Nigerian poets and the inaccessibility of their poetic diction and range of references, was largely misread as making a claim for the referentiality of language and the self-transparency of meaning. The poet was seen to be saying that meaning in poetry is or should be self-evident rather than self-concealing; that meaning is easily and universally accessible; that men (and women) send and receive meanings in an unmediated space free of discursive encumbrances. In spite of the fact that the very metaphorical encoding of the poem belies such a reading, this reading, for misguided ideological reasons, became a truism repeated over and over in reviews and criticism of his work and then in student essays. Leaving aside the multiplicity of metaphorical maneuvers in the poem, a close look at the last stanza shows that Osundare privileges meaning as the mediator between men (forgetting awhile any gender hair-splitting). "Meaning" is proposed as the site of interaction and exchange by its strategic positioning in the poem. Rather than a simple referentiality, what we have here is something even more complex than the Bakhtinian dictum that "the word in language is half someone else's". Beyond this simple dialogism, the foundational Cartesian *cogito* of Enlightenment rationality is reversed and revised in such a way that *meaning* is now seen as central to consciousness because it is meaning that stands between man and the object world and man and other men. To grasp the full significance of this proposition, it is important to link this with the logic of animist conception of the relationship between the phenomenal world and the subjective. Animistic subjectivity is constructed on a relationship between the object world and a self that is mediated by *meaning*, to use Niyi Osundare's term.

The centrality of meaning to the Osundare aesthetic becomes clearer when we look at the poem "The Rocks Rose to Meet Me", a sequence from *The Eye of the Earth*, an anthology which contains some of the most animistic poems he has ever penned. This poem takes as its subject the perennial theme of return-to-the-roots we find in most African writing. Here the prodigal returnee is not welcomed by a mother figure but by the rocks of home village, which clearly represent father figures. The poem presents a parade of these local deities (which inhabit/are the rocks) as they emerge one after the other in their ancient glory to meet the returning son. These rocks imbued with *meaning* by the animistic beliefs of the people become the backdrop against which the poet stages the earth celebration which is the theme of the entire collection. Unmoving and immovable, the rock deities stand unchanging and eternally presiding over the ephemerality of time, the cycles of the seasons and continuity of human life and activity. The poet-persona chants their praise epithets and, as wanderer meets rooted rocks, he places his own 'unbearable lightness of being' beside their solidity and gravity. And then:

> I read the cipher tattooed
> on the biceps of stone
> open like a book of oracles. (p. 37).

As the ciphers yield their oracular meanings to him, his welcome becomes complete. He finds the roots of meaning which link him to the environment and to the people. With the completion of this rite of return, he is now fully empowered as poet and spokesman to read/speak on behalf of the environment and the people. And this he does with zeal marrying an environmentalist fervor and an animistic representational mode to a socialist commitment to change. Even the most secularist of social visions such as Marxism is, in Niyi Osundare's poetry, "re-enchanted" within the world of animist materialism. Readings of his poetry often miss this animistic strategy because of the endless belaboring of the secular in disregard of the animistic code which is its enabling ground. The most rewarding approach to this poetry would be to begin with a recognition of this intertext.

LAST WORD?

To conclude these explorations with an articulated bandwagon sentence in the manner of Melquiades' magnetized ingots, we should simply say that an understanding of animism as-collective-fantasy-as-social-practice-as-cultural-practice is essential to understanding that "something going on in Africa" which outsiders "are uncertain what it is and, what it means" (Chabal,1996: 32).

ACKNOWLEDGEMENTS

This essay is an abridged and somewhat different version of a paper entitled "Explorations in Animist Materialism: Notes on Reading/Writing African Literature, Culture and Society" (forthcoming), originally conceived and written as an elaboration upon the term "animist realism" which I had used in describing the representational strategy deployed in Ben Okri's *The Famished Road* (See "Ben Okri: Animist Realism and the Famished Genre", *The Guardian* (Lagos) 13 March 1993). In his book *Strategic Transformations in Nigeria Writing* (1997), Ato Quayson notes that I use the term "animist realism" without adequately defining it. "Harry Garuba (1993)", he says, "comes closest to providing a new terminology for discussing Ben Okri's later work when he refers to it as dominated by 'animist realism'. Unfortunately, he leaves this highly suggestive term unexplained thereby allowing it to be drafted into other frames of reference without being defined" (p. 148). The original essay and this version seek to redress this by defining the term within the larger discursive framework of animist materialism.

NOTES

1 More sinister is the widespread abuse of this practice by African dictators such as General Eyadema, Mobutu Sese Seko, Hastings, etc.

2 On the publication of Osundare's *Moonsongs*, a younger Nigeria Epaphrus Osondu wrote a poem entitled "Only Ill Bred Poets Bay at the Moon" to protest what he believed was the older poet's abandonment of his poetic creed as supposedly enunciated in *Songs of the Marketplace*.

REFERENCES

Achebe, Chinua. *Morning Yet On Creation Day.* London: Heinemann, 197.

Appadurai, Arjun. *The Social Life of Things: Commodities in Cultural Perspective.* Cambridge: Cambridge UP, 1986.

Apter, Andrew. *Black Critics and Kings: The Hermeneutics of Power in Yoruba Society.* Chicago: Chicago UP, 1992.

Barber, Karin. *I Could Speak Until Tomorrow: Oriki, Women, and the Past in a Yoruba Town.* Edinburgh: Edinburgh UP, 1991.

———, ed. *Readings in African Popular Culture.* Oxford: Indiana UP and James Currey, 1997.

Chabal, Patrick. "The African Crisis: Context and Interpretation." Eds. Richard Werbner & Terence Ranger. *Postcolonial Identities in Africa.* London: Zed Books, 1996: 29–54.

Chakrabarty, Dipesh. *Rethinking Working Class History. Bengal 1890–1940.* Princeton: Princeton UP, 1989.

Cooper, Brenda. *Magical Realism in the West African Novel. Seeing with a Third Eye.* London: Routledge, 1998.

Drewal, Margaret. *Yoruba Ritual: Performers, Play, Agency.* Bloomington: Indiana UP, 1992.

Fisiy, Cyprian & Gescheire, Peter. "Witchcraft, Violence and Identity: Different Trajectories in Postcolonial Cameroon." Eds. Richard Werbner & Terence Ranger. *Postcolonial Identities in Africa.* London: Zed Books, 1996: 193–221.

Gerth, H.H. & Mills, Wright C. *For Marx Weber: Essays in Sociology.* 1948. rpt London: Routledge, 1991.

Garcia, Marquez. *One Hundred Years of Solitude.* Trans. Gregory Rabassa. Picador, 1970.

Gauchet, Marcel. "The Disenchantment of the World. A Political History of Religion." *The HarperCollins Dictionary of Religion.* Trans. Oscar Burge. Princeton: Princeton UP, 1997.

Ladipo, Duro. "Oba Koso." *Three Yoruba Plays* (English adaptation by Ulli Beier). Ibadan: Mbari, 1964.

Ogilvie, John. *The Imperial Dictionary of the English Language: A Complete Encyclopedic Lexicon, Literary, Scientific, and Technological. Vol. 1 A-Depascent.* London: Blackie & Son, n.d.

Osundare, Niyi. *Songs of the Marketplace.* Ibadan: New Horn Press, 1983.

———. "The Eye of the Earth." *Selected Poems.* London: Heinemann, 1992: 30 51.

Quayson, Ato. *Strategic Transformations in Nigerian Writing: Orality and History in the Work of Rev. Samuel Johnson, Amos Tutuola, Wole Soyinka and Ben Okri.* Oxford: James Currey and Indiana UP, 1997.

———. *Postcolonialism – Theory, Practice or Process.* Oxford: Polity Press in association with Blackwell Publishers, 2000.

Ropo, Sekoni. "Politics and Urban Folklore in Nigeria." Ed. Karin Barber. *Readings in African Popular Folklore.* 142–5.

Pike, Roston.E. *Encyclopaedia of Religion and Religions.* London: George Allen & Unwin Ltd, 1951.

Sangari, Kumkum. "The Politics of the Possible." Eds. Abdul JanMohamed and David Lloyd. *The Nature and Context of Minority Discourse.* Oxford: Oxford UP, 1990: 216–45.

Soyinka, Wole. *Myth, Literature and the African World.* Cambridge: Cambridge UP, 1976.

———. "From a Common Back Cloth." Ed. Biodun Jeyifo. *Art, Dialogue & Outrage: Essays on Literature and Culture.* Ibadan: New Horn Press, 1988.

Williams, Raymond. *Marxism and Literature.* Oxford: Oxford UP,1977.

A THEORY OF GROWTH AND MATURATION: THE EARTH AS THE EYE OF OSUNDARE'S POETRY

Titi Adepitan

There are new tasks before modern Nigerian literature, four decades into its emergence on the world literary scene. Rarely has serious thought been given to many of these tasks because, in many ways, Nigerian literature has been exceptionally lucky. In less than a decade of active literary production, it already had at least two major writers who looked poised enough to command international respect. It must be remembered, though, that before Chinua Achebe and Wole Soyinka, Amos Tutuola had already won some ambivalent attention. Soyinka (1988) once called the authors of *Toward the Decolonization of African Literature* "the troika," but perhaps we should first bear in mind that before the troika of critics, there had been a quadriga of writers: between Achebe, Soyinka, Christopher Okigbo and John Pepper Clark Nigerian literature won almost *gratis* a confident start, which later generations of Nigerian writers have since liked to take for granted and sometimes abuse. Yet, the truth of literary history is that traditions do not always take off with strong figures, nor do such figures always appear seriatim or in clusters. If the publication of Achebe's *Things Fall Apart* in 1958 is taken as the point of take-off, Nigerian literature has been able to earn a name for itself in just four decades, winning a Nobel prize after only twenty-eight years and commanding a place on lists for one hundred most important books of the twentieth century at forty.[1] Its achievements rest on the singular fortune of father figures, literary patriarchs on the likes of whom enduring traditions are founded.

On account of this relatively strong start, the tendency has been to take a lot of things for granted. Rarely are debates joined on the principles and parameters for canon formation, for instance, nor are criteria ever proposed by which new Nigerian writers can be deemed relevant or influential to that canon. Simply because their precursors turned out as high quality work, it has generally been believed that the gates are open to all comers in matters pertaining to national literary standards. How should the process of growth and maturation of a new generation of writers be determined before critics begin to take them seriously? How should critics delineate the trajectory of such growth in ways that might enhance the store laid by concepts, such as tradition and canon? In reading Amos Tutuola's last works, for instance, should it not be possible to discern a pattern that coalesces around both continuous productivity and a movement forward in technique and stylistic elegance? Certainly, the author of *The Witch-Herbalist of the Remote Town* (1981), *Pauper, Brawler and Slanderer* (1987), and *The Village Witch Doctor and Other Stories* (1990) can no longer quite remain the old naïve Tutuola of *The Palm-wine Drinkard* whom early critics liked to review just for the belly laugh.

Such movements and patterns of growth are not available to every writer, much less are they bestowed *gratis* on just anyone in a literary tradition that is mindful of its own self esteem and the rigor that should inform its criteria of inclusion. "Let a thousand flowers bloom!," so declared the leaders of the second generation of Nigerian writers in the early eighties. Of course, thousands of flowers do bloom in every literary field; by their nature, there is very little in terms of interference that any single individual, body, or government can do about it outside of totalitarian enclaves, like Mao's China where that statement originated. The crisis and confusion facing Nigerian literature consists, it would appear, quite simply in not being able to draw the line between a million flowers that may bloom and the duty of the horticulturist to insist on picking only the most striking and exceptional for celebration.

Canon formation is not quite the same as the surface flash of a literature in ebullition, and there is not much need to prove the case that what many would extol as ebullition in our literature in the last decade has been dubious. Where growth becomes amorphous and shrubs begin to struggle for space with poplars, the topiarist does not weed out the shrubs, he only designs a grand architectural image, which may best sum up the essential vitalities that should nourish a nascent literary canon. Willie van Peer has recently tried to describe the distinction between the proliferation of literature and the high selectivity of canon formation. He calls his approach, which is "concerned with the search for general principles or patterns in literary history," "nomological" (van Peer, 1997: 113). He formulates two "laws." The first "posits that the number of literary works increases continually over time," so that "at any given moment, the amount of literature within a culture surpasses that of a previous moment, provided that the time differences between these moments are not infinitesimally small" (p. 121). The second law states that: "precisely *because* of the first law, cultures are constantly engaged in selection processes, the outcome of which is a heavily skewed subset of the total number of literary works produced within that culture" (p. 124; his emphasis). The consequence of not "setting such upper limits would be cultural incoherence, and thus potential disintegration" (p. 125):

> The basic insight that the second law reveals is the necessity and the inevitability of canon formation. This is significant, for it means that a *definition* of the canon is dependent upon a prior description of the system of literary production: canons arise as a result of a peculiarity of the literary system, embodied in the first law. (p. 127; his emphasis)

There is something in the character of the pre-occupations and strategies of the poet Niyi Osundare that should inaugurate a debate on the place of a canon in Nigerian literature. Such a debate becomes especially pertinent, to the extent that a significant writer begins to grow and mature before our eyes in preparation for admittance into that canon. There is no doubt that Osundare fits into T. S. Eliot's insistence that every writer who would be different is, indeed, just falling in line with a time-tested pattern (Eliot, 1973). The strains and echoes of Osundare's precursors in African poetry—as well as in the literature in general—are frequently clamorous enough to intrude into our assessment of the poet. Achebe, Okigbo, p'Bitek, Soyinka, and several others pop up in Osundare's poetry with a regularity, which seems to threaten the poet's reputation with the fate of Amos Tutuola's "Complete Gentleman" in *The Palmwine Drinkard*. Nonetheless, the more pertinent observation is that Osundare is not just Africa's most successful poet right now, he also looks set to have given rise to an entirely new way of envisioning our environment and circumstances, radically different from whatever may have come before in modern African poetry.

A fullness of theme and an ampleness of vision underlie Osundare's conception of the craft of his poetry. What might ordinarily bog down a lesser poet in the risks and consequences of prolixity, has become for Osundare an elaborate, involved, and masterfully co-ordinated panoply of sound, structure, words, and gesture that is behind an aesthetic that is unique and sometimes quite intimidating in contemporary African poetry. This vitality has also been aided by the poet's identification with a theme hitherto unexplored in our poetry. Osundare addresses himself to the environment, with its flora and fauna, the air, the rivers, the seas, the oceans, the rocks, and the mountains with a votary's sense of call that we are likely to have come across in the poetry of the West, but which is quite rare in African poetry. The earth, our beloved, beleaguered planet is, in short, the eye of Osundare's poetry.

Osundare's invocations and salutations to the earth enable him the lyrical flourish that may have been encountered, though in a tighter, more subdued form in Christopher Okigbo; they also ensure an all-encompassing trope for his other pre-occupations, both as a poet and scholar of the radical persuasion. Environmental concern for the earth creates an audience for the poet, which cuts across class and racial divides and unites the whole of humanity in an overriding desire to relate to our physical world with enlightened self-interest. The theme was rare in the African poetry before Osundare.[2] In a sense, of course, there is a great deal of attention to the environment in Wole Soyinka's *Idanre*, but much of it possesses significations that are mythic and animist in character. The denseness of the universe that confronts us in Soyinka's poem compels us, willy-nilly, to the metaphysical theatre of war and magical action of ancient stories and legends. It is peopled by "primal giants and mastodons... presences such as dilate the head"; the landscape is the "god-suffused grazing" of *Idanre*, with its "mists and clouds" (Soyinka: 1967, 57), and the poet is not overly preoccupied with the dangers of global abuse and overexposure facing our environment.

It should not appear out of place that Osundare seems different from mainstream Nigerian traditions of poetry. Though born and raised in the country, the greater part of the poet's university education was received abroad, in coincidence with the nascent arrival of groups and bodies concerned with environmental watch. If concerns for the earth have found so much passionate advocacy in Osundare, it is quite certainly because an appropriate soil within which it can blossom has been ensured in the poet. "Farmer born, peasant bred," his formative years in an agrarian environment where even the littlest babes learn to pluck intimations from the rustling of leaves found a perfect complement in an enlightened advocacy for the environment by groups like Green Peace and Friends of the Earth.

In the last three decades environmental awareness has become one of the salutary, truly ennobling concerns of the civilized world. No doubt it arose out of the dire need to check the excesses and depredations to which technology and industrialization had exposed the environment. The struggle to redeem Planet Earth has been made supremely sublime by the voluntary and selfless dedication of environmentalists. That subliminal concern is only matched by the cries of anguish, which tear out of the soul of humankind, whenever, in our sobriety, we are confronted by the environmental horror into which our earth is inexorably turning. Virtually every one of these horrors is man-made or artificially induced. For example, *Time* magazine in its January 2, 1989 issue chose for its cover, "Planet of the Year: Endangered Earth." The expose chronicles a frightful list of natural and man-made calamities of which earth stands in danger. The list is long. It includes over-population, global warming or "the greenhouse effect," pollution, hurricanes, floods, earthquakes, radioactive waste, and the depletion of the ozone layer. The list also cites "the destruction of the tropical forests," which goes on "at a rate equal to one football field a second" and the decimation of rare species of flora and fauna, whose extinction comes with the consequence that "they take with them hard-won lessons of survival encoded in their genes over millions of years" (*Time* 21).

In Osundare's poetry, the earth breathes and talks; the earth, to paraphrase a Yoruba saying, has eyes. "Oju ile" or "the eye of the earth" in Yoruba lore is a metaphysical trope for describing the sensitiveness of world-will, the malice and implacable vindictiveness of the body politic of which the individual within society must be wary lest he impugn it at his own cost. The Yoruba prayer, *K'a ma te le ni bi o gbe l'oju,* (literally, "May we never tread on the earth where it has eyes") really simply expresses a reverent wish to avoid running afoul of the popular will, particularly where this may be expressed in terms of resentment or opposition. In the poetry of Osundare this metaphysical trope has been transformed into the dignity and integrity of the environment and all that adds up to it, which must remain inviolate to the rapacity of modern, technological man and the post-industrial age.

*

For a poet who has finally come into his own in voice and craft, the trope of the eye of the earth has also become the ideational complement of Osundare's initial ideological concerns with Marxism and populist notions of art. Osundare was a staunch member of the leftist vanguard in the Nigerian literary fraternity. These second generation Nigerian writers and men of ideas included Femi Osofisan, Biodun Jeyifo, Omafume Onoge, Odia Ofeimun, and Festus Iyayi. Especially in the eighties, they insisted on the need to re-train the artistic eye in the direction of populist concerns in Nigerian literature and also found a coherent metalanguage for its criticism. Their running battles with Wole Soyinka were for many years the staple of Nigeria's largely tentative attempts at critical theory (Jeyifo: 1985; Amuta: 1988). With the collapse of the Soviet Union, many in the ranks of the Nigerian Left became quiet; some renounced almost overnight the ideological viewpoint they had championed for upwards of four decades. 3 The ascendance of ecological themes has ensured for Osundare an enduring relevance for his populist, materialist concerns without the risk of becoming *passé*, like much of Nigerian Leftist rhetoric. The poet's solicitude for the environment puts the ordinary people at center stage of attention and reminds all of the indebtedness of the metropole to the hinterland.

In his early poetry, the preponderance of the metaphors of want and dispossession ensured for Osundare a reputation as the "poet of the marketplace." The poems of this period were largely mainstream Nigerian literature of dissent: acerbic, vitriolic, and extremely bellicose in tone and messianic intent, as in "Who's Afraid of Marx?"(1983). Frequently, they were offered, though not in explicit language by the poets themselves, as a better alternative to the earlier tradition of Christopher Okigbo, Soyinka and JP Clark. Regardless of the genuineness of their artistic sensibility and the integrity of their humanism, the works of these Nigerian precursors were faulted on the grounds of craft. It is certainly one of the ironies of our literature that Okigbo has since become the looming shadow of the Bloomian precursor that no Nigerian poet of the succeeding generations has been able to shake off; indeed, most would prefer to make obeisance as a due rite of passage! The risk, which may not have been obvious to many at the time, was that Nigerian Leftist poetry was in danger of going the way of its predecessor by proposing to carve an identity for itself by chasing larger-than-life shadows. A few years earlier, a new wave of Nigerian poetry had seized the imagination of academia from America where it first became fashionable. This kind of poetry, championed by Chinweizu, Onwuchekwa Jemie, Ihechukwu Madubuike, among others, attempted to propose a more "indigenous" sensibility, a homegrown poetic language that would eschew the "catholic impedimenta" of Okigbo's poetry, the "Hopkinsian disease" of JP Clark's, and the "Tarzanist" fascinations of Soyinka's. The new young poets produced works that insisted on surface clarity and the demystificatio of experience. The new orthodoxy was later to be articulated in the famous book, *Toward the Decolonization of African Literature* (1980).

The Nigerian Leftist writers who took off from where the authors of *Decolonization* ran out of steam were in many ways more sincere, more unpretentious, and less programmatic and self-serving than the proponents of *bolekaja* criticism in Nigeria's unending literary war of succession. Both, as writers and critics, did not fail to engage the tradition of Okigbo, Soyinka, Clark, and Echeruo in meaningful dialogue. For many years, Jeyifo remained "the last word" on Soyinka. Certainly, the *palace coup, which was topmost on the agenda of the bolekaja troika,* was not the singular metier of Nigerian Leftist criticism; between founding poetry journals and chapbooks and running poetry clubs, Nigerian Leftist poetry served notice of its seriousness.[4] Osundare is in many ways the major and most distinguished product of that experiment.

In chapbooks, journals, and cyclostyled weekly proceedings of the Poetry Nite Series in several Nigerian universities, the Nigerian Leftist poet sought to underline his engagement with art with a more quotidian outlook on the place of the individual in society. It was not by accident that this phase coincided with the peak of Ngugi wa Thiong'o's radicalisation and popularisation of fiction and drama in Kenya with the publication of *Ngahiika Ndeenda (I Will Marry When I Want)* and *Caithaba Mutharaba Ini (Devil on the Cross)*. Soyinka's most memorable opposition to the government of the second republic in Nigeria also occurred around the same time, with the production of his play *Requiem for a Futurologist,* the release of a film, *Blues for a Prodigal,* and a long-playing record, *Unlimited Liability Company,* as well as several "agit-prop" revues and sketches. The Marxist poets Osundare, Osofisan, Femi Fatoba, and Odia Ofeimun were riding the crest of a resurgence of populist literature and political activism by major African writers in the early eighties.

Osundare's early poetry, which was to become dominant into his second volume, was in several ways the programme statement of Nigerian Marxist poetry. The credo of this ascendant outlook was summed up in the poem, "Poetry Is":

> Poetry is
> not the esoteric whisper
> of an excluding tongue
> not a claptrap
> for a wondering audience
> not a learned quiz
> entombed in Grecoroman lore
> (*Songs of the Marketplace,* 3).

The customary attention to the opposition was there in "Who's Afraid of Marx?" The concern with the travails of the ordinary citizen was enshrined in "Plaints of an Unemployed Labourer (Whose Wife Surprised His Fortune with Sextuplets)" (1983), one of Osundare's early masterpieces. The poem, a dramatic monologue, counter-pointed the joy of childbirth with the anguish of indigent parenthood in the refrain, "Mama Sule, why have you done this to me?" Many of such early pieces were occasionally interspersed with folkloric, anecdotal, or epigrammatic transliterations from Yoruba into English, and were more an apprentice versification of wise sayings, traditional quips, riddles, and satirical banter than original compositions, as evidenced by the second volume of poems, *Village Voices*.

Both *Songs of the Marketplace* and *Village Voices*, Osundare's first two collections, are *tours de force* of Nigerian Marxist literature. In the first, the opening sequence "Excursions" is a string of vignettes and snapshots of Nigerian life as seen and, as frequently done in the Nigerian tradition of engaged literature, *constructed* through the eyes of the ideologue himself, complete with all the adjectives and qualifiers:

> We meet babies with chronic hydrocephalus
> squeezing spongy breasts
> on mother's bony chests
> shrivelled
>
> We see village boys' kwashiorkor bellies
> hairless heads impaled on pink necks
> and ribs baring the benevolence
> of the body politic
>   *   *   *
> in city fringes pregnant women
> rummage garbage heaps for
> the rotting remnants of city tables
> above, hawks and vultures hovering
> for their turn
> (*Songs of the Marketplace*, 7–8).

The same concern underlies poems like "Sule Chase" and "A Reunion," although in the latter poem the envisioning of a nostalgic and deeply emotional encounter (Arnold 153–54) through the prism of ideology leaves little room for the flow of the right sentiment and cadences. This, in short, is "the mar of Marxism" in the Nigerian poetry of that tradition, to borrow a phrase from Soyinka. In Agostinho Neto's "Friend Mussunda" one encounters the same rupture between two minds occasioned by a foreign language. In Neto's poem the unmitigated anguish reaches through from the poet's insistence on envisioning and lamenting his experience more as a human being than as a spokesman for a way of seeing:

> To you friend Mussunda
> to you I owe my life
>
> And I write poems you cannot follow
> do you understand my anguish?
>
> Here am I
> friend Mussunda
> writing poems you cannot follow
>
> It was not this
> we wanted, I know
>
> But in spirit and intelligence
> we are!
>
> We are
> friend Mussunda
> we are
>
> Inseparable
> and still advancing to our dream
> (*Sacred Hope*, 83–4).

"A Reunion" is a *cri de coeur* in lamentation of subverted potential. The poet's traumatized voice virtually cracks with emotion as it recalls those days of innocence when the promise of life, its abundance and attainments were the common inheritance of every child. The poet singles it out as "the most important poem in the collection" (Arnold 153), and Wumi Raji ups the ante when he rejects Osundare's reading as "particularly inadequate in my view," and calls the poem "the most important poem in Osundare's output to date.... To put it more bluntly, ... the poem which articulates the theme of Osundare's career" (Raji 65). Both Osundare's and Raji's assessments of the poem are "personal" in its most basic (Matthew) Arnoldian sense. In spite of its autobiographical significance for Osundare (or maybe because of it), "A Reunion" reminds the reader of DH Lawrence's injunction about trusting the tale and not the teller in gauging the interface between authorial intent and stylistic execution. The poem fails to evoke for being overly preoccupied with explicit statements and programmatic declarations; at the end of it all the human subject forfeits the spontaneity of feeling which ought to be the singular appeal and reward of such a poem for a denied and socially wounded soul-mate. The voice in the poem can only share a tenuous sense of brotherhood with his interlocutor: the memories he calls up, the articles of social status he would forsake out of solidarity for his old-time mate, and the overt ideological self-projection all jar in the ear. The poem's weakness is one that no one familiar with Nigerian Leftist poetry can fail to miss—the insistence on ideological *attitude* at the expense of the genuine feeling which remains buried under so much rhetoric. The poem concludes:

> We must smash this wall
> built of the inequities
> of class and crime
> then shake hands
> over the ashes of severance
> (*Village Voices*, 29).

＊

The robustness that this paper argues for Osundare's poetry draws its strength from the poet's stroke of genius in his later works for invigorating his poetry with environmental concerns and drawing greater strength and muscularity for it along with its universal appeal. There is certainly now something quite *passe* in much of Nigerian Marxist literature, but if its populist rhetoric survives so robustly in Osundare, it is because its focus on man's material condition has found an admirably pertinent relevance in the poet's campaign for the environment. In the later poems, the concerns of the marketplace have gradually been made more compelling by the state of the farmstead, the countryside and the environment in general. At the end of it all, Osundare may be guilty of just one act of creative hubris: daring to yoke so many pertinent areas of life and existence together in one grand poetic statement. Osundare is the poet of the marketplace, the farmstead, the brook, the valley, the Olosunta rock faces, the valley, the sun and the moon, the wag-bard out to restore esemplasy to its grandest conception in its claims for verbal art since Sir Philip Sidney.

There are rough edges no doubt, and frequently these are as unsettling as the poet's obvious indebtedness to several African and Nigerian precursors and contemporaries.5 Okigbo's elegiac refrain, "Condolences...Condolences..." ("Path of Thunder") resurfaces in Osundare with a similar contrapuntal effect as

"Tonalities. Redolent tonalities" (*Waiting Laughters*); Ezeulu's prognostication to his son Oduche in Achebe's *Arrow of God* ("The world is like a Mask dancing," 46) pops up in Osundare as "The moon is a mask dancing" (*Moonsongs*). There is also a certain kind of turbulence, a syntagmatic licence, and semantic shifts and fluxes that can be quite disconcerting. When Osundare mounts his "horse of remembrance" not many can keep frenetic pace with the "myriad whisper(s) of yester-voices" (*Eye of the Earth*) that beckon to us from different directions; the loser is not always the reader alone, harmony also frequently limps along a mighty mile behind. Expressions like "scene-tax" or "sin-tax" are likely to pop up in Osundare for no other graphemic reason than that the poet cannot resist the fascination with the alphabetic representation of sound. If the "tale" is "stalled" by such "impertinences of half-way fancies," there may be something unwitting in the poet's self-censure:

> Blame not, then,
> The rapid eloquence of the running vowel
> When words turn willing courier
> In the courtyard of dodging ears
> Can the syllable stall its tale
> In impertinences of half-way fancies?
> (*Waiting Laughters*, 5).

These are extremely little, utterly negligible factors compared to the amazing consistency of Osundare's sustained poetic vision. No African poet since Leopold Sedar Senghor has approached his themes with the same encyclopaedic imagination as has become Osundare's inimitable signature. In retrospect, there must have been something quite understated in the way *The Eye of the Earth* signalled the arrival of the poet's encyclopaedic themes even though the collection made all the difference to Osundare's stature by fetching him the 1986 Joint Commonwealth Poetry prize. The unified vision of a body of poems fired by a sustained, disciplined, and masterfully executed votive imagination was already arguably Nigeria's most enduring contribution to modern African poetry. It was there, in the haunting, unabashedly, priestly poetry of Okigbo, which was honed into an exquisiteness that sometimes threatens to curb the critic's power of self-distancing, and also in the title sequence in Soyinka's *Idanre*. By 1986, many probably regarded that phase as Nigeria's golden age of poetry gone by. The significance of *The Eye of the Earth* in Nigerian poetry is first and foremost that it signalled a return to that brief—perhaps because somewhat truncated—tradition of the unified, self-possessed poetic voice established in the Nigerian poetry of the sixties by Okigbo, Soyinka, and Clark.

There is a lot that invites comparison between Okigbo's *Labyrinths, with Path of Thunder* and *The Eye of the Earth;* there is a whole lot more that makes Osundare's first major collection a distinctive watershed in Nigerian poetry. Quite unannounced, the poet was shedding the toga of the marketplace, *de rigeur* in the first two collections, and its strident populist rhetoric even though 1991 and the fall of the former Soviet Union were still a long way off. In its place, was Osundare's self-discovery as a spokesman for the farmstead and all its pristine associations. Osundare's rejection of mythic concerns in his poetry is insistent; in poems, essays, and interviews, the poet makes clear that the business of writing can subserve more urgent tasks.[6] *The Eye of the Earth* is not a "metaphysical" poem in the same way that Soyinka's *Idanre* is a paean to Yoruba cosmogony and myths of origin, but in many ways anxieties over a kinship of sensibility and theme between the two works may be beside the point. Clearly, Osundare is not overly concerned with myth-making in *The Eye of the Earth*. Nonetheless, is it fair to ask a Yoruba poet to write a whole tome of invocations and salutations in obeisance to the earth without willy-nilly *re*-discovering that mystic, mythic association with the earth for which his forefathers were exemplars? The answer is no—not even for a poet with a materialist outlook. Osundare's most votive resonances derive, quite simply, from the earth energies, awesome in their "redolent tonalities" that he unleashes in *The Eye of the Earth* and again in several sections of *Midlife*. We might debate whether this is animist in intent or execution, but there is no arguing the pristine, autochthonous links that the collection re-establishes in a Yoruba reader who knows that *oriki ile* cannot be just bland, secular poetry.

Of course, there is a deliberate effort by the poet to give short shrift to "mystical" associations in *The Eye of the Earth*, and it is a stance that is very consistent with his ideological standpoint. In the sequence "The rocks rose to meet me," the quester-persona reflects on the gods:

> ... I have killed
> since wisdom's straightening sun
> licked clean the infant dew of fancy
> The gold let us dig, ...

The licence in the last line is a questionable fiat, however, because the poet who would defend the earth cannot afford to permit the exploitation of its riches just so the bogey of godhead can be bluffed. The earth in the Yoruba imagination is both mystical and spiritual. In many ways Osundare in *The Eye of the Earth* is the son of the farmstead who returns to reaffirm the faith of his people in the unifying, regenerative superabundance of nature. This quest comes across as a labour of love, which is not in the least a trip down the road of regression and superstition but a clarion call to a new and enlightened awareness of our human circumstances, earthed in a pact of respect for the environment. It is not animism that unites the farmer from Owo in Nigeria and the founders of Green Peace in Vancouver, Canada, when both take life threatening risks to protect the environment, but instead, it is the knowledge that the gold and other riches in it can not be all there is to the earth.

The quest motif that is central to *The Eye of the Earth* can only begin to acquire its full force when the awe and the encounter with the numinous, which are originary attributes of mother earth, are restored to our conception of it. This may be one of the reasons why *Idanre* is one those poems that every society has to compose, the better that its apprehension of the dynamics of its own world can be held at an objective distance from the lure and dangers of sophisticated ways of seeing. In a large sense, *The Eye of the Earth* is a companion volume to Soyinka's work in this regard. In Osundare's work, the journey is *again* both spiritual and metaphorical, and sustained by a sense of recall—of the days of childhood and work on the farm, "where [his] first faltering steps/ broke the earthworm in the path of dawn." As the flora and fauna are animated in the electric imagination of the poet in "Forest Echoes," the reader forgets that it has all been a flashback, until in one of the finest takes on style and technique in African poetry, the poet announces:

> And now
> memory,
> loud whisperer of yestervoices
> confluence of unbroken rivers,
> lower your horse of remembrance
>
> Let me dismount.

It soon becomes evident in the next sequence, "Harvestcall," that the poet has only been creating a template, an elaborate structure of utterance for the huge possibilities in meaning and metaphor of which the grand construct *Eye of the Earth* is capable. The sequence, like much of the collection, is a guided tour through landmarks but particularly through the vicious interfaces between past and present, plenitude and dearth, the suppleness of natural rain forests and man-made ecological depletion as the poet revisits and re-visions the state of the countryside. He concludes with the poser: "With our earth so warm/ How can our hearth be so cold?"

Osundare is a master of troping, especially in the shorter pieces where the poet's restless eye roves and pulls off sometimes startling, sometimes improbable associations between object and referent. In *The Eye of the Earth*, these vignettes and snapshots, which are basic to any understanding of the poet's craft, also serve as a bridge between what I have proposed as the template (the first segment of the collection, up to "Harvestcall"), and his deployment of its tropes and metaphors as encyclopaedic, co-referential structures of utterance in the two other segments. The build-up actually takes off from this bridge or interlude, titled "Eyeful glances":

> a careless match, a harmattan rage
> our farms are tinder
> for a dispossessing flame; a criminal torch, an incendiary plot
> a blaze conceals the trails
> of the looters of state

The whole of the second segment signals the transition from the dryness and aridity that threatens the world in the first, loaded with poems that celebrate the coming of rain. Earth is transformed as the season of showers and torrents seizes the initiative on life and nature from the blitzkrieg of the harmattan and drought. "Rainsongs," "First Rain," "Okeruku," "Who says that drought was here?," and "But sometimes when it rains" are all united by another of Osundare's main distinguishing features as a Nigerian poet: his insistence on espousing a vision of hope even when his ascerbic indictment of society might otherwise propose him to his reader as an incurable cynic. The perfidy of leadership and the "topsy-turvies" of the Nigerian political culture, in general, have in recent years tended to detract from a perception of literature (and social commentary) as an expression of faith in positive values. Stretched beyond its limits by the moral and political crises of the last two decades, Nigerian literature has become little more than a cudgel that we wield over the heads of "looters of state." The path to a rounded and full-bodied growth for a national literature becomes thereby short-circuited as writers are constrained more and more to assume the role of prophets of doom.7 The duty of social indictment that the contemporary history of the Nigerian nation has all but substituted in the hands of its writers as mainstream art and literature is redeemed a great deal by the tutored approach of a poet like Osundare, who seeks to balance a statement of our dismal circumstances with a vision of hope.

It is this affirmation, which enriches the poems in the final section, "Homecall," almost each of them is a nugget of accomplishment in Osundare's continuing experimentation with a fusion of poetic voices and personas, the individual autobiographical self, and the communal. Its main stylistic accomplishment may not be so readily known, however. It is built on the strong, repetitive rhythm of Yoruba incantatory poetry, as the poet asserts through invocation, and invokes through assertion; his affirmations are rendered through staccato bursts of short sentences, which declaim the positive value of things, as in "Our Earth will not Die":

> But our earth will not die
>
> > Who lynched the lakes. Who?
> > Who slaughtered the seas. Who?
> > Whoever mauled the mountains. Whoever?
>
> Our earth will not die.
>   *   *   *
> > Weeping willows drip mercury tears
> > in the eye of sobbing terrains
> > a nuclear sun rises like a funeral ball
> > reducing man and meadow to dust and dirt.
>
> But our earth will not die.
>
> > Fishes have died in the waters.   Fishes.
> > Birds have died in the trees.   Birds.
> > Rabbits have died in their burrows.   Rabbits.
>
> But our earth will not die
> (*Eye of the Earth*)

*

The poet's claim in an interview with Stephen Arnold that the "autobiography of an African is the autobiography of a place" (Arnold 150) is a very perceptive observation on the relationship between African writers and the literature. It is also likely that the strategy of autobiography has furnished a poet with an emotional intensity that often startles, with an appropriate mode to bookmark his own crucial location in the world that he describes and the sense of siege which he shares with well-meaning people all over the world about the state of our environment. The displacement of the author in New Critical theorizing must be of immense concern to African writers and critics, for whom literature has yet to attain that nirvana of nothing and nothingness where the text constructs and deconstructs itself by the logic of a volition yet to be coherently articulated. On the other hand, "the distrust of autonomous selfhood" that Arnold (p. 145) indicts in the preamble to his discussion of the genre of autobiography in African literature may not be altogether misplaced. In African politics and letters, autobiography had its day as a huge strategic resource for *answering back* to the West; clearly, it was part of a distinctive historical phase that culminated in political independence. Any heavy reliance on the same resource by an African writer would now appear to be quite *passé*. That is half the trouble with Arnold's recourse to James Olney's *Tell Me Africa: an Approach to African Literature* and *Metaphors of Self: the Meaning of Autobiography*, both of which were published in 1973. Simply, the nationalist imperative that drove first generation African writers is no longer available to their successors.

Of course, Osundare pulls it off, even though one suspects that "gets away with it" may be more to the point. In truth, the autobiographical form in African literature accorded eminently well with that phase in twentieth-century African history when, for reasons that have never been investigated, emerging African leaders and men of letters not only embodied the yearnings and aspirations of their communities but also carried names that seemed to be walking billboards for their countries. And we had names like Leopold Sedar *Sen*ghor of *Sen*egal or Jomo *Kenya*tta of *Kenya*, not to mention names that were converted into acronyms for something noble, such as "Go On With One Nigeria!" The joke of such a coincidence (if ever it was one) has since fizzled out before the grimness of African politics and the proportionate shrink in the stature of African leaders. It is doubtful if any contemporary African leader, apart from Nelson Mandela, can conjure with a fly-whisk half the awe that Kenyatta in his heydays would simply have taken as a minor whiff of the divine aura of kings; and certainly, apart from the *Madiba*, no present African leader can call himself the father of his nation and be taken seriously. Similarly, not many of our present-day writers can begin to draw from autobiography as a testimony to the assertion of collective selfhood, which it used to be in the hands of, say, Senghor, Peter Abraham, Camara Laye, or Soyinka. African society has since become a lot more diverse and the place of the writer has shrunken within its orbit.

There is something very exceptional in the way Osundare has employed the form, no doubt. His "I" is not the egotistic one of African autobiography, nor is his "shall" the absolute, programmatic declaration of intent by the man of destiny that first generation African politicians seemed to have lifted from the pages of *Coriolanus*. For that matter, Osundare's poetic persona may not always be taken for granted as the poet's, and there is abundant evidence that the poet himself recognizes this (Arnold 158). It may very well be that we read *too much* autobiography into Osundare because the poet encourages us to establish links and correlations between the experiences he describes in poetry and his background, that good literature and its criticism must sometimes endeavour to transcend.[8] It may be worthwhile to investigate the costs and consequences of this autosuggestion by an author for the risks they may pose as impediments to an engagement of issues of craft. The greater relevance of autobiography to Osundare's poetry is that in him we have one of our few writers who are amenable to any notion of a theory of growth and maturation. The task before Nigerian criticism is to appropriate him into mainstream discourse and rigorously engage his career as a poet who, for all the accolades we would like to drench him in, may not yet have tapped a fraction of his genius. It may then be profitable to use him as a standard for determining how far our writers need to go before we credit them with the phenomenal breath of the long distance runner and the crystallization of artistic vision that is the singular hallmark of major writers. If such a task were undertaken today, Osundare would be assured of a secure place with the best in African literature; if informed criticism accepts, as it should, to play midwife to an unfolding career a little while longer, our poet may yet sit at the very pinnacle of distinction. A good deal of the local criticism on him at the present time would seem to me to be betraying this task, innocently no doubt.

The Eye of the Earth may remain Osundare's most significant, most accomplished work for a long while. This is one account of the seminality of its ecological thesis to the poet's mature concerns and the exemplary, if not quite unique, breath of harmony that homologizes experience and poetic craft. The poet has admitted to an interviewer that he is a "writer of collections": *The Eye of the Earth* is the finest example of such a unique imagination. Its especial grace in Osundare, even in a loosely strung collection like *Horses of Memory* or a problematic and quite hamstrung volume like *Moonsongs*, is that there is always something to marvel at in the tenacity and robustness of a poetic imagination that stretches itself to breaking point in order to establish the remotest associations between experience and metaphor, meaning, and construct.

Of course, *The Eye of the Earth* only canonizes one of the two main planks in Osundare's preoccupations; its dominant trope of the farmstead and the countryside, as we have noted, is something of a poetic blueprint for the environmental concern, which has seized the imagination of the enlightened world. The other is the social or, more appropriately, the socio-political, as encountered in the poet's early work and celebrated in *Waiting Laughters*. *Midlife* is both the poet's full-throated crow at the "plenitude" of his poetic "being" (p. 39), his "peopled imagination," his personic inhabitation of ecological space, and a gathering in of the preoccupations of the two mainstream concerns of the environment and society. Between the three volumes is contained the sum of Osundare's success as a poet to date. Angus Calder's sterling essay on *Waiting Laughters* can hardly be bettered in its judicial grace and its attempt to place the poet in the company of names like Pablo Neruda, Aime Cesaire, and Bertolt Brecht (Calder 1992). It would seem, however, that Calder's approbation is based on a volume, which may turn out to be the chief culprit in Osundare's oeuvre for the conceits, and indulgences we have already remarked. It is quite correct to say that the poetry of social criticism, like efforts in a similar direction in prose and fiction, is not the best premise to found the reputation of African writers; there is almost invariably something brittle about the literature of nonce concerns. The earth is very much the eye of Osundare's poetry.

NOTES

1 *Things Fall Apart* does not feature on the Random House/ Modern Library list of the "100 Best Novels of the Century" (*The Globe and Mail* A13). It is in the 70th position on the Radcliffe list (*The Vancouver Sun* F3). Also, between February and March 1998, the University of British Columbia's bookstore mounted an exhibition of the "100 Most Important Books of the Century" across various disciplines; *Things Fall Apart* enjoyed pride of place on the list, which was compiled by the international association of librarians. Achebe himself cites an inclusion in "The 250 Literary Greats," a list compiled in England of the major books of the millennium, including the *Bible* and the *Koran* (*ALA Bulletin* 15). It is only appropriate to observe that much of this is tokenism, however. The anthropological curiosity, which the West would wish sated on Things Fall Apart, has yet to mature into genuine literary taste for a work like *Arrow of God*.

2 The Yoruba tradition of *Ijala* poetry is the only one to my knowledge, which incorporates such concerns.

3 The late Tai Solarin rejected socialism as soon as the USSR collapsed.

4 Osundare's first outing was in *Opon Ifa*, the poetry chapbook published at Ibadan by Femi Osofisan, in 1981. There was also *Positive Review*, with an "editorial collective" that was a "who's who" of Nigerian Marxism and coordinated between the universities at Ibadan and Ile-Ife. The Poetry Club of the Department of English, University of Ibadan, relaunched in 1981, also played a crucial role for young minds.

5 Osundare's leaning on strong figures is one of the ways by which theories of tradition and influence acquire their pertinence. It is not imitation or plagiarism but the phenomenon of the writer who must first assemble his constituent parts before he can step out, in ways that Harold Bloom and TS Eliot have both made clear and intriguing (Eliot: 1973; Bloom: 1973). There is cause for concern, however, when a writer's claims duplicate another's, in circumstances which have little to do with growth. In *Another Raft* (1988), Femi Osofisan under the pen name Okinba Launko has the epigraph "Show me a single black man/ who is not adrift/ in the land of his own birth..." (v). In *Petals of Blood* (1977), Ngugi wa Thiong'o writes, "Tell me one black man who is not adrift even in the land of his birth" (237).

6 His criticism, on the other hand carries traces of the recognition, if not the endorsement, of myth:

    It was Schlegel who once declared "mythology and poetry are inseparable." This statement may sound too magisterial and perhaps too sweeping in a century like ours when an ever-growing rationalism seems to be punching a big hole in the mythic umbrella. But one fact which has never been in serious doubt is that poetry (and, indeed, literature generally) and mythology are interdependent; hence it has been difficult to resolve the "difference" between Mark Schorer's "myth is the indispensable substructure of poetry" and Richard Chase's "poetry is the substructure of myth."

7 Whichever way the victory goes in this contest between twin brothers, there will still remain the indisputable fact that both myth and poetry owe their survival and sustenance to language, man's most elaborate and articulate mode of making statements and meaning (1988b: 100–1).

I broached the point at the 1992 Association of Nigerian Authors Convention in Abeokuta, Ogun State, Nigeria. The panel of discussants at the symposium on literature and human rights included Niyi Osundare, Festus Iyayi, Harry Garuba and the present writer. The *African Concord* reporter who covered the event later wrote, "Titi Adepitan of Ogun State University couldn't understand what the fuss (about human rights) was all about"(*African Concord* 62).

8 A number of Osundare's interviews invariably deal with autobiographical matters.

REFERENCES

Achebe, Chinua. *Arrow of God*. Second Edition. London: Heinemann, 1974.
ALA Bulletin: A Publication of the African Literature Association. 24.2 Spring 1998.
Amuta, Chidi. *The Theory of Modern African Literature: Implications for Practical Criticism*. London: Zed Books, 1989.
Arnold, Stephen. "A Peopled Persona: Autobiography, Post-modernism and the Poetry of Niyi Osundare." Riesz and Schild 143–65.
Bloom, Harold. *The Anxiety of Influence*. London: Oxford University Press, 1973.
Calder, Angus. "Niyi Osundare's *Waiting Laughters*." *Cencrastus*. 43 Autumn 1992: 27–9.
Chinweizu, Onwuchekwa Jemie and Ihechukwu Madubuike. *Toward the Decolonization of African Literature*. Enugu: Fourth Dimension Press, 1980.
Eliot, TS. "Tradition and the Individual Talent." Kermode and Hollander. 2013–19.
Globe and Mail (Toronto). "*Ulysses* Heads List of 100 Best Novels." Tuesday, July 21, 1998. Eds. Kermode, Frank and John Hollander. *The Oxford Anthology of English Literature*, vol.II. Toronto: Oxford University Press, 1973.

Jeyifo, Biodun. *The Truthful Lie: Essays in the Sociology Of African Drama.* London: New Beacon Books, 1985.

Neto, Agostinho. *Sacred Hope.* Trans. Marga Holness. Foreword. Basil Davidson. London: Journeyman/UNESCO, 1988.

Nichols, Lee. "1998 ALA (Texas) Conference Wrap-Up and Interviews." *ALA Bulletin.* 12–38.

Okigbo, Christopher. *Labyrinths, with Path of Thunder.* London: Heinemann, 1971.

Olney, James. *Tell Me Africa: An Approach to African Literature.* Princeton: Princeton University Press, 1973.

Onoko, Oji. "Struggle for Freedom." *African Concord* (Lagos). 16 November, 1992.

———. *Metaphors of Self: The Meaning of Autobiography.* Princeton: Princeton University Press, 1973.

Osofisan, Femi. *Another Raft.* Lagos: Malthouse Press, 1988.

Osundare, Niyi. *Songs of the Marketplace.* Ibadan: New Horn Press, 1983.

———. *Village Voices.* Ibadan: Evans Brothers, 1984.

———. *The Eye of the Earth.*

———. *Moonsongs.*

———. "The Poem as a Mytho-Linguistic Event: A Study of Soyinka's 'Abiku.'" *African Literature Today* 16 (1988): 91–102.

———. *Waiting Laughters.* Lagos: Malthouse Press, 1990.

———. *Midlife.*

———. *Horses of Memory.* Ibadan: Heinemann Educational Books, 1998.

Raji, Wumi. "A Feast of Reunion." *ALA Bulletin.* 65–7.

Riesz, Janos and Ulla Schild, eds. *Genres autobiographiques en Afrique/ Autobiographical Genres in Africa.* Berlin: DietrichReimer Verlag, 1996.

Soyinka, Wole. *Idanre and Other Poems.* London: Methuen, 1967.

———. "Neo-Tarzanism: The Poetics of Pseudo-Tradition." Ed. Biodun Jeyifo. *Art, Dialogue and Outrage: Essays on Literature and Culture.* Ibadan: New Horn Press, 1988. 315–29.

Tutuola, Amos. *The Palm-Wine Drinkard.* London: Faber and Faber, 1985.

———. *The Witch-Herbalist of the Remote Town.* London: Faber and Faber, 1981.

———. *Pauper, Brawler and Slanderer.* London: Faber and Faber, 1987.

———. *The Village Witch Doctor & Other Stories.* London: Faber and Faber, 1990.

Vancouver Sun. "Literary Lists: the Invidious Enterprise." Saturday, July 25, 1998.

van Peer, Willie. "Two Laws of Literary History: Growth and Predictability in Canon Formation." *Mosaic.* 30.2. June 1997: 113–32.

GREEN ORANGES & ANTHILL CASTLES: AN ALIENATED LITERATURE?

Femi Oyebode

In this paper, I shall be asking whether it is ever possible for a North European language, such as English, to be domesticated, colonized, or even naturalized by an African writer to the degree that the language can be said to properly speak about the smells, the acuteness, and bitterness of the alkaloids that materialize in *ewuro*, for example. Can this imported language describe the moods of an intemperate climate, of the rocky out growths, of the mysterious noise of mosquitoes, of the peculiarities of dancing, of polygamous unions, of ancestors who parade the homestead and partake in feast of spirits and demons, of unnamed trees, animals, ants, and flowers shaped like vulvas and unashamed in the midday sun? Can a language manufactured and manicured for cursing at sea, for mowing green lawns, for ordering slaves and the underclass, and for articulating gravity and relativity, sing and infect the arteries with lust and desires for pleasure? Can it ululate or, in grief, wail and, in wailing, fill the soul with a hush that is already blue, and bluer still, in the very presence of death and the grossest orchestration of sorrow? And why should this language be asked to do these things, and why should it be able to do these things?

In raising these questions in the context of Osundare's poetry, I am suggesting that his poetry is a clawing after the warmth of the womb's sounds, the well marked syllables of Yoruba set several tones down, the drop of pebbles in a pond reverberating circular and concentric circles, amplitudes of the tribe, and one's identity. This is a qualitatively different vegetation with Yoruba; this is the geography of sounds and tempo that Osundare is attempting to re-create, to recapture, and he is in need of a baroque and gilded style, a repetitious and static enunciation of our way of being, and an elaboration of every curve and detail in the process of seeing the world. His model is Yoruba *oriki*. But can he succeed; can any of us approach the sun dressed in wax? Can the treasure, which we can only expose in the faintest light, seek the glare of rude and extraordinary armory of alien air? There is no doubting the fact that our poetry, and I mean here, African poetry written in English or French, is a failure of the sense, one's own uniquely awkward life, to speak its own color. I am not concerned to argue against writing in English or any other alien language. Nor am I interested in justifying our practice. I am stating the obvious. A language in which one's deepest instincts are converted into the rough shape of breathing must, by definition, be the language in which the profoundest descriptions of emotional life can be articulated. Language is no mere tool to converse in or communicate with; language, in so far, concerns poetry as the medium, like clay, in which the art itself is rescued from death. A tool is a chisel that scrapes and cuts the world. In poetry, the language is the blood and bones, the viscera coursing with pain and delight in which the poet steps out, always to reorganize the invisible architecture of our perceiving the world. Fiction can escape the impracticality of using an alien tongue. Conrad and Achebe (whatever the perceived differences between them, have more in common than most realize) have both shown us that a certain detachment from the language is a precondition for serving fiction's gods well. There is no example of extraordinary poetry written in a language alien to the poet. I mean alien to the writer in the same way that English is to an African, like Osundare, I.R.S. Thomas, and Heaney. They mourn nearly lost languages and have mixed feelings about writing in English, and our relationship to the language is complex and impossible. For a poet not to be able to say that he *loves* or at least *cares* very much for the language in which he writes is problematic for his poetry. To say that one has an affection for this foreign language in which one writes is not without grief. For, it is to say that one prefers someone else's mother to one's own. A profound sense of disloyalty, of sadness, of shame, of guilt, of anger, of helpless "victimhood" surrounds such an utterance. You will by now see that for an African poet writing in English, his sense of self is compromised in the very process of creativity. I do not believe that we have here the best grounds for creative imagination, except if the subject of the poetry, itself, is problematic of disloyalty or of identity. This point has not been made clear, as far as I know, in criticisms of African poetry in English or French. The problem of identity is usually thought to pertain solely to our cousins in the Caribbean or North America whose identities are grossly under siege, and more explicitly so. The African writer is usually not asking the question, "Who am I?" We are embedded in the rich and dense network of myths that anchor us firmly to a place, a language, a climate, a customary way of being and belonging. Quite often, the daring questioning of our identity is regarded as superfluous. We know who we are. Only if that previous statement were true! The problem for the African poet with regards to his identity is as serious as that of our Caribbean or North American cousins, if somewhat different. I do not think that this problem is as acute for the writer of prose as it is for the poet. But, this is only a matter of degree. Ultimately, all art explores our notions of ourselves and either re-affirms what we wish to be true or undermines the undeserved complacency of our daily lives. The terrain of art is that of the personal. It is constantly traversing the foundations or our inner world, creating new illusions to live by, explaining and justifying, contradicting and goading, all the time surveying the territory of our dreams. Identity, as a subject matter for art, is never far from the surface. In approaching Osundare's poetry in this context, I will first examine his poetic projects and his solution to the problems that writing in English poses for us. I will then turn my attention to the future of African poetry in English.

In *Village Voices*, Osundare declared his literary project: here is an example of committed literature; here is a writer who has read and imbibed his Neruda. He identified with the ordinary folk, distinguished between them and their leaders, attributed all the failure to the leaders, and painted pictures of the ordinary folk as victims of the emotional and intellectual poverty of their leaders. It is easy to see these characteristic features as Osundare's signature. This is not the place to rehearse the arguments for and against committed literature. But as Berlin said: "Art for art's sake may be a fallacy, but if a work of art is not art, if it does not pass the aesthetic test, and no amount of morally worthy sentiment or intellectual acuteness will save it (p. 205)." And, furthermore, Tolstoy says:

> The majority of the public… think that the task of all literature
> consisted only in denouncing evil and discussing and correcting it… that the days of the story and of verse have gone
> forever, and that the time is coming when Pushkin will be forgotten and will no longer be read, and that pure art is impossible, that literature is only a tool for the civic development of
> society and so forth… How could one think about poetry when
> for the first time a picture of the evil surrounding us was
> being unveiled before one's eyes, and when the possibility of
> putting an end to it was being presented to us? How could we
> think about the beautiful as we fell ill? The literature of a peo-

ple is its full, many-sided consciousness, in which must be
reflected equally the national contemplation of beauty in a
given epoch of development, and also the national love for
goodness and truth (pp. 222–3).

Berlin and Tolstoy are, I think, arguing that we judge literature in terms of
whether it is good literature or not. It is a separate matter whether as well as
being good or great literature; it also edifies or argues for morally superior positions and so on. I am broadly in agreement with this position. There is a temptation in modern Africa for the parlous state of contemporary life to dominate
and distort the purpose of art. And, for artists to feel compelled to enunciate
political views without consideration to the artistic merits of the work itself, it
is as if the political depths of a given work can rescue its lack of merit. I am not
arguing here against a socially committed literature. Our reality is pervaded by
the grossness of political negligence and ineptitude that art could not possibly
ignore politics. But art, however committed, will first of all be valued for being
art. In approaching Osundare's poetry, I have concerned myself with what he
does with language. In a sense, I am sidestepping the issues that flow from his
politics and, some might say, from his radicalism. I have already argued above
that for poetry, language and the use of words is the very essence of the task. It
is the capacity of the poet to undermine our natural assumptions about language, his ability to alter or prejudices about the self-evident meaning of a word,
his ease at taking risks with rhythm, with tempo, with modulating the organic
music that is poetry, the use of melody and the harmonies of the language that
determines a poet as a worthy poet or not.

In *Village Voices*, Osundare captured the speech patterns and the verbal mannerisms of Nigerian English. He also displayed for all to see the rhetorical
devices of Yoruba form of speech and the techniques of repetition and parallelism common to Yoruba poetry. In the poem, "A dialogue of the drums," he
introduced and explored the possibility of drawing into the reserves of English
the facts of the Nigerian environment, the variety of drums, and the distinguishing shapes and sounds of these drums. The overall effect, however, is of
a language treating its subject as alien to the integrity of the language itself.
There is a problem here of how to successfully integrate Yoruba words within
a body of English words without drawing undue attention to the Yoruba words
so that they do not seem out of place. The stress pattern of Yoruba words is distinct enough to render this task thankless. Also, the pitch in which Yoruba is
spoken is different from the pitch in which English is set, so a definite change
in register is required in reading a composite sentence made up of English and

Yoruba words. These are technical problems, which need to be considered if the overall effect of the insertion of Yoruba words into a poem is to be regarded as a success. All this is only of relevance if you regard poetry as an aural art form—how one hears sounds and whether the organization of these sounds is effective or not—instead of a visual one determined by what one sees on a page. Osundare succeeds in his transposition of the subtleties of the rhythmic changes of Yoruba diction into English. In this regard, the English poet who he most resembles is Gerald Manley Hopkins, whose "sprung" rhythm accommodates the irregular meter of speech. Osundare's gift is to insinuate the complexities of uneven stress patterns, the canter of jollity strewn amongst the slow dirge like profundity of elongated vowels are stretched syllables and to pace the rhythmic drive holding together the lines and ideas.

In contemporary English poetry, in its British and American forms, poets attempt, with varying success, to remove the patina of poetic references from words that already have a surfeit of use in the poetic context. The wish is, of course, to refresh the language—to re-invigorate it so that we are not lulled into a sense of complacency, thinking we know what we mean because we so casually use the same words. Poetry and language, I believe, sicken and die if not constantly challenged. Modern poets attempt this difficult task either by eschewing the use of "poetic" words or by introducing new, somewhat prosaic words from everyday use, such as "bottles," "condoms," "plastic bags," "coca-cola," and so on. The same effect can be achieved by distorting the use of "poetic" words such as "roses," "daffodils," "moon," and "sun," in order to refresh their connotations. For any of this to succeed, however, the poet needs to turn the door on a stable and secure hinge; evolution is only possible if we are sure of our ground. Modern poetry succeeds to the degree that it steadies the nerves of the reader even as it proceeds into foreign territory. We can only appreciate the Martian terrain if we have some (definite) notion of our own. In Osundare's case, the risk is that the leap, which the language is being asked to make, is too great. New and unusual words are introduced to the language at the same time as the inner framework of the language, the skeleton that sustains it, is also being deformed. The result of Osundare's daring poetic instinct can sometimes, but not always, read like a translation. It is very reminiscent of the effect of the translation of Neruda, or some other Spanish American poet, such as Avallejo, into English: beautiful poetry, which is patently not English in origin but is, nonetheless, great poetry. The language simply becomes a mode of expression rather than the medium in which the poetry is worked out. Part of the problem here is to do with whether the language is merely denoting something, which the poet has in mind, or whether the language is, itself, being formulated in the process and thereby helping to clarify what the poet has in mind. You will notice that I have been referring to languages as if they were living, organic beings with purpose and independent of the poet's will. This approach, in a sense, is liable to treat language as a mystical entity existing in the world separate from its use by human agents. I have no wish to create a Popperian disembodied world of human artifacts independent of human consciousness. But, there is a way in which language is like an invisible plasma with a palpable life extending beyond the brief interlude in which anyone of us is suspended within its lattice. To this degree, language permeates our consciousness as if alive and distinct. It is, of course, dependent upon its anchorage in a human brain for its sustenance. To come upon Osundare's poetry is to confront an alien form, familiar in its superficial paraphernalia but obtruding into consciousness because of its shape and size. The weight of its character is reminiscent of grief—a lost world or a yet to be perceived world of images and thoughts.

In *The Eye of the Earth*, Osundare dissolves the problems I have described above. In creating, albeit, in a nostalgic mode the richness of the Nigerian, in particular the Ekiti, countryside, Osundare was able to twist and turn the language so that it came to accommodate the vastness, the colors, the lushness, and the imposing audacity of the material and organic world. The abstract infrastructure of this volume of poetry was the hyperbole and ornate architecture of Yoruba *oriki*. But, I think that in order to domesticate an alien language, like an animal or plant more used to a different climate, you may have to feed it the most delicious delicacies, overburden its sensory pores, immerse it without respite in the hothouse of its new niche. Osundare utilizes this approach. He forces the language to come to terms with a new environment, he wrenches the language from its complacent posture and situates it in a pulsating aromatic world that the language itself comes alive, refreshed and enchanted—practically invigorated.

But, there is something missing. The picture we get is a poetic portrayal of life. Where is the mud, the fly, the dust, the pain and the dying, the tangle of energy that is rude and abrasive? Above all, where are the people, the drama of envy and jealousy, the pettiness and sourness, the demanding contrariness, the acquisitiveness, the aggression and vulgarity of people? Osundare's own voice, the narrative voice, is carefully in the shadows, the morality is again of the virtuous priest, not the sinful poet, inhabiting and participating in a world of imperfect and often undesirable—a poet who is not a member of a class or a nation necessarily, but a vulnerable, human being struggling to do what is right like the rest of us. The emotional charge that has yet to explore the fullness of our moods is the multi-layered and differentiated services of our feelings.

Neruda, who is Osundare's model, especially in his (Neruda's) love poetry, was able to combine the positive life-affirming emotions with the heartbreaking despair and disillusionment that characterizes our tragic place in life and was always as a participant, not merely a detached observer, who derived his moral authority from his virtue. Of course, Osundare, in life, has been on the barricades. But the poetry in *The Eye of the Earth* does not speak to the poet's own vulnerability, nor does it portray the people at all. This is a landscape painted without recourse to the inhabitants. I admit that a single volume of poetry cannot aspire to several disparate goals. *The Eye of the Earth* is a successful volume, no matter how you look at it. One can sound peevish and petty in asking for some of this and some of that. Osundare's achievement is that forcibly and irrefutably he has drawn a picture of a particular corner of Nigeria. It is a compelling and truthful picture. It is also memorable.

In *Moonsongs*, Osundare moves into an abstract mode. This volume is sheer indulgence in artifice. The poems serve only language's purpose. Language, here, is a vehicle for adorning itself. The intricacies of expression, the accretions of qualifying terms, of adjectival flourishes, and the retreat into lyricism and clever imagery do not enhance the poetry—that is, if poetry is distinct from the devices that give it life. Jarrell writing of Wallace Stevens said:

> The immediacy and precision and particularity, the live touch
> of things, the beauty that exists in precarious perfection....is
> lost in rhetoric, in elaboration and artifice and contrivance, in
> an absolutely ecumenical Method of seeing and thinking and
> expressing, in *craftsmanship* (pp. 126–7).

These comments on Stevens' later works could just as well be true for Osundare's *Moonsongs*.

In *Waiting Laughers*, there is an almost absence of narrative voice. The poetry approaches the oracular. There are flashes of inspired symbolism and imagery. The poetry has acquired a fundamental opacity, a recognizable mannerism of expression, and easy facility with poetic effects, an absence of the concrete enactment of danger, a disengagement from the reader. Like Miles Davis in his later period, the music has moved away from the solidarity with the structures that made it at once exceptional as well as understood. There is a danger in saying all of this, of my being interpreted as denouncing or being unappreciative of the highest calling of the poet, which is to experiment with words and language. In the two volumes under consideration, Osundare's gift for vivid imagery, for earthy humor, and for grand and rich expositions is ever present.

But, there is a way in which his artistic project has not been moved forward. Both volumes confirm the very distinctive style, the mannerisms of expression that mark the poetry as his. These poems become almost a parody of Osundare.

Osundare's project is only partly completed. He has colonized this alien language, showed the language how to describe new experiences, how to speak in strange accents and tempo, and how to adapt to previously uncharted phenomena. But, there is still a gap to fill; the language has yet to describe the people, their awesome beauty, their ugliness, the varying shades of their color, their size, their manner of walking, their terror, their sins and sinfulness, their lusting for power and for hope, and all the intricate secrecy of their dreams. There is little inferiority here. It is only in the poem, "A Reunion," in *Village Voices* that we get to know the poet as a living being, a being with feelings that transcend mere indignation at our socio-political situation. It is as if the personal is so trivial, so petty in comparison to the enormity of our desperate situation, that the only appropriate tone is the oracular. The intensely personal is as important if not more so than the public affects that pre-occupy us. It is the personal in all its myriad forms that sustains the spirit, and there must be a place for its expression in poetry. If a Martian were reading African poetry in English today, he would have very little sense of our emotional life. There is a void waiting to be filled. I am speaking about the superficial, confessional poetry that characterizes modern American Poetry. I am referring to the need for personal sensibility to infuse the poems with vigor. Yoruba poetry in its vast range does not deal exclusively with the grand and portentous. It has space for the fullness of life. Osundare has the gift of language to appropriate these spaces and to populate them with images specially suited to their temperament.

In Hountondji's *African philosophy: myth & reality* he concluded:

> The most important thing today is not to study African cultures but to *live* them, not to exhibit them to ourselves or dissect them with scrupulous scientific objectivity but to practice them, not to digest them passively but to transform them.... Instead of suing French or English to discuss the structures of Yoruba or Fon, we would do better to use yoruba or Fon to discuss the structures of French or English and, more generally to use African languages in advanced word in the various sciences [and one could add, in the humanities] (p. 169).

Hountondji, of course, recognized that this is an enormous task. In arriving at the same conclusion that Hountondji asserted, I am persuaded not by Ngugi's declaration of a need from decolonization of our psyche (although this is also necessary, but can be achieved by other measures) but by a subtler argument not widely put forward. I have already hinted, that in literature, and here I refer specifically to poetry whose demands I believe to be different, in order to produce the greatest possible words, the writer has to breathe the language and have an uncomplicated relationship with the language. His use of the language must not be at one remove; the ability to enunciate or declare must be automatic, organic, and effortless as breathing is to us all. My understanding of Yoruba as I am sure Osundare's is, is total and unpremeditated. The emotional resonance of words, their natural and specified meanings, the anchorage of their sounds in the network of other noises, the very trajectory and velocity of their passage through the private and secret, the utterly opaque plasma of another person's soul, these are more clear, more like judging what is transparent, to me than any manifestation of English, either in print or spoken. Our tragedy is that a disjunction has occurred in our education to dislocate the continuous progression of our use of our own languages. To understand is one thing; to use a language with high proficiency, with the fluency, which is required in the making of this thing called poetry, is another. And, Yoruba poetry is a highly formalized art, departure from which demands a command of the formal and implicit rules, an appreciation of the history and tradition that must underlie any reformation. Unfortunately, most of us do not have the facility of this language. Before long, the poetry that is rightfully ours will have become a relic, a ruined castle, and an example of how houses were built rather than a living, breathing animated culture housing us.

Osundare's poetry is an attempt to re-engage us with the precepts of our own poetry, a very good attempt at re-connecting us with the modes of singing, crying, and laughing, which instructs how we walk, how we look at others, how on moonlit nights we sit close to each others, huddle and then sigh, and how a community derives pleasure and wisdom from a simple story or other. But, it does this in an alien language. His gift has been to construct out of this alien language a unique style, recognizable even in the dark, his shadow and profile stamped on the lines. Great poetry demands this, that the words be purely a signature tune, uncorrupted by any other voice. In this respect, Osundare has succeeded, but at what cost?

I have been arguing that our very best poetry, from Okigbo, Soyinka, and Osundare, even if applauded, would have already failed, by the simple fact of its alliance with an alien tongue. I am led to conclude that this literature, which has flourished in this brief and transitory period in our long history, is a temporary aberration. I am a contributor to this aberration, and I regret it but have little power to alter my fate. Poetry has everything to do with the tribe, with the affirmation of the tribe's identity, with the orchestration of the self's wish to belong to a named and recognizable group and to understand how the world is, how to live the good life, and how best to die. I must not be misunderstood as advocating *tribal poetry*. I am pointing out the role of all art, but in particular, the role of poetry in defining and consolidating our sense of self in terms of group membership. The myths, which hold together the possibility of survival in a human community, the implicit rules, which govern and facilitate our communion with others, the modal expressions of success or failure, the insignia of moral worth, the unpardonable sins—these are all inscribed on the soul's slate by art, by the voluble stream of poetry. This is what I mean by poetry's tribal essence. Poetry also instructs the soul how to listen, how to modulate sounds such that the meaning flows out of the music. Poetry is pre-eminently an auditory art, a verbal, aural art. These multifold aspects of poetry demand a precision of usage, a complex yet audaciously simple line of reasoning, an emotional life rendered free of illusion and then covered over with distraction and beauty, spaciously separated silence, but in the end, poetry demands modesty and self-confidence all at once. All this in the service of language.

What Osundare and others like him are doing, I hope and believe, is preparing the ground for the re-emergence of true poetry in our own languages. The stylistic contributions to the English language, which Osundare can rightfully claim as his own and that must be seen as daring excursions into how Yoruba *oriki* can be wrenched from its moorings and pushed to serve others purposes. His pursuit of alliterations must signal the introductions of this technique into Yoruba poetry. Our aim must be to have this poetry translated into Yoruba and then taught in Yoruba classes, so that it can inform the artistic urges of others. It may be that it would also profit poetry in other languages, such as Hausa, Igbo, Or Efik. Laying the foundation for something, which whilst not visible today, can become like coal, compressed and converted to diamond by the sheer weight of its underground status. It would be fitting if the poetry of Osundare, especially as it derives most from traditional Yoruba poetry, were to be the first in the process of giving birth to a feeding back to the sources of all our creative urges.

My criticism of Osundare's poetry and his recent progression into abstract poetry is aimed at those who I hope will one day write the modern poetry—the true poetry that our hearts yearn for, in our own languages. Our contribution to the literature of another culture and another language, no matter how noble or accomplished, must be a transitory phase. It is an illusion to regard our current literature as anything other than alien.

REFERENCES

Berlin, I. "Artistic commitment." *The sense of reality.* Oxford: University Press, 1996.

Hountondji, P.J. *African Philosophy: myth & Reality.* Trans. H. Evans. Indianapolis: Indiana University Press, 1983.

Jarrell, R. *Reflections on Wallace Stevens Poetry and the Age.* London: Faber and Faber, 1953.

POETRY AND COMMITMENT

STILL DARING THE BEAST: NIYI OSUNDARE AND CONTEMPORARY NIGERIAN POETRY*

Stewart Brown

Arguably the defining characteristic of Nigerian poetry in English has been its confrontational attitude to authority: from the poets of the high colonial period like Dennis Osadebay who used their verse to oppose the deculturing practices of imperialism, most famously in his poem 'Africa's Plea':

> Don't preserve my customs
> As some fine curios
> To suit some white historian's tastes'[1]

through the labyrinth of Christopher Okigbo's mythologising to that strand of his work, in 'Path of Thunder', where – in no uncertain terms – he declares his opposition to a power-elite which is set on the destruction of the new Nigeria's potential for national fulfillment:

> parliament has gone on leave
> the members are now on bail
> parliament is now on sale
> the voters are lying in wait[2]

and through to Achebe's and Soyinka's responses to the civil calamity of the Biafran war in direct and pointed verse, and to J. P. Clarke's commentaries on the state of the nation in the 1970s. But it is among the generation of poets who began publishing in the 1970s and 1980s that the notion of the poet as being duty-bound to confront the political events of the times, or more particularly the antics of the country's rulers, has become axiomatic. Of course across the continent writers have argued over the extent to which they should become, in Nadine Gordimer's phrase, 'more than writers'3 and the arguments about *commitment* and *responsibility* are well rehearsed, not to say well worn, but in Nigeria – as with much else – the issues are felt and expressed in extreme terms. Several poets have incurred the wrath of the politicians or soldiers in power, victimised in one way or another for their outspoken criticism, although it is still hard to believe that Nigeria's presidents and generals spend much time reading poetry.

In 'The Emperor and the Poet', a lucid and passionate introductory essay to his book-length poem *A Song from Exile* (1992), the much-lauded young Nigerian poet and artist Olu Oguibe – compared by Chinua Achebe to the young Christopher Okigbo – describes the circumstances of his 'exile' from Nigeria and the strength of his feeling about the state of the country. He lists intellectuals, artists and writers who, like himself, have been effectively forced out. He is full of praise for those few, including Niyi Osundare and Tanure Ojaide,4 who stayed and risked speaking out, 'daring the beast' as he puts it. His poem *A Song from Exile* is a lyrical account in eight parts exploring feelings of anger, shame and despair at being away from the society which both abuses and yet feeds his creative spirit. Outside Nigeria, Oguibe's poetic persona feels that his

> tongue is blunt
> The songster has journeyed
> Without his voice.5

Oguibe acknowledges both anguish and a sense of guilt over his exile status, aware of the relative comfort of his situation as a doctoral student in London, considering himself, in one mood, 'A coward fled home and the battlefront'. He is unable to accept that there can be any 'peace away from home' and is tortured by a conscience that:

> makes my bed with a quilt of thorns
> Ah, conscience that leashes a man to his past
> Conscience that stakes a man in the open courtyard

and pelts him with rain
(A Song from Exile, 13).

A Song from Exile is a moving expression of the author's dilemma and distress. If it reads as rather gauche and heart-on-sleeve in places that is to some
extent proof of the authenticity of its sentiments. But what does such a poem
do, beyond establishing Oguibe's sense of his own commitment to Nigeria and
the pain of his exile? And why have so many Nigerian poets persisted in pitch-
ing their writing against successive regimes in this way? It can seem, after a
while, like nothing more than a self-aggrandising *style,* a relatively safe way of
asserting one's radicalism. In 'The Emperor and the Poet', Oguibe addresses
the issue himself:

> It is arguable to what extent the artist can influence or turn
> the course of history, and we in Nigeria have had so long a his-
> tory of battles between the artist and the state that we have
> even greater reason to be doubtful ... we are simply saying
> what we see, for it is seeing and not saying, our people say,
> that kills the elder. It is hearing and not heeding that will kill
> the child. That, for us, is the fate of the Emperor and the poet.
> (A *Song from Exile,* 7).

That recourse to the oral tradition and its proverbial lore as validation for the
poet's literary practice is another familiar assertion about contemporary
Nigerian poetry in English, that there is a filial relationship between that body
of writing and the oral traditions of the region. Quite how the influence of the
one tradition is expressed in the other is not always clear. Oguibe, though, is
calling up the notion of the oral poet as the literal spokesman for the common
people in the courts of the powerful. In some West African traditions poets were
indeed 'licensed' to air grievances or criticisms of the rulers in praise-song or
at communal gatherings when those being criticised were obliged to hear and
to react. Perhaps, as Odia Ofeimun has suggested, by their responses to the
poets' critiques the generals have just been acting out their part in the cultural
transition![6]

Certainly in claiming that traditional duty to speak out and in challenging the
politicians' contempt for the alter-native[7] poetic licence so openly, Oguibe joins
a throng of contemporary Nigerian poets[8] who have often seemed more concerned with that public role, and with the political content and effects of their
poems, than they have been with the techniques of their craft. Their engage-

ment with this role has perhaps resulted in neglect of the wider implications of writing a hybrid 'English poetry', or of ways in which that borrowed role might be more effectively underpinned by an adaptation of the oral poets' techniques.

One defence against that charge has been the urgency of their situation. For Tanure Ojaide, confronting the desolation of Nigeria's civil society by successive corrupt governments is a sacred duty, and words, given appropriate poetic shape by the very pressure of the circumstances, are the only weapon available to him. As he writes in 'Before Our God':

> Neither bullets nor other savageries can arrest words
> that have already been aired –
> paper is witness to the lone mind.
>
> ....
> These words file out on the dirt road
> to stop nerve-wrecking waves of despots;
> they are the charms worn before battle9

That poem answers the question of 'why write at all' and in terms of Oguibe's presentation of the necessary opposition between the Emperor and the poet in Nigeria, Ojaide's poem 'What poets do our leaders read' is unequivocal in its condemnation of poets who take a less critical, less forthright stand than his own. They are, he says:

> Perjurers of the Word,
> drummers of bloated drums,
> carriers of offensive sacrifice;
> fanners of vanities.10

Over six collections now Tanure Ojaide has practised what he preaches, using his poetry to expose the perceived evils in his society and imply the necessity of a different morality. His poetry is much admired and has won prestigious Nigerian and international prizes. His work has been compared with that of David Diop, Pablo Neruda and Mayakovsky, and certainly he shares their socialist commitment and values. In plain-spoken, interventionist poems like 'When soldiers are diplomats', 'The levelling rule' and 'Song for my Land', he chronicles the destitution and despoliation of Nigeria in recent times:

> More and more the land mocks my heart.
> Where are the evergreens of my palm;

why is the sun of salvation eclipsed
by coups and intolerable riots?

Wherever I pass, mockery of the land;
naked trees flaunt sterile bodies at me
('Song for My Land', *The Fate of Vultures* 41).

There are other, gentler, strands in Ojaide's poetry – he has written some fine love poems for example – but for the most part his poems are blunt 'messages from the front', sacrificing imagistic complexity or formal musicality for a rhetorical outrage that – arguably – overwhelms the 'poetry' – insofar as we equate poetry with subtlety, ambiguity and linguistic cunning.

That is a charge which might be levelled at the work of many of Nigeria's contemporary poets, particularly when their work is read *en masse*. While there can be no doubting these poets' sincerity or the depth of their anguish, the unending self-righteousness of the narrative voice, the artless predictability of the sentiments and the clichéd language of 'protest' undermine, at least for this reader, the force of so many of these poems, *as poems*. But that 'at least' is, of course, an immense qualification. Where, in cultural and ideological as well as in geographical terms, is such a response coming from?

Nigerian poets and critics – not noted for their reticence or the gentleness of their own critical judgements – have been loud in their assertion of the particularity of African and especially Nigerian circumstances which have aesthetic and cultural as well as economic and social aspects. Indeed another explanation of the younger Nigerian poets' obsession with social and political commentary, advanced most eloquently by Funso Aiyejina[11], is that it stems precisely from their engagement with – and continuing reaction – to that most cataclysmic event in recent Nigerian history, the Biafran war. This is the generation of writers who saw as children or young men (they are almost entirely men) both the horror and the passion that went into that war and understood most vividly what it cost their peers who were caught up in and killed by it. Their collective vision of a better society is, Aiyejima argues, as much a consequence of that historical experience, that memory, as it is a reaction to the reality of the corrupt and ineffectual governments that their country has since endured. So that 'alter-native' aesthetic, informed both by that sense of an historical duty and notions of poetic function in some way derived from the oral tradition, seems largely to foreground content over form, to value accessibility above linguistic or imagistic subtlety and to prefer 'statement' to 'song'.

And yet the poet who was effectively the founder of that alter-native tradition, Odia Ofeimun, whose poems are as uncompromising as Ojaide's, as outraged as Oguibe's, is very much concerned with both form and the power of wit and startling imagery as poetry's most effective agents. Ofeimun is set apart from many of his contemporaries too in the grounded experience that underlies his political vision. He was not always part of the society's educated elite. For several years after leaving school he worked at a variety of manual and petty clerical jobs, including three years as a factory labourer with the West African Thread Company in Apapa. Then after studying political science at university and a spell spent teaching and working as a civil servant he was Chief Awolowo's private secretary for several years. That broad working experience clearly shapes the moral agenda that drives all his poetry.

Paradoxically the withdrawal of the original 1980 edition of *The Poet Lied* by Longman when J. P. Clarke decided that the title poem pointed a finger too uncomfortably at him and threatened to sue for libel – that 'scandal' ensured that Odia Ofeimun's name would be well remembered even though few people, even in Nigeria, had had the opportunity to read much of his work. 'It put my name on the literary map in a way that I find intimidating,' Ofeimun has remarked.[12] Several poems were well known of course, from journal and anthology publications, and his reputation as a powerful performer of his own work was well established from his days at the University of Ibadan. That original edition of *The Poet Lied* was a very slim volume indeed and it was clear that the selection of poems included there represented a very thin trawl of Ofeimun's work up to that point. His second collection, *A Handle for the Flutist* came out in Nigeria in 1986 to wide critical acclaim – if to some political discomfort – and quickly sold out. In 1989 a new, much expanded edition of *The Poet Lied* appeared in Nigeria (Update Communications Ltd, Lagos). It was effectively a provisional Collected Poems, including all that was in the Longman collection plus many of the poems of that period which were edited out of that volume, all the poems in *A Handle for the Flutist,* and, significantly, a long interview with Onwuchekwu Jemie, which explores many of the philosophical and political ideas that underpin his poetry.

The interview provides a very useful context for a reading of the poems, establishing that the heart of the book is indeed the poet's consideration of the events and ramifications of the Civil War, or rather, as Aiyejina suggests, what that dreadful experience meant for the artists of the society in terms of their understanding of the roles and functions of art. Ofeimun's ambition in 'The Poet Lied' was to establish – by parodying its opposite – a moral position for the 'committed' poet of the post-war Nigeria into which he spoke. So the lying poet asked only:

to be left alone
with his blank sheet on his lap
in some dug-out damp corner
with a view of the streets and the battle fields
watching the throngs of calloused lives,
the many many lives stung by living.
He would put them in his fables
sandwich them between his lions and eagles,
between his elephants and crocodiles.
('The Poet Lied' 40–1).

Ofeimun weaves echoes, half-quotations and some well-known literary posi-tions into the ironic fabric of his poem, and for those who felt themselves thus identified it must have been a painful experience. But as Ofeimun makes clear in the interview, that was not the main intention of the piece. It was rather to construct a manifesto for himself and his generation of writers against which their own integrity might be measured.

Clearly Ofeimun takes the business of writing seriously, this is no therapeu-tic, leisure-time activity. His ambition is to make a poetry that is both commit-ted and crafted, relevant and resonant. He cites Salvatore Quasimodo, Rilke and Martin Carter among his formative influences and his work does read – in a way that much contemporary Nigerian poetry in English pointedly doesn't – as if it, too, acknowledged a notion of poetry that transcends regional and even cul-tural boundaries. You feel that the language, not just the writer, is under pres-sure:

She whose tongue could coil
a rig of pythons to break oaks
She whose fire could raze
palaces to dust in rainstorms
She whose hands could wield pestles
to make miscreants footloose with dread
She was always the first
to call the doves to witness
('Our Wild Christian' *The Poet Lied* 87).

Robert Fraser in his book *West African Poetry* characterises Ofeimun as 'a manic harlequin' in the courts of post-independence Nigeria's corrupt leaders. Fraser reads the poems in the 1980 edition of *The Poet Lied* as seething against 'the pure absurdity of injustice it (the poetry) knows itself powerless to redress' (p.307). But Ofeimun sees himself rather as a literary guerrilla and, certainly with the later poems, he clearly feels that such poetry *can* make things happen. In societies where the written word is still regarded with some suspicion[13] and where the formalised spoken word has long been one of the accoutrements of power such poetry must resonate and will be attended to. As he puts it in 'A Handle for the Flutist', a poem rich in literary allusions and yet located very precisely in contemporary Nigeria:

> the worshipped word is enough
> to expiate crimes and to lay honour
> upon whom the pleaded grace of song has fallen.
> *(The Poet Lied,* 118).

Indeed Ofiemun argues in that poem that it is the very fear the generals – 'the executives' – have of poetry's loaded words, more potent than the loaded guns of more familiar kinds of guerrillas, that has lent poets such authority as they have in Nigeria. Echoing that image of the oral poet able to make 'gods crumble to their knees/questioned by simple images', Ofeimun declares with characteristic irony, and with an awareness of the paradox in what he, the scourge of the tyrant, is saying:

> so let us praise those who will track down
> folksongs with police dogs
>
> They will not live with poets
> in the Peoples' Republic
> ('A Handle for the Flutist' *The Poet Lied,* 119).

If Ofeimun is the voice of the harlequin, the goad, the wit puncturing the pomposities of Nigeria's rulers with his ironic barbs and bells, then Niyi Osundare is the high priest of the 'alter-native' vision. Perhaps it is significant that, like Ofeimun, he is not from a traditional elite background – 'farmer born peasant bred' he asserts in an early poem. He is the one poet whose lyrical and critical intelligence seems to offer both an alternative politics *and* a notion of poetics which suggests a real way forward for Nigerian – indeed African – poetry in English. Osundare's work is at once aware of both the cultural traditions that feed its roots and of the potential for a unique flowering in the fertile hybridities of an 'African English'. Much of his poetry addresses issues of global significance although his poetry speaks directly into the topical debates of modern Nigeria. There is a gravitas and weight about Osundare's poetry that, while the reader is aware of the characteristic quality of anger that is so prized in this 'alter-native' tradition, makes his arguments seem the more considered, the more measured. And indeed they are measured, for the other quality of Osundare's poetry, which might seem at odds with the notion of gravitas and weight, is its musicality, its lightness of touch. One never feels that Osundare is preaching, nor that – as reader – one is being harangued, yet the effect of much of his poetry is both to teach and to inspire a critical rage against the global inanities that are the targets of much of his own wit and anger.

These general comments are true of Osundare's work as a whole, from his first collection, *Songs of the Marketplace* (1983), through to his most recent book, *Horses of Memory* (1998),[15] but I would like to look at the two volumes that to me best exemplify, on the one hand, the philosophical and political ideas that underpin his work, and on the other, the techniques and cultural resources that so distinctively shape his poetry.

The Eye of the Earth (1986), his third collection, is as much a celebration of the natural world and the peasant traditions of his Ikere people, as it is a critique of the geo-political and economic forces which he feels threaten the earth's very existence. Osundare's commitment is not exclusively to one race or to one nation but rather to an ecological vision of an ideal harmony between Man and Nature. But despite the urgent passion of his concerns, Osundare seems always conscious of the priorities of his craft. *The Eye of the Earth* is by turns lyrical and declamatory, carefully structured and yet rich in bold, original imagery. The sequence is broken into three movements. It begins autobiographically by delving into Osundare's childhood memory of peasant life in Ikere, and then, by contrasting that seemingly idyllic past with the present circumstances of his people and their land he draws out the political criticisms that are the heart of his concern.

The sequence opens with 'Forest Echoes', an extended praise-song to the Nigerian forest, drawing vivid portraits of its trees and creatures. The poet's intention here is more than just to celebrate the landscape of his childhood: it is to demonstrate the balance in nature, the reliance of each element on the others in maintaining the ecological harmony. So the Iroko, the ironwood tree that defies the 'sweating sawyer' and 'champion machet' is king of the forest, but even he will fall eventually to the 'block-headed termites' and the 'scalpel-toothed' squirrel, that 'adzeman of the forest'.

The poem goes on then to consider the land itself, and the balance Osundare's ancestors understood between harvesting its mineral and vegetable wealth and paying due respect to the earth mother as the provider of such riches. He contrasts that traditional honouring with the cynical and short-sighted way today's entrepreneurs exploit the earth's gifts. Addressing Olusunta, one of the gold-bearing rocks sacred to his Ikere people, he asks, 'how dig the gold/without breaking the rock?'[16] Of course the rock is not just the mountain itself, it is the community, the whole social system that has developed around it. For the poet recognises as perhaps only a modern Nigerian could, how easily sudden wealth, if not carefully managed, can turn from a blessing into a curse.

In 'Rainsongs', the second movement of the sequence, the poet celebrates the gift of rain as nature's 'arbiter between plenty and famine, life and death'. The seven poems in this movement focus on different aspects of the experience of the rainy season. First comes a prayer for rain, 'Let Earth's Pain be Soothed' but soon enough, looking at the lush transformation of the countryside after the first rains, the poet can ask 'Who says that drought was here?'

'Homecall', the final movement of the sequence, brings Osundare's political argument into focus. The decline of his people from that balanced lifestyle he remembers as the world of his childhood is used as a metaphor for the experience of the whole nation, indeed of the whole Third World. The life of the child who was 'Farmer born and peasant bred' was rich in spiritual experience that helped sustain his community, in material as well as religious terms. But the culture was not strong enough, the poem argues, to resist 'alien' ideas and values, unadapted to local circumstances, that began in school and ultimately produced a national culture of materialism, envy and corruption which resulted in a whole people being reduced to dependence on imported food for its very subsistence:

> Farmer-born peasant-bred
> classroom-bled
> I have thrown open my kitchen doors
> and asked hunger to take a seat,
> my stomach a howling dump
> for Carolina rice
> (*The Eye of The Earth*, 44).

That decline inspires Osundare's rage, not only in *The Eye of the Earth* but throughout his work, and in essence, is the source of Osundare's political vision. As I've described it Osundare may seem something of a romantic, a reactionary figure even, lamenting the passing of a golden age. Rather his poetic and political vision spring from a profound awareness of African history and the debilitating effects of the long-term contact with Europe which has disrupted the mechanisms of balance he sees in the experience of his own people. What, in human terms, most disrupted that balance was the Atlantic slave trade, and Osundare's bleak, passionate but restrained poem 'Goree', responding to a visit he made to the notorious Senegalese slaving station in 1989, establishes the force of his historical imagination. Elsewhere in his work, and in common with the other poets of the alter-native tradition, he is not averse to pointing out the injustices of 'traditional' as well as contemporary governments. So he is no reactionary. And while the notion of a balance, in nature and in political structure, that sustains the community, may be idealistic, as one critic has remarked,[17] it does represent an *imaginable* alternative to both the brutalising crude capitalism of post-independence Nigerian governments and the crude ideological socialism of the intellectual 'opposition'. Osundare's alternative political vision, as it is enmeshed and expressed in his poetry, is both pragmatic and practical, informed by an essentially optimistic view of humanity's ability to change and a belief in the fundamental instinct of mankind to both respect and nurture the earth and its resources.

That pragmatic optimism is evident, too, in *Waiting Laughters,* which won the 1991 NOMA award for poetry. It is this collection – and Osundare's books usually seem to have been conceived as extended poems – which seems to me to best represent Osundare's notion of poetic craft and his relationship to the oral tradition. Subtitled 'a long song in many voices', it is broken into six sections, each of them announced by a different musical setting. For example the opening, 'Some laughters are very significant', has the instruction *flute and/or clarinet; medley of voices.* As a mere reader one has to try and 'hear' the poem in that performance context in order to get a sense of how effective the words off the page might be. As straight text, sections of the poem occasionally seem over-ornamented, particularly in the first section where there is an almost baroque quality to the language, *every* noun encrusted with adjectives, *every* line an image. But it is clear Osundare knows what he's doing, and knows what effect he is striving for. A note to the poem explains that the sequence:

> is about waiting in different and often contrasting circumstances, and the behaviour of time in the waiting process. But more than anything else, it is a poetic response to the gloom and despair which seems to have gripped contemporary African society.[18]

The opening section of the poem establishes various 'levels' of waiting; from the political:

through the elemental:

Oh teach us the patience of the Rain
Which eats the rock in toothless silence

to the cosmic:

Waiting
on the stairs of the moon
creaking up and down
the milkyways of fastidious comets
(*Waiting Laughter, 25*)

In such contexts, the poet seems to imply, there *is* time to indulge in the playfulness of a language rich in puns, alliteration and the mannered laughter of literary wit. In section two of the poem, 'The freedom of any society varies proportionately with the volume of its laughter', the social and historical context of African, particularly Nigerian, history is drawn, and issues like those he explores in *The Eye of the Earth* are considered. So is the fundamental question, for a poet, of language:

The tongue is parrot
Of another forest

......

A white white tongue
In a black black mouth

....

And the tongue hangs out its blade
blunted
by the labyrinthine syntax of ghostly histories

....

History's stammerer
when will your memory master
the vowels of your father's name?
(*Waiting Laughters,* 40).

It is in his brilliant use of that 'borrowed tongue' – as he calls it elsewhere – breaking and remaking English, capitalising on the tension set up by that confrontation of language and culture, that Osundare answers, for his generation, the question of authenticity-in-English that dogged the previous generation of African writers. Osundare is doing for African poetry what Derek Walcott did for Caribbean poetry, claiming and maiming the language for his own ends. No English poet *could* use the English language in the way Osundare does. He uses it to confront the same outrage and distress that Oguibe and Ojaide lament, but with an understanding of the power of wit, of mockery, of laughter, to both discomfort its targets and revitalise its users.

Aderemi Bamikunle has usefully pointed to the close relationship between Osundare's techniques and the devices of the Yoruba oral tradition – from the more or less literal 'translation' of certain poems of occasion[19] to the more subtle adaptation of forms and functions and, as with *Waiting Laughters*, the incorporation of music into the fabric of the poem's 'event'. The notion of the poet *speaking for* a community is as important to Osundare as to the other poets of the 'alter-native' tradition, but this need not be the overt assertion of that right and duty that Oguibe and Ojaide claim, but can be expressed rather in that nuanced adaptation of the oral poets' devices which signal his awareness of the responsibility that accompanies those forms. This is apparent in the ways he has used both aspects of the praise-song tradition, on the one hand to genuinely praise the person or even object that is its subject, as in 'Sowing':

> When a long-awaited shower has softened the pilgrimage of the
>   dibble, corn-grains sing their way to germinal roots
>
> of lying ridges. Seedlings dream truant tendrils in the mois-
>   tening bed of unpunctual heaps; the tuber is one patience
>   away,
>
> climbing through stalks
>
> through pinna-leaved groves
> through vines which twine the moons like wayward pythons
> (*Waiting Laughters,* 88).

or to be bitterly ironic in debunking its subject's hypocrisies:

>   Waiting,
> like the corpulent clergy
> for his tithes
>
> like the white-wigged judge
> for his turkey

like the hard-faced don
for his chair

like the policeman
for his bribe
waiting
(*Waiting Laughters*, 48).

Neither of those examples takes praise-song forms as a literal template for the English-language poem, but the effect, within the sequence as a whole, is to recall that dual function of praise-song in Osundare's tradition, and the risks that the praise singer who was more than just a sycophant always took.

Similarly his use of proverbs – and by all accounts his poems are rich in echoes of Yoruba proverbs – is a matter of subtle adaptation rather than a simplistic translation. Even for the reader without knowledge of Yoruba proverbs, much of Osundare's work bears the cast of proverbial utterance. Indeed some of the more obvious echoes are from proverbs that exist in English:

The plough has no share in
the malady of running swords
(*Waiting Laughter*, 53).

And in a sense it doesn't matter about such origins. Osundare's sources, his technique, like his language, are hybrid, and his poetry is inevitably *about* crossing boundaries. 'Peasant born and farmer bred' but, in Walcott's words 'with a sound colonial education', Osundare's genius is in welding his several inheritances into a unique and appropriate voice for his times. That quality is evident at the conclusion of *Waiting Laughters* where Osundare uses the 'traditional' techniques of poetry, traditional across boundaries of culture and race: unusual imagery, a rhythmic surge, a concise, considered use of a language crafted to produce more of a sense of threat to the status quo than any number of ranting, breast-beating statements of the kind he satirises in the opening couplets of this quotation:

Our laughter these several seasons is the simper-
ing sadness of the ox which adores its yoke,

The toothless guffaw of empty thunders
In epochs of unnatural drought

The season calls for the lyric of other laughters

New chicks breaking the fragile tyranny
of hallowed shells

A million fists, up,
In the glaring face of complacent skies

A machet waiting, waiting
In the whetting shadows of stubborn shrubs

A boil, time-tempered,
About to burst.
(*Waiting Laughters,* 96–7).

Unlike some of his more outspoken contemporaries, Osundare 'dares the beast' not only at the level of rhetoric but also in terms of ideas. If the generals would object to his poetry they must first *read* it; they cannot skim the surface for the obviously offensive word but must explore the metaphor, understand the irony, consider the ambiguities, discover its measured 'beauty'. Beauty and the Beast! Now that would be, in Oguibe's words, for a poet to 'turn the course of history'.

NOTES

1. Donatus Nwoga, *West African Verse,* London: Longman, 1967: 17.
2. Christopher Okigbo, *Labyrinths,* London: Heinemann, 1971: 68.
3. Since this essay was first published both Ojaide and Osundare have taken up teaching posts in the USA.
4. Gordimer, Nadine. "The Essential Gesture: Writers and Responsibility." *Granta,* No. 15 1989: 137–5 1.
5. Oguibe, Olu . *A Song from Exile.* Bayreuth: Boomerang Press, 1990: 9.
6. See the discussion of Ofeimun's poem 'A Handle for the Flutist' later in this essay.
7. 'Alter-native' tradition – the term seems to have derived from Femi Osofisan's *Guardian* essay 'The Alternative Tradition: A Survey of Nigerian Literature', but is used by Funso Aiyejina in its broken form in his essay 'Recent Nigerian Poetry in English: an Alter-Native Tradition' (see note 10 below) to draw attention to the alteration of the consciousness in the work of the younger generation of Nigerian poets who are self consciously *native* - with all the ramifications of that term – in their language, their cultural orientation and their concerns. It has become reviewers' and critics' shorthand for the writers of that generation.
8. See, for example, the work of Femi Fatoba, Funso Aiyejina, Fred Agdeyegbe, Silas Obadiah, Emevwo Biakolo, Femi Osofisan, Eman Shehu; and see the Association of Nigerian Authors' anthology, edited by Harry Garuba, *Voices from the Fringe,* Lagos: Malthouse Press, 1990.
9. Ojaide, Tanure .*The Blood of Peace,* London: Heinemann, 1991: 28.
10. Ojaide, Tanure .*The Fate of Vultures,* Lagos: Malthouse Press, 1990: 9.
11. Aiyejina, Funso. "Recent Nigerian Poetry in English: an Alter-Native Tradition."Ed. Yemi Ogunbiyi. *Perspectives on Nigerian Literature: 1700 to the present,* vol. 1. Lagos: Guardian Books (Nigeria), 1988.
12. Jemie, Onwuchekwa. "A Conversation with Odia Ofeimun." *The Poet Lied,* Lagos: Update Communications Ltd., 1989: 148–76.
13. Fraser, Robert. *West African Poetry,* Cambridge: Cambridge University Press, 1986.
14. Jemie, Onwuchekwa. 'A Conversation with Odia Ofeimun'.
15. For a full bibliography of Osundare's work – and a useful bibliographical essay – see Don Burness' essay on Osundare in *The Dictionary of Literary Biography.* See also Jeyifo, Biodun. "Niyi Osundare" Ed. Yemi Ogunbiyi's *Perspectives on Nigerian Literature,* vol. 2.: 314–20.
16. Osundare, Niyi. *The Eye of the Earth.* Lagos: Heinemann, 1986: 14.
17. Aderenii Bamikunle, "Niyi Osundare's Poetry and the Yoruba Oral Artistic Tradition." *African Literature Today* 18 (1988): 49–61.

18. Unattributed jacket note to *Waiting Laughters*. Lagos: Malthouse Press, 1990.
19. Aderemi Bamikunle, "Niyi Osundare's Poetry and the Yoruba Oral Artistic Tradition" pp. 52–3.

* This essay is a revised version of 'Daring the Beast: Contemporary Nigerian poetry' first published in *Essays on African Writing 2: Contemporary Literature*, ed. Abdulrazak Gurnah. Oxford: Heinemann Educational Publishers: 1995.

"COURIER WITH A LIVE COAL IN HIS RUNNING PALM" (MIDLIFE): NIYI OSUNDARE AS WITNESS TO THE HUMAN IN NIGERIAN PUBLIC LIFE.

Jane Bryce

"Animal can't dash me
Human rights."

– Fela Anikulapo-Kuti.

In this chapter, I am concerned with a particular aspect of the work of Niyi Osundare—his writing for the Nigerian press—and what this indicates about his view both of the role of the poetry and that of the writer. My interest in Osundare's relationship with the popular press arises from the fact that, at the time I first met the man and came across his work, I was a researcher at the (then) University of Ife and making a precarious living from freelance journalism. In 1986, I interviewed four poets in Ife and Ibadan (Niyi Osundare, Femi

Fatoba, Funso Aiyejina, and Odia Ofeimun) for an article in *West Africa* magazine, which came out under the title "Dreams and bullets." Osundare was at this time lecturing at the University of Ibadan, writing a poetry column, "Songs of the Season," in the Ibadan based newspaper, *The Nigerian Tribue,* and commentaries for the weekly magazine, *Newswatch.* That article reads today as a kind of marker of the political situation in Nigeria as it affected writers then, and as it has continued to affect them subsequently. The difficulties then were nothing to what they became; Osundare's comments at the time, however, have remained true through all the vicissitudes of ever more vicious militaristic dispensations, and the article bears looking at as evidence of his tenacity and faith in his own and his country's powers of survival.

In the article, I wrote: "If poetry is indeed 'emotion recollected in tranquility,' you wouldn't expect to find much of it in Nigeria. Emotion, yes; life, noise, confusion, risk and squalor, yes—but tranquility, no. The mullah's grotesquely amplified call from the minarets at dawn expunges the image of dreaming spires, deemed essential to poets of a quieter place and time. Here and now, the question is how to keep alive the fires of creativity in a study too dark and too hot to work in because 'they've taken the light.' In a political situation of extreme instability, where should one look for repose when writing, itself, is seen as subversive?"[1] To the list I gave then of writers who had suffered or died in Nigeria for political causes—Wole Soyinka, Christopher Okigbo, Odia Ofeimun, Mamman Vatsa—we now know we have to add the journalist Dele Giwa, killed by a letter bomb in 1987; Wole Soyinka (again), driven into exile in 1994; Ken Saro-Wiwa, executed in 1995; poet and human rights activist Igaga Ifowodo, detained in 1997; along with the routine harassment of journalists and the incarceration, twice, of the outspokenly critical musician, Fela Anikulapo-Kuti. "In the light of this roll call, my question in 1986: 'Where daily survival is a full-time occupation, how does anyone find the surplus energy to write?' now sounds quaintly naïve." Writing has, indeed, shown itself to be one of the primary sites of resistance to political repression in Nigeria, and writers have demonstrated ever greater ingenuity in terms of how they get their work read in the face of a collapse in the once thriving publishing industry. In this, the press has played a crucial role, in terms of providing an outlet for creative writing and a forum for discussion of literary issues, and Osundare was prescient in his explanation in 1986 as to the reasons behind his own journalistic engagement. First, he said, "There is a redemptive job to do, to let the people know poetry is for them, not restricted to the nauseatingly arcane communities of the ivory tower." Second, there is the poet's role: "In a society like ours where we have so many pressures, where human rights don't exist, where you have people suffering all kinds of injustices, a writer can't just keep quiet. Poetry affords me the opportunity of commenting. It's not cowardice. It may be a kind of discretion. You're able to say your mind without necessarily running into the trap of the powers of the moment." The example I gave to illustrate the use of this facility of "strategic subterraneity,"[ii] was Osundare's response to the recent crisis engendered by the shooting of students and workers at Ahmadu Bello University, Zaria—the poem "For the slain of Samaru." It expressed both the countrywide revulsion at the security forces' action and the tenacious belief in the possibility of change. "If the present" (I wrote, glossing Osundare), "is the "season of cannibal carnage/ Jackboots / Starched visions/ Brazen bullets Incontinent cannon," then, dialectically, "We are the dream/which survives the night/The bird/on tomorrow's tree.'" Today, after fourteen years, another military coup, an annulled election, the death of a dictator, and the return to pluralism—have we indeed survived the night? Is tomorrow's tree ready at last to bear fruit?

Wiser, perhaps, than I was in 1986, I don't pretend to answer these questions. My task is the easier one, of considering Osundare's evolving role as a self-appointed spokesman for his people and how his writing has kept faith with his own perception of the writer's role. At the time of the earlier article, Osundare had published only *Songs of the Marketplace* (1983) and *Village Voices* (1984). *Eye of the Earth*, which was to win him the Commonwealth Prize for Poetry, appeared later in 1986, along with *A Nib in the Pond*, a collection of early work. Since then, there have been seven more volumes, with more forthcoming. The bird has not stopped singing. Even more remarkable, this output has been achieved at home in Nigeria, where he has continued to teach at the University of Ibadan, one of the few of his generation who has refused to be forced overseas. While Wole Soyinka's coruscating account of the years of military rule following the overthrow of the Second Republic in 1983, *The Open Sore of a Continent* (1996), could perhaps only have been written outside the country, Osundare has maintained his oppositional stance from within. It is no doubt inevitable that he has met with the criticism of having backed away from his earlier "revolutionary" position and clarity of expression, taking refuge in a more elaborate, less accessible style as time has gone by. Aderemi Bamikunle traces a diminishing of the "overtly political" content of his poetry with succeeding volumes, so that "Even less apparently political than *Eye of the Earth* is *Moonsongs*," which has become "more abstract, and...has ceased from making concrete statements about social and political events." (Bamikunle, 1995: 122). In fact, judged by his own definition of the function of poetry as "man/meaning/to/man" as opposed to "the esoteric whisper/of an excluding tongue" (*Songs of the*

Marketplace, 3), Bamikunle commends *Village Voices* as "the best of the poet's works" (p. 123). *Moonsongs* (1988), on the other hand, uses "a metaphoric framework for un-revolutionary philosophic statements," and its "beautiful metaphors and symbols" have become "a labyrinth through which the political message has to labour" (p. 122). In an earlier assessment, fellow poet Funso Aiyejina saw the development of Osundare's work somewhat differently. While in agreement that it becomes "less overtly political," he maintains that "the political dimension...becomes even more potent" with the poet's greater assurance of voice and deftness of expression. Though his review stops with *Eye of the Earth*, for Aiyejina, Osundare is "the fulfillment of the public poet—the towncrier— glimpsed briefly in (...) Okigbo." (Aiyejina, 1988: 124). For Biodun Jeyifo, introducing a later edition of *Songs of the Marketplace*, "In Osundare we confront both poetry of revolution and a revolution in poetry, in terms of forms and techniques." The question of what constitutes "political poetry" is what interests me here, and the expectation, based on the earlier volumes, that Osundare should continue to perform in a particular way in order to merit the tag of "revolutionary."

It is necessary to remember that the poems published as a collection in *Songs of the Season* in 1990 were written over a period of five years, between 1985 and 1990, for the explicitly public purpose of communicating to a newspaper readership, and taken together with *Eye of the Earth* (1986), *Moonsongs* (1988) and *Waiting Laughters* (1990), published within the same period, they demonstrate the poet's ability to adapt his poetic voice to different purposes and different media. The South African writer, Njabulo Ndebele, winner of the 1984 Noma Award for Publishing in Africa, attending a Symposium on African Literatures in Lagos in 1988, spoke these words: "Writers should not be afraid of extending their imagination and experimenting with form. The struggle is not only limited to protesting in the streets...After protesting, all of us go home to parents, children, and something happens there which feeds into your life."[iii]

The comparison with South Africa is not fortuitous. Fela Anikulapo-Kuti, speaking during a recording session in London in 1989, made the connection explicit in his summary of conditions in Nigeria under Babangida: "I am now convinced that the Nigerian government has no moral right to condemn the Botha regime for violating the rights of our brothers and sisters in South Africa. For instance, in both South Africa and Nigeria, progressive organizations are proscribed; law-abiding citizens are detained without trial; police attack and kill innocent people at night, destroy their homes and rape the women; patriots are labeled 'radicals and political extremists,' or 'anarchists and terrorists'; trade unionists are jailed for life...there is not enough to eat... there are no medicines, everything is expensive."[iv] Despite attempts to silence him—Operation Silence Fela, for example, when over a thousand armed police descended on Abeokuta, where Fela was scheduled to perform to a student audience of 20, 000 in April 1989, surrounded the stadium and threatened to shoot anyone who went near it—Fela continued to take on the authorities until his death in 1997. He spoke and sang on behalf of millions who were voiceless, but Niyi Osundare was one of those who spoke on *his* behalf: "What has made Fela a world famous figure is not just his music...there are many people in the world who have heard about Fela's politics...particularly the role he played as a conscience of his country and the egalitarian impulse that he showed." This was a week after Fela's death, with the same cadre he had dubbed "beasts of no nation" still firmly in power (at this stage, under General Abacha), and Osundare criticized the hypocrisy of those who bewailed his death while mutilating his message. While Fela's music was being played on the airwaves, he noted that government owned stations "stay away from the biting lyrics...They are selective in the kind of (Fela's) music they play. We weep too loudly in this country...this is a country of tears, a country of hypocrites. You caused this tragedy over several years...and when the result of your tragedy comes, then you hold your head in your hands and start crying." In this interview, Osundare uses the occasion of Fela's death both to defend his "eccentricities" and to claim him as an artist, one whom the excesses of the regime drove to self-abuse. "I am an artist myself," he declares, "and I know the trauma we go through. Everything you create comes out of intense labor. Every artist goes through that torture...so I understand perfectly why some artists take to drugs...I believe personally that the best thing to do is to train yourself, discipline yourself so much that, when that tension comes, you would be able to handle it."[v] This comment, conventional enough in tone, conceals more than it reveals, for here an artist gives a clue as to what sustains him in the face of the same forces that drove many of his fellows to flight or death. The easy flow of words, a kind of organic fecundity of language, issuing from his pen in the form of political comment, literary criticism, and poetry, belies the struggle for expression he describes as "torture." How to explain this, except that writing, itself, is the salve that makes existence possible, the line linking the artist to the anonymous and voiceless millions of his fellow countrymen? In an essay, "Bard of the Tabloid Platform," Osundare explains his use of the newspaper medium in terms of his desire to "articulate many of the ideas which populate the consciousness of his contemporaries, struggling for verbalization" and of its "enormous potentials for reaching the people whose joys and sorrows, whose lives and deaths, whose triumphs and travails formed the crux of the songs."(Osundare, 1990). In this respect, the impetus for Osundare's writing

arises from the same indomitable spirit and will to survive of those he writes
for and about, as here, in his poem for Fela:

> Your song is the drizzle of dawn
> Sparing no roof, however tall;
> So when monsters hurl down
> Their spears of death, the PEOPLE
> Are your shield...[vi]

Poetry, says Osundare, "has helped me to survive. And in a way I hope I have
been able to use my use my voice and my songs and my poems to help our people survive, too" (Nichols, 1998: 35).

This at first sight, ill-matched marriage of poetry and the press turns out to
be in the tradition of the best of Nigerian journalism. *The Guardian*, for many
years the benchmark of serious journalism in Nigeria, led the way in the early
1980s in creating a space for dialogue on literary issues in its pages. Of this initiative, Stanley Macebuh, then managing director of the newspaper group,
explains: "Among the other dislocations caused by the economic slump, the
severe decline of the book publishing industry was probably likely to have the
most long-lasting effect...The idea at the *Guardian*...was to step in where the
book publishing companies could not, and offer, on a weekly basis and in our
newspaper, a series of critical appraisals of the works of Nigerian writers."
(*Perspectives* vol 1, 1988: viii). And, introducing the second volume of these collected appraisals, ex-Ife lecturer and member of the editorial board, Yemi
Ogunbiyi, states: "It was clear to the founding fathers that the literary pages of
a serious national newspaper had an abiding duty to participate, initiate and
even stir up debate in the all-important area of literature and culture."
(*Perspectives* vol 2, 1998:xi). This role has been taken up and continued by other
newspapers in the Abacha years, notably *Vanguard* and *Post Express,* which in
the 1990s provided an outlet for creative writers without other access to publishing, while also creating a context for the discussion of each other's work.
Niyi Osundare's perception of the opportunities afforded him by *Tribune* for the
wider dissemination of his poetry, and for public comment and critique, may
therefore be seen as part of this ongoing dialogue.

There are a number of further points of connection with Fela, which are
worth exploring. While both artists have chosen English as their medium of
expression, it is an English inflected by a first language renowned for its elas-
ticity, sonorousness, depth of meaning, subtlety, and Yoruba performative qual-

ities. Fela's songs, indeed, draw freely on a linguistic continuum from Standard English to pidgin to Yoruba, while Osundare repeatedly cites his parents and his origins in Ikere-Ekiti as his formative influences as a poet. "I come," he tells us, "from a culture where the word matters a lot." He considers that he grew up among artists, "and everywhere around me people told me you must respect the word. Because when a matter is too hard for a gun to kill or for a cutlass to cut, put all those lethal weapons away and use a much more lethal weapon, which is the human tongue." (Nichols, 1998: 35). For both Fela and Osundare, the word "human" appears to have a particular connotation beyond its usual English meaning, and it is this special significance that I now wish to explore. vii

Interviews with Osundare are peppered with references to "human," "humanistic," and "human rights," as in this one with *Amnesty* magazine: "Human beings without human rights are like animals. I stand for human rights. I would like to see human beings live their lives to the fullest—free, fulfilled, and self-respecting."viii A preoccupation with the rights and obligations of human beings is a recurring theme of Osundare's poetry, as of his public statements. In an interview after his fiftieth birthday, he described himself as "fascinated by the meaning behind the meaning," and therefore impelled to respond quickly to events around him. "Something pricks you and you want to respond to it...you grab your pen and scribble some verses and you keep working on it until it becomes a poem." This response correlates with a sense of optimism, a belief in the possibility of change and the power of the individual to bring about that change, which infuses his work with urgency. As he concludes, "We have vowed not to allow silence to take over this country. Every dictator needs silence of the graveyard type. We are not going to oblige the dictator, the spirit killer. To speak out is to be human and speaking out is one of the conditions of humanity."ix His poem for incarcerated editor, Kunle Ajibade, written "in solidarity with Ajibade and other political prisoners in Abacha's dungeon," testifies to this determination. Not only was it published in *The Guardian* and *Post Express* in 1997, it was also smuggled to Ajibade in prison. In the poem, Osundare refers to a "jungle of silence," ruled by a tyrant, served by hyenas, while:

> The country is a lie
> Told with a crooked eye
> By power-pimps
> And their cannibal imps ("For Kunle Ajibade")

Besides the poem, Osundare employed the names of the detained as a mantra or a kind of reverse praise-song, constantly repeating them on the basis that: "Nothing scares a despot more than the names of those he is trying to destroy." (*Amnesty*, 18). This name-calling is a feature of both Fela and Osundare's work. The newspaper poems in the "tributes" section of *Songs of the Season* reads like a roll-call of the country's human rights and democracy activists: Chief Adenıran and Tai Solarin, educators; Femi Falana and Gani Fawehinmi, radical lawyers; Dele Giwa and Ray Ekpu, *Newswatch* editors; Ayodele Awojobi, professor who exposed the theft of 2.8 billion Naira under Shagari; Obafemi Awolowo, nationalist politician; Fela; Tanure Ojaide, poet. Besides these, he sings also of the unnamed, the ordinary people—street-sweepers, drivers, jobless graduates, tax-gatherers. In short, he sings to those who

> ...have been trampled
> Like penny carpets
> Spat upon
> Like a dunghill
> Chewed, then spat out
> Like a hapless root...("Shout of the people," *Songs*, 35)

In the same vein, Osundare is proud to decode his own name, as "Osun has declared my innocence, or the goddess of the river is on my side" (*Source* profile, 1997, 49). Again, this is a clue to how he perceives his responsibility as an artist, and as a human being marked by a national identity, which confers on all who hold it a social obligation. As we know, Yoruba names all have meanings, and those meanings encapsulate an essential aspect of the individual. Karin Barber's work on *oriki* points to the device of "nominalization" as one of their key features, so that "phrases and even whole sentences are turned into nouns through the use of prefixes such as –a and –o..." (Barber, 1991: 71). Osundare, now a surname, could arguably be said to belong in the category of *oriki orile*, since it was given to his father at birth as a sign of a successful future (*Source* profile, 1997: 49), and refers to "the ancient place of origin by which his extended patrilineal kingroup is defined... emblematic...often taken from nature" (Barber, 1991: 68), as here with the river Osun, which crosses Niyi's father's farm. Though in a different context, Osundare himself can be seen as a performer of *oriki*, since his name-calling has a related effect to that described by Barber: "When a performer utters *oriki*, she addresses herself intensely and exclusively to the subject...Uttering a subject's *oriki* is thus a process of empowerment. The subject's latent qualities are activated and enhanced" (Barber, 1991: 75). While in the traditional setting, *oriki* are a means of enhancing reputation and paying tribute to "big men." Osundare calls on the same process of enacting "a concentrated regard and acknowledgement, calling attention to the relationship between herself as admirer and him as object of admiration" (Barber, 1991: 184), to demonstrate his support and admiration for the victims of "big men," power brokers, and the perpetrators of injustice. In so doing, he concurs with what another poet, the Malawian Jack Mapanje, perceives as the artist's obligation: "...to sing the song of reparation of the names of those heroes and heroines that our despotic regime has obliterated from our history" (Mapanje, 1997: 230).

None of this is new, and both Osundare's role as spokesman for the oppressed and his debt to oral tradition have been repeatedly acknowledged. Fellow poet, Ezenwa-Ohaeto, calls him "the poet for the suffering man" (1991: 160), one who "manipulates not only English words but also Yoruba thought-patterns as he further teases symbols out of their normative order through a complex use of images and personae" (p. 162). In this, as another poet, Tanure Ojaide, points out, he is of his generation, in the sense of drawing on African culture, not to showcase its materiality, but for the very form and substance of the utterance. "The writers," he says, "are taking up cultural poetic techniques of parallelism, topicality, indirectness, repetition, and others to express their contemporary feelings." (1995; 13) To this list he adds *oriki* and *ijala* as used in particular by Soyinka and Osundare (p. 13). The English poet, Stewart Brown, speaking about contemporary Nigerian poetry, draws attention to the pitfalls of " the notion of the poet as being duty-bound to confront the political events of the times" (Brown, 1995: 58), which all too often leads to poetic craft being supplanted by political outrage. Of Osundare, Brown says: "He is the one poet whose lyrical and critical intelligence seems to offer both an alternative politics and a notion of poetics which suggests a real way forward for Nigerian – indeed African – poetry in English" (p. 67). Where Bamikunle laments Osundare's view of history as "anti-climactic and disappointing" (Bamikunle, 1995: 126), Brown suggests that "his poetic and political vision spring from a profound awareness of African history ...Osundare's alternative political vision, as it is enmeshed in and expressed in his poetry, is both pragmatic and practical, informed by an essentially optimistic view of humanity's ability to change and a belief in the fundamental instinct of mankind to both respect and nurture the earth and its resources"(pp. 67–8). This comment brings us back to the point I started from, the use of "humanity" as a touchstone and its special meaning within a Yoruba linguistic and philosophical context. The title of Brown's essay, "Daring the

Beast," pinpoints one essential aspect of this meaning, which is its mode of signifying, by way of binary opposition, a lack of humanity—hence, of beasthood. Animal images are frequently used by Osundare to point to the inhumanity of Nigeria's power elite, whether generically or specifically, as in his poem for Ken Saro-Wiwa:

> The hyena has murdered Thunder's son...
> Viper-belts caress their oily waists...
> Seething serpents on every branch...
>
> A cockerel crows out its throat at noon...
> A goggle-eyed viper hatches the eggs
> Into serpent streets and crocodile lakes
>
> The mongoose has stolen the monkey's tail...
> Crocodile warlords trade swords with salamander monarchs...
> The Tortoise-General smiled, tooth-gapped...
>
> Who are these reptiles from forgotten ages?
>
> ("The Man Who Asked Tall Questions")

In a *Newswatch* column, entitled "Crocodile tears," Osundare takes this image further in castigating the mourners at the death of Chief Abiola for their hypocrisy, calling them *asenibanidaro*, "those who, after killing their victim, fly into weeping tantrums at his graveside."[X] He describes Nigeria as "a moral jungle," and "a country with no moral center, no stable positive values, a place where the dividing line between wrong and right is perilously thin, where the person who insists on principle and healthy consistency is regarded as either mad or stupid or both" (Osundare, 1998). Again, on the occasion of the execution of Saro-Wiwa, he asks: "How 'free' can the imagination be in an unfree continent, how uncommitted can it afford to be in a place which commits the writer to death?" He goes on to articulate "the writer's almost divine mission" to create a space for the "manifestation of the soul and collective imagination of a people."[XI] Here, Osundare indirectly answers Saro-Wiwa's question when the gallows failed four times to hang him, and on the third or fourth attempt he cried: "Why are you people doing this to me? What sort of a nation is this?" (Soyinka, 1996: 149) This is not a nation, but a jungle; they are not human, but beasts—the beasts of no nation.

In an essay, "*Eniyan*: the Yoruba concept of a person," Segun Gbadegesin addresses the question of what constitutes personhood for the Yoruba, and this article, I believe, helps to illuminate, for those of us who are not Yoruba, the special significance of "human" as used by Osundare and Fela in their references to "human rights." *Eniyan*, he tells us, "has a normative dimension as well as an ordinary meaning," hence the expression "he/she is not a human being," delivered as a moral judgment on someone perceived "as falling short of what it takes to be recognized as such." (Gbadegesin, 1998,149) Since the Yoruba concept of a person encompasses various distinct attributes—*ara* (body), *okan* (heart, mind), *emi* (breath, spirit) and *ori* (head, destiny)—"the question whether a human person is all body or something else is not seriously raised by Yoruba thinkers because it appears too obvious to them that there is more to a person than the body." Hence, the human quality of selfishness: *imotara-eni-nikan*, is conceptualized as being an inordinate concern with the body, at the expense of the spirit. "This suggests that if human beings were to be concerned with their spirits, they would not be selfish" (p. 150). This definition has some fascinating implications for the concept of human rights and what is taken as "normative" human behavior in that it suggests that anyone who abuses the human rights of another forfeits his or her own right to be considered human. Since every individual is inspirited with the divine breath of Olodumare, human rights abusers may be construed as an abomination equivalent to other religious abominations in Yoruba society. *The Webster Dictionary* definition of "human" posits it in opposition to "divine," as in "to err is human, to forgive divine," whereas we can see that the Yoruba concept of "human" embraces the divine. Osundare's name is one example of this close interrelationship between divine and human, spirit and flesh, with its personal claim to the protection of the goddess Osun, who, moreover, "has declared my innocence." This confers on the bearer a special kind of authority, giving him a touchstone whereby to judge the behavior of others. This is not, of course, a merely individual perspective, but a moral system rooted in the collective psyche, to which the language acts as signpost. Fela's chosen name, *Anikulapo*, meaning "one who has death in his pocket," points in the same direction, suggestive of the artist's responsibility to speak out regardless of the consequences.

It is, however, *ori* which Gbadegesin sees as "the distinctive aspect of the Yoruba concept of a person" (p. 157), being the aspect which determines the individual's personality and their destiny. The key thing here, of course, is that (according to the most popular belief) we each choose our own *ori,* and we are therefore responsible, to some extent, for our own destiny. As Gbadegesin says, this suggests "that human beings are not on a purposeless mission in this world, that they have a mission to fulfill, a message to deliver—which is the meaning of their existence—and that this mission has been fully endorsed by the creator" (p. 161). For the poet, then, delivering his personal message is to fulfill his destiny, and therefore to be human. To fail to do so would be to forfeit his humanity, in the same way that the perpetrators of human rights abuses forfeit their humanity. This phenomenon is commented on by Abiola Irele in his essay on Yoruba tradition, which seeks to trace a line of connection between writers by pointing to the philosophical underpinning of a shared cultural and linguistic background. Yoruba religion and myth are marked, he suggests, by an "intense organic feeling for the universe which the myth expresses," and what differentiates Yoruba society above all, is "the discernible cult of intense vitality that permeates every aspect of the culture and its social articulations, in the active celebration of the sense of a constant and forceful connection of man with the springs of life latent in the universe" (Irele, 1981: 195). I take this to mean that destiny is not something to be passively accepted, but actively engaged with, with the aim of accomplishing *meaning* for human existence. This meaning is a collective enterprise, which "cannot be separated from the social reality of which (the individual) is just a part," so that "personality is rendered meaningful by appeal to destiny *and* community" (Gbadegesin, 1998: 168).

This discussion clarifies for me the underlying reason for the recurrence of the term "human" in Osundare's writings and utterances, and his vision of his role as writer as being one of social responsibility. Recognition was given to this particular dimension by the award, in 1998, of the Fonlon-Nichols Award "for (his) literary achievements and (his) dedication to the struggle for human rights in (his) country and all of Africa." (Nichols, 1998: 32). In response, Osundare said it recognized "what has always been central to the spirit of my creative and my literary and cultural dispositions: an attempt to balance the integrity of art with the imperative of social and cultural relevance" (p. 33). The fact that Osundare is not alone in holding this view of the function of art only strengthens the efficacy of his position. In an article published in one of the earliest of the *Post Express* literary pages, Dan Izevbaye points to the increasing importance of the media in promoting the humanities, and describes the new relationship of academics to the press as "a third phase in the transformation of humanities scholarship in Nigeria...offering a simpler, more direct form of intellectual service."[xii] Osundare was, as has been demonstrated, one of the first to perceive and avail himself of the possibilities afforded by the popular press. Fela, operating in the field of popular music, performed a similar feat, with striking similarities of thought and expression. In his 1987 release, *Beast of no nation,* he attacks African leadership in similar terms to Osundare's cited earlier:

Which kind talk be that?
Animal talk be that,
Animal in human skin
Animali putu tie-o
Animali wear agbada
Animali putu suit-u

If the purpose of human existence is "to contribute to the totality of the good in the universe...by a life of selfless devotion and sacrifice to the communal welfare" (Gbadegesin, 1998: 168), what can be said of Africa's leaders, who devour and consume the people they are supposed to serve? If they cannot be said to accede to a philosophical definition of humanity, then what? "Animal-i," of course. Fela's anthem, like Osundare's poetry, like his political commentary, like so much of the writing, which has continued to be produced in Nigeria in the 80s and 90s, reiterates this fundamental and sustaining fact:

I beg-i mek you hear me well-i-well
Human rights na my property
So therefore you can't dash me
My property
Animal wan dash us
Human rights

Animal CAN'T dash us
Human rights.
Human rights na my property.

I began by asking a question I also declined to answer: is tomorrow's tree finally ready to bear fruit? Can we detect any real change in the wake of the 1999 elections and the return of so-called democracy to Nigeria, or are its artists and intellectuals, as well as those for whom they speak, condemned to repeat forever the vicious cycle of inanity and deprivation that has come to characterize their country? Guests at Wole Soyinka's fiftieth birthday celebrations at Ife in 1984 received a typewritten, cyclostyled statement from the celebrant, entitled "Reflections of a member of the wasted generation" (Soyinka, 12/7/1984, unpublished). My copy of that document, yellow and dog-eared, is before me now and I turn to it as another marker, another writer's position paper on the

events of an era. In it, Soyinka concludes his review of "a quarter century of wit-
nessing and occasionally participating in varied aspects of our social struggle in
all their shifting tempi," by confessing himself "in a state of near-total stupor"
and asks: "Is it not pardonable that, given the wearisome repetitiveness of this
malignant frustration of individual and collective efforts...that our generation
should begin to feel more than a little burnt out?" Soyinka was writing six
months after a military coup had ended Nigeria's second short-lived spell of
democracy, in a context, as he put it, "devoid of politics, devoid of a popular man-
date or private desire to oust the then existing government..." At a major turning point in his personal odyssey, he paused and took time to ask the fundamental questions, which still today go unanswered. He challenged the country's
rulers "to commence a genuine, productive dialogue with the ruled...the trade
unions, the professional bodies, the market associations, student and teachers'
unions—all the human elements which contribute to the uneven pulse of this
over-abused nation."

If that dialogue has never really begun, its absence has continued to be noted,
lamented, and challenged, not least by the poets who followed him, Osundare
among them. In one of his *Tribune* poems, Osundare dramatized another
debate, between *olowo* ("there is money") and *talaka* (the people), to whom he
gave this claim:

> We put the hum in your factories
> We are the blast in the furnace
> Of your minting forge...

(*Songs of the Season*, 40).

Then, he also made this challenge:

> Money Man...
> Your tinsel dreams squat
> On the volcano of an abyss
> An abyss which ticks like
> The heart of a million bombs.

(*Songs of the Season*, 46).

True to his self-appointed vocation as town-crier, in August 1999, shortly after
the election, he speaks in his own voice through the medium, once again, of a

Guardian editorial, entitled "The New Masquerades," in which, like Soyinka, he reviews events from the perspective of one who has participated in "varied aspects of our social struggle" (Soyinka, 1984). Refusing to join the party, to dance with the masquerade procession, Osundare insists on asking the awkward questions: "How many times will a people be taken for a ride before they finally gain their bearing? We have seen these masquerades before...(and) should be able to identify them by the craters left by their footprints."[xiii] Fifteen years, almost to the day, after Soyinka made his deposition, Osundare's enunciation echoes that of his precursor: "It is we, the people, the perennial victims of political predators, who must refuse co-optation and corruption and insist on justice...refuse to be carried away by the coated tongue or the greased palm, and reject this perpetual assault on our common will and dignity as human beings and citizens of Nigeria...We must not stagger into the next millennium with the same Sissyphean burden" (Osundare, 1999). Political change may not have truly arrived in Nigeria, but the voice of criticism has not been stilled. As Osundare wrote of another poet:

> We find in his many and varied songs
> Voices of his and other times.
> ("Song for all seasons": for Tanure Ojaide, in
> Songs of the Season, 148)

NOTES

i   Jane Bryce, "Dreams and bullets," in *West Africa*, 21 July 1986, 1524–1525.
ii This expression is taken from Mpalive-Hangson Msiska's Introduction to *Writing and Africa* (Longman, 1997), 6, in which he is speaking of Malawian poet, Jack Mapanje's call for "the sort of strategic subterraneity that is evident in his poetry, in which subversive agency relocates itself frequently in order to disable the mechanisms of censorship."
iii Njabulo Ndebele, interviewed by Jane Bryce in "Writing as resistance in South Africa," *The Guardian* Sunday Supplement, August 28, 1988, pB2.
iv Fela Anikulapo-Kuti, interviewed by Jane Bryce in "Animal can't dash me human rights," *Index on Censorship*, 9/1989, 12.
v   Interview with Festus Adedayo: "Fela's Essence," *Omega Weekly*, August 22, 1997, 2.
vi Niyi Osundare, "For Fela Anikulapo-Kuti," *Songs of the Season* (Heinemann, Nigeria, 1990), 95–6.
vii *Webster's Encyclopaedic Unabridged Dictionary* gives the following definition: "...having the nature of human kind...of or pertaining to the social aspect or character of man...sympathetic, humane...a human being." It states further, "...human may refer to good and bad traits of man alike. When emphasis is placed upon the latter, *human* is thought of as contrasted to *divine*.
viii Interview with Omowunmi Segun, "Writing against repression," in *Amnesty*, 18—19. *(Dates)*
ix Interview: "'I am an incurable optimist' says Osundare," in *The Guardian on Sunday*, March 16, 1997, pB5.
x   Niyi Osundare, "Crocodile Tears," *Newswatch*, August 24, 1998, 38.
xi Niyi Osundare, "The Longest Day," *Newswatch*, November 18, 1996.
xii Dan Izevbaye, "Critical Engagement: Developments in African Literary Theory and Criticism," *Post Express*, Saturday November 30, 1996, 12.
xiii Niyi Osundare, "The New Masquerades," *Guardian* editorial Sunday 15/8/99, taken from online website: *http://ngrguardiannews.com/editorial/en758103.htm*

BIBLIOGRAPHY

Aiyejina, Funso. "Recent Nigerian Poetry in English: an Alter-native Tradition." *Perspectives on Nigerian Literature, vol one, 1700 to the Present*. Lagos: Guardian Books Nigeria Ltd, 1988: 112–128.
Bamikunle, Aderemi. "The Development of Niyi Osundare's Poetry: a Survey of Themes and Technique." *Research in African Literatures* 26.4 Winter (1995): 121–137.

Barber, Karin. *I Could Speak Until Tomorrow: Oriki, Women and the Past in a Yoruba Town*. Edinburgh University Press, 1991.

Brown, Stewart. "Daring the Beast: Contemporary Nigerian Poetry."Ed. Abdulrazak Gurnah. *Essays on African Writing*. UK: Heinemann, 1995: 58–72.

Gbadegesin, Segun. "*Eniyan:* the Yoruba concept of a person." Eds. P.H. Coetzee and A.J.P. Roux. *The African Philosophy Reader*. New York: Routledge, 1998: 149–168.

Ezenwa-Ohaeto. "Dimensions of Language in New Nigerian Poetry." Eds. Eldred Durosimi Jones, Eustace Palmer and Marjorie Jones. *African Literature Today*, vol. 17. UK: James Currey, 1991: 155–164.

Irele, Abiola. *The African Experience in Literature and Ideology*. UK: Heinemann,1981: 174–197.

Mapanje, Jack. "The Changing Fortunes of the Writer in Africa?" Eds. Mpalive-Hangson Msiska and Paul Hyland. *Writing and Africa*. UK: Longman, 1997: 16–233.

Msiska, Mpalive-Hangson. Introduction to *Writing and Africa*. Eds. Mpalive-Hangson and Paul Hyland. Longman, 1997: 1–9.

Ojaide, Tanure. "New Trends in Modern African Poetry." *Research in African Literatures* 26.1 Spring (1995): 4–19.

Osundare, Niyi. "Confessions of a tabloid bard." Eds. S.Arnold and A. Nitecki. *Culture and Development in Africa*. Trenton, New Jersey: Africa World Press, 1990: 1–47.

————.*Songs of the Season*. Nigeria: Heinemann, 1990.

Soyinka, Wole. *The Open Sore of a Continent: a Personal Narrative of the Nigerian Crisis*. Oxford University Press, 1996.

OSUNDARE AND POETRY FOR THE PEOPLE

GD Killam

Osundare wants his poetry to be accessible to the generality of people. In his first volume, *Songs of the Marketplace*, he chooses as one of his models the poet and diplomat Pablo Neruda, and uses the Chileans words as the epigraph to the volume: "I made an unbreakable pledge to myself/ That the people would find their voices in my song." In the first poem, "Poetry Is," he asserts his artistic purposes in conjunction with his populist theme of social obligation. For Osundare, poetry is:

> Not the esoteric whisper
> Of an excluding tongue
> Not a claptrap
> For a wondering audience
> Not a learned quiz
> Entombed in Grecoroman lore
>
> Poetry is
> A lifespring
> Which gathers timbre
> The more throats it plucks

Harbinger of action
The more minds it stirs

Poetry is
The Hawker's ditty
The eloquence of the gong
The lyric of the marketplace
The luminous ray
On the grass's morning dew

Poetry is
What the soft wind
Musics to the dancing leaf
What the sole tells the dusty path
What the bee hums to the alluring nectar
What rainfall croons to the lowering eaves

Poetry is
No oracle's kernel
For the sole philosopher's stone

Poetry
Is
Man
Meaning
To
Man
(pp. 3–4).

The reference to "Grecoroman lore" is crucial to Osundare's poetic, for through it he asserts that the uses to which the pre-civil war generation of Nigerian poets, such as Wole Soyinka and Christopher Okigbo, put their postcolonial education inheritance are no longer appropriate to his purposes. These poets, according to Osundare, brought "the whole mechanistic apparatus of European poetry the modernist pretensions to African soil. That was why Soyinka was difficult. And Okigbo too. And this comes from the poetic practice and canons of people who believe that poetry must be difficult" (*Vanguard*, Lagos, 10 February 1985, p. 4). In an essay entitled "Words of Iron, Sentences of Thunder: Soyinka's Prose Style" (in *African Literature Today*, no. 13, 1993), Osundare describes what for him makes Soyinka's work obscure. Through his criticism of Soyinka, Osundare reveals his ideas about the appropriate form and content of poetry. In an article in *West Africa*, he urges Soyinka "to find a middle ground between his journalistic and his creative styles of writing. He should work towards greater 'audience consciousness' and towards achieving a 'transparency which is simple but delicate'" (6 August 1984, p. 1579). The two poems Osundare wrote each week – "as a matter of policy and challenge" – in his popular Sunday column in the *Nigerian Tribune*, "Songs of the Season," are devoted to demonstrating that "verse journalism" – poetry for the general public in the popular presses – can

> Convince the audience that poetry can be accessible,
> enjoyable and relevant at the same time.
>
> (A grandly ironical occupation in a culture whose very vein is
> lyrical and artistic!) In other words, my experimental verse
> journalism
>
> is part of an on-going attempt to rescue (Nigerian) poetry from
> the "labyrinths" and "crypts" of the frustrating obscurity into
> which it
>
> has been pushed by the Soyinkas and Okigbos.
> (*World Literature Written in English* 29, 1989, p. 3)

For Osundare, "the greatest dilemma the Nigerian writers faces today is how to marry these two: the mass-oriented kind of literature and the so-called serious literature" (as reported by Sina Odugbemi, in *Vanguard*, Lagos, 10 February 1985, p. 4).

In "The Poet," from *A Nib in the Pond*, Osundare extends his populist theories about the function of poetry to include the role of the poet, who

> Is not a prophet,
> God's hollow ventriloquist,
> auguring past futures
> in dated tongues
> the poet's eyes are washed
> in the common spring
> through seeing beyond

the hazy horizon
of lowering skies
who says the poet
should leave the much
Unranked?
in a land of choking mud
how can the poet
strut
clean
in feathered sandals
and
pretend to the world
he never smells
(p. 10).

Although he eschews the obscurity and arcane language of the pre-civil war poets, Osundare has in common with his peers (including most of those of the first generation) a political purpose in writing that makes it potentially revolutionary and transformative. Like the novelist Chinua Achebe in *Anthills of the Savannah* (1987), Osundare wrestles with the problem of making literature accessible and available to the masses and dissociating it from the socioeconomic processes that make it elitist. He does this by drawing on the oral tradition of his agrarian roots. In the stories, songs, and rituals of this tradition, as well as the forms, moods and tones, he finds a model from making his verse accessible to the oppressed people in Nigerian society, who are victims of a self-serving political and economic leadership. Coincident with this search for an appropriate poetic model is his desire to revitalize poetry and prompt his audience to action.

Osundare's poetry combines the meditative with the rhetorical and displays a wide range of topics such as the cultural influence and poetry of Europe, with issues relating to the abstractions of love, pride, humility, honesty, cowardice, misery, and corruption. His moods – lyrical, celebratory, ironical, satirical, humorous, and bitter – are equally various as he exposes the many reasons for the disfunctioning of Nigerian society in his generation.

His principal concerns are with the larger issues of Nigerian public life as they affect and compromise the well-being of society as a whole. And these concerns are apparent from the first publication.

Osundare admits that his first volume, *Songs of the Marketplace* (1983), is the work of an apprentice: "It contains all kinds of poems. Some of the poems I wrote when I was in high school. I just polished them up. Inevitably that collection is eclectic" (Ajibade, 1991: 44). Yet in this volume there is a range of reflection and comment on popular issues that are more and more consolidated in subsequent verse. For example, he ironically evokes the plunder of Africa during the colonial period in "on Seeing a Benin Mask in a British Museum," written for the art festival FESTAC 77:

He stilted on plastic
A god deshrined
Uprooted from your past
Distanced from you present
Profaned sojourner in a strange land

Rescued from a smoldering shrine
By a victorianizing expedition
Traded in for an O.B.E.
Across the shores
(p. 39–40).

There are also angry occasional poems for people, such as "For Bob Marley" and "Prisoners of Conscience (for Ngugi wa Thiong'o)," and for events, such as "Mamibia Talks" and "Soweto. "Soweto" expresses anger at the South African government's brutal violence against black protesters in Sharpeville in 1960 and in Soweto in 1976,and it prophesies the end of apartheid in that country:

First
SHARPEVILLE
Now
SOWETO

These murdered flowers
Blossoming
Will fruit in freedom
These rising shoots
Will tree into fee spaces
Beyond tomorrow.
 (p. 48).

Most of the poems in the volume, however, assert and reinforce Osundare's connection with his rural roots and nature. This connection occurs in poems throughout the volume and specifically in the nine poems in the section titled "Songs of Dawn and Seasons," in which he presents nature as a guiding principle and metaphor for human life. Osundare's willingness to return to and even embrace agrarian traditions suggests that education did not alienate him from his people and their concerns. Rather he uses his literary background and skills as a writer to enhance his connection with and commitment to the downtrodden, oppressed, and dispossessed. In the process of asserting this allegiance in his writing, he consistently repudiates those in power who effect these conditions and the ramifications of their actions.

In his second volume of poems, *Village Voices* (1984), Osundare portrays the activities, concerns, and attitudes of peasant farmers. For example in "Eating Tomorrow's Yam," he details the concerns of a farmer; in "The Prisoner's Song," he convincingly portrays the bluster of a prisoner; and in "Alarinka," he captures the listlessness of a wanderer. Although Osundare sympathetically enters the lives and minds of his characters, he avoids naivete and sentimentality in his characterizations.

Here for the first time in his poetry, Osundare projects a clear revolutionary proletarian consciousness. His abhorrence for the duplicity of the political establishment is found in such poems as "The New Farmers Bank" and "A Farmers on Seeing Cocoa House, Ibadan." "The Politician's Two Mouths" ends with a warning to the reader:

> The politician's mouth has two edges
> Like Esimuda's sword
> It is murder both ways
>
> When the man of power
> Tells you his tale
> Ask him to wait till
> You bring a sieve (p. 57).

In affirming his understanding of his sources, Osundare castigates other poets whose claims to connections with the common people are spurious:

> You singer of royal songs
> Your drum, dumb in the marketplace
> Only talks in the palace of gold

You songs extol those whose words
Behead the world (p. 2).

In his third volume of poems, *A Nib in the Pond* (1986), Osundare repeats and elaborates the material of Songs of the Marketplace. In "calling a Spade," he declares:

No need hiding
In the tabernacle of words
So easily swept off
By the storm of anger

No need camouflaging
Behind a flimsy jungle
Of occult id-ioms
The metaphor of protest
Flips every leaf
In the book of change

There is no petname for
Injustice
Poverty
Has no bank for nicknames (p. 9).

In his preface to *The Eye of the Earth* (1986), Osundare declares the origins in rural-oral societies of his poetic material: "Farmer-born, Peasant-bred, I encountered dawn in the enchanted corridors of the forest, suckled on the delicate aroma of healing herbs, and the pearly drops of generous moons. Living in those early days was rugged, but barns brimmed with yams fattened by merciful rains and the tempering fire of the upland sun. Earth was ours, and we earth's" (p. ix).

The affirmation in this passage proceeds no solely from "passionate nostalgia" (p. x), but from the determination that "looking back becomes on of the weapons against a looming monster For in the intricate dialectics of human living, looking back is looking forward; The visionary artist is not only a rememberer, he is also a reminder (p. x). The nineteen poems in the volume, which is divided into a prefatory poem—"Earth"—and four subsections—"back to earth," "eyeful glances," "rainsongs," and "homecall"—trace the history of humanity's association with the land. Osundare writes of humanity's association with the land. Osundare writes of the structure of the book:

> The "forest" in the first movement is echoes of an Eden long departed when the rainforest was terrifyingly green though each tree, each vine, each herb, each beast, each insect, had its name in the baffling baptism of Nature "Rainsongs" is a logical continuation of "forest echoes," it being a celebration of the giver and sustainer of life" "Homecall" raises vital queries, amplifies crucial fears about the state of the earth, our home. (pp. x,xi.xii).

In this volume, Osundare depicts the collusion of Native farmers with "the virulent advent of Europe's merchants" in betraying the land for the sake of a "cancerous god called MONEY" (p. ix); he continues by adumbrating the wider implications of this betrayal. Treatment of the land, which Osundare considers the most important natural resource, becomes a marker of human myopia, venality, and treachery, which will in the end, he warns, destroy the earth. The poems present a vision of a dying earth proceeding from the act of the "rich and ruthless [who] squander earth's wealth on the invention of increasingly accomplished weapons of death, while millions of people perish daily from avoidable hunger" (p. xii).

The poems in this volume and in the next, *Moonsongs*, are more carefully articulated and precisely focused in their concern with nature, landscape, and rural life than the poems in earlier volumes, which makes these collections more unified in approach and sustained in achievement. The poems *in The Eye of the Earth* and *Moonsongs* also present Osundare's revolutionary agenda with greater precision, clarity, and force than in the earlier volumes by showing what nature has been, has become, and might become again, through language that is at once simple and highly allusive.

The agent of Osundare's meditation in *The Eye of the Earth* is memory, which allows him to traverse both past and present in his reflections and meditation. The order of the poems reflects the chronology of his life, and a poem titled "Farmer-Born" captures the movement through time that organizes the volume. He returns to his childhood and moves forward to the present. He recalls the past without sentimentalizing it, specifying that its essentially pristine quality contains with in it "loric fear" and Leaves wounded / by the fists of time," and environment where one treads "soft-soled, the compost carpet / of darling jungles" ("Forest Echoes," p. 3). Poems in the volume move through the forest and describe encounters with natural phenomena, animate and inanimate; with the divinities and near divinities of the Yoruba pantheon, including Ogeere Amokoyeri, Agbegilodos, and Ogbese, Osun's rebel daughter; and with a modern deification in the form of NEPA (National Electric Power Authority) as it has come to humanize and caution nature.

The volume's closing poems, "They Too Are the Earth," "What the Earth Said," "Ours the Plough, Not to Plunder," and "Our Earth Will Not Die," are apostrophes to earth and to its potential for restoration. The final poem is intended to be read "to a soleman, almost elegiac tun" (p. 50). The volume's last words are assertions: "Our earth will not die" (p. 50); "Our earth will see again / this earth, OUR EARTH" (p. 51). Given Osundare's concerns throughout most of the volume, one can only hope that his optimism and faith in the links he sees between his poetry and such international movements as "The Green Peace, The Women of Greenham Common, Operation Stop the Desert, and The Save the Amazon Committee" are not misplaced (p. xii).

Osundare told Ajibade in the 1991 interview that he believed that "the source of artistic excellence is variety and progress There is no way you can read without being influenced by what you read one way or another. I myself have discovered that I am getting rather philosophical" (p. 45). He was responding to a comment that his later poetry was moving toward an obscurity of language that contrasts with the directness and simplicity of his first three volumes and leaves *The Eye of the Earth* and *Moonsongs* open to the same charges that he leveled at

Soyinka's poems and Okigbo's early works. The poems of *The Eye of the Earth* and *Moonsongs* are structurally and linguistically more complicated and make a greater demand o n the reader. To be fully understood and appreciated, the volumes probably require a thorough grounding in Yoruba cosmology. Osundare's increasing poetic complexity seems inevitable: as a poet finds an authentic strophe, he or she discovers how to make the craft sustain the vision.

This understanding in Osundare's case results in the creation of a more comprehensive and complex cosmology. To the elemental physical landscape—earth, forest, rocks, and rivers—he adds the animate universe, to which he attends in the minutest detail—animals, birds, and even insects. The earth bec mes a microcosm within the celestial macrocosm that include the sky, stars, sun, and especially, the moon.

Osundare places this extended inanimate and animate universe in a traditional—or imagined traditional—community. As he envisions this community, it retains its traditional assumptions and values, and therefore allows him to stage its encounter with and modification by extraneous forces. Drawing on his foundation in oral traditions, he stages these later poems as communal performances. In his early volumes, Osundare indicates that his poetry should be understood as an "oral aural" experiences and performed to the accompaniment of traditional African instruments.

In *Moonsongs* the communal and participatory element in the poetry is more insistent. He includes enjoinders to some poems: "To the accompaniment of lively woro drumming, the follow songs, in call-and-response" (p. I); "To the accompaniment of the songs: Osupa o I yuwa mi o, osupa o, I yeyin mi" (p. 8); "IN the background throughout, a persistent sound of pestle in mortar, supplying a rhythm to the poem and the accompanying song" (p. 29).

Moonsongs (1988) is organized in three parts: "Phases 1–14"; "Further Phases 15–24"; and "Moonechoes: Shadows Across the Path," a final section of twelve poems. (The twelve poems in the final section, as its title suggests, are adjunct to rather than integrated into the main text.) The moon, as the containing metaphor of the volume, is a reflection of the life-giving force of the sun, and Osundare use it to reflect on the uses to which humankind puts the sun's creative and restorative energy. The phrase "the moon is a mask dancing" resonates throughout the volume and helps to create a connection between the real and the quasicorporeal:

> The world is a mask dancing
> Mask dancing
> Mask dancing (p. 34).

Osundare takes the phrase from Achebe's novel *Arrow of God* (1964), in which implies that to perceive the illusiveness of human experience as embodied in the mask, one has to view it from different positions and perspectives. Osundare equates his discoveries about human experiences to the phases of the moon. He also imagines how the moon perceives human activity. The temporal and universal, which he conveys in the moon's songs in "Phases" and "Further Phases," are contained by time:

> Time
> Time never runs its race
> Like a straight, uncluttered road
>
> Time the seasons
> Seasons the times;
> The forest sprouts, blooms
> And rots into seed

The seed mothers the mountain
The mountain mothers the river
And the river springs green flowers
In Edens of unsinning apples

I heard moonsteps in the corridors of
Seasons
The sky is aflame with dusts of hurrying
Dials ("Shadows of Time," p. 72).

The behavior of personified time reflects Osundare's own apprehension and, in turn, accounts for the ordering of the poems in the volume. Osundare establishes the moon as his muse in the opening poem of the first section, "Phases":

Spread the sky like a generous mat
Tell dozing rivers to stir their tongues
Unhinge the hills
Unwind the winds
The moon and I will sing tonight (p. 1).

The volume then goes on to explore and communicate the reflections on human experience that the contemplation of the moon can evoke in the poet. *Moonsongs* is concerned not only with conditions in Nigeria and not only with the opulence of Ikoyi, where the moon

Is a laundered lawn
Its grass the softness of infant fluff;

The ceiling is a sky

Of pampered stars

Ikoyi contrasts with Ajegunle, where

the moon
is a jungle,
sad like a forgotten beard

And undergrowths of cancerous furry:
Cobras of anger spit in every brook
And nights are one long prowl
Of swindled leopards (p. 42).

The disenfranchised and despised are found everywhere by
        the moon:

With its ears the moon sees the Soweto of our Skin
And painfields so soggy with the sweat of a
Thousand season

In Grenada where Sunset nurtures freedom
With bayonets and cackling cannon

In Mnagua where reddening flares
Brave the breath of Twilight storms

In the sorrows of our South deep, so deep
Like scars of millenial [sic] lesions. (p. 40).

Through all of the pain, the spirit of humankind, Osundare says, will endure:

No, not yet a knell

We shall not go till we have eaten the elephant
Of the moon
We shall not go
Till our scrupulous eyes have stitched the broken tendons
Of the sky
We shall not go
Till our green dreams spawn golden suns
In the chronicle of stubborn trees (p. 52).

Osundare understands the contending ideologies that shape the lives of ordinary people in his society; therefore, the range of tones in *Moonsongs* moves
from the exuberant through the humorous, the absurd, and the grotesque. He
castigates and caricatures members of the ruling class while enjoining his readers to embrace his sympathetic portrayal of the people.

Waiting Laughters (1990) is, as Osundare says in the subtitle, "a long song in many voices." The song has four movements that all relate to the themes implied in the title—waiting and humor. The poems have the experimental character of those in the earlier volumes and call for accompaniment by musical instruments: "flute and/or Clarinet; medley of human voices" (p. 1); "kora and/or gojr; medley of voices" (p. 28); "gangan, bata, ibembe in varying accents; medley of voices: (p. 44); "flute, kora, gangan, sekere; voices in final flourish" (p. 76).

Osundare draws his subject matter for the most part from Nigeria, specifically from his Yoruba inheritance, but there are poems that relate to events in other parts of Africa and throughout the black world, references to the Niger, the Nile, the Limpopo, and the Atlantic of the middle passage. Some poems celebrate agents and martyrs in the cause of African and black freedom—such as Thomas Sankara, Nelson Mandela, Steve Biko, and Walter Rodney; while others recall apostates to the cause of freedom—such as Adlof Hitler, Marcos, and Idi Amin. A poem begins:

> The innocence of the Niger
> Waiting, waiting
> Fourhenderedseasons
> For the proof of the prow
> Waiting
> For the dispossessing twang of alien accents
> Waiting
> For scrolls of serfdom, hieroglyps of
> Calculated treacheries (p. 37).

References to Sharpeville, Langa, and Soweto suggest that these are not isolated experiences but rather encompass the history of black peoples.

In these poems Osundare extrapolates extended meaning from familiar words and phrases, such as "Robbing Island" and "passports are pass ports" (p. 38). Whatever the subject matter, the poems move toward providing answers to the series of rhetorical questions posed at the end of the volume.

> What happens to the song which waits too long
> In the labyrinth of the throat
>
> What happens to the prayer which waits too long
> Without an amen

What happens to the face which waits too long
Without the memory of a mask

What happens to the LAUGHTER which waits too long
In the compost of anguished seasons?

What.? (p. 94).

Songs of the Season (1990) is gathering of poems from a project Osundare launched in the Nigerian newspaper *Sunday Tribune* in 1985. In the preface, Osundare explains that the project

> Has been empowered by a definable style and purpose: to cap-
> ture the significant happenings of our rime in a tune that is
> simple, accessible, topical, relevant and artistically pleasing;
> to remind kings about the corpses which line their way to the
> throne, to show the rich the slums which fester behind their
> castles, to praise virtue, denounce vice, to mirror the triumphs
> and travails of the downtrodden who ever so often the big
> books forget; to celebrate the green glory of the rainy season
> and the brown accent of the dry, to distil poetry from the dust
> and clay of our vast, prodigious land. (p. v)

Osundare notes that "written poetry has remained an alienated and alienating enterprise in Nigeria – a painful irony in a country where every significant event is celebrated in song, drum and dance, where living still has a fluid rhythm and the proverb is one huge tome of uncountable wisdom" (pp.v–vi). Osundare's success in this project may be measured by the fifty-seven poems in the volume under five general categories: "songs," which includes "not for the poor," "song of the street-sweeper," and "shout of the people"; "dialogue," which includes "a the senior service club" and "retiring into farming"; "tributes," such as "for the women of Greenham Common" and "for chief Obafemi Awolowo"; "parables," such as "slaves who adore their chains" and "the king and the poet"; and "sundry strivings," with poems entitled "songs for children's day" and "songs for all seasons." The volume begins with an invocation to *isi-hun* (voice-opener) and "a song for my land," in which the poet celebrates his central experience of connection with the land, the sources of the poems in this volume.

There are, as well, praise poems denoting the various contributions by Nigerians who have had a vision of Nigeria embracing the whole of the population. There is also a section of thirteen poems entitled parables containing such poems as crying hyena, those who praise the knife and the king and the poet, poems of the once upon a time kind where the moral fable contains a moral lesson. *Songs of the Season* is the product of a project Osundare launched in the newspaper *Sunday Tribune* in 1985. In the preface to the volume Osundare says that the project

> Has been defined by a definable style and purpose: to capture the significant happenings of our time in a tune that is simple, accessible, topical, relevant and artistically pleasing; to remind kings about corpses, which line their way to the throne, to show the rich the slums which fester behind their castles, to praise virtue, denounce vice, to minor the triumphs and travails of the downtrodden who ever so often the big books forget; to celebrate the green glory of the rainy season and the brown accent of the dry, to distill poetry from the dust and clay of our vast and prodigious land.

Whatever the tone and mood of the poems, ranging from the panegyric/lyric to the abrasive and satiric, the volume is encompassed by a political purpose either directly stated or implied. Osundare notes further that "written poetry has remained ... an alienated and alienating enterprise in Nigeria, a painful irony in a country where every significant event is celebrated in song, drum and dance, where living still has a fluid rhythm and the proverb is one huge tome of uncountable wisdom" (pp. v–vi).

Midlife (1993) is a monumental celebration of poetry by a poet who recognises at midlife that he a poet, a member of that panoply of poets who sum up a totality of experience and convey their summations in ways which can shape worlds. Osundare places himself, comfortably, reasonably and without embarrassment in the company of such poets as Soyinka, Gervog Emin, Ai Qing and Wal Whitman (all mentioned on the Dedication page p. viii) to whom are added Guillen, Brathwaite, Neto,Walcott, Heaney, Mayakowshy, Okigbo, U Tamsi, Okot pBitek, Neruda, Elytis, Vallejo, Octovio Paz, Maraka, Tagore, Cesaire. The multitudes that Osundare contains, their sources and their consequences in the affairs of his life, are the sole subject matter of the poetry in this volume. The political context in which the poems are presented is the same as in the recent past volumes:

Sirens, buntings, and billowing banners
Sirens, bugles and rolling cannon.
And enter Hitler with the burning bush
Of his shifty moustache
Enter Bokassa with infant skulls
In his imperial pot.
Enter Pinochet with Allende's blood on his iron bow
Enter Botha, Bikos brain under his spiked boot
Enter the Iron Lady with five testicles like a Joba squirrel
In his rigid gaze.

Enter the Horseman, a sanguinary twilight.

These are the people and the values which poetry confront and surmounts, recognising that

Empires rise, decline, and fall, from their ashes new
           juggernauts and
new swords and conquistadors who sail the skies with vassals
           on every
coast, marching through tender dreams,
pillaging distant lands to prosper their own.

The lessons of history are that the world goes round like a giddy mask. The poet has a vision of the world which says

No to the dirge of coffin-makers.

Osundare sums up his purposes in the volume in what he calls Foreline where he writes:

This volume ... is informed by an inescapably panoramic
Vision where voices are many, protean, even kaleidoscopic. In
keeping With the oral poetic tradition whose inexhaustible
lifespring I am ever indebted to, poetry here is confession,
declaration, reflection, play, struggle, vision... It is exchange,
an unwavering engagement with the world, a dynamic treasury of poetic probings and rooted voyagings mediated through
epic syntax and experimentation in the choric blend of rhetoric and song.

These lines sum up the achievement of the volume. They speak with an utter clarity not only about the sources of the poetry, the manner in which the poetry is expressed but all with an absolute confidence about the ability to realize the poetic mission. "The world I see is bent," says the poet. "I am mode and medium for its straightening" (p. x). The poetry is pantheistic and metaphysical. I am human in every sense: lover of life without regret (p. 37) But beyond this,

> I am light
> I am shadow
> I am the luminous covenant
> Of short and tall spaces (p.3).

> I am a running river Sundering lands, coupling nations,
>   Winking here, dimpling there, 20

> Coiling like a patient cobra

> Round the foot of the towering hills
> Deserts stretch out their breathless hands
> But my memory charts a path
> Of cooler wanderings. (p23).

The heightened language is maintained throughout the volume the mystical vision does not tire, the energy level is unrestrained and unconfined as the poet coveys his certainty that he draws his understanding and his energy from his immersion in the physical and metaphysical world in which he resides but which provides him with a profound understanding of historical causation and a capacity for prophetic vision.

And with the recognition of the special capacity with which his birthright has endowed him there is, as the volume closes, a recognition by the poet of his place in the great scheme of things:

> I have left the prints in the laughter
> Of fragrant dust,
> wayfarers, do not dig my heels for rodents,
> there is a quarry of gold in the pit of my sole.
> Touched, touching,

> I have hawked steaming songs
> In the streets of hungry ears
> Broken the emperor's sword at its gilded hilt
> For me tears which share the borders
> Of waiting laughters
> For I am a stubborn thread in the loom of being
> Indigo song, yarn of purple weftings
> I
> Wear the suns sweat like a garland blu harvests
> I am the caller at noon.

Horses of Memory (1998), is dedicated to the memory of the poet's father and celebrates the fathers artistry and the relationship between the artist and the earth: poet, singer, drummer and farmer. The poetry is more reliant than previous volumes on local Yoruba materials. The integration is greater between the English and the Yoruba. And this enriches the poetry. Osundare writes:

> these poems are composed for orchestration and incantatory
> spectacle: part choric, part threnodic, designed as they are, to
> achieve full celebratory energy and with the accompaniment
> of singing and drumming.

But the meaning is not lost on those readers who do not have the Yoruba. The English language poetry is as trenchant as in earlier volumes and the political/public stances as uncompromising. This is in character with the commitment African poets have had to using their genius to expound notions of public responsibility.

But here and unlike the earlier verse there is a tone of optimism that had been lacking in the earlier volumes. Then there was oppression and human capacity while known and celebrated was shackled by successive military regimes which put the general public good in abeyance while self-serving interests where cultivated.

Now there is optimism in the new regime, a public and elected regime that holds out promise for the future. But this optimism is not found without a profound recalling of what has lead up to the present. And history must be used judiciously. Osundare cites Kwei Armah in this regard:

> There is no need to forget the past. But of each piece of the
> past

That we find in the present, it may be necessary to ask: will it
    bear me
like a stepping stone, or will I have to bear it, a weight around
    my neck?

Osundare further cites Faulkner, Adumaradam and Ewidayepo to indicate his own purposes: History is not was, "it is, Roots, proclaims the Tree, and The song is the memory of the poet." The volume is in seven sections, contains 81 poems and early on establishes the central image of the volume (an image derived from or perhaps, better, inspired by Kofi Awoonor):

The word was your horse:
You rode it through fire, through frenzy
Through waters of silver depths

The word was your horse
You rode it through echoing hills
Through valleys of flowering songs

. . . .

You were the word which fell from the sky
And, touching earth , broke
Into a thousand truths.

There is optimism here but it is a cautious optimism. On the one hand:

The yams you planted last season
Have burst into bloom:
Efuru has sprung muscular tendrils
From the womb if a faithful soil:
. . . .

A thousand seeds are sprouting, sprouting
A thousand tendrils are wandering, wondering

And yet:

Where are the hands which mulched their roots
With a ring of green moons?
Where are the hands which piloted their journey
Up the stairs of the stake?

The poems in the successive sections of the volume provide various specu-
lations and answers to these rhetorical questions in a range of moods and tones
speculative, doubting, celebratory and finally affirmative, the poets tracing
Africa's colonial history as a rape of artistic artifacts Ife in Bonn, Benin in
London, Zimbabwe in New York – robbing the poet in part of his history, a continuity celebrated by the poet/griot.

Everywhere in the poems the poet's strength is anchored in his recollection
of the gift of art his father gave him:

Yours, too,
Is a peopled imagination:
I can summon those lost arks

In the covenant of your palm,
Fearing no angry prophecies
Nor floods of partial gods
. . . .

Courier of First Lights
Who gave my myth, and then a mask
I will comb Memorys forest
For the chosen tree .

Moments of uncertainty and confusion I, too, /am victim/
        of a map/
which forgets its land./ are balanced by moments of pure
        affirmation:

The poet routs the snore
Of a tribe committed to slumber
. . . .

I am a poet:
My memory is a house
Of many rooms

The volume concludes with the longest poem, "Horses of Memory," in which the poet consolidates the imagery of the horseman and poet/artist/griot, recognizes the experience encompassed by memory, in history and in the present, collective and personal, and affirms the need to draw on the lessons and the wisdom that rationalizing memory provides.

The latest volume of poems, *The World is an Egg*, (2000) has, like all of Osundare's previous collections, a containing metaphor. Here it is the adumbrated meaning of Egg, the source of life and by extension the source of poetic inspiration. Coupled with this is the assertion, given as paradox, not that In the beginning was The Word but rather In the Word was the Beginning. The Word, the Word, is an egg/ From the nest of Hawk and Dove. Only through the word is it possible to articulate the myriad meanings of experience and to convert this experience into comprehension. Here, too, as with the earlier volumes, the poems describe the plight of the disenfranchised and the poet stands opposed to those responsible or irresponsibly accountable – for the disenfranchisement:

> There is poverty in the land
> Screams the village wag
>
> The Emperor rolls out his armoured tanks
>
> The Bishop shoots it with the Cross
>
> The Imam binds it with his beads
>
> The Politician drowns it with a torrent of words
>
> And, slapping each other on the back,
> They strut back to their feathered roost,
>
> Considering all the problems
> SOLVED

The conditions among the general populace which prompt this fierce condemnation of those in offices which should respond to and ameliorate the conditions prompted by the seer, the village wag (the irony here is not misplaced) are revealed in all of the poems in the four sections of the volume and display the metaphor of the egg in connection with the power of the word as an avatar of new beginnings.

SELECTED BIBLIOGRAPHY

Adejuwon, Femi. "Singing for the Oppressed." Rev. of *Song of the Marketplace*. *Nigerian Tribune* (Ibadan) (5 March 1986).

Ajibade, Kunle. "My Vision, My Styles." *African Concord* (9 September 1991).

Arnold, Stephen. "The Praxis of Niyi Osundare, Popular Scholar-Poet." *World Literature Written in English* 29 (1989).

Bryce, Jane. "Dreams and Bullets: Nigerian Poetry." *West Africa* 21 July 1986.

Bolaji, Sanni. "Osundare's Songs of Sorrow and Hope." *Punch* (Lagos)1 November 1984.

Jeyifo, Biodun. "Niyi Osundare." Ed. Yemi Ogunbiyi. *Perspectives on Nigerian Literature: 1700 to the Present*, vol. 2. Lagos, Nigeria: Guardian Books, 1988.

Nwahunanya, Chinyere. "Osundare's New Esotericism: The Genesis of Poetic Disintegration." Ed. E.U. Ohaegbu. *Language, Literature and Social Change. Acts* of the 7th annual conference of the Modern Languages Association of Nigeria, 8–11 February 1989. Nsukka: University of Nigeria, 1989.

Oni, Sanya. "Osundare: The Poet of the Market Place." *National Concord* (Lagos) (24 June 1988).

Osundare, Niyi. *Songs of the Marketplace*. Ibadan, Nigeria: New Horn Press, 1983.

———. *Village Voices*. Ibadan, Nigeria: Evans Bros., 1984.

———. *The Eye of the Earth*. Ibadan, Nigeria: Heinemann, 1986.

———. *The Nib in the Pond*. Ife, Nigeria: University of Ife, 1986.

———. *The Writer as Righter*. Ife, Nigeria: University of Ife, 1986.

———. *Moonsongs*. Ibadan, Nigeria: Spectrum Books, 1988.

———. *Waiting Laughters: A Long Song in Many Voices*. Lagos, Nigeria: Malthouse Press, 1990.

———. *Songs of the Season*. Ibadan, Nigeria: Heinemann Educational Books, 1990.

———. *Selected Poems*. Oxford, U.K.: Heinemann, 1992.

———. *Midlife*. Nigeria: Heinemann Educational Books, 1993.

———. *Horses of Memory*. Nigeria: Heinemann Educational Books,1998

———. *The Word Is An Egg*. Nigeria: Kraft Books, 2000.

MEANING, TRANSLATION, AND THE POET'S LITERARY ASPIRATIONS

MORPHOLOGY AND MEANING IN NIYI OSUNDARE'S POETRY

Adeyeye Samson Dare

Niyi Osundare's is the clearest, loudest and most attention-getting poetic voice from the Anglophone Africa today. A new generation poet, following the earlier established poets such as Okigbo, Soyinka and Clark, Osundare has, through enormous productivity, elegance of style, and currency and consistency of thematic concern, succeeded in drawing the world's attention to himself. To date, this celebrated poet has published ten volumes of poetry: *Songs of the Marketplace* (1983), *Village Voices* (1984), *A Nib in the Pond* (1986), *The Eye of the Earth* (1986), *Moonsongs* (1988), *Waiting Laughters* (1990), *Songs of the Season* (1990), *Midlife* (1993), *Horses of Memory* (1998), and *A Word Is an Egg* (2000). The Ikere-born poet has been in the international spotlight as a result of the many prizes and awards he has won. On the merit of *The Eye of the Earth*, Osundare jointly (with Vikrarm Seth of India) won the Commonwealth Poetry Prize in 1986. Similarly the *Village Voices* received Honorable Mention by the Jury of the Noma Award in 1986. In manuscript, *Waiting Laughters* won the ANA/Cadbury Prize in 1990. When it was published in 1991, the book won for Osundare the Noma Award. The poet was the recipient of ANA/Cadbury Prize for 1994 on the merit of *Midlife*. These factors account for the keen interest that critics, reviewers and stylisticians have in his poetry.

In this chapter, I shall discuss four of his works from a morphological point of view. The works are: *The Eye of the Earth* (1986), *Moonsongs* (1988), *Waiting Laughters* (1990) and *Midlife* (1993). All page references point to the editions indicated in the Bibliography. Readers might notice that these four works represent the later efforts of the poet. It is hoped that an insight into them will enhance an appreciation and understanding of the other works.

It is demonstrated that a linguistic reading of poetry as imagistic and symbolic as Osundare's can be highly stimulating and rewarding. I am not proposing a linguistic reading as an alternative to a "purely" literary evaluation. Rather, my current reading is meant to be complementary to other forms of reading. When a linguistic evaluation is carried out jointly with other forms or levels of appraisal, semantic minutiae are likely to emerge.

There is a brighter prospect for a linguistic appraisal of Osundare's poetry. We have noted elsewhere (Dare, 1998) that Osundare is an extremely conscious artist endowed with extraordinary linguistic sensitivity. He enormously enjoys working with words. Biodun Jeyifo (1988: 316–317) once noted:

> Words and images delight and excite Osundare in the way that a painter in love with his calling delights in colors, and a sculptor who works in molten bronze enthuses in the plasticity of his medium ... Osundare ... has kept his metaphoric and semantic range copiously and wide.

The poet sometimes appears to be under some pressure to purge his soul of words.

It may be observed that his passionate love for words is made acute by his training in linguistics and literary studies and his poetry has also been immensely enriched by his cultural backgrounds. Our poet continues to pay his debt to his training as a linguist and literary stylist by employing metaphors, images and symbols derived from linguistic structures. In many places the meta language of linguistic and literary studies becomes an effective medium of poetic communication. (for example, "I am the ubiquitous *and* in the broken/*scene-tax* of a stammering *discourse,*/ the *but* which tempers the flame/ of volcanic *clauses* ..." *Midlife*, p. 58).

However, the focus in this chapter is on the morphological pattern in his poetry. Attention is drawn to the symbolization and imaging achieved by the means of innovative morphological structures. Space limitation does not permit the inclusion here of the negation morpheme "-less" which is a major stylistic and poetic strategy in his poetry. Readers who belong to our poet's discipline have a greater advantage in apprehending his meaning and enjoying his poetry. Sometimes "outsiders" are excluded.

MORPHOLOGICAL INNOVATIONS

Morphological innovations constitute the central concern of this chapter and graphological features are brought in only when they enhance or illuminate the poetic and stylistic functions of morphological "maneuvers". To be sure, Osundare often seeks the collaboration of morphology and graphology in the pursuit of stylistic effects and poetic communication. Often, the analyst does not find it expedient, even sometime finds it impossible, to describe these two features in isolation from each other.

In an exciting and attention-compelling manner, Osundare causes major morphological dislocations and innovations, sometimes for their own sake but often in the service of particular themes or ideas. As in all instances of reiteration noticed in Osundare's poetry, sometimes it is the idea, meaning, and theme, sometimes it is the structure and the structural principle that are allowed to recur and draw attention to themselves. In this chapter I demonstrate that the forms, the structures and the principles behind these are given pre-eminence in the morphological innovations.

ANALYSES

On the analogy of "yesterday" and "yesteryear", in which "yester-" occurs as a pre-fix (a bound morpheme), the words

> yester-morrows
> yester-voices
> yester-showers

are formed. The poet writes

> ... the map
> is history's whisper
> in the ears of yester-morrows
> (*Moonsongs*, p. 68).

Out of context, the word "yester-morrows" makes little sense, but in the context before us, we can understand the paradox conveyed by the two bound morphemes yoked together by the use of a hyphen. As it were, the word has one "leg" in the past ("yester-") and the other in the future ("-morrows") with a bridge provided by the hyphen. The possessive word "history's" sets up the philosophical tension in the word: the poet sees history as a dynamic interaction between the past and the future linked by the present (which the hyphen may be said to represent). With the word "yester-voices", we have one bound morpheme and one free morpheme, having unrelated meanings. The import is made clear in context:

> Memory,
> loud whisper of yester-voices (*The Eye*, p. 12).

The action of "memory" is conceived of in terms of a "loud whisper", a whisper that comes from the store of information belonging to the past. The first morpheme represents the past, the second represents "loud whisper". In other words, "memory"" is to ''yester-" what "loud whisper" is to "-voices".

Again the second morpheme in "yester-showers" is a free one. The poet writes:

> The rain fell in June
> and December licked it brown
> with its feline tongue
> they who marvel the sinews of our dust
> let them ask what happened to the offspring
> of our yester-showers
> (*Moonsongs*, p. 34).

We are told that "the rain" which fell "in June" was "licked" "brown" by "December". What is left is "the sinews of our dust", a bad memory of "the rain". As in other compound words in its class, "yester-" in "yester-showers" stands for the past while ''showers" of course refers to the rain.

Excited by the morphological relationship between "king" and "kingdom", the poet creates the word "darkdom" occurring in the following contexts:

> ... the night
> in the gloomy alleys
> of NEPA's darkdom
> (*The Eye of the Earth*, p. 25)

Sing to us about the glow-worm's treason,
in the darkdom of night
(*Midlife*, p. 44)

Since the word "kingdom" containing the final bound morpheme "-dom" denotes the sway or dominion of a monarch, the word "darkdom" is meant to convey the notion of a state in which "darkness" holds sway. It is useful to note that the morpheme "dark" now occupies the position in which "king" occurs in the original word. The implication is that in this position, the word (or morpheme) "dark" has assimilated the semantic values of "king" in addition to its own.

In the lines from *The Eye*, the word "night" and the adjective "gloomy" overlapping semantically with the morpheme "dark", prepare the reader for the neologism "darkdom". Perhaps the poet's chief stylistic interest resides in the word NEPA, in its possessive form. The National Electric Power Authority (of Nigeria) charged with the responsibility of providing energy and light has come to symbolize darkness. The lines present a picture of the kingdom not of light but of darkness; hence "darkdom".

In the extract from *Midlife*, the word "darkdom" has implications similar to those discussed above. The noun "treason", signifying the illegal overthrow of lawfully constituted authority, anticipates the notion of "kingdom" that we encounter in "darkdom". The "glow-worm", that insect which punctuates darkness with its light, is said to have committed "treason". For practical purposes, the word "kingdom" can replace "darkdom" in the prepositional phrase "in the darkdom of light" which intimates the idea of a state dominated by ''night''.

The manipulations employed for stylistic ends in "*mal*eficent", "execu*thieves*" and "ultra*violent*" are partly morphological, partly phonological, partly lexical and partly semantic. While retaining the idea of maliciousness in "*mal*eficent", the poet seeks to draw attention to the involvement of the *male* gender in the lines:

women battling centuries of
*mal*eficent slavery
(*The Eye of the Earth*, p. 45).

The poet presents women as "battling" to free themselves from "centuries" of "slavery". To underscore the destructive evil in the servitude, we have a premodifier "maleficent". With the help of a visual impression, the poet segments the word into "male" and "ficent", the former having an autonomous lexical existence whose meaning is alien to this word, the latter a bound morpheme, altogether meaningless except as it occurs in the normally inviolable structure of the word. The morphological segment, "male", looks back semantically to the item "women", to which it is antonymous. The theme of female domination by men is adroitly communicated in these two lines. This remarkable economy of presentation hardly has a better alternative.

Relying on the phonological and orthographic contrasts between a part of the word "executive' and the word "thieve", our poet produces the form execu*thieves* in the line:

> native executhieves hold fort for alien wolves
> (*The Eye of the Earth*, p 46).

The second part of the word "executives" in which the voiceless alveolar plosive /t/ occurs is replaced with the word "thieves" containing a voiceless dental fricative /Ø/. With this phonological grafting and additional adjustments in spelling, we have a queer word, which communicates the impression of "thieves" in high places, or highly placed "thieves". The phonological, orthographic and semantic super-imposition on the word "executive" producing "executhieves" is in harmony with the import of the final word "wolves". The contrast is located in the pre-modifier of each of them: "native" and "alien". The economy of presentation is also remarkable.

Again the manipulations in "ultraviolent" are partly phonological, partly lexical, partly morphological and partly semantic. We read:

> February has come
> also come is the sun's ultraviolet rays
> in the tropical chapter
> of our riddled cravings
> (*Moonsongs*, p. 55).

Two words are virtually collapsed into one with minor phonological and orthographic adjustments. The words are "ultraviolet" and "violent". Of course "ultraviolet" is made up of two morphemes: "ultra-" and "violet". It is the phonological and orthographic resemblance between the second morpheme and the adjective "violent" that partly inspired the merger. It may be safe to argue that the adjective "violent" and its semantic implications are transferred to the second morpheme in "ultraviolet". But the super-imposition is facilitated by the similarities between them.

There are intimations in the neighboring words that the primary connotations of "ultraviolet" before the super-imposition are still retained. The preceding word "sun" (in its possessive form) and the word that follows, "rays", confirm these residual semantic implications coexisting with those of "violent". Even the adjective "tropical" indirectly furnishes this contextual information. With the yoking together of "ultra-" and "violent", we do not only have an idea of "sun" and "rays" but also of violence. The complex manipulations made explicit above have been pressed into the service of economical stylistic effect.

From *Moonsongs* (p. 3) comes the following lines:

> Fiery scales, fiery scales
> So eloquent in the manhood of the sun
>
> Oh sea
>   Season
>   season . . .
>
> The sun which blues the sea,
> Which tones its flesh ...

Obviously the poet is interested in three elements: the "sea", the "sun" and the "season". The visual arrangement of "sea', "season" and "season" into a terrace-like structure helps in emphasizing the relationship among them. The poet seems to suggest that the "season" is the result of the interaction between the "sea" and the "sun". This is the implication of the lines:

> The sun which *blues* the sea,
> Which *tones* its flesh

That interaction is morphologically symbolized by the concatenation of these two linguistically unrelated free morphemes ("sea"" and "sun") producing the neologism "Seasun" occurring last in the terrace-like structure. Between "sea" and "seasun" in the terrace-like arrangement occurs "season", a position suggesting that "season" comes into being as a result of the interaction mentioned above. The neologism "seasun" is produced on the analogy of "season" and the phonological resemblance between "son", the final morpheme in "season", and the noun "sun" must have in part inspired and facilitated the fashioning out of the neologism "seasun".

Let me dwell a little longer on the word "season". This is clearly a regular English word, unlike the word "seasun", a product of contextual and stylistic exigencies. The line:

So eloquent in the manhood of the sun

provides the contextual pressure that suggests a co-existence of another meaning with the obvious import of the word "season" The noun "manhood" intimates not just physical maturity, but possibly sexual' maturity. So we can infer from "manhood" the notion of "fatherhood" or "parenthood". The complete phrase is "the manhood of the sun", having the implication that the "sun" can have a "son". In its marriage with the "sea", a marriage consummated in the word "seasun" (a kind of morphologically symbolized marriage), the "sun" produces a "son". The "son" lives, not separately from the spouse of the "sun"; it lives in the bosom of the "sea"; hence "season". There is another reason to assume that the "son" is sired by the "sun": there is a striking phonological and orthographic resemblance between them. In addition to the idea of mere natural, physical interaction between the "sea" and the "sun" producing "season", the metaphor of generation is involved.

Just as he collapses two or more words into one, Osundare habitually breaks a word into two or more meaningful lexical items, which can sometimes be read as phrases, clauses or sentences. Some examples are:

eyebrow : I - brow
man-slaying : man slaying
mangoes : man goes
winnowing : we - knowing

From *Moonsongs* (p. 9) we have:

The iron I-brow of the foaming tyrant

Certainly the form "I-brow", two words forced to appear to be one through the use of a queer hyphen, owes much to the pronunciation and, to a limited extent, orthographic representation of the word "eye-brow". But the indebtedness of "I-brow" stops at that; nothing can be said in favor of semantics about their relationship. For the semantic and stylistic considerations, we must turn to the context in which the linguistic novelty occurs. The new formation is preceded by the word "iron" which defines the character of the "foaming tyrant'.

The item "I", forming part of the neologism, must be cast in "iron", so perpendicularly unbending, reflecting the graphological character of the letter. In so far as the "I" represents the ,'will" of a person, we can say in the common parlance that the !'foaming tyrant" has a "will" of "iron". The "brow", the other aspect of the novel creation, speaks of the physiognomy of the implacable "tyrant" which is as severe as his "will" is unbending. The derivation of the two words, "I" and "brow", hyphenated, from a single item "eyebrow", far from forfeiting verbal economy, is both stylistically fruitful and semantically rewarding.

In a section of *Waiting Laughters* (pp. 12, 13), we have a subject matter dealing with the frustration, perspiration and desperation in the "visahouse". Here people present their "passports" for authorization to travel abroad. The poet then tells us that:

Passports are passports

Characteristically, the poet offers his own definition of "passports" involving the separation of the single word into two morphemes: "pass' and "ports". The two words so produced indicate that "passports" involve traveling from one port to the other; and movement from one port to the other is not very easy as the experience in the "visahouse" shows. The pun and the re interpretation may be a poet's way of trivializing the painful process of obtaining a visa. A "passport", the poet seems to be saying jocularly, cannot "pass" until it has been "passed".

On page 105 of *Midlife*, the poet presents the following lines:

Man-slaying monsters
man, slaying monsters
man slaying monsters

The compound word "man-slaying" in the first line becomes two words: "mar" and "slaying" - in the two other variants. The compound word is a modifier to "monsters" in the first line, making the construction a nominal phrase. That nominal group means that "monsters" kill man. However, the second line, in which the first word, "man", is separated from the present participle "slaying" by the use of a comma, has an elliptical relative clause:

the man, (who is) slaying monsters

The third variant also has an elliptical relative clause but the clause is a restrictive one, unlike the previous one, which is non-restrictive. There is another major semantic difference between the first variant and the last two: the first one implies that monsters slay man, while the last two mean that it is man that slays monsters.

Writes the poet:

> the mortal murmurs of musing mangoes
> of crude climbers and missiles
> from starving quivers;
> and suddenly, each fruit a toll
> of expiring winds
> each toll a tale
> each tale a tail of coiling snakes
> ah! mangoes man goes. Man
> Goes in so many lives hanging green
> on racks of ripening branches
> (*Moonsongs*, p. 50).

With the assault "of the crude climbers and missiles" launched by "Starving quivers", the "musing mangoes" make "mortal murmurs". The repetition of the determiner "each", the alliterative recurrence of the lateral /l/ and the voiceless alveolar plosive /t/ accentuate the calamity of the "mangoes" whose experience was first that of "a toll", and then that of "a tale" and then "a tail of coiling snakes". The fall of the "mangoes" and the fatalities they suffer attract the exclamation, "ah! mangoes".

But suddenly the plural noun, "mangoes", becomes a sentence containing one long adverbial (or prepositional) phrase:

> ah! mangoes man goes. Man
> Goes in so many lives hanging green
> on racks of ripening branches

Initially, the reader encounters the ordinary sense of noun, "mangoes", fruits that are being harvested out of season possibly as a result of excessive hunger (cf. "starving quivers"). But when the poet moves from the referential import of that noun to the sentiments of "so many lives hanging green", he separates the noun into two morphemes: "man" and "goes". Luckily for the poet, the "-es' plural morpheme coincides with the third person singular morpheme in the verb "go". Taking advantage of the happy coincidence our poet produces a sentence out of a plural noun. (By the way, "man goes" is a prominent reminder of

Soyinka's memorable sentence, "The man died", which is also the title of his prison notes).

Next we consider an apparently unwieldy creation, "we-knowing-season", derived from two words "winnowing season":

> Winnowing season: we-knowing-season
> The chaff know their hell,
> grains thresh a handsome pilgrimage
> to the Jerusalem of the jaw ...
> (Waiting Laughter, p. 20).

The "winnowing season" marks the difference between the "chaff" and "grains" and the activity involved in separating them. The present participle "winnowing" pre-modifying "season" provides the orthographic and phonetic information used in forming and feeding "we-knowing-", the first two segments of the structure. There is absolutely no connection, semantic or etymological between "winnowing" and "we-knowing-". But the poet, labors, as usual, to establish a relationship.

"The chaff", the outcome of "winnowing" (a gerund, not a present participle) are said to "know" (a segment of the neologism) "their hell' as they are burnt off. Similarly the "grains" are on a "pilgrimage" to 'the Jerusalem of the jaw". The poet intends a relationship of contrast between "hell" and "Jerusalem". The possessive pronoun "their" pre-modifying "hell" is also intended to stand in a relationship of contrast with "we" (a segment of the newly formed expression). It is *their* "hell" and not "ours". Furthermore "pilgrimage", in a sense, is an exercise in "knowing", not just "Jerusalem" (or Mecca) but certain profound spiritual truths - a kind of epiphany. "We-knowing-season", then, is a season of knowing, of discovery, of enlightenment, of epiphany. There may be no serious semantic justification for the fashioning out of the neologism, but there is certainly abundant contextual and, to a limited extent, poetic justification for it.

Habitually, Osundare breaks a word into two morphemes, which stand on separate lines, giving the impression of a run-on line. One of the morphemes may not make sense apart from the other, but the one that makes sense independently of the other usually carries much more semantic and poetic "load" than it does in its union with its "partner". The fact is that the morphological union is not altogether violated, for the poetic experience created for the reader is such that enables him to see simultaneously a morphologically unbroken word and a morphologically separated one. In reality, there is only one word whose morphological structure is taken unusual advantage of for stylistic and poetic ends. In the end, neither the word nor its morphological nature is lost. The semantic and contextual gains are often enormous.

Here are some lines from *Waiting Laughters* (p. 6):

> Wait
>   ing ...
> And the hours limp a
> long,
> with
> band_
> ages
> of fractured moments

The words which have gone through morphological cleavage are:

> waiting
> along
> bandages

It is useful to bear in mind that the lines quoted above introduce the dominant theme in *Waiting Laughters* – that of "waiting". And of course in waiting, the element of time lag, of delay, of tardiness is involved. This fact is morphologically symbolized. The separation of the present participle "waiting" into its ""root", "wait" and the "-ing" ending, with the two morphemes appearing on two separate lines in a visually created tier, symbolically captures the psychological processes of "waiting". The eye rests first on "wait" before it moves to the "-ing" occurring below it to its right. The slowness involved in capturing the morphologically separated word into one integrated whole is deliberately achieved. Significantly, the word 'waiting" is so crucial to the theme of the collection of poems when it occurs for the first time. The morphologically achieved tardiness sets the tone for the entire work.

The word "hours" is a clear indication that tine is under consideration. We are told that "the hours" "limp", a word that pictures impeded or uneasy motion as well as physical deformity. Then comes the word "along" separated into the meaningless morpheme "a_" and the accidentally meaningful morpheme "-long". The morpheme "-long" in the word "along" has no meaning except in its union with the other morpheme. But luckily the morpheme "-long" coincides in form with an adjective in English' "long", an adjective signifying extensiveness in time or distance. The word agrees with the idea of slowness set in motion by the word "waiting". While the adverb "along" agrees with the notion of movement suggested by the verb "limp", the adjective "long" is in harmony with -the notion of tardiness conveyed by true word "waiting". Thus, the poet has adroitly offered us two words simultaneously: "along" and "long'.

The word "bandages" is similarly separated into two morphemes, "band-" and "-ages", both of which are accidentally meaningful for different reasons. The noun "bandages" is congruent with the sense of injury conveyed by the verb "limp" and the participle "fractured". Since "moments" are "fractured", "the hours" are bound to "limp along". And "bandages" are needed to "band" the "fractured" parts. Thus, the word "bandages" is a collocational necessity.

The morpheme "band-" is meaningful as the root of "bandages" signifying an element or stuff with which things are held together. In other words this morpheme to a very large extent retains the sense of the entire word "bandages". But the final morpheme ".ages" is, ordinarily, meaningless without its root. Fortunately, there is a completely semantically unrelated word in English, which has a form similar to the morpheme "-ages". That word is "ages" (in its plural form) which is collocationally harmonious with the words "hours", "moments", and even "waiting", those indices of time. The last part of the poem may be read as:

ages/ of fractured moments.

In other words while the morpheme "band-" is in the right company with "limp" and "fractured", "ages" looks back to "waiting" and "hours" and forward to "moments". Thus, we have two words in one; "bandages" and "ages" actively involved in the reading and re-creative processing of the poem.

The word "baggage" is subjected to a similar cleavage in the lines:

and the stars depart with a bagg
age of silent seasons across
their ancient shoulders?
(*Moonsongs*, p. 16).

The word "baggage" is necessitated by the verb "depart", since departure is associated with that word. The complete idiom is "bag and baggage". At a level, the poet may be seen as creating a memory of these two words by breaking "baggage" into two queer morphemes running into each other on separate lines. The two morphemes, "bagg-" and "age", are hardly meaningful out of their morphological union. The only point against the morpheme "bagg-" being interpreted as a substantive word in English is its orthographic oddity; it has two instead of one final "g". In spite of that slight orthographic anomaly, the mind is able to identify a core of meaning in the morpheme. It can in other words be allowed to pass for "bag". Without any loss or twist in meaning the line can read:

> and the stars depart with a bag.

Note that we have canceled both the anomalous second "g" and the hyphen. A "bag" still collocates with the verb "depart".

The morpheme "-age" does not require as much labor before we can recognize in it a substantive word of English. Granted, we are dealing no more with the final morpheme of "baggage", "-age", which, alone, is semantically vacuous. But that morpheme happens to coincide in form with a substantive word in English, "age", a noun having to do with time. This word enters into a harmonious collocational pattern with the noun "seasons" and the adjective "ancient". The two lines can read,

> age Or silent seasons across
> their ancient shoulders

without any significantly altered meaning. Thus we have a co-existence of lexical items, "baggage", "bag", "bag and baggage" and "age", impinging simultaneously on the consciousness of the sensitive reader. We might note that the morpho-graphological rupture of the items discussed in this extract is an attempt by the poet to show a symbolic and sympathetic connection between the "fractured moments" - the temporal disturbances - and the broken words.

The word "ill-literate" ostensibly formed on the basis of the morphological structure of "illiterate" is subjected to a morpho-graphological cleavage in the text:

> Rumor slaps the tabloid face of illiterate
> mornings
> bleeds screaming headlines like a noisy leech
> (*Waiting Laughters*, p. 16).

To understand the difference between "illiterate" and "ill-literate" we must recognize that the "-il" in illiterate and "ill" in "ill-literate" are totally unrelated. The item "ill" is normally an autonomous word in English connoting "evil", "bad". Thus we have: "for good" or "for ill"; "ill-governed"; "ill-conceived"; "ill-motivated"; "the ills of the society"; "speak ill of"; "ill-advised"; "ill-gotten gains"; etc. The word "ill" should therefore not be confused with the use of "i' and an additional "l" to form negation in English: "literate" = illiterate; licit = illicit; legal = illegal.

It becomes apparent that in offering us the two morphemes "ill-" and "literate" the poet is working both on the structure of negation morpheme in English and the compounding involving the substantive lexical item "ill".

The breaking of "ill-literate" into two morphemes on two separate run-on lines is emphatic. It is a way of drawing attention to the fact that the word is not being used in the ordinary or usual sense. The perniciousness normally associated with illiteracy is foregrounded and lexicalized, as it were, in the initial morpheme at the end of the first line, "ill-".

The idea of "ill" or evil is suggested by the "rumor" which "slaps" the "face" of the "tabloid". Everywhere "rumor" is associated with ruinous information or defamation (or slander). "Rumor" often connotes verbal assault intended to malign a person. The verb "slaps", suggesting physical violence, conveys this idea of verbal assault. It would seem that the poet is suggesting that "assault and battery" is not different in character or impact from slander. The verb "bleeds" and the participle "screaming" advance this theme of physical violence is being no less destructive than verbal attack.

There is linguistic evidence that the poet is not interested in non-literacy. Since news reporting, news printing and news publishing are involved, the question of illiteracy or non-literacy in its very literal sense does not arise. That, we suspect, is why we have the morpheme "literate", also a substantive lexical item in English, separately from the morpheme "ill-". At a level, we have "literate mornings"; at dawn people are assaulted with "screaming headlines" which are as "noisy" as "leech".

There is an irresponsible sensationalism involved, a sensationalism that is pernicious, inspired by reckless mercenary desire. That inordinate, amoral pecuniary drive is captured by the nominal phrase "noisy leech" and the verb "bleeds".

In a sense, then, the morphemes "ill" and "literate" are separate and yet united. They constitute one word and yet they are two. The community and their newspaper producers are "literate", yet they are 'ill-literate'; they are "literate", they are "illiterate". The pervasive and far-reaching evils perpetrated by the "tabloid" and the "headlines" are such that require many words to describe: "literate", ''ill-literate'', "ill" and "illiterate". This in our view is one of the skills that make Osundare such a successful, unique and exciting poet.

The noun "geography" provides another exciting morphological manipulation in Osundare's poetry. Writes the poet:

> And the sun traces the geo
> graphy of History on my glistening brow:
> tell-tale creases, rippling like water snakes
> into the dense foliage of the head
>
> The nose is a heaving island
> in the ocean of the face
>
> The sun knows the geo-graphy of history
> (*Midlife*, p. 81) .

The morphemes running into each other in two lines are "geo" and "graphy" It is remarkable that the poet does not use a hyphen to indicate compounding. Conscious of the fact that the reader is familiar with "Geography" as an academic discipline, the poet feels the need to caution the reader against regarding it as such in this context. The temptation to think of it as a subject (or an academic discipline) is heightened by the presence of "History", a related academic discipline, having its initial letter capitalized. The substance of what is involved in "Geography" as a subject, is being applied by the poet, but the classroom orientation is rejected.

The poet's method of achieving this is to separate the word into two morphemes, "geo" and "graphy" where "geo" represents the face or "brow" and "graphy" stands for the lines, "tell-tale creases" and snakes". It is the "sun" that "traces" the "geo graphy". The word "History" here stands for the "age" of the poet. The point is that it is possible to read the "age" of a person from the lines and wrinkles on his face. Perhaps in addition to age, it is possible to discern the intensity of experience and the level of maturity of a person from his or her physiognomy.

The "sun" is involved because time is measured in the traditional African society by the position of the sun. Besides, since the "sun' "looks" down directly at the earth and "sees" everything as it happens or as it is, it is understandable that the "sun" traces the "geography" of "History". The "sun" not only "traces", it also "knows the geography" of "History". It would seem that the "sun" is employed as a symbol of nature that is all-seeing and all-knowing. It is interesting that although the l 24 two morphemes in question occur first on two separate but successive lines, when they occur the second time on a single line, they are presented as a single, compound word, brought together by a hyphen. It is, therefore, extremely important to note this second appearance serves to underscore the fact that the poet deliberately presents the word as containing two separate morphemes. This insistence on two morphemes is an emphatic way of saying that the word before us does not signify the academic discipline we are so familiar with.

The adverb "finally" is split into two morphemes i˜i the service of stylistic effectiveness:

> ... The circumcising sun
> hangs between the sky,
> deliberate, cruelly kind
>
> > A! a grey-hot edge has fine -
> > Ally breached the prepuce of the rnist:
> > the day knows now the dialect
> > > of the knife.
>
> (*Midlife*, p. 78).

The image is predominantly that of circumcision , the instrument that accomplishes the feat is the "circumcising sun" whose action is described as "cruelly kind". "The circumcising sun" is also described as "a grey-hot edge". Now we come to the two morphemes, "fine_" and "Ally". Even when these two morphemes are brought together, it takes more than ordinary sensitivity to recognize the result as the adverb "finally".

The poet seems to be under some curious pressure to pass a favorable comment on the action of "the circumcising sun" or "grey-hot edge". Not satisfied with the paradoxical judgement, "cruelly kind", he has already passed, the poet feels the need to disrupt the morphological structure of the adverb "finally" in order to commend the "action". The first morpheme, "fine-", totally unrelated to the adverb, is a complimentary remark on the action of "breaching" the "prepuce" of the mist. Ordinarily, circumcision, circumlocutory referred to in the phrase "breached the prepuce", is a painful but beneficial experience. The adjective "fine", the first of the two morphemes, affirms the beneficial nature of the exercise. The adjective may also refer to the cleanness or "fineness" of the cutting, made possible by the sharp "grey-hot edge" or "the dialect of the knife".

The second morpheme is "Ally". The oddity of the neologism is all the more remarkable when we notice that the second morpheme comes at the beginning of another line. And since it begins another stanza, its initial letter is capitalized, a deliberate effort to draw attention to its existence as a substantive word of English. Clearly semantically unrelated to the adverb "finally", the form "Ally" is a word (a noun or a verb) signifying cooperation, connection or unity.

With that meaning, the form "Ally" both semantically and symbolically serves as a link between the two stanzas. Besides, the participle "breached" is balanced semantically and ideationally by the word "Ally". What the poet is saying is that the "sun" has "cut the day" into two, an extended metaphor for midday. (Compare this with, "Ticking mountains *fine-ally* strike their hour", *Moonsoongs*, p. 18).

CONCLUSION

We have attempted in this chapter to draw attention to one significant poetic and stylistic strategy in Niyi Osundare's poetry: morphological experimentation. We can see, through these analyses, that the poet takes extreme liberties with his language. An extremely conscious artist that he is, Osundare seeks to register deep impressions through fine morphological points and wonderfully adventurous morphological innovations.

His training in stylistics and literary studies, we have hypothesized, may have equipped him with an unusual linguistic sensitivity, and readers who share this background with him have a special advantage over others in processing Osundare's poetic compositions. His indebtedness to his basic training can be demonstrated at all levels of linguistic description--syntax, phonology, semantics, etc.

Osundare's poetry is so rich that only a multidisciplinary approach can come close to revealing its value in full. The effort in this chapter does not represent more than a tiny aspect of the linguistic dimension of Osundare's poetry.

REFERENCES

Primary Sources:
Osundare, Niyi.*The Eye of the Earth.* Ibadan: Heinemann, 1986.
————. *Moonsongs,* Ibadan: Spectrum Books Ltd., 1908.
————. *Waiting Laughters,* Lagos: Malthouse Press Ltd., 1988.
————. *Midlife,* Ibadan: Heinemann, 1993.

Secondary Sources:
Achebe. Chinua. "The English Language and the African Writer" *Insight* . 1966. No. 14.
Adegbonyin, A.S. *Niyi Osundare.* Ibadan: Sam Bookman, 1996.
Aiyejina, Funso. "Recent Nigerian Poetry in English: An Alternative Tradition" *Perspective on Nigerian Literature.* Vol. One. Ed. Ogunbiyi. Lagos: Guardian Books Nigeria Ltd., 1988.
Ajayi, R.O. "Two Of a kind? Art and Politics in the Poetry of Niyi Osundare" M.A. Thesis, Obafemi Awolowo university, Nigeria, 1987.
Banjo, Ayo. "The Linguistic Factor in African Literature" *Ibadan Journal of Humanistic Studies.* No. 3. 1983.
Boulton, M. The Anatomy of Poetry, London: Routledge & Kegan Paul. 1953.
Carter, R. and Burton' D. *Literary text Language Study.* London: Edward Arnold. 1982.
Chapman, Raymond. *Linguistics and Literature: An introduction into Literary Stylistics.* London: Edward Arnold. 1973.
Cluysenaar, A. *Introduction to Literary Stylistics.* London: Batsford. 1976.
Combes, H. *Literature and Criticism.* Middlesex: Penguins Books Ltd. 1953.
Dare, A.S. "Linguistic Reiteration in Niyi Osundare's Poetry" Ph.D. Thesis, University of Ibadan. 1998.
————. "Communicative Symbols and Images in Garuba's *Shadow and Dream* and Osundare's *Moonsongs.* M.Phil. Thesis, University of Ibadan. 1993.
————. "Rhetorical Interrogatives and Imperatives in *The Eye of the Earth* in *GEGE: Ogun Studies in English,* Vol. 1. 1990.
————. "New Wine in Old Wine Skin: Dead but Quickened Expressions in Osundare's Poetry" in *Oye: Ogun Journal of Arts.* Vol. II. 1989.
Epstain, E. L. *Language and Style.* London: Methuen. 1978.
Fowler, Roger. *Linguistic Criticism.* Oxford: Oxford University Press. 1986.
Halliday, M.A.K. "Language Structure and Language Function" in John Lyons (ed.) *New Horizons in Linguistics,* Middlesex and New York: Pelican. 1970. 140–165.

———— and Hassan Rugauiya. *Cohesion in English*. London: Longman. 1976.

Halliday, M.A.K. "Linguistic Function and Literary Style: An Inquiry into the Language of Williarn Golding's *The Inheritors* in *Explorations in the Functions of Language*. London: Edward Arnold. 1973. 103–140.

————. *Language as Social Semiotic: Social Interpretation of Language and Meaning*. London: Edward Arnold. 1988.

Jakobson, R. "Linguistics and Poetics" in T. Sebeok (ed.) *Style in Language*. Cambridge Mass: MIT. 1960.

Jeyifo, Abiodun "The Language Factor in Modern Nigerian Literature" in *Perspectives on Nigerian Literature*. Ed. Ogunbiyi. Vol. One. Lagos Guardian Books Nigeria Ltd. 1985.

————. "Niyi Osundare" in *Perspectives on Nigerian Literature*, Vol. Two, Lagos: Guardian Books Nigeria Ltd. 1988.

Leech, G.N. *A Linguistic Guide to English Poetry*. London: Longman. 1969.

————. "Linguistics and the figures of Rhetoric" in *Essays on Style and Language*. Ed. Fowler. Henley: Routledge and Kegan Paul. 1966. 135–156.

Milic, L.T. "Rhetorical Choice and Stylistic Option: The Conscious and Unconscious Poles" in *Literary Style: A Symposium*. Ed. Seymour Chatman. London and New York: Oxford University Press, 1971.

Minot, Stephen. *Three Genres: The Writing of Poetry, Fiction ard Drama*. New Jersey: Prince-Hall Inc. 1965.

Mukarovsky, Jan "Standard Language and Poetic Language" in *A Prague School Reader on Aesthetics, Literary Structure and Style*. Ed. Paul, L.G. Washington: Georgetown University Press, 1964.

Ngara, Emmanuel. *Stylistic Criticism, and the African Novel*. Ibadan: Heinemann. 1982.

Olaogun, Modupe. "'Niyi Osundare! Poet of the Market Placet". (unpublished Ms, 1986)

Olatunji, O.O. *Features of Yoruba Oral Poetry*. Ibadan: University Press Ltd., 1984.

Ong, Walter. Orality and Literacy: Technologizing the Word. London: Methuen, 1982.

Osoba, G. "Graphology as a Communicative Device in Poetry: The Example of Niyi Osundare's Songs of the Marketplace" in *Gege: Ogun Studies in English*, Vol. I. 1991.

————. "A Stylistic Analysis of 'Nliyi Osundare's Songs of the Marketplace." M.A. Thesis, University of Ibadan. 1985.

Osundare, Niyi *Songs of the Marketplace*. Ibadan: New Horn Press. 1983.

————. *Village Voices*. Ibadan: Evans, 1984).

———. A Nib in the Pond, 1986.

———. Ife Monographs on Literature and Criticism. 4th Series, No. 6.

———. "The Writer as Righter" in *Ife Monographs on Literature and Criticism*, 4th Series, No. 5. 1986.

Osundare, Niyi. *Songs of the Season*. Ibadan: Heinemann, 1990.

———. "Bilingual and Bicultural Aspects of Nigerian Prose Fiction." Ph.D. Thesis, York University, Toronto. 1979.

Richards I.A. *Principles of Literary Criticism*. London: Routledge & Kegarl Paul. 1924.

———. *Practical Criticism: A Study of Literary Judgement*. London: Routledge & Kegan Paul. 1929.

———. "Poetic Process and Literary Analysis" in *Style in Language*. Ed. Shbeok. Cambridge, Massachusetts: M.I.T. 1960. 9–23.

Sinclair, McH. J. "Taking a Poem to Pieces" in *Essays on Style and Language*. Ed. Fowler. London: Routledge & Kegan Paul, 1966. 68–81.

Spencer, J. et al. "An Approach to the Study of Style" in *Linguistics and Style*, London: Oxford University Press, 1964. 59–105.

Taylor, T.J. *Linguistic Theory and Structural Stylistics*. Oxford, New York, Ontario, Potts Point, Paris and Hammerweg: Pergamon Press Ltd., 1980.

Thorn, J. "Generative Grammar and Stylistic Analysis" in John Lyons(ed.) *New Horizons in Linguistics*. Middlesex: Penguin. 1970.

Turner, G.W. *Stylistics*. Middlesex: Penguin. 1973.

BEYOND "THE ROPE OF A SINGLE IDIOM": TRANSLATING AFRICAN POETRY

Christiane Fioupou

The phrase in my title, "the rope of a single idiom," is a quotation from the opening poem of Niyi Osundare's *Waiting Laughters*:

> And laughing winds
> So fugitive in
> Our harried seasons
> > Who can tie
> > Them down with
> > The rope
> of a single idiom   Who dare? (p. 4)

I thought these lines would be appropriate to suggest the many facets of Niyi Osundare's both anchored and elusive poetry whose "hybridity" is encapsulated in the author's now classic autobiographical lines from *The Eye of the Earth*: "Farmer-born peasant bred / classroom bled" (pp. 43–44). This shift from "bred" to "bled" not only conveys a kind of transfusion, as it were, and even some contamination from one sound to another, but also the cross-fertilization of two languages and two types of education: the Yoruba oral tradition of the poet's "farmer-peasant" family and the English literary tradition of the "classroom."

Osundare himself has explored the problems of conceiving a poem in Yoruba and writing it in English in his article "Yoruba Thought, English Words: A Poet's Journey Through the Tunnel of Two Tongues" in which he asks: "If language is truly the dress of thought, how would deeply Yoruba ideas look and feel in English coat and tie? What adjustments must be made in size and style to prevent the tie from turning into a noose?" (2000: 25).

But then, when an "African" poem written in English is translated into French, which is neither a tonal nor a stressed language, what strategies can be chosen to recapture and recreate the sense and sound of the "original," its polysemy and polyphony, to go beyond the "rope," the "noose," or the "tie" of a single idiom? In this paper, I propose to use my experience as a translator to suggest some answers to these questions.

First of all, I have to say that I do not speak Yoruba. My knowledge of the culture and the workings of this language comes from my having been steeped in the works of Wole Soyinka and his constant references to his Yoruba "aesthetic matrix." Indeed, my interest in literary translation was triggered off when Samuel Millogo and I translated Soyinka's *The Road* into French; because of the many idioms and language registers used in the play (standard, Biblical, pidgin and American English, Yoruba…), translating these different levels was an exhilarating challenge.

I later drew upon what Soyinka had written about his own translation—from Yoruba into English—of D. O. Fagunwa's *A Forest of a Thousand Daemons* and the problems connected with the translation from a tonal language (Yoruba) to a non-tonal language (English). We know that in tonal languages, each syllable must be pronounced with the proper tone. In Yoruba, "syllables consist usually of one consonant followed by a vowel or a vowel by itself" (Beier, 1970: 12). As there are seven vowels and as each syllable can have a high, mid, or low tone, we can infer that, for a European ear and mouth not used to the subtlety of tones, it amounts to having to master twenty-one different vowels. For instance, a word like *agbon,* depending on the tone used, has five distinct meanings (respectively chin, coconut, basket, wasp or the heat of pepper) (Beier, 1970: 11).

The title of Wole Soyinka's adaptation of Bertolt Brecht's *Threepenny Opera*—*Opera Wonyosi*—is revealing as to the kind of puns that are made possible through the play on tones. As we learn through the characters, "Wonyosi" was the name of a very fashionable and expensive material—costing five hundred dollars a yard—during the Nigerian oil-boom of the 1970's. At first reading, the English title seems to imply that it is an "opera" worth five hundred dollars rather than three pence. But as Yemi Ogunbiyi explained, when "freely translated into English from Yoruba with appropriate accents, 'Opera Wonyosi' means 'the dupe buys the Wonyosi cloth' " (Ogunbiyi, 1979: 3). Within the limited space of a title, this bilingual pun based on tone variations gives us an insight into the highly satirical stance of the play and the tonal punning potential of Yoruba. At a more down-to-earth level, and to illustrate how pertinent (and impertinent) tones can be, one often hears stories from West Africans who, as children, would go to church to listen to sermons for the sheer pleasure of catching European priests using the wrong tones and uttering obscenities. More seriously, the use of play upon words and tones is basic to the Ifa divination poetry of the Yoruba, in all its complexity, ambiguity, and sophistication (Yai in Fioupou, 1994: 346).

Dan Izevbaye's article on Akin Isola's translation of Soyinka's *Death and the King's Horseman* into Yoruba gives us other interesting insights into the shuttle movement between one language and another, as it analyses the "translinguality of *Death and the King's Horseman*—that is, the power to communicate Yoruba experience through English words" (p. 157). Izevbaye's conclusion that "Soyinka's text is not really either wholly English or wholly Yoruba, but the product of a new discourse at the interface of both languages" (p. 168) is an echo of the cultural and linguistic transfusion to which I alluded at the beginning of this paper. Also, in his English translation of Fagunwa's *Hunter's Saga*, Soyinka was very much aware that a departure from the Yoruba original was necessary to remain true to its spirit and its music. In his introduction, he reports that a passage he had translated for *Black Orpheus* had aroused some protest from a critic because he had used "toad" for an animal that was "more a member of the lizard's species." Soyinka vindicates his choice:

> Fagunwa's concern is to convey the vivid sense of events, and a translator must select equivalents for mere auxiliaries where these serve the essential purpose better than the precise original. In what I mentally refer to as the "enthusiastic" passages of his writing, the essence of Fagunwa is the fusion of sound and action. (Soyinka, 1968: Introduction)

Soyinka goes on to explain "the most frustrating quality of Fagunwa for a translator is the right sound of his language. This most especially has been responsible for my resorting to inventive naming ceremonies for some of his unfamiliar beings."

Dapo Adeniyi acknowledged his indebtedness to Soyinka for his own translation of Fagunwa's *A Journey to the Mount of Thought:* he appropriated his predecessor's "equivalents of precise tonal and semantic constructions" and "inventive naming ceremonies" (Adeniyi, 1994: vii–viii). Adeniyi feels that, because Fagunwa "insists here on a more farcical edge that enables him to drum more with words than in any of the previous works," he has "the responsibility of not merely translating meaning but of translating tones" (p. ix).

In his turn, reviewing Adeniyi's adaptation, Osundare praises the two writers' achievement of having translated Fagunwa, "a relentless verbal fabricator and punster, a conscious even mannered stylist whose uniqueness rests on his achievement of a fusion of sound and meaning" (1994: 1529). For when it comes to translating from Yoruba into English, all these authors insist upon its being a forbidding task because: "while English is a stress-timed language, Yoruba is a syllable-timed one operating through a complex system of tones and glides. In this language, prosody mellows into melody. Sounding is meaning, meaning is sounding" (Osundare, 2000: 20). Beier and Osundare quote a Yoruba organist describing his language as "the missing link between music and speech" (Beier, 1970: 11), hence the impossibility of finding English equivalents for musical words like *kolokolo*, meaning "stealthily," "circuitously," "muddy," or "fox," depending on the tone pattern used (Beier, 1970: 11). In Osundare's words:

> Meaning is sounding, sounding is meaning. But how have I been meaning in Yoruba and sounding in English? Through phonological approximations exemplified in the generous use of alliteration, assonance, and consonance in the English text. Through the use of repetition and various reiterative strategies which may sometimes look (but hardly sound) pleonastic in the eye of some readers. (Osundare, 2000: 26–27)

For we are dealing with poetry here, which adds to the problem of not only having to find equivalents from a tonal to a stressed language but also of remaining faithful to the structure of a densely-packed form. Fortunately, English poetry can easily accommodate alliteration: *Beowulf,* the first known English poem (transcribed from the oral tradition around the 10th century) was based on Germanic prosody with two or three stressed syllables alliterating in each line. Ruth Lehmann recently proposed an interesting "imitative translation" of *Beowulf* from Old English into Modern English to reflect the alliterative pattern of the original poem, avoiding French and latinate vocabulary and using Germanic words as much as possible:

> Hrothgar spoke out, he reached the hall,
> stood on the steps, saw the steep gable

gleaming golden and Grendel's arm.
(Lehmann 95. 925–928)

Gerald Manley Hopkins's achievement in his attempt to revive the rhythm of Old English alliterative verse and folk poetry became a model for many African poets. We know that what the Victorian writer called "sprung rhythm" has given rise to controversial debates in Nigeria, launched by Chinweizu et al., in their *Decolonizing African Literature,* where they accuse Wole Soyinka and other Nigerian poets of "voluntary moral servitude" (Chinweizu, 1985: 171) in their imitation of "Hopkinsian syntactic jugglery" (p. 192). Soyinka's scathing answer to those he calls "Neo-Tarzanists"—for their clichéd understanding of the African poetic landscape—dismisses the basis of Chinweizu's disparaging remarks: Soyinka grants that though some writers can be accused of apishness because of their superficial and contrived borrowings, "a distinct universal quality in all great poets does, on the other hand, exercise ghostly influences on other writers—however different in background—at moments when a similarity of experience is shared." (Soyinka, 1988: 99). Thus, Soyinka sees "sprung rhythm" as the best way to describe the musicality of some Yoruba poems, which are deliberately staccato, because of its capacity to render "the allusive, the elliptical, the multi-textured fullness of what constitutes traditional poetry, particularly *in recital*" (Soyinka, 1988: 319). He therefore suggests Chinweizu should listen to a good Yoruba reciter and in the process, "make the discovery that Gerald Manley Hopkins did not invent 'sprung rhythm,' nor is its exploitation forbidden to modern Africans who use his language because he so uniquely made it his tool" (p. 319). In other words, to adapt Osundare's own quotation, why not wear Hopkins's English coat if it fits Yoruba styles and sounds?

The issues evoked so far have been those concerning the passage between two languages. "When two languages meet, they kiss and quarrel," says Osundare (2000: 15). But then, when three languages meet—as in the case when an "African" poem written in English is translated into French, neither a tonal nor a stressed language—what devices can be used to conjure up the multifaceted sounds and meanings of the original? I now propose to illustrate some of the problems involved in translating Osundare's verse into French by way of a few concrete examples.

In Osundare's poem concerned with "the bitter-sweet clamour of initial beds" (*Waiting Laughters,* 8), the initiation into sexual experience is suggested through echoes of "initial," "dawn," "first," and "portals." The first lines of the fourth and last stanza mark a definite passage into adulthood:

> The deed was dawn
> and we watched a tutored childhood
> slip off in ripples of purple noons
> Wisdom removed its veil, tucking it gently
> in the belly of Time's uneasy shadows. (*WL* 8)

At this juncture, "dawn" can be read both as an unexpected substantive chosen to convey the newness of the experience but also as a pun based on the implicit shift from "done" (performed, accomplished) to "dawn," a new beginning leading to "noons," then to "wisdom" and "Time's uneasy shadows." Moreover, it seems highly probable that the partial homophony of "done" and "dawn" could be linked with the recurrent associations of "deed" and "done" throughout *Macbeth*, for instance, in "If it were done when 'tis done" (pp. I, vii, 1) or "I have done the deed" (pp. II, ii, 15). In both cases, the "deed" is connected with real or symbolic death: in Shakespeare's play, the accomplishment of a crime, "this more than bloody deed" (pp. II, iv, 22); in Osundare's poem, the "deed" implies having killed the old for the new to be born as it refers to the death of childhood "slip[ping] off in ripples of purple noons" for the "dawn" of adulthood to be possible. Of course, the alleged intertextual reference to *Macbeth* is perhaps a mere coincidence of which the poet himself was unconscious. And in any case, is it possible to find a French equivalent for the pun and simultaneously hint at the reference to Shakespeare? After re-reading *Macbeth* and looking through various French translations for the many "deed... done" passages in the play, I reached the conclusion that the task was impossible, particularly since the compactness of the line, its alliterative pattern, and the pun had to be rendered as well. At least—and this was one consolation—I would not be accused of reading into the text and over-translating.[1] And yet, inevitably, one could see in the "deed was done" another pun on "Donne," as John Donne himself was fond of playing with his name. Again, as we know that Niyi Osundare wrote a poem "Merry Metamorphosis: for John Donne" (*A Nib in the Pond*, 27–28) with intertextual references to Donne's "To his mistris going to bed" and "The Flea," one could infer that "The deed was dawn" could also be read as "The deed was Donne" or "The deed was Donne's." But, of course, at this point, there is no question of translating the name of this English Metaphysical poet who is so popular among Anglophone West African writers.

I then embarked upon trying to respect the concentration of meaning and sound contained in "The deed was dawn," but I soon realized that the alliterative pattern would be lost in the process and would have to be compensated for in the following lines. And yet, I had the strong feeling that the pun on "dawn" and "done" was very much in the spirit of the poet's trying to add Yoruba tones to English to revitalize it, striking the reader or listener into an awareness of "Yoruba thoughts, English words" at work, with an intentional edge of strangeness to it. The final outcome of this long but fascinating search was a string of sounds that could be divided and read in at least three different ways (three different tones?): as "dawn" means sunrise or "the birth of the day," "The deed was dawn" was translated as "*L'acte était né-sens*," *né-sens* being homonymous with *naissance* (birth) but also suggesting *né aux sens* (the awakening of the senses) and *né au sens* (pregnant, as it were, with meaning). I am aware, of course, that *né-sens* is some kind of eye-pun difficult to render orally, except through a pause meant to make the poetry performer ponder over the incongruity of the hyphenated word:

> *L'acte était né-sens*
> *et nous regardions une enfance chaperonnée*
> *se perdre dans les ondes empourprées de midi.*
> *La sagesse retira son voile, le glissant avec douceur*
> *dans le ventre des ombres énigmatiques du Temps.*

One could object, however, that the problems that arise in translating puns are not specific to stressed and tonal languages, or to poetry. We only have to refer to the article that Henri Parisot, the translator of *Alice's Adventures in Wonderland* and *Through the Looking-Glass*, wrote about his strategies to find acceptable French equivalents to eighty odd English wordplays contained in the ori‚ inals—without having to rely on footnotes saying, "untranslatable puns" (Parisot, 1987: 69). Parisot's translations of *Alice* have acquired the status of "authorized versions," but his rendering of *The Rime of the Ancient Mariner*, though a classic, is not so successful since it lacks much of the musical energy of Coleridge's original poem. My model for translating poetry into French is rather Pierre Leyris: his skilful adaptation of Gerald Manley Hopkins's sprung rhythm comes close to a *tour de force*, recapturing the interplay of various levels of meanings and powerful bursts of sounds, conjuring up the "Hopkins disease" of which, we have seen, African poets nurtured on tone-based languages are so fond, to the anger of hide-bound "Neo-Tarzanists"!

The issue of having to render elaborate alliterative poetry is omnipresent in African poetry written in English, and very much so in Osundare's works; in this kind of Yoruba-English-French *ménage à trois*, I constantly had to keep in mind that the poem I was translating was not an "English" poem: indeed, Stewart Brown has written that "No English poet *could* use the English language in the way Osundare does" (Brown, 1991: 44). So I, in turn, had to use poetic license and rely heavily on assonance, consonance, and alliteration to project at least some facets of the context, content, and acoustics into this multicultural palimpsest. And after all, as the poet himself stated: "I am more of an ear than an eye poet. On certain desperate occasions when a quarrel erupts between the sounding and the meaning of a word, I often tilt the scale in favour of the formemer" (Osundare, 1997: 15). I feel that this can be interpreted by the translator as special permission to do the same on such "desperate occasions."

An example of the necessity to be faithful to certain recurrent sound echoes can be found in the highly rhythmical "The Rocks Rose to Meet me":

> The rocks rose to meet me
> like passionate lovers on a long-awaited tryst.
> The rocks rose to meet me
> their peaks cradled in ageless mists.
> *Olosunta* spoke first
> the eloquent one
> whose mouth is the talking house of ivory
> *Olosunta* spoke first
> the lofty one whose eyes are
> balls of the winking sun
> *Olosunta* spoke first
> the riddling one whose belly is wrestling ground
> for god and gold. (*The Eye of the Earth*, 17)

The author's note tells us that *Olosunta* is "a huge imposing rock in Ikere [the poet's home village], worshipped yearly during the popular Olosunta festival; reputed to be a repository of gold" (17). The recurrence of "god" and "gold" is central to the poem both as sense and sound. Thus, because the line could not be merely translated as "*terre de lutte / pour le dieu et l'or* " if the basic sound echo between "god" and "gold" were to be respected, I integrated some elements from the author's note into the two words: "*Olosunta l'énigmatique dont le ventre est terre de lutte / pour le dieu adoré-minerai d'or.*" "As *le dieu adoré*" means "worshipped [or adored] god," and as it can also be heard as "*le dieu à dorer*" (the god to be gilded), the homophony anticipates the second element of the line, "*mine rai d'or*" (gold ore), and also the debunking process of the following stanzas:

> *Olosunta* spoke
> his belly still battle ground of god and gold.
> The god I have killed
> since wisdom's straightening sun

licked clean the infant dew of fancy.
The gold let us dig
not for the gilded craniums
of hollow chieftains

Olosunta *parla*
le ventre toujours champ de bataille du dieu adoré-minerai d'or.
Le dieu adoré je l'ai tué
quand le soleil réparateur de la sagesse
a léché l'ultime rosée des mirages infantiles
Le minerai d'or laisse-nous le chercher,
mais pas pour couvrir de dorure
la boîte osseuse de chefs creux (p. 18)

In the same vein (no pun intended), and still in connection with gold, another poem (*WL*, 20–21) refers to Croesus and "his breath a gail of gold." Apparently, "gail" is a portmanteau word coined by Osundare to evoke a surfeit of gold—a whole "gale" and "pail" of it—and to stress the proverbial wealth of Croesus provided by the gold-bearing sands of the Pactolus River. As the poem starts with the interplay of syllables in "Winnowing seasons we-knowing-seasons" (rendered as "*saison de vannage sait son vain âge,*" which, translated back, literally means "winnowing season knows its vain age"), and as "*un van*" is the French word for a winnowing basket, homonymous with "*un vent*" (wind), I felt that keeping to the lexical field of the opening lines would convey both the king's breath loaded with gold, and the implement used to collect the precious ore from the river. Hence, the translation proposed: "*Son souffle un van de sables aurifères,*" with a view to respecting the ambiguity—more written than oral—of "gail/gale" through the "*van/vent*" adaptation. In the process, the "g" alliteration in "a gail of gold" is replaced by the "f" sound of "*souffle/aurifères*"—imitating the potent breath of Croesus—and by a sequence of sibilants *(son/souffle/sable)* suggesting the swish of gold in the winnowing basket (or pail!).

The constant search for equivalents in the target language, and at times the necessary departures from the source language, make it preferable to publish the translation in a bilingual edition; the reader with some knowledge of English can then have direct access to the original poem, appraise the poetic loss, and decode some of the intricacies (and the apparently far-fetched transpositions) of a translation that is desperately trying to adjust to the English (Yoruba English?) poem and remain faithful to its spirit. It must also be stressed that the research done to capture the background of Osundare's text not only steeps the translator in the "farmer-peasant" culture of the African poet but also leads one back to the roots of one's own culture: I was reminded, when sifting the evidence to be able to translate a pun about Croesus's wealth, that a very common French word, *"pactole,"* meaning "riches, profit, jackpot," was in fact the name of a river.

In the poem dealing with waiting in the visa office:

> Exile, pilgrim, tripsters of feathered heels,
> there is a baggage of patience
> in the missionary temper of wanderlust (*WL* , 11),

"Tripsters" is another portmanteau word combining tricksters and trippers. "Tricksters" spontaneously evokes trickster tales and also Esu, the Yoruba Trickster god, the god of crossroads and chance, the "elder brother" of the Greek god Hermes, himself, the patron of travellers, merchants, and thieves, represented with wings on his sandals ("of feathered heels"). I consequently coined *"aventouristes"* by fusing adventurers (or adventurists) and tourists, a weaker telescopic word in French than in the source text. But this loss was compensated for in *"aventouristes aux talons ailés,"* thanks to the double meaning triggered off by the choice of winged (*ailés*) as an equivalent of "feathered": the homophony of *"talons ailés"* (winged heels) and *"talons zélés"* (overzealous heels), which just happened by chance, actually creates a pun that projects the tripsters' legerdemain, as it were, onto their heels.

Similarly, in the opening poem of *Waiting Laughters:*

> Blame not, then,
> The rapid eloquence of the running vowel
> When words turn willing courier
> In the courtyard of dodging ears
> Can the syllable stall its tale
> In impertinences of half-way fancies (p. 4)

One can sense the polysemy of "stall its tale," "stall its tail," and "stall it stale," each reading making sense within the poem itself. The least I could do was to reconstruct an optional equivocation in French: to translate "its tale," I chose "*la fable*"—rather than "*le conte*" or even "*sa fable*"—simply because "*la fable*" (the fable, the tale) is homonymous with "*l'affable*" (what is affable or friendly). Thus, "*La syllabe peut-elle immobiliser la fable / Sur des impertinences de rêves mi tigés?*" leaves open the possibility of hidden meanings.

To take another example of this type of ambiguity, in the stimulating satirical texts on rumour,

> Rumour is the faltering step of a practised mask
> the delicate gold of budding palm fronds
> the raffia tattle of thickening groves
> where silence is silver
> and shibboleths court the tongue
> with ashen scabbards (*WL* , 16),

The fifth line evokes the "shibboleths [that] court the tongue" but could also "cut" the tongue with scabbards,' the rumour of a sword. What seems to be needed here is a word that could cover both meanings:

> *La rumeur est le pas hésitant du masque chevronné*
> *l'or fragile de la palme naissante*
> *le babil de raphia des bois touffus*
> *où le silence est d'argent*
> *et les mots de passe fleurettent la langue*
> *de leur fourreau cendré*

In French, the verb "*fleureter*"—akin to the English verb "to flirt"—is old-fashioned now and has been replaced by "*conter fleurette*," i.e. "to court somebody." But since "*fleurettent*" is also close to "*fleuret*" (a fencing-foil), "*fleurettent*," "*fleuret*," and "*flirtent*" fuse in sound and meaning, simultaneously cutting and courting, generating whistling echoes and rustling rumours when in contact with "*fourreaux*," "*raphia*," and "*touffus*."

These examples, among many others, are representative of the challenge met by the translator in every poem, if not every stanza or line. Again, I could be accused of over-interpreting, but I cannot help trying to capture what is unwritten yet deeply felt and implicit through the recurrent rhythmical and polysemic patterns of the text: when I translate, I cannot forget the poet's words that "in Yoruba, poetry is song and chant" (Osundare, 1997: 14); that in his village illiterate women chant "*oriki*" (praise poetry) "with a virtuosity that would make a university professor of poetry go blank with envy" (p. 15) and that hunters can sing "*Ijala*" (hunter's songs) from dusk to dawn; that his father was a singer who, with other villagers, composed satirical songs "as a metaphorical guillotine" that prompted the king to abdicate (Osundare in Arnold, 1996: 151). Hence Osundare's words:

> So poetry for me is song, performance; it is utter-ance.[...] The Yoruba syllable is a unit of music. To reflect its glides and slurs in English, I often go for long-drawing words, hence the ubiquity of words with the -ing ending in my verse. (2000: 26–27)

The problem is, if the "-ing" ending is a strategy for the Yoruba poet to reflect "the glides and slurs of the Yoruba syllable in English," on the contrary "-ing" endings—be they verbal nouns or present participles—sound rather ponderous when translated directly into French. Furthermore, the use of a relative clause and an active verb instead of a present participle often lacks the compactness that is needed in poetry; hence, the need to find apt equivalents or suitable transpositions. To take an example, there are twenty "-ing" endings in the opening poem of *Waiting Laughters* (pp. 2–5), most of which will have to be turned into adjectives or nouns in the French version, for fear of sounding trite and awkward:

Tonalities. Redolent tonalities

Of wandering fancies yeasting into mirth,
Yeasting into glee, in the crinkled lanes
Of giggling cheeks,
Lingering aroma of pungent chuckles,
The rave of ribs which spell the moments
In latitudes of tender bones. (*WL* , 2)

These lines set the tone of the whole collection, *Waiting Laughters,* which aims at capturing the process of waiting in its various forms through humour, wit, irreverence, and laughter. Not only is the composition punctuated by rhythmic repetitions of key lines or words but a musical accompaniment is also suggested in each section, for instance "flute and/or clarinet; medley of voices" (p. 1). This implies that the poems can become chanted performance, and it is in this spirit that I endeavored to translate this "difficult" stanza:

Tonalités. Imprégnantes tonalités

De rêves errants dilatés en levain de joie en
Levain d'allégresse dans les gloussantes rigoles

Des joues déridées,
Arômes persistants de petits rires épicés,
Côtes en délire qui épellent ces instants
Sur les latitudes sensibles de leurs os

I attempted to include certain features that could reflect the various ways of laughing by using staccato "d," "p," and "g" sounds as well as liquid consonants and the "i" assonance throughout, hopefully recreating the "redolent tonalities" of giggles. "To giggle" (and to a certain extent "to chuckle") are tricky words to translate into French if one wants exactness, compactness, and musicality. I could not use the words that instantly came to mind such as *"rigoler"* (to have laughs, to joke, to have fun) because they were too colloquial for the register of the poem. I therefore played on the homonymy of *"rigole"* (I/you/he/she/they laugh[s]) and *"rigole"* (either a furrow or a rivulet), to render "crinkled lanes." As *"dérider"* is both "to cheer up" and "to unwrinkle" and *"se dérider"* is to brighten up, I thought the gist of the lines would be respected by using *"déridé"* as an adjective that could qualify the furrows (*rigoles*) of the cheeks (*joues*) as they are "unwrinkled" and as they "brighten up" through giggling and chuckling (*gloussantes rigoles*).

Kissing and quarrelling, chuckling and bickering: this, indeed, is the vocabulary used by Osundare when he refers to the impassioned relationship between his mother tongue and his acquired language:

> Yoruba and English. I do not only write in these two languages. I also live in them. I am close enough to hear their amorous chuckles and bitter bickerings. (2000: 30)

The poem "Waiting / like the crusty verb of a borrowed tongue" is a poetic rendering of this fight when "Thoughts draw battle lines with Words / and the wind is loud with the deafening tower / of pidgin babels":

> Here, my tongue
> But where, the mouth?
>
> The tongue is parrot
> Of another forest [...]
>
> A white white tongue
> In a black black mouth

> Here my mouth
> But where, the tongue?
>
> And the tongue hangs out its blade,
> blunted
> by the labyrinthine syntax of ghostly histories
> In the lore of the larynx,
> in the velar enclave of orphaned probings,
> Thoughts draw battle lines with Words
> and the wind is loud with the deafening tower
> of pidgin babels.
>
> History's stammerer,
> when will this tongue, uprooted, settle back
> in the pink peat of the mouth? (*WL*, 40–41)

And yet, he who apparently calls himself "History's stammerer" admits that Yoruba and English are "locked in creative scuffle" (Osundare, 2000: 18). And even though he grieves that "the tongue hangs out its blade, / blunted / by the labyrinthine syntax of ghostly histories" (*WL*, 40), he paradoxically expresses the loss of music with the very musicality of a "white white tongue":

> Yoruba is a sound-based, sound-powered tongue replete with onomatopoeia and ideophones whose communicative essence lies in what Wole Soyinka has called the "fusion of sound and action," the sheer pleasure in weighing words on the scale of the tongue, savouring their cadence and resource, making the matrix of meaning so contingent upon the mathematics of sounding. (Osundare, 1994: 1529)

To conclude, these lines written in English stressing the sensuousness of Yoruba words are just another reason why the French translator should be steeped in the very mood of *Waiting Laughters*, embrace the rich texture of a multi-layered language "beyond the rope of a single idiom," play with its hybridity and its strangeness, squeeze out the potential ambiguity of words to compensate for the lack of tones or the lack of stresses in the French language, "weighing words on the scale of the tongue," and in the process, experience what Denis Slata calls "The Joys of Homonymy":

Homonymy sparks off word-playing which, by arousing laughter, liberates the mind of two fearsome scourges: over-seriousness and its sad spouse –foul mood.[2]

Or, as it were, let us try and translate puns to stop the pains. And I leave it to the reader to translate this last pun without pain...

NOTES

1 I went through a similar experience when I translated "The Rocks Rose to Meet Me" (*The Eye of the Earth* 34), wherein I noted a conspicuous link between "craniums," "princes," and Hamlet, or rather, "hamlets." The French for hamlet is "*hameau*," so the link between "prince" and "hamlets" is lost in French translation. The point remains, of course, that some Shakespearean references that sound almost hackneyed to English-speaking readers (Poyet) are unknown to many French readers who have read Shakespeare in one of the many different French translations. "To be or not to be" is an exception, known to everybody in the original.

2 My translation of Denis Slata, "Les joies de l'homonymie," *Le Monde*, 2 July 1993: 29: "...L'homonymie allume le calembour qui, en suscitant le rire, libère l'esprit de deux redoutables fléaux : l'esprit de sérieux, et sa triste épouse, la méchante humeur."

REFERENCES

Adeniyi, Dapo. *Expedition to the Mount of Thought*. (The third saga, Being a free translation of the full text of D. O. Fagunwa's Yoruba novel *Irinkerindo Ninu Igbo Elegbeje*). Ile-Ife (Nigeria): Obafemi Awolowo UP, 1994.

Arnold, Stephen. "A Peopled Persona: Autobiography, Post-modernism and the Poetry of Niyi Osundare." Eds. Janos Riesz & Ulla Schild, *Autobiographical Genres in Africa*. Berlin: Dietrich Reimer Verlag, 1996: 142–165.

Beier, Ulli, ed. *Yoruba Poetry: An Anthology of Traditional Poems*. Cambridge: Cambridge UP, 1970.

Brown, Stewart. "Review: Niyi Osundare's *Waiting Laughter*." *Wasafiri* 14, Autumn, 1991: 43–44.

Chinweizu et al. *Toward the Decolonization of African Literature*. London: KPI, 1985.

Coleridge, Samuel Taylor. *Le Dit du vieux marin*. traduction française de Henri Parisot. Paris: José Corti, 1988.

Donne, John. *Selected Poetry and Prose*. Eds. T.W. and R. J. Craik. London: Methuen, 1986.

Fagunwa, D. O. see Adeniyi, Dapo (*Expedition to the Mount of Thought*) and Soyinka, Wole (*The Forest of a Thousand Daemons*)

Fioupou, Christiane. *La route: réalité et représentation dans l'oeuvre de Wole Soyinka*. Amsterdam-Atlanta: Rodopi, 1994.

Hopkins, Gerald Manley. *Poèmes accompagnés de proses et de dessins*, Choix et traduction de Pierre Leyris. Paris: Seuil, 1980.

Izevbaye, Dan. "Elesin's Homecoming: The Translation of *The King's Horseman.*" *Research in African Literature* 28-2 (1997): 154–170.

Lehmann, Ruth P. M.. *Beowulf: An Imitative Translation.* Austin: The University of Texas Press, 1988.

Ogunbiyi, Yemi. "Opèra Wonyosi; A Study of Soyinka's *Opera Wonyosi.*" *Nigeria Magazine.* 1979: 3–14.

Osundare, Niyi. *A Nib in the Pond.* Ifé Monograph on Literature and Culture, University of Ifé 4–6 (1986).

———. *The Eye of the Earth.* Ibadan: Heinemann, 1986.

———. *Waiting Laughters.* Lagos and Oxford: Malthouse, 1990.

———. "Tale across the wall: Review of *Expedition to the Mount of Thought* by Dapo Adeniyi." *West Africa.* 29 August–4 September 1994: 1529.

———. "Yoruba Thought, English Words: A Poet's Journey through the Tunnel of Two Tongues." *Kiss and Quarrel: Yoruba/English Strategies of Meditation.* Ed. Stewart Brown, Birmingham University African Studies Series 5, Centre of West African Studies, 2000: 15–31.

Parisot, Henri. "Pour franciser les jeux de langage d'Alice." *L'Herne: Lewis Caroll.* Paris: Editions de l'Herne, 1987: 69–84.

Poyet, Albert. "Métamorphoses poétiques et effets dramatiques des clichés dans *Macbeth,*" *Le cliché,* Ed. Gilles Mathis, Interlangues. Littératures, Toulouse: PUM, 1998: 263–278.

Shakespeare, William. *Macbeth.* Ed. Nicholas Brooke. *The World's Classics.* Oxford: Oxford UP, 1994.

Slata, Denis. "Les joies de l'homonymie," *Le Monde,* 2 July 1993: 29.

Soyinka, Wole. *The Forest of a Thousand Daemons, A Hunter's Saga.* Trans. D.O. Fagunwa. *Ogboju Ode Ninu Igbo Irunmale.* Lagos: Nelson Panafrica Library, 1968.

———. *The Road.* Ibadan: Oxford UP, 1965.

———. *La route,* traduit de l'anglais par Christiane Fioupou et Samuel Millogo. Paris: Hatier, 1988.

———. *Opera Wonyosi.* London: Rex Collings, 1981.

———. *Art, Dialogue and Outrage (Essays on Literature and Culture).* Ibadan: New Horn, 1988.

METAPHOR: NIYI OSUNDARE'S DOMINANT LANGUAGE

'Demola Jolayemi

This chapter attempts to do a stylistic analysis of Niyi Osundare's poems in *Village Voices* with the aim of establishing his foregrounded use of metaphorical language. Various types of metaphors are identified and discussed; among which are anthropomorphic metaphors, animal metaphors, concrete and abstract metaphors, synaesthetic metaphors, organic metaphors and telescoped metaphors. I have selected ten poems from *Village Voices* for analysis; and discovered that there were 475 lines altogether from where I have identified 263 metaphors. I concluded that Osundare works with a formula whereby from every two lines in his poems, there must be, at least, one metaphor. Furthermore, I have tried to test this hypothesis of two lines- one metaphor on some other poems of Osundare. I have selected for analysis the first and the last poems in the *Eye of the earth*, and my thesis has been vindicated. Thus, my paper presents Niyi Osundare as a master metaphorist.

INTRODUCTION

A reader encountering Osundare for the first time, will perceive an "indirect" use of language analogous to the language of the talking drum, understood only by the initiates. An "indirect" language in the sense that Osundare has a way of circumventing his target of discourse, and in its place uses suitable corresponding images. This is done in a way that a verdant reader does not know from where the arrows fly. For instance, in the last stanza of 'New Birth' in *Village Voices*. he writes:

> *A new river* is here
> *Beckoning boatmen* for new *boats*.
> A new moon enlightens the sky
> Dismissing the tired darkness
> Of yester-nights. (p. 43).

The tenor of this poem is the birth of a new child, but it carriers three vehicles: *river*, *boats* and *moon* which at first do not collocate with 'birth'. But when one stops to think, one realizes that the three concrete nouns are objects that 'move'. The river flows, that suggest movement; the boat, when rowed moves and 'the coming and going' of the moon, in its phase, suggests a kind of movement. All this denotes living or being alive. Coupled with the adjective 'new' that modifies 'river' 'boats' and 'moon', the reasonable conclusions one draws is that *new river, new boats* and *new moon* do not represent any other but something that is new or young and that is alive. Thus, *new river, new boats,* and *new moon* represent a *new birth*.

Apart from the tenor and the vehicle there are other lexical items in the poem that are metaphorical. For instance, 'New birth' has actually been compared with a full grown human being, this is manifested in the use of three active verbs in a stanza of four lines. Thus, we see 'New birth', like a man, 'beckoning', 'enlightening', and 'dismissing'. The last source of metaphor in that short piece is the unusual syntactic rendition of 'tired darkness'. 'Tired', an adjective used for animate objects, is not a conventional modifier for 'darkness', an inanimate object. But when one remembers that the transition between dusk and dawn has different degrees of darkness, 'Young' darkness may be referred to as the time that darkness is barely apparent, while 'tired' darkness may be likened to that time which marks the end of dusk and which welcomes the approach of a new day "tired darkness", therefore, is another connotation for the arrival of a New Birth. Viewing it from this perspective, one may be tempted to conclude that, Osundare presents his readers with unconventional usages and leaves them confused. However, the labyrinth is easily resolved by the simple and familiar images that the poet juxtaposes with his intent as we shall come to realize before the end of this chapter.

THE NATURE AND FUNCTIONS OF METAPHORS

From available literature, six main types of metaphor have been identified. These are anthropomorphic metaphors, animal metaphors, concrete to abstract metaphors, synaesthetic metaphors, organic metaphors and telescoped metaphors (Ullmann, 1977). Each of these metaphors shall be fully discussed, and attempts shall be made to see alter whether or not Osundare's metaphors fit into any or all of these varieties of metaphor.

The origin of the word metaphor can be traced to the Greek word 'methophore' from meta' and phorein' which means 'trans' and 'to carry' respectively both of which jointly literally mean 'transfer'. *The Advanced Learners Dictionary of current English* (1963) defines metaphor as 'the use of words to indicate something different from the literal meaning' (p.16). The dictionary goes further to give two examples of metaphorical use of language:

(1) I will make him eat his words
(2) He has a heart of stone.

In (1), the complement, 'eat his words' has been likened to the action of making something to disappear by swallowing, or more aptly, when a dog vomits at an unexpected place, like in a living room, it is forced to eat back the vomit. Thus 'words' has now become food to be eaten. The act of making one to be apologetic, regret, or to withdraw one's words or action has now been compared to eating something up. Example (2), a complement too, directly compares a heart with a stone, known for its hardness. A person that, therefore, possesses and indefatigable will is said to have a heart of stone. In (1) and (2), a metaphor each has been established, viz, making one to regret one's action is compared to 'eating up' and a person that possesses manly attributes, represented by a synecdoche (heart), has been compared to a 'stone' because of its strength of will.

In *Dictionary of Literacy Terms*, Cuddon (1977) explains that the word "metaphor" is derived from two Greek words that mean carrying from one place to another. Cuddon goes further to inform that metaphor is a figure of speech in which one thing is compared implicitly with another, as in the former examples when a strong heart is compared with a stone. A metaphor can thus be regarded as the basic figure of speech in poetry.

Richards (1924) in his book *Principles of Literacy Criticism*, has three main-descriptions of metaphor. First, he says

A metaphor maybe illustrative as diagrammational, providing

a concrete instance of relation which otherwise would have to be stated in abstract terms (p. 188)

Then he goes further to explain that 'metaphor'

...is the supreme agent by which desperate and hitherto uncommon things are brought together in poetry for the sake of the effects upon attitude and impulse which spring form their collocation and from the combinations which the mind then establishes between them (p. 189).

Lastly, Richards adds some more information:

'metaphor' is a semi-surreptitious method by which greater variety of elements can be wrought into the fabric of experience (p. 190)

Oliplant (1959) talks of metaphor as an implied or condensed simile stressing that the likeness is put forward as if it were the plain and literal name for the fact. For instance "The news was a daggar to his heart" carries the implication that the news was as painful in him as pushing a dagger through his chest to his heart. Such pain as experienced by the subject of the sentence needs no further description since the imagery 'a dagger in his heart' has aptly captured the experience. Therefore, in the unusual collocation of the news as a dagger, a metaphor has been established because the pain of the "news' has been implicitly compared with the pain of a dagger in the heart.

Moody (1970:9) defines 'metaphor' as "the descriptive application of qualities from one thing to another" (p. 20). Also, Fatiregun (1981) explains that a metaphor is like a simile but, the only difference being that the words introducing the comparison, (e.g 'as ....as' like', etc.) are omitted, and we speak as though the two things compared are identical.

He quotes Shakespeare's Macbeth as an illustrative material for metaphor.

'Life's but a walking shadow, a poor
` player that structs and frets his
hour upon stages, and
heard no more (P. 27)

Here, life has been implicitly compared to a walking shadow, and man, a poor player. This position seems to be shared by Kreuzer (1995) who describes metaphors as

> figures that fuse the comparison so completely
> that one of the two element that one of the
> two elements compared is either equated with
> the other or spoken of in terms of the other (P. 163).

Ullman (1977) also refers to 'metaphor' as 'similarity of senses' and a condensed comparison positing an intuitive and concrete identity.

From the above, a metaphor can safely be defined as a linguistic device that employs a word or phrase that literally denotes one kind of idea or object used instead of another by presenting an analogy between them. A metaphor is different from a simile in the sense that the latter compares directly with the use of 'like', 'as', etc, while the former's comparison is implicit or indirect.

In the early part of this discussion, two terms 'tenor' and 'vehicle' were introduced. These are the two sectors on which a metaphor operates. These terms have been introduced by Richards (1924), Cuddon (1977) and Ullman (1977). By "Tenor", we mean the object that is being compared in the message, the line of thought, idea or image under discussion that is to be compared while "Vehicle" is the object used for comparison. In other word, a tenor is that thing we are talking about while the vehicle is that to which we are comparing the tenor, and the feature or features that they share make the ground for the metaphor. Indeed, tenor and vehicle are aptly described by French critics as "le compare' (the compared) and 'le comparant' (the comparing).

ANALYSIS OF OSUNDARE'S USE OF METAPHORS

Niyi Osundare's *Village voices*- a collection of forty poems-has been chosen for study. Ten (10) out of the forty (40) poems (40%) have been selected, studied and analysed in detail. These poems are the first two, the last two and six (6) randomly selected others in the collection.

Antrhopomorphic Metaphors

Anthropomorphic is a term from two Greek words: anthrop(man) and morphe(form). Anthropomorphic metaphors are therefore those metaphors that involve human attributes (Ullman 1977). One of the early scholars who identified this type of transfer was Giambattusta Vico- an Italian philosopher, who in Ullman (1977) supports that:

...the greater part of expressions referring to inanimate
objects are taken by transfer from the human body and its
parts, from human senses and human passions (p. 214)

In *Village voices,* Osundare makes use of a wide range of anthropomorphic metaphors. For instance, in 'A Dialogue of the Drum' (pp. 5–8), we find:

the talkative face of the drum
the language of the leather...
Speaks with two elegant mouths...
Your drum, dumb in the market place
Only talks in the place of gold...
Your song extols those whose words
Behead the world,...
the neck of the palm;...
the laughing sun...

From the above pieces, 'faces', 'mouths' and neck' are parts of the human body that have been transferred to an inanimate thing- the drum. While human attributes- 'talkative', speak's, talks, 'dumb', 'behead', and 'laugh' are actually attributed to an inanimate object. Other anthropomorphic metaphors identified in Osundare's poems, are: 'youthful breeze', 'footsteps of words', 'barren forest', 'the moon puts a smile on the aescant. 'Lip of the sky', ' the moon's face is well of tears' 'oblong face of time', and 'its elusive cheek', others are "of the sea's lips" and sand caresses". Furthermore, "the forest is barren" while the moon "puts on a smile"; season and sky each has a pair of "lips; the moon has 'face' that is full of 'tears', time has a cheek and 'oblong face', and it 'caresses' and the star like a sad adult, actually 'sobs'. Without any doubts, there are anthropomorphic metaphors in great display and these have been used by the poet to convey, most strikingly, his preoccupations.

Animal Metaphor
These are metaphors that derive their images from the animal kingdom. In normal conversation we often make direct comparison between our daily activities, or objects or ideas and some animals. For instance, we say, 'the man is a lion', or 'misfortune dogs his steps,' 'will you stop dogging me about, or 'Don't be so sheepish'. In addition we talk of 'the tail of the story,' 'elephantiasis,' and 'wings of my desires.' In the above metaphors that have human beings as intangible objects and as tenors respectively carry vehicles from the animal kingdom.

Thus, Osundare explores the animal kingdom for a wide range of metaphors. Examples of such metaphors in the poems under investigation are 'hippo hands' ('hippo is from hippopotamus); 'Wakeful ambush of the second cock;' and more (see *Village Voices*):

    (a) 'fangs of facts' (p. 7)
    (b) 'roaring foams' (p. 34)
    (c) 'gull rockets in the sky' (p. 34)
    (d) 'eye bats its lid' (p. 47)
    (e) 'Our man becomes a locust' (p. 48)
    (f) 'I am a snake' (p. 43)
    (g) 'wasped its tail' (p. 6)
    (h) 'the wasp power-stung, enterers a race of waist (p. 48)
    (i) 'before this moon hears the first cock' (p. 42)

From abstract phenomena to Concrete metaphors
The goal of every writer is to communicate effectively. In order to do this, a metaphorical use of language becomes inevitable because some metaphors help to translate abstract ideas into concrete and tangible terms. Thus, we find in Village voices such metaphors as : 'mountain of distance', 'foot steps of words' 'torrent of self-praise', 'my coiling words', 'fang of facts', 'aluminum clarity', and 'tree of words'. Aptly, these metaphors have helped in the concretization of abstract ideas and experiences.

Synaesthetic Metaphors
Synaesthetic 'is from Greek 'Syn' ('together') and 'aistesis' ('perception'). This category of metaphors is on transpositions from one sense to the other out of the five commonly know senses. So, a metaphor may move from sound to sight, from touch to sound from taste to sight, etc. Hence, in 'I wake up this morning,' Osundare employs synaesthetic metaphors to convey his preoccupation. This is evident in 'a youthful breeze harps the leaves' and 'rising feet drum the road.' Two senses are involved in these two metaphors. The first metaphor has a transposition of the sense of feelings ('a youthful breeze'), and sound ('harps'), while the second transposes from sight (rising feet') to sound ('drum the road'); 'Ears shall bend my way' moves from the sense of hearing (sound) to that of movement (kinetics); Fart chokes the village nose' transposes from smell to touch, and in 'foot steps of words' the movement is from sight to sound. Other examples of synaesthetic metaphors in Niyi Osundare's *Village Voices* are:

(a) 'My word will climb the tree of wisdom,' (p.2)
(b) 'talkative face of the drum;' (p. 5)
(c) 'two elegant mouths carry a high pitched' (p. 6)
(d) 'face of the drum;' (p. 5)
(e) 'majestic accent,' (p. 6)
(f) 'those whose words behead the world,' (p. 7)
(g) 'caught in Sorrow's trap' (p. 35)
(h) 'armed with sweet words' (p. 47)

The use of synaesthetic metaphors lends pictureque-ness to Osundare's message through a multiple sensory appeal.

Organic Metaphor
This type of metaphor is also known as functional-structural metaphors. In this figure of speech, the vehicle is symbolic, and it carries an implicit tenor (Cuddon, 1977). In other words, an organic metaphor is established when the imagery or the object of comparison is symbolic and has an implicit undertone. Example of such metaphors are numerous in the text under study, and some of these are:

(a) 'a youthful breeze harps the leaves.' (p. 1)
(b) 'rising feet drum the road' (p. 1)
(c) 'farts Choke the village noses' (p. 1)
(d) 'the chains echo across the world' (p.)
(e) 'when red rays are bidding farewell to the western sky'
    (p. 47)
(f) 'Esuru grows swollen head and outgrows the prostegeous
    belly of the mortar.' (p. 48)

Telescoped metaphor
This type of metaphor is also know as 'complex metaphor', because the vehicle of one metaphor becomes the tenor of another. A piece of Osundare's poem used in the introductory part of this chapter readily comes to mind. In the poem, the tenor which is 'New Birth' has given rise to three vehicles: 'new river', 'new boats and 'new moon'. Thus, the vehicle of one metaphor develops to become the tenor of another. Other examples in the text are:

fat Cars: juicy damsels;
world of softness; consumes; fat salaries (p. 48).

From the above, it can be solely concluded that Osundare uses a wide range of metaphors that are classifiable into the various categories in the literature. To indicate the stylistic import of this preponderant reliance on the metaphorical channel, the following statistical analysis indicates the regularity and frequency of metaphors in the text under study:

Table 1
Analysis of metaphor-Line Ratio in Ten (10) selected poems from *village voices*

Poems	No. of Lines	No. of Metaphor	Ratio
1. We have waited so long	56	31	.6
2. I wake up this morning	105	25	.6
3. A dialogue of the Drum	25	14	.6
4. I Rise now	42	19	.5
5. To A passing year	45	37	.8
6. The Stars sobs	46	36	.8
7. A Villager's protest	63	20	.3
8. The Bride's song	40	17	.4
9. New Birth	18	12	.7
10. A farmer on seeing cocoa house Ibadan	35	17	.5
Total	476	263	.6

From the above data, we can arrive at the facts that:

(1) The metaphor-line ratio in Osundare's poem is .6 and
(2) the ratio is thus approximately 2 metaphors to 3 lines of a poem.

This result is applicable to the whole of *Village Voices*.

A replication of this study on another of Osundare's collections, say *The Eye of the Earth,* for which he was joint winner of the 1986 commonwealth poetry prize, may even prove a stronger vindication of my thesis. The first three lines of the first poem in the collection reads thus:

A *green* desire, *perfumed* memories
a *leafy* longing *lure* my wandered feet
to this *forest* of a thousand wonders. (p. 3).

These first three organic metaphors listed above are set of metaphors that work, like human beings, to lure 'my wonderer feet' to the forest. Here, we have identified five metaphors in a three line poem; let us end our little experiment with the poem that ends the volume, "Our Earth Will not Die."

> Lyched
> > The lakes
> Slaughtered
> > The Seas
> Mauled
> > The mountain's
> But our earth will not die (p.50)

In these seven lines, four anthropomorphic metaphors are discernible as indicated. They help to drive home the point that whatever atrocious attempts are made to maim the earth, "Our earth will not die."

METAPHORS FOR WHAT STYLISIC ENDS?

One striking thing about metaphor as figure of expression is its unusual collocation. Thus, Osundare achieves surprise and pointednesss by drawing unexpected parallels between unrelated objects. For instance, in 'A Dialogue of the Drums' Osundare writes:

> I hail from a line of drummers
> And understand perfectly
> The language of the leather...
> Bata speaks with two elegant mouths...(p.5)

In this short piece, at least, three metaphors are identifiable as indicated in the quotation 'language of the leather.' There is a striking evidence of unusual collocation of lexical items. 'Language,' for instance, does not share any form of syntagmatic relation with 'leather.' Further, *Bata* is said to speak and with two mouths! Thus, the poet has employed unusual tropes to foreground his message. This is the height a poem can reach. Richards (1924) argues that:

> As the two things put together
> are more remote, the tension
> created is of course greater... (p. 190)

Breton, in Ullmann (1972) shares the same opinion when he posits that:

> To compare two objects as remote
> from one another in character as possible,
> or by any other method put them together
> in a sudden and striking fashion this remains
> the highest task to which poetry can aspire (p. 214)

Another way Osundare has effectively communicated with the use of metaphor is in bringing closer real but hitherto elusive experience or abstract ideas. He captures this in his poems by concretizing such abstracts ideas. Thus, he talks of:

> mountain of distance (p.2)
> torrents of self-praise (p.6) and
> fang of facts (p.7)

Taking these metaphors one after the other, distance is a thing that tasks the brain when we want to imagine it; distance is spatial and it entails some mental exercise to properly conceptualise. But a concrete object, 'mountains,' has been used to modify 'distance'. Torrent denotes force at which the ocean wave moves. As used here, an emotive upsurge of a base desire, "self-praise". In fang of facts, fang has no syntagmatic relationship with facts. Fangs are the long, sharp, frontal teeth of carnivorous animals such as a dog, snake or lion. Facts, abstract concept, which are now concretized in a most inspiring way by using 'fang' as measure. Facts have therefore been concretized.

In his metaphorical artistry, Osundare has found synecdoches and metonyous quite handy. These devices help the poet to say a lot within a short period and in a few words by talking about wholes in parts, and by relying heavily on innuendos and other forms of associational meaning. Below are some examples:

(a) 'ear shall bend my way' (p.1)
(b) 'fart chokes the village nose' (p.1)
(c) 'those whose words behead the world.' (p.7)
(d) 'plant new vows' (p.34)
(e) 'the death of an old skin' (p. 34)
(f) 'tears only water your farm' (p. 35)
(g) 'a chest that bribes' (p. 47)

(h) 'the best of his sweats' (p. 47)
(i) 'my belly will be round' (p. 42)
(j) 'children between his groins' (p. 42)
(k) 'a penis stronger than an iron bar' (p. 42)

CONCLUSION

An effective use of metaphor is a sign of ingenuity and a creative force in the use of language. To this, Aristotle, in *Ullmann* (1972), attests to the strength of metaphor as a stylistic device by saying:

> the greatest thing by far
> is to have a command of
> metaphor... it is a mark
> of ingenuity (p. 212)

The French stylist, Proust (1920), corroborates that

> Jecrosi que la metaphorre seule peut donner
> une sorte d'eternite au style (p.75):
>
> I believe that metaphor alone can give style
> a kind of eternity.

While Sir Herbert Read, in *Ullmann* (1972), concludes that 'we should always be prepared to judge a poet... by the force and originality of his metaphors' (p. 212), Osundare's choice of metaphorical mode cannot be divorced from his membership of a generation branded 'emergent poets' (with a positive connotative sense) who bears the mission and vision of demystifying poetry in the African context. Part of their stylistic goal is to discourage obscurity as much as possible by adapting and adopting oral traditional resources into the crafting of modern poetry in the medium of a new English (or European language), still rich and vibrant, but less turgid and elusive. This is corroborated by Jeyifo (1988),

> Niyi Osundare's central looming position in the new poetry
> that derives first of all from this issue of language poetry
> "demystification"...his 'revolution in attitude to receive poetic
> diction assumes the character of the informing aesthetics, the
> defining poetics of Osundare. (p. 316)

It is therefore no wonder that Osundare makes a copious use of metaphors from the flora and fauna reminiscent of the traditional folklore.

Furthermore, recently, Mowah (1997) compiled and published an anthology of poems having been, evidently influenced by Osundare's use of metaphors. He acknowledges this at the opening page of the book in this dramatic and poetic stunt:

> Gratitude!/Acknowledgement
> To
> Niyi Osundare for 1989, and
> For the wallet of metaphor (p.6).

To sum up the thematic and technical import of Osundare's copious use of metaphors of a multifarious topology, we rely on the memorable words of Jeyifo (1988):

> You will always read Osundare's volumes...sometimes humerous, often searing, occasionally bitter and satirical but always vividly and metaphorically arresting evocations of episodes from our recent history and the upheavals, triumphs and defeats of struggle in Nigeria (p. 318)

The effect of all this is that there is great beauty in the works of Osundare as exemplified in *Village Voices*; a kind of beauty that is glaring, vivid and concrete. A kind of concretization that is, in fact, cinematic. Osundare, wielding metaphor as a linguistic tool, has been able to communicate clearly and effectively to people and on issues of great diversity. It is upon this note that I regard Niyi Osundare as a master metaphorist.

REFERENCES

Burton, S.H & Chacks field, C.J.H. (1979). *African poetry in English: An Introduction to practical criticism.* London: The Macmillan press Ltd.

Cuddor J.A. (1977). J.A. (1997). *Dictionary of literary terms.* Dentsch: Andre Publisher.

Fartiregun, V.A. (1981). *English literature: Unseen poetry and prose.* Ilesa, Nigeria: Fartiregun Press and Publishing Co. Nig. Ltd.

Gatenby, E.V. Hornby, A.S. and Wakefield, H. (1967). *The Advanced Learner's Dictionary of Current English* London: Oxford University Press.

Jeyifo, Biodun (1988). Niyi Osundare. In Yemi Ogunbiyi (ED), *Perspectives on Nigeria Literature 1700 to the present* Vol. (2) Lagos, Nigeria: Guardian Books Nigeria Ltd.

Kreuzer, J.R. (1958). *Elements of poetry.* New York: The Macmillan Company.

Moody, H.LL.B (1968). Literary Appreciation: London: Longman Group Ltd.

Mowah, F. U. (1997). *Eating by the flesh.* Ibadan: Kraft Books Limited.

Osundare, Niyi (1984). *Village Voices* (Poems). Ibadan, Nigeria: Evans Brothers Nig. Ltd.

Osundare, Niyi (1986). *The eye of the earth.* Ibadan: Heinemann Publishers.

Proust, E.M. (1920). A props du "style" de Flaubert. Nouvell Rerue Francaise, XIV (1) 72–92.

Richards, I.A. (1924). *Principles of Literary Criticism.* London: Routheledg and Kegan Paul.

Ullman, Stephen. (1977). Semantics: *An introduction to the science of meaning.* London: Oxford or Basil: Black Well.

SHAFTS OF COMING SONGS: NIYI OSUNDARE AND THE POETIC OF UTOPIA

Emma Ngumoha

> ... in the house of memory...
> doors open into the backyard of
> time, and widows bare their breasts for the
> knowing shafts of coming suns.
> - Niyi Osundare.

There comes a time in the lives of millions of persons when the past becomes a memory and the future looms as a serious question mark. Such is the situation in Nigeria today as millions of Nigerians feel depressed vis-a-vis the present harsh economic crisis. The present gloomy national mood contradicts the glorious expectations of the early nationalists. The incentive that encouraged them to face their several challenges was the fact that the future was quite definite and appealing and in every way alluring. They had no doubt about the joy, the happiness and prosperity that awaited the people if they could cross the great abyss of colonial imperialism. It was this picture of a future prosperity and the enjoyment of the greatest blessings in life that inspired and strengthened them in their determination to work for political independence. Today, after many years of independence, the projected prosperity is elusive. Most of the millions who wallow in the poverty of economic depression of today do not have the enviable picture that was earlier envisioned by the nationalists.

In the present-day world, the accelerated socio-economic development of a country is linked to its technological capability. Many nations the world over have exploited the resources of science and technology to foster development. Science makes and continues to make life very comfortable for man. But what counteroffers can the humanities make? Can the poets defend themselves and their calling in a world where science and technology are, more or less, sacrosanct fetishes? What are the functions of a writer in a technological age and what is the role of the poet in a milieu of economic problems?

The questions above are relevant, especially in these days of austere aspirations when the poet has to defend his art by showing his relevance and commitment to the predicament and future of a despondent populace. Percy Bysshe Shelley (1792–1822) wrote his "A Defense of Poetry" to oppose the view held by Thomas Love Peacock among others, that the advance of civilization would inevitably render poetry obsolete. The occasion of Shelley's essay was the publication, in 1821, of Thomas Love Peacock's *The Four Ages of Poetry*. In a polemic, which Shelley undertook to defend his calling, he declaimed that far from being deteriorated and made powerless by the advance of civilization, poetry is actually the decisive and even the sole reason of civilization. Definitely, poetry cannot be content to survive as a picturesque anachronism or a sentimental self-absorbed escapism. Poetry is not withering away in the scientism and technology of modern life; it is not going to wither away, as long as men feel the necessity for expressing themselves on the highest level.

May we now journey along with the poets and other Creative artists to another world, another life, another civilization called Utopia. Some poets and other writers record, in their imaginative creations, man's longing for the seemingly unattainable. Man naturally longs for a perfect state of eternal bliss, a situation where all his problems are solved; man is in dire need of a world of supreme felicity and delight, a pleasure garden. This has given rise to a sub-genre of works known as Utopian Literature. Derived from Thomas More's *Utopia* (1516), Utopia is an imaginary place of ideal perfection, and by extension, implicates a scheme of total social reform.

The two operative words in Utopian Literature are transportation and transformation. Utopian works transport suffering humanity to another world of beauty full of the delights and satisfactions denied him in this harsh world of reality. Utopian transport functions at the level of imagination for after many years of suffering and privation while on earth, man recreates, repaints and rebuilds the mental picture of what the future holds. In his days of hunger, illness, unemployment and intense suffering, he eases his body and mind by rejecting the present and the past and living mentally in the beautiful picture of the future which his mind preserves and holds before him as a rich reward for all suffering and effort.

Having been mentally transported to that ideal state of affairs by his creative imagination, man begins to seek out ways to ameliorate the shortcomings of his condition; he tries to transform his life in order to approximate that which he envisioned and to which he transported himself. This is the background of all social reforms, the root of progress and development, the beginning of all innovations in science and technology.

The history of civilization proves that there is no limitation to man's material creation of the things he has anticipated. The entire history of man's achievement from time immemorial points to the fact that what man has mentally created, he can bring into actual realization. The dreams of great men in the past, which seemed value and impossible are surprisingly, presented to us today as concrete realities. Thus, Francis Bacon's *New Atlantis* (1626) stressed the role of technology in bringing about the happiness of society. Bacon's ideals of a new civilization, as magnificently expressed in that Utopian dream, are realized in our modern world. Jules Verne, in *From The Earth to the Moon* (1865), transported his countrymen to the moon in a rocket launched from Cape Canaveral in America. That "impossible" imaginative futuristic projection in the nineteenth century was realized, one hundred and four years later when Neil Armstrong stepped on the moon on July 21, 1969. Also, Verne's *Twenty Thousand Leagues Under the Sea* (1870) is an imaginative penetration of the depths of the sea. That dream was realized seventy years later through the invention of the submarine during World War II. Thus it is seen that man needs literature of transport to a better future which would function as a prop to help him seek out the possibility of transforming his environment. Imaginative anticipation via creative projection is a major achievement of the humane letters.

One of the greatest exponents of the need for Utopian Literature on the African scene is Professor Charles Nnolim. He reminds us that while the Western concept of utopia is futuristic, reflecting a future oriented worldview, African concept of utopia is backward looking, reflecting a backward-looking world view. Furthermore, he states that "while science fiction which is, in the main, futuristic, crowds modern fiction writing in Europe thus ensuring a more scientific, technologically oriented future for Europe and the West, African utopia continues to be backward looking"(13). Nnolim has raised a very serious alarm, and our concern should be that present day Nigerian fiction writing, especially the Pacesetters Series, lacks futuristic prophetism, which is essential for progress.

However, in Nigerian poetry today, Niyi Osundare stands out as a creative

future-conscious poet who responds to specific events in ways that are characteristic of our fundamental human needs and the course of our evolution. His
deep-rooted attachment to the social problems of his native environment is fine-
ly crafted in his poetic quartet: *Songs of the Marketplace, Village Voices, The Eye of
the Earth*, and *Moonsongs*. Osundare prefers using imaginative projections when
he wants to foster a deep understanding of knotty empirical and social problems to when he seeks to set forth his deepest convictions.

"Songs of home and around" is the first movement of *Osundare's Songs of the
Marketplace*: it takes a panoramic look at our society's vice and problems. The
poet takes us on "Excursions" to different shades of poverty; there are "babies
with chronic hydrocephalus" and "village boys' Kwashiorkor bellies" (p. 7). The
poet also looks at the predicament of the mendicants whose

> ... sightless sockets
> burn indictory gazes into
> heavy pockets
> and vaults of hoarded loot.
> (*Songs of The Marketplace*, 12).

Furthermore, the mounting discontent moves over to the secretariat where
the civil servants are nothing but civil, where files are lost and found at the whim
of office messengers. There is also an indictment of the dysfunctional aspect of
Nigerian bureaucracy. As the poet put it:

> The correspondence tray
> is the coffin of ailing democracy
> Pending is heavier than out.
> (*Songs of The Marketplace*, 12).

Finally our "Excursions" end in the university corridors and the streets. The
alienation and anomy of our tertiary institutions also balance the apparent
degeneration in the social and bureaucratic environment. Our universities are
said to be full of "threadbare gurus" who recycle "worn traditions/dreading
change like despots/... pawning wives for chairs/then slouching in glamorized
mediocrity/breeding flat minds...."(p. 713) In the streets we encounter the masses who cry out against the ruling class that lacks vision and humanistic sympathy' one that stocks "dissident throats/with bullets from foreign friends" (p. 14).

From the foregone "Excursions," it becomes obvious that it is difficult to
become an optimist in our country these days, for wherever the poet looks at -

in the street, motor-park, in the schools or the secretariat - the portents are neither pleasant nor reassuring. However, it is interesting to note that against the
backdrop of the dark pessimism of "Excursions," Osundare transports us to a
new "Dawn" which is the "time to recall the future/and foretell the past" (p. 81).
Finally, in his characteristic way of "closing" each volume of his poetry,
Osundare celebrates a futuristic imaginative utopia, and poetry flashes fire in
such contexts:

> Hear him:

> I sing
> of the beauty of Athens
> without its slaves

> Of a world free
> of Kings and Queens
> and other remnants
> of an arbitrary past

> Of the end
> of warlords and armories
> and prisons of hate and fear

> Of deserts treeing
> and fruiting
> after the quickening rains

> I sing of a world reshaped.
> (*Songs of the Marketplace*, 89 –90).

It is this same spirit of the need to change the human condition for the better that, to a great extent, inspired The *Eye of the Earth*. The last part of this collection, "Home call," is our major concern. The poet raises questions about the
future of planet earth and "tomorrow's children" in a world of nuclear arms
build-up, which threatens human existence. He shows this concern in a highly evocative poem entitled "Our Earth will not Die."

> And the rain
> the rain falls, acid, on balding forests

> their branches amputated by septic daggers
> of tainted clouds
> Weeping willows drip mercury tears
> in the eye of sobbing terrains
> a nuclear sun rises like a funeral ball
> reducing man and meadow to dust and dirt.
> *(The Eye of The Earth*, 51).

But our poet is an "incurable optimist" who does not want his auditors to yield to any intimation of a possible catastrophe. He reassures us that:

> Our earth will see again
> eyes washed by a new rain
> the western sun will rise again
> resplendent like a new coin....
> The sea will drink its hearts content
> when a jubilant thunder flings open the sky gate
> and a new rain tumbles down
> in drums of joy.
> Our earth will see again
> this earth, OUR EARTH.
> *(The Eye of The Earth*, 51).

The vision and informing spirit of this piece, according to the poet, is akin to that which has fired The Green Peace, The Women of Creenham Common, Operation Stop the Desert, The Save the Amazon Committee, and the millions of human beings who frequently troop out in European and American cities, urging that we give the human race priority over the arms race (p. xii). Once more, Osundare presents a clear optimistic picture of a world free from "nuclear dust" where tomorrow's children would grow up rather than blow up.

This forward-looking anticipation of human fulfillment is, invariably, a permanent feature in the poetry of Niyi Osundare. The same pattern of projection is reflected in *Moonsongs*, which is divided into three parts, namely "Phases," "Further Phases" and "Moonechoes." In the third movement of "Phases" the mast heading, "I must be given words to refashion futures like a healer's hand" is by Edward Kamau Brathwaite and is quoted by Osundare. This is a special part to the fact that "refashioning futures" is an all-consuming central concern in Osundarean aesthetics.

In *Moonsongs*, the poet uses the moon as the central symbol and, with it, looks at the community, the folklore, the poverty, starvation, oppression and love. The moon is used as a means of social commentary especially in "Phases" and "Further Phases." Of Ikoyi he says:

> The moon here
> is a laundered lawn
> its grass the softness of infant fluff
> silence grazes like a joyous lamb.

And of Ajegunle he says:

> here the moon
> is a jungle
> sad like a forgotten beard
> with tensioned climbers
> and undergrowth's of cancerous fury.
> (*Moonsongs*, 42).

"Moonechoes," the third part is about the poet's personal experience. However, the last two poems of this section, "Back to the Future" and "Shadows of Time" (Anniversary of a future remembered) reflect the already set Pattern of Osundarean futuristic projection. In "Shadows of Time," the poet laments lack of vision in a changing world of widespread opportunities. As he put it, "The chameleon joins eyes/with owls of luminous nights/But the forest still cannot see the bird/ On tomorrow's tree." (*Moonsongs*, 1988: 72). Finally, Osundare uses the metaphor of time to demonstrate that society and culture are dynamic. He propels us from the inertia and lethargy of the Past and present to the dynamism and hope of the future. Time lives in our dreams; time is the drum of tomorrow's ear; time is the unborn dinosaurs/ fossil of coming moons/ Energy of blazing ashes/ flame of foetal fires," (*Moonsongs*, 68) time compels and propels:

> Time is the robe
> Time is the wardrobe
> Time is the needle's intricate pattern
> In the labyrinth of the garment...
> Time the season
> Season the times;
> The forest sprouts, blooms
> And rots into seed
> The seed mothers the mountain

> The mountain mothers the river
> And the river springs green flowers
> In *Edens* of unsinning apples.
> (*Moonsongs*, 72).

On the strength of the foregoing discussion therefore, it is obvious that Osundare stands out as a poet who leaves the past and present out of his consideration and makes a new life, a new social order, beginning with tomorrow his central concern. By projecting his auditors into the future, the poet indirectly inspires their creative instincts. That Nigerians are, like older peoples, endowed with creative abilities, largely latent at the moment, cannot be faulted. Nigerians possess enough knowledge and abilities to make this plundered country a utopia. According to A. O. Anya:

> Given the physical and human resources of Nigeria, it is inconceivable that this nation will remain forever a footnote on the pages of history. The endowments are far too profligate from a most beneficent nature to expect the squalid present as the only harbinger of our future and destiny. The experience of history teaches that a new dawn always precedes the darkest night of the human condition. (p. 157)

As we analyze the creation of man and his accomplishments, we are impressed with one outstanding fact namely, that achievement of whatever kind is the crown of effort, the diadem of imaginatively projected thought. Those who question the role of the humanities in present day science-biased world should note that Jules Verne, whose *From The Earth to the Moon* was a precursor to the American landing on the moon, was not a scientist; he was a visionary creative writer like Niyi Osundare.

I, therefore, join Professor Nnolim to call on African writers who should be Africa's bearers of utopia, to effect a turn-about in their vision and challenge all of us to facing the future rather than dwelling in the past, by writing futuristic literature to redirect our vision and make all of us forward-looking.

REFERENCES

Anya, O. A. "Traditions, The pursuit of Intellectual Life and Nigeria's Future." *Nsukka Journal of the Humanities* I(1987): 141–159.

Nnolim, Charles. E. *Ridentem Dicere Verum: Literature and The Common Welfare.* Port Harcourt. PUP, 1988.

Osundare, Niyi. *Songs of the Marketplace.* Ibadan: New Horn, 1983.

———. *The Eye of the Earth.* Ibadan: Heinemann, 1986.

———. *Moonsongs.* Ibadan: Spectrum Books, 1988.

Shelley, P.B. "A Defiance of Poetry." Eds. Frank Kermode and John Hollander. *The Oxford Anthology of English Literature,* 2 vols. New York: OUP, 1973: 746–762.

POETRY AND PEDAGOGY

TOWNCRIER
IN THE CLASSROOM –
NIYI OSUNDARE'S
SEIZE THE DAY

Don Burness

When he was a young man Chinua Achebe canvassed the racks one day in a bookstore in Lagos looking for appropriate children's literature. What he found did not please him – at best most of the books for children lacked imagination; at worst they carried dangerous messages for African children, including racism. Not being one to sit by while harmattans of pollution blow from distant lands, Achebe took upon himself the task of writing children's stories for his own children – and for Nigerian children.

Other distinguished Nigerian writers have also written literature for children. These include Cyprian Ekwensi and poets Ossie Enekwe and Gabriel Okara. Niyi Osundare's *Seize the Day and Other Poems for the Junior* published in 1995 brings poetry into the classroom, awakening if not stimulating the imagination of young people and also teaching them the gospel of hope, the evils of corruption at a personal and public level, love of the earth and the vast greatness of Africa.

There are thirty poems in *Seize the Day* followed by explanatory notes and exercises which include vocabulary building, suggested essays based on images and themes from specific poems, geographical and historical questions and subjects on which students are to write their own poems. All these exercises were prepared by Agbo Areo. In addition, the teacher is invited to purchase from the publisher an audio cassette of Osundare reading the poems in the book.

Accessibility has always been a major concern of Niyi Osundare' s poetry. Twelve years earlier in *Songs of the Marketplace* (1983), the poet presented his credo:

> Poetry is
> not the esoteric whisper
> not a claptrap
> For a wondering audience
> not a learned quiz
> entombed in Grecoroman lore
> ....
> Poetry is
> man
> meaning
> to
> man.[1]

Several of the poems in *Seize the Day* tell a story. These narrative poems include "story of the Lion," "The Fallen Statue," "The Master Barber," "The Pot and the Pan," and "Poverty's Offense." These story–poems, like traditional folk tales, serve to teach a moral or make a specific observation. The lion in "Story of the Lion" believes that he is invincible. We know that the lion had a particularly effective praise singer who ran from village to village proclaiming the lion as the king of Jungle. Surely there is a gap between myth and reality, for the brave self-important lion flees at the sight of Elephant. And he is a lazy fellow to boot, somehow convincing his wives that they should kill his food for him. Osundare's lion believes the propaganda of his praise singer:

> "I will rule for ever!"
> Boasts the Lion, King of the Jungle,
> "For as long as rivers flow
> Towards the sea
> And night closes the eye
> of the day"
>
> Hearing this, the wise person remembers
> The story of a favourite toy which fell
> From the hands of a sleeping child,
> And the hungry fire which took off
> The robe of the arrogant corn

It is the Lamb's eternal luck
That even Lions are not immortal.[2]

The Lion's pride results from a combination of ignorance and arrogance. The Lion, sure of his eternal position, cannot conceive of a world where he does not dominate. Like beautiful teen-age girls, like healthy people, like rich people, like powerful people, the Lion is a prisoner of a particular kind of stupidity. The Lion refuses to see that time is the eternal masquerader and that around the corner lies a season of loss.

In the "Story of the Lion" Osundare makes a quantum leap from an African to a symbolic world that William Blake would have recognized. For Africa is not the continent of the Lamb. The weak animal might be the dik dik or the suni or the duiker. The Lamb is a Christian symbol and Osundare's lamb of meekness also represents those ordinary Nigerians, those without wealth or power, who have proclaimed the kingdom of the self. The poem conclude with an observation, a statement, that the harvest of Kongi will not endure forever.

Other poems in *Seize the Day* refer to social and political oppression. In "Ode to the Tongue," Niyi Osundare challenges those who would erect statues to silence:

> The tongue in your mouth is a faithful bridge
> Your freedom tool, your right to speak
>
> The tongue is also
>
> One long morsel that fills the mouth
> Foe of silence from north to south[3]

The allusion "from north to south" invariably would suggest to a student Nigeria itself. In another poem "Snappy Line 3" the poet continues his metaphorical observations:

> The tongue is a machet
> The mouth is its sheath
> It cuts both edges[4]

Through *Seize the Day*, Osundare reiterates one of the principal themes in all his poetry – the creative role of language in challenging those who would rule the world by fear and force. It is clear that he believes children as well as adults must not be hood-winked, must not surrender their souls to those who rule and lionize themselves. In so doing, Osundare is returning to a traditional Yoruba belief that language is a tool to unmask false masqueraders: Language is the light that enables people to see the thief who robs the blind man in the night.

But this is only one side to Osundare. There is the planter-harvester of crops of joy and hope, a friend to the sun and to the waters, to the squirrel and to the rocks of Ikere-Ekiti, and mostly a friend to man. The drumbeat of affirmation echoes throughout *Seize the Day*. It is as if the poet looking at a fragmented Nigeria, a Nigeria where the wounds of civil war have not completely healed, refuses to give in to despair. Surely the greatest challenge facing the youth of Nigeria at the end of this century of squandered opportunity is to reject the moral and economic pollution of their elders and build a more humane society. This can only be done with a positive attitude and Osundare the town crier cries out to children – "despair not, the world is filled with flowers of hope." The poems, "Let Us Thank the Sun" and "Birthday Wish" sing of seasons of hope. The former, rooted in images of the earth, is among other things, a love song to the world:

> Let us thank the sun
> For the glory of the day
> let us thank the cloud
> For the blessings of rain
>
> Let us thank them
> Who make our world
> A garden of smiles,
> Who till the land
> With a happy hoe
> Seed the ridges
> With bushels of laughter
> And ripen the rows
> With a skyful of suns
>
> Let us thank them
> Who water our droughts
> With drums of faith,
> Who bloom deserts of doubt
> Into loams of supple trust
> Where Hope thrives on sturdy roots

And the future is one sure song
In the fruiting branches of Tomorrow's tree

Let us thank them
Who mine our dusts
For hidden nuggets
Let us thank them
Who thresh our tears
For gladdening grains
Let us thank them
Who plumb our dreams
For deepening truths

Ours is a world
Of making minds and caring hearts
Of endless rainbows and deathless dreams

No matter what, its several nights
Ours is a world of living days

Ours is a world of beautiful people.5

Osundare here knows the psyche is fragile and that children need to believe in a productive future. Like traditional oral poets Osundare sees himself as a teacher, a teacher of responsibility, a teacher of brotherhood, a teacher of hope. Whether he is writing for adults or children, the poet's mission remains constant.

Recognizing that he was a student of noble teachers, Niyi Osundare has chosen, both as poet and professor, to carry on the task of educating the mind and the soul of those who will listen. In *Songs of the Season* published in 1990 Osundare pays tribute to Chief Samuel Fai Adeniran, as the great teacher "who sowed seeds that continue to grow." In *Seize the Day*, Niyi Osundare's "The Teacher," dedicated to "G.O. Bezi, my unforgettable teacher," seeks to let students know that teachers despite their low pay, are to be respected, for they teach the alphabet of hopeful future, bringing visions of light in the darkened skies of a long suffering land.

In other poems as well such as "I come from a Continent," a praise song for Africa, images of the teacher are present.

> I come from a continent
> Of searing days and mellow nights
> Where the sun stands in the center of the sky
> Ferocious like a schoolmaster
>
> I come from Africa.[6]

Reading *Seize the Day*, Nigerian students are present at a literary festival – there is movement, there is a gaiety and there is also a sense of the presence of a rich, necessary and socially helpful tradition. After all Osundare the poet of the written word is a descendant of Yoruba poets of the spoken word who for centuries have carried their wares to young and old gathered in the village to hear the guardian of the word.

NOTES

1 Niyi Osundare, *Songs of the Marketplace*. Ibadan, New Horn Press, 1983: 3–4.
2 Ibid., *Seize the Day* (Ibadan, Agbo Areo Publishers, 1995), p. 15.
3 Ibid., p. 8.
4 Ibid., p. 26.
5 Ibid., p. 22–3.
6 Ibid., p. 35.

POETRY AND SOCIAL MOBILIZATION: THE TEACHINGS OF NIYI OSUNDARE

Aderemi Raji-Oyelade

Speech, next to reason, is our greatest gift,
and verse is the highest form of speech.[1]

FIRST WORDS

Sir Philip Sidney's statement, which opens this brief essay, is without doubt a true but idealistic view of the nature and character of that special genre we call poetry. At its refined best, poetry should be advanced speech therefore dialogical, accessible and readable. However, in practice in contemporary Nigeria and most other African nations, written poetry is regarded as rather insignificant, irrelevant or impregnable by a generality of readers who include students under the rigors of formal examinations, "non-students" in the scarce option of informal reading, and ironically, publishers who are indeed unwilling marketers of this literary form. This notoriety of obscurity is a challenging commentary on poetry's possibility of social mobilization. The positive basis of promoting a virile reading culture, especially of poetry, lies with both the writer and the readership whose main responsibility shall be highlighted in the later part of this essay.

In Nigeria today, Niyi Osundare is a major poet and teacher who is using the lyrical strategies and the oral resources of traditional African poetry for mass appeal in written texts. Several critical commentaries have been made on the creativity, craft and vision of the poet as a significant, distinct and influential voice in terms of the message and, more so, the form of his poetry. I do think that perhaps the most insightful as well as expository location of Osundare within the widening field of recent Nigerian poetry has been attempted by Biodun Jeyifo in his "Introduction" to *Songs of the Marketplace,* Osundare's first volume of poetry[2]. In that introduction, Jeyifo had predicted that the poet "will attract attention or achieve recognition" both for his poetic expression and thematic substance, "his radical utopian views" (pp. xiii–xiv).

Ten years after, Osundare has gained huge popularity as a literary pathfinder of a new poetry of performance accessible to a larger percentage of the Nigerian readership. In "A Dialogue of the Drums," the poet promises:

> When I raise my voice
> The world will be my chorus
> I, owner of the throat for pleasing songs,
> ....
> But there are some people I know
> People whose names I will not mention
> Whose hippo hands slap the drum
> Like a slab of flabby flesh
> Flogging mere noise from
> Its tuneful belly[3].

The discerning reader would understand here that the poet is using the traditional African mode of indirect attack to accuse a certain section of the literati of linguistic obscurity on poetic composition.

IN THE FORGE

To understand the social relevance of Osundare's works more intimately, it is necessary to understand briefly his ideas of the function of poetry, the character of the poet, and his conception of poetic language. Two critical essays, apart from his declaratory poems, affirm clearly and extensively the Osundare vision as a writer.

The first essay is "Bard of the Tabloid Platform: A Personal Experience of Newspaper Poetry in Nigeria"[4] – in which he stresses the functionality of art and the responsibility of the artist as a mediator of his people's sensibilities:

> The writer is, ...able to make language do more than was ever deemed possible. He is able to articulate (not just express!) many of the ideas which populate the consciousness of his contemporaries, struggling for verbalization. (p. 6)

Osundare believes that by appropriating the lyrical qualities of traditional African verbal art, written poetry "could be made not only alive and well, but also to help keep society so" (p. 9). This belief is the actual basis of his experiment with newspaper poetry in *The Sunday Tribune*, a demonstration which lasted over five years, between March 1985 and September 1990, and which led to the compilation of a representative volume of the poems under the title *Songs of the Season*. At that time, Osundare chose the newspaper medium because in his own words, unlike learned journals and poetry magazines, "it possesses enormous potential for reaching the people whose joys and sorrows, whose lives and deaths, whose triumphs and travails formed the crux of the *Songs*" (p. 12).

The second essay, entitled "From the Closet to the Marketplace: Popular Poetry and the Democratic Space in Nigeria[5]" also dwells on the need for clarity and inventiveness of expression in poetry if it must serve but not *alienate* the people:

> A vital condition for popular art, then, is popular participation, the ability of the people to comprehend and appreciate the artistic offering, to hear the voice and recognize themselves in the songs. It is no etymological accident that the words "popular" and "people" share the same ancestry. (p. 3)

OSUNDARE: THE POET IN THE CLASSROOM

To turn to his *oeuvre* of creativity, it is important to note the declaratory meaning of a much-quoted poem – "Poetry is" – which is generally considered the manifesto of the Osundare text. This poem serves as the introit to *Songs of the Marketplace*:

> Poetry is
> not the esoteric whisper
> of an excluding tongue
> not a claptrap
> for a wondering audience
> not a learned quiz
> entombed in Grecoroman lore

....

> Poetry is
> the hawker's ditty
> the eloquence of the gong
> the lyric of the marketplace
> the luminous ray
> in the grass's morning dew

....

> Poetry
> is
> man
> meaning
> to
> man. (pp. 3–4).

Here, it is important to note that the primal vision of Osundare's creativity is an effect and complement of his responsibility as a teacher imbued with an intense desire to teach his students in a most delightful way. Between the publication of *Songs of the Marketplace* and the most recent of his works, I can say, *a la* Okigbo, that I was a "sole witness" to his homecoming as poet and teacher. I was one of three students who formally attended the Creative Writing classes taught by Niyi Osundare during the 1982/83 academic session at Ibadan. Olakunle George, Cheng Oazutelegheife (a Cameroonian) and I, with eight others, had spent our first year aspiring to become prose writers under Isidore Okpewho, eminent professor of classical and oral literature. In our second year in the Department of English, the three of us opted for the poetry class which Osundare managed to transform into an interesting and elastic space for multidisciplinary, cultural, political and aesthetic discourses. He was very pragmatic and frank; he would give an assignment and do it himself as a way of challenging or relieving the student of funny alibis; and on certain occasions, Osundare would insist on direct experience before artistic production.

I remember vividly our discussion of such canonical Nigerian poems as Christopher Okigbo's "Heaven's gate", Wole Soyinka's "Abiku" and J.P. Clark's "Abiku" and "Ibadan" and his recommendation that we must read as many canonical works from other literary traditions, including Asian, Latin American and American, to complement, query and balance our traditional familiarity with European and modern African poetry. But Osundare would not forget to add that a working knowledge of the properties of oral African poetry is the beginning of wisdom and relevance for any aspiring poet amongst us.

The most memorable assignment given by Osundare was what I call "the Ibadan at night" project: we were asked to re-read Clark's "Ibadan" and do an individual composition, with rhythm, metaphor and all, in twenty lines of poetry entitled "Ibadan". To realize this, we were required to stand on one of the legendary seven hills of the ancient city and come away with the piece in 72 hours. We chose night and the balcony of Premier Hotel on the crest of Mokola Hill, some ten minutes drive from the University of Ibadan campus. Being an indigene of the city, I thought I knew how well Ibadan should be imagined but the teacher thought otherwise. In fact, we were all noted as unsuccessful and bad imitators of J.P.Clark's classical work; and I was specially accused of using arcane and polysyllabic words in that and other compositions. In an earlier assignment, Osundare had noted that I was "too Soyinkaesque" in diction, a subtle admonishment which I took as rare compliment! As implied, the serious writer must move beyond the imitation of traditional/modern poets and develop his own distinct voice; a writer who seeks relevance within and beyond his community must strive to be accessible to a larger percentage of the reading public. These are the two ground rules of Niyi Osundare, the Creative Writing teacher.

MEMORY'S CHILD

Outside the formality of the class, the most influential gathering of writers and readers at the University of Ibadan during the glorious eighties was The Poetry Club which used to hold regularly every Thursday evening inside Room 32, the Faculty of Arts' small lecture theatre and, on special occasions, in the building's quadrangle. The Poetry Club was the practical, informal ground where unresolved and specific ideas are discussed in the characteristic freewheeling and irreverent atmosphere of the literary circle. Osundare used to submit his pieces to close and eager scrutiny of the club whose membership included students, staff and other enthusiasts from the Faculty of Arts and other departments including Physics, Mathematics, Agriculture and Anatomy. I recall that many of Osundare's poems which were later published in *The Sunday Tribune "Songs of the Season"* column and his award-winning *Waiting Laughters* were first presented on the floor of The Poetry Club. A major hallmark of his presentation was the practice of revising traditional songs and the recreation of folkloric atmosphere as background to many of the songs and poems. Metaphorically speaking, Osundare loves rendering poetry on a canvass of performance. As a self-avowed public poet, he prefers to read his poems to a chorus of apt folk songs. He has done this many times, nationally and internationally, to appreciative ovations.

By the sheer power and beauty of his poetry, also reflected in his social essays, Niyi Osundare has endeared himself to many; an unforgettable conversationalist, he can only be compared, in varying degrees of stature, with Femi Osofisan, Odia Ofeimun and Harry Garuba in terms of influence among the so-called third generation Nigerian writers.

A memorable moment in my early contact with Osundare was on the occasion of the 50th anniversary of the birthday of Professor Wole Soyinka on July 13, 1984.

Soyinka was then teaching at the University of Ife and one of his notable critics – Professor Dan Izevbaye, Head of the English Department at Ibadan – had secured a 3-day break for staff and students of the department, thereby making it possible for some of us to participate in events marking the birthday of the literary giant. I chose to accompany my Creative Writing teacher to Ife, a trip which still remains indelible in my memory.

That one hour drive offered me the closest insight into the Osundare mindset, his vision of and frustration about the "alter-native" tradition of African poetry that was gaining ground then. We discussed poems after poems, the metaphoric essence of the word in Yoruba language, the problem and frustration of translating words, metaphors and poems from Yoruba into English. This was the period when Osundare was actively immersed in the writing of his widely acclaimed work, *The Eye of the Earth*. I remember vividly how he was eager to find the correlative word in English for particular specie of fruit the name of which I cannot remember again.

But I know that he was engaged in a process of acquiring the vocabulary of the plant and the animal kingdoms. He actually visited the university's Botanical Garden and some members of "Nigerian Field", a prominent academic association of environmentalists on campus, in his quest to find parallel linguistic/scientific terms for local objects of Nature. Yet, in many of his poems, Osundare would use rare Yoruba words with mythical and deep historical connotations in order to retain the freshness and originality of meanings.

The typical Osundare poem is a well researched yet accessible text; he studied the history and witnessed many of the traditional festivals of his Ikere-Ekiti hometown which eventually served as the grand pretext of the sequence of poems inspired by the distant myth of Olosunta, the father/god of rocks and hills in Ikere-Ekiti.

A cursory analysis of the entire range of Niyi Osundare's poetry reveals him as an artist committed to the social, political and psychological interest of his people, a poet who has chosen to be the voice of many other unheard voices and therefore has carved for himself the image of a scribal town crier. His definition of the functionality of art and the artist can be found in "The Poet", a rarely quoted poem in which the artist is conceived of as an ordinary but endowed mechanic of change, the custodian of that semantic detergent which must purge "a land of choking mud."[6]

In many of his works, the reader would find, transparently so, an imaginative exposition of the problems of material and moral corruption in contemporary African society. But underneath the clarity of expression in many of his poems is a combination of wry humor and a painful satire of society. Social events like petty pick-pocketing as in "Sule Chase", display of power as in "Siren" and establishments or parastatals like "The Nigerian Railway" (all in *Songs of the Marketplace*) and the banking hall, "The New Farmer's Bank" (in *Village Voices*) are brought into focus; also topical historical events and experiences contained in "Udoji", "On Seeing a Benin Mask in a British Museum," "Soweto" and "Namibia Talks" *(Songs of the Marketplace)* are treated in a very enduring manner.

Osundare's works are *volumes*, not collections, in the sense that they are deliberately composed to have central themes or controlling patterns of expression. Therefore, *Village Voices* is so titled for its dependence on the articulation of the customs, values, wisdom and above all, the consciousness of traditional "village" society. *The Eye of the Earth* is a seminal affirmation of the poet's closeness and sympathy or rather empathy with Nature. The most lyrical of Osundare's works to date, this volume marks the watershed of a new Nigerian poetry, of the "alter-native" tradition; it shows a poet who is alive to his responsibility as a moralist, mobiliser and revolutionary both in his use of language and in the seriousness of his vision.

Of all his works, *Moonsongs* has been the most ambitious with language, surreal and dense; this perhaps is responsible for its lack of popularity among the increasing readership of Osundare poetry. *Waiting Laughters* is a successful experiment, "a long song in many voices", about the possibility of hope in the gloomiest of situations, while *Midlife* is composed around the poet's reflections at the age of forty. This collection is second only to *The Eye of the Earth* in its inventive directness, its lyrical energies and in its evocatively oral accents.

A closer reading of Osundare's works would show that his populist aesthetics, which encourages a large and intimate readership, is informed by his use of the folktale technique in poetic narration, his use and extension of traditional proverbs, and most importantly, his employment of the performance mode both in writing and reading his works. It is noteworthy that Osundare talked about devising four modes of articulating his message – *parables, direct address, dramatic exchange,* and *hymn-like lyric* apart from eulogies and tributes.7

For a literate, Western-educated writer, the art of poetry-as-performance (or rather, *poetry-in-performance*), which Osundare has chosen, is a difficult but not impossible task. An understanding of the fact that a reading culture in Africa is secondary to oral culture would go a long way to enhance the strategies of accessibility in the production/reception of any work of art. According to the teacher, if much of traditional African poetry is predicated on performance, then written poetry deserves nothing less if it must be relevant now. But above all, the poetic expression in terms of imagery and symbols must derive from the totality of the people's consciousness (of which the writer is a part). A poetry that demands effective reception and mobilization deserves a *mobilizing* expression; Osundare confesses:

> As much as possible, the vocabulary stays close to the marketplace, the public square, the crowded motor park, the festival crowd, the seething slum, the opulent districts, the sun, the moon, the rivers, the mountains, the green glory of the rain forest, the copper glow of harvested fields.8

Perhaps it is a knowledge of this populist aesthetics and confession that prompted Stephen Arnold to say that the poet "is not an Anglophone African poet; he is a Yoruba poet who writes in English."9 I should add that the essential Osundare poem reads much as a written extension of the verbal artistry of the typical African oral performer. The poet himself talked about the necessary and inherent "interface" of the native tongue with the acquired tongue of the English language.10 He has further explored this point in an essay poetically titled "Yoruba Thought, English Word: A Poet's Journey Through the Tunnel of Two Tongues."11

From this brief discourse, we realize that oftentimes a poet determines his own relevance, or the lack of it, to his society not *only* by his vision but much so by the exactitude of his poetic expression, by the privilege and power of communication. But does the reader owe the society any responsibility in the development of a virile reading culture? Whose responsibility is it to effect the right channel for poetry's power of social mobilization? As stated before, the onus is on the poet who must deploy certain creative strategies in order to break the barrier of mis-reading, misunderstanding and mis-representation in culture.

Equally, the readership must be aware of its constructive capacity through criticism and feedback on a literary work. It is through this symbiotic relationship of writer and reader that a culture of reading could be created and sustained. This, in simple terms, has been the subject of Niyi Osundare's aesthetic as well as ethical engagement as writer and teacher. In bare reference to the dialectic or dichotomy of form and content in literary presentation, he would always tell the listening ear: *what* you write is as important as *how* you write it.

LAST WORDS: A CYBER-DIALOGUE

Below is the text of a recent, distant, electronic-aided conversation with Osundare. This further confirms the pedagogic and pragmatic character of the teacher and poet. Osundare's responses to my predictable questions (the same questions which I have earlier tried to resolve in my own terms) give concrete testimony to the eloquence of his 'Poetics'. When I wanted to know why he would practically attempt every assignment he gave his Creative Writing students, the poet replied:

> That practice which I still engage in even over here (University of New Orleans) springs from a basic principle: my belief that a good teacher is also a good student and vice versa. I have always seen teaching as a two-way process, active and transitive both ways. The teacher, for me, is not an oracular dispenser of knowledge, while the students are reduced to the status of ciphers and receptacles. For teaching and learning to take place and progress meaningfully, a certain democratic spirit and demonstration of humility become necessary. The classroom becomes a level playground of a kind (though highly disciplined and devoid of cheap populism). Working on the assignment I have given to students strengthens my bond with them. It helps students see that their teacher is afterall a human being like them — capable of some lofty lines and at times some phrases that need further work. It also makes it possible for me to feel out, think out, the peculiarities of given topics so as to be able to appreciate the problems they pose for students. Personally and professionally, that policy provides me with a useful practice ground and is very much in aid of my belief that a poet must write (or read) something useful everyday!

Here come my other questions and Osundare's responses to them:

So, were you trying to present a model for the class, especially to challenge the lazy ones?

No, I never presented it as a model to the class, because my policy is always to encourage a diversity of voices, to help the student discover his/her own well and offer instructions about how best to dig that well. If through this process my students took something away from my classes, it would be interesting for them to know that many of them have left something for me too to remember: I still hear across the vastness of time and space the voices of Remi Raji, Kunle George, Cheng (the irrepressible bard from Cameroon), Afam Akeh, Chiedu Ezeanah, Akin Adesokan, Bisi Adeigbo, Frank Ikhimwin, Yebo Adamolekun, Jumoke Bamgbose, Foluso Henry, Osama Ighile, Dayo Olumide, Lolade Bamidele, Femi Lawani, etc, etc. I, too, work on topics I have assigned to my students because I believe teaching, like life itself, is an endless learning process.

In those preliminary classes, you used to read or chant lines of poetry to improvised beats; and you almost insisted on a "working knowledge" of the properties of oral (African) poetry. Why that insistence?

No doubt I do this because I know that no major poet has ever achieved greatness without some intimate knowledge of the oral sources of poetry: Pushkin, Chaucer, Shakespeare, Milton, Whitman, Eliot, Neruda, Elytis, Tagore, Walcott, Brathwaite, Hughes; and Africa: Okot p'Bitek, Soyinka, Clark-Bekederemo, Kofi Awoonor, Ama Ata Aidoo... All these are poets who value the primal, oral sources of their art, and whose style and sensibility are closely shaped by those sources.

Our situation in Africa is rather peculiar. Colonialism and its evil collaborators made sure they tried to devalue everything African in an attempt to devalue the African person. Our religious symbols were condemned as heathen, pagan; our beautiful songs as crude babblings of Conradian natives. The

African colonial education arrangement was designed to prop-
agate this destructive fallacy. Many Africans, writers included,
fell into the colonial pit and have not been able to pop out of
it. Remember, many African writers cannot write one correct
sentence in an indigenous African language; some cannot
even pronounce their own names well. Isn't it a rhetorical
question asking what attitude such writers are likely to show
towards oral literature and oral tradition? Now, I can already
hear some triumphal "postmodernists" bellowing "nativism",
"essentialism", etc. I am not pushing the point that African literature is merely a conglomeration of raffia skirts, ankle bells,
and traditional chants. But I do know that knowledge of these
traditional modes wouldn't hurt our appreciation and practice
of the so-called modern literature. Often I ask: where would
many of Shakespeare's plays have been without his knowledge of the oral and written lore of his people and other
Europeans of his time?

Could we have had *Song of Lawino* etc without p'Bitek's deep
understanding of Acholi language and culture? Walcott code-
switches between the most intimidating register of English
and the earthiest of the Caribbean fisherman's lingo. And, of
course, what has given *Death and the King's Horseman* that
prodigious universal appeal if not its Yoruba oral-cultural deep
structure?

Alright, the interesting observation is that your stress on orality is very deep and almost
palpable in your writing.

If my stress of African oral literature, especially its poetry, is
an ever-increasing one, it is because as a result of my upbringing and political education, I have come to realize the inexhaustible treasure trove that African oral poetry is. I have seen
traditional artists perform with consummate skill and originality and renewed my reverence for the strength and depth
of our songs and fables. Take Alabi Ogundepo, Ologundudu,
Adepoju, or an oriki chanter or chantress. Fancy how "ewa ete"
(the beauty of the lips) gives such eloquent vent to "ewa inu"
(the beauty of the mind). Consider the enviably effortless

sweep of the music of their poetry. Listen to the riveting foot-sounds of their ongs. Isn't there something in these supple lines that can give much-needed sustenance and vitality to our written verse? Oral poetry is for me a stabilizing anchor against the drift into mindless imitation of foreign modes and the deracination and ventriloquism that this invariably entails. And so constantly, everywhere I have taught, I tell my poetry workshop members to develop and sharpen their vernacular sensibility and allow it to help their scribal practice.

This is also tied to the relationship between music and poetry. At different times, you've talked about the inevitable connection of poetry to music. Is it given that all poetry must be musical?

Poetry and music are like heart and blood; one cannot do without the other. Without some vital damage. In our scribal triumphalism, we often forget that the spoken word came before the written, and that the spoken word cannot do without its music. Human language is basically music whether it is the click of the Xhosa, the syllable isochronicity of Yoruba, or the elaborate stress pattern of English. Human beings hardly talk without singing. And how can we read, recite, perform poetry without singing it. In Yoruba, in Igbo, in Edo, in Urhobo, in Hausa, in Igala, and in Effik, etc? Of course, poetry can do without music to that extent and with that success that honey can do without its sweetness. This is not to say that every poet must be a musician; but a good ear and consummate sense of rhythm are the best friends of a poet.

Let's go back to the class. I recollect that you were very precise about the number of lines to be written per poem. You used to recommend 20 lines for each of those weekly assignments. Why were you so specific about the volume of presentation? Is there something magical about twenty lines?

There's nothing magical about it. It was all in a bid to sensitize students to the constraints of space and volume. Remember each poem was discussed in class; the shorter the poems the longer the time we had available for a discussion of each offering. Besides, as beginners it is always better for students to test the water with shorter pieces before graduating to longer ones.

I am not sure if you still remember our trip to Ile-Ife on July 13, 1984 for the fiftieth anniversary of Professor Wole Soyinka. At that time, you were about writing or completing The Eye of the Earth *just as you were engaged in acquiring and establishing the English translation or the scientific names of plants and animals (of the Yoruba world). I could recollect your comment that you preferred to retain or introduce native/Yoruba words and phrases where the other language would not serve the purpose. What strategic function does this serve?*

Yes I remember that trip and occasion: three cheers to your memory! Some English translations of Yoruba words and expressions sound absolutely absurd, out of place. So do the foreign names for some Yoruba flora and fauna. The problems of names and naming have always confronted me in my writing, but in no other work are those problems more acute than *The Eye of the Earth*, a volume that is so primal, so telluric. I agonised several times over the best way to express words such as iroko, oganwo, ayunre, elulu, patanmo etc. Do I go for the botanical, zoological nomenclatures? How will they sound in a poetic text? Well, eventually, I decided to leave these words in their original baptism, then proceed with the arduous task of footnoting and glossing. This was not done to add the so-called "local colour" (there is something artificial and forced about that phrase), but to deepen the indigenous thrust of the work and its purpose and vision. I haven't done anything remarkably novel here: People like Achebe, Soyinka, Armah, Ousmane (Sembene), Ngugi, etc have led the way. It is one method of perching, albeit precariously, on the bridge between the indigenous language/culture and the foreign.

In your other classes, it was typical of you to start the day's lecture with a 5–10 minutes "political chats" on "burning" national issues, what Fela Anikulapo-Kuti would call "yabis".

For many of your students at Ibadan, it was a memorable insight into the political side of Osundare, the fearless teacher; at that time, the fearful slogan of the military government then was that the prison, not the university, should be home for those of you who were "teaching what you were not paid to teach". The teacher as an ideologue, what do you think about this?

> I think the best thing for any conscientious teacher in those dark days of the Babangida/Abacha junta was to teach exactly what he/she "was not paid to teach". (That infamous phrase came out of the Abisoye Panel of 1986). I mean, there was so much oppression, so much plundering, so much killing of the Nigerian dream going on, but those dictators and their venal collaborators would rather have university teachers look elsewhere and busy themselves with their "teaching." Teaching what? In what context? In what country? For what purpose? Towards what future? Subversive confrontation is the conscientious person's response to a tyrannical situation. I see the classroom as a hallowed space: useful and urgent; a platform for the production, propagation, and exchange of knowledge; the generation of the kind of education that humanizes and liberates, the kind that encourages the asking of questions, that emboldens us to take a stand and maintain it while respecting the right of the other person to differ or disagree as the case may be.

The artist in Africa has been severally referred to as a moralist, the custodian of his/her people's mores, the teacher per se. In your own views, what is the art/act of teaching?

> I have said this times without number: teaching is the most important vocation in the world (it's not just a job). When I am in the classroom, I consider myself having no money but possessing something that the millionaire does not have; having no gun but possessing something that a General, no matter how many his stars, does not have. That is the opportunity to interact with the minds of the future, influence them positively while getting influenced in the process, learn with and from them, share dreams with them, break bread with them, relieve them of some of the burden of false consciousness that our neo-colonial and inhuman education has placed on our shoulders if not in our heads, point out alternatives to cynicism and despair, get them to know the dangers of igno-

rance and appreciate the value of knowledge. One of the lines I often share with my students is: Ignorance is a disease; but fortunately, it is a curable disease.

Curable by the present structure of education as we have it now?

Our educational systems in Nigeria, in Africa, are not designed to educate, but to load the mind with all kinds of ill-digested "facts", rubbish more lethal than arsenic. A good teacher must find a way of installing a system that liberates and humanizes. Ignorance is one of the oft-ignored diseases in Africa today. It is more virulent than malaria or AIDS. In fact, these deadly plagues are in large part a consequence of ignorance. Dictatorship of all kinds, and the ease with which people collaborate with or surrender to it, are also members of the brood of the foster father of ignorance. And it is most dangerous in its manifestation in the so-called educated person. Time there was when we used to berate our universities for turning out "educated illiterates"; the ones we turn out now are both uneducated and illiterate. I mean, how would you describe the attitude of a student who tells you with expansive fanfare: *I haven't read newspapers for six months; I don't watch TV; it is not my business who rules the country as long as I can just come to the classroom, copy the teacher's dictation, regurgitate his notes at exam time, grab my certificate (or 'Let My People Go' as it goes in student parlance), hit the world and hustle for a job?* An ill-trained person is worse, more dangerous, than one without training. No disability could be more pernicious for a country!

In a brief moment, how do you see yourself as a functionary in that 'most important vocation in the world': teaching?

I have always seen myself as part of the cure of the disease called ignorance. I believe that by the time my students and I have interacted even if only for one semester, they should be able to know where they came from, where in the world they are, and where their dreams are heading. There should be that raising of consciousness without which both Self- and Other-knowledge is impossible. My areas of specialization, Creative Writing, Applied Linguistics and Literature, stand me squarely within the core of the humanities. As a "book buff" and voracious reader, I am constantly trying to widen and deepen my knowledge in my so-called areas of specialization and explore the inevitable connections that these have with other areas of human learning. I am a devotee at the altar of knowledge without frontiers. I try to "infect" my students with some of this enthusiasm. Practising what I teach is teaching what I practise. I see the classroom as one of the most important places to commence the re-humanization of our society, of our world. The classroom has also been kind to me: many of my lifelong friends I met in that space. I treasure my memory of my former students the same way I cherish my memory of my former teachers. {Ibadan-New Orleans Dialogue via e-mail, 24/10/99}

Finally, I feel that this discussion would not be complete without some commemoratory lines for Olosunta, the teacher, the poet who has always suggested that the richness of art is indeed in the number of ears its song can pluck. Perhaps the poem I've written, titled "This Garland Too Light Yet On Creation Day," will get close to Osundare's ears (see "Poems For Osundare" section).

NOTES

1 Sir Philip Sidney, "*From* Defense of Poesie." In *The Oxford Anthology of English Literature Vol. I*. Frank Kermode and John Hollander, et al. New York: O.U.P., 1973: 643.

2 Biodun Jeyifo, "Introduction" *Songs of the Marketplace* 1983. Ibadan: New Horn Press, 1987: vii–xv.

3 Niyi Osundare, *Village Voices*. Ibadan: Evans, 1984: 5.

4 Paper presented at the 1987 Canadian Association of African Studies Conference in Edmonton, Alberta, Canada; now published as "Confession of a Tabloid Bard." Eds. S. Arnold and A. Nitecki Trenton. *Culture and Development in Africa*. New Jersey: African World Press, 1990: 1–47.

5 Paper presented at the Conference on Art and the Development of Civil Society in Nigeria: The Role of Literature in the Democratic Process, organized by the Friedrich Ebert Foundation, 13–15 May, 1996.

6 "The Poet", written in 1984, is contained in Osundare's *A Nib in the Pond*, an Ife Monograph Series (1986).

7 See "Bard of the Tabloid Platform."

8 Quoted from "Bard of the Tabloid Platform: A Personal Experience of Newspaper Poetry on Nigeria", pp. 16–7.

9 Stephen Arnold, "A Peopled Persona: Autobiography, Post-modernism and the Poetry of Niyi Osundare" Eds Janos. Reisez and Ulla Schild. *Autobiographical Genres in Africa*. Berlin: DVR, 1996: 147.

10 Osundare used the term "interface" in his response to a question at a public performance in Bad Homburger, Germany in August, 1993. The poet Odia Ofiemun also performed with Peter Ripken as "rapporteur."

11 This essay is Osundare's contribution to a seminar organized in his honor at the University of Birmingham in October, 1995 under the theme *Yoruba and English: Strategies of Mediation*.

POET, BEHOLD THY TIE!

Akin Adesokan

The Nigerian poet, Niyi Osundare, one of Africa's best, prefaced his first volume of poems, *Songs of the Marketplace*, with an epigraph from Pablo Neruda:

> I made an unbreakable pledge to myself
> That the people would find their voices in my song.

The collection was published in 1983 when Osundare had already obtained a doctorate degree and settled down to teaching in the department of English at the University of Ibadan. Nigeria was under the four-year-old elected but practically fascistic National Party of Nigeria-led government of Alhaji Shehu Shagari, which was overthrown on the last day of the year by a military junta. *A pinnu 'yaa!* Nigerians cheered that cold Saturday morning, punning on Happy New Year. Those Yoruba words translate as *We resolve against suffering!* In February 1999, citizens of Nigeria had just voted to expel the last of a succession of military regimes for sixteen years, a record on the continent.

Ten years after his debut Osundare had published eight volumes, including a selection. His fourth book, *Eye of the Earth* came out in 1986; he was an acclaimed major voice. The volume shared that year's Commonwealth Poetry Prize with Vikram Seth's verse-novel, *The Golden Gate*. He was still teaching in

Ibadan, traveling and writing, maintaining a weekly poetry column that later became *Songs of the Season* (1990). Winning Noma Award in 1991 for *Waiting Laughters*, an experimental "long song in many voices" came as an Of-Course; he would soon issue *Selected Poems* (1992) through Heinemann in London, upon returning from a two-year teaching stint in the US as a Fulbright scholar. In 1993 he published *Midlife* which he had written during a residency at the Iowa Writing Program in 1988, the year of the publication of *Moonsongs*.

Osundare chose his camp well. Or, as Biodun Jeyifo, the Marxist scholar wrote in the introduction to *Songs of the Marketplace*, "the dialectics of revolution have found a habitation in his poetry." The former president of the radical Academic Staff Union of Universities continued: "In all modern African poetry, *all*, I repeat, only in the poetry of Agostinho Neto and David Diop will you find the same depth and passion and lyricism in solidarity with the oppressed, the down-trodden, the dispossessed, and a corresponding faith in their aspiration and will to revolutionary change as we confront in Osundare's poetry."[1] (Original emphasis.) That introduction was published in the volume's second impression of 1987, a renewed interest partly generated by the success of *The Eye of the Earth*.

RIVER PETRARCH MEETS RIVER TROTSKY AT THE FEET OF OLOSUNTA

I studied poetry under Osundare in the late Eighties. I had a friend then, Henry Foluso, who read my poems and commented on them, and gave me his to read in return. Henry was ahead of me by three years. I knew that he took Creative Writing courses under Osundare, and that he wrote a eulogy for his teacher when he won the Commonwealth Prize. A line stuck in my mind:

> *O sun dare shine...*

During my second year, I had registered for the Creative Writing course in Fiction taught by Harry Garuba. The rule was unambiguous: you either took poetry *or* fiction. I had always felt very strong about writing fiction, but like most undergraduates, I found the pull of poetry equally irresistible. Like Henry I was studying Theatre Arts, and editing the students' magazine, *The Masque*, which published poems, opinions and reviews every Monday. Encouraged by Garuba's very flexible approach to teaching, and hoping to write better poetry, I registered with Osundare. I noticed the differences between the two tutors very quickly. Garuba instructed us to write a story about anything, providing it was set on the campus. His friends sat in on some of the tutorials, and I remember one funny incident, when a short story appeared, and one student directed his criticisms at one of the teacher's friends. The criticisms were so personal and direct that the other fellow had to say, But *I* didn't write it! The story was "That Sunshine Girl" by Kole Omotosho.

On the contrary Osundare took every class alone. I wondered then whether this was because the course level was more advanced than the previous year. He focused on subject matter, rather than setting, believing that a subject matter might choose its own setting. In February, when it was St. Valentine's Day, he asked for poems about love. Then he showed us a drawing by the artist Obiora Udechukwu, *The Road to Abuja*, and asked us to write a poem on it. There was another assignment on rocks, for which a student was suspected by his colleagues of "undue influence" from *The Eye of the Earth*. One criticism of this style that I remember held that it limited the imagination. Those who thought that it was good for artistic discipline had a more eloquent argument.

Osundare was concerned about punctuality, in attendance as well as in turning assignments in. A defaulter might suffer no more than a rebuke, but the fault never went unremarked. This quality extended to his manner of criticizing a poem. He hardly condemned a poem outright, preferring the use of expressions like 'experimental', 'statemental'. I have nothing against experimentation, he would say, pointing to his own varied poetry, but it has to be done consciously. He was teaching another course in Stylistics, but my own experience was limited to the poetry class.

Of course, there was always the sense of humour. In the year before mine, reports say, he had jokingly singled out a student from the drudgery of writing a St. Valentine's Day poem because the tough-looking student didn't seem the romantic type. Once upon a discussion on the use of appropriate words, he told the story of a laundry machine operator, an Indian who, unable to identify the flowing gown agbada, simply said, And here's a parachute!

In Osundare's office on the top-floor of the Faculty of Arts building there were inspiring sights. It was an office full of books, files, and manuscripts; on the blackboard, pieces of words—not as poems interrupted by teaching, but as study-aids: enjab-ment; run-on-lines; collocations; CAESura; magnificɛnt as opposed to magnificient. Langston Hews. Ted Hews. Nerroodah. Mahmood Door-wish. The poet loved the sound and texture of words; you could actually hear him caress them. On the walls, there were several legends, including two Positive Poem posters. One, from *King Lear*, said

That distribution undo excess
And each man hath enough.

Another was unattributed:

When Mark Anthony had spoken,
the people said How well he spoke.
When Demosthenes had spoken, they said Let us march!

Perhaps the most engaging was the poster illustrating a moral from Tolstoy of the religious writing phase. A man with tattered pants was shouldering another who was shouldering a third man smoking a cigar and holding a whip. The quotation was something like: "I sit on a man's back, and claim that I feel pity for him and would like to reduce his burden by any means. Except by getting off his back." For a long time, if I recall correctly, a corner of the blackboard was kept sacrosanct with a quotation from Amilcar Cabral, also available on a red strip of cloth in the office of his friend, the playwright Femi Osofisan, on the other wing of the same building: "In the great dialectics of human struggle, looking back is also looking forward. The activist is not just a reminder; he is also a rememberer."

That was Osundare's office at the time: a confluence of River Petrarch and River Trotsky. A student leaving this office would want to go and read *The Penguin Book of Socialist Verse* and any of the spruce but dauntingly-written *What is Dialectical Materialism?* Series, fresh from Progress Publishers and sold on the frontage of the Students' Union Building. Osundare appeared and spoke at seminars organized by campus journalists; he was sighted at the SUB on February 11, the Kunle Adepeju Day—the anniversary of the 1971 police killing of a student who was the poet's undergraduate contemporary. And his weekly column in the *Sunday Tribune* was as regular as the Lagos traffic jam. In late May 1989, after General Ibrahim Babangida's police had taken over virtually all the university campuses in the country following the nation-wide protest against the Structural Adjustment Program, SAP, and all students were advised to go home, I went to return Osundare's copy of *The Heights of Macchu Picchu*. I had done this rather reluctantly, having only borrowed the book two days before. He was so engaged listening to a student's philippic on "the Bolsheviks and the Mensheviks" that I was convinced he'd not remember to ask for his book. But he did.

In the October 19, 1987 issue of *Newswatch* magazine Osundare, one of the weeklies' columnists wrote an indignant piece titled "Where Is Your Tie?" After a talk given by the writer, Kole Omotosho, Osundare and a couple of friends and colleagues had sought to retire to the exclusive Ikoyi Club in the most elitist part of Lagos. As usual they had dressed casual, but casual for Osundare was most likely a short-sleeve shirt, a pair of trousers and a pair of sandals. The Aluta outfit. Dress code was not a casual matter at Ikoyi Club, so the restaurant's supervisor insisted the poet put on a tie before he could sit down to the meal. It was the clash of two opposing and deeply held brands of etiquette, in the end Osundare and his colleagues left the club in protest. I quote from his riposte:

> "The sartorial regulation of Ikoyi Club is an eloquent testimony to the Nigerian's craving for outward appearance. A people often too vain to dive beyond the surface, how frequently we allow appearance to supplant reality, while glittering externalities subvert the core of genuine probings. Our cavalier superficiality, our frequent pastime of cutting corners to false truths has made us a country which stands logic on its head, a land where science is conquered by superstition, and urgent problems earn a plater of easy nostrums."[i]

This was late 1987, months before the first wave of the wind that scattered the Soviet Republics and blew the Iron Curtain to tatters.

What's the connection? In that article, Osundare linked his anger to the need for a cultural liberation. This was almost always synonymous with the "total liberation of the oppressed world" to which Omotosho's talk had alluded earlier that evening. Although not a joiner of associations, Osundare here gestured toward a political attitude that was (and remains) leftist. Jeyifo had made this clear in his appreciation of Osundare's poetry.

Before the fall of the Berlin Wall, with the exception of a few who were close enough to the trends in the Soviet Union to make sectarian distinctions, leftist politics in Nigeria consisted largely of an academic or moral interest in utopia socialism. (Fortunately, the Political Bureau set up by General Babangida's junta in 1986 recommended a socialist political system, and for a long while, Nigerian newspapers hosted scores of articles on the merits or otherwise of the proposed system. Discussions did little to make socialism *marketable*, but they progressively drew attention to the incongruities at the heart of the Nigerian state itself; incongruities that nevertheless have a material basis. Instructively Edwin Madunagu, a notable Marxist on the Bureau resigned for reasons of principle, long before the report was submitted.) University teachers with a social conscience and genuine interest in literature were almost invariably left leaning. Osundare numbered among this crop of teachers. In that spirit did he expect his piece, like most polemical extensions of his poetry, to be read.

In 1993 I published a review of Osundare's eighth volume, *Midlife*. That piece, published in the then clandestine Nigerian *Tempo* newsmagazine, was titled "The Poet as Everything." It was an autobiographical volume, and for the first time, the front cover of an Osundare collection featured his photograph. The general tone of the book is of tempered idealism, the reality of middle age. Osundare projects himself as a moderate human being who partakes of the plenitude of being. "In this poem ('Human in Every Sense') river banks burst and the Niger flows into the Mississippi, the Zambezi into the Danube. Walls disappear; the sand dunes of the desert shift for the Tuareg to trade salt for pepper in the heart of Africa", was how I wrote of the collection's most ambitious poem. For me then, *Midlife* represented an explicit definition of a public persona already foreshadowed in *Moonsongs* where "the moon is a mask dancing". There are very interesting conjunctions around this volume, and they indicate a political rather than an artistic attitude.

The great Nigerian novelist, Chinua Achebe uses that phrase, 'a masquerade dancing' in the novel *Arrow of God*. Ezeulu is advising his son, Nwoye, to embrace modernity because "the world is like a masquerade dancing, and in order to see it clearly, one has to keep moving." After Ezeulu, another wise character in a later Achebe novel, the journalist Ikem Osodi in *Anthills of the Savannah* quotes Walt Whitman with approval:

> Do I contradict myself?
> Very well, I contradict myself.
> I am large, I contain multitudes.

In *Midlife*, Osundare quotes the same verse; in fact the entire collection pulsates with a Whitmanian fascination with the elements and seasonality. This image of a wise person who sees with the whole body, tendentious as it may seem in a poem of middle age, a poem about growth, has a good deal of value. Politically Osundare is a moderate; artistically he is a risk-taker, a compulsive experimentalist albeit within the traditional mode. This essay is about Osundare the political writer, whose concern for human rights is informed by his poetic sensibility.

Nigerians' resolve against suffering in early 1984 refused to materialize as soldier after soldier after arrogant soldier ruled the country as a huge barracks full of sheep, whose only value was in being whipped in line. To disassemble the New Year cheer altogether, what they did was to 'pin new *iya*'—they got allocated new kinds of suffering. It was like the declaration by the Old Testament king of Israel, Rehoboam: "My father chastised you with whip, but I will chastise you with scorpions." Shagari's government was elected, but it was clearly fascistic, instructing policemen to shoot people at sight if they protested the "moon-slide victory" of the ruling party in the August 1983 elections. But the military junta of General Muhammadu Buhari, which overthrew Shagari, proved worse: it tried corrupt politicians, which was good, but the selection of those to be tried was absurd. The big fish escaped the net full of wide holes, but the terrapins got trapped. More absurd, the military tribunals handed out sentences only an apartheid regime could better: life plus 252 years with hard labor; 144 years to run concurrently; 210 years, etc. Listening to his own sentence in 1984 a former governor laughed till he cried. General Ibrahim Babangida created political parties and a new breed of politicians, only to annul an election he had taken five years and an estimated two billion dollars to organize. General Abacha's Rehoboamic vow was contained in the terse statement: "Any attempt to test our will be ruthlessly dealt with." He detained Moshood Abiola, winner of the elections that Babangida had annulled, and when Abiola came out in July 1998 after Abacha's death, it was as a corpse. Abacha ordered the hanging of the writer Ken Saro-Wiwa and eight of his companions. He served raw coup as a four-course meal at breakfast, lunch and dinner, roping in General Olusegun Obasanjo, a former head of state, and General Shehu Musa Yar'Adua, his old second-in-command. He shut down newspaper houses, torched others, arrested or exiled journalists, charged Nobel laureate Wole Soyinka and his co-activists with murder. Members of an opposition group, the National Democratic Coalition, NADECO, became the usual target; 'NADECO agent' became the catchall name for whoever dared speak out against the regime. Abacha successfully got Nigeria quarantined from civilized quarters. He even eliminated his own deputy through entrapment in a coup he himself originated.

Meanwhile, soldier after soldier lined his own pockets and those of his friends and family, while public utilities went to seed. A proud and flamboyant exporter of petroleum soon began to import for domestic purposes. Nigerians were thoroughly brutalized; they had never had it this bad. Rehoboam's scorpions not only stung, they stuck their tails in. Much of Osundare's published poetry was born in these years but as I said, the concern here is with his public commentary.

THE PRINT MEDIA

The involvement of the Nigerian intelligentsia with the print media became quite pronounced with the arrival of *The Guardian* in February 1983, when university teachers, poets, and dramatists took to writing editorials and opinion columns. The founding of *Newswatch* magazine the following year began similar trend; when Osundare and Adebayo Williams, then teaching English Studies at Obafemi Awolowo University, Ile-Ife, began writing fortnightly columns for the magazine, they reminded most readers of their university colleagues at *The Guardian*. Before now Osundare had been writing reviews and commentaries for the magazine *West Africa*. These two teachers were also writers (Williams had published a novel), and were only playing a social role in an industry whose original masterminds were intellectuals. (Elsewhere I have written that the Nigerian press canvasses interests that go beyond the control of the political society. This is an obvious point; scholars of the Nigerian press have identified the country's pluralistic nature and the adoption of a federal constitution before independence, as the structural origins of this autonomy. Williams, who later left *Newswatch* (apparently disillusioned at the editors' closeness to the Babangida regime), put it more dramatically when he wrote that while Alhaji Ahmadu Bello, the Sardauna of Sokoto who was the first Premier of Northern Nigeria encouraged young men to enlist in what was called the Nigerian Army, Chief Obafemi Awolowo, Bello's counterpart in the West encouraged young men—and women—to go to school. When the tyranny of the gun hijacked political authority in Nigeria the press—or the pen—became a natural opposition.)

It was this intellectual bias of the print media that attracted the likes of Osundare. He and Williams wrote every other week, alternating with the magazine's three editors—Ray Ekpu, Dan Agbese and Yakubu Mohammed—so that every week, two opinion columns ran. Osundare's column appeared fairly regularly since 1987, even when he took long breaks from his post at the University of Ibadan. His articles were informed by the same humanist temper of his poetry; shorn of the mediating subterfuge of art they clarified his political disposition and sited him on the out-side of the picket line. The articles are still not collected; besides this is not an attempt to analyze them individually. But some, like "Where's Your Tie?" and "For Thomas Sankara" (a passionate tribute to the assassinated military leader of Burkina Faso) are representative of his social allegiance: the grand historical desire to wrest the destiny of decolonized societies from the grip of every type of overlord—local, national and multinational.

He was not alone. Decolonization theorists and Pan-Africanists mounted this same horse. Cabral had been there; Walter Rodney and Cheik Anta Diop were obvious inspirations; deploying different methods, Ngugi wa Thiong'o and Ayi Kwei Armah remain at the forefront.

The imperialism thoroughbred was gored in the late 1980s. The Warsaw Pact collapsed, a phenomenon at once attributed to the diligence of the trio of Pope John Paul II, Ronald Reagan ('the Seventh Horseman'—a phrase from the newest volume, *Horses of Memory*) and Lady Margaret Thatcher ("his beautiful paramour"), and the imperatives of internal dissension in the communist bloc. If the universal rumble did not quite shatter the faith of every anti-imperialist in the 'Third World' it left palpable disillusion in its wake. The West claimed the victory, trusting in the wisdom of the World Trade Organization. It was a truly mesmerizing time: Osundare would want to consecrate both Neruda, a communist, and Vaclav Havel, an anti-communist, as his own guardian angels.

But thank goodness for Nigeria! It left immense dark spots—it was one huge dark spot. Elsewhere on the continent, a monotony of Conradian darkness. On the eve and in the wake of 1990, the wind of change blew across the Equator line, but rustled few major wings. Sergeant Doe was out, but Blaise Campaore was in. The balls of the ancient *Ofwe* of Yamoussoukro were only swinging, they didn't look certain to snap. To the South, of course, the release of Nelson Mandela from twenty-seven years of incarceration was major. But it would take some more years to rid the continent of some more of the vestiges of the "Aminian theme": Kenneth Kaunda, Hastings Kamuzu Banda, Mobutu Sese Seko. If the "triumph" of capitalism was wearisome because it meant something different to Osundare, the intransigence of Africa's "Atlantic ulcer" was doubly so. He sufficiently ventilated his anger on these issues in his column.

MODERATE'S GESTURES

Osundare's vision is continental. There are few truly passionate African writers who can afford not to take the continent's case. In March 1998, at the height (but also toward the end) of Abacha's terror in Nigeria, Osundare was awarded the Fonlon-Nichols Prize for contributions to the struggle for human rights and excellence in creative writing. Past winners included Mongo Beti, Assia Djebar, Werewere Liking, and Ken Saro-Wiwa, who only spent two months in freedom after he received his award in Accra on March 23, 1994. (He was arrested in Port Harcourt on May 20, remained in detention until October 31, 1995 when he and eight others were wrongfully condemned to death for the killing of four Ogoni chiefs, and murdered on November 8.)

A year before the award, Osundare had produced at the University of Ibadan "The State Visit" a satirical play on corruption and irresponsible leadership. He left Nigeria in August 1997 for a two-year teaching contract at the University of New Orleans. According to a report he himself confirmed, the same security agents who stopped poets, journalists and other activists from coming into the country or getting out of it put him through some ordeal at the Murtala Mohammed International Airport. In 1997, there was a real possibility that his name featured on some arbitrary list of "NADECO people". The speech he gave at the award ceremony was titled "Freedom and the Creative Space", dealing with the ways in which totalitarian rule prevalent in Africa posed serious threats to the lives and works of artists.

> "A state which parades prisons full of writers and graves lit-
> tered with the bones of visionary thinkers and activists is
> telling prospective writers and thinkers in no unmistakable
> terms: 'Behold these, therefore, and learn; do what they have
> done and suffer their fates'."3

He could have been speaking of Nigeria. But he was clearly speaking about Africa; it was the moderate gesture of a passionate conscience. He said later in an interview with Lee Nichols, one of the two people for whom the prize was named, that "to narrow my anger and frustration down to just one person or just one ruler or just one government would be cheapening myself and cheap-ening the amplitude of my vision."4 Other people might argue with justifica-tion that speaking specifically about Abacha's tyranny did not amount to self-debasement; on the contrary, it would seem to agree with Osundare's preference for a vision that's at once local and global. After all, Wole Soyinka wrote a book, *Open Sore of a Continent* as "a personal narrative of the Nigerian crisis" and still dwelt on the national identity of the Basques.

VI

He correctly recognized that award as one that would "throw even more chal-lenges on my way." It was a recognition that sought to draw Osundare to deploy-ing more than symbols in his engagement with the quotidian issues that poet-ry is inadequately fitted to grapple with. It sought as much to reward him for what he had done to link his art with his politics as for getting him to do so much more of the same. For a poet who began by swearing to an unbreakable pact with the people as the sum of his songs, this was a worthy bequest. The title of Osundare's 1987 dress-down article in *Newswatch* was an attempt at rib-bing on the silliness of a colonial mentality. But I find it a quite fitting and col-orful garment for a different kind of code, this time moral. He is the poet of Olosunta, the rooted child of rocks, the free-moving child of rivers. He speaks and writes approvingly of Kenzaburo Oe's rootedness and cosmopolitanism; quotes Shakespeare's *A Midsummer Night's Dream* to the effect that every work of art must have a place and a name.5 When Osundare talks about the existence of pan-human attributes all over the world, as he often likes to do, he is making a very profound gesture: James Joyce was always writing about Dublin. Saro-Wiwa struggled for the Ogoni.

NOTES

1 Jeyifo, Biodun. "Introduction." Second Impression of *Songs of the Marketplace*. Ibadan: New Horn Press, 1987: ix

2 Osundare, Niyi. "Where Is Your Tie?" *Newswatch* October 19, 1987: 54.

3 Osundare, Niyi. "Freedom and the Creative Space." *ALA Bulletin* 24.2 Spring 1998: 52–56

4 Ibid., p. 37.

5 Adagbonyin, Sonnie Asomwan; NIYI OSUNDARE: *Two Essays and an Interview*. Ibadan: Sam Bookman Educational and Communications Services, 1996: 69.

Niyi Osundare
photo © Marianne Fleitman

Admiring the Noma Award plaque (Lagos, 1991)
photo: Ray Ekpu of *Newswatch*

With Kole Omotoso, left; Justice
Akinola Aguda, middle.

With Amiri Baraka (Dakar, 1989)

With Breyton Bretenbach (Rotterdam, 1996)

Reading: Tokyo, 1993

Niyi Osundare and Odia Ofeimun in conversation with Berlin's Minister for Culture, Roloff Mormin and Dr. Anke Wiegand-Kanzaki, Secretary General for the House of World Culture, Berlin. 1993

With students of the University of Ibadan, Nigeria.

With S'eamus Heaney
(Rotterdam 1996)

From left: Niyi Osundare, Njabulo Ndebele, Micere Mugo, Tiyambe
Zeleza, Kole Omotoso (Tokyo 1993)

From left: Odia Ofeimun, Tanure Ojaide, Niyi Osundare,
Festus Iyayi. (Cape Coast Castle 1994)

With Dennis Brutus (Dakar 1989)

With members of the Association of Nigerian Authors (ANA) Abeokuta, 1992
(Festus Iyayi 2nd right, Ken Saro Wiwa 2nd left)

With Sipho Sephamla

With the Master Kora player Papa Sosso
(Morocco 1999)

From left: Romain Gaignard, Niyi Osundare, C. Fioupou, Wole Soyinka,
O. Yai, René Souriac, Université de Toulouse-le-Mirail

With Ken Harrow and Abiola Irele.

With Wole Soyinka, Université de Toulouse-le-Mirail

Being conferred with the honorary doctorate by
Professor Romain Gaignard, President of the
Université de Toulouse-le-Mirail.
Photo: Daniel Avril

With Kamau Brathwaite
(Barbados 2000)

ORALITY, NATURE AND MARKET-PLACE CREATIVITY

NIYI OSUNDARE'S VILLAGE VOICES AND THE ORAL ART: A STUDY IN AESTHETIC TRANSFER AND LINKAGES[1]

Charles Bodunde

INTRODUCTION

The processes and movements of decolonizing provoke a literary response that interprets orature in terms of the medium for the African artist to re-enter the essence of his culture to draw inspiration. Sometimes, this position is stretched to its passionate limit, in which case, it presents an approach that tends to prescribe an aesthetic principle for the production of African literature and its criticism. Boniface Obichere reflects the signature of this breed in offering that orature

> is the incontestable reservoir of the values, sensibilities, aesthetics and achievements of traditional African thought and imagination... it must serve as the ultimate foundation, guidepost, and point of departure for a modern liberated African literature. It is the root from which modern liberated African literature must draw its sustenance.[2]

It is already established that orature is a premise of linkages. It connects the artist with the aesthetic forms available in his culture and provides the ground for establishing literary relations among African writers, including those in the diaspora.

As current critical atmosphere indicates, the debate has moved beyond the simple call to employ oral resources. With Osundare, the relation with orature is informed by the more demanding purpose of constructing coherent modes to express new ideas and vision. The subjects of the works of the poet derive from his aversion to the pervasive atmosphere of state terror and repression around them. Osundare raises alarm against what he describes as the "over-whelming physicality of (the tyrant's) weapon and strategies of violence"[3] and restates the role of literature in this regard:

> And how can literature help to conquer that fear, rupture that silence, and neutralize that violence? By constantly, intelligently exposing the lie which lies at the root of every violence; the lie which feeds and strengthens it.[4]

The oral art has a role in this engagement and it is the purpose of this chapter to examine Osundare's *Village Voices* (1984) in order to find out the ways in which oral forms like songs, icons, dirges and myths are deployed to construct social vision. Osundare's transfer of oral forms can be viewed in the context of a wider practice which involves some other contemporary poets. It appears necessary therefore to draw examples of aesthetic transfer from a poet like Jack Mapanje whose *Of Chameleons and Gods* relates with Osundare's *Village Voices* in content and form.

FABLES, WITS AND POETIC MEDIATION

Needless to say, oral forms have their own existence and they serve various functions within the culture. They are used in written literature to perform similar social purposes. The act of correlating the artistic and social functions of oral genres with creative possibilities in written poetry for instance makes sense because these forms have succeeded through the ages in conditioning certain valuable means of cognizing and humanizing the society. Daniel P. Kunene expresses related view in his argument that allegory, parables and other genres can be seen as a continuation of the tradition of oral narrative, particularly of the use of the fable as a commentary on human affairs. Allegory owes its effectiveness perhaps largely to the fact that some commonly accepted experiences of life, with their related consequences or associations, are used as a surface argument for closely parallel situation which would seem to be incontrovertible once the surface or illustrating argument is accepted.5

Osundare uses oral sources in a fascinating way to reflect his social vision. For instance he uses the chicken fable to raise questions on the compensatory order of nature:

> Who does the chicken think
> it is deceiving?
> It eats pebbles
> and swallows sands
> yet complains of toothlessness
> the goat which has teeth
> the dog which fortifies its mouth
> with the strongest of ivory
> dare they eat pebbles in the morning
>
> and still walk about at noon?6

This can be related to Jack Mapanje's use of folkloric elements like fable and wits to express experiences and extend meanings. In *Of Chameleons and Gods*, the poem, "Song of Chicken" is a fable which incorporates wits to expose the ambiguity in human actions. As a fable, the poem relies on the critical voice of the animal figure to create effects:

> Master, you talked with bows,
> Arrows and catapults once
> Your hands steaming with hawk blood
> To protect your chicken.
>
> Why do you talk with knives now,
> Your hands teaming with eggshells
> And hot blood from your own chicken?
>
> Is it to impress your visitors?7

This fable contains metaphors which allow for a wide range of interpretations. One of such is the ambivalent position of certain political figures in dealing with the crucial question of leadership in Africa. Mapanje alludes to the tragic irony in which the freedom fighters of yesteryears, who "talked with bows, arrows and catapults" (p.4) to liberate the land from colonial hold, now "talk with knives" of plunder against the same land.

ICONS, IMAGES AND MEANING-MAKING

Osundare expresses a concern for the social situations within the rural set up. He exposes the contradictions that exist between city life and the rural, bucolic tradition. This dichotomy is often used as a metaphor for the decadence and affluence of the ruling elite as against the communal but impoverished agrarian people.

Although we find, in *Village Voices*, (especially in "Akintunde, Come Home"), the romanticist metaphor of the city as a destroyer, Osundare's picture of village life is not in any way idealized, if we define the term in the sense and spirit of the Wordsworthian romanticism in a poem like "Michael." Images in "Akintunde, Come Home" show a village of natural disaster inhabited by the exploited poor:

> Come back here
> where the walls are mud
> and meatless meals quiet
> the howling stomach
> come back here
> where dreams spun on campaign promises
> snap in the noisy bellies
> of belching parliaments
>
> Come home son,
> through our thatched roofs
> we can see the devouring deluge
> of looming clouds (pp. 22–23).

Osundare engages the metaphor of racing and the symbol of a monster city to express the devouring savage culture of modern life:

> Akintunde, I have told you to come,
> come home from the land
> where life is a race in which
> the strong trample the weak, dashing
> for the fluttering fragments

of stolen trophies
Come away from bubbles
which melt like wax
before a raging blaze (p. 22).

In this poem, meaning depends strongly on creative deployment of images and icons borrowed from the oral art. The iroko tree, which is an icon in many Yoruba rituals and poetry, is employed here to portray a power rage in which the weak becomes the sacrificial object:

Come home, son,
for we cannot be all iroko
slapping the sky's face
with imperious boughs
while the lower forest
dies a sunless death
at our unfeeling feet
come away from the fold
of sun stealers (p. 22).

In its original form, within the context of the Ifa poetic corpus, the iroko tree reveals the allegory of serious life struggle involving sacrifices and conquest. Osundare's imaginative transfer connects the original in form and in content as the following local equivalent collected by Wande Abimbola indicates:

Awon ota ni nda Iroko laamu...
Won ni ebo ni ki o wea ru...
Igba ti o rubo tan
Ni Esu ba lbo pe awon agbe wa
Pe ki won o mea san igbo
Ti Iroko mbe ninuu re
Gbogbo awon igi lomba Irokoo sota
Ni awon agbe be lule.
Igba ti won de idi Iroko,
Esu niwon ko gbodo ge e
Nitori pe igi abami ni.

(Enemies were worrying the Iroko tree of the city of Igbo...
He was told to perform sacrifices,...

> After he had performed sacrifices,
> Esu went and called farmers,
> And ordered them to start clearing the forest
> Inside which the Iroko tree was.
> All the trees which were the enemies of Iroko
> Were cut down by the farmers.
> But when they got to the foot of the Iroko tree,
> Esu commanded that they must not cut him
>
> Because he was not an ordinary tree.)[8]

Of course, Osundare's vision of contemporary life in Africa is shaped by this kind of borrowing which carries the qualities of its own imagery to influence meanings in the poem it is made to inhabit.

One finds in Mapanje's poetry a similar reflection. The poem, "Messages" (in *Of Chameleons and Gods*) reflects on the decay of city life and its consuming effect on the village youth. The technique of the collective voice which Osundare employs to indicate the communal vision typical of the traditional social and aesthetic practices also occur in Mapanje's "Messages". Here, a mother speaks in riddles and in a collective voice to condemn her daughter's adoption of city life:

> Tell
> Her besides, a cat sees best at night
> Not much at noon and so-when time
> Comes, while she eats and drinks
> While she twists and shouts, rides
> And travels, we shall refuse
> To reach her our stuff of fortune
> Even if she called us witches!
> We swear by our fathers dead! (p. 14).

Here, the "stuff of fortune" is a mother's traditional gift (to a daughter) symbolizing and acknowledging Filial piety. Mapanje weaves this icon into poetry to express two levels of disconnection: the girl's disconnection with her traditional origin and then, in a more specific sense, the severance of tie with life source, in this case, her mother. The poet's description reflects the typical image of the archetypal ruined maid:

Her back swirls off me
Gassed by reeking perfumes, sitting:
Tattering curtains, doors to bathrooms
Couples in corners unabashed

She comes back thick-lip-cigaretted
The chest jutting into the world generously
The lashes greased bluer (p. 14).

She loses the opportunity of a link (through the speaker) and darts off "float-ing to the next customer" (p.15) unable to respond to her "navel name", As⌐wilunda. This action, rendered in the technique of drama-in poetry, express-es the girl's decadent and fragmented self. As noted earlier, Osundare employs poetic images and symbols to create a contrast between the city and the rural setting. A similar pattern of contrast is reflected in Mapanje's "Messages". In this poem, contrasts of setting and social practice are made using the images of hunting and war. Images reveal the survival of the communal values of the tra-ditional social formation even within the most competitive context:

Did you think it was a hunting party
Where after a fall from chasing a hare
You laughed together an enemy shaking
Dust off your bottom, a friend reaching
You your bow and arrows? (p. 15).

The city is pictured as a battle ground where everyone wages "a lonely war" (p. 15) to "hack (his) own way singlehanded/ To make anything up to the Shaka of/ The tribe!" (p. 15) Like the Iroko icon in Osundare's "Akintunde, Come Home", the Shaka symbol in Mapanje's "Messages" works intertextually, con-necting the Zulu epic on Shaka to amplify meanings in Mapanje's poem. This means the referent, Shaka, evokes an existing oral poetic form; an epic, part of which Jack Mapanje and Landeg White include in their book of oral poetry:

Ferocious one of the Mbelebe brigade,
Who raged among the large kreals,
So that until dawn the huts were being turned upside down...
He who beats but is not beaten, unlike water,
Axe that surpasses other- axes in sharpness;

> Shaka, I fear to say he is Shaka,
> Shaka, he is the chief of the Mashobas.
> He who armed in the forest, who is like a madman,...
> He who while devouring some devoured others
>
> And as he devoured others he devoured some more;[9]

This epic symbol (as used in "Messages") affects the poem with the meanings it carries in the original epic, part of which is the struggle for domination in the world of warlords. In a more political sense, this may just be Mapanje's cryptic response to the devouring politics of the Banda era.

SONGS, DIRGES, MYTHS AND AESTHETIC MEDIATION

Songs, dirges and myths occur in the poetry of Niyi Osundare as transferred-forms imaginatively used to comment on contemporary social situations. As we have argued earlier, there is a similarity between the functions which these forms perform within the oral culture from which they are transferred and the social purpose they are made to serve within the written tradition and the new culture into which they are relocated. Speaking about the value of the song, Osundare casts the broad perspective in which the song manifests itself in the oral context:

> Traditional, oral Africa thrives on the song; every occasion has its lyrics, even trivial incidents provoke a ballad. There are songs which mark the inexorable cycle of human existence-birth, puberty, marriage age, and death. There are songs for praising, songs for cursing, songs of abuse; songs which wax purple in the King's palace,... The towncrier talks in song,... I have seen old people weep in poetry...[10]

In Osundare's *Village Voices*, the song is the medium for biting satirical lashes against the corrupt ("Not in my Season of Song") and for raising social consciousness ("The Prisoner's Song"). There are at least two levels of creative transfer of songs. There is a physical transfer that involves the use of songs in their original indigenous forms. This mode of transfer is often accompanied with what Osundare himself calls "mediated translation." This song type improves the rhythm and the communicative power of the poem especially when read as performance poetry. The following song, taken from Osundare's *Waiting Laughters* (1990) is a good example of this kind of transfer:

Omi i lo o, iyanrin lookun rode
Omi i lo o, Iyanrin lookun rode
Aye mo re de, e emee jami lo loona o o o.

(The water is going
Going going going

The water is going)[11]

The song expands on the dialectics of motion and stillness; the passage of time, history and the patient workings of those who intervene in these structures to create new forms of social commitment. In the main poem, images are structured to convey the opposing possibilities of visionary creators who, like rare flowers, "cling, still,/ To the beard of the valley/ ...dancing in the whistling wind" (p. 67) and visionless men who "sharpen dark knives/ For our fledgling voice" (p. 67). The poet constructs moral justice in the model of a life taker becoming "drowned in the deluge of the echoed" of "A village of rolling hills"(p. 67) and the man who waits for life while humanizing society survives the deluge for his "heels are strong" (p. 67). The song helps to reveal the deeper meanings of the poem because its images and sense are analogous with the intended message of the poem. So the song illuminates by replication.

The other level of transfer of songs works through the technique of close trai slation, a mode which Aderemi Bamikunle finds to be basic to the composition of "The Prisoner's Song" (in *Village Voices*).[12] Osundare uses this technique in "The Bridal Song". The poem is a direct rendering of the traditional bridal song which normally incorporates oral genres like praise poetry and lamentation to present the theme of departure. In mood and imagery, Osundare's English rendering is close to the original:

Baba, thank you today
For the kindness of many years
Going am I now to my husband
The son of Efurudowo whose yams
Wrestle heaps to the ground
Owner of the powerful machete
Whose maize drills the molars
Like seasoned warriors
My calabash tray will give way
Coming back from his farm (p. 42).

The choice of this genre makes sense against the background of the decaying of values signified in Osundare's "Akintunde, Come Home" and Mapanje's "Messages". The poetic figure in "The Bridal Song" symbolizes moral virtues and therefore functions as an alternative to the lost child archetype in both "Akintunde, Come Home" and "Messages".

There is a slightly different mode of transfer in Osundare's "A Dialogue of the Drums". Here, Osundare creates a performance atmosphere with voices of poet-singers, audience and the sound of the drums. The poet defines his origin in the tradition of songs and drums:

> I hail from a line of drummers...
> I was born with a song in my throat
> And my handson the face of the drum...
> Whatever song you raise
> Is what the world sings after you (p. 6).

Osundare exploits the traditional poets-in-dialogue mode to define the nature of his art. He distances himself from the palace singer whose drum is "dumb in the marketplace" and whose royal song "extols those whose words/ Behead the world" (p. 7). The song and the drum, for the poet, make sense only when they are employed to tell the truth, "the fangs of facts" (p. 7) even as state apparatuses are organized against the artist to silence him. Osundare insists that the great task of the artist is in sustaining "the audacity to keep telling the emperor: Your majesty, thou, indeed, art naked" even as tyrannical rulers "send dissident writers to the gallows with... medieval equanimity"[13]

In "A Dialogue of the Drums", Osundare recreates the confrontational atmosphere typical of the traditional song of abuse to cast a diatribe against the artist who jettisons critical intervention to take up the role of the palace artist:

> Where were you when adan filled the night
> With the shame of Apeloko
> Who proved too sharp with the neighbour's yams?
> I know where you were
> You were in the palace, running endless errands
> Like a shuttle in the loom
> Your eunuch drum a dumb stool
> For harem buttocks (p. 7).

For the poet, "the people always outlast the palace" (p. 8) and to be on their side is to unite with the most stable arena of creativity.

The dirge form occurs occasionally in Osundare's poetry but this is not in the magnitude with which Kofi Awoonor and Kofi Anyidoho handle the genre. Again, like "The Prisoner's Song" and "The Bride's Song", Osundare's "The Star Sob" is a close translation of the Yoruba dirge form:

> You who kill kings
> as if they had no crowns
> you who snatch the rich
> from vaults of gold
> like beggars hauled from
> a heap of backstreet garbage
> you who kill a physician
> as if his art were a moonlight trick (p. 35).

As the following example shows, traditional dirge emphasizes the sense of loss by locating parallel image of death in nature:

> Ko seni ti o ni dale bora ninuu wa
> B'eruun ba yan,
> Gbogbo kooko a keru, a re 'wale aja.
>
> (Without exception, everyone shall make a wrapper of ground.
> When dry season is severe,
>
> All grasses shall pack up and die.)[14]

Osundare translates this relation of art and ecology into a creative force leading to the dirge form, "The Stars Sob":

> you who go up a tree
> coming down with the juiciest fruit
> Ah! the stars are sobbing
>
> Forests drop their tuft of green
> vegetables go pale
> on the market stall (p. 36).

Quite often, Osundare uses Yoruba myths to help build ideas. In *Waiting Laughters* for instance, he imagines a revolutionary situation in which the people, fed up with the "garnished sand from the kitchen/ of heartless season" (p.

22) take the "screaming stone" (p. 22) and "the humble axe" (p. 22) to termi-
nate the reign of a tyrant. There is a vision of the revolt of the people in
Osundare's allusion to Orogodo, an Ikere (Yoruba) myth which he describes as
"a remote place of banishment for dishonourable rulers" (p. 22):

> behold the wonder,
> the crown is only a cap!
>
> Orogbdodo Orogodo...
> Oba ba ti beyi
> O'mo d'Orogododo o o o o
>
> The king's brave legs are bone and flesh...
> The castle is a house of mortar and stone (p. 22).

The significant import of the lines is the unraveling of the powerlessness of
the king or ruler once he loses the people's support. Furthermore, the myth is
used to reveal a new possibility, which is the capacity of the ordinary people to
discover the force of their collective action, a phenomenon which is stronger
than the power of a ruler. Osundare sustains this pattern of demystification in
his poetry, borne here by the metaphor of discovery in the line, "the crown is
only a cap!" This kind of pattern amplifies the revolutionary force of Osundare's
poetry.

It is important to mention that the proverb is a vital sub-genre in the poetic
modes discussed. Osundare uses this form to achieve a more coherent articulation of vision. There is an interesting relation of the form to setting in "A
Villager's Protest" where a villager speaks in proverbs, the form he is most
acquainted with to express his anger against corrupt politicians:

> Esuru grows swollen-headed
> and outgrows the prestigeous belly
> of the mortar
> the wasp power-stung
> enters a race of waists
>
> Men of deep unwisdom
> knowing not that
> power is the bird of the forest

which nests on one tree today
and tomorrow pitches its tent
on another. (p. 48).

CONCLUSION

I must emphasize that oral art forms are not static or fossilized materials. They are constantly being reconstructed to assume new roles even in the oral cultures in which they are found. This implies that, as creative products, they have their own recreative force and the adaptability that will always make them, to use Osundare's words, "persist without greying."[15]

As it appears, the appeal in Osundare's poetry lies in the capacity of the borrowed forms to reveal new social vision conceived in the ambience of a literary intention that tends the global space: "When I raise my voice/ The world will be my chorus". Osundare shares this creative vision with a number of African poets and the link between him and a poet like Mapanje is hinged on this concern. However, he does more than most of his contemporaries in the sense of reinterpreting oral aesthetic to create a form of poetry which is revolutionary in terms of contents, form and medium of dissemination.

NOTES

1 The paper is part of a sponsored research on oral traditions and aesthetic transfer in contemporary Black poetry. This writer will like to acknowledge the assistance of the Alexander Von Humboldt Foundation Germany in carrying out the study.

2 Boniface Obichere, ed. "Introduction." *Journal of African Studies* 12.2 (1985): p. 52.

3 Niyi Osundare, "Freedom and the Creative Space" *ALA Bulletin: A Publication of the African Literature Association.* Vol. 24, No. 2 (Spring, 1998), p. 54

4 Ibid.

5 Daniel P. Kunene, "The Crusading Writer, his Modes, Themes and Styles", in Mineke Shipper-de Leauw (ed.), *Text and Context: Methodological Exploration in the Field of African Literature* (Leiden: Afrika-Studie Centrum, 1976), p. 197.

6 Niyi Osundare, *Village Voices* (Ibadan: Evans Brothers Ltd., 1984), p .14. Subsequent page references occur in the text.

7 Jack Mapanje, *Of Chameleons and Gods* (London: Heinemann, 1981) p. 4. Subsequent page references occur in the text.

8 Wande Abimbola, *Ifa Divination Poetry* (New York: NOK Publishers Ltd., 1977) pp. 76–77.

9 Jack Mapanje & Landeg White, *Oral Poetry From Africa* (New York: Longman, 1983), pp. 25–26.

10 Niyi Osundare, "Bard of the Tabloid Platform: A Personal Experience of Newspaper Poetry in Nigeria", *Canadian Association of African Studies Conference*, Edmonton, Alberta, Canada (1987), p. 11.

11 Niyi Osundare, *Waiting Laughters* (Lagos: Malthouse Press Ltd., 1990), p. 67. Subsequent page references are made to this edition and occur in the text.

12 See Aderemi Bamikunle, "Niyi Osundare's Poetry and the Yoruba Oral Artistic Tradition", *African Literature Today* 18 (1992), p. 56.

13 Niyi Osundare, "Freedom and the Creative Space", p. 53.

14 Bade Ajuwon, *Funeral Dirges of Yoruba Hunters* (Lagos: NOK Publishers International, 1982), p. 59.

15 Niyi Osundare, "Bard of the Tabloid Platform: A Personal Experience of newspaper Poetry in Nigeria," p. 3.

OSUNDARE AS NATURE POET: A SIMPLE SENTIMENTALITY

Kofi A.N. Mensah

Niyi Osundare's *The Eye of the Earth*[1] is in one sense something of a rarity, a volume of poems by a modern African poet that constitutes a sustained meditation on the theme of nature. Indeed modern African poetry written in the languages bequeathed by Europe has paid some regard to the natural environment and phenomena. Who can forget Senghor's magical evocation of nighttime in his Nuit de Sine"[2] or David Rubadiri's recreation of the frenzy of an African thunderstorm in his much-anthologized poem of that title? Osundare's collection goes beyond the rather occasional character of the African poet's reflection on nature and offers a very intimate relationship with nature that is deliberately sustained in order to lead to a cautionary message for the reader's benefit. This paper is, however, not centrally concerned with Osundare's message in *The Eye of the Earth*: the poet himself offers a very clear statement of his concerns in the splendidly lyrical preface to the collection. Rather, this paper will, in a brief discussion of Osundare's language, try to show how the poet's attempt to recapture an intimate, simple, African relationship with nature is deeply coloured by his education in English language and literature. Thus it seems the persona in this volume speaks in a mixture of two voices: an "African" voice which describes nature in a style derived from traditional oral poetry, and a modern voice that has been schooled in English studies.

Perhaps we can begin this discussion by noting the different approaches to nature found in the two poems by Senghor and Rubadiri. Rubadiri's nature is vividly evoked and the reader may wish to acknowledge poet's skill and achievement, but the poet/persona is *not* present in the poem. He paints a picture for the reader's attention, but stays out of it. Senghor's evocation is different: the persona's voice permeates the description so that the picture we get, we feel, is more how he wishes the scene to be than how it really was. Thus, while every evocation is inevitably something of an interpretation, Senghor's poem is more emphatically so, more of an idealization than Rubadiri's. Rubadiri says: "This is how it is!" Senghor says: "This is how *I* see it - in retrospect!"

In 1795 with rise of Romanticism in Europe, the German literary theorist, Friedrich von Schiller, distinguished two kinds poetry based principally on the poet's relationship to nature3. The *simple* poets, writing in the early stages of European culture, are at home with nature. In their writing they paint nature's details with great care, yet, at the same time, they seem detached from nature. The simple poets, in the words of Schiller, "do not attach themselves to nature with that depth of feeling, that gentle melancholy, which characterises the moderns". The simple poet, as a child of nature, is bold, direct, imaginative, and yet takes nature a little for granted because it is there. Not so the other kind of poet whom Schiller characterises as *sentimental*. This second kind of poet represents a time when "nature is no longer in man, and we no longer encounter it in its primitive truth". Writing at a time when the mode of existence is "in opposition" to nature, the sentimental poet tends to idealize nature and, as a result, to produce a quality of poetry which is more reflective, presenting nature with greater intensity of feeling than does the simple poet. What the sentimental poet expresses with regard to nature is precisely that sentimental intensity of feeling which we attach to something we can no longer take for granted. The movement from simple to sentimental poetry is, as Schiller conceives it, a movement from reality to the ideal in the presentation of nature.

Schiller's essay was, of course, part of a specific polemic taking place a time when some scholars thought European poetry had changed fundamentally for the worse. His essay was an attempt to justify the new, "sentimental" poetry as arising from more complex social conditions and to caution against judging that poetry by the expectations arising from the earlier, "simple" kind. However, despite arising from very specific circumstances, Schiller's essay provides a useful approach to African nature poetry and to Osundare's *The Eye of the Earth* in particular.

We noted briefly at the outset the different ways in which Rubadiri in "An African Thunderstorm" and Senghor in "Nuit de Sine" relate to nature. Using

Schiller's categories, we might characterize Rubadiri's poem as simple and Senghor's as sentimental, though the writers belong roughly to the same generation. What is important is the absence of homesickness for nature in the simple poem; and conversely, the presence of homesickness for nature in the sentimental poem. The sentimental poet expresses a deep yearning for a natural environment from which he feels separated or which he believes is no longer available. Rubadiri suggests that African thunderstorms are always available for the poet's contemplation, but there is a sense of the elegiac in Senghor's poem, a sense of an Africa that is past or quickly passing.

The persona who speaks in *The Eye of the Earth* gives us enough clues to enable us construct a life history for him; and though we may with justification identify him with the poet himself, it is useful to see him as speaking for a certain kind of African who, born in a rural culture, has through formal education been removed from the simple life of the village. He is, he tells us, "farmer-born peasant bred" and has "frolicked from furrow to furrow" and "sounded kicking tubers in the womb of quickening earth" (p. 43). Born to farming people, the fields have been his playgrounds and he has grown up with intimate knowledge of the fertile richness of nature. However, he has subsequently been removed from this happy intimacy with nature. By and large, the persona sees this separation from his rural background and his upbringing within the more scientific traditions introduced from the West as entailing a diminution of his ability to appreciate nature's divinity - an attitude which is instinctive in traditional cultures. This, for example, is how he presents himself as an adult returning like a prodigal son to his native terrain and its imposing rocks:

> Olosunta spoke
> his belly still battle ground of God and Gold
> The god I have killed
> since wisdom's straightening sun
> licked clean the infant dew of fancy. (p. 14).

The suggestion here is that the passage into adulthood, and the "wisdom" that has come with it, has destroyed the wonder and mystery that nature held for him as a child. For the persona, the removal from nature has practical consequences as well: it has led also to the loss of the traditional agrarian skills and a new dependence on imported "Carolina rice" (p. 44), and the subsequent impoverishment of his nation. Also of course, the loss of the sense "the divinity" in nature has led its being over-exploited and laid to waste by a greedy few who see in the environment only the gold and not the god. Thus in a sense the persona's mission is to call a halt to the destruction of nature by restoring its wonder.

We begin then to see the dual character of Osundare's persona which leads logically to the dual quality of his voice. He is not simply the westernized modern African pining sentimentally for a rural environment he has never known and which he is afraid is fast disappearing. Such a persona would tend towards a total idealization of nature, converting its real objects into artificial symbols of his or her desires and longings. This is for example, what the English Romantic poet, Shelley, does in his famous poem, "To A Skylark" in which he will not even allow the bird to be a bird but converts it into a figure of his poetic aspiration[4]. The persona in *The Eye of the Earth* does know nature at a deeply personal level. At the same time, however, the regard this persona pays to nature is not entirely simple. It is a backward glance at something which, like himself, has been impoverished by materialism. The earth for this speaker is not just the bountiful mother of the million udders; she is also the damaged planet whose pristine beauty can only be called into being by the magic wand of the poet's pen. The persona regards nature with a glance which at once both simple and sentimental: he may speak with an educated and modern awareness of the degradation of the environment, but his appeal gains its strength from a powerful evocation of nature's wonderful bounty and variety which comes from direct and intimate interaction.

We turn now to the central, though brief, discussion of the quality of Osundare's poetic language. The poet informs us in the preface that the volume is conceived in three movements: `back to earth', `rain songs', and `homecall'. Together the movements represent, firstly, a looking back to a time" when the earth's head stood on its neck and a hand sprouted but five fingers" (p. xii) - images which suggest a living, healthy, normal state of mother earth; and, secondly, a looking forward to a time when the earth will be restored to its prim. al health, and the injustices accompanying its ruin redressed. I shall restrict my discussion of Osundare's language to passages taken from the first section `back to earth'. It is in this section, after all, that he is most centrally concerned with recalling the scenes of his boyhood.

I consider this section one of the finest tributes to the majesty and variety of the rain forest ever achieved in writing. It is a detailed portrait which includes a variety flora: tall trees which seem to touch the sky and keep out the sun; trees with different hardiness of wood - *iroko, oganwu, ayunre*; the less hardy palm with its gifts of nuts, kernels and wine; the coquettish *patonmo* which shyly closes its leaves when touched. The portrait also includes glimpses of the different fauna: antelope, partridge, weaverbird, squirrel, chameleon, monkey and even the skeleton of a dead snake. Mention is made also of the carpet of leaves, the smell of "budding herbs" and "ripening roots", the majesty of an anthill, and the awesome but protective mien of the rocks surrounding the poet's native village: altogether a splendid tapestry of nature in the tropics.

In his portraiture of the environment of his childhood, Osundare depends largely on the devices of orature, particularly of praise poetry, the Yoruba *Oriki*, as is amply demonstrated in this portrait of one of the hardiest trees of the rain forest, the *iroko*:

> Iroko wears the crown of the forest,
> town's rafter, roof of the forest
> ironwood against the termites of time
> Iroko wears the crown of the forest
> its baobab foot rooted against
> a thousand storms.
> Iroko wears the crown of the forest,
> scourge of the sweating sawyer
> the champion matchet assays a bite,
> beating a blunted retreat to the whetting stone.
> The ironwood wears the crown of the forest. (p. 5).

This is virtually a traditional panegyric to the tree with its familiar pattern of repetitions (sometimes with variation) to serve as linkage, of personification, praise epithets, hyperbolic imagery and copious alliterations. It reads like a very skilful *translation* into English of a Yoruba poem. In doing this, the poet is continuing a poetic tradition, but in the context of this paper he is also attempting to reclaim an ethos -- a way of regarding nature which, like the poem, is traditional. Despite the verbal dexterity the focus in this passage is on the natural object rather than the persona. Nature is presented with reverence but not without humour, witness the hasty retreat of the champion matchet rather like a bloodied boxer. The speaker intimately knows his subject and has grown up around it.

Generally, this is the idiom in which Osundare wishes to offer the earth to the reader's attention. The very title of the volume, *The Eye of the Earth*, is suggestive of the simple rural outlook. The eye is the term used in many West African languages for the node on a root or stem from which new leaves or growth spring. To trample the eye of the earth, which the volume cautions us against, is to render it incapable of producing or supporting new life.

However, the attempt to present nature in this essentially "simple" manner, in which attention is directed at the object rather than the persona in an idiom that is basically traditional, is not always maintained. The first sign of the move from the simple to what might be called the sentimental is the very intrusive and indeed autobiographical presence of the persona as if to emphasize that this is a very personal recollection:

> A *green* desire, perfumed memories
> a leafy longing lure my wanderer feet
> to this green forest of a thousand wonders. (p. 3).

What, for instance, does "green" mean here? Does the persona merely yearn for the rich green of the forest? Or is the desire "green" as in Greenpeace, ie, imbued with an activist aspiration to prevent the further degradation of the earth? Either way, a profound homesickness motivates the poem and is emphasized by the use of "perfumed" to describe the persona's memories of the forest. There is here the honest admission that this account of nature is sentimentalized. This is done in the way things often are when they are played back in the mind. Thus at the end of the section, the speaker, as if to remind the reader once more that the glorious account of the forest has been the rapturous outpouring of a nostalgic mind, concludes as follows:

> And now
> Memory
> loud whisper of yester-voices
> confluence of unbroken rivers
> lower your horse of remembrance
> Let me dismount. (p. 12).

Secondly, scattered through the description of the forest, which, as I have suggested, is done in the manner of a traditional African poet, is evidence in the diction and imagery that this speaker has been schooled in English literature and other Western ways. Of this, one of the most striking is the epithet, "Coy Mistress", which the poet uses to describe *patonmo*, a plant whose small leaves fold up when touched (p. 11). The expression is a fanciful characterization that probably originates from the poet's knowledge of Andrew Marvell's poem, "To His Coy Mistress"[5]. It has the effect of an in-joke that offers something extra to those speakers who can catch the allusion. All allusions of course function in this way, proffering a significance only to those who spot them, but an African poet employing this particular kind of allusion in a description of nature that is predominantly oral in form confesses his alienation through his very rhetoric. Nature for him is not as it was or is for the untutored peasant.

There is more evidence of this hybrid rhetoric. As he contemplates the forest in its present condition, the poet remarks on the wounds inflicted by time's axes and particularly by the activities of loggers, and describes the gap left by felled trees and the tiny shrubbery crowding to fill the vacant place

> like a finger missing from a crowded hand
> swarmed by struggling shoots
> unapparent heirs to fallen heights. (p. 5).

The witty play on the English expression, 'heir apparent', to express the absence of majesty that characterizes the tiny shrubbery that seeks to replace the colossal tree which has been cut down is indeed delightful. However, while the image of the hand with a missing finger is consistent with what we have characterized as a simple presentation of nature, objectifying its subject and placing it out there for the reader's contemplation, 'unapparent heirs' is clever in a different way. It betrays the writer/speaker's mastery of the English language as such: the delight we feel in this turn of phrase is not entirely in the picture it creates, but in the verbal play itself. A similar effect is achieved when, in this encyclopedic portrait of the variety of the rain forest, the poet sings

> silent requiems
> to the vertebra of expired snakes
> *lying unstately* on the roadside turf. (p. 11). (my emphasis)

The play is on the expression "to lay in state": the skeleton of the dead snake is enjoying no such ceremony.

Beyond these instance in which the scholarly poet plays upon an English expression, there are instances where whole sections depend for their effect on the poet's learning, as in this description of an anthill:

> My parting eyes arrest the anthill,
> pyramid of the forest,
> with a queenly Pharaoh swollen
> with stony orders,
> block-headed termites building
> moatless castles, brittle turrets
> ceaselessly wounded by the arrows
> of the rain. (p. 10).

293

Here Osundare depends for his evocation of the scene not only on his knowledge of the landscape and history of Egypt, but also of medieval European architecture and warfare such as one might encounter in historical fiction such as Sir Walter Scott's *Ivanhoe*. This portrait of an anthill and its occupants is not such as a traditional Yoruba poet might paint; rather it is refracted through a prison of learning. A bookish wit and an alienated perspective are elements of Osundare's portrait of the rain forest despite the obvious effort to present it as a simple villager might. The poet's language, taken together, reveals him as a sentimental nature poet who tries to express an intimacy he had once with nature, but which is impossible to recapture. The traditional elements in his verse belong to a way of life and a relationship with nature which the educated poet can sustain only at the risk of sounding falsely traditional and of denying part of his authentic voice as a spokesman for a modern time and a modern concern with nature. The other elements of his diction which are not derived from traditional poetry indicate a different and more personalized relationship with and view of nature in which the poet directs attention away from the object described towards the beliefs and mannerisms of the speaking subject.

Finally, what overall impression of nature does the poet leave us with, given the dual perspective from which natural phenomena are viewed and the duality of the poetic voice? Perhaps in clarifying Osundare's view of nature, we might gain by recalling the example of the English Romantic poet, William Wordsworth, who like Osundare employs the recollection of boyhood scenes as a central device in his presentation of nature. For Wordsworth, nature was imbued with an in-dwelling presence which as a child he experienced without understanding, but which people, himself included, felt less and less as they grew older or as they became engaged in the furious pursuit of material well-being, what the poet called "getting and spending"[6]. A major concern of Wordsworth's work was to arrest and hold up for the reader's gaze particular scenes and moments from nature in order to reawaken wonder and joy.

As we move to summarize Osundare's nature, this may very well be a good moment to invoke Aldous Huxley's well-known comment on Wordsworth's pantheism:

> The Wordsworthian who exports...pantheistic worship
> of Nature to the tropics is liable to have his
> religious convictions rudely disturbed. Nature, under a
> vertical sun, and nourished by equatorial rains, is not
> at all like the chaste mild deity who presides over...the prettiness,
> the cosy sublimities of the lake district.[7]

Surely anyone familiar with it, knows that the rain forest is nothing if not a cathedral with the strong presence of a divinity whose face is, of course, very different from the one which is revealed in the lake district of England. One is reminded of the magical words of another famous nature poet who reflecting, as he often did, on the great variety of nature's aspects, declared that "Christ plays in ten thousand places"[8].

Not surprisingly, therefore, Osundare's nature shares with Wordsworth's the aspect of the neglected godhead. For the Nigerian poet too there is a divinity in nature to which the western educated African tends no longer to respond. Consider this vision of the rocks of his native town, Ikere, in which the massive stone is pictured as a powerful fetish priest advancing:

> The rocks rose to meet me
> with ankle bells of
> ploding pods
> and seeds scattered like a million beads; (p. 17).

or again the equally awe-inspiring personification of the earth as "the one that shaves his head with the hoe" (1), an epithet which the poet expresses directly in Yoruba. And yet the poet suggests that nature's awesome and sometimes terrifying power is unleashed only on the puny but insolent mortal who fails to show proper respect:

> Olusunta spoke first
> the elephant hand which hits the haughty man in the head
> and his testicles leak to the wondering earth. (p. 14).

But Osundare's nature is also a reservoir of many delights which he, like Wordsworth, holds up for the reader's appreciation. As is to be expected, when it comes to expressing the many delightful and fanciful aspects of nature, it is the witty and erudite language which the poet employs. We have already seen an example of this in the picture of an anthill cited earlier. Another instance is this humorous and endearing account of a stream flowing eventfully to the sea,

> tunnelling through coy caves
> descending on lowing rocks
> with the youthsome clatter
> of capering cascades
> spanning bridges of fallen mahogany

throbbing with fishlets and tadpoles
temporary semicolons hastening to
the unpunctuated period of the looming sea. (p. 7).

The cleverness here is like that of a metaphysical poet. This may not be the serenity of Wordsworth's "lake district" but it is delightful nevertheless, and the divinity revealed here is not Ogun, but a daughter of Osun. Thus in the end, the poet's two voices work together to reveal a nature which is at once imbued with awful power and delightful coyness, the tiger and the kitten, a confluence of many facets, which we destroy at our peril.

NOTES

1 Osundare, Niyi. *The Eye of the Earth*. Ibadan: Heinemann Educational Books Ltd., 1986. Subsequent page references are indicated in the text of this essay.
2 Senghor, Leopold Sedar. *Poems*. Editions du Seuil, 1964: 14.
3 von Schiller, Friedrich. "On Simple and Sentimental Poetry." Ed. W.J. Bate. *Criticism: The Major Texts*. New York: Harcourt Brace Jovanovich, Inc 1952: 408–412.
4 Shelley, Percy Bysshe. "To A Skylark." Ed. David Perkins *English Romantic Writers*. New York: Harcourt Brace Jovanovich, 1967: 1033–1035.
5 Marvell, Andrew . "To His Coy Mistress." Ed. M.H. Abrams et al. *The Norton Anthology of English Literature*, vol. 1. New York: W.W. Norton & Co., 1962: 1387.
6 Wordsworth, William."The World Is Too Much With Us." Ed. M.H. Abrams et al. *The Norton Anthology of English Literature*, vol. 2. New York: Norton, 1962: 220.
7 Huxley, Aldous. "Wordsworth in The Tropics." *Collected Works of Aldous Huxley*. London: Heinemann, 1970: 117.
8 Hopkins, Gerald Manley. "As Kingfishers Catch Fire..." Ed. W.H. Gardner *Poems and Prose*. London: Penguin, 1953: 51.

RECONSTRUCTING THE FORGOTTEN NATURE & HISTORY:APPROACHING OSUNDARE AND HIS
Horses of Memory

S. Louisa Wei

Niyi Osundare's poetry is famous for its constant praxis in poesy, its deep concern for people and its tireless meditation on Nature, words and history. His poems have been considered as "a poetic revolution or renaissance." This revolution is not only in the poet's relationship with poetic language, but also in his attitude towards poetic creation. As a new poet who rose after the civil war, Osundare takes it his responsibility to speak for/to people of Nigeria, of Africa and of the third world. His initial intention, however, remains unfulfilled, even after gaining laurels outside Africa as one of leading African poets. Since his writing is mainly in English, his poetry can hardly achieve the goal of wakening the sensibility of African people. Osundare is fully aware of this contradiction and his own limitation. Nevertheless, his poetic creation raises larger questions concerning a new definition of poetry, as well as the (im)possible reconciliation between the memory/history of Africa and western cultural hegemony.

The goal of this essay is threefold. First, I shall examine Osundare's ideal and praxis of poetry. Then I will analyze Osundare's reflections on memory and poetic vision of history. Finally, I will demonstrate how, by taking the artistic stance of "people's poet," Osundare returns poetry to his people and makes a statement against the postcolonial cultural invasion. My arguments will be mainly based on a reading of Osundare's 1998 collection, *Horses of Memory*.

NATURE ON SURFACE AND IN STRUCTURE: A "TOTAL" POETRY

The first thing that impresses readers of Osundare's poetry is probably its pervasive use of natural imageries. Osundare depicts the many faces of Nature in vivid personifications while constructing his reflections of history, nation and words. His imageries create a lyricism that is as nostalgic as it is anticipating, carrying a special flavor that is enchanting to modern readers, regardless of their country of origin. Osundare's poetic language not only includes a large vocabulary related to the rural-agrarian culture and natural phenomena, but also a number of proverbs and metaphors taken from the African languages and traditions. His expression of the "green desire" and his concern for the endangered earth as well as the endangered people also reveal a great compassion that can be shared by a global readership.

Indeed, Nature has been the most inspiring source for all great poets in the world. Osundare's delineation of Nature stands out not only through a unique vision that links sensitivity to sensibility, but also by adopting metaphors and proverbs from the oral literature (or orature) of Africa. Compared to his forerunners such as Soyinka and Okigbo, Osundare comes closer to the African tradition in his emphasis on the lyricism. His desire to produce poetry that is close to traditional poetry and to reject poetry that is too intellectual, erudite and elitist, comes early in his poetic career. In "Poetry Is", the opening poem of his first published collection, he rejects the kind of poetry written by his predecessors on the Nigerian poetic scene as too inaccessible to be good poetry. Let us look at how Osundare uses natural imagery to describe his ideal of poetry and reject the "learned" poetry.

> Poetry is not
> the esoteric whisper
> of an excluding tongue
> not a claptrap
> for a wondering audience
> not a learned quiz
> entombed in Graeco-Roman lore
>
> Poetry is
> A life-spring
> Which gathers timbre

The more throats it plucks
Harbinger of action
The more minds it stirs

Poetry is
The hawker's ditty
The eloquence of the gong
The lyric of the marketplace
The luminous ray
On the grass's morning dew

Poetry is
What the soft wind
Music to the dancing leaf
What the sole tells the dusty path
What the bee hums to the alluring nectar
What rainfall croons to the lowering eaves

Poetry is
No oracle's kernel
For a sole philosopher's stone

Poetry
Is
Man
Meaning
To
Man.

This poem is often read as a manifesto of Osundare's poetics. It illustrates his ideal of poetry at three levels. First, as the "luminous ray/On the grass's morning dew," poetry is the language that speaks through lyricism, through the images of Nature: "What the soft wind/Music to the dancing leaf." This language is direct, elegant, and accessible to all, revealing the appreciation of natural landscapes to which we often turn a blind eye. Second, poetry is not "an excluding tongue" just for the learned, but rather, the "hawker's ditty," the "eloquence of the gong" and the "lyric of the marketplace" about our daily life and meditation. Osundare assumes the role of a "people's poet" and determines to return poetry to people. Third, poetry should aim at a communication, at stirring more minds: it is "man meaning to man." In order to achieve this goal, the poet often includes dialogues between his poetic personae and employs many sequences of questions and answers. The following is a more detailed analysis of Osundare's poetic traits.

As we can see in *Horses of Memory* and other collections, Osundare frequently uses two types of figures of speech to structure his poems. One is the sequence of question and answer. The other is parallel. While his very short poems often contain a single metaphor or one sequence of question and answer, his long poems are generally a combination of restless parallels and question-answer sequences.

The use of parallels is perhaps the most distinct formal feature of Osundare's poetry, which provides his work with a compelling vigor. Natural images are "structured in parallels," just as colors and images are painted on the canvas to create a landscape with a contemplation, pointing to the deeper meaning of words while celebrating the power of poetic form. Parallels allow the poet to elaborate on his senses and thoughts and to fully disclose the depth and many faces of feelings. The following stanza is a proof of the formal perfection that Osundare's parallels achieve, which is comparable with the strict and neat parallels that can only be found in early Chinese poetry.

Dawns of eastering suns	Twilight of hurrying moons
Dawns of inchoate beams	Twilight of capricious fires
Dawns of mysty dreams	Twilight of bearded visions
Dawns of umbilical lairs	Twilight of mellow-dies (p. 7).

Osundare's parallels are not only neat in form but also metaphorically gracious. The restraint of form in his parallels sharply contrasts to his question-answer sequence(s) where voices of interlocutors burst out. For the poet, the path to truth lies in the constant dialogue between heaven and earth, between river and road, between man and Nature: where the surface of natural images subsides, the urge in truth seeking takes over. Thus, there is a sensual and/or rational strength that comes through the parallels, with no less power than the heart racing drumbeats or the "voiceover" in the biblical poems.

Besides transforming traditional proverbs, metaphors and other devices of prosody into contemporary usage in language, the poet also introduces poetry in performance, achieving what some have called "a poetic revolution or renaissance." At the beginning of many poems, he gives instructions on the construction of a "soundtrack" as a way to reinforce his vision, indicating an accompaniment of gongs, drums and strings, with male and female vocals or a chorus with many voices. Osundare said that when he performed at home, he has an orchestra.

The audience hears the music in the background but the words coming from the poet are not lost. People come to the performance because they want to be entertained. The music entertains them but the words of the poem educate them. The two go hand in hand. One of the richest things that Africa has is music or lyricism.

Yet, readers with no experience of African oral performances may not be able to bridge the gap between the poet's version of the performed poem and their own marriage of his vision and sound, but the gap is part of the text that stimulates various possible readings. In other words, how the "soundtrack" incorporates with the poet's vision is largely left to the reader, evoking a rather demanding yet interesting act of reading which requires readers to literally "break the silence." In a similar way, words or lines in Yoruba language within Osundare's English poems also create a special voice, which is like a distinctive solo vocal floating on top of the chorus. This vocal enhances the musical quality of his poems no less than the music instruments, providing a unique experience to readers. Although it is not clear which lines are sung or recited by what kind of voice or chorus, the participation of many voices also calls for the encountering of what Bakhtin calls polyglossia and/or polyphony.

Therefore, the "revolution" in Osundare's poetry is actually a returning to the root, to the oral tradition of Africa. The choice of writing in English, however, does not make the "return" or the "revolution" an easy task. Osundare observes that when "poets read their work, in Yoruba, for example, they get a kind of reaction from the audience which is really electrifying;" but when using the English language, poets such as him "are cut off from this reaction." On the other hand, "oral literature is at its best when it is oral and when participants are face to face. Once we write, there is an intervention. Then one is not creating oral literature as much as using its resources to fit the conventions of written literature." Like many artists from the third world, Osundare is facing a dilemma in the era of postcolonial culture. As I will argue later in my concluding section, his limitation is as well where his strength comes from.

Concerning what poetry is, and, how it should be performed, the Chinese and western traditions seem to stand at opposite poles. In the "Great Preface" of *Shi Jing*, the first collection of Chinese poetry often translated as *The Book of Songs* or *The Classic of Poetry*, poetry is defined this way:

> The poem is that to which what is intently on the mind goes.
> In the mind it is "being intent"; coming out in language, it is
> a poem. The affections are stirred within and take on form in
> words. If words alone are inadequate, we speak them out in
> sighs. If sighing is inadequate, we sing them. If singing them

is inadequate, unconsciously our hands dance them and our
feet tap them.

While ancient Chinese critics assert that poetry comes from within, they set the
tone that the intent deserves more respect than the words. Following this vein,
later poets gradually started to emphasize on a praxis that can help to catch the
"spirit" of Nature and feelings. Aristotle's definition of poetry in his *Poetics*, on
the other hand, emphasizes the action as the primary form of expression:
Now, epic and tragic poetry, as well as comedy and dithyramb (and most music
for the pipe or lyre) are all, taken as a whole, kinds of *mimesis*. But they differ
from one another in three respects: namely, in the *media* or the *objects* or the
mode of *mimesis*.

Aristotle not only defines arts as different kinds of *mimesis* but also evaluates
works of art according to how well the *mimesis* works. For instance, he thinks
tragedy is better than epic since it allows more than one voice and thus represents reality in a better way. In this vein, art is perfection in imitation.
Osundare points to a poetic that comes between the Chinese and Western traditions. As Chinese lyrics, his poems juxtapose natural images with human feelings, transforming the images as expressions of the heart. Meanwhile,
Osundare uses personifications extensively and creates dialogues between his
poetic personae. As in the western tradition, the interaction between the poet
and the audience is explicitly encouraged. Therefore, without sacrificing the elegance and sentiment of lyricism, Osundare's poetry involves rather dramatic
dialogues and question-answer sequences that are as eloquent and powerful as
biblical poetry.

Osundare's poetic ideal, as he reflects in "Poetry Is" and other poems, is one
of a "total" poetry. As most poets of the new "alter-native" tradition in Nigeria,
Osundare has "adopted the diction of ordinary speech" in place of the "learned,
allusive pedantry of much of the poetic diction of the pre-Civil War poets." What
is extraordinary about Osundare's poetry is that he "has kept his metaphoric
and semantic range copiously wide" without losing the clarity and simplicity of
his poetic language. This makes his poems very translatable and thus they have
the potential for a larger global readership. Readers from various cultural backgrounds can always identify certain elements from his poetry, either aesthetic
or thematic, either his deep concern for people of Africa or his celebration of
poetry as a "peopled history," as I will further demonstrate in the following discussion.

HORSES OF MEMORY: A POET OF HISTORY

Osundare's poetry collection, *Horses of Memory*, has many poems that ponder upon memory, remembrance and history. Although thematically speaking, these poems are hardly one of a kind, Osundare marks his difference by reflecting history around the image of "horses." For him, "Word" is the vehicle of poetry, a horse that a poet can ride on; poetry is also a vehicle of history, a horse that leaves traces of remembrance. As some subtitles of the book suggest, the horse can "gallop," "canter" or "kick" on its path that leads to truths, resembling various rhythms in poetry and reconstructing a poet's vision of history. Furthermore, as Osundare indicates in the opening poem of the collection, "For the One Who Departed," even when the poet dies and the dust settles under his feet, the horse of his Word will continue to run from the past to the future.

As a scholar poet, Osundare has a "preoccupation with artistic quality" and an "obsession with 'playing' with language, with words and metaphors." His frequent reflections upon Word are best illustrated in the following stanzas taken from "For the One Who Departed:"

> The Word was your horse:
>> Your rode it through fire, through frenzy
>> Through waters of silver depths
>
>> The Word was your horse:
>> Your rode it through echoing hills
>> Through valleys of flowery songs
>
>> The Word was your horse:
>> You rode it through bristling seas
>> Through lakes with merciless shells
>
>> The Word was your horse:
>> You rode it through zebu-humped clouds
>> Through streets of dripping knives
>
> The Word was your horse:
>> You rode it through rock through steel
>> Through quarries of dreaming metal

> The Word was your horse:
>> You were the Word which fell from the sky
>> And, touching earth, broke
>> Into a thousand truths
>
> You were the Word
> Which shot the deer
> Before the hunter's gun

In this poem, "You" refers to the poet's father. Osundare's feelings toward his late father are expressed again through paralleled imageries. The father is indeed another poet, and thus, the memory of the father also becomes one poet's memory of another, casting the light of self-reflexiveness with a nostalgic sentiment. The poem summarizes his father's life journey as well as his poetic one. During both journeys, he rode the horse through "echoing hills" and "flowery valleys," through times of "fire" and "frenzy," through "streets of dripping knives" and "quarries of dreaming metal," observing the sharp contrast between beautiful natural landscapes and ugly social realities. After five stanzas of parallels starting with "The Word was your horse," the poet claims twice that "You were the Word," making a powerful statement that the poet is the Word and thus the horse.

In another excerpt from "Memory Chips," the poet further explores the concept of Word by declaring that,

> Words, too, have memory:
>
> A pinnaful of verbs labouring
> Up the precipice of the head
>
> A canoe of nouns in the promontory
> Of forgotten seas
>
> Silence's echo is
> Louder than thunder (p. 57).

For Osundare, Word has a life and memory to its own right, and what are left from history are, sometimes, merely words. His tireless reflections on words are not only due to his awareness of the power of words, but also because of his sense of responsibility as "the public poet [and] the town-crier." Osundare is an artist who makes every effort to construct an "ideological creed." He is never overtly didactic since he never attempts to pin down the meaning of words. He lets his words seek their own meaning and emphasizes the perfection in his poetic praxis.

The entire *Horses of Memory* is constructed around the pole of the memory/history, which is shaped and reshaped through oral poetry, written history and simple remembrance. Osundare's "horses" are running through a matrix of reality with its own complexity and integrity. The concept of history serves as the axis of this matrix, relating to other types of narration such as songs, stories, and memories. Osundare often uses indicators such as "road," "river," "heaven" and "earth" to locate a path that leads to the truth in search of lost memories. In his poetic world, memory rotates with the sun and the moon, extends along the roads and the rivers, fills the hearts and the valleys, expands between the sky and the earth, and, speaks of life and death. The turning of seasons lends the poet an eye on the turning of pages of history.

As the poet points out more than once, human remembrance is often defeated by oblivion and thus, the history repeats its most unpleasant plots and details. The poet cries for remembrance, laments on the forgotten history and expresses regrets towards the oblivious nature of human beings, as we can read in "Memory's Street:"

> The rain has beaten us. The rain has beaten us
> Not once. Not twice. Not thrice.
> The rain has beaten us a million seasons
> Now the cloud has eaten the sun
> The sky is carnival of bleeding sharfs. (p. 38).

Osundare believes that the "future is/ a past/ we often forget to re-/member" (p. 45). He faces the cruel reality of Africa, but still keeps the hope for people. As he said in an interview, that is the duty of an artist.

> There are yet those who, because they have been beaten by the rain for such a long time, do not believe it is possible for them to get a place to dry their clothes, and themselves, and their spirit. I think these are the people the artist is really trying to touch, to let them know about the possibility of change, to let them know that, although our sky is overcast at the moment, there is some sun, some rainbow, possible in the firmament. I think this is the role of the artist.

Osundare assumes the role of such an artist by putting together the picture of a past that is often forgotten. He hopes to waken those who were "beaten by the rain" and to encourage in them the idea that the sunshine is not just a dream. For Osundare, history is not just in the past tense. It is an event, a moment, or even a persona that may come to meet us at any time with different faces. In a poem titled "Metamorphosis," the poet warns us that,

> Sometimes
> History enters the night
> As a sheep,
> Waking up
> As a wolf (p. 114).

In another poem written "For Festus Iyayi," the poet describes history as "an actor/ in a room/ with a thousand mirrors."

> And so
>
> Tyranny
> may be long,
> History is
> Always
> l
> o
> n
> g
> e
> r (p. 115).

Thus, in a sense, history is a continuation from the past to the present, from the present to the future. History will outlive any tyranny and injustice. Osundare often personifies history as the persona "History," who is both male and female and reincarnates even after experiencing the grave. In "End of History," he wrote:

> Old truths tumble—
> On the compost of newer Truths
>
> And sunset pundits swear
> They have climbed the mountain

And see History's grave
In the elbow of misty valleys

...

Today I look History in the face
His/her brow a taut membrane
Of inexhaustible riddles

Today I look History
In the face
And I remember the child in the tale
Who touched the elephant's tail
Vowing he has seen everything
About the giant of the forest (pp. 51–2).

In the same vein, the poet challenges History's true value and existence by inter-rogating it in the face:

We shall look History
in the face,
probe every pore
of its shadows,
thresh its depths
for nomadic grains...

Inter
rogate its silences (p. 116)

The last and title poem of the collection, "Horses of Memory," summarizes both the issues with which Osundare is concerned and his poetic traits. Inspired by Kofi Awoonor's line, "Ride me, memory," he once again portrays memory with his most eloquent lyricism, blending expressive imageries with a dialogic diction—a sequence of questions asked by the "Grey One." The poet claims, "the rain is/ memory of the drought," "the desert is/ the memory of the sea," and "the egg, is/ the memory of the hen." He suggests that the fifth or last sec-tion of this poem should be performed with "strings, horns, drums, and voices in final flourish" (p. 130). He calls the reader to ride with him, with words, and with horses of memory. Images such as "echoing hills" and "bristling fires" reappear in this poem, making us missing the moments when we were touched by his depiction of very usual things that possess an unusual beauty, such as the laughter of a golden bell, and a nightscape of the moon and stars. In other words, we already have a nostalgic feeling towards reading the poems before the book comes to an end. This is how Osundare invites participation of both his life experience and his poetic journey. It is for the "demystification" qualities that Osundare's poetry is considered a "peopled history," or, the history written by a people's poet.

RECONSTRUCTING THE FORGOTTEN NATURE AND HISTORY

Before I conclude, I want to further discuss a question raised earlier in the essay. Namely, how should we look at the contradiction between Osundare's intention to write for Nigerian people and his choice of writing in English? This issue has become one that concerns both the artistic and ideological stance of any serious artist (especially those from the third world) who wants to have his/her own place in the postcolonial discourse. Writers before Osundare had already been facing the dilemma, as he observes closely:

> Our pioneers were very hard working. They promoted literature in English but, at the same time, they undermined the potentiality of that literature by the kind of medium which they chose. ... Some of these poems were extremely difficult, particularly those by Soyinka and Okigbo. [When reading them, our] enthusiasm soon fizzled out. When I started writing, this negative influence was in my mind and I felt it was the duty of the new generation of Nigerian poets to bring poetry back to people. Since everything about our culture is lyrical and musical, how come, when we put this in written form, we alienate the people who created the material in the first instance?

What we can read between the lines here is that a poet like Osundare has to face more than one choice. First, he has to choose a "medium" of communication. Osundare chooses one that comes closer to the orature tradition, using not only metaphors, proverbs and parables from African tradition but also certain traits or prosody. He writes about and for African people, taking sources of inspiration from them rather than showing off his erudition of western literature or celebrating its narcissistic intertextuality. His preference in oral poetry is an artistic stance that is also political: he does not want to alienate the people from his own culture just as his forerunners did not attempt to avoid it. Second, the poet has to choose a language. Osundare chooses English although the decision is not an easy one.

It seems that within the specific genre of poetry all the problems of a literature, which arose from the womb of colonial society and is still struggling to free itself from the ambiguous legacies of its origins, achieve their most concentrated form.

Poetry cannot speak through images as films can. It needs a vehicle of language. Even though Osundare's English poems cannot reach a majority of African people, and it seems that his strong audience consciousness is largely unfulfilled due to his choice of English, his strength also comes from this choice. If he writes in Yuroba, for example, he would not achieve what he has achieved outside Africa, and he would not be able to help in attracting attention to African literature. Thus, the poet is acting as a culture translator, besides playing the role as the town-crier in Nigeria by devoting to a "verse journalism" that keeps the poetry in touch with people's daily life and concerns. As if to compensate for the loss caused by his choice of writing in English, Osundare writes a column in *Nigerian Tribune* to show this strong commitment to people in Africa.

If we understand Osundare's artistic and ideological stance, we can better understand why he never stops writing about the forgotten Nature and History. In Osundare's poetic world, History is versus Nature in the sense that Nature is an eternally unchanged reminder of the latter, while History has to fight for its true existence to maintain the well being of Nature. Therefore, when Nature is forgotten due to industrialization and other causes, part of our History is also forgotten. For the poet, memory can take numerous shapes, from road and river, to sea and mountain, and to words that possess the sheer joy of experiences. In this sense, no matter which language Osundare chooses to write, his poetic depiction of Nature and History will remain as part of the new tradition. He writes about forgotten Nature and History so we will not forget our past, which will meet us again in the future.

REFERENCES

Aiyejina, Funso. "Recent Nigerian poetry in English: an alternative tradition" *The Guardian* 11 April 1985: 9.

Arnold, Stephen H. "The Praxis of Niyi Osundare, Popular Scholar-Poet." *World Literature Written in English*, vol. 29.1 (1989): 1–7.

Bamikunle, Aderemi. "Niyi Osundare's Poetry and the Yoruba Oral Artistic Tradition." Eds. Eldred Durosimi Jones, Eustance Palmer and Marjorie Jones. *Orature in African Literature Today*, No. 18, 1992.

Birbalsingh, Frank. "Interview with Niyi Osundare." *Présence Africaine* 147 (1988): 95–104.

Ezenwa-Ohaeto. "Survival Strategies and the New Life of Orality in Nigerian and Ghanaian Poetry: Osundare's *Waiting Laughters* and Anyidoho's *Earthchild*." *Research in African Literature* 27.2 Summer 1996: 70–82.

———. "Dimensions of Language in New Nigerian Poetry." *The Question of Language in African Literature Today* 17 (1991): 155–64.

Halliwell, Stephen. trans. *The* Poetics *of Aristotle: Translation and Commentary*. Chapel Hill: UP, 1987.

Biodun Jeyifo. "Niyi Osundare." Ed. Yemi Ogunbiyi. *Perspectives on Nigerian Literature: 1700 to the Present*, vol. 2. Lagos: Guardian Books, 1988.

J.O.J. Nwachukwu-Agbada. "The Language of Post-war Nigerian Poetry of English Expression." *The Question of Language in African Literature Today* 17 (1991): 165–75.

Owen, Stephen. *Readings in Chinese Literary Thought*. Cambridge: Harvard UP, 1992.

NIYI OSUNDARE'S
PERFORMANCE NOTES

Abdul-Rasheed Na'Allah

INTRODUCTION

Almost every critic of Osundare extols how wonderful a performance poet he is, usually citing the involvement of oral traditions in his poetry. If asked several times, the Canadian Steven Arnold is likely to repeat that Osundare's involvement in performance poetry comes from his consciousness of civic responsibility, and from Osundare's efforts to remain at the same level as his people. He might also add, though, that Osundare's people's sense of poetry is fulfilled through performance (Arnold "A Peopled Persona"). British scholar Stewart Brown would go further to say that Osundare is celebrating the Yorubanness in his English writing. Osundare wants to tell the British that he is beyond being domesticated in Britain (Na'Allah, 1999: 63).

It is practically impossible for Osundare to suspend dancing, beating of drums, playing flutes, or *goje*, when performing his poetry – even when his refrains are not written in Yoruba language, as they often are not, like in his "Songs of the Season" column in the *Tribune* newspaper ("Bard" 1–47), or when Osundare does not add any refrain at all. Yoruba musical rhythm is the blood that flows in his veins, as it does in African traditional drumming, fluting, and dancing. Osundare and many of his contemporaries, Tanure Ojaide and Kofi Anyidoho to name only a few, have demonstrated what it means for modern

African poetry to get fulfilled through song and performance, and unfulfilled in being read or recited! Yet, as Biodun Jeyifo once asserts, Osundare's poetry "is a distinct revolution within the new poetic revolution" (p. 315). Tanure Ojaide, in explaining why their generation of poets break away from the mystic past (what has been termed the mysticism of the Nigerian poetry in English), says that as a new generation, they must recognize the need for dialogue with the people, to tell Nigerians that poetry in English is sweet and beautiful, and that it belongs to the people (pp. 17–31). Ojaide says the new poets heavily adopt voices of village singers, and sing about the common problems of ordinary persons. Although the poets still speak and write in the colonial language, they want to reduce the gap between themselves and the ordinary African. This is what Addison Gales would call the de-Westernization of African poetry (Ojaide, 1996: 17). Funso Aiyejina calls it the "Alter-native tradition" ("Niyi Osundare" 315. See also several papers in this volume, including Abdel-Malek).

Ojaide's explanations of the performance quality in oral poetry clearly define the aesthetic composition of modern African poetry:

> The inherent performance quality of oral poetry has bearing on the aesthetic composition of modern African poetry. As I have mentioned of the Urhobo udje practice, the poet and cantor, composer and performer, may not necessarily be the same person but are likely to be. Even when they are different, they are mindful of the other's presence. In other words, verbal composition and performance are intricately related. Since the modern poet is more likely to perform his/her own poetry, these performance qualities are built into the poem... The story told in a poem engenders its own dramatics. Much extemporization is still a part of written African poetry as songs or refrains are extended in poetry readings. The relationship between audience and performer which is controlled in the West is more spontaneous in Africa. Modern African poets attempt to involve their audience, and this also influences the compositional process. (pp. 24–5)

In other words, contemporary African poetry tells stories, uses refrains, and often involves audience participation. Ojaide is right when he says that the poems engender drama. Like the modern African dramatists' exploration of African tradition of the total theatre where songs, mime, drumming, dance, and dialogue are sythesized on stage, contemporary poetry of Osundare, Ojaide, and Anyidoho, is a total theatre performance. Says Ojaide, "Though the post-independent generation of Awoonor, Okigbo, Clark, and Soyinka was indebted to the oral tradition, it is with the new generation of poets that orality has become a distinctive mark of West African poetry" (pp. 34–5).

Osundare is a lucky man![1] He was born into a peasant community, by a peasant mother, to a peasant poet-father. Osundare schooled in oral performance as an apprentice under his own father. Similar to a Dadakuada apprenticeship process (see "Dadakuada as Oral Art of Ilorin"), he earned his "oral degree" from his father's oral poetry and cultural institution, singing, drumming and performing to his father's admiration: *Omo eni nju eni lo*, one's child does grow to be greater than one. Osundare constantly demsontrates his oral poetry skills, and carries his Ikere-Ekiti performance signature around the world. His native roots have continually been a source of strength to him, and like all of his contemporaries, he produces masterpieces of what Ojaide describes as "oral" poems (Ojaide, 1996: 3).

Osundare is also influenced by the English dramatic tradition because from a young age, he acted on stage at High School. He still has a strong interest in drama (see "The Plays of Niyi Osundare"). He has written some plays, including *The State Visit* — performed for his fiftieth birthday in March 1997 (see "L'Etat Cest Mois") –*The Wedding Car*, and *The Man Who Walked Away*. It is therefore easy for Osundare to dramaticize and visualize himself as dramatist even as he writes poetry. He said to me during a recent interview, "When poetry came to dominate (my work), it came in dramatic terms. And for me, poetry and music cannot do without the other."[2] Just as playwrights use stage direction to give producers hints, clues, and descriptions of settings, actors, costumes, etc., Osundare adopts what I call "performance notes," usually in parentheses immediately following poems title or as parenthetical statements between poetry lines or stanzas or as footnotes or endnotes.

CHARACTERISTICS OF OSUNDARE'S PERFORMANCE NOTES

Drama critics often complain about complications, confusions, and inefficiencies of stage directions. Some stage directions leave producers confused about what meaning to place behind a character's action. When reading from a text, one starts asking questions about what has led to a particular action suddenly noted on stage direction. In Alan Dessen's *Elizabethan Stage Conventions and Modern Interpreters*, Dessen remarks on some of Shakespeare's stage directions. He writes,

> To work with these stage directions, however, especially in the best known plays, is quickly to encounter frustation and con-

fusion. Thus, many scenes in which meaning is closely linked to decisions about staging have no directions whatsoever (as in the nunnery scene in *Hamlet* where the reader today can never be certain when Hamlet becomes aware of the eaves-droppers, if, indeed, he notices them at all). Moreover, the signals that <u>are</u> provided often are uninformative or confusing or inconsistent (as with the many situations where a character is given no <u>exit</u> but nonetheless is directed to <u>re-enter</u> — e.g., Osris at the close of *Hamlet*. Such murkiness is characteristic not only of printed text ... but also of those texts and manuscripts that actually may have been used as the basis for performance. (p. 23)

However, as Dessen later noted, some dramatists try to be as clear as possible in their manuscripts, but the editor or the playhouse director imposes his/her own conventions and alters some of the playwright's specific directions (Dessen, 1984: 23). In other cases producers over use their initiatives and creativity by portraying a meaning different from the one intended by the playwright. Wole Soyinka's protest about an American producer's rendition of *Death and the King's Horseman* is a good example (Soyinka 5–6).

Niyi Osundare and other modern African poets may not have to face imposition from playhouse practices or over anxious producers. Performance notes are very minimal in African poetry books, and the performer has a greater responsibility to use his or her initiatives to bring the poetry alive. However, the performance note is the most cogent and authoritative piece of information about a particular poem. Often it is the detail in the process of performance which the performer is called to implement. This may be the modern African poet's way of showing that the performer of African written poetry is an innovator, like the African oral poet, and should employ performance skills in such a way that makes every performance unique. Performance notes are often a sentence or two, or short phrases in parentheses. The notes basically do the following:

1. give hints and define the type of performance modes required
2. performance tools such as musical instruments, etc.
3. locate the cultural roots of the poem
4. indicate poet's dedications, and sometimes give epigraphs
5. provide translations and explanations of uses of non-European words and concepts

Performance notes often show the poet's commitment to his people's cultural requirements, and indicate the poet's desire for the performer to follow his own recommended performance modes. In my discussions[3] with Niyi Osundare, he identifies that his intentions for using performance notes include the desire to show the following:

1. the mood expected for the performance of his poems (e.g. happy, sad)
2. particular situations addressed in the poem, (e.g. oppression, drought)
3. occasions addressed by the poem, (e.g. new yam festival, raining season, court trial)
4. philosophical beliefs and postulations of the poem

It is very crucial for the performer of a modern African poem, whether in classrooms, or in open public forums, to respect the poet's notes in order to realize the full impact intended for the performance. The Yoruba art theory is very relevant here[4]:

a kìì wo batà
ba won jo batá

One does not wear shoes
to dance to bata drumming

To understand some implications of the above poetics, it is useful to go back to Tanure Ojaide:

> Most traditional African songs/poems are composed for specific events and therefore relate some ideas. The impact of the meaning of the song is always a primary consideration. The traditional African poet is generally a communicator of ideas in a musical way ... while in America and British poetry, musicality can be in-built at the expense of meaning in the rhymes and other figures of sound such as alliteration and assonance, in traditional African poetry musicality is not expected to be in-built in the verbal structure. Rather, it is an addition, an ornament, left for the falsetto voice to intone ... The emphasis is ... on the meaning rather than the musicality of words.

The parallelism in *batà* and *batá* adds color to the poetic rendition of the adage – the change of tone from *batà* to *batá*, and the play on words from *batà*, shoes, to *batá*, a kind of musical drumming, increases the musicality and artistic richness of the adage. Yet, Yoruba culture places more importance to its meaning over its "musicality." In a way, this is an artistic law, and a cultural philosophy.5

To dance to the *batá* ritual music, one of the rules is not having *batà* on. Now, does batá music have any metaphysical or spiritual significance? How important is wearing shoes or not wearing shoes when dancing to music among the Yoruba? I have heard stories that the *batá* drum is made of a special kind of skin. There are some myths and mysticism about the process of the drum's production. If a person dances to *batá* music with his/her shoes on, will that result in tragedy? Or is it just a way to show that shoes are an impediment to a free, artistically and culturally involving dance?

The *batá* adage shows that expectations are clearly laid out in Yoruba poetics for the artistic responsibility of the Yoruba poet. Although the poet enjoys some freedom to innovate, specific guidelines exist for organizing and identifying every performance. For example, there could be rules such as, "this is how we dance this dance," "this is the drum pattern we beat to this song," "we use only *bembe* drum in this dance," "flute is the appropriate musical tool to this song," "*sakara* and *goje* are the main tools we use here," and so on.

Respecting the instructions in the performance notes is one way that a performer can respect African cultural and aesthetic requirements during every performance. Like in stage direction, the writer knows his or her culture well and gives a clearer picture of his intentions and expectations in the performance of his poetry. The musical tone for the expression of grief among the British may not be the kind the Yoruba use for grief. The kind of calculations that warn the French dancer to change to another dancing step may be nonsensical to the Hausa dancer. The Russians may not have a provision for a change in the guitar tune to change to new dance modes, but the Zulus on the dancing floor listen closely for such an artistic signal. Here is a Yoruba musical theory,

> B'orin bati yi,
> Ki'lu naa yi pada
>
> Once the song changes
> The drumming has to change

There are expectations that mood does change in the peak of performances. New seasons come in as old ones bid their "Now Let us Depart." Oral performances and musical sounds must change to fit new seasons, and drumming tempo must change to fit changes in songs. When the drumming changes, the dancing steps must also change. The *b'orin bayi* adage is thus another example of the artistic conventions of the Yoruba, and like the *batá* adage, it provides a guiding principle for artistic creativity as the musical current rises up and down. Later in this paper, I shall show that Niyi Osundare is very mindful of all these artistic laws as he composes his poems and uses performance notes to guide future performers. Most modern African poets use performance notes to reduce the gap between traditional oral performance and the written text.

I have already explained that the modern African poetry teacher still uses his/her wisdom and artistic judgment whenever he/she teaches modern African poetry in the classroom. For example, if the poet recommends *gangan* for performing a particular poem, and this type of Yoruba drum is not available in the classroom, students can be told what *gangan* drum is (perhaps a picture of *gangan* drum may be brought to class), and they may then be asked to beat their tin-canes from under their armpits or on their tables pretending they are making music from *gangan* drum. However, it is most important that teachers of modern African poetry should have *goje, iyalu, fere, gangan, dundun, bembe, agogo, sakara, batá*, and other kinds of African musical tools in their school's resource room. Wherever active dance, opera-like performance or more than one voice is required, every performance of modern African poetry must strive to satisfy these requirements. A call and response poem requiring audience participation should not be performed by a single performer, or worse, be recited as if it's an English sonnet. Even where a performer can use voice modulation, it is still preferable that a call and response poem is given its right due of audience participation. Changing one's voice, though a great artistic talent, does not satisfy the requirement for audience involvement.

SAMPLE PERFORMANCE NOTES IN OSUNDARE'S POETRY
The following are sample performance notes from some of Osundare's poetry collections.

A Nib in the Pond:
Very few performance notes are used in this volume:

    1. "Shaping Clay" Footnotes: "GRA – Government Reservation Areas(exclusive, privileged)." (*Selected Poems*, 6–7).

2. "Like the Bee" Parenthesis: (after Francis Bacon) – dedication. The poet focuses on the qualities of the bee, comparing it to the spider and the wood-insect; perhaps celebrating what Francis Bacon is, and refuting what he is not (p. 8).

3. "Atewolara" Parenthesis: (for Tunde Odunlade) – dedication. Footnote: "atewolara – the hand is the best companion" (p. 13).

4. "The Worrior of Change". Parenthsis: (for Balarabe Musa) –- dedication. The poet celebrates the steadfastness of Balarabe. Perhaps written in the Nigerian second republic when Balarabe dared the NPN House of Assembly and was impeached from office as Governor of Kaduna State (p. 19). Footnote: "iroko" – "large tree found in the forest; also called 'the African oak'"

5. "Noon Yet" Parenthesis: (for Femi Ogunmola) – dedication. Perhaps the poet is also praying for Ogunmola – that he will not die young.

The Eye of the Earth
More performance notes are used here. Only a few will be discussed:

1. "Earth" Footnote: "ogééré amókóyeri – the one that shaves his head with the hoe" Without this note, it may be extremely difficult for a non-Yoruba speaker to know this meaning, or the image intended by this phrase (*Selected Poems,* 30).

2. "From Forest Echoes" Parenthesis: (with flute and heavy drums). A mixture of flute and heavy drum perhaps signifying celebration of the fertile earth – harvest? If flute alone, the mood could be solemn or sad, but the introduction of heavy drumming to it reflects more the festive nature of the poem (p. 32).

3. "The Rocks Rose to Meet Me" Parentheses:
I: (To be chanted with agba drum throbing in the background).
II: (The drums quieting)

In the first performance note, the specific drum required is mentioned. The fact that it should be in the background is important – obviously the message of the poem must not be overwhelmed by the music.

The second note shows a performance note giving hints of quieting the drumming in the middle or peak of performance. The sudden quieting of drumming will create some important effects. Perhaps the performance is getting highly spiritual or the poet just wants the quieting of drumming to enable the voice of the performer to be heard more boldly.

Footnote: "Olosunta -- a huge, imposing rock in Ikere, worshipped yearly during the popular Olosunta festival; reputed to be a repository of gold"

Footnote: "Oroole -- a pyramid-shaped rock; also in Ikere"

4. "Harvest" Parentheses:
   I: (To be chanted to lively batá music). This is definitely a hint about a festival – celebration of the eating of new yams. II: (Music lowers in tempo, becoming solemn). Here the poet is introducing a sad mood – sadness for the disappearance of food in the farms, at home – perhaps drought, perhaps uncultivated lands, etc. The changing of the drumming tempo creates multiple dramatic effects. A similar note can be seen in the poem "Our Earth Will Not Die" (p. 50), with tune changing, but this time becoming louder in the peak of performance, (music turns festive, louder) indicating a happier situation. This is a good example of how Osundare observes the Yoruba's *b'orin bayi* poetics.
   Footnote: "efùrù – the king of yams"
   Footnote: "aróso, fèrègèdè, ò tíí lí, pàkalà all four are types of beans"
5. "Let Earth's Pain be Soothed" Parentheses:
   I: (For the one who brought rainy news Under-the-Rock) – dedication; invocation. This poem is an invocation for rain. It is an exploration of the earth's pain when the earth is without rain that soothes its womb. "Our earth has never lingered so dry/ in the season of falling showers" (pp. 41–2).

The poet's use of "rainy-news" in this note indicates a dedication to one who brings food during drought, who gives others hope when everyone is hopeless, or who mobilizes others for a positive change, when it's almost impossible to find any responsible leadership genuinely mobilizing others for change – one who can go "Under-the Rock" to get water to assuage the people's thirst.

II: (To the accompaniment of a flute and/or the rain drum). Performance hints: Here the writer gives the performer an option – a choice between using one or both of the instruments. With flute alone, the performer might have chosen to retain a sad and solemn mood throughout the piece. However, if the performer chooses to mix-up the instruments, the mood could be a little bit different.

Moonsongs
There are several performance notes in this volume. However, only a few will be discussed.

1. "I" Parenthesis: (To the accompaniment of lively *woro* drumming. The following song in call-and-response).
   Pèreé O Péré yoju l'órun
   > Agbamúréré
   > (2 times)
   Asèsèyo osù óda bi egbin
   > Agbamúréré
   Ka kósu kóbi ka lo mú saya
   > Agbamúréré
   Kátódébe ó ti b'ójó lo
   > Agbamúréré
   Kirìj kírìjì pepelúpe
   > Agbamúréré

   Celebration, moonlight, and lively woro drumming indicate it's a very happy occasion. Audience involvement is required in this call-and-response performance. This work is also celebrating the new season.
   Footnote: English translation of "Pere" refrain (pp. 54–7).

2. "III" Footnote: "àdòko – a bird noted for incessant songs" (p. 60).

3. "Monday Morning" Parenthesis: (at Ibadan University)

information, perhaps about the place where the poem was composed. The performance note here hints that the poem may be discussing life at the Ibadan University.
Footnote: "Crisbo Garden a popular nightclub in Ibadan" (p. 76).

Waiting Laughters
A hamonious performance, with performance notes at the beginning of the book, and across the poems. The main one is in parenthesis at the first page of the volume, and the minor ones are in footnotes across the poems.

> Main performance note:
> "Throughout, to the accompaniment of drums, horns, and stringed instruments, if possible the *kora* or *goje*. Medley voices."

We may infer the following from the above note:

1. that all the performances, like the book's title suggests, are done in a happy, sometimes, philosophical mood. *Goje* is often used for philosophical performances.
2. The performer is given the choice to decide what instrument to use between *kora* and *goje*, for philosophical poems. Note that there is no flute here, and there may not be any sad or solemn moments throughout the performance.
   Footnotes: used throughout the poems. Only examples shall be cited here:
   • "Onibanbantiba no specific semantic meaning, used here as a tonal counter-point"
   • "awodi kite" (88).
   • "okro – vegetable with long green pods; sometimes called okra"
   • "Sokoyòkòtò – make-the-husband-robust: a favouraite Nigerian vegetable" (95).
   • "Oṛògòdo Oṛògòdo – A king who dances with a dizzy swing"
   • "Oṛògòdo – straight he goes (Oṛògòdo in Ikere mythology is a remote place of banishment for dishonorable rulers)"

323

It would have been extremely difficult for a performer outside the poet's Ikere native culture to know some of the concepts and meanings explained in these footnotes if the poet
had not explained them.

Seize the Day

The "Explanatory Notes" provided by Agbo Areo are useful for the cultural, ethical or didactical preoccupation of the poems written for young readers. The
book here includes exercises. However, Niyi Osundare provides his own performance notes to many of the poems. I will discuss only a sampling of them.

1. "Seize the Day" Parenthesis: (Accompanied by drums or
   hand clapping)
   This is the first time that hand clapping is given as an option
   in place of drumming. This gives every child an opportunity to participate in music for the performance. However, it
   is also done with the realization that the teacher, who might
   use this poem in the classroom, may not have access to a
   drum, so hand-clapping easily replaces the drumming (p.
   1).
2. "The Spirit of Light" Parenthesis: (To the accompaniment
   of flute) This poem doesn't seem to be a sad song, although
   perhaps a bit solemn. It seems that the choice of instrument
   here is more for the convenience of the classroom situation
   than to create a sad or solemn mood (p. 2).
3. "Beauty" Parenthesis: (To the accompaniment of the drum)
   There is no specification of the type of drum here. However,
   a high sounding drum would be for a happy, celebration
   mood, while a low sounding mood could establish a reflective mood.

   Generally in *Seize the Day*, the writer offers the performers
   more options so that the performances can be easily done
   in elementary or high schools. Another examples of extra
   options in this book includes (with a solemn song) "Ode to
   a Fallen Tree" (p. 5) without specifying a particular melody.
   Also, (with any song in praise of mother) "Eye-lash" leaving
   options open. Another one, (to the accompaniment of a
   drum) "Ikere-Ekiti" without mentioning any specific drum.

And again, (with an African Drum) "Riddle" gives the performer wider options to choose from, could be from any part of Africa. This performance note also helps to introduce children to other parts of Africa, since the continent is their constituency. Yoruba and Hausa children using songs from each other's cultures, or Nigerian Ibibio children using a South African Xosa song will take pride in African heritage outside their immediate ethnic groups. Another example of options is (to the accompaniment of a popular African Song) "Life" only specifying "popular." Among other performance notes in "Seize the Day" are (with hand clapping) in "Ode to the Tongue"; (to the accompaniment of a real mouth-organ); and (for G.O. Bezi, my unforgettable teacher)!

Footnotes: There are a few footnotes across the poems, as usual, serving as English translations of Yoruba words, phrases, sentences, songs, etc.
• "omi iye – water of life" (p. 12).
• "konkoloji kogbakoji konkolo Jikogbakoji konkolo" – Musical sounds, often semantically meaningless.
• "Timer lorry; also it's a driver, and by extension, all those responsible for the felling of a trees" (p. 17).
• "Usukuma – An ethnic group in East Africa" (p. 19).
• "Olosunta – The largest rock in Ikere-Ekiti; an important festival is celebrated in its honor" (p. 21).
• "Dar-es-Sallam – The capital of Tanzania in East Africa, situated by the Indian Ocean" (p. 34).

This poetry book also contains pictures, and has poems generally written to teach moral lessons. Through the performance notes, children are given hints about what musical tools to use and what performance mood to create. English translation of Yoruba words also provides very good education to children performers. There are also opportunities to know names of cities and places in other parts of Africa.

Horses of Memory
There are several performance notes in this volume, in parentheses and footnotes. Only a small sampling will be discussed.

1. "For The One Who Departed" Parenthesis: (Heavy drums, occasional ululation). Performance hints (p. 5).
2. "Memory's Road" Parenthesis: (for many voices, in orchestra). Hints.
3. "Scars of Unremembrance" Parentheses:
   a. (for Harry Garuba) - dedication.
   b. (to the accompaniment of kora, bata, and/saxophone) Performance hints.
4. "Skinsong (1)" Parenthesis: (for George Laming) – dedication.
5. "New Drum" Note: *The Drum invites us to new steps – Tanure Ojaide.* Epigraph.
   Footnotes: "Used for its sound effect; no specific semantic 'meaning'" (p. 62).
   See more footnotes on pp. 84, 101, 104, & 115.

Most of the parentheses are hints about performances, and two of them are dedications to different individuals. There are also several other parentheses (see pp. 68, 70, 98, 99, 103, 108, 119, and 127). This is the first time we have an example of an epigraph: the poet uses a quotation as a guiding spirit of his poem, "New drum" (p. 54). There are other epigraphs, in "Stiltdancers" (36) and "Horses of Memory" (p. 127). All these performance notes put more life into the performances, and help to further define the poems for their readers and performers.

The Word is an Egg
This book has five sections, and the footnote is used more often, almost on every page. Parentheses are also given as performance hints in a few places. Whereas some sections hardly have any such information, other sections have several parenthetical performance notes.

Section I: "Abùùbùtán"
   a. "Invocations of the word" Parenthesis: (to be performed

with full musical accompaniment). There is a refrain in this poem, and the audience is expected to be heavily involved. The hint for using a "full musical accompaniment" could even suggest that a festival performance is expected. Full music among the Yoruba may include instruments such as *gangan, agogo, sekere, omele,* and perhaps a few more. This shows that the mood is happy, and perhaps the performance is a celebration of the power of word.

Section II: "The Word is an Egg"

a. "The Kingdom of the tongue" Parenthesis: (to Bill Furlong) – dedication.

Footnote: on the dedication – "A precocious, inspiring member of my 1992 summer session literature class at the University of New Orleans" (p. 17).

b. "Words which" Parenthesis: (Music; various voices). This is an opera performance – especially the suggestion of "various voices".

c. "In praise of little things" Parenthesis: (Accompanying music with tempo   varying as the mood and meaning of each stanza demands. A medley of voices). Again, a fulfillment of another *b'orin bayi* artistic convention. This tells the performer to change mood and tempo according to the meaning of each stanza. This has also encouraged the performer to be creative, and to pay closer attention to the meanings of the poems.

Section III: "Silence"

Again in this section, there are very few performance notes.

a. "Words Underground" Parenthesis: (To the brave souls of *Tell, The News, Tempo, The Punch* locked in costly combat with Nigeria's brutal dictatorship). – dedication. The poem, obviously, is about the Nigerian journalists' struggle against the brutal Nigerian regimes.

b. "Sighlens" Parenthesis: (an elfin song).

Footnote: "Alùpàyídà – metamorphosis"

As if indicating silence, there is no drum or music introduced to any of the poems in "Silence" section. Only "an elfin song," a fairy tale song, and just once towards the end. Footnotes are also quite sparse.

Sections IV & V

There are very few performance notes in these two sections. Section IV has only one parenthetical note, and Section V has only two. However, both ofthe sections have several footnotes.

    a. Section IV: "Words Catch Fire" Parenthesis: (many voices – in orchestra) (p. 59). This is another opera-like performance.

    b. Section V: "Omolétí" Parenthesis: (Inexhaustible, Fish of the Ocean); (Inexhaustible, Fish of the Lagoon) (p. 83). Both translations from Yoruba.

Every performance in *The Word is an Egg* is like "actors on stage," is like a performance in orchestra! In many of the other poems in sections IV and V, refrains are involved, and the audience is expected to participate.

CONCLUSION

Performers and teachers of Osundare's poetry must not ignore the performance notes because only by following them could they create the type of mood, atmosphere, and performance structure that the poems require. Since modern African poets want to be identified through their African native cultures and community aesthetic approaches, the wisest critic respects the poets' wishes by following strictly the poets' prescriptions in their notes. Modern African poetry teachers should not behave like the over-imposing drama producers who portray meanings that are far different from those of the playwrights. The era of Eurocentric criticism for African poetry is over. Osundare and his peers have dug the final graves for any remaining colonial approaches to modern creative writing in Africa.[6] Contemporary African poetry needs innovative and loyal teachers always anxious to learn how best to realize the expectations of the poet's performance notes. One important characteristic of the notes is the use of modifiers to show the actual tempo of musical accompaniment needed (e.g. "solemn song," "full musical accompaniment," "heavy drums," and "lively bata music,") thus helping to show the performers how far they could go to create and retain the culturally relevant effects.

    Osundare does not limit his choice of musical instruments to his Yoruba culture. He often recommends Hausa, Igbo, and many other non-Yoruba (even non-Nigerian) cultural instruments. This clearly helps to identify the poet as a pan-Africanist, who is very eager to explore African cultural heritage and to mobilize Africans for mutual sociopolitical and literary advancements. This pan-Africanist approach is one of the hallmarks of *Seize the Day*, Osundare's poetry for junior readers.

Finally, Osundare's poetry fully realizes its potential when performed on stage. The stage, for Osundare, is a melting point for a dedication to the African culture of performance and the socialist ideology of mobilizing the grassroots. He sees it as a symbol for action and the non-silence tradition that he is always eager to provoke in society:

> The poet's pen is
> the cactus by the stream
> (shorn of its forbidding thorn)
> each stem a nib
> towards the field of action
> its sap the ink of succour
> when doubt's drought
> assaults the well
> (a stanza from "The Poets," *A Nib in the Pond*)

NOTES

1 Osundare had said during his eulogy for Soyinka at Lawrence, Kansas, in April 2000, shortly before Soyinka was conferred with the 2000 Forlon-Nichols award, that Soyinka was a "lucky man," citing, of course, a different reason.
2 Personal interview with Niyi Osundare, April 10, 2000.
3 Ibid.
4 I am still researching into this theory's wider implications.
5 Perhaps this African cultural concept defines artistic beauty, however great, as being subservient to meaning. It reiterates most African writers rejection of the philosophy of an art for art sake.
6 Read Chinua Achebe's "Colonialist Criticism," *Hopes and Impediments*. New York: Doubleyday, 1988: 68–89.

REFERENCES

Chinua Achebe. *Hopes and Impediments: Selected Essays*. New York: Doubleyday, 1988.

Arnold, Stephen. "A Peopled Persona: Autobiography, Post-Modernism and the Poetry of Niyi Osundare." Ed. Ulla Shield. *Autobiographical Genres in Africa*. Bayreuth: Mainz – Africa Studien, 1996.

Dessen, Alan C. *Elizabethan Stage Conventions and Modern Interpretations*. Cambridge: Cambridge UP, 1984.

Gayle, Addison, ed. *The Black Aesthetic*. New York: Doubleday, 1971.

Jeyifo, Biodun. "Niyi Osundare." Ed.Yemi Ogunbiyi. *Perspectives on Nigerian Literature*. Guardian Books Nigeria Limited, 1988. 314–321.

Na'Allah, Abdul-Rasheed & Michelin Rice-Maximin. "Thresholds: Anglophone African Literatures Conference in Toulouse." *ALA Bulletin*. 25.3 (1999): 61–73.

———. "Dadakuada as One of the Oral Art Forms of Ilorin" African Notes, 18.1&2 (1994): 29–50.

Ojaide, Tanure. Poetic Imagination in Black Africa. Durham: Carolina Academic Press, 1996.

Osundare, Niyi. "Bard of the Tabloid Platform: A Personal Experience of Newspaper Poetry in Nigeria." Ed. Stephen Arnold. *Culture and Development in Africa*. Trenton: Africa World Press, 1990: 1–47.

———. *Selected Poems*. Ibadan: Heinemann Educational Books, 1992.

———. *Seize the Day*. Ibadan: Agbo Areo Publishers, 1995.

————. *Horses of Memory*. Heinnemann Educational Books, 1998.

————. *The Word is an Egg*. Ibadan: Kraft Books Limited, 1999.

Raji, Wumi. "The Plays of Niyi Osundare." *The People's Poet: Emerging Perspectives on Niyi Osundare*. Ed. Abdul-Rasheed Na'Allah. Trenton: Africa World Press, 2002.

THE PERFORMATIVE
CONTEXT OF
NIYI OSUNDARE'S
POETRY

Sunday Enessi Ododo

Niyi Osundare is called "a major voice" as well as "one of the foremost" poets. The Nigerian new poetic tradition is no longer a contestable issue (Jones 3, Bamikunle 49). He has experimented in style and technique with several books of poetry: *Songs of the Marketplace* (1983), *Village Voices* (1984), *A Nib in the Pond* (1986), *The Eye of the Earth* (1986), *Moonsongs* (1988), *Songs of the Season* (1990), *Waiting Laughters* (1990), *Horses of Memory* (1998), and *The Word is an Egg* (2000), and has established his uniqueness as a poet. The resourcefulness of Osundare's poetry can be measured by the number and quality of critical writings his poems have invited, such as works by Jayifo (1987 and 1988), Aiyejina (1988), Ngara (1990), Jones (1992), Bamikunle (1992 and 1995), Bodunde (1995) and innumerable seminar papers and theses. All these works undertake discourses on Osundare's materialist and political visions, poetic style and technique, poetic language and cultural elements.

What cannot be taken away from him, however, is his creative, re-creative and dexterous use of materials from the store house of oral tradition. He has done for Nigerian Poetry what Femi Osofisan has done for Nigerian Theatre—reinterpreting myth, legends and carving out new meanings from 'Oratural' heritage in tune with contemporary social dialectics. This indeed has been the experimental preoccupation of most modern African artists, using oral tradition and relying on their aesthetic codes to rewrite history and to fashion a unique artistic format that is distinctively African, thereby freeing themselves, to a remarkable extent, from the clutches of western aesthetic canons of literary execution. Through this a new process of cultural validation is enunciated and this Abah sees as "affirming the positive cultural practices of the people and making use of them in a new context by addressing contemporary issues" (p. 84). This is where the resilience of Osundare's poetic distinctiveness in style and technique lies. Bamikunle amplifies this, insisting that "his judicious use of elements of the African oral tradition, has produced poetry that is distinctively African" (p. 61). Aiyejina also concurs that aside from the social relevance of Osundare's poetry, "his work is distinguished by the sustained lyricism, and the use of the dramatic tone, both of which are reminiscent of the oral traditions of Africa" (p. 123).

However, the use of oral tradition in creative literary activity, particularly poetry, has often been evaluated from a social standpoint, with less articulated attention on performative values in the overall poetic design. This explains why Bamikunle is obsessed with a recurring notion that in the hands of Osundare "traditional social vision has become a weapon for very incisive criticism of contemporary political economy" (p. 60), and locates Osundare's "distinct voice as a poet" in "his revolutionary use of the oral traditions" (p. 136). Aiyejina also bases his admiration for *The Eye of the Earth* (a collection of poems that also, to some extent, utilizes core traditional elements) on "the political dimension in this volume" which is explored "through nature metaphors and imagery" and the poet's "lyricism" and "linguistic competence," all derived from the oral tradition art form (p. 124).

It is an incontestable fact that the essence of oral tradition artistic forms can only manifest more meaningfully and be better understood in performance. A number of authorities agree on this. Ruth Finnegan maintains,

> Oral literature is by definition dependent on a performer who formulates it in words on a specific occasion—there is no other way in which it can be realized as a literary product. . . if we take forms like a play, a sermon, jazz poetry, even something as trivial as an after dinner anecdote—in all these cases the actual delivery is a significant aspect of the whole. . . they only attain their true fulfillment when actually performed. (pp. 2–3)

Maclean uses a wide range of recent theories (Bakhtin to Deleuze, speech act theory from Austin to Felman, theories of allegory, the strategies of desire and the entropic and energetic models of Michel Series) to contextualise the significance and dynamics of performance in narratology. Thompson extenuates further that oral telling involves a stock of motifs, formulas and historical traditions which are drawn upon to produce a performance text. Using some specimen from African art, such as masks, musical instruments, hair dresses and costumes, Epskamp reasons convincingly that the meaning and function of these art forms in a social cultural context can only be truly derived in full utilization and colour through performance. It is for these reasons that this essay seeks to examine the performative values of Osundare's poetry via their structure, execution of contents and the theatricality of the traditional art forms utilized in his poems, as a corollary to the fact that the true values and aesthetic effectiveness of these art forms can only be assessed in a performative context. This is further validated by the understanding that in "the performing arts of Africa almost all theatrical means are integrated" (Epskamp, 1992: 47), and as such isolated assessment of these "theatrical means" may be misleading.

The justification for this study stems from the awareness that poetry is not traditionally recognized as an individual art form but as a collective artistic experience that is performed and shared with an abiding communal spirit. This understanding most likely informed the stately formality (especially in rendition) of the poetic verse in Greek tragedy, which has in turn had a telling influence on the succeeding dramatic traditions. Poetry thus can be seen as a formal feature of the narrative art which also has greater capacity to coordinate other traditional art forms (masque dramaturge, drumming, singing, dancing, mimicry, etc.) within the oral performance art. Even for written drama, poetic verses can be better appreciated in performance rather than when read privately.

It is also instructive to note that most great and successful playwrights in history also recorded recognizable achievements as poets. Williams Shakespeare, T.S. Eliot, John Millington Synge, Bertolt Brecht and a host of others were great poets. In Nigeria, most of our foremost playwrights have also had successful careers as poets, such as Wole Soyinka (a Nobel laureate), J.P. Clark, Bekederemo, Femi Osofisan, Olu Obafemi, and a few others. It is therefore not a thing of coincidence that the successes these dramatists have attained as playwrights rests largely in the involvement of poetry in their drama. Interestingly, Osundare, whose poems are being considered here, is also a playwright, even though unpublished. This further underscores how the creative elements of these two distinct art forms can influence the creative outlook of one another, as we shall soon see in the poetry works of Osundare. If "a play is a poem" as Hodge ingeniously puts it, then a poem can also pass for a play (v). Therefore, considering Osundare's poems under a performative context is in order. This exercise will generate fresh awareness on the dynamics of African performance concept.

Of all Osundare's books of poetry,[*] *Village Voices* exhibits more sustained elements of performance with a synthetic romance with oral traditional art forms. Bamikunle affirms this, stressing that "the strength of Osundare's poetry" in this collection "comes from his exploration of the rich store of rural life both for material for art" and "also for poetic technique"(*Orature* 55 and *Development 132*). Jeyifo is more pointed in his submission that in *Village Voices* "the poet celebrates the rural communities as sturdy producers, witty raconteurs, singers, jesters, satirists," which are all latent kernels of the performing arts (319). It is for these reasons we have chosen *Village Voices* for our discussion.

THE PERFORMATIVE CONTEXT

Osundare's creative approach in *Village Voices* gives the work a kinetic aura that unlocks its literary qualities and relocates it within the vibrant performative context of oral poetry, which imaginatively coordinates a variety of traditional art forms in a communally participatory experience. This further reinforces the African holistic philosophy of the performing arts—music, dance, drama and associated theatrical appendages (scenic presence, costumes, props, lighting, drumming, movements, gestural conduits, etc.)—which involve a sign system (index and icon) for proper understanding of the poems as performance before an audience in the manner specified (Epskamp 55). He says that the indexes and icons in a narrative experience are tied to conventions of performing, and are thus symbolic in nature. This appeals more to our imagination than what is physically seen, but all the same, they are there and can be pictured in our mind's eye. Let us now proceed to the work of poetry and attempt to validate all these claims.

Village Voices is divided into five sequences "rising voice," "voices in dialogue and banter," "voices about coming and going," "voices of anger and indictment," and "closing." The first and the last sequences contain one poem each, "I wake up this morning" and "I Rise Now" respectively. One introduces the poem while the other closes it. The other three sequences, with fourteen, nine and thirteen poems respectively, form the main body of the poetry collection. A closer look at this collection foregrounds a picture of drama text with an episodic structure, bound together with a single thematic concern (decrying societal vices) and a unifying production concept, a celebration of communal ethos. "Rising voice" thus becomes the prologue, "I Rise Now" becomes the epilogue. All the other poems within the body represent different episodes conceived with a very high sense of music and other performance attributes. Each poem title becomes a guiding metaphor through which the ideas of the poet can be decoded in performance. This involves Brechtian performance style which is rooted in the concept of epic theatre. 1 Interestingly, Brecht is considered a major influence on the creative style of some radical Nigerian dramatists with socialist vision (Gbilekaa 72–75). The most prominent of them are Femi Osofisan, Bode Sowande, Kole Omotoso and Olu Obafemi, all personal and ideological friends of Niyi Osundare.

Bamikunle claims that *Village Voices* is influenced by the traditional notion of poetry as song, which resulted in the "musical song-like rhythm" as "framework for all the poems" (pp. 131–2). This notion is also firmly rooted in Yoruba Oral Poetry, which Osundare is very familiar with as a Yoruba indigene. Writing on the "Yoruba Oral Poetry: Composition and Performance" Olajubu maintains that a "poem in Yoruba is essentially a song and its performance is a musical dramatic opera" (pp. 72–4). He adds that "it is meant to be sung, chanted or intoned in performance in the presence of an audience" and concludes that the poet in Yoruba oral poetry is a performer whose activities involve "a combination of singing, drama, dancing, masquerading and costume parade" while backed up by an orchestra of soloists, chorus singers and drummers. Drawing inspiration from these robust positions, we want to establish that in *Village Voices* a versatile poet/performer using all the resources of oral performance art starts the performance and ends it. In between both poles he introduces other personae to animate his poetic narration with boisterous theatrical elements, giving the collection performative qualities.

The prologue opens with the poet arriving at the market square, bringing with him an orchestra of musicians, drummers and dancers as he sings in "I wake up this Morning" to the mammoth crowd waiting for his performance (p. 71). Indeed, the whole collection is nothing but a song interspersed with dramatic actions involving members of the community and thereby engendering collective spirit in addressing communal issues. The poet confirms, "I wake up this Morning / with a song: in my throat" (p. 1). All the other poems in the collection therefore form the contents of that song. As an introductory song to the performance that is a social event where personalities and issues are often satirized to check excesses in the community's conduct, "I Wake Up this Morning" details the readiness of the poet to perform his duties to the community as a 'seer' and a 'prophet,' and also hints at what to expect within the trunk of the performance. For artistic readiness, the poet informs that he has "borrowed the earful clamour/ of the towncrier/ gained the unkillable clarion/ of the gong/cushioned" his "throat with the velvet feathers / of the dove" and charged his "words with the fiery urgency / of the thunder" so that when he sings "ears shall bend" his way. On what to expect he proclaims,

My words will not lie like a eunuch wind
My words will climb the tree of wisdom
feed multitudes with fruits of thought
and plant the earth with potent seeds.
(p. 2).

For those who might doubt his courage to address the excesses of the high and low of society, he declares that he wears "courage Iike a shield/ and see, reusing to hide, / those who pour poison/ in the village stream" and has the courage to tell kings that their "fat chokes the village nose."

The execution of this first poem (prologue) encourages boisterous a u d i - ence participation as chorus, which is an exciting way of starting a performance of this nature. Every stanza of this poem starts with the voice of the first person narrative, except two of them, which are cast as responses to what the voice is saying. To illustrate, the poet sings

I wake up this morning
with a song in my heart
a youthful breeze harps the leaves
rising feet drum the road
to meet the upland sun
my sole treads the dew
rousing my body
to the virgin cool of earth

The audience choruses,

The day has woken from night of sleep
time for the spinner too spin the spindle
The day has woken
time for the smith to fan the smiling coals
into hissing steel

This is repeated after each of the next four stanzas which all start with "I have," "I wear," "I wear," and "I wear," respectively. However, on the eighth and ninth stanzas the starting lines change to "My voice" and "My words" and the refrain for each of these changes:

He who has not seen the sea
let him taste salt in the stew
he who does not know fire
let him watch a forest blaze
in the season before it rains
he who does not know the poet
let him listen to the footsteps of words

And the final stanza ends as follows:

for
I have woken up this morning with a song in my throat
the chorus echoes across the world

This is a recapitulation of the first stanza of the poem, which is also a technique used in music. The first and second refrains can be sung together at this moment for the maximum effect of the phrase "echoes across the world." Similar features are apparent in "The stars sob" (p. 35), "Unequal fingers" (p. 60), and "The Cock's comb of Fire" (p. 39).

From here the poet moves straight into the first episode of the performance, which is fittingly titled "voices in dialog and banter." From this moment until the last poem, the poet goes into role-playing as in "A Dialog of the Drums" (p. 5), "Search for a Wife" (p. 18), "The Politician's Two Mouths" (p. 57), "The Padlock and the Key" (p. 65), etc. At other times he comes before the audience telling tales and moralizing, as in "Killing with a Sword" (p. 13), "Chicken Story" (p. 14), "Eating Tomorrow's Yam" (p. 16), "Advice" (p. 19), and "Akintunde, Come Home" (p. 22), assuming the role of a narrator preparing his audience's mind for the next episode of his narration. Sometimes he disappears entirely to become part of the audience, as can be deciphered in "The Prisoner's Song" (p. 24), "A Reunion" (p. 27), "A Villager's Protest" (p. 47), "Dying Another's Death" (p. 55), "We Have Waited So Long" (p. 66), etc. There are some instances where his poetic narrations are best accompanied with built up actions in mime and movements as could be done with "An In-law's Message" (p. 17), "Feigning Rebel" (p. 20) and "The Cock's Comb of Fire" (p. 39). Some of these poems also come across like dramatic monologues.

The epilogue, which is tagged "Closing" is where the poet/ performer reemerges as at the beginning of the performance to end the plot:

> I rise now
> for it is time to go
> . . . the vanishing sun has rolled up the mat
> of our play
> but not the mat of our fertile throats
> which neither sleep nor snore
> like waters of a young river
> I should rise with tomorrow's sun
> and plant more songs in the ears
> of a waking world.

This further establishes that Osundare probably intends this poetry collection to be performed and not just read. The word 'play' and 'songs' as used above are very significant to this submission. Plays and songs are meant to be performed and with their performance other theatrical elements are introduced. The use of 'play' and 'songs' in this context also suggests that the best way to realize *Village Voices* as a performance is through the folk operatic mold. This is a performance style that can adequately coordinate equal proportions of dramatic elements and music as found in this poetry collection. Some of these dramatic elements and other performance features foregrounded in the text deserve some attention.

DRAMATIC AND PERFORMANCE FEATURES

Dialogue:

This is an important feature of any dramatic experience because it is through dialogue that dramatic actions are suggested and sustained. Some instances of conversation between two or more people can be identified in the poetry collection, and this is exactly what dialogue means. Its essence however is to be *heard* and not just read, even though it is written on printed pages. What makes the dialogue in this collection more effective than in most plays with straight dialogue is the compact language that is used. This substantially intensifies feelings and high actions. In Hodge's view, the impact of poetic language is described as "often as potent as physical body movements simply because verse conveys intense inner feelings in a compact and heightened way. It thus has the capability of direct contact with the audience" (pp. 28–29). He adds that this accounts for the reason why most playwrights who write dialogue in prose try to find a language somewhat more elevated than what is used in everyday life.

In the hands of Osundare, dialogue takes a fresh turn using traditional stylistic devices of symbols, images, proverbs, myths as well as the evocative language of the drum. More striking is how he engages eight different drums (bata, omele, gangan, gbedu, ibembe, reso, ogbele and adan) in a musical dialogue in "A Dialogue of the Drums" (p. 5). Drum rhetoric is harnessed while contributing immensely to the overall design of the poetry collection as a musical performance. The drums concretely present a picture of an actively engaged musical ensemble, which the audience responds to in dance, movements and gestures. This spells out another level of dialogue between the drummers and the dancers.

It is also useful to note that some of the poems where dialogue occurs can actually be reconstructed into dramatic episodes (texts). These poems include "Eating Tomorrow's Yam" (p. 16), "Search for a Wife" (p. 18) and "The Padlock and the Key" (p. 65). Let us illustrate with "Search for a Wife":

> *In Anke's Parents house. Other members of the family are present. Idowu has just finished presenting his request to take Anke's hands in marriage.*
>
> Anke's Mother: You are a good-looking young man, well-mannered and strong-armed, any family will be proud to have as a son in-law, but there is a problem why we cannot.
>
> Idowu: Problem? *(looking worried)* What problem?
>
> Anke's Mother: I sympathize with you young man, but the fault is not the hunchback's but that of his hunch: Idowu, your mother is a great curser.
>
> Idowu: My mother?
>
> Anke's People: (In unison) Yes, your mother. *(Idowu is puzzled by this revelation and strong agreement by the others on this point. He remains speechless as light fades out.)*
>
> *Idowu's home. His mother is sweeping the living room when Idowu bursts in furious and angry. She jerks shouting*

Idowu's Mother: Tani mose? Who have I offended? *(trying to strike with the broom in her hand, realizing it's Idowu she relaxes)* Idowu, what explanations do you have to offer for this manner of entry?

Idowu: Mother, I went visiting a young woman today, but her mother vows her daughter will never he wife to a curser's child.

ldowu's Mother: *(Infuriated)* Me, a curser? The lairs are at it again! Whoever says I am a curser may he see his own ears without a mirror, may *Soponna* turn his house into a furnace, may *Sango. . . (getting more frenzied and bringing out afose – a medicinal object from her brazier).*

Idowu: *(cuts in calmly)* Now mother, I can see what liars Anke's People are. *(He walks out, leaving her in self realization and looking stupid. Black out.)*

Characterization:

A variety of characters are also foregrounded in *Village Voices* through which the dramatic actions inherent in the poetry collection can be sustained in performance. Their variety also fittingly captures the different shades of personalities and nuances in attitude that can be found in a societal set up. More importantly, these are characters that are actively engaged in expressing their desires. Their moral stance and decorum are what the poet uses to his advantage in registering his materialist and social vision by decrying want, poverty, injustice, maladministration, political deception and man's inhumanity to man. Some of the distinctive characters that can be found in the text are narrator, musicians, poet, kings, politician, protesters and prodigals. Others are in-laws, suitors, brides, prisoners, warders, farmers, academics, students and a host of villagers representing different interests. On a more creative level Aiyejina articulates the ingenuity of Osundare by observing that "the various drums in 'A Dialogue of the Drums' become characters in a well-orchestrated symphony of the pains, poetry, prophecies and hopes of the people" (p. 123). This gives physical presence to the musical dialogue of the drums we have already discussed.

Music and Dance:

Wherever music exists, dance is implied. As a merry making nation, the Yorubas attach a lot of importance to music and dance. Of all the eight drums used in "A Dialogue of the Drums" only two (*gbedu* and *adan*) are not used for entertainment. Gbedu is a royal drum which also has ritualistic connotations, while adan is a satirical drum found in Ikere-Ekiti, Osundare's home village. The names of all the eight drums are also names of dances associated with them. The presence of all these drums in the orchestra of this poetic performance is therefore indicative of a variety of dances that are foregrounded in the artistic experience. The following lines from "A Dialogue of the Drums" are also affirmative:

> I have thrilled royal steps
> With *gbedu's* majestic accent
> And learnt why *egiri* turns thick ears
> To the hunter's feeble arrows
> I have put a stick to *ibembe*
> Urging virgin brides to dance to
> The virtue between their legs
> (p. 6).

"The Bride's Song" is another poem that naturally calls for music and dancing because it captures the procession of a bride to her husband's house (p. 41). This is one rite of passage that the Yorubas celebrate with a lot of fanfare. The *oriki* used in this piece to narrate the farming prowess of the son of Efurudowo, the bride's husband, further enhances its performative qualities. Olajubu asserts that the "Yoruba tradition enjoins an individual whose *oriki* . . . is being chanted to react promptly by giving the artists gifts of money and materials according to the strength of his purse" (p. 79). Indeed he is joined in this money-spraying exercise by his friends and close associates, which serves to magnify the social event while making it more colourful. "I Rise Now," being the closing poem, will definitely elicit a high level of audience participation in singing and dancing (p. 71). This can turn into a carnival as everybody present will also rise with the poet/performer to parade home while still in performative mood.

We have said so much about music in the course of this discussion. What remains to be said, however, is that it will be very challenging to turn these poems into songs. An easy way out might be an adequate study of the original Yoruba pieces where most of these poems are either derived or gained inspiration from. Bamikunle also affirms that the poems actually translate or transliterate known Yoruba songs (p. 135). The lyricism that already exists in most of the poems will be an advantage. More challenges await a prospective director who might be willing to perform the poetry, because the melodies inherent in them are invigorating and vivacious. If not carefully controlled this may over

Emerging Perspectives on Niyi Osundare

sensitize audience participation into standing in the way of the performance as rehearsed. This has happened before on the Yoruba popular traveling theatre stage, especially with the plays of Hubert Ogunde (See Adedeji *Dynamics*).

Osundare's strongest forte as a poet is his sound musical sense which is ever present in varying degrees in all his poetry books. To date, in our own estimation, *Village Voice* enjoys the best of this sense of sound. In *The Eye of the Earth* he couches his lines with sweet-sounding rhythms. In *Moonsongs and Waiting Laughters,* Osundare also foregrounds the accompaniment of the poems with a variety of musical instruments. They also exercises in musical composition. In all, Osundare's musical mellifluous rhythms are informed by the highly tonal nature of Yoruba language and a consistent clever ability to string out musical notes from his words in a vibrant poetic enterprise that has evolved a poetic style that is '*Osun*-daring.'

Staging and Scenography:
The locale for this performance as can be inferred from "I Rise Now" is the market square full of baobab trees, which cast enough shade for the comfort of the audience present. The setting is communal and is better achieved through arena staging. Even though a number of scenic elements are suggested in the text, they cannot be given realistic vent in arena staging. Props and costumes can enhance the performance better in this instance. Because of the different subject matters explored in all the episodes of this work, there are also numerous and varied characters. Therefore a lot of props and costumes would be required for a successful performance. Every episode has its own peculiar requirements. Perhaps the best way to deploy these props and costume in performance is through the use of a property man as used in *The Marriage of Anansewa* by Efua Sutherland. The poet/performer may assume this role since he is in charge of the performance event. In terms of lighting, general illumination of the performance area is mostly required while some specific lighting effects can be used to enhance the stage picture of some of the dramatic moments in the poetry. Strobe lighting, effectively combined with sound effects, can be used for instance, in "A Villager's Protest" to create a state of pandemonium that usually goes with protest (p. 47). "A Dialogue of the Drums" is very rich in spectacle and sound. A lighting colour mix can heighten the aesthetic features of this carnivalesque display of dance and music (p. 5). Generally, the text has a lot of potential for creative lighting.

In all, *Village Voices* is an ingenious exercise in African Concept of "total theatre" which Adedeji describes as "an ensemble where the conscious and the unconscious, the real and the unreal, poetry, song and dance, intermingle with elements of traditional theatre both sacred and secular" (*Profile*, 1971: 3). It forces the audience to participate in the artistic experience while conjoining spatial and temporal frames into seamless experimental essences. These are attributes that can make an exciting performance in every poetry collection. Its production as stage performance will definitely lure many stage directors to do more experimentation with poetry performances. It has its own distinctive stage values which are quite different from that of a play performance. These can only be discovered in a production process.

NOTE

1 Most plays by Bertholt Brecht begin and end with prologues and epilogues respectively. See *The Three Penny Opera, The Good Woman of Setzuan* and *The Caucasian Chalk Circle*. Their episodic structures and the use of music and story telling format are also useful to our claim. However, it should be remarked that Ukala (286) and Gbilekaa (181) have sufficiently debunked the notion that the so called Epic style is essentially Brechtian and thus recover most of the features of this style back to African indigenous oratural tradition which predates Brecht.

REFERENCES

Abah, Oga S. "Perspectives in Popular Theatre: Orality as a Definition of New Realities" Ed. Eckhard Breitinger. *Theatre and Performance in Africa.* Bayreuth: Bayreuth Africa Studies Series, 1954.

Adedeji, J.A. "A Profile of Nigerian Theatre, 1960–1970." *Nigeria Magazine.* August to December, 1971: 107–109.

Adedeji, J.A. and Hyginus Ekwuazi. *Nigerian Theatre: Dynamics of a Movement.* Ibadan: Caltop Publications (Nigeria) Limited, 1998.

Aiyejina, Funsho. "Recent Nigerian Poetry in English: Alternative Tradition." Ed. Yemi Ogunbiyi. *Perspectives on Nigerian Literature, 1700 to the Present,* vol. 1. Lagos: Guardian Books Nigeria Limited, 1988 .

Bamikunle, Aderemi. "Niyi Osundare's Poetry and the Yoruba Oral Artistic Tradition." Eds. Eldred Durosimi Jones, Eustace and Marjorie Jones. *Orature in African Literature Today 18.* London: James Currey Ltd, 1992.

———. "The Development of Niyi Osundare's Poetry: A Survey of Themes and Technique" *Research in African Literatures 26.* 1995 .

Bodunde, Charles A."Oral Traditions & Modern Poetry: Okot p'Bitek's Song of Lawino & Okigbo's Labyrinths." Eds. Eldred Durosimi Jones, Eustace Palmer & Marjorie Jones. *Orature in African Literature Today 18.* London: James Currey Ltd, 1992 .

———. "The Sociology of New Nigerian Poetry in English" Ph.D. Dissertation, University of Ilorin, 1995.

Brecht, Bertolt. "The Good Woman of Setzuan" and "The Caucasian Chalk Circle" *Parables for the Theatre.* London: Penguin Books, 1966.

———. *The Three Penny Opera.* London: Methuen, 1979.

Epskamp, Kees. *Learning by Performing Arts: From Indigenous to Endogenous Cultural Development.* The Hague: CESO, 1992.

———. *On Printed Matter and Beyond: Media, Orality and Literacy.* The Hague: CESO, 1995.

Finnegan, Ruth. *Oral Literature in Africa*. London: Oxford University Press, 1970.

———. *Oral Poetry: Its Nature, Significance and Social Context*. Cambridge:Cambridge University Press, 1977.

Gbilekaa, Saint. *Radical Theatre in Nigeria*. Ibadan, Nigeria: Caltop Publications Limited, 1997.

llodge, Francis. *Play Directing: Analysis, Communication and Style*. Englewood Cliffs, New Jersey: Prentice-Hall, 1971.

Jeyifo, Biodun. "Introduction" *Song of the Market Place* By Niyi Osundare. Ibadan: New Horn Press, 1987.

———. "Niyi Osundare" Ed. Yemi Ogunbiyi. *Perspective on Nigerian Literature: 1700 to the Present,* vol. 2. Lagos: Guardian Books Nigeria Limited, 1988 .

Jones, Eldred D. "Myth & Modernity: African Writers and their Roots." Eds. Eldred Durosimi, Jones, Eustace Palmer & Marjorie Jones. *Orature in African Literature Today 18*. London: James Currey Ltd, 1992.

Maclean, Marie. *Narrative as Performance: The Baudelairean Experiment*. London: Routledge, 1998.

Ngara, Emmanuel. *Ideological Form in African Poetry*. London: James Currey Ltd, 1990.

Olajubu, Oludare. "Yoruba Oral Poetry: Composition and Performance" Eds. Uchegbulam N. Abalogu, Garba Ashiwaju and Regina Amadi-Tshiwala. *Oral Poetry in Nigeria*. Lagos: Nigeria Magazine, 1981.

Osundare, Niyi. *Songs of the Marketplace*. Ibadan, New Horn, 1983.

———. *Village Voices*. Ibadan: Evans Brothers, 1984 .

———. *A Nib in the Pond*. Ile-Ife: Ife Monograph Series 4.6, 1986 .

———. *The Eye of the Earth*. Ibadan: Heinemann,1986.

———. *Moonsongs*. Owerri: Spectrum,1988.

———. *Waiting Laughters*. Lagos: Malthouse, 1990.

Sutherland, Efua T. *The Marriage of Anansewa*. London: Longman, 1975.

Thompson, Stith. *Motif Index to the Folktale*. Copenhagen: Rosen, Kilde & Bagger,1995–8.

Ukala, Sam. "'Folkism': Towards a National Aesthetic Principle for Nigerian Dramaturgy." *New Theatre Quarterly* XII 47 (1996): 279–287.

* *Horses of Memory* and *The Word is an Egg* had not been published when this article was completed, and so they were not considered in this determination. Editor.

OSUNDARE: COMPARATIVE PERSPECTIVES

THE POETICS OF THE "ALTER-NATIVE"[1] TRADITION: THE CASE OF NIGERIA'S NIYI OSUNDARE & EGYPT'S AHMAD FUAD NIGM

Kamal Abdel-Malek

Despite their different native traditions and personal backgrounds, both the Nigerian poet Niyi Osundare and the Egyptian poet Ahmad Fuad Nigm share a remarkable commitment to their respective peoples. In the case of Osundare, he employs a diction that is derived from the oral performances of his native land mingled in a fascinating manner with the poetic rhythms of the English William Wordsworth and the American Walt Whitman[2]. Nigm's diction is similarly derived from the vernacular poetry and folk tradition of his native Egypt, reflecting the tenor and color of the folk poet/singer and the city vernacular poet. Both poets celebrate the earth and the common folk and both attack the corrupt politicians, charlatans, selfish businessmen, both local and foreign, and the "fat cats" of their respective societies. In what follows we will situate each poet in his native literary and social tradition, assess their poetic innovations, and make some comparisons between the two in the hope of appreciating more what is so peculiar to each and what is shared by the other.

NIYI OSUNDARE

Niyi Osundare is considered as one of the most prominent and prolific new Nigerian poets (writing in English) of the post-1967 Nigerian civil war period. He belongs to a group of new Nigerian poets who veered away from "the obscurantism and eurocentrism of most of the first generation of modern Nigerian poets."[3] He was born on March 12, 1947 in Ikere-Ekiti, a small village in western Nigeria. He grew up in a peasant family, "farm-born peasant-bred" as he calls himself in his poem, "Farmer-Born".[4] He was influenced by both his grandfather who was a diviner-physician and by his father who was a farmer and an accomplished drummer and singer. We are told that his grandfather used to take him to the forest where they would collect herbs and roots for medicinal purposes. The grandfather would then recite incantations over the herbs and the roots to stir the healing powers in them. A childhood that witnessed the beauty of the Nigerian forests, the power of the spoken/sung word— be it the grandfather's incantations or the father's songs—must have molded the poetic sensibilities of the young Niyi and must have conditioned his future poetic vocation.

Osundare's education is marked by the excellence of his academic achievements. After his graduation from a local Christian school, he went on to the University of Ibadan where he finished his Bachelor's degree with honors. In 1974, he obtained his M.A. in English literature from the University of Leeds and five years later in 1979 he received his Ph.D. in English from York University in Ontario, Canada. He returned to Nigeria where he began his academic career at the University of Ibadan. Between 1990 and 1992 he was awarded the prestigious Fulbright scholar-in-residence fellowships which enabled him to take residence at the University of Wisconsin and the University of New Orleans. His poetry collections in the English language, include the *Songs of the Marketplace* (1983), *Village Voices* (1984), *The Eye of the Earth* (1986), *Moonsongs* (1988), *Songs of the Season* (1990), *Waiting Laughters* (1990); *Selected Poems* (1992); *Midlife,* (1993), *Horses of Memory* (1998), and *The Word is an Egg* (2000).

AHMAD FUAD NIGM

Ahmad Fuad Nigm is Egypt's most celebrated vernacular poet. He composes in colloquial Egyptian Arabic as opposed to standard Arabic. Because of his harsh anti-establishment overtones, his protest poems/songs have cost him his freedom for he was jailed for several times. The fact that his work is composed in the colloquial causes it to suffer scholarly neglect; after three decades of uninterrupted productivity, Nigm's work has received very scant critical attention both in his native Egypt and abroad—in fact the only studies in English of Nigm's work were published in 1988 and 1990 by this author.[5] Such scholarly neglect, some may call it despise, is regrettably due to the tendency among the "overwhelming majority of Arab scholars and Orientalists to define Arabic literature as encompassing only the literary works written in standard Arabic, a language which has maintained by and large the syntax of the language of the Qur'an if not its vocabulary."[6]

Nigm was born on May 22nd, 1929 in Izbit Nigm, a small village, north of Cairo.[7] It is ironic that the populist poet who now writes to the poor was born to a "feudalist" family which did not only own thousands of acres but also had its home village named after it. In contrast to the poet/scholar Osundare, Nigm never had a formal education. Apart from attending for a short while the local Quranic school in his village, he probably never went to school. He tried a variety of odd jobs, and at one point in his career he was accused of fraud and embezzlement and was jailed for a few years. Once out of jail, around 1963, he met a blind singer, Shaykh Imam, with whom he had a partnership that lasted for over two decades. Nigm would compose poems that Shaykh Imam would sing to the melodious tunes of his 'ud (Arab equivalent of European lute).

The songs of Nigm-Imam became popular in the aftermath of the devastating Arab defeat at the hands of the Israelis in 1967. They sang about the agony of defeat and the hope of restoring Arab strength to regain the Israeli-occupied lands, and to restore with that Arab dignity. The poems/songs suggest that only force and a prolonged people's war can redeem Egypt's honor. This would be Nigm's *leitmotiv* in his post-1967 poems. At this point, Nigm's *engagement* had just begun in earnest. It is in this sense that Farida al-Naqqash is wrong to portray all of Nigm 's work, from 1964 onward, as revolutionary.[8] Indeed, one cannot ignore the shift in Nigm's work from a quietistic social and political awareness of Egypt's causes before 1967, to a strident revolutionary *leitmotiv* both in theme and tone after 1967.

Nigm was involved in several major demonstrations in Egypt since 1967, particularly the student uprisings which characterized the 1970s. The common denominator in those uprisings was the students' and workers' demand to liberate Israeli-occupied Sinai and to change the no-war no-peace state that prevailed at the time. Battle was the demonstrators' outcry and many—especially the students—called for a people's war.[9] The battle eventually took place in 1973; the result of which parts of Sinai were liberated and a momentum for peaceful negotiation was created.

Nigm's work was for over two decades banned in Egypt and although many Egyptians were familiar with it, they were not able to see it in print until a few years ago. Nigm and Shaykh Imam managed to have hundreds of revolutionary *chansons* recorded on cassette tapes which were surreptitiously making the rounds in Egypt. Their first record was produced in France by *Le Chant Du Monde*. To date, Nigm has published over thirteen collections of poetry and a two-part memoir in colloquial Egyptian Arabic.[10]

For twenty years, from 1968 till mid-1980s, Nigm was jailed by the Egyptian authorities several times for his "subversive" poetry. Long periods of incarceration, however, helped grind to sharpness his poetic craft and enhanced his popularity in and out of Egypt. Despite the authorities' attempts to curb his activities and break him, Nigm managed to become the spokesman and the eloquent dreamer of Egypt's simple and unlettered folk.

POETRY BETWEEN IVORY-TOWERISM AND COMMITMENT

What is the function of poetry for Osundare and Nigm? Does one compose poetry to "express" one's inner feelings or to "reflect" one's societal concern? For Osundare, poetry is

> not the esoteric whisper
> on an excluding tongue
> not a claptrap
> for wondering audience
> not a learned quiz
> Entombed in Grecoroman lore
> ....
> Poetry
> is
> man
> meaning
> to
> man.[11]

Osundare believes that poetry should not be the exclusive property of the elite but rather an affordable commodity in the marketplace of the common folk. It is not the vehicle of the private whisperings of self-meditation but the mouthpiece of the common concerns of the simple and the unlettered.

He attacks the inequality that causes the crooked politicians and the corrupt middlemen to squander the national wealth while the wretched peasants are left to fend for themselves, eking out a miserable existence. The crooked ones

> They want more yam
> for the city stomach
> more maize for the bottomless boot
> of the glittering Mercedes.[12]

For Nigm, authentic poetry is the guide to the perplexed. The words of a poem that authentically reflects the concerns of the poor and the unlettered can be the only way out for them. Words for Nigm have eyes through which people can see the road ahead when oppression reigns supreme,

> When the sun sinks in a sea of mist
> When a wave of darkness blankets the universe
> When vision dies in sights and insights
> When the road is lost in winding lines and circles
> Then, you mindful wayfarer,
> Will realize that you cannot see the road ahead
> Except through the eyes of words.[13]

In his poem, "Ya'ish Ahl Baladi" (Long Live the People of My Country), Nigm paints a satirical picture of Egypt's social pyramid where the rich few sit securely on the top and the poor masses at the base (the pyramid is the Egyptian form *par excellence*). The poem's date is 1968, a mere year after the Arab defeat in the 1967 Arab-Israeli war, the implication may have been that the unbridgeable class gap in Egypt was one of the causes of Egypt's defeat in the war. The poem's date leads us to believe that David Hurst and Irene Beeson, in their biography of the late Egyptian President, Anwar al-Sadat, were wrong to assume that Nigm's poem was written in reaction to al-Sadat's *infitah*, open-door policy—started in earnest after 1973—which created a class of *nouveaux riches* and middlemen.[14]

In his poem, Nigm lampoons the rich who live off the work and the sweat of the poor. They live in Zamalik, Cairo's middle-class neighborhood, and own large estates in poor Upper Egypt. The social gap between them and the down-and-out is hopelessly wide. Nothing seems capable of bridging the ever-widening gap between the two classes—not even Nasser's *tahaluf,* alliance of the working classes, slogans.

> The people of my country live
> Not knowing one another,
> No bond among them
> To allow the "alliance" to live on.[15]

The gap between the poor and the intellectuals is also wide. The intellectuals are chided for turning into state-salaried bureaucrats who write what the rulers want them to. They do not mix with the "masses" but they sit in their fashionable haunts where they meet and engage in idle talk.

> The intellectual lives in Café Riche
> (Long live the intellectual!)
> Pedantic, slippery and talkative.
> He lacks experience
> He dislikes the crowd,
> With one empty word here
> And a hollow term there,
> He quickly fabricates solutions.[16]

In terms that remind one of Osundare's poetry, Nigm describes the rich in his society as individuals who have their own quarters—like Zamalik—where they savor their wealth and the satisfaction of their consumer appetites.

> Walk and you may see them
> In downtown
> If a car as big as a ship passes you by
> Their necks are thick and pasty,
> Bellies are fat
> Skin is gleaming
> Mind is obtuse.[17]

The poor languish in their misery, their arms are thin and their frame is frail and yet they possess native cunning that helps them survive. Rather sarcastically, Nigm advises the poor to tend to their life and not to heed the hollow slogans of politicians.

> Poor of our country;
> Fellah and laborer;
> You're the lubricant of the waterwheel
> The coal of the factory
> Teach your children contentment
> For we are, of course, all the slaves of Fate:
> Your livelihood, mine
> And the livelihood of the dogs
> Are issues postponed until the Day of Reckoning.[18]

Nigm's sardonic style betrays a sense of momentary despair, a despair that stems from lack of faith in change under such oppressive conditions. That despair is, however, rare in his poems.

If Nigm's cause is the struggle for class equality and freedom from fear over one's safety and wellbeing, what is Osundare's?

Osundare draws a comparison between the blissful old days of his childhood and the oppressive hardships of the present. In his *The Eye of the Earth* (1986), Osundare tells us about his childhood and from his very evocative preface, we see a nostalgic poet remembering happier times in his village:

> Farmer-born, peasant-bred, I encountered dawn in the enchanted corridors of the forest, suckled on the delicate aroma of healing herbs, and the pearly drops of generous moons. Living in those early days was rugged, but barns brimmed with yams fattened by merciful rains and the tempering fire of the upland sun. The cock rang the bell of dawn, promptly aided by a lone and distant corn-mill which hummed into action, making sure it carried the village along. Earth was ours, and we earth's. We grew what we ate and ate what we grew. [19]

This was the case in the distant past, before the onslaught of foreign domination and the irulent advent of Europe's merchants who turned the native farmers into cocoa-coffee-cashew croppers, while yamfields succumbed to weed and granaries rang out like mourning shells. A cancerous god called MONEY crashed in from across the seas, with a blind sword and a crown of noisy gold, smashing old customs, assailing the very core of ancient humanistic ethos. To acquire it on Europe's terms, Africa abandoned what she ate, committing her fertile soil and rugged energy to those alien crops which cushioned the

European stomach. (Whoever still doesn't know the roots of Africa's hunger should run a rapid eye back to these uneasy epochs).[20] ... For in the intricate dialectics of human living, looking back is looking forward, the visionary artist is not only a rememberer, he is also a reminder."[21]

Like Nigm, Osundare's concern is with the poor peasants and workers

> Village boy's kwashiorkor bellies
> hairless head impaled on pin necks
> and ribs baring the benevolence
> of the body politic.[22]

The affluent and the corrupt politicians are on the other hand seen as

> bloated millionaires
> hostaging us to slave makers
> exporters
> importers
> emergence contractors
> manufacturer's representatives
> buying cheap
> selling dear.[23]

In depicting effectively the plight of the poor and how the class inequality deprives them of the essentials of life, Osundare utilizes imagery that is derived from his native environment. Take for example these lines in which the forest with its tall trees (*iroko*) and small shrubs and saplings stands for Osundare's society with its structured class hierarchy:

> "Come home, son
> for we cannot be all *iroko*
> Slapping the sky's face
> with imperious boughs
> while the lower forest
> dies a sunless death
> at our unfeeling feet
> Come away from the fold
> of sun stealers..."[24]

The shrubs and saplings are deprived of their sustenance (the sun rays) which in turn is stolen by the tall trees—dubbed the "sun stealers", in the same way the rich and the powerful "hog" the national resources depriving the poor of their due share. Osundare's *iroko* are Nigm's rich residents of the posh Zamalik district.

And like Nigm, Osundare indicts the pseudo-revolutionary intellectuals (the "Pedantic, slippery and talkative" in Nigm's words); one finds this in poems with telling titles such as "Feigning Rebel," and "Listen, Book Wizard".[25] He finds "the intellectual revolutionary posture as a ruse, the intellectuals are eager to step into the shoes of the corrupt politicians."[26]

But unlike Nigm, Osundare directs much of his attention to the fate of mother earth, to the environment and the depleting effects of pollution on it. His is a concern for landscape as well as "humanscape."[27]

Osundare's poem "Our Earth Will not Die" declaims the triumph of hope over despair, the belief that sooner or later the earth will overcome its woes and become alive again. In the beginning despair reigns supreme as the earth faces utter desolation and death of hope:

> Lynched
> > the lake
> Slaughtered
> > the sun
> Mauled
> > the mountains[28]

It is the environment that is being despoiled by the earth's inhabitants: acid rain defoliating the forests, and the ozone seriously depleted. But hope can still be spotted before the end of the tunnel:

> The westering sun will rise again
> resplendent like a new coin.
> The wind, unwound, will play its tune
> trees twittering, grasses dancing.
> hillsides will rock with blooming harvests
> the plains batting their eyes of grass and grace.
>
> The sea will drink its heart's content
> when a jubilant thunder flings open the skygate
> and a new rain tumbles down
> in drums of joy.[29]

For Osundare, hope and optimism about the future are essential to one's own existence, for without hope "life crumbles like a clay doll in the tropical rain."[30] For Osundare is the kind of man who "... dreams of a frog when he sees a tadpole, he dreams of rain when he sees a cloud.[31]

Both Osundare and Nigm use similar techniques such as the use of humor, use of folkloric forms and poetic diction and in what follows we will discuss the ways in which each poet uses these techniques.

USE OF HUMOR
Both Osundare and Nigm employ humor in their poetry in order to dramatize their message. In "Song of the Nigerian Driver" Osundare satirizes the Nigerian driver who does not seem to care even about his own vehicle "So, flog it like a fatherless donkey."[32] In his "A Tongue in the Crypt," Osundare satirically calls on his people

> Patriots
> Thinkers
> Countrymen,
>
> Behold your tongue
> Sealed up in this iron cage
> For public safety
> And the national interest
>
> For permission to use,
> Apply to:
> The Minister of Whispering Affairs
> Dept. of Patriotic Silence,
> 53 Graveyard Avenue,
> DUMBERIA.[33]

Notice that "behold" in "Behold your tongue" may also suggest "Hold your tongue". Silence, being later described as a patriotic duty, is enforced by formidable "Minister of Whispering Affairs" who is located on "Graveyard Avenue," a name which conjures up the silence of the grave. This is all happening in the imaginary land of "Dumberia" a coined name that does not only evoke silence, muteness and voicelessness, but also stupidity. Osundare seems to suggest that under the oppressive political regime the motherland, Nigeria, has become "Dumberia", a land that is eerily devoid of both sound and sense.

Likewise, the oppressive rulers are often the butt of Nigm's humor. With simple and biting colloquial Egyptian Arabic, Nigm satirizes his targets, revealing a highly refined sense of humour.

In mock-heroic style, Nigm ridicules Nasser and three prominent figures who served under him and who were primarily blamed for the defeat in 1967: Abd al-Hakim Amir, Shams Badran and Abbas Radwan:

> According to my Master the hash-smoking rip-off
> These four people will be tossed in Hell:
> Shams ibn Badran who, without preparation,
> Entered the war;
> Abd al-Hakim ibn Amir
> Who fell in love with Warda (famous singer);
> Abbas ibn Radwan who stole the gold and silver
> And Abd al-Lazi' Ibn al-Mitabbit, sticky son of the pasty one
> Who has stayed the longest in power.34

Notice that Abd al-Lazi', the sticky, is assonant with Abd al-Nasir, the name of the late president Nasser. Ibn al-Mitabbit, son of the pasty one, alludes to Nasser's long stay in power. The opening, "According to my Master " is usually the way some medieval Arabic texts begin, especially works of Hadith or Qur'an exegesis. Muslims might find such imitation disrespectful but Nigm uses it somewhat lightheartedly. To enhance the humor, Nigm juxtaposes colloquial phrases alongside terse literary ones. In this fashion, the diction fluctuates rather absurdly from the stilted classical to the out-and-out colloquial.

Other examples, among many other, of humor in Nigm's poems include a reference to a minister in the government who was also a novelist as a "self-made ignoramus" who writes works better left unread; the Egyptians, Nigm states, won the war against the Israelis in 1973 with not only "technology" but also with "nukta-ology"—*nukta* being Arabic for a joke, a reference to the characteristic Egyptian humor which Egyptians often employ to devastate their oppressors.

FOLKLORIC FORMS AND EXPRESSIONS

Osundare acknowledges his indebtedness to the oral tradition of his native land. "Prominent at the back of my mind," says Osundare about this work, "are the traditional roles of the oral poet to whom I owe a lot: to entertain, to inform, to satirize, and to warn."35 He cites also the folktale and its technique as having been "enormously useful" to his work. "Casting new happenings in old modes, couching the here-and-now in the form of once-upon-a time," says Osundare, "I have discovered that the poem could actually be an everlasting proverb."36

Osundare utilizes some folkloric genres such as folk songs, proverbs, maxims, and anecdotes, in which "tradition has encapsulated its understanding of life, its worldview and social preferences."37

> Sigidi thirsty for a dance of shame
> Craves a festival in the rains
> Bees hum peacefully in a following farm
> A restless boy punctures their hive
> with a crooked stick.38

As Bamikunle notes these lines are based on "two common images in Yoruba by which the combatants threaten their opponents in the way the poet threatens to carry the fight to the enemies of society."39

> Your mates wrestle in the village square
> you grapple massive morsels
> in your neighbour's kitchens
> where a bowl of yam
> puts you flat on your slothful back.40

This is a reworking of a Nigerian wrestling song, a traditional taunt to the opponent, utilized here by Osundare to depict a political leadership that "reaps without sowing, leading the country through twenty-five years of socio-political and economic impasse."41 Likewise the traditional anecdote about the chicken that "eats pebbles and swallows sands yet complains of toothlessness,"42 is made to refer to the fraudulent rulers add insult to injury in their oppressive and deceitful dealings with their people. In this act of "reworking" the traditional, Osundare does not hand down the traditional as it is but rather he alters it to suit his poetic/revolutionary purposes, making it an "alter-native" tradition.43

Much like Osundare, Nigm's identification with the causes of his country's simple folk is dramatized not only in his use of their everyday idiom but also in his use of the different forms of their orally transmitted literature. He employs such forms as the *mawwal* (narrative ballad), children's songs, lullabies, songs celebrating the seventh day after a child's birth, wedding songs, folk proverbs, folk riddles, cries of the peddlers.44 The following selected examples will illustrate Nigm's dexterity in rendering these forms malleable to his political message.

Here is one of Nigm's poems in the form of children's lullabies,

> H u u u h, ninna huuuh
> Huuuh to you who are Mother's song
> In her comings and goings
> Huuuh to you who are always the dream of longing
> Huuuh to you who are the balsam for wounds,
> Ninnah huuuh.
>
> When they said the baby was a girl
> Henna grew out of my hands
> A sun rose in the evening
> Go away, darkness of loneliness, go away
> Ninnah huuuh.
>
> When they said the baby was a boy
> My back sprang up and found support
> I complained of the homeland's conditions
> To my offspring, I was able to speak up
> Ninnah huuuh.45

Nigm, in the above, adapts a line from a traditional lullaby in which the mother clearly favours the male offspring singing:

> When they said the baby was a boy
> My back firmed up and found support.xlvi

In the same lullaby, there is no mention of female offspring. But in his poem Nigm goes beyond these anti-female traditions and makes the mother joyfully sing for her baby girl.

Although the elements of Nigm's imagery are mainly derived from folk wisdom and wit, they are not always employed in their conventional sense but rather are adjusted to fit Nigm's particular purposes. The "eloquent chick" in the popular proverb *"il-katkut il-fasih mi l-beda yisih"*xlvii (the eloquent chick cries out at the moment it hatches), is used in "il-Hawi" (The Juggler) as the symbolic correlative of hope for oppressed Egypt. And to point out the treachery of the oppressive ruler, Nigm writes:

> When the low-bred ruled
> He could let (you) go—but wouldn't,xlviii

Instead of the conventional meaning in the famous *mawwal*, "When the dog (low-bred) rules, the lion calls him master,"[xlix] notice here how Nigm makes explicit the debasement and the vile nature of the oppressive ruler but drops any reference to the demeaning behaviour of the once proud oppressed (the lion being the symbol of the oppressed folk). In other words, Nigm here utilizes the form and even alludes to the folk symbols but rejects the values included therein if these values prove obnoxious to his revolutionary message. In this way, Nigm, much like Osundare, alters the native tradition, making it an "alternative" tradition.

To what extent is the work of Osundare or Nigm popular/populist? In comparing Osundare to his fellow Nigerian poet Chinweizu, A. Bamikunle[l] observes that while both poets are "very readable", Chinweizu achieves this "readability" not by employing popular African artforms, as Osundare does, but by assuming "the poetic posture that depends for effects on maintaining a clear distance between him and his audience. His attitude to the public, whether it is mankind, Africans or Nigerians, is one disdainful disgust." Again, unlike Osundare, Chinweizu "is the sage who is on the periphery of society and laughing at the absurdities of that society." This is how Chinweizu sees the Black world:

> Black curious freak
> Mind expropriated by settler concepts
> Mind dislocated by hostile mindsmiths
> Patch work contraption... [li]

But one wonders if Bamikunle's observation needs some qualification. One finds examples of Osundare's harsh criticism of his countrymen's acquiescence to oppression and lack of initiative—in fact in terms that are not dissimilar to those of Nigm. In his poem "Ignorance" Osundare condemns his rural countrymen for being ignorant for letting themselves be led like sheep by cruel rulers—the wolf,[lii] and in "Song of the Sudden Storm," far from standing with the masses in their struggle against corrupt rulers he turns on them calling them

> Fickle like a fart
> Forgetful like a tale-less tribe,
> People of our land,
> Our memory is a lazy dust
> Washed easily off our land
> By showers of arbitrary seasons.[liii]

In laughing at the absurdities of his society, Osundare shares a measure of similarity with the Egyptian Nigm who too satirizes the shortcomings of his fellow countrymen in somewhat harsh terms:

> Revolt, people of my country
> Revolt, may a calamity strike you dead!
> Revolt, uproot the causes of your malaise
> Your rulers the "Free Officers" are but
> A gang of vampires sucking your blood.[liv]

One is perhaps more accurate to state that Osundare, much like Nigm, changed his attitudes to the masses over time. Osundare's indictments of the masses in his 1983 *Songs of the Marketplace* gave way to more confidence in them and their worldview in his 1984 *Village Voices*. Likewise Nigm's indictments were included in a 1969 poem, in the aftermath of the bitter Arab defeat at the hands of the Israelis in the 1967 war, and while Nigm was in jail.

POETIC DICTION

In his collection of poetry, *Moonsongs* (1988), Osundare's language is a mix of English interspersed with Yoruba phrases acting as refrains. The first poem, Osundare calls it a song, in the collection starts this way:

> Spread the sky like a generous mat
> Tell dozing rivers to stir their tongues
> Unhinge the hills
> Unwind the winds
> The moon and I will sing tonight
> > Kiriji kiriji kiriji pepelupe ...
> Oh moon, matron, master, eternal maiden,
> The bounce of your bosom
> The miracle of your cheeks
> Your smile which ripens the forests,
> Your frown which wrinkles the dusk
> The youth of your age
> The age of your youth
> All, all await
> The echoing thunder of my riddling chants
> > Kiriji kiriji kiriji pepelupe ...[lv]

In "Buka Banter" in his collection, *Songs of the Season* (1990), Osundare mixes standard with pidgin English for humorous purposes. "Whetin you go chop?" (What are you going to eat?), thus begins the poem. Various answers are given, but none includes meat. "Mba, Mba' my pocket don loss im teeth," the speaker in the poems says. "Mba" is "No" in Igbo, not Yoruba. And in his *Midlife* (1993), Osundare frequently uses long Yoruba phrases that are not always translated into English. Osundare includes his audience and their utterances and responses to his voice in his work. In so doing, he shows himself "committed to exploring the transitional links between oral and written poetry."[lvi] By choosing to utilize Igbo in addition to Yoruba, Osundare, who is a Yoruba, shows his identification with all communities in his society.[lvii]

Nigm's choice of colloquial Egyptian Arabic as his vehicle of expression highlights the differences between Standard and Colloquial Arabic and, in fact, exploits them. For merely by choosing the colloquial over standard Arabic, he has made a statement on the prestige and literary heritage not only of the colloquial language but also of popular culture and sentiment that is not lost on the reader. The grammar and lexicon of colloquial Arabic also share in this statement of purpose, but of course go much farther than that, extending Nigm's freedom and range of expression and rendering his poetry more effective in voicing his concerns in terms that are much more meaningful in the ears of the common folk.

It should be noted that Nigm's colloquial is not just another level of language in the same way that the language of the courtroom is different from that of the souk. Nor can the colloquial be adequately rendered in Standard Arabic. To cite some examples from Nigm's poetry, take for instance, words like *bakash* or *awanta*—words Nigm often uses to describe the activities of politicians—which can be translated into English as hocus-pocus or monkey-business; or take the creatively coined verbs *yi'afyin*, to take *afyun* (opium); *yi'anfis*, to take a *nafas* (literally a breath but here the equivalent of a "drag", i.e. to smoke hashish or some other narcotic); and other words which are out and out colloquial and almost untranslatable.

Another characteristic of Nigm's poetic diction is its raciness. He sometimes uses words that would definitely be considered unprintable by the elite writers. When he describes how American products inundate the Egyptian market and how the Coca Cola advertisements fill the Egyptian color television sets, he says:

COKE IS IT!
Drink, O congenial one

Cut the nonsense
About all that patriotism and the bull's ass.[lviii]

About a character in a "trashy" film, a sign of Egypt's cultural poverty, Nigm calls him, "goz tant marika il-labwa"[lix]) (the husband of the ever-horny Auntie Marika). The official journalists, who are state-salaried, are respectively called "il-mumisin" (the prostitutes) and "il-arsagiyya"[lx] (the pimps): they either prostitute themselves to the rulers or they act as pimps while the rulers "screw" the helpless masses.

CONCLUSION

As we have seen throughout, the Nigerian Osundare and the Egyptian Nigm hail from different native traditions and personal backgrounds. Osundare is a poet/scholar composing, in English, verse in which he shows commitment to the common folk in his country and to conserving the wellbeing of "mother earth". His imagery and choice of diction betray his long association with the Western poetic tradition, especially of the Romanticists (Wordsworth and Whitman among others). But he interweaves his work with the lyricism and pithy idiom of his folk tradition, making use of the indigenous artforms and the wisdom lore of his native land.

Nigm, on the other hand, hails from a modest background with no formal education to speak of, and no known profession other than being a people's poet. In contrast to the scholarly and the lecture-hall demeanor of Professor/poet Osundare, Nigm comes across as now a bohemian artist now a street-wise ruffian. He composes protest poems/songs that are couched in the Arabic vernacular of Egypt and, much like the case with Osundare's work, these are framed in folk poetic forms. Unlike the case with the poetry in standard Arabic, Nigm's vernacular poetry is in a language that is closer to the mind and heart of the great majority of Egyptians, a language that is earthy since it is, by and large, derived from the racy witticisms of the Egyptian street.

Both poets, however, do not mechanically make use of their respective native tradition in order to curry favor with "the masses". Rather, they interweave strands of the native lore with their own modern revolutionary voices. They charge their indigenous tradition with the dynamic rhetoric of their revolutionary stands on issues relating to the rights of the poor and the oppressed, Third World liberation movements, and the preservation of the earth's natural resources. If the native tradition tends to reconcile the common folk to their lot in life, however miserable, and to the status quo, however static and unbearable, the potent poems/songs of Osundare and Nigm proclaim in familiar idioms and artforms the advent of something new: something that goes beyond the frontiers of the native tradition. A revolutionary "alter-native" tradition that adopts a double critique that rejects both the "conservatism" of the folk tradition and the obscurantism of the elite.

AUTHOR'S NOTE:
I would like to express my gratitude to Dr. Abdul-Rasheed Na'Allah for having invited me to contribute this article to this volume, therefore giving me an opportunity to enter the poetic universe of Nigeria's great poet Niyi Osundare and compare him to Egypt's noted poet, Ahmad Fuad Nigm. I am also grateful to A. Skuba-Pincock for having read and provided important comments on this article.

NOTES

1 I owe this coined term to Funso Aiyejina who uses it in his article, "Recent Nigerian Poetry in English: An Alter/Native Tradition," *Komparatistische Hefte*, nos. 13–16 (1986–87): 49–64. I do not however define the term in the same way he does in his article.

2 Don Burness, "Niyi Osundare (12 March 1947–)." Eds. Bernth Lindfors and Reinhard Sander. *Twentieth-Century Caribbean and Black African Writers*, Third Series. Detroit: Gale Research, Inc. 1996: 287.

3 Funso Aiyejina, "Recent Nigerian Poetry in English: An Alter/Native Tradition," *Komparatistische Hefte*, nos. 13–16 (1986–87): 61.

4 In his collection, *The Eye of the Earth* Heinemann Frontline Series, 1986, rep. 1988: 43–44.

5 See my article "The Khawaga Then and Now: Images of the West in Modern Egyptian Zajal." *Journal of Arabic Literature* 19 (1988): 162–178, and my book *A Study of the Vernacular Poetry of Ahmad Fuad Nigm* (Leiden: E.J. Brill, 1990). See also the Arabic study Jalal al-Mukhkh, *Ahmad Fuad Nigm min al-Thawra ila al-Khayba* (Sousa, Tunisia: Dar al-Maarif, 1990). Most of my statements on Nigm are derived from my published studies cited here.

6 See my *Ahmad Fuad Nigm*, 4. For a detailed treatment of this scholarly neglect of vernacular literature, see my "Introduction", 1–5.

7 Ibid., 13.

8 *Baladi wa Habibti*. Beirut: Dar Ibn Khaldun, 1973: 9.

9 David Hurst and Irene Beeson, *Sadat*. London: Faber, 1981: 150.

10 *Suwar min il-Haya wil-Sign*. Cairo: The Supreme Council of Arts and Literature, 1964; *Baladi wa Habibti*. Beirut: Dar Ibn Khaldun, 1973; *Ya'ish Ahl Baladi*. Beirut: Dar Ibn Khaldun, 1973; *'Iyun il-Kalam*. Cairo: Ash'ar al-Thaqafa al-Jadida, 1976; *Ughniyat il-Hubb wil-Haya*. Cairo: Madbuli, 1978; *Ana Fen*. Baghdad: Dar al-Hurriyya lil-Tiba'a, 1979; *Ishi ya Masr*. Beirut: Dar al-Kalima, 1979; *Tahran, Ughniyat wa Ash'ar lil-Thawra*. Beirut: Dar al-Kalima, 1979; *il-'Anbara*. Cairo: Madbuli, 1982; *Aghani min il-Mu'ta'al*. Montreal: Le Cercle de la culture arabe du Quebec, 1980; *Five Poems By*

Ahmad Fuad Nigm, tr. Miriam Lowi. Ottawa: Jerusalem International Publishing House, 1982; *Sandu' il-Dunya.* Cairo: Madbuli, 1985; *Kalam 'ala Safar.* Cairo: Matba'at al-'Uruba, 1989; Ahmad Fuad Nigm, *Diwan,* Part I & II (Damascus: Dar Tlas); *il-Murgeha.* Cairo: Madbuli al-Saghir, 1993; *Mudhakkirat al-Sha'ir Ahmad Fuad Nigm al-Fagumi.* Cairo: Dar Sphinx, 1993; *Mudhakkirat al-Sha'ir Ahmad Fuad Nigm al-Fagumi,* Part II. Cairo: Madbuli al-Saghir, 1993.

11 Osundare, "Opening" in his collection, *Songs of the Marketplace.*

12 Cited in Don Burness, "Niyi Osundare (12 March 1947–), 287–288.

13 Nigm, *Diwan,* Part II.

14 David Hurst and Irene Beeson, *Sadat,* 218.

15 Nigm, *Ya'ish,* 71.

16 Ibid., 72.

17 Ibid., 73.

18 Ibid., 75.

19 *The Eye of the Earth,* 1986: xi.

20 Ibid.

21 Ibid., xii.

22 "Excursions," *Village Voices,* 7.

23 ibid., 14.

24 *Village Voices,* 22.

25 See Osundare's *Songs of the Marketplace.*

26 Bamikunle, "New Trends," 83.

27 I am grateful to my 13-years old daughter, Amira, who advised me to change my original "manscape" to the present "humanscape".

28 *The Eye of the Earth,* 50.

29 Ibid., 51.

30 Don Burness, "Niyi Osundare (12 March 1947–), 291.

31 Ibid.

32 Ibid., 292.

33 In Osundare's *Songs of the Season,* cited in Don Burness, "Niyi Osundare (12 March 1947–), 292.

34 This piece is taken from a tape of Nigm-Imam songs. See my *Ahmad Fu'ad Nigm,* 64–65.

35 Osundare, "Tabloid Poetry." Eds. S. Arnold and A. Niecki. *Culture and Development in Africa.* Trenton, NJ: Africa World Press, 1990: 5.

36 Ibid.

37 A. Bamikunle, "New Trends in Nigerian Poetry: The Poetry of Niyi Osundare and Chinweizu," *Literary Criterion,* 23, nos. 1–2 (1988): 84.

38 Ibid.

39 Ibid.

40 Ibid., 85.

41 Ibid.

42 Ibid.

43 See Funso Aiyejina, "Recent Nigerian Poetry in English: An Alter/Native Tradition," *Komparatistische Hefte*, nos 13–16 (1986–87): 49–64.

44 For full treatment of the use of these forms in Nigm's poetry see *my Ahmad Fuad Nigm*, 89–104.

45 Nigm, *il-'Anbara*, 156–157.

46 As recorded in *The Folk Music of Egypt*, collected by Tiberiu Alexandru and Emile Wahba. Cairo: Ministry of Culture, 1976(?).

47 Samya Atallah, *al-Amthal al-Shabiyya*. Beirtu: al-Watan al-Arabi, 1984: 32.

48 Nigm, *Baladi*, 50.

49 See Ahmad Mursi, *al-Ughniyya al-Shabiyya*. Cairo: Dar al-Maarif, 1983: 399.

50 A. Bamikunle, "New Trends," 78.

51 Ibid.

52 *Songs of the Marketplace* , 34.

53 Osundare, "Tabloid Poetry," 5.

54 Nigm, *Diwan*, Part II, 744.

55 Osundare, *Moonsongs*, 1–2.

56 Don Burness, "Niyi Osundare (12 March 1947–), 294.

57 Ibid.

58 Nigm, *Sandu*, 96.

59 Ibid., 82.

60 Nigm, *Tahran*, 64.

POSTCOLONIAL CONTEXT, POSTMODERNIST PERSPECTIVE: N. OSUNDARE'S WAITING LAUGHTERS & Y. ANDRUKHOVYCH'S "CARNIVAL" POETRY

Irene Sywenky

Any juxtaposition of the postcolonial and the postmodernist is bound to be ambivalent. Centrifugal orientation of the postmodernist epistemology away from the centre (subject, truth, history) runs opposite to the largely centripetal efforts of the post-colonial recovery of history and (re)construction of national/ethnic identity of de-colonized communities. Although the notions of both postmodernism and postcolonialism lack definitional clarity and precision, it is specifically within the area of the latter that we feel the need to elaborate before proceeding with the main argument. One of the more significant developments in the area of postcolonial studies has been the recent negotiation of its scope to include the study of peripheral cultures, whereas the problematics of the very condition of cultural peripherality[1] is slowly moving into the focus of academic attention (it also overlaps with the area of our present interest, the so-called marginal/peripheral post-modernisms[2]). Acknowledgement of the condition of peripherality not only expands the limits of postcolonial studies[3]: it reaches beyond the traditional dichotomy of the colonizer vs. colonized towards the centre vs. periphery/margins, a binary opposition that is more complex and universal. It implies reading and being read in the context of the world culture in relation to the imperial/central "other." The geopolitical tensions of postmodern epistemology in the context of post-colonialism and peripherality produce literature that is a battlefield of implicitly coded desires to participate in the global discourse and to continue within and for the purpose of the reproduction of a particular cultural paradigm. As I. Hassan implicitly argues, the resolution of double claims of the local and the global, national and international lies at the very heart of marginal literatures (p. 13).[4]

The significant move towards the emphasis on the condition of peripherality goes along with a recognition of the fact that the term "postcolonial(ism)" cannot adequately cater to the very scope and heterogeneity of the condition it refers to. The ambiguity of the concept, particularly because of its emphasis on certain temporal/chronological boundaries it implicitly constructs, has been justly noted and challenged (cf. McClintock). The root of such discussions, however, extends beyond the ambivalence of the mere term to the complexity and diversity of the postcolonial realities themselves. As an Australian scholar observes in relation to East European societies, true postcolonial consciousness steps over the original dichotomy of the colonizer vs. colonized to accept the history in its totality, to realize the teleological nature of both colonial and anti-colonial systems of thought and their ideological power and purpose (see Pavlyshyn). This leads to a possibility of theorizing epistemological closeness of the postcolonial and postmodernist pluralisms and a necessity of differentiation between the post-colonial and anti-colonial (ibid.). In all its obvious pragmatic value, such a differentiation, however, fails to account for the virtual impossibility to draw any distinct demarcation line between the both, and, further, it assigns certain holistic and "cathartic" values to the postcolonial, implying that it actually steps over the limitations of the "anti-colonial" consciousness. The "post" in "postcolonial(ism)" (at the present stage) largely remains the signifier of certain geopolitical changes on the map that do not necessarily correlate to the state of affairs in the world order. The post-independence euphoria necessarily evolves into the realization that breaking away from colonial hierarchies merely leads to the discovery of more complex and subtle power structures. Where the dichotomy of the colonizer vs. colonized is (or might seem to be) overcome, a new dichotomy comes into play — periphery/margin vs. centre, and, thus, anti-colonial may re-emerge in the context of new (neo-colonial) cultural, economic and political practices.

In the discussed context it cannot be overlooked that, although postmodernist consciousness does intersect with postcolonial pluralism, the postmodernist project itself was initiated, generated and theoretically validated at the "centre," and as such might be viewed as representing cultural expansion from the centre. However, to talk about postmodernist experimentations at the periphery in terms of a passive reception or a certain artificial "transplantation" of an alien discourse on the soil of the local tradition (cf. Ilnytzkyj) would be a huge simplification of the matter. "Processing" of postmodernism by any postcolonial culture is also its appropriation for its own uses and ideological purposes, including participating in the construction of the national self. As Jusdanis argues, a peripheral culture presents an "experiment on the margins, which, having internalized the tensions between dominant and minor, periphery and center, prototype and copy, imitates and also *creates*, follows but *resists*" (p. xii, my emphasis).[5] The present paper examines the construction and self-exploration of the national self through geopolitical tensions at the crossroads of postcolonial and postmodernist and the internal conflicts of implicit process of writing oneself into the world culture while maintaining a distinct cultural identity.

The two cases, that we find are representative of these processes, provide an interesting comparison between two essentially different cultures, contained within similar power structure relations — Nigerian/West African and Ukrainian /East European. Whereas it is hardly necessary to introduce Osundare in the context of the present volume, a few words should be said about Andrukhovych. Yuri Andrykhovych (together with Oleksandr Irvanets and Viktor Neborak) belongs to the trio of poets and prose writers self-named as "Bu-Ba-Bu" that appeared in the late 80's in the atmosphere of the newly awaken national self-awareness, great cultural upheaval on the eve of the collapse of the totalitarian structures and the coming independence of the nation[6] (the era of the "quiet revolution," as defined by one of the poets, "Interview" 73). Written in the spirit of the predominantly carnivalesque mode complete with its subversion of hierarchies, norms and canons, Andrukhovych's poetry and prose stirred a lot of controversy at the time when the national consciousness was dominated by nostalgia for mythic origins and cultural essentialism. Similarly to Osundare, Andrukhovych engages in a largely controversial discourse of re-evaluation and re-contextualization (both explicit and implicit) of traditional values and discourses.

What yields a particular interest to the comparison is the framework of laughter that unites the discussed oeuvre. Although generally laughter (and carnivalesque, as in the case of Andrukhovych) can be regarded here as a certain liberating space, an inner jubilating outcry of the nation, it also has other dimensions and cannot be treated from a unifold perspective. The condition of suspended expectation is what unites both spaces of laughter. Osundare's imagery generally tends to be extremely opaque (one of the better examples would be the symbol of the moon in his *Moonsongs*, where the elusiveness and fluidity of the image renders it almost impossible to pinpoint the ever sliding signified; the image of the moon also reappears throughout *Waiting Laughters*). The metamorphosis of laughter in the discussed collection is of the similar quality. The very title of the cycle significantly tones down the potential *jouissance* of it. The space of waiting creates temporal disturbance, the condition of suspension. The ambiguity of the title leaves it open to various potential connotations: laughters that are waiting to come to life? laughters suspended in the middle of the process (of jubilation)? laughters that are being awaited? The plurality of the noun is just as significant, the form being implicit of both the variety of meanings and realizations of laughters and the potential multiplicity of voices. If the opening verse explicitly resorts to the literal meaning of laughter and plays around various modes of its expression (mirth, glee, giggles, chuckles, pp. 86–87), the following poems of the cycle manifest a noticeable shift to the key word "waiting," and more seldom references to laughter acquire a range of more ambiguous associations. *Waiting Laughters* is about expectancy with its promise that might or might not come fulfilled. It is about certain void space, waiting to be filled. The characteristic plural form of the laughter in the title also adds to the various plural modes (truths, histories, voices etc) explored in the collection. Osundare's laughter is a laughter stripped of innocence and burdened with the centuries-old wisdom of the nation: "[l]aughter's parable explodes in the groin / Of waking storms / Clamorous with a covenant / of wizened seeds" (I, 86).

Similarly, Andrukhovych's poetry, belonging to the "carnival" period of the Bu-Ba-Bu group (from the mid 80's to the beginning of the 90's, with the potential applicability of this designation to the whole range of cultural phenomena of the time), reflects both the authenticity of the jubilation spirit of national liberation and a critical detachment of a spectator of the "show." Andrukhovych's "laughters," which are both light-heartedly playful and soberly ironic, are more diffused and create a framework for a wide range of the play and transgressions that involve literary hierarchies and national mythologies, intertextuality and parody. On the more particular level there is a distinct dialogue with Bakhtinian *carnivalesque* (which is also manifested especially clearly in his novel *Recreations*). In the cycles such as "Circus 'Vagabundo'," and "Medieval Zoo" Andrukhovych creates a trans-historical fair, where history collapses to a zero point of time and space. This fictional space of make-belief reinforces everything that is not sanctioned on the societal level: overt eroticization, breaking of taboos, masking and de-masking, bringing down of sacred topics and elevating of the trivial. Carnival is also a powerful liberating space where the nation is reborn and re-affirmed. What creates a strong irony about this allegory is the implicit characteristics that go along with the "carnival" — it is staged, it is temporary, it is an illusion and it inevitably comes to an end. As the "carnivalesque" cultural phenomenon was retrospectively examined in an interview with one of the poets of the group in 1995 (see the "Interview"), it was nostalgically conceptualized as an indispensable but naive stage, which was bound to take place but was also bound to come to an end. The transition to the sobering "post-carnival" period comprises a paradigmatic condition of the "post-independence" nation in the broadest sense it also applies to African literatures (cf. Na'Allah).

The ambiguity of laughter, as an unfulfilled promise and unrealized desire in Osundare, and the ambivalence of the carnivalesque in Andrukhovych invades the space of geopolitical dimension. The ever present shadow of Nigeria's haunted past in Osundare and the totalitarian structures in Andrukhovych is only part of what constitutes the impossibility of breaking away from the dichotomies of power. The looming of the "more central" centre after the collapse of the colonial administration dominates the political subtext of the both poets' oevre. If for Andrukhovych it is generally the West (as designated by Western Europe, North America, etc.), for Osundare it is exclusively the other side of the Atlantic (which is partially rooted in his autobiographic experiences[7]).

The complex movement and fluidity of the anti-colonial vs. post-colonial paradigms can be easily discerned in both Osundare's and Andrukhovych's works. Although all of Osundare's poetry manifests the complex dialogics of the "post-independence" consciousness, it is *Waiting Laughters* with its rich irony, allegory and imagery, complex discursivity and opaqueness of meaning that present a particular interest in the context of the present essay. Osundare perpetually oscillates between, on one hand, the colonial past and the totalitarian present of the colonial legacy, representing the narrower defined limits of the post-colonial, and, on the other hand, the inevitable dichotomy of the periphery versus centre, the "other" of the West. The poet's concern with the still unhealed wounds of his native land expands beyond the Nigerian context to that of the whole Africa (the kaffirs and the Boers, African despot, the Nile, the Niger, the Kilimanjaro, cf. poem X). Osundare's concerns with the West, on the other hand, are grounded in the present and projected in the future. One of the more powerful evocations of the Western unattainability, detachment (and simultaneous desirability) comes across in the topos of the visa office (or "awe-ffice," through one of Osundare's wonderfully precise word-plays), where hierarchies and dichotomies come alive more vividly than anywhere else (poem IV). Western multifacetedness comes across through potentially different perspectives; it is both alluringly paradisiacal and welcoming ("the hangings [in the visa office] stoke wondering dreams / with their tourist havens," p. 93) and hostilely closed ("[t]he Atlantic is a wilderness of barbed walls / brooking no windows, its door of deafening steel // The key fell into spaceless water...," p. 94). The visa becomes an implicit object of desire, a tool of conquest ("Passports are pass ports / Knock still ye who may..." p. 94), a key to the "door of deafening steel" (p. 94). Ironically, the seemingly liberating space of the visahouse also becomes the beginning of the new imperial space ("the walls, / high, imperiously white," "imperial hiss" of the visaman, p. 93), a medium of exercising new power structures. The quintessential symbol of patriarchy and power, and by transference, of imperial control, the phallic image ("seals pompous like a mad phallus," p. 93) dominates the scene. The polysemantics of "mad" contains the whole range of implications that could be equally meaningful here — from the absence of reason, un-reason, to blind, animalistic fury, uncontrollable rage. The empire of phallus becomes the universal context for all the trans-historical empires. There is a certain irony, however, about the poet's play around the connotations of openness/closedness, entry/door/window and the general implication of the reversal of process of conquest.

Andrukhovych's situatedness between the ghost of the colonial past and the encroaching Western paradigm is explicitly less evaluative, although it contributes to an equally strong statement. His archeology of the imperial history repeatedly re-contextualizes and displaces the national self. Recovering layers of the colonial past is actualized on various levels: thematic, allegorical, linguistic (lexical). This comes particularly strong in "Three Ballads" where the Austrian period comes alive through three scenes in the life of the city. Through the casual description of the collapse of the city tower in "1. Lemberg[8] Catastrophe of 1826" as a "minor apocalypse" of the "tragic city" with not so significant human losses (one trumpeter, two soldiers and several labourers, p. 18), the poetic focus is on the connotation of the "minor" and "small" — in terms of the city's and people's insignificance both in the general course of history and in the system of imperial hierarchies. Repetition of the archival words through the German accent enhances the perspectival "side-glance" in the poem. The elaborate matter-of-factedness of the "Lemberg Catastroph" extends into "Whispering Across the Ages" where the figure of the Austrian Emperor Franz-Joseph — significantly referred to as just (Emperor) Joseph — becomes not only symbolical of any known imperial power, but is also implicit of another Joseph to come (Stalin). Ironically framed into a form of praise/eulogy and playing around the notion of a "happy nation" (p. 20), the poem contains particular allu-sions to the empire of the not so distant past. Andrukhovych's direct references and allusions to the Marxism philosophy (e.g., "Faustian Celebration," p. 22), intrusions of other languages (Polonisms, Russian) create subtle and not so sub-tle subtexts of power structures of the past. The invasion of the modern Western cultural values comes across in a more elusive way. After the decades of virtual isolation from the West, which holds particularly true for the ex-Soviet ethnic republics, the sudden exposure and "accessibility" of the Western way of life and Western values at all levels (through material goods, travel, as well as massive media exposure) the culture began to experience an invasion of Western realia. In Andrukhovych's poetry the acknowledgement of this phenomenon is both ironic and serious, a parody of the culture of bad taste and mass consumption, and a play of intertextuality. The fabric of his verse incorporates the actual resort to English, the network of various allusions, as well as a general tendency towards the globalization (or internalization) of the local. Thus, in "The Monument" his incorporating of Iaremcha (a town in the western part of the country) in one row with Hollywood, Hong Kong, Geneva and San Remo (p. 75) is facetious, consciously pretentious, ironic and serious all at once (also see below for the discussion of "Cossack Jamaica").

The points of tension at the crossroads of the postcolonial and postmodernist concerns can be situated primarily around the issues of the history, the truth and the subject. The issue of history, instrumental to the reproduction of nation-al identity, is central to the paradigmatic postcolonial narrative. It also closely relates to the positivistic concept of the truth. The recovery of the (objective) his-tory and reinstallment of the (historical) truth constitutes one of the political purposes of the postcolonial discourse. The eternal (post)colonial desire for the recovery of one's identity clashes with the postmodernist dismantling of the notion of history as a narrative construct and dislodging of the logocentric truth. Osundare's various modes of plurality create the impossibility (and refusal) of grounding the epistemic centre. 9 The subtexts of "fleeing truths" (I, 87), the repetitive associations with "elusive," "fugitive," "running" and dream-like qual-ities refer not only to the forever escaping layers of meaning but also to the poet's and Africa's search for destination. Osundare's history is an ailing sore waiting to be opened with "[e]very minute / heavy like an expectant rock, / the eyes labouring through / a century of winks" (II, 90). The historical space con-stitutes a gap to be filled: "... waiting / for a history which snails towards the coast, / a delta of meandering dreams... (X, 102). The poet's elusive treatment of subjectivity has been justly noted (cf. Arnold) and it is manifested particu-larly strongly in *Waiting Laughters*. The impersonality of much of his verse and multiplicity of voices is counterbalanced by an occasional emphatic "I." This negotiation is largely a reflection of the movement between the contemporary discursive practices and the authorial stance on the issue of the poet's function in the society and his role in the advancing of the national history, traditionally ascribed to the poet as a civic figure. One of the poems from the earlier *Moonsongs* features E.K. Brathwaite's words as an epigraph that reflect such a movement: "I must be given words to refashion futures like a healer's hand" (p. 60). This quotation is interesting both in its acknowledgement of the narrative's impact on the societal development, the discursive character of culture, history, etc., and, a distinct allusion to the messianic role of the artist. Osundare's fluctuation between the both poles gravitates strongly towards the postcolonial demand of history and truth and assertion of the poet's role in this project. The dislodged time-space, shattered in a myriad of fleeing moments, with "band- / ages / of fractured moments" (II, 90) ultimately comes together in the powerfully assertive "we-knowing" season ("winnowing season," VI, 96). Osundare's refusal to bury Nigeria's and Africa's past of tyranny and its tortuous road to democracy seeps through the fabric of his verse, which cannot escape the memory of the "scrolls of serfdom" (X, 102), tyrants and despots, blood and "hieroglyphs of calculated / treacheries" (ibid.), "the bleeding anthem on the lips of wounded kraals" (X, 103), and "green graves" that "cluster like question marks" (ibid.). The imperial/dictatorial "I proscribe the tale / I proscribe the TRUTH / I proscribe HISTORY!" (p. 106) constitutes the negation of the quintessential postcolonial desire. The nation's need and yearning to be spoken for, the yearning of "the mouth for its fiery tongue" (p. 107) also translates into Osundare's assertion of the civic duty of the African poet.

Significantly less dramatic and more playful than Osundare, Andrukhovych employs the similar thematics on a more low-key level. According to him the time of artistic messianism is unmistakably gone (he is perpetually ironic towards himself and his colleagues as poets and their oeuvre, cf. "The Monument" p.75, to quote just one example). His acknowledgement of the history and the unwitting resort to the haunting realia of the past is consistently informed by the postmodernist perspective. He dislodges the positivistic view of history and questions the very possibility of knowing the past. The construction of the jigsaw puzzle of history is never completed and the poet openly plays with its pieces, whether it is a liberal retelling of a historical fact, however, complete with the reference to archives for that touch of authenticity (in "Lemberg catastroph of 1826"), a search for his love lost "somewhere between renaissance and barocco" (p. 10) or generally an examination of the confused societal condition where the nation is unable to cope with the collapse of the many established structures. The medieval city of his dreams and many affections (the actual city of Lviv), where he locates many of his poetries of the time, becomes a point of departure on the scale of history where many time-spaces come together. The poet's love affair with the city also translates into his essential need for history. His union with the past is wholistic and cathartic. However, the search for the eternal wisdom through the glass of the centuries is often a disappointing exercise. His character "collected impressions / of castles, dungeons, monasteries, / ruins, stairs, monks' cells and yards, / and listened to what the stones will say at last... // But they remained silent..." (p. 12). The problem of the collective memory as the carrier of historical knowledge and the impossibility of its recovery presents one of the more significant issues in Andrukhovych. Viewed through the usual for him symbolics of urban topoi, knowledge through memory becomes a failed project through human subjectivity and an impossibility in itself: "it is only through us that cities pass / to un-memory.." (p. 46), "[t]here are cities that are impossible to enter through a gate. / There are cities that are impossible to enter // And they bring a huge key, and they look for a place to insert it, but / there is no gate, the guards all crumbled / to dust. Seven winds are sweeping / across squares and halls" (p. 44). Although less explicit than Osundare on the related issues and more elusive about politicizing his discourse, Andrukhovych's assertion of the past is no less significant. His writing of the national history ultimately consists in the impossibility to view the contemporary national space in ways other than through the prism of the multiple historical layers, where each contributed to the complex self-perception of the contemporary national self.

One of the more significant aspects of the both poets' oevre, so characteristic of the condition of postcoloniality, is the constant negotiation between cosmopolitanism and nationalism, or, put in more neutral terms, between the larger and the local. As Ojaide has justly noted, "the conflict of allegiance between one's immediate national society and the larger world" creates a constant tension in the text (p. 91). One of the manifestations of this tension in the discussed poetic spaces is the combined use of the elements of *folkloric forms* (be it a specific traditional poetic form, a system of folkloric images, or intertextuality drawing on oral/traditional narratives) with the *postmodernist techniques*. Let us examine the first part of this proposition. The use of traditional poetic forms and elements of folklore undoubtedly "ha[s] a cultural validation" (Ojaide, 86), which embraces not only the emphasis on the "local," national cultural space within the bigger poetic space, but also the redefinition of the ethnic as inherent part of the modern national identity. [10] Osundare's resort to the tradition of oral literature complete, in *Waiting Laughters*, with the performative element of musical accompaniment, establishes a very strong national voice. The poet uses various forms of oral tradition: prayer (XVIII), elements of chant (VII), oral folktale/parable (XIV), as well as a variety of folkloric images, stylistic models and nature-oriented, formulaic tropes (particularly epithets). The oral literary form is traditionally a public one, presupposing the fact of a performance, and, hence, the fact of an audience. It communicates to the listener/reader important concerns and issues. Thus, the use of oral tradition implies a doubly significant factor: resort to the national model of cultural expression that establishes a distinct identity, and a tribune-like position (enhanced by a medley of voices in *Waiting Laughters*) that demands an audience and proclaim issues of didactic importance. The source of national awareness or nationalism is the poet's conscious or subconscious projection of his culture (cf. Ojaide p. 34). As Ibrahim Tala comments, new African writers "include oral tradition to link their past with their present experience (as a group), to localize the content of their works, to educate fellow Africans and give them confidence in their cultural heritage and to enlighten outsiders and help them get rid of the false impression about African culture acquired from years of cultural misrepresentation" (I.K. Tala, *An Introduction to Cameroon Oral Literature*, Yaounde: SOPECAM, 1984, pp. 95–96, qtd. from Ojaide, p. 34). What is significant in this observation is the statement of both inward and outward orientation of such cultural products: they are geared towards the re-inforcement of national values, and, at the same time, presentation of the particular culture at the global market.

The same holds true for East European cultural commodities. Andrukhovych displays similarly significant use of tradition through folkloric images, topoi, archaic poetic language of the traditional folkloric poetry. The theme of the fair or travelling performance (which assumes different variations on the topic), various folk celebrations, play with and around images of the Christian tradition throughout his verse, re-contextualized use of the prayer (e.g., "The Song of Mr. Baz'") and lamentation (cf. "Lamentation or the Patriarch's Cry...") constitute an important basis to his creativity. It is interesting to note that the topos of the street performance assumes two distinct manifestations: as a globalized, cosmopolitan, trans-national and trans-historical circus, and as a localized, grounded in national traditions image of the fair, Christmas street performance, or a folk celebration. Andrukhovych's extension of the local, national into the larger, international context and his resort to the topoi of the West acquires several meanings in the framework of his poetry. It cannot be read outside the context of: 1) the juxtaposition of his peripheral culture *versus* the "other" of the West, 2) the simultaneous placement of it *alongside and together* with the West, 3) the possibility of subtexts of unconscious nostalgia for the pure and "untouched" authentic beauty of the "essentially" national which can no longer be read in the restrictively narrow context of the national culture (cf. "Shepherd..." or the ending of "Cossack Jamaica"). This process is particularly explicit in his "Cossack Jamaica" — the poet plays around the original name of cossack Mamaj — where the latter comes to meet the West. The wonderfully colourful image belongs to the quintessentially Ukrainian folkloric character (borrowed from a well-known painting). He is given a non-Ukrainian name and becomes an eternal time-traveler, cutting across the ages and crossing the cultural borders. Ironically, here Jamaica and generally tropical topoi (Bahama and Haiti), themselves the battlefields of post-colonial tensions, become representative of the exotic landscapes associated with the quintessentially Western ideas of luxury, leisure and consumerism. Cosmopolitization of the paradigmatic national character and his displacement through the introduction into the global context comprises a significant statement: it is both a break from the tradition and the tradition's continuity; it is the desire to be part of the world yet to retain the identifiable national features. Situating of the traditional national self (closed, conservative and solidly rooted in the past) in the contemporary scene (open, cosmopolitan and eclectic) manifests the ultimate negotiation of the centre versus periphery relations.

This double facetedness (or universality) of the "local" constitutes precisely the implicit subtext of the both poetic projects. Both Osundare's and Andrukhovych's use of folklore material is very far from the naive and simplistic glorification of the national: it is a re-contextualized and critically distanced repetition of the folkloric inventory and it cannot be other than that, given both the intellectual sophistication of the poets' oeuvre and the complexity of the socio-cultural context. Proceeding from Linda Hutcheon's redefinition of parody, in particular postmodern parody,[11] it is helpful to adopt this concept for the discussed cases here. What is important in the suggested interpretation of the use of folklore as parodic is its double-directedness: assertion of the tradition and the past as an inherent and essential part of the national psyche (through the very fact of the "quotation" of original material) , and simultaneous re-thinking and re-configuring of the national tradition within a new context and from a qualitatively different perspective, which potentially arises from the mere factor of a poet's situatedness in the end of the 20th century. Both poets are concerned with the construction of the modern national identity within a larger context. Osundare's "quoting" of the traditional Nigerian/African poetic forms and images for a potentially global readership and Andrukhovych's dislocation of what was locally rooted for centuries constitutes re-contextualization in itself. Another level of re-contextualization, however, is actualized through the *means* and *techniques* of writing the national "text" into the global context, and this brings us to the issue of discursive practices.

The discussed above postmodernist displacements on the epistemic level also correlate with the purely technical experimentations of the both poets' works. Postmodernist means of expression here include focus on discursivity, multiplicity of meanings, play with words and contexts, negotiation between the reality and fiction, and some cases of complex intertextuality (particularly in Andrukhovych). Osundare's remarkable feel for the word translates into the reader's acute awareness of the language as, in fact, one of the undeniable "truths" of his poetry and sometimes climaxes into almost perceptual, tactile experiences ("I pluck these words / From the lips of running winds..." p. 89; "The rapid eloquence of the running vowel / When words turn willing courier ..." ibid.). Playing with discursivity can unexpectedly take shape of rather material terms: "My song is space / beyond wails, beyond walls / beyond insular hyeroglyphs / which crave the crest / of printed waves" (VIII, 100). One of the more important features of Osundare's *Waiting Laughters* is this collection's particular emphasis on the syntactic dislocations as well as graphic effects (cf. poems II, X, XI). The alluring beauty and power of forever changing and escaping meanings and the fluidity of his symbolism do not yield easily to any attempt at a meaning-centered reading; it is a paradigmatically open text, which resists an attempt at closure.

Qualitatively different from Osundare, Andrukhovych is utterly explicit about the playful and "consumer friendly" quality of his poetry. Incorporation of low-style jargon and the general "mass culture" appeal of his work, however, does not erase the unmistakable sophistication of his poetry, which layers subtexts and meanings, potentially accessible only to more informed readers. The inventory of his postmodernist techniques should probably begin with his use of parodic intertextuality as one of the more important aspects of his poetic oevre. It embraces not only themes, images and generally models of folkloric texts as it was shown above, but also biblical contexts, and more particular and subtle cases of intertextuality. Particularly significant are his re-workings of the experimentation models of national historical avant-garde (cf. the ending of "Shepherd...," p. 53, based on the play of the sound-image of the word). The poet explicitly plays around the notions of illusion versus reality (cf. Circus "Vagabundo", IV, 70, where the lyrical character is the creator of his own show, i.e., reality, which he can close or open at will; by transference, the author also manipulates his own discursive reality). In a self-reflective way fictional worlds intersect allowing his characters to travel between them. The selected works of Andrukhovych in the cited collection are organized as a retrospective overview of both his poetry and prose, where prosaic quotations serve as a cohesive framework or commentary (through his characters' eyes) on his poetry. This elaborate structure is concluded by the ironic "side-glance" at one's own oevre, where the spectators, characters from one of the poet's novels, for a moment become the audience for his poetic show ("I have understood almost nothing," - confessed Marta. "I don't get it all either," agreed Khomsky, " but somehow I like it very much,"p. 76).

Osundare's subtle and hard to pinpoint lyrical postmodernism and Andrukhovych's elaborate flaunting of his more technical and narrative-grounded postmodern-ness (dated by the late 80s - early 90s) is as true as the secondariness of the both undertakings, i.e., their drawing on the Western literary models and theory. Put in the context of the above observations, the writing of the national body into the posmodernist discursive mode undoubtedly constitutes a re-contextualization. Notwithstanding the differences of their poetic expression both Osundare's and Andrukhovych's situatedness is defined by analogous power structure relations, and their poetry manifest some paradigmatic relations within the space of the post-colonial culture. Discussed in the beginning "reception" and "processing" of postmodernism becomes more than a passive reception of Western cultural models. It is an appropriation of the "other's" discourse to produce one's own counter-discourse, it is a statement of writing oneself into the world context, and it is undoubtedly endowed with ideological subtexts common to any peripheral and/or post-colonial culture. Hostility towards postmodernist experimenations on the ground of "authentic" cultures often stems in misunderstanding or overlooking of these important factors. Resorting to the voice of an "insider" may be useful here. Talking in particular of Central and East European societies (although the implications are much broader), Halina Janaszek-Ivanickova, in her emphasis of the political significance and social involvement of postmodernism in these cultures, condemns the failure "to realize that it is not permissiveness, escapism, mannerism, and secondariness that are decisive in postmodern conquests of the world.... What is decisive is anti-fundamentalism and pluralism, the victory of the so-called 'weak thought' which is by no means weak but merely conscious of its limitations, ... and a final departure from 'great narratives'" (1995: 810). Similarly, in her preface to the collection of published proceedings of a Central and East European conference on postmodernism Janaszek-Ivanickova also placed main emphasis on the "significance of the postmodern breakthrough for changing the social and philosophical consciousnesses of these countries" (1996: 10) through its contribution to the postmodern anti-fundamentalism.

NOTES

1 Although, so far, the notion of cultural peripherality has not been sufficiently conceptualized, it drew enough attention in academic scholarship to refer to it as a term in its own status. Among more serious attempts at defining the concept is Tötösy de Zepetnek's, particularly in his preface to the special issue of the *Canadian Review of Comparative Literature* on post-colonial studies. He argues for expanding the area of post-colonial cultural studies (with its focus on the traditional dichotomy of the colonizer versus (de-)colonized) towards the inclusion of less obvious cases of the centre/periphery relations, which may manifest equally paradigmatic representation of the distribution of power. Such cases may include centre/pheriphery relationships, for instance, between "immigrant populations and mainstream societies *within* the *a priori* post-colonial situation of Canada and Britain" (p. 400, emphasis in text), or the peripheral position of such literatures as Portuguese, Catalan etc., within the context of European cultural hierarchies (p. 401). As the argument follows, a change in the political power structure can often indicate movement from one (post-)-colonial/peripheral situation to a different one (such, for example, would be the case of some Central and East European countries, which, upon having set free from the totalitarian domination of the Soviet Union, found themselves facing a new "other" — the West. The notion of cultural periphery is also closely approached by Jusdanis in his examination of "the formation of culture on the periphery of Europe" (the case of Greece, p. xi). For the elaboration of this concept in relation to the condition of post-coloniality also cf. Trinh, Mukherjee. The two literatures discussed in the present essay fit both frameworks by being post-colonial in the established sense of the term and peripheral in the system of hierarchical power distribution in the areas of politics, economy and culture.

2 In the context of the above discussed notion of peripherality, peripheral manifestations of postmodernism deserve particular attention. The recent volume entitled *International Post-modernism. Theory and Literary Practice* (see Bertens and Fokkema) comprises a comprehensive overview of cultural postmodernism as an increasingly global phenomenon. Although it does entertain certain points that remain open to argumentation, it also contains the most coherent up-to-date attempt to conceptualize peripheral postmodernisms. Both African and East European postmodernist experimentations of the last two decades can be situated within the latter category. It is characteristic that these peripheral manifestations of the quintessentially Western (or North American, according to Bertens and Fokkema) phenomenon are examined in the section significantly entitled "Reception and Processing of

Postmodernism." Although this largely definitional title implicitly designates peripheral cultures as potentially passive recipients of the "ready-to-wear" goods, the editorial introductory note to this section does refer to the "diffusion and *transformations* of the concept" (p. 298, my emphasis), and stresses that "[i]t would be an unwarranted simplification ... to study the diffusion of postmodernism as one-way traffic" (p. 303). Notwithstanding these promising allusions they remained largely unexplored on a theoretical level (although each national manifestation of postmodernism was explored in a separate article of the section). According to the editors, the feasibility of constructing an international concept of postmodernism lies in two potential areas: 1) "... writers and critics seem to consider it tactically advantageous to borrow ideas and techniques from abroad for bringing about change in a literary or cultural situation at home" (p. 299); here the idea of change seems to be confined to the novelty of form and the authors prefer not to venture into the realm of ideological structures and their significance for, e.g., such a largely political project as the formation/construction of national identity through literary narratives; 2) an arbitrary aspect of the borrowing of literary conventions that might have an "effect of a pleasant surprise" (ibid.). The discussed section, however, also included Western European postmodernisms, and this significantly narrowed down the range of potential theoretical elaborations that could present a common basis for such a wide range of regional representations.

3 Or should the order of inclusion be reversed here with the study of peripherality as more general and, thus, subsuming post-colonial studies as its particular manifestation?

4 Although the concepts of peripherality and marginality are often used as interchangeable, it is worthwhile to differentiate between them. We agree with Tötösy de Zepetnek that "the notion of margin is too radical and only applicable to a limited set of situations" (p. 404).

5 Although Jusdanis talks about modernity of Greece and the project of modernization with literary narratives as its essential component, the relational centre/periphery paradigm of cultural development remains largely applicable within a wide range of peripherality.

6 Ukraine is a quintessentially postcolonial (as well as peripheral) society. It went through several centuries of colonization and was under Austrian, Austrian-Hungarian, Polish and Soviet rule.

7 See Arnold for the examination of the autobiographic material in Osundare's poetry.

8 Lemberg is a German name of the present-day city of Lviv in Western

Ukraine, given to it during the period of the Austrian empire.

9 In his article on post-modernism and the poetry of N. Osundare, S. Arnold emphasizes the anti-post-modernist stance of the Nigerian poet and argues for the value of history and subjectivity in his creative work, admitting, however, the possibility of reading his oevre as "almost postmodern" (p. 160). Fully agreeing with the line of Arnold's argumentation, we need to emphasize that in the context of this article we are talking not about certain conscious stance or philosophical perspective, but rather about the impossibility to be outside the context of postmodernity, which becomes in part a way of reading the world culture and participating in it. In this sense "processing" the postmodern in all its manifestations becomes an important step in any peripheral culture's negotiation between the tradition and modernity, the local and the global.

10 The use of folkloric material deserves special attention in the context of the present essay. Cf. Ojaide who emphasizes the significance of the incorporation of the folkloric tradition into the present-day culture to meet the demands of the modern society (p. 34). Also, the study of Balinska-Ourdeva based on one of the prose writings of Andrukhovych, where she argues that the disattached, critically distanced use of folklore is ultimately embodied in the process of re-discovery of the modern national self. The folkloric texts are denied "the elevated status of being the ultimate embodiments of the national psyche," and are "subjected to a consumable ... revival that leads to their irrevocable transformation and modernization" (p. 211). Thus, the oral tradition is being "appropriated without excessive 'nationalist' sentiments" (p. 211).

11 In her *Theory of Parody* and later in *A Poetics of Postmodernism*, Hutcheon argues that there are no transhistorical definitions of parody and the very concept has significantly evolved since the medieval and renaissance imitation with the purpose of the traditional mockery or ridicule of the original material. Postmodern parody in its "trans-contextualization" is a "repetition with difference" (1985: 32). "A critical distance is implied between the backgrounded text and the new incorporating work, a distance usually signaled by irony" (ibid.). The irony, however, is not always belittling or destructive; it can be playful or critically constructive (ibid.). Such irony simultaneously marks a rupture and a connection with the past (1988: 125) through parodic intertextuality. This type of parody both embraces the past and questions it.

REFERENCES

Andrukhovych, Y., O. Irvanets', V. Neborak. *Bu-Ba-Bu. T.v.o./.../ry.* Lviv: Kameniar, 1995.

Arnold, Steven H. "A Peopled Persona. Autobiography, Post-modernism and the Poetry of Niyi Osundare." *Genres autobiographiques en Afrique/Autobiographical Genres in Africa.* Eds. Riesz-Janos and Schil-Ulla. Berlin: Reimer, 1996. 143–65.

Balinska-Ourdeva, Vessela. "The Act of Reading as a Rite of Passage: Iurii Andrukhovych's *Rekreatsii.*" *Canadian Slavonic Papers* XL.3–4 (1998): 209–31.

Bertens, Hans, and Douwe Fokkema, eds. *International Post-modernism. Theory and Literary Practice.* Philadelphia: John Benjamins Publishing Company, 1997.

Hassan, Ihab. "Marginal Literature at the Exploded Center: An Okinawan Instance." *World Literature Today* 71.1 (1997): 13–21.

Hutcheon, Linda. *A Poetics of Postmodernism. History, Theory, Fiction.* London: Routledge, 1988.

———. *A Theory of Parody. The Teachings of Twentieth-Century Art Forms.* London: Methuen, 1985.

Interview with Victor Neborak. "Proshchannia z karnavalom v ukraiins'kij literaturi" ("Farewell to the Carnival in Ukrainian Literature"). *Svitovyd* II.19 (1995): 73–82.

Janaszek-Ivanickova, Halina, and Douwe Fokkema, eds. *Post-modernism in Literature and Culture of Central and Eastern Europe.* Katowice, Slask: 1996

Janaszek-Ivanickova, H. "Postmodern Literature and the Cultural Identity of Central and Eastern Europe." *Canadian Review of Comparative Literature* 22.3–4 (1995): 805–11.

Jusdanis, Gregory. *Belated Modernity and Aesthetic Culture.* Minneapolis: U of Minnesota P, 1991.

—-. "Is Postmodernism Possible Outside the `West'? The Case of Greece." *Bizantine and Modern Greek Studies* 11 (1987): 69–92.

McClintock, Anne. "The Angel of Progress: Pitfalls of the Term 'Post-Colonialism.'" Eds. Patrick Williams and Laura Chrisman. *Colonial Discourse and Post-Colonial Theory: A Reader.* New York: Columbia UP, 1994: 291–304.

Mukherjee, Meenakshi. "The Centre Cannot Hold: Two Views of the Periphery." Eds. Stephen Slemon and Helen Tiffin. *After Europe.* Sydney: Dangaroo Press, 1989: 41–48.

Na'Allah, Abdul-Rasheed. "African Literatures and Postcolonialism: Projections into the Twenty-First Century." *Canadian Review of Comparative Literature/ Revue Canadienne de Littérature Comparée* 3–4. 22 (1995): 569–85.

Ojaide, Tanure. *Poetic Imagination in Black Africa. Essays on African Poetry.* Durham, North Carolina: Carolina Academic Press, 1996.

Osundare, Niyi. *Selected Poems.* London and Paris: Heinemann, 1992.

Pavlyshyn, Marko. "Post-Colonial Features in Contemporary Ukrainian Culture." *Australian Slavonic and East European Studies* 6.2 (1992): 41–55.

Tötösy de Zepetnek, Steven. "Post-Colonialities: The 'Other,' the System, and a Personal Perspective, or, This (Too) Is Comparative Literature." *Post-Colonial Literatures: Theory and Practice /Les littératures post-coloniales. Théories et réalisations.* Eds. S. Tötösy de Zepetnek and Sneja Gunew. Special issue of the *Canadian Review of Comparative Literature/ Revue Canadienne de Littérature Comparée* 22.3–4 (1995): 399–407.

Trinh, Minh-Ha T. "No Master Territories." Eds. Bill Ashcroft, Gareth Griffiths, and Helen Tiffin. *The Postcolonial reader.* London: Routledge, 1995: 215–18.

LONG LOST KIN: NIYI OSUNDARE THROUGH AN AFRICAN AMERICAN LENS

Kamau Kemayo

> Words...are a gift from the Almighty, the Eternal Wisdom.
> ...it is folly to misuse words or not to know how to use them well.
> —Njabulo S. Ndebele[I]

AKOBEN
[Presented with the accompaniment of mbira or talking drum;
light but insistent rhythm builds during recital,
but does not overpower the Voice.
Music continues and fades after the poem is over]

<pre>
              Sing
            praises   .
            for the   .
          executioner   .
         brother take   .
          your s words   out
          of my heart   blades
          twist my soul   bleed in
</pre>

<pre>
        hot/cold facets   strobes
       a base in emotion   leaves
      stub born rings   don't stab
      in the back face talk   me joy full
        stitched to my long lost brothers
             thank you, thank   you
                how like a lover
            telling joyful things that
                  hurt how   you
               make blunt words
          cut jagged edges from life
             a cymbal won't draw
                blood   surgical
              wounds bathed with
           the hole atlantic heal me
</pre>

This poem functions as an introduction to a critical essay. It is a mirror image of the shape of a traditional Adinkra symbol, "Akoben." The words are a reflection of the solid symbol. Akoben is a call to collective action—a call to arms. Yet, in this poetic context, the community is called to arm ourselves with sharp minds and strong commitment to rebuilding the ancient links between and within communities that have both common bloodlines as well as common enemies. Niyi Osundare represents both the call—as a politically inspiring poet—and the arms because his words are incisive and help to remove or eliminate various problems from the community. A comparative approach will be used in connecting Osundare to an African American poet/activist whose commitments, ideals, and even artistic expressions are strikingly similar. In his prefatory notes to one of the texts I will juxtapose to Osundare's work, Haki Madhubuti stresses the same point as AKOBEN, "Words cut and heal. I am not a doctor, however I would like to think *Earthquakes and Sunrise Missions* is preventative medicine." The kind of poetry Osundare writes inspires and motivates, also providing a preventative function. His words go beyond preventing social ills. By being so concise and directed, they help to heal the African society. *brothers, take your swords out of my heart...you make blunt words cut jagged edges from life, loud symbols that won't draw blood. bathing my wounds, crossing the hole filled by the Atlantic, your words heal me*

Houston Baker talks of the autobiographical moment of Black writing.[2] As a poet, I have experienced it myself and used it as a creative foundation or spark. Yet, that moment also extends into the idea of literary criticism. As critics, we bring our own baggage to the process of analysis and interpretation. Critics, perhaps too often, say more about themselves than about their subjects. This "auto-biographical criticism" begins with the reading of the piece. My first exposure to Niyi Osundare's poetry was a rare pleasure, one of those golden firsts where one realize that this text/poem/song is a true work of art and will become a treasured friend. Ayo Banjo credits Osundare with believing that "the authorial first-person should be restored to literary works." Banjo's statement points to a dual responsibility. The author's intent cannot be forsaken to the critic's perspective. Neither can the critic's perspective be ignored in his or her interpretation. I can only acknowledge that this essay consciously addresses what it says about me. I trust that I am not too unusual or idiosyncratic that few will share my feelings about or experiences with Osundare's poetry. Adagboyin's interview of Osundare serves as a foundation to help maintain the poet's authority over his own work. At the same, it points in the direction I want to go within this work. The attempt to "realize the import of the first person in literature." Yet like Osundare, *I* believe that the "I" in Afrikan literature is really a "we."[3]

Osundare's sense of a conscious artistry balanced with academic intellectualism and commitment to sociopolitical change is impressive as demonstrated in A. S. Adagbonyin's interview. His pain at the political situation in contemporary Nigeria is further evidenced in "Not and Internal Affair."[4] His pedigree of influences was not particularly exceptional or surprising for one of his talent and accomplishments. I was intrigued, however, that he did not acknowledge any exposure to contemporary African American influences.[5] This seems discordant to me because I hear so many echoes of the Black Power poetry of the 60's and 70's, both in his poetry and his own words describing it. Perhaps this is because my own development, poetic and intellectual, began during that time frame. My experiences with Jones/Baraka, Sanchez, Cruz, Evans, Lee/Madhubuti, Shange, and others perhaps parallel Osundare's with Keats, Whitman, Donne, and Wordsworth; these are the poets I read and the poetry I learned in college and high school. Premed, psychology, and African American Studies curricula did not expose me to the classic poets of English literature that someone with Osundare's educational background in Nigeria would have encountered.

Ultimately, though, I believe we—Africans and African Americans, as well as others throughout the Diaspora—have much in common. *Stitched to my long lost brothers.* Surely the revolutionary ideologies of Civil Rights and Black Power can be compared to the various strategies in African independence movements. The contradictions and hypocrisies in post-colonial African nation-states are not too much different from the tensions between nationalist, assimilationist, liberal, or conservative sociopolitical patterns in African America. African cultural survivals notwithstanding, the number of African scholars being educated or teaching in the US, and the conscious reinsertion of African cultural structures into US lifestyle by the Afrocentric movement bridge the Atlantic in a manner heretofore impossible. Contemporary global society encourages cultural transmissions, interactions, and exchanges beyond academic and intellectual arenas. Films like Amistad, Sankofa, and Daughters of the Dust bring a greater awareness of the Diaspora to larger numbers in mainstream African America. A popular Afrocentrism expresses itself in fashion—headwear, diverse uses of kente, Kwanzaa, and an increasing exposure to Ma'at. *hole atlantic heal me* The cultural distance between Africans and Black Americans has shortened, as has the physical distance. The passage that once took weeks or months is now a plane trip of only hours. The physical obstacle has collapsed. So, too, the imposed hegemonic structures of mental colonization. Figurative imagery becomes obsolete. I now reclaim my lost heritage in a literal sense. The kinship I feel in Niyi Osundare's poetry is among the things that give me the right.

As an individual, I can take this prerogative. Yet, my audacity is to assert a birthright of more than ancestral memories and tribal traditions; today's Africa, and its people are also mine! Of course, I realize (sadly from my perspective) that some elements of US society, even many of its Black intellectuals, will not endorse this claim. Nevertheless, my heart and soul tells me it is legitimate. But the scholarly context demands more proof than assertion, fact than fancy, logic than emotion. As individual readers, accept what proofs you will, or will not. This is probably not a new topic to any scholar of African/African American issues. If you have already made a decision, I will only be preaching to the choir or to deaf ears. Nevertheless, my goal is to demonstrate the community of African and African American poets. Should any *one* accept and be satisfied with my arguments or merely give them serious consideration, the effort will have been worthwhile.

Jane Bryce's suggestion that poetry could be "emotion recollected in tranquility" is hardly applicable to much of contemporary African poetry, as the remainder of her article attests. Unfortunately, for the people who must live the lives poets document, the soils of political and social unrest are fertile nutrients for the poetic muse. African societies, with their strong oral flavors, and positive valuation of performance and music will see its art forms stimulated by a "political situation of extreme instability." Certainly, similar themes run through Soyinka, Achebe, Ngugi, Sembene, Armah, and others' novels and plays. South Africa's apartheid stimulated a generation of music dedicated to popularizing the revolutionary movements. Oftentimes, this music is based in everyday experience, like Masakela's, "Stimela." Or it is more overtly political, like Manu Dibango's "Biko" and the numerous references to Mandela. Social environments and lifestyles, in interpersonal and political manifestations, are catalysts for Black creativity.

Poetry in Africa has strong oral performative dynamics that take it further away from both recollection and tranquility. Poetry is immediate, often surfacing as a means of direct communication between two or more individuals in a public context. Poems in this genre breed poetic responses. The poetry may be of a conflictual nature or merely friendly banter, like the variety of uses of signifying. While content that consists of a creative or cogent message is expected in this tradition, virtuoso expository improvisation is a more qualitative issue. The recent Rap/Hip Hop music phenomena in the US and around the globe can be traced on a straight line back to these roots in Africa. Likewise, the traditions of African American toasts and the "dozens" are interactive, dynamic poetic constructions that go back to Africa. Static poetry on a page, for both Africans and African Americans, even though it may conform to other more Western norms, nevertheless demands linguistic innovations like the oral traditions of Africa.

Assuming that any good poet or poem has a relevant message, such innovations often function to distinguish Black poets as exemplars. Asomwan S. Adagbonyin's *Niyi Osundare: Two Essays and an Interview* identifies Niyi Osundare as a stylistic innovator with few if any peers in contemporary poetry. Darwin Turner describes Haki Madhubuti as powerful and original, a virtuoso performer, and an artistic prophetic educator.[6] He references Dudley Randall's label of Lee (Madhubuti) as "one of the most interesting of the revolutionary young black poets."[7] Though separated by the Atlantic and a few years—Madhubuti the elder—these poets are masters. Their artistry is incisive and thoughtful. *sing praises to the executioners*

When Soyinka speaks of "the duality of knife as bloodletter and creative implement" one need not be a sculptor, or see one in action, to sense that statement's inherent accuracy.[8] The knife appears outwardly such an everyday and common implement. Its multiple functions transcend easy categorization as a mere kitchen tool. So, too, with poet and his or her words: love songs/poems can be directed to mates or kin, or *freedom*. The creativity of nommo is self-evident and the dangerous effects of words are sharper than in-laws' tongues.

Madhubuti's arsenal includes slashing satire as well as more reasoned, descriptive or philosophical works. A central metaphor in my tribute to Osundare is the poet as executioner/surgeon. Undeniably, too many innocent people have been victimized by executioners or their masters—people in both colonial and postcolonial Africa, people in the pre-and post-emancipation Americas. Even some whose innocence is questionable have paid prices too steep in relation to whatever "crimes" they may or may not have committed. Yet, maybe the executioner's blade has removed some real threats to real People, not just questioners of the abuse of autocratic authority. With one sweeping polemic text, a social cancer is targeted. Poets lack the surgical precision to remove the cancer, but they move people intellectually and emotionally to seek health, such movement as can topple kings. Of course, the questions arise: "Who defines what is a social cancer?," "What is health at the level of a community?," and "Whose health is enhanced by the poem in its diagnostic or surgical functions?"

If, as Osundare asserts, "public humiliation was an effective social sanction," public poetic outcry is an effective political medium. 9 No doubt, the wave of regressive and repressive policies of killing the messengers proves the effectiveness of poetic voices that have been silenced. While not as bloody, economic and media factions in the US essentially eliminated the conscious Black artist from the public eye. Yet Black art in the US remains one of its most critical arenas. Perhaps in both the US and Africa, public attention or awareness does not translate to "public sanction." Or perhaps the powers-that-be simply do not care and feel no obligation to respond to artistic or public sanction. Neither apathetic publics nor evasive and negligent governmental or media institutions have thwarted Osundare or Madhubuti from publishing and criticizing negative factors inside and outside their communities.

Two particular and specific comparative analyses will be presented. First, a general thematic analysis of Madhubuti and Osundare's poetry will afford the opportunity to assess each poet's significance in terms of his political, social, and entertainment values. Each poet rejects the idea of an overwhelming aesthetic impulse. There is certainly beautiful language in some of their poems. Osundare says "...art must say something and say it beautifully." (Adaboyin, 1996: 91). Madhubuti essentially agrees,

> in this universe
> the magic the beauty the willful art of explaining
> the world & you;
> the timeless the unread the unstoppable fixation
> with language and ideas;

the visionary the satisfiable equalizer screaming for
the vitality of dreams interrupting false calm
demanding fairness and a new new world are the
poets & their poems [10]

...art becomes artifice when it is not backed by cogent content.
—Niyi Osundare

In spite of various structural and physical devices, meaning and relevance to the community stands out as a more dominant component in these men's poetry. In fact, this appears to be the driving force behind their writings. Their themes of constructive resistance, rejuvenation, and reclamation of a dissipating culture are similar. Osundare makes more use of stylistics and physical presentation. This factor influenced the appearance of "Akoben." Yet, Madhubuti also rejects strict formulaic structures. He rarely uses metered lines and/or rhyme schemes. Madhubuti eschews a narrative or prosaic structure. His lines may be chopped, interrupted, cut, or extended as in the example from "Poetry: A Preface." Yet, the style of his poetry, and this poem in particular, is not its most significant aspect. Magic, beauty, and a fixation with language and ideas are the poetic charges. When Madhubuti applies the label of a "satisfiable equalizer," or describes the tasks of "explaining the world & you" as "interrupting false calm demanding fairness and a new new world," he clearly situates himself in the realm of activism and social conscience. Adagboyin's interview with Osundare definitively documents his reputation as a "socially obligated writer."

Madhubuti publishes African-centered and conscious literature with Third World Press. He lectures, teaches, writes, edits, and distributes a variety of Afrocentric texts. Osundare is a teacher, writer, and critic. Both write with strong social consciousnesses, yet maintain powerful individual voices. Their writings evoke a sense of immediacy. This immediacy is structural in the sense that they use the first person. Each poet uses the singular "I" as a means of proclaiming his or her individual vision. It opens an implied dialogue, creating the performative aspects of the African oral tradition by subjecting the reader as audience in direct relationship to the poet. Yet, neither poet loses their sense of connection to their people. The audience is pulled into their vision by the inclusive plural "we." Madhubuti uses the plural form substantially more than Osundare. He also utilizes a "they," which further contextualizes an in-group/out-group dynamic, which further clarifies the community of "we-ness." This I/we tension is evident in Osundare's poetry as he embraces the autobiographical moment. He affirms the personal pronoun "I" but in the African communal context.[11]

The poems in Haki Madhubuti's *Book of Life* and *Earthquakes and Sunrise Missions* resonate with Osundare's structural approach to poetry. Adagboyin's essay on Osundare's neologisms is significant and instructive; directly to Osundare, yet its formulas can be applied to Madhubuti as well. Adagboyin's analyses need only be reiterated here. Osundare creates new words in different ways: compound words, suffixes, or prefixes. An African usage of a nonindigenous language, English in Osundare's case, implies that such language could be twisted or fractured to reveal an alternate world view. In this regard, Madhubuti suffers from indoctrination into the English language and a Western dominated society. While the British influence in Nigeria is still strong, it is counterbalanced by a numerical majority of African peoples with competing world views and linguistic heritages: traditional Yoruba, Igbo, Fulani, or Hausa peoples maintain values and realities that daily challenge the idea of a Western cultural dominance. This linguistic/cultural phenomenon was not lost on the Black Power ideologues, or the Pan-Africanists. Changing names, naming institutions with terms from African languages, and embracing alternative value systems like Kawaida (Kwanzaa or the Nguzo Saba,) Ma'at, or rites of passage organizations combined with various fashion choices/statements that reject mainstream viewpoints. The world views embraced were not as local as the Igbo or Yoruba, but the work of Karenga, Nobles, and others points African Americans away from the Western world toward a distilled cultural product that I refer to as "Afrikanity."[12] Thus the neologisms in Madhubuti's—and one must also remember that Haki Madhubuti had changed his name from Don L. Lee— poetry exemplifies a restructuring of reality and an assertion of Africanist [at the very least non- or anti-Western] perspectives, even in the more local New World US context. Osundare's responses to Adagboyin's question about his creation of new words point in this direction. He acknowledges that new words are always coming into the indigenous languages. It is a reasonable step to assert that new words can come into the nonindigenous languages, especially when they are created by the perceptions and needs of the indigenous.

Neologisms in Madhubuti s poetry:

realpretty, Afrikanwomen, ungettable (*Life*, 14).
pig-eaters (*Life*, 15).
kneeknot (*Life*, 16).
eachother (*Life*, 17).
moonlounge (*Life*, 20).
renurtured, styler, newrisin (*Life*, 23).

blackworld, Afrikanlove, spacesun (*Life*, 24).
steelness (*Life*, 6).
illusionize, refix (*Life*, 29).
Dr. Clearhead Knowitall (*Life*, 31).
trafficful (*Life*, 51).

hueless (*Sunrise*, 38).
nobackbone (*Sunrise*, 47).
middlenoon (*Sunrise*, 56).
brakelight [verb](*Sunrise*, 57).
unsilent, peacefulgivings, waterclear (*Sunrise*, 59).
riverlike, springlove, oceandeep, glowingover (*Sunrise*, 60).
overneeded (*Sunrise*, 64).
firetone (*Sunrise*, 67).
suntimes, lovesong (*Sunrise*, 68) .
softrose (*Sunrise*, 70).
Womenblack, yellowblack, darkearth, joyscreams, lifegiver (*Sunrise*, 71).
berryblack (*Sunrise*, 72).
lifeforces (*Sunrise*, 77).
hungerless, falsesong (*Sunrise*, 85).
berrycolored, nappyheaded, rustykneed, widehipped, biglipped,
    cherrybrown (*Sunrise*, 92).
malepractice, maleabsence (*Sunrise*, 98).
trackman (*Sunrise*, 108).
Blacklife (*Sunrise*, 109).
menblack (*Sunrise*, 113).
screamingly (*Sunrise*, 118).
earthrise, deepblack, sunbaked, rootculture (*Sunrise*, 119).
realenemy, blackpoem, realpeople, doubleblack, purpleblack, x-black
    (*Sunrise*, 185–186).[13]

This list compares favorably with the following, which is borrowed from Adagbonyin. Especially note the many incidents of compounding seen in both poets' work.[14]

kinsvice (*SMP*, 33).
crabprints (*A Nib*, 38).
hillsteps (*WL*, 24).
harvestide (*SS*, 41).

noonfields (*VV*, 71).
painfields (*M*, 40).
mindprints (*ML*, 56).
after disco (*A Nib*, 28).

Osundare makes greater uses of suffixes in his neologisms.[15] Madhubuti makes more use of the form of compounding. This can easily be seen in a review of Madhubuti's list juxtaposed with the chart of Osundare's compound word creations. A direct word for word comparison will not be necessary for this category. Madhubuti's other neologisms, however, can be fit into a chart that compares the two poets.[16]

Niyi Osundare	Haki Madhubuti
teacherly, earlessly (*ASA*, 40).	screamingly, riverlike
leaplessness, winkless (*ASA*, 40).	hungerless, hueless, steelness
unsilence, beclamoured (*ASA*, 37).	unsilent, renurtured, ungettable, refix
beltful, streetful (*ASA*, 39).	trafficful, overneeded
preyer (*ASA*, 42).	styler, lifegiver
hostaging, tongueing (*ASA*, 38).	illusionize, newrisin,
peacefulgivings (noun)	

I recognize that some of my statements are out of line with mainstream ideologies and viewpoints about the relationship between contemporary Africans and their descendants generations removed in the US. Some Black American scholars reject the idea that we (they) are African, except in the undeniable brown-skinned phenotype and the genetic fact of ancestors from Africa. They would not agree that the state of contemporary African American society or African American cultural expressions or the group's political and economic realities has anything to do with Africa. For them, Africa was left behind when the coast could no longer be seen from the deck of the slave ship. For them, slavery is indeed a thing of the past, relegated there by the Emancipation Proclamation, or at latest, the XIIIth Amendment. For them, Civil Rights are a reality and not merely guaranteed by legal decree. For them, Affirmative Action discriminates against White people. They consider themselves brown-skinned White people (even though they often possess enough race pride to deny such an obvious assimilationist label) because they acknowledge nothing of African survivals remaining in New World society to be an influence on their behaviors or perspectives. They have $ouled out. Their jobs, their well-being, self-respect, and self-esteem are linked to affirming Euro-American culture and appeasing the White power structure. African American or Afro-American are misnomers applied to them. They are Negro. But the African community also has its share of those who identify more with Europe than Africa. There are certainly those in Africa who view the American of African descent as crazy kin better left locked out of sight in the cellar or an attic bedroom. Whether because of the sting of being rejected, or basic repulsion at the blatant "Americanness," for some Africans, Black Americans have no legitimate claims of kinship, cultural, or otherwise. I would not have these people change their identity for me. I would let them know that some of *us* believe otherwise. If they do not want me to speak for them—and I don't—by proclaiming them "Africans" or by letting Black Americans claim Africanness, I would ask that they refrain from making blanket statements that disavow me of my heritage and antagonize my cousins from across the Atlantic. Though I personally make these claims, they are not idiosyncratic. "Long Lost Kin" through out the Diaspora have agreed with me and validated this perspective. *Hot/cold faucets bleed in basins of emotion—facets that blink on/off leaving stubborn rings*

Though lacking the nation/state implications, the Civil Rights/Black Power struggles of the 1950s, 60s, and 70s were no less struggles for freedom and independence than the anti-colonial movements toward freedom and independence that swept across Africa over the same time frame and continued into the 90s. Unfortunately, those temporary successes leave many confused in the light of regressive politics and continuing oppression, especially where Blacks, Africans, or African Americans seem to be those wielding the power. We, Africans on both sides of the Atlantic, must look closer at each other, our political battles, and cultural expressions in order to bring about a new, better world harmony. *don't stab me in the back brothers & sisters. face me, talk with me. we can be joyful, once again* We have won some battles over the last half century. Nevertheless, our struggles continue. We have lost many battles, too—more battles and more recently than most of our so-called leaders care to admit. The year 2K is already upon us. If we sincerely want positive social change, we must listen and respond to the many voices of the people. If our leaders do not take us where we want to go, listen to our artists. Osundare and Madhubuti constantly remind and goad us. The struggle goes on, and on.....

AMANDLA!

NOTES

1 "The Prophetess" in *Contemporary African Short Stories*. Achebe, Chinua and C.L. Innes (Editors) page 14.

2 See "There is no No More Beautiful Way" in *Afro-American Literary Study in the 1990s*.

3 See Osundare's response on pages 103–107 of *Niyi Osundare: Two Essays and an Interview*. His commentary on the critical as well as creative use of I/we in literature is both descriptive and prescriptive.

4 His contribution to *Ogoni's Agonies: Ken Saro-Wiwa and the Crisis in Nigeria..* Ed. Abdul-Rasheed Na'Allah. Trenton, NJ: AWP, 1998: 105–108.

5 Hughes is later listed as someone he has read, but the influential link is missing or unstated. Clearly Hughes is one of the most oral of poets. His language is also among the most accessible. Osundare readily admits his debt to the oral traditions and/of folklore and his belief that the common man/woman should be able to read it "no matter how big a word is the tongue cuts it, not a knife."

6 See the Afterword in *Earthquakes and Sunrise Missions*.

7 See the Afterword in *Earthquakes and Sunrise Missions*, p. 182.

8 Soyinka, Wole. p. 53.

9 This quote is actually Bryce's interpretation of Osundare's recollections of signifying poetry in the village life of his peasant upbringing. (Bryce,1986: 1325)

10 From "Poetry: A Preface" in Earthquakes and Sunrise Missions pp. 13–14.

11 See Adagboyin pp.103–107.

12 This is not a completely original term. Nobles have developed it substantially. The advent of substituting a "k" rather than the "c" in Africa is detailed in Lee's (Madhubuti's) *From Plan to Planet* as well as Thompson's *Flash of the Spirit*. Many poets and activists in the 1960s and 70s adopted this convention.

13 This poem uses numerous nouns and adjectives as prefixes for –black. An exhaustive list of them would not contribute substantially to demonstrating my point about Madhubuti's neologisms.

14 Once again, I acknowledge an indebtedness to Adagbonyin's superb scholarship. His analyses are of a quality that it would be difficult, as well as unnecessary, to duplicate. This list includes his table 3 on compounding and a few other examples from the essay "Run-in Towards the Communicative Core" that is the second chapter in *Niyi Osundare: Two Essays and an Interview*.

15 Please see Adagboyim's Table 2 pp. 38–41.

16 Again, I am indebted to Adagbonyin's scholarship. I do not provide an exhaustive list of the words he documents, only enough to demonstrate the similarities between Osundare and Madhubuti.

APPENDIX 1
A Review of Osundare's *Horses of Memory*

when blue songs erupted
from the memory
of your mouth
black and painfully proud
from "The Sun's Workman's Hands"

Niyi Osundare's latest publication, *Horses of Memory*, was published during the period this essay was written. I had wanted to include this collection of poems in the essay. Rather than revise the existing text to incorporate the latest book, I chose to review it in an appendix. After careful consideration, this pathway seems to have been the best because *Horses of Memory* is such a unique work it should stand alone instead of on the shoulders of its predecessors. It forges new directions for this poet. Osundare's imagery is, as always, concise and insistent. It deviates substantially from the structural analyses proposed by Adagboyin. This is not to say it is of a lesser quality. Instead, Osundare demonstrates his versatility and depth. He makes minimal use of the convention of the neologisms that lend uniqueness to his articulation. In this collection of poetry, Osundare seldom physically manipulates the words on the page beyond fairly common patterns of stanzas and indentation. He maintains the characteristic oral and performative dynamics by giving orchestral directions, which evoke the presence of drums and choral voices, even when the simulation (what he labels "celebrative energy") is left largely to the imagination of the reader. To the extent that these characteristics set his poetry apart from other poets, his voice is nevertheless distinct and powerful.

Horses of Memory gives a more focused philosophical vision because of the common thematic glue that binds the poems together. The vast majority of the poems center on issues of memory or images evoked in the poets experience, remembrances, and reminiscings. The collection is dedicated to his late father. Though just published in 1998, the majority of the poems were written during 1986 and apparently none after 1991. The first and longest poem, "For the One Who Departed," is a celebration of his father as musician, father, farmer, griot, and inspiration. This initiates a consciousness that pervades the collection. Memories of people and their lives, of places and events are not static. Such memories, through their being remembered, lamented, and celebrated, constitute a living history that unfolds in the daily present that welcomes the future with greedy embrace. Though written more than a decade ago, these poems have a timeless sense of personal import bordering on urgency.

Beyond the theme of memories, the word itself, "memory," a derivative (remember, remembrance,) or a form of "forget" appears in most of the poems. Of the approximately sixty individual pieces, fourteen have one of these words in the title. Three others have "history" in the title. Similarly, the texts of the poems themselves utilize this vocabulary. Only six poems, and two of those very short, do not have one of these words in their texts. These are more than buzzwords; they restate and reiterate the common theme. Although separated into chapters with individual titles for the poems included in them, *Horses of Memory* reads more like one of Whitman's epics, "Passage to India" or "Song of Myself." The poems and chapters merge, like movements or sections, into a broader conceptual whole. They easily could be numbered or outlined to fit into a larger, complete and insular text. Osundare's orchestration of individual poems transcends the singular poem, and brings a symphonic sense to the collection.

Musical analogies to *Horses of Memory* fit Osundare's own interpretation of the African poetic arts. His structural approach is less physical than the forms discussed in Adegboyin's work. Instead, the structural approach in this collection is more in line with a jazz/blues concerto. He invokes a variety of repetitive and/or call and response techniques. Osundare utilizes a traditional AAB blues motif but also elaborates and improvises on the B-line like a jazz solo. "For the One Who Departed," "Memory's Road," "We Shall Remember," "Africa's Memory," "New Drum," "I Met History Today," and "Horses of Memory" are a few examples of this blues motif. He improvises on a stated theme in "Memory Street" [The juggernaut has broken the teeth of the street], "Scars of Unremembrance" [We summon our scars], and "Who's afraid of the proverb." In most of the longer poems, Osundare improvises and "worries the line" both across and within stanzas.

The varieties of repetition and improvisation transcend the individual poems. With the use of memory as a consistent, restated and revised theme, and given the structural similarities among the poems, Osundare engages the reader in the epic unfolding of this reflective period of his life. In this regard, the analysis of the separate and paradigmatic images, the dedication of this work to his late father is of critical importance. The celebration and sorrow he feels for his father are both fuel and vehicle for this book. Niyi Osundare rides the horses of memory not until they tire and balk at the effort, but only until they glisten, shine, and snort with beauty. This is an excellent collection of poetry, worthy of the honor of one's ancestors. Ariyoosu Osundare has not laid down the machete. Proudly, he has passed it down to the son who wields it deftly.

BIBLIOGRAPHY

Achebe, Chinua and C.L. Innes. *Contemporary African Short Stories*. London: Heinemann Educational Books, 1992.

Adagboyim's, Asomwan S. *Niyi Osundare: Two Essays and an Interview*. Ibadan: Sam Bookman, 1996

Ani, Marimba. *Yurugu: An African-centered Critique of European Cultural Thought and Behavior*. Trenton NJ: Africa World Press, 1994.

Asante, Molefi. "The Search for an Afrocentric Method." In Hayes, Floyd (Editor.) *Turbulent Voyage: Readings in African American Studies*. San Diego: Collegiate Press, 1992: 24–37.

Baker, Houston "There is No More Beautiful Way." Eds. Baker, Houston, Jr., and Patricia Redmond. *Afro-American Literary Study in the 1990s*. Chicago: The University of Chicago Press, 1989.

Bryce, Jane. "Dreams and Bullets." *West Africa*. Jul 21, 1986: 1524–1525.

Gates, Henry Louis, Jr., ed. *Black Literature & Literary Theory*. New York: Routledge, Chapman and Hall, Inc., 1984.

———. *Figures in Black: Words, Signs, and the "Racial" Self*. New York: Oxford University Press, 1987.

———. *The Signifying Monkey: A Theory of African-American Literary Criticism*. New York: Oxford University Press, 1988.

Gayle, Addison, Jr., ed. *The Black Aesthetic*. Garden City: Doubleday, 1971.

———. ed. *Black Expression*. New York: Weybright and Talley, 1969.

Henderson, Stephen. *Understanding the New Black Poetry*. New York: William and Morrow Co., Inc., 1972.

Madhubuti, Haki [Lee, Don L] *Earthquakes and Sunrise Missions*. Chicago: Third World Press, 1983.

———. *From Plan to Planet*. Chicago: Broadside Press, Institute of Positive Education, 1973.

———. *The Book of Life*. Detroit: Broadside Press, 1973.

Maja-Pearce, Adewale. *The Heinemann Book of African Poetry in English*. London: Heinemann International, 1990.

Na'Allah, Abdul Rasheed. Editor. *Ogoni's Agonies: Ken Saro-Wiwa and the Crisis in Nigeria*. Trenton: Africa World Press, Inc., 1998.

Ngugi Wa Thing'o. *Moving the Centre*. London: James Curry LTD, 1993.

Ndebele, Njabulo S. "The Prophetess." Eds. Achebe, Chinua and C.L. Innes. *Contemporary African Short Stories.*

Nobles, Wade. *Africanity and the Black Family: The Development of a Theoretical Model*. Oakland: Black Family Institute, 1985.

Osundare, Niyi. *Horses of Memory*. Ibadan: Heinemann Educational Books [Nigeria PLC], 1998.

Radhakrishnan, R. "Postcoloniality and the Boundaries of Identity" *Callaloo* 16.4 (1993): 750-771.

Soyinka, Wole. *Myth, Literature and the African World*. London: Cambridge University Press, 1976

Thompson, Robert Farris. *Flash of the Spirit: African & Afro-American Art & Philosophy*. New York: Vintage Books, 1984.

ART, VALUE AND EVALUATION IN NIYI OSUNDARE'S "BENIN MASK" AND JACK MAPANJE'S "KABULA CURIO'S SHOP"

Olufemi Ibukun Dunmade

Iya ja je ji l'Egbe
Ile eni l'eso ye'ni[i]

The Yoruba epigraph above restates the subject of my study in this paper. Niyi Osundare deploys it as an element of style in his poem, "On Seeing A Benin Mask in A British Museum" (For FESTAC 77),[ii] hence "Benin Mask." Osundare translates the proverb in the poem thus: "Suffering afflicts the stranger in an alien land/One is most valued in one's own home." The epigraph metaphorically reflects issues central to art, value, and evaluations. The proverb questions the reader about value and evaluation in the second clause, and talks about philistinism in the first clause. Art, however, is not an important focus in Osundare's translation of the proverb, although it is implied in *teso*, a Yoruba word for "adornment," or "object d'art." To underscore the relevance of the epigraph to our study, the proverb could be represented thus: "Suffering afflicts the stranger in an alien land, his object d'art is valued in his own home."

Issues centering on value and evaluation recur wherever literature and art or other forms of cultural activity are discussed. Often, the cultural forms are the focused in these issues. But, other interests and approaches have been generated from these issues, sometimes even outside literary or artistic values. Niyi Osundare's "Benin Mask" and Jack Mapanje's "Kabula Curio-Shop"[iii] demonstrate such interests. Artistic value and evaluation are central to them. In addition, these issues are used to recognize other social issues.

ART, VALUE AND EVALUATION

Art is simply the creation or expression of what is beautiful. The object so expressed or created is itself an art or a work of art. The materials of creation could be any language, paints, wood, concrete, and so on.

"Value" is, however, a complex term. It has been defined in at least three ways.[iv] But its currency in everyday speech, and as it is relevant to our study, maintains two related but more or less distinct senses. In a sense, "value" means the material or monetary equivalence-in-exchange of something. In the other broad sense, "value" is not monetary and not obviously or necessarily material but underlines the extent to which something is held in esteem or appreciated because of its relative effectiveness in performing some function or meeting some need.

Evaluation is a specific act of correctly identifying the objective value of something or accurately describing features that are related to its value. Persons make the most valid judgments with certain appropriate qualifications or an adequate understanding of the object being evaluated.

Acts of evaluation take many forms. It can be in forms of verbal statements, such as "it is a good work of art..." It can also be in the treatment given to the object, or in the exchange of value—in cash or in kind. Evaluation could be the more explicit, overt verbal judgment, or the implicit, largely non-verbal one.

OSUNDARE AND MAPANJE

Osundare and Mapanje are poets from Nigerian and Malawi respectively. They have the same strong feeling for art. This strong feeling has been sustained variedly by each of them in various poems. But the poets sustain their meditation on art other than poetry. Osundare's "Benin Mask" and Mapanje's "Kabula Curio-Shop" establish an ambience of the poets' concern with an art other than poetry. Osundare's poem is on a Benin mask while Mapanje's is on a lioness carving.

Both Osundare and Mapanje are social critics. They are human rights crusaders. They always seek humanistic ends with their poetry and decry every negative vocation through their works. I will exemplify with two of their poems.

OSUNDARE'S "BENIN MASKS" AND MAPANJE'S "KABULA CURIO-SHOP"

The two poems, "Benin Mask" and "Kabula Curio-Shop" are apparently different cultural forms. The poems derive more immediately from the concern of two poets for different themes, and they deploy different poetic elements to realize their themes. "Benin Mask" focuses on the theme of exile and displacement, while "Kabula Curio-Shop" is on the theme of labor and its abuse.

Osundare realizes the theme of displacement and exile through a cluster of images of dislocation and exile. He addresses the mask in Benin museum in the following words:

> Here stilted on plastic/...
> Uprooted from your past
> Distanced from your present

The poet emphasizes this theme in other images like those of estrangement. The mask is described as a "Sojourner in a strange land"; she is surrounded too by "alien ears."

Mapanje's concern with labor is best illustrated in the poet's repeated attention to the long toil, the skill and the concentration involved in carving. He underlines this concern in a series of repetition:

> The sharpening of axes, adzes, carvers the chopping, the whittling and such carving such scooping and scooping then the sandpapering and smoothing.

The labor involved is emphasized further in the breaking strain image of the carver's "eyes red over bellows."

Osundare conceives the artwork anthropologically and presents an otherwise material force in symbolic, spiritual and religious terms. The mask is variedly presented as a "deity," a "god deshrined," "profaned." Mapanje's conception of the lioness carving is materialist. The artwork is repeatedly described only as "Black wood."

"Benin Mask" demonstrates a poet's fascination with proverbs, while "Kabula Curio-Shop" is evidently built greatly on contrast on cryptic images. Osundare places one proverb over another in the poem and accesses each proverb through different poetic figures. He laments in a proverb, the humiliating treatment meted out to the mask, the god:

> Iya jajeji l'eghe
> Ile eni Iteso yetni

He decries in yet another proverb, the oddness and impropriety in the treatment:

> Only what becomes is becoming
> A noose does not become a chicken's neck v

Mapanje contrasts the first stanza of "Kabula-Curio-Shop" with its second stanza. The first stanza depicts the artist, the carver hard and careful at work. The second presents the product of his work as carelessly abandoned in the tiny corner of the Curio-Shop, "broken legs, broken neck, broken udder."

But despite the apparent differences observed between the two poems, the two share some profound similarities. The poems are appreciably concerned with art, value, and evaluation. They deploy issues in their poems to comment on some specific social relations also.

VALUE AND EVALUATION IN THE POEMS

"Benin Mask" and "Kabula Curio-Shop" examine art, their value and evaluation. They are on carvings, and they condemn the treatment the carvings are subjected to. They share many poetic figures, such as rhetorical question, images of commerce, and of destruction and irony to explore this shared perspective.

"Kabula Curio-Shop" points to some images of commerce, and to the poet's pre-occupation with the issue of value. It is implied in the poem that there is a monetary equivalence-in-exchange for the carving. This value, however, is not fulfilled. There, it is suggested that the artist was exploited and did not get his labor's worth:

> Black wood between carefully boned legs
> Such energy release and the price bargained away...

Also, "Benin Mask" underlines, in an image of "commerce," Osundare's concern with the issue of value. It is implied further in the image, however, that the mask might only have been, in truth, bartered for an order of the British Empire. According to the poet, the mask is:

> Traded in for an O.B.E.;
> Across the shores

There is suggested a form of exploitation; the mask attracted no (monetary) value.

Osundare and Mapanje disapprove of the treatment of the carvings. They both express their disapproval in rhetorical questions. Mapanje is visibly angry and almost indignant at the treatment of the black carving. He expresses his anger and disbelief rhetorically:

> would you imagine (that carving) now a broken symbol
> thrown careless in the nook of a Curio-Shop a lioness broken
> legs, broken neck, broken udder

Osundare expressed displeasure at the sad spectacle when the mask is turned. In a rhetorical question, no less linked with a Yoruba adage, Osundare expresses his sympathy for the mask, his admiration for her endurance of suffering, and her anger at those revelers surrounding it. Osundare asks:

> Whoever saw a deity dancing langbalangba (vi) to the carious
> laugh of philistine revelers?

"Benin Mask" and "Kabula Curio-Shop" implicate the modern tourist industry and tourists in the bad treatment meted out to art. The modern tourist industry commercializes art, and the two poets frown at the industry's evaluation of art as dependent only on what amount of money it might fetch in some market or as dependent on its performing some material functions.

Osundare and Mapanje frown at the philistinic attitude toward art. In "Kabula Curio-Shop," this attitude is reflected in both the under-costing and the careless abandonment of the carving broken into pieces in a corner of the shop. The carving is regarded by the trader only as an unusual wood decoration. It is not the valued, the poet laments, as embodying another person's labor.

Osundare perceives the attitude of the tourists to the mask as philistinic. He achieves this perception through an ironic rhetorical feat. While one is led initially to believe that the mask was rescued from "a smoldering shrine," it is ironic to point it out that the mask was rescued only to be sold into a strange land. Further, to the earlier ironic twist in the fate of the mask, the poet foregrounds another irony in the philistinic attitude to the mask. There is a note of irony in the scrupulousness with which curious tourists analyze the mask. Their interest is material. They savor, in the poet's words:

Paralleled lines on your forehead
Parabola on your cheek
Semicircles on your eye brow
And the solid geometry of your lips

But tourists' evaluation is both a denial and an inversion of the spiritual sense that the mask's features carry.

SOCIAL RELATIONS IN THE POEMS

"Benin Mask" and "Kabula Curio-Shop" also implicate some social relations. The poems suggest the poets' awareness of some relationships into which people must enter or are forced into with each other. The poems reproduce such social relations and interrogate them.

Two apparently different forms of social relations circumscribe both poems. But these relations are indubitably facets of the same coin. Mapanje reproduces class relation in his poem, while Osundare presents racial relation. They both, however, reflect relations as imperfect and as being at the expense of one of the other parties involved.

"Kabula-Curio-Shop" focuses on a socio-economic relation between a class, which owns and controls capital, and another, which depends for its survival on selling its labor. The Curio-Shop operator represents the first class and the carver, "the other." The carving is both an artifact and an industry. It is a structure of meaning and also a commodity sold on the market. But the carver did not sell his art at a profit, nor did he get a fair treatment for the work from the shop operator.

"Benin Mask" hints at racial relation and at two groups of people who "display" a difference in their attitudes toward the mask. Belonging to a kind are the Benin's, whose presence is accessed in metaphoric and synedocheic terms that derive from a Yoruba proverb - Eniyan l'aso mi[vii] telescoped in the lines,

Here you stand, chilly
Away from your clothes

The warp and weft of the clothing of Benin mask are a people. The mask's "trade of living" is the Benins.

Belonging to the "Other" are the tourists, understandably white and Britons. Osundare uses this poem to underline this racial perspective in many ways. In a euphemistic term, the poet alludes to history, draws in white imperialist government, symbolized by Queen Victoria, as suggested in the image in "a victorianizing expedition"[viii] and that in the 'O.B.E.'[ix]

The mask is both an art and an integral tradition of the Benins and was produced by them. Traded for the order of the British Empire into Europe, the mask is not evaluated, per se, by the whites according to its own principles. The mask underscores for the Benin an African philosophy on the interdependence between things (material or matter) and spirit (gods and deities), the mask underlines for the Britons western thought of an airport art, a high pressure European type commercialism, which does not give the mask a fair treatment.

CONCLUSION

"Benin Mask" and "Kabula Curio-Shop" are two poets' meditation on art. The poets access different themes in their respective meditations on a carving and a mask. But they are both preoccupied with art, value, and evaluation. They decry the fact that art is ill-valued and devalued. They also implicate social relations in their concern. They indict certain consumers of art portraying them as philistinic.

NOTES

1   The epigraph is a Yoruba proverb; it is deployed by Niyi Osundare in "Benin Mask."

2   Niyi Osundare, *Songs of the Marketplace* (Ibadan: New Horn, 1982) pp. 3

3   Jack Mapanje's *Chameleon and Gods* (London: Heinemann 1981) pp. 3.

4   Barbara Hernstein Smith "Value/Evaluation" ed Frank Lentricchia and Thomas McLaughlin *Critical Terms for Literary Study* (Chicago: Chicago University 1990).

5   The lines formulate another Yoruba proverb - Ohun to yeni lo yeni, okun orun ko ye adiye.

6   The question is a translation of Agbalagba kii se langbalangba'.

7   The proverb is another Yoruba adage; it is 'telescoped' in the poem.

8   History has it that in 1897 a British expeditionary force carried away to Europe Benin art pieces conservatively estimated as numbering 2,400.

9   O.B.E. is an abbreviation in the poem; it is interpreted by me as Order of the British Empire.

REFERENCES

Appiah, Kwameh Anthony. "Race." Eds. Frank Lentricchia and Thomas Laughlin. *Critical Terms for Literary Study*. Chicago: University of Chicago Press, 1990.

Awoonor, Kofi. *The Breast of the Earth*. Enugu: Nok, 1975.

Belsey, Catherine. *Critical Practice*. London: Methuen, 1980.

Bourdieu, Pierre. *Distinction: A Social Critique of the Judgment of Taste*. Trans. Richard Nice. Cambridge: Harvard, 1984.

Ellis, J. "Art Culture and Quality." 19 *Screen* no. 3, 1978.

Gates, Henry Louis Jr. *"Race," Writing and Difference*. Chicago: University of Chicago Press, 1986.

Mapanje, Jack. *Of Chameleon and Gods*. London: Heinemann, 1981.

Mukarovsky, Jan. *Aesthetic, Function, Norm and Value as Social Facts*. Trans. Mark Suino. Ann Arbor University of Michigan, 1970.

Olaniyan, Tejumola. *Scars of Conquest: Masks of Resistance*. Oxford: Oxford University of Chicago Press 1990.

Osundare, Niyi. *Songs of the Marketplace*. Ibadan: New Horn, 1983.

Smith, Barbara Herrnstein. "Value/Evaluation" Eds. Frank Lentricchia and Thomas McLaughlin. *Critical Terms for Literary Study*. Chicago: University of Chicago Press, 1990.

Wolff. *The Social Production of Art*. New York: New York University Press, 1984.

CONSUMMATE POETS OF TIME: OSUNDARE AND MEMBERS OF HIS GENERATION

Tayo Olafioye

Writing beats a feat that measures eternity; only giants of the mind achieve it. This assertion, perhaps, resonates the significance of poetry as an exaltation of humanity. To affirm this belief, Confucius once said to his son: Poetry can serve to i.ispire emotion, to help you in your observations, to make you fit for company to express your grievances. (Liu Hongbin, Pen International 65)

Thus, Osundare, along with a few significant members of his generation of new African poets—Tanure Ojaide of Nigeria, Jack Makpanje of Malawi, and Kofi Anyidoho of Ghana, for example—fits eloquently into the ascription above. These sweet, bitter-spoken poets of contemporary Africa make majestic pronouncements to denote the poet's ambassadorial responsibilities, the arbitrary snapshots of African realities. They use poetry to paint archetypes of dichotomies: the rich and the poor, the ninny and the smart, the green and the arid landscapes, the mighty and the minion, the humane and the beastly, the witches and the wizards, the filial and the prodigal. Thus, the poets swing between angst, melancholy, satire, and hope. How complete or inadequate swell the truths that they emote? How eloquently colloquial or flexibly demotic rise their writings? How will their poetry outlive their time? How does their poetry influence the collective or personal moralities of their respective societies? Finally, on what scale score their political and social criticisms in universal dream events, dreamscapes, and dream histories of their time? Most of the above are the kilometers by which we are going to measure Osundare and his contemporaries. How timeless is his impact, and how substantive is his content?

Decidedly, Niyi Osundare's "College" in his *A Nib* shares multiple attributes with Ojaide's "The fate of vultures." Both poems so sharply inveigh national and international political malpractice in their country, Nigeria, or Africa as a whole. Both poets, however, operate from two different cultural approaches. One, Ojaide imbibes Urhobo tonality, while on the other hand, Osundare trails Yoruba praxis. Their mission remains undoubtedly the same—correction of the human and political meandering of their society. In so doing, they depend on prosodic deployments, tones, echoisms, anaphoras, repetitions, alliterations, synecdoches, onomatopoeias, puns, parodies, oxymorons, satires, and sarcasms—all of which generate impudent humors much as they aim to ameliorate and soothe pains. Kofi Anyidoho of Ewe, extraction from Ghana, and Jack Makpanje of Malawi, wear similar garments of concerns and cultural influences.

Ojaide, militantly and straightforwardly appeals to his god of memory, Aridon, to retrieve for society through him, the loot which politicians stashed away.

> Aridon, bring back my wealth from rogue-vaults; legendary
> witness to comings and goings, memory god, mentor...
> (The Fate of Vultures, 11).

Not only does the poet pursue the moral crusade of retrieval but also savagely vilifies the protagonist-predators of social comfort, economic remunerations, political probity, and the national moral health. As Osundare will soon demonstrate, Ojaide plunges into a display of puns, through alliteration, which depicts the mood of the nation as well. Many international awards attest to the poet's talents. The poet appropriates his Urhobo Deltaic Udje song and dance to criticize openly and insultingly. Here, Ojaide moves, measure for measure, with Niyi Osundare, a compatriot and the famous Nigerian Poet, both contemporaries at the University of Ibadan. Thus, in the poem, "Collage," below, Osundare puns, reverses, and evokes double meanings that parallel Ojaide:

> Comrades or comraids
> trail-blazers or blaze-trailers
> demask or the mask.
> *(A Nib, 35).*

Conceptionally, "Collage" presents a series of fragmented thoughts, philosophies, and social engineering united by a psychological process of disconnectedness. It creates a broken picture of instability and mayhem held together by tenuous and evil idealisms.

The poet scoffs at the socialist tendencies that inundated the land. Do the indigenous, political, and visionary pretenders pose socialist comrades sculpted in the image of their Soviet mentors, now defunct? Hence, the rhetorical curiosity: are they truly socialist comrades, or are they the ideological elite who "mask" their corrupted salivation for wealth and fraud? Are they and their foreign mentors aid givers to destitute nations only here to raid the national treasury, values, and conscience? They wear masks of immoral disguise. From any angle they reflect "comraiders," notorious as trailblazers or blaze-trailers in the artistry of unprecedented moral dilapidation, corruption, and thievery. They raid all constituencies of decency and progressive culture.

Here, the two poets use their art to express national and personal grievances, and hence they fit, in absentia, into the minds and company of the world. After all, a good writer holds a conversation with the world in his own absence. They both cultivate deeply and intensely into the dynamics of language to generate the politics of ideas. They also invest in the ambivalence of fluctuations or oscillations between anger, demand, hope, and retrieval. Osundare towers step by step with his contemporary, Ojaide, as, for example, Osundare, bastardizes words for effect in criticizing or satirizing social ills. On democracy, corruption, hypocrisy, and religion, he writes:

> from praying ground to preying ground from democracy to
> demoncrazy from conscience to con-science
> (*A Nib*, 36).

The play on words in this poem akinly approximate that of Ojaide's Shamgari in "The Fate of Vultures." Words are twisted to generate ominous meanings, using alliterations and sound effects, vitriolically assailing the hypocrisy of the elite through a dark humor. They oscillate between "praying ground" and "preying ground." Ostensibly, therefore, people superficially proclaim their Christian or Islamic faith and professions for the world to see and appreciate their righteous living. Pointedly, however, this fabricates a ruse. As soon as the same unsavory characters leave their daily activities, they turn their turf into "preying ground." Here, they lie replete with fraudulence and countless corrupt practices: farming money, influence, greed, and acquisitions out of individuals and national treasuries. These animals prey upon economic and moral victims and hope.

Second, the type of democracy Africa practices under various guises of originality of peculiar African circumstances is actually demon-driven, imbued with
demon craziness, political crassness, incompetent technology, boldface thievery, and chameleonic performances. These political or social operatives possess
neither conscience nor expertise that belies education, values, sensitivity and
civilization. Rather, the poet indicates that they practice the science of trickery,
fraudulence, and manipulations without conscience. They are con artists, con-
scientists, and specialists of deceit, myopia, shallowness, and incompetence.

Similarly, there are puns in the catchwords or buzzwords that politicians spew
during electioneering campaigns to rally their political troops or adherents:

> Vote for me
> Vote for reliability
> Vote for re-liability Vote for re-liar-bility
> (A Nib, 37).

They blazon on the psyche of the populace are the very attributes that they
lack. They provide no reliability, yet they claim reliability as one of their strongest
suits. Once they infest in the office, they become liabilities, preying on national resources and the people. Only a beast preys on others, its victims. Like the
dog, we have given them bones to watch, but they chew them to smithereens.
They loom up as pathological liars, clever political despots, sit-tight office hold-
ers, and engineers of political ruses who refuse to limit their tenure in office.
They burrow in for life.

Both Ojaide and Osundare inventively craft the titles of their poems. "The
Fate of Vultures" bemoans the predators of society. The corrupt elite of any hue
decidedly describes vultures, preying on the economic, social, and political car-
casses or intentions of their people. The vulture apotheosizes decadence, dirty
death, and evil. Its actions merit death, in a revolutionary backlash from the people. To Osundare, "Collage" presupposes misapplied education. The "Collage"
manifests a psychological process of uniting irreconcilables, which imagistically
paint the inimical problem of contemporary Africa. These portray the images
of stifled growth or progress and political philosophies gone aberrant. Corrupt
forces of life take away the values that some of these corrupt entities learned in
college.

They live in liberating formless mass. Thus, Nigeria has become a penal
colony of discomforts and an Agbarha where not much works. The leadership,
therefore, forms a collage of moral misfits and psychological mish-mash of inadequacies.

KOFI ANYIDOHO

Sometimes, uncertainties or inaccurate measurements threaten great artists or budding ones when their good works start to boom. Time often earns them their respects for the insightful penetration that they display of their time. The less talented writers, however, remain immune, receiving a considerable measure of trust as a consolation prize for their limitation. So do these poets become subject to artistic scrutiny all over the world to test their talent and worthiness? Kofi Anyidoho of Ghana shares in the portrayal of the manifestly deadly realities of most African societies of today. He affirms the observations of his contemporaries—no man made, counterfeit social engineering, can or will always succeed. They often fail under the pressures of alternatives, scrutiny, conscientiousness, and probity. Mindless specialists overloaded Africa in political or social engineering. His poem, "Renegade," in his *A Harvest of Our Dreams* attends to his assertion.

Here, the poet agonized the crucifixion of the conscientious critic of social mismanagement. The sitting powers, possibly the military, salivate over the orgy of bloody recriminations against their opponents:

> Prior hideouts in the carnage groves
> the vultures smell rumors
> of blood flowing in open fields
> They purge themselves against
> the feast of rot but grief shall be
> the only testimonial for their greed
> (A Harvest of Our Dreams, 52).

The poet engages similar graphic lyrics and images of power, as did both Ojaide and Osundare. Some African powers, like those in Ghana, decimate their people in open killing fields with blood flowing as rivers. The ignoble social mismanagement of these vultures of decay and dirt invites other vultures, which scented the rotten carnage far away, to gorge themselves with rot. The society constitutes the rot. The governing body defecates it with corruption, dishonesty, and dishonor.

Indeed, "They purge themselves against the feast of rot" (p. 52). Their attempt at self-ritualistic cleansing arrives belatedly. The people have started to make recriminatory steps against the vultures, the predators of social good. Thus, the poet imposes a curse on the evil authorities, just as Ojaide did in many poems: "But grief shall be the only testimonial for their greed" (p. 52). Curses often symbolically follow the tethered end of African jolting endurance of pain and disgust. Ojaide had sought the help of cultural pantheons to wreck vengeance on authoritarian and elitist misfits of Africa. He had summoned "Sopono," "Ogun," "Amadiora," and "Sango" to carry his deleterious angst to punish evildoers. He had also used similar words as Anyidoho's in "bloodpool chlorinated for bath," "Safari of poachers" (greed), "corpses," and "all the spear-tongued critics fed roaming hyenas." Both poets respectively communicate the grim circumstances of their societies.

The renegade in the poem assumes an oppositional pose. Society reacts riotously to the social mismanagement. Hence, the renegade becomes "hooked out/for dishonorable mention in official bulletins," just as the military in Nigeria bayoneted Ken Saroikiwiwa, perfunctorily expended him, however imperfect some of his activities appeared. Power crucified the renegade, a leader of consciousness and social justice, nailing his name, like that of Jesus Christ, to a upas tree. The renegade represented a leadership of conscience:

> From Memory of the rioting mob
> they hooked him out
> for dishonorable mention in official bulletins
> His name they nailed
> to the upas tree on our public square
>
> The crows will come and peck
> at the vision in the renegade
> But the harvest of his dreams
> will not belong to the vampire
> (A Harvest of Our Dreams, 52).

Thus, the renegade rose as a sacrificial offering to the gods of corruption, on the cross of recklessness. The crows of the country pecked out the vision (eyes and imagination) of the renegade who refused to share in the national loot. In killing him, they pecked out his mind, existence, and usefulness. They assassinated his aspirations and hopes for society. Exempli gratis: Ken Saroikiwiwa.

In pain, therefore, the poet wishes the authorities a crop of ill wills. "But the harvest of his dreams/ will not belong to the vampire." Power suffers negative ascription which Osundare and Ojaide clearly showed. In this poem, corrupt and inhumane power masquerades as vampires, crows, and vultures.

The renegade's tree of vision will blossom across the land. Its harvest will enrich the common man but not those behind the plow of management.

As does Osundare and Ojaide, the poet Anyidoho, advertises hope:

> Our doves will come gather his words
> into secret barns of souls
> whose insurance against decrees of death
> (*A Harvest of Our Dreams*, 52.)

The dove represents the image of peace, writers, or conscientious people. They will gather the renegade's ideas and plant them in the minds of society as an "insurance" against dictatorship. Publication, therefore, immortalizes art, truth, and resistance.

Anyidoho concentrated on political matters as the most pressing of his time. Ojaide does too, because they both live in a time of turmoil in their respective society. The emerging countries form implacable jungles of human misery.

> And now with our own hands
> we offer our hearts for safe-keeping
> to the Panther prowling round
> the outskirts of our lives
> reclining under ancestral communal trees
> laying ambush in the midday snooze
> in which even dreams
> take on the density of fear.
>
> Let us not deceive ourselves
> believing the future is
> but a photocopy of the past.
>
> If the wisdom of the elders
> were proof of the elders
> their hopes would not have lost
> their looms in the noonday
> spark that set the sea ablaze
> (*Ancestrallogic and Caribbean Bluess*, 84).

Here again, in "History and blindness," the poet depicts the hubristic stranglehold of society, the past and the present. Power is the panther that prowls the ground of the people's security "the outskirts of our lives."

Anyidoho recalls history and legend, as did Osundare many times in his creativity. The future cannot reflect the innocent past because the characters involved in today's governance have lost innocence and, consequently, have stripped themselves of honor. The elders of the past in their venerable wisdom managed disasters, and their heritage—heirlooms—were destroyed at sea. The panthers (authorities) ambush communal happiness and security. The people live in the density of fear because of the national misery and wrong-headedness that they inflict on society.

The poem "Sound of Silence" in Anyidoho's *Earthchild* corroborates the poet's pains for his people, just as Osundare deemed himself a spokesperson for his country's poor and cheated. The poet indicates in his poem that he lives a silent hurt as much as his nation, a love that he cannot extravagantly display by kissing so wantonly in the open a symbol of prostituted importance and fakery.

> Because because I do not scream
> You do not know how bad I hurt
>
> Because because I do not kiss
> on public squares
> You may not know how much I love
>
> Because because I do not swear
> again and again and again
> You wouldn't know how deep I care
> *Earthchild* 23.

This poem that is akin to Langston Hughes in both style and content; the poem states:

> Because my mouth
>
> Is wide with laughter
> And my throat
> Is deep with song,
> You do not think
> I suffer after
> I have held my pain
> So long

Because my mouth
Is wide with laughter
You do not hear
My inner cry
Because my feet
And gay with dancing
You do not know I die.
Langston Hughes

Thus, the poet preaches the pains of silent hurt and the virtues of silent love and silent care. He contends against so much grief unnecessarily hatched for the people. He decries empty, vociferous gestures, or hollow programs that hold the people on the leash. He scorns their placebos and rejects those who undermine the integrity of the people and nation.

The poet masks his frustrations in introspection. That he does not swear against predators does not preclude an abiding care and a deep hurt. He represents the constituency of the destitute and rejected. The poet appears too civilized in his language. That the crocodile closes his mouth merely hides his teeth, not pull them.

Anyidoho does not become truly silent. His poetry speaks volumes. He realizes that to remain quiet in the face of mayhem commits a fatal mistake. In concurrence, Ojaide interposes here in "The Fate of Vultures":

I would not follow the hurricane,
nor would I the whirlwind
in their brazen sweep-away;
they leave misery in their wake.
I would not spread my ward's wealth
in the open and stir the assembly to stampede;
I would not smear my staff
with the scorn of impotence.
(The Fate of Vultures, 11).

The poet would rather stand exemplary by hoisting an unblemished national flag of character, honor, and harmony.

Anyidoho uses an almost Haiku typeset with striking repetition of "Because because" to intimate emphatic reasons and meanings embedded in his filial love and care. Similarly, the poet denounces the society's lascivious and ostentatious display of its symbols of success, chieftaincy titles, wealth acquisition, multiple marriages, fleet of cars, rows of houses, off-springs, and pyramids of influences, mostly acquired by corrupt means. Such signposts, or symbolism, speaks to the heart of corruption, superficial values, and myopic and effete elitism. All of these concerns resonate in the echo chambers of written modern African poetry:

> You keep saying
> how somehow our world must live by signs
> But see how much we give away
> Doing time in pursuit of signs
> deprived of all meaning
> and of all purpose
> We break our words in two. Then we
> Split each half into sounds and silences
> (*Earthchild*, 23).

By implicit reference, the poet decried "how much we give away" in a wasteful spending of our national resources. This "we" (which embodies entirely too many Nigerians and too many Africans) creates white elephant projects that hire, at great costs, the technical, foreigner "know-how's" If only it could generate qualitative, internal management, and constructs instead of wasting national resources. Such "pursuits of signs" become "deprived of all meaning and purpose." Thus, in Anyidoho, we hear the echoes of Osundare and Ojaide's itchy complaints about the frivolous Nigerian nation that nobody wants, loves, or claims.

A poetic quip qualifies "Newspeddler," ostensibly the Minister of Misinformation and bad news. The poet mocks the government's myth of action that they scrupulously attend to the people's desires "at least they picked the venom from our voice." They attempt to stifle dissent and discontent. Consequently, they pretend to solve the problems of inadequacies and social misery; they pretend to be socialists and to cast spells that would remove the people's disillusionment. They play Nanny, bleating that they have the answers to the nation's hiccups. Playing their mythical god-like roles, they cast the people's social problems and meaning of pain "into stainless tubes well corked with seals of state." Mere decrees without good intentions and resources bear no fruit. Their seals of state, whirlwind, and delible promises of intention degenerate from the genesis. Theirs has become a government rich in placebos:

Last night newspeddler told us how
at last they picked the venom from our voice
into stainless tubes well corked with seals of
state.

And we will glide through life with all sorrows
transformed into beautific visions of excess joy

So help us Dog!
(*Earthchild* , 28).

In their self-effacing delusions, they promise to transform the people's predicaments into visions of excessive joy. The poet would only ridicule their falsehood, redeemer metaphysic and intestinal incompetence with a contorted jibe of "God's" name reversed as "Dog" so help the people.

The satiric jab-ascription of "Dog" testifies to the authority's crassitude. "God" forms a name of exaltation and supernatural essence. In all religions, God holds a place of eminence in the minds of most people and most societies. The psychological sustenance and prayerful security that such omnipotence gives humanity does not breed in a conclave of dogs. They only bark. Like a dog, the rulers love their people to a minimal extent and live for self-interest only. On the whole, a dog is still an animal: subjugated, domesticated, and subservient. God is God, and a dog is a dog—even spelled backwards. Both God and dog do not describe the same and equal entities, "So help us Dog" (p. 28).

Other political poems in Anyidoho arise in "Food for Ghosts," "Republican Dominican," and "Our Fortune's Dance," the latter of which captures Ojaide's similar poetic evocation:

The raw energy of a certain rolling stone
came rumbling throughout will-carved dreams.
Our master hunters had climbed up trees
to pluck berries. They fell in love with Moon.
So Sdelploviawo must wield machetes
and face the panther's wrath

My singer has sent a song of how
today the land is ruled by monstrous things
with huge dense beards. They had no head.

> My people how soon again in our hive
> shall we swarm around our honey comb?
> ("Our Fortune's Dance," 47).

Monstrous creatures rule the land—monsters that sport huge dense beards that symbolically emblazon their evil image. Thus, Anyidoho raises alarm if only to rouse the people. These beards form masks of indignity and dis-ingenuity that reflect the razzmatazz of self-importance gone vacant and of cultic and spurious self-projections.

> My people how soon again in our hive
> shall we swarm around our honey comb
> (*Earthchild* , 47).

The hive describes the people's choking existence. They live in squalor, jousting for measly crumbs to survive. The poet yearns for the good old days and pre-Imperialistic eras to alleviate their misery. They need again the honeycomb of life, which the powerful now appropriate.

THE ROLES OF WRITERS

Niyi Osundare's "A Nib in the Pond" reflects the spirit of Ojaide in his "Naked Words." Both poems extrapolate the scope of responsibilities that a poet's talent can cover or expose. Osundare asserts:

> We read your lines
> opening up the earth
> like a book of paths
> hear your voice
> melting the wax of a thousand seasons
> (*A Nib,* 10.)

Here, Osundare upholds the responsibility of the poet as one who "opens up the earth/like a book of paths" (p. 10). The people and, indeed, the world hear his voice and read his lines. He opens the paths of ideas for society to follow. Thus, the poet is effectively and influentially raising the people's level of action and awareness. Literature, after all, offers an expression of metaphysical truth, "melting the wax of a thousand seasons" (p. 10) because the earth that the poet opens up provides the world with information on Africa's political and inhumane continental disorientation. The writer intercedes by painting the images of the national condition, if only to educate. The writer's role in political arguments is the mark of history. He cannot stay silent or afford to remain apolitical; he must record the social history of his time:

> shut the closet on
> plebeian skulls cracking
> under patrician heels
> (ANib , 10).

The poet must not and cannot watch the military perfunctorily crack the skulls of ordinary citizens (plebeians) without complaining. The poet must use silent creativity to speak volumes of reasonable noise to defeat misguided blueprints of governance:

> You who throw a nub
> in the pond of silence
> ripples in your pond
> convulse barracks and power brothels
> overturning plots of plunder
> dying on calculating cables
> in the mirror of every letter.
> (A Nib ,10).

The poet dips the nib in the pond of silence that ripples and echoes around the world. It rattles, or tremors, the seats of military power (barracks) and the enclaves of convenience (brothels), where plots profligate the looting of the national treasury. The writer acts as the El Zorro of national conscience and sledgehammer against corruption. For the poet to be silent constitutes a grave mistake, no matter how grim or unspeakable the national condition or invincible the power of authority. If he holds his tongue, the enemy speaks and sets the agenda of the debate. The national condition will surely get worse. Thus, the poet "must overturn plots of plunder" (p. 10), which power-dispensation crafts in cloakrooms. The polity becomes enamored when it "reads the word," "hears its voice," "in the mirror of every letter."

On the other hand, Tanure Ojaide tackles the same problem of the writer's role through integral metaphors of national unity and purposefulness through the immanent logic of culturally induced linguistic harmonies. Hence, the "Naked Words" announce the role of the poet in the appropriation of the vitality of culture, national, and ethnic distinctions:

This is a family ceremony
to which the whole world has come.
Outsiders understand
let them imbibe our wisdom and secrets
but we will not change our songs
because of their presence,
we will not sing their songs here
to show that we have heard them sing
about themselves.
Let us not learn from teachers
who have no love from our land.
We must speak the truth
about ourselves to ourselves
without interpreters, middlemen.
Abet those who come to us
listen with more that their ears.
This is a family ceremony
to which the whole world had come.
We will be very true to ourselves.
      (*The Eagle's Vision*, 11).

This poem summarizes Ojaide's poetic mission to "speak the truth about our-selves without interpreters, or middlemen" (p. 11). The mandatory imposed attentions to self culminate the "family ceremony" of words, cultural tonalities, and linguistic atmospherics that change the Eurocentric tenor of the English language. The poets write in English syntax, but their contents and props engender African familiarity and particularities. The English language no longer belongs to England alone but has now become a world heritage that magnetiz-es gems and peculiarities in universal diversities. Ojaide determinedly affects English with his African tonalities, props, and artifacts to achieve this familiar-ity and peculiarity. Clearly, "The literature of one's own country in education is the best introduction to the pleasures and significance of literature as a whole" (Paul Scott). Without doubt, English girds a political belt, a vehicle of democra-cy or unity in disconnected phantoms of national tribes. It creates an open soci-ety in which most understand one another.

Ojaide lampoons intellectuals—such as professors, Odebalas, and gover-nors—who vainly launch community funds for communal projects but are poised to reap its benefits. In a similar exposition, Osundare also questions the honor and probity in the pandering poet or elite. He demands commitment on the side of the people, in his "Questioning A Pandering Poet":

428

What is the poet doing
in the corridors of power:

romping to the ravaging rumblings
of constipated stomachs

nodding to the killsome lies
of reptiles of state

swaying to the rustling silk
of state fops

festering on the sputumed remains
of political tables

clappingfor the airy rambling
of ghosted tirades

peeping at the eunuch beds
of noisy children

licking the bloodies boots
of goose steppers?
(*Questions A Pandering Poet,* 12).

The poet thus denounces pandering to establishments and corrupt regimes, accommodating kills some lies that the smuts spew, embracing state fops or caricatures of dignity, collecting crumbs from political tables of benefactors, abetting airy rambling of the ignorant leadership, and licking the boots of bloody soldiers, tyrants, or miscreants. Both Ojaide and Osundare take the same side, just as they side with the people, the logically mandatory constituency to which a poet should belong:

Of man and mammon
duty and diadem
nous and nescience
who still argues
which side the poet should be?
(Osundare, 1992: 12).

The poet needs not agonize on his choice between mammon (demon, earthly god) and his self-image-man. The poet applies a biblical reference as Ojaide did in his "The Fate of Vultures" in parodying Shadrack, Meschach, and Abednego. He also applies alliteration in "man and mammon" and "duty and diadem." Diadem symbolizes truth and commitment; "diadem" represents ostentatious and shallow display.

In this debate, we hear the voices of Osundare and Ojaide, find a thoroughfare of continuity and sameness, divergent as some of their details may appear; however, they both share in their people's predicaments in their ongoing social intercourse with polity and the world. This becomes Ojaide's implication when he asks the world to "imbibe our wisdom and secrets/ but we will not change our songs/ because of their presence" (p. 11). He thus invites the world to share in the festival of African linguistic creativity in laying out its progress, values, difficulties, and human limitation. The world must penetrate the tongue with which the African writers speak our self-truth and self-revelations, good or bad, because a society needs its own distinctiveness for its self-identity, as well as its culturally vital contribution to the world in any language. The poet provides the vehicle of transmission, a responsibility that rests on Osundare and significant members of his generation.

Osundare's "We read your lines/ opening up the earth" (p. 10), as well as Ojaide's "This is a family ceremony/to which the whole world has come" (p. 11), invites the intellectual world to share their woes and glories with open minds, free borders, and unrestrained cross fertilization in diverse mutualities of their humanity. Both poets open up the earth of their time, the secrets of their home, the wisdom of their heritage, and the distinctiveness that their backgrounds contribute to the world of ideas. Thus, critics measure Ojaide's success and relevance to his time with the comparative embrace, which his works share with Osundare's ability—for example, to ring the bells of human miseries and hopes in their compatriot landscapes.

Olu Obafemi, a critic of the socialist bent, puts into clearer summations Osundare's writing that also found equal description and identity in Ojaide:

> All these elements make Osundare's poetry exude life and vitality. The content is popular and so is the medium. The poetic metaphor as it has been poetry summarizes Osundare's commitment as a poet. The procimal relationship to oral performance mode, the familiarity of the images, the simplicity and lucidity of the language combine to make his works distinctive from those of early Nigerian poets and in fact in

advance of his own contemporaries. This is so especially when the popular medium is in the true tradition of popularity as a dialectical preoccupation of rooting the poetic vision in the needs, hopes, attitudes, and aspirations of the ordinary people in society, the working people and peasantry in constant and conscious struggle against the forces that oppress them. No doubt, these qualities are only steadily maturing in the poet's creative enterprise and endeavor. But they set him confidently on a path of creating a stature yet unconceived in the annals of poetic creativity in Africa.
(Olafioye, 1989: 36).

Idowu Omoyele, a literary critic for *The Nigerian News* also renders a penetrative perspective on Osundare, Ojaide, and Ghana's Anyidoho—three poets who best define Ojaide's generation and his importance in their midst:

Niyi Osundare in his *Selected Poems* and Tanure Ojaide in *The Blood of Peace and other Poems* tape the resources of oral tradition to explore their social vision. Both are notable poets of the After-Okigbo generation, a generation which began to appear on the Nigerian Literary scene in the aftermath of the civil war which Christopher Okigbo, incidentally, foretold in *Path of Thunder* and in which he was killed, again true to his prophesy, in 1967. Like the Ghanaian poet, Kofi Anyidoho, both Niyi Osundare and Tanure Ojaide perceive poetry as song and they employ a variety of rhetorical and sound devices, which seem to enhance, albeit with varying degrees of success, the lyrical quality of their verse.
The Nigerian News, June 24th, 1996 15.

In "Not Standing Still" in his *Selected Poems*, Niyi Osundare parallels Ojaide's sermon of patience and hope. He couches his hope in Yoruba cultural profundities:

Not standing still
is the beginning of battle
he will never pluck the fruit
whose back caresses the earth

> The circle which has a beginning
> also has an end
> a little patience is what it needs
> that stammer
> will call
> his father's name.
> *(Selected Poems , 9).*

The stammer traditionally dims hope of an early possibility to enjoy elementary family discourse, talk less of calling his father by name—a seemingly ordinary task to the tongueloose. Anyone who has raised a child would appreciate the intuitive feeling of fulfillment and gratification, which children generate, when they lovingly call the father—by the social, culture-designation—dad. Thus, Nigeria, the child with hiccups and elocutionary-limitations will overcome his political, social, and economic disabilities. Niyi Osundare declares that the downtrodden must never give up. Brighter days are looming in the horizon: "Not standing still/ is the beginning of the battle/ he will never pluck the fruit/ whose back caresses the earth" (*Selected Poems,* 9). Thus, the poet encourages society to react to despotic rules and smash them ruthlessly.

Thus, Ojaide gains preeminent stature as a result of his depth, perception, and elan. He has consistently distributed accusation, charge, and hope in the raging national morass of impurities. The blind world, for example, never expects Nigeria to resuscitate. Hence, it collapses into the fits of wonderment when the poet's prescription of hope works. The world sees blindly, perhaps because it has not responded strongly enough to the maniacal despotism assailing the land. Many nations collaborate with the regime on economic fronts for their own convenience at the expense of the Nigerian masses. The poet thus remains the traditional scope, minstrel, and griot of his time. He serves as a committed reminder of the gaieties of doom, falsehood, self-glorification, and leadership embroiled in myopia. His people's insignificance resonates in their imagistic dubbing as ants—restless and foraging for survival. In spite of antsy behavior, they dream of the day of deliverance. Thus, the poet excites and stimulates their forlorn hope.

Anticipating the difficult roads ahead to reach harmonious national reconstruction, the poet—Osundare—clinches his message with a metaphoric allusion to the stammer's overcoming his involuntary speech pauses and repetition. Thus, Nigeria will regain normality to the relief of all. No troubled individual or society can afford to be complacent, pleasure-seeking, relief searching, merely by caressing its itchy back with the roughage of the concrete earth or walls of tree-barks. This philosophical observation and nudging of society into action parallel Ojaide's eternal apothegms that ring a poetic alert that no one sits idle with a cobra coiling at his or her doorstep. The Nigerian masses must work for, fight for, and crusade for the peace, progress, stability, justice, fairness, harmony, and the fruits that they seek. Because power concedes nothing without struggle, Nigerians must never allow it to wear them down. It cannot put a period where God has put a comma. The people have borne too much for too long—pains in the silence of their hearts.

Osundare strides in step with his age. The similarity in his works with those of his astute contemporaries' disconsolate differences certifies his relevance. Thus, Osundare proclivity measures well without those half-baked, half broiled, half cooked, and ill-digested lunch that some critics made of poetry. His metaphorical style has always evinced a bold erudition—a highly palatable repast. Many poems from Osundare and his contemporaries are so brilliant that they have become timeless expressions of their generation.

REFERENCES

Anyidoho, Kofi. *A Harvest of Our Dreams*. London: Heinemann, 1984.

———. *Earthchild*. Accra: Woeli Publishing, 1985.

———. *Ancestrallogie and Caribbean Blues*. Trenton: Africa World Press, 1993.

Ezenwa-Ohaeto. *Commonwealth*, vol. 16. No. 12. Ed. DavidMalouf, 1993.

Ogede, S. Ode. *New Trends: African Literature.*, vol. 20. Ed. Eldred Durosimi Jones. Trenton: Africa World Press, 1993.

Ojaide, Tanure. *The Fate of Vultures*. Lagos: Malthouse, 1990.

———. *Daydream of Ants*. Ikeja, Lagos: Malthouse, 1997.

Olafioye, Tayo. *Critic As Terrorist*. San Diego: Advantage Books, 1989.

Omoyele, Idowu. *The Nigerian News*. 24 June 1996.

Osundare, Niyi. *Selected Poems*. London: Heinemann, 1992.

INTERVIEWS WITH OSUNDARE

"I AM ONE OF AFRICA'S ACCIDENTS": INTERVIEW WITH NIYI OSUNDARE

Stephen Arnold

Niyi Osundare, born in 1947, teaches literature and creative writing at the University of Ibadan, and he is today generally held as Nigeria's most important poet. He won the first of his almost innumerable literary prizes in the 1968 Western State literary contest, where he was awarded first prize in the senior section for poetry. On graduating from Ibadan University, he received a scholarship at the University of Leeds and later completed his PhD at York University in Toronto. In 1981, he was one of the principal winners of the BBC Arts and Africa Award; in 1986, he won the African area award of the Commonwealth Poetry Prize and was joint winner of the overall award. In 1988, he was invited to the Iowa International Writers Workshop. In 1991, he won the Noma Award, the most prestigious award for African literature, for his collection *Waiting Laughters*.[1]

STEPHEN Arnold: *On January 10, 1987, thugs attacked you in Ibadan and left you for dead. The poetry you have published since then has been labeled by critics as surrealistic and existential, not poetry for the masses as before. Was your near-death experience traumatic for your poetry? Have you abandoned poetry for the masses?*

Niyi OSUNDARE: It's true; the experience was traumatic in many ways. This was a negative milestone, indeed. It was a life experience that created a stylistic change that people have noticed in my poetry. It started with *Moonsongs*. *Moonsongs* came to me right from the time I regained consciousness in my hospital bed. Every night when everybody had left, the only friend that remained was the moon, whose rays came through the curtains and bathed me in my bed. On nights when the pains were great, the moon looked like a terrible enemy and its rays were red. On other nights when I was relatively relieved, there was a kind of silver luxuriance about its rays. So the moon, itself, put me through different moods.

One of the first things I did when I regained control over my hand was to ask for a pen. The doctor wouldn't allow it, but as time went on I was able to grab a pen and a few sheets of paper. So I began writing *Moonsongs* right from my hospital bed. But its writing didn't start when I put pen to paper. It started forming in my mind soon after I regained consciousness. I got tired of the hospital. I had to learn to walk again at age forty. And eventually when I was sent home to convalesce, I discovered that my brain had reversed the diurnal range. I was getting the little sleep I could get in the daytime and I was up at night. So most of *Moonsongs* were written at night. I believe that the drugs I was asked to take because of the severe concussion I suffered, and a loss of balance, must have affected my brain and made much of *Moonsongs* surreal.

The moon is a complex of masks. People have misunderstood this. They compare what they see in *Moonsongs* with what they discover in *Village Voices* and *Songs of the Market Place*. Now, this is answering the second part of your question. But I think a little bit of patience is what is needed. *Songs of the Market Place*, my very first collection, had a different task. Its task was to actually revolutionize the matter and manner of Nigerian poetry, to show people that it is really possible to write poetry, to read it and enjoy it and profit by it at the same time. This was closely followed by *Village Voices* and *A Nib in the Pond*, which is the collection in which I spell out what I consider to be the functions of the artist in society. And then came the *Eye of the Earth*. So when I started writing *Moonsongs*, it wasn't that it was born out of some kind of lunacy, and that it was born out of some kind of dream existence. No, I was conscious of what I was doing some of the time.

I am scared of monotony. Variety is the sauce and source of art. I have a lot to say and I believe that if I'm going to produce a dozen volumes of poetry, each must be different but related to the others. So I will agree, there is a lot in *Moonsongs* that is different from what I was saying before. I think my readers were just shocked. "Oh, is it possible for Osundare to write this kind of condensed poetry?" And I also changed style from a conscious perspective. The kind of simple poetry people had asked for was degenerating into a simplistic doggerel in the hands of many people, and it was rather embarrassing being cited as a weapon of defense by a number of people who were really not writing poetry. Well, it has been said that poetry is for the people, so "after all so and so is doing poetry for the people," so I wanted to do something a little different — if obscure, certainly not obscurantist. If condensed, certainly not alienating.

Because, for example, if we look at the moon in *Moonsongs*, in the final analysis what I am saying is related to what I was saying before, only this time I have taken a leap to the surreal realm, and the moon becomes for me an icon and a symbol. The moon is, itself, a mask and I wear that moon as a mask and dancing in that mask my audience has to see me from different angles if they want to gain a full hold of what is happening. I owe this metaphor to Chinua Achebe; one of his characters says, "The world is like a mask dancing; if you want to see it you don't stand in one place."

> *Time is the robe*
> *Time is the wardrobe*
> *Time is the needle's intricate pattern*
> *In the labyrinth of the garment*

This was a proverb song I learned in primary school. *Moonsongs* is an updated translation, a transmutation of that proverb, so it's got to be abstract. So for people who have been used to me in the marketplace singing about unemployment and so on it must be a surprise to them, but if they look at the moon really properly they will see that the moon is different things in different places. The moon you see in the slum is not the moon you see in the Government Reserved Areas. The moon you see when you are happy is not the same that you see when you are sad, although it's the same material phenomenon in the sky. But what we see is shaped and conditioned by what we are, and what we mean is a function of what we have been processed or programmed to be. A student wrote to ask if I had gone from the earth to the sky, to the heavens in *Moonsongs*. I wrote back to say what I have done is bring the moon to the marketplace, to bring the sky to the earth.

The history of the Diaspora is there, the suffering of black people, particularly in "Mooncantation," "The Slave Castles," and "Ikoyi," " Victoria Island," and the "Rags of Time," as they affect the rags of human beings. And people must also know while I was writing *Moonsongs*, I was also writing my *Songs of the Season* for the *Tribune*. These were and still are designed to be topical and to be accessible to and to touch the lives of the people. So it's actually a way of using all the hands at my disposal because I believe that the hands of the artist must of necessity be more than two.

Your defense of Moonsongs *as taking a new social direction rather than an abandonment of social direction, is convincing, but I suspect your critics are going to welcome your next two collections,* Waiting Laughters *and* Midlife, *with the same complaints as those they leveled at* Moonsongs; *that is, that you have abandoned social poetry for personal poetry. Can you remember some passages which refute this?*

The guys who attacked me in 1987 didn't take social responsibility out of my brain with the axe. My way of perceiving life has matured. It is less complacent, but the compassion I have for the suffering and the underprivileged and the anger with which I view the rulers is still there. What I am trying to do in *Waiting Laughters* is to say that although the situation in Africa is grim today, although despair seems to have descended upon the continent—and I am saying particularly what I see in new writing in Nigeria shows such a stifling cloud of despair; people are literally saying "the sun will not rise tomorrow, the sea has eaten up the land and we shall die of hunger." My vision is different. There is a certain ebullient, optimistic side to my vision because I believe in the rational side of humanity, without forgetting the irrational side. For every bad human being you have 1000 good ones. When I was attacked, it was the good ones who helped my recovery. So there is no way I will ever succumb to despair. What I am saying in *Waiting Laughters* is that our laughters are actually waiting.

The two important phenomena in that collection are waiting and laughters. I think what is emerging from my writing more and more is a certain kind of mature complexity. In the past, especially in my early collections, I was rather too enthusiastic about life and I tended to stress the positive sides too often and too much. The positive sides are still very much theirs now, but the monster to be demolished is there; but it is not all of us who are actually working to demolish the monster. Some among us are bad. I have pointed them out while at the same time putting into the picture the good ones and the good visions that they represent brings in a certain level of paradox, contradiction, and therefore a certain level of complexity. My vision has become more complex. Every fiction has its fact and every fact has its fiction, and night is not the exact opposite of day; between black and white there is the gray zone and there are times when the gray zone is more luminous than either of the colors that actually make it up. So it is this kind of complexity that has come with middle age and that has informed *Waiting Laughters* and *Midlife*.

The introductory poem of *Waiting Laughters* is a kind of prologue that the problems of our world are so complex and so diverse. Who can presume to capture them in one idiom—who dare?! So I think that instead of seeing the world as a phenomenon that is monolithic, I am seeing it as essentially pluralistic. It's a world that disperses in our consciousness, and for us to catch up with what is happening, we have to devise a non-monolithic, rather flexible and dynamic, but not opportunistic and *a priori and ad hoc* way of apprehending the world of the last 10 years of the twentieth century.

In *Waiting Laughters*, of course, I talk about waiting in different situations. I owe a lot here to Shakespeare. *As You Like It* was one of my childhood romances: "Time ambles in diverse places with diverse persons"—I actually mention these lines in *Waiting Laughters*. The question I am asking is what is waiting and what is time—to a well fed man and to a starving man, to the judge who pronounces the sentence "I now declare that you be hanged until you be dead" and to the felon on death row expecting the news at any time. Is time really the same with this man as it is with the judge? Then a man walking up and down the platform of a railroad station, a home bound person who hasn't been home for a long time, a person for whom home is nostalgia, a nostalgia that is just about to be confronted, and what is going to lead to this confrontation and to this eventual realization is something to take him across the bridge. What is time to a husband who is pacing up and down the corridors of a labor ward? What is time to a groom who is waiting for a bride on the first bridal night? What is time to the moon? What is time to the sun? What is time to the seed which germinates in the earth? What is time to the green blade of grass in the rainy season? What is time to the brown sponge that is left in the dry season?

The idea of color is also very important in this collection. The most important colors are green, brown and yellow; and, oh yes, crimson! In fact, the long poem "Crimson Twilight" in *Moonsongs* I was writing while in the hospital bed. The poem actually captures the night I was attacked, because when my wife showed me the shirt I wore that night, I wasn't able to recognize it. It was a white shirt, soaked crimson red. So crimson represents the kind of violence I experienced. But it also goes back to the color of birth when the placenta breaks. So life and death are united in the color crimson.

So *Waiting Laughters* is there, showing waiting in different circumstances, then, the laughter. In the past, I would have represented that laughter as a unidimensional phenomenon. Now, I'm interrogating that laughter. What happens to a song that waits too long in the labyrinth of the throat? What happens to laughter which waits too long on the lips? Does it dry up? And of course I owe the whole interrogative tenor to Langston Hughes: what happens to hope deferred? But at the same time I am saying, "Grant us the patience of the lamb which slays the lion, but without inheriting its claws." This is very important. So I think that in the last few years my poetry has become more philosophical. More existentialist in tenor? I agree. But more personal? I don't think I'm more personal than I used to be. The "I-factor" has always been in my poetry, and this is something that I owe inevitably to the oral poet.

In *Waiting Laughters*, waiting is the key because now we are a queue country. The cornucopia of Nigeria has dried up so that people queue up for virtually everything. When I asked the artists of the publisher for a concept for *Waiting Laughters*, the first drawing they gave me was a long, interminable queue. But I quarreled with it because waiting as I see it is not eternal; there is some ray of light at the end of our tunnel. So it's not waiting that bottoms out into pessimism. No. But what I'm trying to grapple with in *Waiting Laughters* and also in *Midlife* is a certain kind of rationalized, problematic optimism.

Now, with *Midlife* the "I" has to be there, because *Midlife* is autobiographical. I turned forty, and it occurred to me that it should be marked. I actually did a poem for my Sunday Tribune "Songs of the Season" column called "Forty Hearty Cheers," but it wasn't just for me; it was also for all of my colleagues and friends who turned forty at about the same time I did—my generation.

When I got to Iowa in 1988, it occurred to me that this was an idea really to be developed. I must say that I owe a lot to Walt Whitman. I picked up a copy of *A Song of Myself* and re-read it. What I wanted to do was to put finishing touches to "Drum Talk." But I discovered that that had to wait because there was a more urgent idea on my mind. I wrote the first poem and the second and the third, and before I knew it, the idea of a collection was already gathering in my mind, and it possessed me. I used to get up at 4 a.m., and I wrote from 4.30 a.m. to 2 p.m., with a thirty minute break from 7:30–8:00. So the "I" in *Midlife* is Niyi Osundare. But it is also more than that. I see myself as a citizen of the world and a being in our universe. But, talking about political commitment, oh yes, both *Waiting Laughters* and *Midlife* are politically committed. In fact, the question I am asking in *Midlife* is, "Now I am forty, but how old is my continent Africa?" I am forty, but my continent is still a baby! I am at noon. The image, the metaphor of the sun dominates the poem. But it appears that with Africa it is still dawn, it is still darkness. So I am interrogating Africa and the world.

So many of the poems are remembering things my father and mother said to me when I was young. My mother used to say, "It is only a fool that has two eyes. For a real human being the whole body is his eyes, so see with your whole body." That idea came to me. And another very crucial idea: "Humanity is a river; when it flows back it also flows forth." So don't pollute this river at any point in its course. So certainly in *Midlife* and *Waiting Laughters*, I am not talking directly about unemployment, about oppression and so on, but I think I am making a very useful comment by engaging other icons and other symbols in turning the side of these problems and showing the world another dimension of them and moving on the other things.

The metaphors of the sun, of the rock, of the river—these are the three metaphors in *Midlife*. I come from Ikere Ekiti, a town that is very rocky. I celebrate it in *Midlife* and also in *Eye of the Earth*. In more than any other collection I have done, the river in *Midlife* takes an important place. My name is Osundare. The first morpheme of the name of the river that flows through our back yard is Osun. It also crosses our path to the farm, so we are surrounded by the river. So my father's name was Osundare, which means, "The Spirit of the River has vindicated my innocence." I grew up seeing people singing and dancing in praise of Osun. But it's not just a river. It is also water. Because it is water it has its own dialectics. Green is a very important color in *Midlife* because if we talk of the water and the river we also talk about the rain. The rain is also an icon I use frequently. Because for me the moon unites the earth and the sky—in a way, when the rain is falling, it is as if the sky was making love to the earth. This again I owe to Yoruba cosmology because the sky is the husband of the earth. So when you have a quarrel between the two, you have drought. At times when you have excessive love you have the flood; the river overflows its banks. So the river is life, but at the same time it is death—what I call the red rage of the flood. When I was growing up, I saw people carried off by the flood. But I also saw the entire community go to offer sacrifice to the rock, Olosunta, and they had to climb seven hills to make the sacrifice. Before they got back to the town, the whole town was dissolved in a flood because it rained heavily. And, of course, so many songs were composed. It may have been some kind of coincidence. It happened that they offered sacrifice and the rain fell. After some time, another sacrifice had to be offered because it rained too heavily and the crops were being ruined and many people had disappeared into the flood. So I have seen both sides of the river; it is life, but it is also death. The same water that replenishes our system can also choke us.

In a way *Midlife* ends the way my first collection *Songs of the Marketplace* ended, as in the last poem, "I sing of change," where I'm projecting my vision of a world that is reshaped. In *Midlife*, I had finished writing the collection before I discovered that the tone is very reminiscent of the Book of Revelation, but a revelation without an Apocalypse. I behold a world that is different but where people have to work toward this difference. So, my style has changed because I believe variety is very important, and I have a fairly restless artistic impulse. I am always experimenting. There are times when I pick up one theme and I write about four poems around that theme. And I also write prose on that same theme, just to test myself—mainly for my column in *Newswatch*. You have one theme; it appears somewhere else; it's possible to ask, "Is that mask dancing again?" and to look at that mask from different angles. But the philosophical question I ask myself is, "When I see a mask at point a, point b, and point c, am I sure that it is the same mask that I am seeing?" Our world is changing; it is so kaleidoscopic.

I believe that different things have to be said, and even the same thing has to be said in different ways. One other factor that has helped me is my training as a linguist. I like playing with words, breaking them up like scientists do atoms, fusioning them, reuniting them, making them explode, dispersing them. But one abiding feature with me, it's more than a habit, it's a passion, is Hope with a capital H. We need it in the world today. It is organic to me. I have studied history and discovered that every human collectively has gone through one kind of trauma or another. We black people are going through it, but it is not going to be forever. As a Chinese poet, whose name I have forgotten, says, "Who says every night must end in day?" I do.

Your surname is iconic too. What does your first name, Oluwaniyi, mean to you and to your community? Is it expressive in any way of your socialist beliefs?

Oluwaniyi means "God has honor." "Oluwa" means God, "Niyi" means "has honor." Something I haven't revealed to anyone before is in my name: My first name was "Oluomi," and it means the "owner of water," or of the "water spirit," or "friend of water," or "one for whom water is the essence of life," and this is crucial, especially for understanding the second movement of *Midlife*, "What the River Said." I asked my parents why my name was Oluomi. I was told I was a fairly cooperative baby. I rarely fell ill. I remember—at the time I was born there wasn't any hospital, there wasn't even a court of law in Ikere. My father was an herbalist, a drummer, a farmer, and a singer—so many things in one. So Osun, the water goddess that is worshipped in my area, is my father's and my family's god, or goddess, depending on what kind of emanation you see. Before people discovered my connection with this goddess, my mother said whenever I was ill, usually with a high fever—there was a time I was ill and nearly died—they went to all kinds of herbalists. Nothing worked. Even herbs produced by my father didn't take. Then they just tried water, ordinary water, cold water. They gave me some to drink, used some to bathe me, and poured the rest on what is called *awoje*, the very centre of the head, which is usually very soft when one is young, and within hours I was laughing, smiling, and playing. So that was the last time I ever went to the herbalist. After, whenever I was ill, the medicine was water. I think the modernists call this hydropathy. Because of this, my mother became a strong devotee of the river spirit. Before me, there had been three babies, all of whom died in infanthood. So my parents were so surprised that I lived. So, of course, naturally, they named me Oluomi, "the one for whom water is the essence."

Now, father and I were working on the farm one day and my father said, "You may be going to school soon. The white man may not like the name Oluomi, because they may call it pagan, so I am thinking about another name for you." I started asking about what name they were going to give me. One day we were working on the farm again and he said, "It's going to be 'Oluwaniyi.'" Oluwaniyi is not a very common name. There was only one person bearing that name in the area. He was a very responsible, successful farmer who had many wives and many children—the traditional values. I hope I am not going to disappoint that man. My first name stuck to me as a result of the way I was healed. The two names were still used, but as time went by, Oluomi dropped. Christian education—or mis-education—saw to that. The Christian teacher just struck Oluomi out of the school register before I knew how to read and write. I've shortened Oluwaniyi to Niyi because having grown up, as I mentioned in *Eye of the Earth*, I now see the gods: I think the infant dew has been licked clean by the sun of maturity. I grew up and became rational. I'm not a church person. I'm not a shrine person. Of course I believe in the essence of all these gods and in the freedom of people to worship. It's just that you won't find Niyi in church.

How is your rejected, so-called pagan, name still with you?

It's my essence. "Oluwa," meaning "the Christian god has honor," was shortened by my pre-university friends to "Olu"—God. I shortened it to the humble Niyi—"has honor."

When and how did you become a socialist?

I think I have always had the tendency. This is the first time I have been asked this question. But this is not the first time I have thought about it. I think I had practiced the socialism that I grew up to read about, even before I was literate at all. I grew up in a communal situation. I never saw anybody starve. I never saw anybody have too much while the other person had nothing. And besides that, in Ikere-Ekiti community lived a very vibrant, hardworking, no-nonsense

445

people. There is a poem in *Waiting Laughters*. This is another reason that people should know that my recent social message is equally strong as in the early poetry.

Waiting Laughters has a social message. There is a poem there, "The Storming of the Bastille," which I did in honor of the bicentennial of the French Revolution. The supreme metaphor of that poem comes from an experience I had at five or six years old. When I was still at her breast I used to surprise my mother with tales. I remember things that happened when I was very, very young. For example, in our area there was once a king who was very tyrannical. People didn't want to visit violence on him because they had built the palace he lived in, and they wouldn't set it on fire. Political action took an artistic form. A song was composed; I still remember my father singing it. It was sung around the palace of the king just for him to hear. It was a parable of course. He heard it and still refused to leave. People started singing it every day. Somehow the District Officer heard about it, and he knew there was going to be some kind of revolution. So the District Officer stepped in and the tyrannical Oba was banished. He was taken to Orodogo—a mythical place of dishonor. "A king doesn't dance with a dizzy spell." That was the first time in my life I saw a motorcar, when the Oba was taken away. "The king who doesn't behave with dignity deserves to go to Orodogo for life." Another Oba was put in his place.

When I grew up and read about the French Revolution, I noticed a lot of similarities between what happened at home and the French Revolution. The only difference was, the height of our king was not reduced by his head. There was no guillotine. The song was a metaphorical guillotine. So I grew up in that kind of climate—people questioning, challenging communal life, the life of the individual flowing into the community, and vice versa. Nobody starved. If anybody committed an infringement against the social ideal, the judgment was immediate. It wasn't violent, but it had its own violence. Satire was very potent.

My father was a composer, and I accompanied him to many meetings where songs were composed, where people were supplying the ideas and my father supplied ideas and a tune and the drum to go with it. As I grew up, the country grew with us. Colonialism introduced capitalism into Africa. I am not saying that the African society I grew up in was perfect—no. It had its superstitions, its wars, its slavery, insecurities, its ignorance, too. So many people died from sheer ignorance, from preventable diseases, from trial by ordeal, asked to drink poisons when they were called witches and so many died. And it had its kings, some of whom could be tyrannical, terrible, some insisting on human sacrifice; it wasn't a perfect society at all. But as far as the economic arrangement of the society was concerned, it was a far cry from what I grew up seeing.

After primary school and secondary school I discovered that sixty-five of us had finished primary school, but only three entered secondary school. It is true I was about the best in the class, but there were so many others who were so good. What made the difference was that my father grew cocoa in addition to yams. The ones who merely grew yams didn't have anything to sell. My father was able to sell cocoa and make some money, and that was what made the whole difference in my life. He was able to send me to secondary school. The others just disappeared, into nothingness as it were. This is actually the kind of situation I lamented in "A Reunion" in *Village Voices*.

I ran into a friend who was my classmate who couldn't get into secondary school and had disappeared for a long time and we didn't see him. The next time I saw him was when I was at the University of Ibadan as a teacher after I came back from Leeds in 1974. A friend came to see me, and he wanted a beer. When we sat down to order the beer someone came in who looked like somebody I knew. He bowed for me and took my order and "Sir-ed" me, saying "Yes, Sir." He went away. When he came back I looked at him again. He used to have a scar on his cheek and that is what I saw. And I went to him and I said, "Are you so and so?" And he said, "Yes." "Do you know me?" I asked. And he said, "Yes, you are my Oga now." It was a very, very emotional moment. We used to wear the same clothes. At times when I wore my own clothes into rags, we took turns and wore the same trousers. And look at what had happened. He wasn't the dullest in our class. So this is why I made this unbreakable pledge to myself, that I would never forget such people. It is not play-acting; it is something that is organic to me, that what I am today is an accident. I am one of Africa's accidents. There are so many mute, inglorious people wasting away in the wilderness of our beleaguered continent.

So I don't think I became a socialist by reading socialist books. It has always been in me, and I believe that this is what you apply to everybody. You have to have a socialist tendency. Compassion is important. You must have fellow feeling before you can become a genuine socialist. Unfortunately, in our world today, there are many textbook socialists.

I then discovered that whoever had the white man's power became the chief; he could send his kids to school. The other ones became irrelevant. Our values changed over night. The chiefs have no power now. Another set of chiefs took over, the ones who sold crops to the white man and took money also derived power from the white man because of their connections, and I started observing that the same Christians who brought us the love of god, humility, were the same people who brought us this terrible economic system. I have never felt comfortable where other people are hungry, and this is something I have inherited from my parents and from the community from which I have grown.

Everybody was everybody else's concern in that community. There was a time when you would leave your yams by the roadside, and whatever coins you wanted for one was represented by the numbers of pebbles you put by them. So whoever took the yams would leave the coins, and at the end of the day you would count the remaining yams and the number of coins would correspond to the number of yams taken away. Now, the white man came and introduced "everybody for himself and the devil take the hindmost," and it is this hindmost that is primary in my ideology and my concern. So, I didn't become a socialist all of a sudden. But reading socialist books has enriched my theoretical grounding and expanded my horizons to let me know what is happening in the rest of the world.

As a socially committed poet who calls himself a socialist humanist and occasionally a Marxist, you must have been affected by events since 1989 in the so-called socialist world. What has been the impact of these events on you and your poetry, and what are the implications of these events for Africa?

The events in Eastern Europe did not come to me as a surprise. Every ideology is a confederation of spectral entities, from the mildest to the most dogmatic tendencies. I believe that the more dogmatic an ideology becomes, the drier it becomes. Like the branch of a tree it is extremely brittle, and it breaks very easily. The milder it is, the more malleable and flexible, and therefore the more amenable and responsive it is to changes to the lives of people. The USSR had moved to bureaucratization of life. Stalin died, and Stalin remained. I didn't know Ceaucescu was so repressive until recently. But each time I meet writer colleagues from Eastern Europe, they are so skeptical about socialism. So, in that sense I think socialism had problems of dogmatism and a certain kind of reification. And the irony is that alienation, which is a very powerful concept of socialism itself, became a descriptive metaphor for the kind of socialism which has emerged over the past forty or fifty years, because the system alienated the people, and at the time George Orwell's rather sardonic vision in *Animal Farm* began to acquire more and more authenticity. This is why I say that what was happening was not a surprise, and I want to enter a very important *caveat* here because I wouldn't want us to throw out the baby with the bath water. I don't think I want to join the halleluiah chorus who are singing all over the world today "Down with communism, out with socialism, oh welcome good day, the new dawn of capitalism!" I believe that a lot of what is being said is simplistic and reductionist.

The people in Eastern Europe may be tired of communism, but from what I have seen, they are not clamoring for the extreme other side, which is a kind of cannibalistic capitalism. Shortly after the fall of the Berlin Wall, I remember reading that some of the people who, out of sheer euphoria, fled East Germany to West Germany started trooping back a week or two later and they said: "We discovered all of a sudden we had to look for jobs, a place to live." One of them said he wasn't prepared to exchange socialist barbarism for capitalist cannibalism." This is a very important point. It was Said who said "Every grammar leaks." Likewise, every ideology leaks. The leaks in communism are being seen everywhere today. But this doesn't mean that capitalism is *the* system.

There is something inhuman about capitalism. The profit motive, the fact that you enslave other people to increase your profit, or that you put out a book not for cultural and spiritual enrichment but to add to your bank account, and as Ngugi says, "it is a society where you are either eating other people or being eaten."[11] This is not how human beings should live. We are more or less living like those beasts that Shakespeare portrays in *King Lear*—that humanity must live like monsters of the deep who perforce must prey on one another. I don't believe in a system that encourages people to prey upon one another that way. This is not saying that capitalism does not have its own advantages. The encouragement of initiative without allowing it to degenerate into extreme and rapacious individualism is important. We must care for the individualism. Even in communal African society, every individual had his own trademark as it were. So what I see is a blend of the best of capitalism and the best of socialism. It is not a matter of either/or; we have played the either/or-game for a long time, and this is why we have ideological anarchy today; the world is in a disturbing flux because the left is falling apart and the right does not have enough moral strength and ethical energy to seize the initiative. I believe that we will reach some kind of golden mean. It is not that socialism has failed completely, no! In 1981, when I was putting *Songs of the Market Place* together, the last poem in that collection was titled "I sing of change," where I use certain lines from Yeats: "Sing on/ Somewhere at some new moon we'll learn that sleeping is not death/ Hearing the whole earth change its tune." The third stanza in my own poem goes: "I sing/ Of Earth/ with no/ sharp north/ or deep south/ without blind curtains/ or iron walls."

I still remember some friends accusing me of utopianism; that "East will always be the East and the West will always be the West." This was in 1981. In 1988, when I was doing *Midlife*, one of the movements was called "Breaking Walls." I had the Berlin Wall physically in mind, although I had to develop all kinds of ancillary metaphors because that wall is also metaphorical, even today. Reading history told me that the world will have to do something about one city divided into two—one people into two. So the fact that the wall has fallen today does not mean so much that capitalism has succeeded as that the world has reached a certain stage of rationality that such walls will have to fall. I believe that other walls will replace them, and they will also fall because what Lenin calls the state of permanent revolution is also crucial. What we are seeing is not the demise of socialism.

How does all this affect Africa? As I put it in my essay on the release of Mandela, a powerful wind of change is blowing across the world. All orthodoxies are falling over each other like ninepins. Indeed, 20th century humanity is showing an unmistakable abhorrence for dictators and their murderous antics. Africa has some of the cruelest dictatorships in the world today, from south to north, from east to west. The wind of change that is sweeping South Africa today is traceable not solely but to a large extent to what is happening in Eastern Europe. And now in West Africa: Gabon, Ivory Coast, Benin, Liberia. But we have to be visionaries about this. I think a world where two powers are balanced against each other is better for Africa. It will be a sad day indeed if we wake up one day to discover that the whole world has one ideology. I prefer a dialectical development of the world, for socialism to renew itself and get stronger and for it to be able to counter capitalism.

Do you think that Mandela's release from prison holds more significance for Africa than the dissolution of the Soviet bloc?

I would say that the two are related. The racists in South Africa must have been learning a lot from what has happened to the Ceaucescus. It must bring chilling echoes of the French Revolution to them. And the dictators know that they are sitting on a keg of gunpowder. The two events—one leads to the other. I wouldn't say that the sole reason leading to Mandela's release is events in Eastern Europe, but those events play a contributing role.

Let's return directly to literature. You often seem willing to supply interviewers with names of poets whose work you admire. I recall Neruda, Whitman, Brathwaite, Wordsworth, Soyinka, Vallejo, Anyidoho, Walcott, Baraka, and many others. But you've also said you don't like the words "influence" and" borrowing." Why not?

The reason I am scared of these two words is due to the abuse they have sustained when used by critics, biographers, and gossip hunters. Every writer is influenced by other writers, and every artist borrows. But I want to separate the two terms. Now, when we talk about influence, it may be conscious or unconscious, or perhaps even subconscious. Reading and writing are complementary correlatives. The more a writer reads, the more he writes. And the more he writes, the more he wants to read. Given the nature of the human mind, there is no way a writer can write without being influenced by what he has read. What the writer has read has a way of settling at the subconscious level of the writer's mind. So, influence may reside at this level of consciousness. At this level, it is possible for the writer to make use of the tone, the tenor, the material, the manner, a substantial stylistic property of the other writer without knowing it. I have witnessed cases of borrowing, which were pointed out and the affected writers said they never did it, even when these cases were clear.

Borrowing is more deliberate than influence, though it has its own subterranean import. You borrow an idea when you feel that there is something you are doing that can be helped by something that has come before. Borrowing is very common in this part of the world. For example, Fela Anikulapo-Kuti, the Afro-music king is one of the victims of what has been borrowed. I can count at least three of the Nigerian musicians of the juju brand who have borrowed this from Fela. But they didn't just borrow it. They borrowed it and infused it with words, so that the tone is still Fela's, but the words are not his. And I think the communal ownership of artistic property in traditional Africa is responsible for the excessive, obvious borrowing that we have in Nigeria today. Who can tell me the owner of a proverb or the author of an idiom or a folktale? These are communally owned cultural archetypes.

A culture moving from oracy to literacy confronts the problem of ownership. So latent things are patented and copyrighted. But there are still many people who want to treat them like artifacts of oral culture whose ownership is flexible and anonymous. So—every writer borrows. Whichever artist says he doesn't borrow must either be a liar or an impostor. Originality is good, but none is absolute. Every giant stands on the shoulders of other giants and is therefore able to see more of the horizon. But I am not using borrowing and influence here in the Renaissance sense of the words. No, originality is still possible, though human effort is cumulative. Space science would not be possible if somebody had not split the atom.

So, when we discuss literary originality today, how far down the stream must we go before we discover the source? So originality as far as I am concerned is a relative term. I borrow expressions from other people and borrow heavily from oral literature. In fact it's my inexhaustible source of inspiration. There is what I call primary order of originality, and there is secondary order of originality. I am not defending my own originality because I also have problems with pastiche, with montage art and art that is mere collage. In fact, this is one of the problems with post-modernist writing, where you bring things from all kinds of sources without any attempt to make them cohere, without any attempt to make them into an organic whole. So, I am certainly indebted to many writers, from many continents and countries.

But coincidences do happen. I still remember very well in 1985, I did a poem to mark 25 years of Nigerian independence, which was published in two installments in my column "Songs of the Season." I titled it "A Song for my Land." The first two issues were already published when I sauntered into the University Bookshop at Ibadan, and what did I see but a book of poems by the most prominent Chinese poet in modern times. The first poem I read in his collection reminded me so much of the poem I did earlier on. Anybody who has read his poem and mine would probably say, "Oh, yes, Osundare was influenced." And "Of course there are a panoply of historical reasons which Osundare could use to justify himself." He is older than I am. He lived and wrote before I was born. And, most important, he wrote his poem before I wrote my own. But, how many people would know that I never read him before I wrote my own poem? So I am very very skeptical about influence criticism. It becomes tiresomely speculative.

I owe a lot to oral literature and to musicians. Sunny Ade. I also acknowledge my debt to plastic artists. Each time I see sculptors working, I am inspired. In fact one of the poems in *Waiting Laughters* is on sculpting. Another one is on painting. And another on molding, particularly the type of molding you do with clay. I am fascinated by the clay—its suppleness when it is wet and the dry, rigid finality it obtains when it passes through the kiln. This, for me, is a parable for the creative work itself. So, the influence on the writer is inexhaustible. I owe a lot to so many of the people who have come before me, and I am not afraid to acknowledge it.

In conversations and in your drama criticism you frequently mention Bertolt Brecht. When did you first start reading Brecht, and hasn't he been an influence on your writing?

Brecht has been a very powerful figure in contemporary Nigerian writing. I first came across him when I was an undergraduate, majoring in English and minoring in Theatre Arts. But I was much more into theatre arts. I was frequently on the stage, acting, dancing, singing. This is where I came across Brecht in so many respects—in dramatic literature, in dramatic theory and criticism, in improvisation, even in technical theatre. I discovered that Brecht was a great artist, very versatile, and that there was a lot that we could gain from him. Now the first feature which captured our minds—my and my classmates'—was Brecht's theatre, his dramaturgy. We were particularly fascinated by his use of the alienation effect. Here was a man who revolutionized theatre practice. He is the greatest dramatist since Shakespeare. He introduced so many innovations into the theatre. He was irreverent with old traditions. He either jettisoned them completely, or he altered them in such a way that you still had glimpse of their old self. He has given you something that is essentially fresh and essentially different. His idea of the epic theatre approximates very significantly to our idea of the African total theatre.

One of the problems with the theatre in Africa is the proscenium stage. But African theatre is different. The African audience doesn't just want to see your face. The African audience wants to see the totality of you, not just your profile, but all your profiles. Therefore, the theatre in the round is more popular in Africa. It is the theatre of the market-city-village square, of the palace, of the moonlight entertainment. So epic theatre afforded us the opportunity of bringing the totality of African theatre on stage, complete with mime, dance, drumming, singing, and of course dialogue and verbal repartee. Brechtian theatre is rich in all of this. And in his theatre there is proverbial lore. Brecht touched me in many ways in which other Europeans didn't touch me. There was something essentially African about his theatre: his use of proverbs, of epigrams, of epithems; these were very useful to us in the move from oral lore to written lore. There was also something about his politics which fascinated us. He was irreverent and revolutionary in many ways. He was on the side of the poor. He didn't offer simple solutions. He problematized issues. With the alienation effect he is telling us that theatre is not magic, that the actor is a human being before he becomes an actor at all, and he will become a human being again after he puts down his mask. His use of masks was also very important at the time we were undergraduates. So I saw the theatre of Brecht as an essentially revolutionary theatre. He broke loose from the unities and created some kind of epic. He deconstructed theatre practice and theatre theory as he met them and introduced his own. We were fascinated by this as we were growing up in a colonial and neo-colonial era, where freedom was not there and where people lived in poverty while a few lived in affluence. We saw a lot in Brecht's theatre that was parable. The drama of my friend, Femi Osofisan, is heavily influenced by Brecht. I still remember the first essay I did on Osofisan's theatre. I commented on his use of Brecht and predicted that he was becoming the Brecht of Africa. Many have worked on the topic of convergences between Soyinka and Brecht. There is also a similar study on the work of the Tanzanian writer Ebrahim Hussein (see *Kinjeketile*) and Brecht. So Brecht has given African theatre aesthetics a lot.

What I like about Brecht's poetry is his simplicity. His simplicity is so forceful, effective, and unignorable in its thrust. What Brecht writes is what I call the statemental type of poetry—essentially declarative. This is what is happening and what will happen. There is a lot of sarcasm and irony. In the end, the oppressor will feel like committing suicide. His poetry is essentially satirical, and satirical poetry is very common in Africa, especially in our literature of the oral mode. And I like the way Brecht takes up old ideas, refurbishes them and makes them shine even brighter than in their original form. Not just me—many of us owe a lot to Brecht, and among us his art lives.

You read Brecht in English translation, so you miss one of his most important techniques, which is to take proverbial language, which supports the status quo, and to turn it inside out, rendering it subversive. I suspect that you may do the same thing with Yoruba expressions that you translate into English. Do you do this?

Yes, I do it a lot. As I said earlier on, African culture is very rich in proverbial lore. But proverbs come in different shapes and forms. Many of them are very oppressive, reactionary, retrogressive. One of them is the proverb, "The fingers are not equal." I still remember that each time the oppressors who have stolen our money and have mortgaged our national patrimony, each time they are asked, "How come you are so rich and others are so poor?" The ready answer is always, "The fingers are not equal." I have therefore devised a means of capturing this kind of very dangerous norm. My way of doing this is to ask questions which interrogate the proverb itself. So while we say, "Fingers are not equal," we have to look at the fingers again and see what is happening to the individual fingers. If the smallest finger is so small because of the position it occupies, and if the thumb is the largest because of the position it occupies, we can then say, just as it is impossible for the little finger to pick up for example a needle all by itself, so is it impossible for the thumb to pick up anything all by itself. What this means is that the fingers must all work together to get anything done, and in working together they must work in equanimity and in equality. So, in one of my poems one of the villagers says: "They stole all our money and when we asked them and they told us 'the fingers are not equal'. Then we asked if the fingers are not equal, why have some decided to be the smallest finger while the others are the biggest finger which really monopolizes the honor of the hand?" I have also developed this into a poem, "The parable of the fingers" in which each of the fingers is trying to succeed, to reach the top all by itself, but it discovers that it couldn't do anything, so in the end all of the fingers come together in order to defeat their enemy.

Now, the animal kingdom is also very useful here. Most of our legends and idioms of proverbs are built around animals. I categorize animals into three: the aggressive, cannibalistic type, which live by eating other animals—the lion, the hyena, the cheetah (for me a pun, the cheetah and the cheater), and the wolf. The second category comprises animals which are big and strong, but they are not as powerful as the first category—the elephant, the buffalo, the bison, and many others that live in the forest. The third category is animals which are small and relatively powerless. I usually talk about the hare and the hyena as the opposite extremes. And I often say that if lambs unite, they will lead the lion. What I am trying to do is to reverse the order. Usually people concede the supremacy of the jungles straight away to the lion. But I say the lion can be defeated if the smaller animals come together. So I arrogate power to those that have no power at all.

Another way that I carry out this subversion is in the tree kingdom. The iroko is the highest and sturdiest tree in the forest. Many proverbs are built around it. Many praise names have the iroko as their corner stones. But I am rather ambivalent towards the iroko. I see it as a symbol of imperialism, of dictatorship, of autocracy, and of a rather unctuous misuse of power. It monopolizes the sun and the sky, so the shrubs under it are pale. In fact, this was in the back of my mind when I wrote "A grass in the meadow" in *Village Voices*: "I do not want to be an iroko ... Let me be a grass in the meadow ... Let me be an active grip in a hand of equal fingers ..."

I believe that many of the proverbs we have today can be reshaped to create a new awareness. After all these proverbs were created when the consciousness of our society was different. Our society has developed since then. And our proverbs must develop with us. This is why I disagree with many of the proverbs in Achebe. There is one in *Arrow of God* where a character says, "You stand in the compound of a coward to point fingers at the ruins of the house of the brave."[iii]

To another interviewer you recently said that the substructure of your poetry is Yoruba, and its superstructure is English. I find it frequently frustrating to come upon patches of Yoruba in your poems for which no translation is provided. Why don't you write in Yoruba and translate into English? And do you sometimes write in English and then translate back into Yoruba?

I'll begin answering from the last part of the question. I haven't tried to translate my poems back into Yoruba. But I write in both Yoruba and English. I write more in English. When we were growing up it was a sin to speak Yoruba on the school campus—in fact, [it was] one of the most serious crimes one could commit. At the end of each week, the prefect read out the names of the Yoruba speakers. They were thrashed and given grass to cut. Perpetual offenders—that was the phrase—were sent home for two weeks. And if they still persisted, their records were endorsed. Many of us grew up disparaging our own language. The only language that mattered—and I must say alas that still matters—was the English language. So this is how many people lost literature in their mother tongue. As if I knew what I was going to do later in life, I insisted upon learning Yoruba, on studying and taking exams in it. My best subjects were English, Latin, and Yoruba, where I topped the list.

So this contradiction was always there. I would like to write in Yoruba. But problems arise. Because if I write in Yoruba, I am freer in my expression, and I am culturally freer too because English, whatever else one may say about it, was the language of colonial imposition. It was the language in which the first decree was drafted for Nigerians. But writing in Yoruba would definitely limit my audience. Call it the Achebe syndrome if you like, to moderate the Yoruba as much as possible, to mediate it into English. This is why there are so many expressions and phrases in my poetry that you say you find it difficult to understand.

I must say that I don't just put any expression into my poetry without explaining it in a glossary or footnote. As a stylistician who has studied to a great extent the strategies of expressing an indigenous experience in a foreign language, I know that there is something happening called "cushioning." Cushioning is a stylistic, creative effort at easing the difficulty of indigenous expression in a target language. In other words, if an expression is difficult in English, I must have a way of making it intelligible to an English audience. Soyinka does this a lot. For example, in *Kongi's Harvest* we find, "He commenced a rapid dialogue with his legs."[iv]

You are known for socialist poetry, but in my opinion, you are at your artistic best as a love poet. I am curious about why your 1986 collection Daughter of the Rain *has not come out?*

Well, I actually have been told this several times. At times, when people discover a love poem by me they are surprised because they have almost stereotyped me into a political poet, and they have forgotten that every public person has a private side to him. And not only that, that love in its most universal, holistic sense, also involves the other kinds of love—erotic love, emotional love, and so on. I write love poetry quite frequently. I am particularly helped by this in my love of nature. Nature expresses a lot of love for me. A lot of crisis is created each time I hold a reading and read love poems. Before you know it, people come asking me, "Who was that poem for?" Many people even read love notes into my political poetry. I think I am a little shy about that private side. I must also tell you there are ones I love whom I don't want to hurt. I don't want suspicions here or there and don't want people asking questions. But this is not to say this collection is not going to be published. Actually, it is not solely because of the embarrassment. I think one of the prices one pays as an artist is this kind of exposure, and one should be able to take it.

It's not that I'm not bold enough to take it. I was thinking that I was too young to really do a categorical collection of my love poems. It is true there are people who actually started with love poems. Pablo Neruda, for example, with *Twenty Love Poems and A Song of Despair*, which shot him into fame. But he grew up with a different tradition, the Spanish *amour courtois*, courtly love tradition is still very much there. I think I want to know more about the world, savor more of the richness and complexity of human relationships, see more types before I settle down to make a collection of my love poetry. When I look at some of the things I would have published in the past, most of them look to me to be very melodramatic, slush; they cry all over the page and tears drip from every edge. I want to be in a position to discipline my feelings into respectable verse. I believe that now after *Midlife*, on the other side of forty, one begins to think about this. As a matter of fact, I write love poems all the time. They afford me the opportunity of expressing a type of feeling that I wouldn't consider private. Love is not an absolutely private affair. It involves more than one person and it is something in the air. What each of us does is to grab his own share of it. Certainly, the collection will be published, soon.

Another major reason it hasn't been published is the supremacy of the political imperatives here. We live in Africa, in a world that is in a constant state of turmoil, where at times you really have to struggle to be able to love. When you live in a continent where you are struggling every day and you don't know where the next piece of bread, the next piece of yam, the next drop of water is going to come from, you really have to struggle to be able to love. So these are the urgent realities of our existence which are taking priority over these private matters. With Nelson Mandela in jail—thank goodness he's released now—I am more inclined to write a poem about appetite and picking their conscience than hiding away in some closet writing about the size of my mistress's bosom.

What effect did the award of the Commonwealth Prize for Poetry have on your work?

A lot. Most of it is positive. A little bit is negative. Remember the axe man came and shattered my skull ten days after I came back from receiving the prize. The Prize gave me a lot of exposure. It was ironic; I was in Canada, working on a new project when the prize was announced, and I never heard about it until I came back to Nigeria. But so much had happened. Maybe had I been around for the announcement, I would have moderated the kind of publicity that went with it. My publishers were very happy, and understandably they went to town. Virtually every television house in Nigeria carried the news. So, by the time I had returned from Canada, everybody was rushing to interview me. I don't think it was just because of this prize. Before the prize, I had been some kind of public person, writing for newspapers and magazines and so on. And many people saw it as the culmination of my effort at popularizing poetry in the newspapers in Nigeria. So it brought a lot of publicity.

I received so many letters, so many good will messages. This has been very stimulating and inspiring indeed. Another side to it, as far as my art is concerned, it has confirmed to me that there are people outside my immediate sphere who understand what I am talking about and who also share my vision. One of the letters I got was from a friend, a poet of my own generation, and another one from Tanure Ojaide. They said they were happy for me, but they were also happy for themselves because the prize vindicated the kind of poetic tradition that our own generation is trying to establish. Another side of it is that it has made publishers more accepting of my work. When I tell people that my first collection was ignored and then was rejected, people won't believe it. New Horn didn't even acknowledge receipt. But now I know if I write I will be heard. I will be listened to if I talk. So the Prize has been a great inspiration for my writing. But I have also taken it as a kind of plateau for my work. I know that complacency sets in with this kind of award, so what I have tried to do is to forget the award and keep on working.

When *Moonsongs* came out, critical opinion on it was divided. Some people said they preferred it to *The Eye of the Earth*, which won the award. Others said *The Eye of the Earth* was better. So somehow *The Eye of the Earth* has become a reference point for me. Now people compare what I am writing or what I am likely to write with *The Eye of the Earth*, and they go back to the archives to compare what I wrote before *The Eye of the Earth* with the book.

What makes me happiest is the message of the book itself—apart from the artistic experiment which one tries to carry out—the fact that our earth needs to be saved. At the time I was writing those poems, it was like a voice in the wilderness. I'm really glad that ecological problems now occupy center stage in our world. Green Peace is coming closer and closer to center stage in European politics. When I wrote this collection, they were a kind of deviant group—the Women of Greenham Common, too. So the Commonwealth Prize has been a really great advantage. But I must also tell you that it has put me so much in the limelight that I have become the victim of that success. I hardly have a single minute to myself now. I am swamped by letters and manuscripts and all kinds of calls and interviews lasting far into the night and morning. But I think the good sides far outweigh the bad sides.

I wonder if there is a question you have never been asked that you have always wanted to be asked, and if so, what might it be?

I have been asked so many questions before and have been passed through so many grills, but some of these have not been asked before. If I may subvert your question, I am glad you have not asked certain questions like the myth of origin and like questions that many have asked me, "and what is the meaning of this line or phrase in your poetry?" You didn't ask whether I have also made any effort in other fields than poetry. I have suspended my activities in drama, but I hope to take it up again. I do creative writing more or less in my tired hours, because the pressure of work is so much and my commitment to my students is so great. All these responsibilities are important, but I hope to do more playwriting someday, and also some children's literature. I already have informal contracts from Nigerian publishers who want something genuinely African and indigenous to substitute for Humpty Dumpty and Bah Bah Blacksheep. It's something I'm interested in, because my own kids are growing up, and I don't like what they are being fed. So I want to do some creative writing—prose and drama—but I will certainly continue writing poetry.

NOTES

1 This interview was held in Ibadan, 16–17 March, 1990. It has not been submitted for publication until years after its recording because at the time of the
  interview, many of the questions were based on works which were available
  only in manuscript. Today, with *Midlife* finally in print, the interview should
  bring light to what would otherwise be obscure, a major period in Osundare's
  work, spanning the period of 1987 to 1992, a period which saw the publication of *Moonsongs*, of the Noma Prize winning collection *Waiting Laughters*,
  and the retrospective *Selected Poems*. With these publications, readers around
  the world finally have access to both the famous public poet who is known as
  the tabloid bard, and to the more private poet who, with the 1988 collection
  Moonsongs, began to baffle readers, many of whom have feared that Osundare
  has abandoned his embrace of socialist ideology.

  This interview was originally schedulled to appear in *Matatu* and later offered
  to *The People's Poet*. It is still expected to be published in *Matatu* perhaps
  under a different title. Editor.

INTERVIEW WITH
NIYI OSUNDARE

Cynthia Hogue and Nancy Easterlin

Oluwaniyi (Niyi) Osundare brings to his writing a consciousness shaped by his varied experience and infused with a deep-seated and infectious optimism that endures in spite of the close quarters he has kept with human injustice. It is this breadth and resilience—personal, intellectual, moral, and spiritual—that have led to his recognition as Nigeria's most distinguished poet.

The author of eleven collections of poetry, including *Horses of Memory* (1998), *Seize the Day* (1995), *Midlife* (1993), *Waiting Laughters* (1990), and *The Word Is An Egg* (2000), Osundare has been twice awarded Nigeria's highest poetry prize, the Cadbury/ANA Poetry Prize (in 1989 and 1994), and was the 1991 recipient of the Noma Award, Africa's most prestigious book award. The recipient of numerous other commendations and awards, Osundare recently received an honorary doctorate by the Universite de Toulouse-Le Mirail (February 1999). The University has conferred this honorary doctorate in literature only twice in this century, last to Somerset Maugham in 1947.

Born into a Yoruba village to a cocoa farmer and a weaver, Osundare received compulsory education as a boy in a British colonial school; thus, the revelation of the power of written language merged early on with the sensuous and physical reality of village life and of a vital culture of songs. After receiving a bachelor's degree from the University of Ibadan, Nigeria (1972), Osundare's studies took him to the University of Leeds (M.A. in English, 1974), and then on to Toronto's York University (Ph.D. in English, 1979). Since completing his doctorate, Osundare has taught in Nigeria and the United States. Currently, he is Professor of English at the University of New Orleans.

One look at Osundare's poetry demonstrates that, in spite of his many years of Anglo American education and residence, the folk traditions of his early life alongside the urgency of Nigeria's political situation provide its energizing impulse. The profound romanticism of Osundare's sensibility, evinced in his faith in political transformation, in the unity of man and nature, and in the power of poetic language to catalyze change, derives first from village life and is further enriched by his knowledge of British and American romanticism. His use of repetition and of a collective speaker, so strongly reminiscent of Whitman for the contemporary Western reader, in fact, have their source in tribal oral modes similar to the ancient traditions that influenced the Bible, upon which Whitman drew for his own poetical voice. Thus, Osundare's aesthetic affirms the continuity between written literature and folk traditions. The impression of unity between nature and humankind created by Osundare's abundant use of natural imagery recalls Wordsworth, as well as Whitman, reminding us of the wisdom, the plainer and more emphatic language, that that poet attributed to humble rural folk.

But finally, Osundare's profound belief in the transformative power of the written word serves as a timely reminder that poetry can be something more than polite, meaningless words. Indeed, the concerns that compelled him to undertake a political-cultural column for *Newswatch*, Nigeria's foremost newsmagazine, and brought him to the fore as a voice of resistance are the same concerns that inspire his poetry. The unifying, universalizing voice of his poems memorializes the spirits of those who have suffered under state terrorism, ensuring their perpetuity as it joins us to them and encourages us to envision a better future.

The following text-combined interview was conducted on two separate occasions: in 1992 at the University of New Orleans, where the two interviewers and Osundare taught together during the 1991–1992 academic year, and in 1999 at the University of New Orleans and by conference call to Bucknell University, where Cynthia Hogue is now on the faculty. The interviewers wish to thank Stacey White for her crucial and timely help in transcribing the interview that follows.

* * *

Q. We want to start by asking you about your personal history as a writer.

A. I often say I started writing before I ever put pen to paper. Oral modes held complete sway in my childhood experience and it was at this stage that the foundation for my future literary career was laid. I grew up recognizing the intricacies of the song, the dramatic nature of indigenous festivals, and the structure of the folktale, and the moral, didactic content of them all. I also learnt very early in life the art of "writing" them all in my memory. The faculty of remembrance is highly valued among the Yoruba.

My contact with written literature didn't occur until I started school; and, of course, I immediately recognized the power of the written word. But I saw it as a useful addition to the oral word, not a replacement for it. The culture I was born into and socialized in is a very vibrant one—so vibrant indeed that colonialism, ruthless as it was, could not obliterate it. This is a culture rich in all kind of rites and rituals, festivals, and ceremonies, complete with their theatrical possibilities. I soaked myself in as many of them as possible, and they gave meaning and purpose to my young life.

My father was a farmer, a drummer, and a singer, a composer of songs, and a community leader, and my mother was a cloth weaver, so I grew up with the rhythm of work and the seasons. I remember my mother sitting at the loom erected against a wall while she sat on a low stool facing it, slotting in the shuttle, and hitting home the thread with a long, blunt-edged wooden stick. Seeing those threads with their different colors merging into a common strip of cloth, and watching that cloth transform into new robes later, was an experience almost magical in my young eyes. Then, there was the poetry of the dyeing pot, the color of indigo on my mother's hands, the smell of indigo in the house, the song and banter of the women of the dyeing yard—all this left me with a riveting sensuous impression.

The rhythm of the seasons became a pattern for me. In my part of Africa we have two seasons, the dry season and the rainy season. The dry season is from November to March and the rainy season from late March/early April to about the end of October. Each season has its own set of activities, its own way of regulating human life and even human thoughts, and has generated a number of riddles, sayings, and proverbs.

And the smells that come with each season. In the dry season the high winds come from the Sahara, and then the humidity rises. When the grass has lain a long time, dry and withered, and the first rain arrives, there is a kind of ripple, which rises from the earth and strikes you right in the nose, and this affects your whole being too! Of course, within a few days you begin to see green things all around you. Within two weeks what used to be browned-out and wilted brush springs into green.

I think this experience of nature has the very first impact on my sensibility as a writer and even on my ideal of art. That death comes but it is only temporary, life is an ongoing experience.

Where I was born, there were no law courts, as we know them. But the traditional ethos made sure people knew the difference between wrong and right. And whoever violated those laws was dealt with in a certain kind of way, sometimes through a battle of songs. Songs were rendered, and the guilty one fled town, even without being told. So the indirectness in those songs, the ability to name without naming—all these things taught me early in life that art matters, that songs have a sting. Without this combination of circumstances, *Village Voices* wouldn't have come to be.

Q. Was it very important that your imagination was protected from colonialism that you grew up in the Yoruba culture without its influence?

A. Yes, but colonialism is a two-edged sword, and it cuts rather sharp with both edges. No matter how negative colonialism is, I see it not only as a preface to but also as a catalyst of change. No matter what happened, Africa was reacting, not just against but also with another culture. It's just a pity that that culture turned out to be very exploitative and dehumanizing in many ways. So many changes actually took place in Africa, which I think are natural to every culture. When the Romans got to Britain many centuries ago, that culture was never the same again, so I think every human culture has a way of affecting another. Colonialism brought western education, and western education introduced the written word, and the written word empowered the spoken medium. My father was only able to compose songs and rely heavily on memory; he had a phenomenal memory. In fact, he used to tease me that I forgot things because now the pen has replaced the brain. But there is a great advantage in being able to put down what was once a volatile and highly transient set of images floating in the wind.

Colonialism affected us even at the time we were growing up because I had to attend a missionary school by force. The kind of missionary school you attended in those days depended on your the religious sect your family belonged to, or was forced to belong to. Because it was the missionaries who set up the schools, you couldn't go to a Catholic school if you were Anglican. I attended an Anglican school. The schools tried to keep the two cultures apart, to destroy the indigenous culture. But at home, the left hand must reinforce the right hand and vice-versa; the family would say, "We haven't sent you to school to come back with a warped mind." So what the schools tried to undo was redone at home, and I maintained some kind of balance.

There were advantages to both cultures. African culture, as I have always said, is not the totally glorious, utterly romantic kind of entity that people imagine; it was and still is a human culture with its vices and virtues. What colonialism tried to do was destroy the virtues and play up the vices. The ideal was to strike the "golden mean" between Western culture and African culture.

Q. Since you were educated in the English language by force, could you talk to us a bit about your choice to write and publish in English?

A. In the past twenty years, I don't know whether there is any African conference I have attended that hasn't raised the issue you just raised. This is now called the "language question": How do you define authentic African literature in English, Portuguese, or French? Is it possible? Some people say it isn't, others are saying, "Well, we shouldn't just look at the linguistic medium; we also have to look at the ideational aspect and content."

As far as I'm concerned, I think I'll again appeal to this balance, this "golden mean" I tried to achieve right from the time I was introduced to the two cultures. I never learned English anywhere other than the classroom—that is why my English is sometimes bookish. Our first contact with English was the grammar book, the blackboard, and the teacher's cane.

Of course, Nigeria has so many languages; my own language is Yoruba. My father, my mother, my immediate family never spoke English. When I got home I had to remove that cloak and take on another one. It was a very complex system of "coat-switching." This language control led to a kind of linguistic schizophrenia for some people. Many people were not able to switch that easily, and it led to problems. I remember very well one of the most serious offenses one could commit in school in those days was to speak the indigenous language, which was described as "uncivilized." The action could at once get you suspended from school, and if you kept on repeating the offense, speaking the indigenous language, you could in fact lose the whole term.

Right from the beginning, colonial education impressed upon the African that his or her culture didn't matter, the language didn't matter; English was the important culture, the important language. Most Africans who react against French and English and Portuguese today are doing so from the memory of that past. I think it's a genuine thing to do. There are two major schools of thought here. There are writers like Chinua Achebe that say, "Well, I was given this language so I'm going to use it." The English language will be able to carry the weight of my African experience, but it will have to be a different language, bent to a certain degree but not broken beyond recognition.

The second position is championed by people like Ngugi wa Thiong'o, a very prominent Kenyan writer and political activist who has said goodbye to English. He made a pledge in a book appropriately titled *Decolonizing the Mind* that from now on it's Gikuyu and Kiswahili all the way.

Many African writers don't know their mother tongues. I was lucky. It was a battle to study Yoruba in high school, but at least indigenous languages were allowed to coexist with English. The English didn't try to make English men and women out of Africans. They maintained an imperial distance. The French wanted to make French men and women out of Africans, to assimilate them.

As far as I'm concerned, I'm for the indigenous languages, because I have studied the history of English. English didn't start off as an international language. I remember Francis Bacon spent his last days translating his literary works into Latin so they might "live." He wasn't confident about the future of the English language because at that time Latin ruled the academic and diplomatic domains. But English was able to survive and flourish.

So what should Africans do now?

Many African writers use European languages, though they are fully aware they should be using the indigenous languages. As long as that awareness is there and as long as we keep deliberately developing the indigenous languages, I think the time is going to come when they will come into their own. And, in fact, many indigenous languages in Africa have a long tradition of written literature. My language, Yoruba has its own solid oral poetic tradition, for example, and Kiswahili has highly formalized conventions for writing poetry. I write in both languages, and when I write in English I keep making use of idioms and cultural echoes from my mother tongue. What I foresee is a multilingual Africa. It is said, "Whoever has two languages has two souls." The two souls should be adequately taken care of, with the indigenous enjoying a well-deserved priority.

Q. It's a paradox that one of the things that English gives you is not only a broader audience in Africa, but an international audience. Is this one of your reasons for deciding to write in English?

A. Yes. It is very important to reach across, very important particularly for an African writer. I have discovered that one of the reasons that people are so intolerant on both sides of the color divide is that we don't get to understand one another. If I understand you and am friends with you, it is likely I will be more sympathetic to your failings and more generous with your strengths. But it appears history has kept us apart, there is a gulf, and I believe very much that literature has a role in putting a bridge across this gulf. When you are African and come across text after text saying all kinds of things about you—the African is not human, has never contributed anything toward civilization Africa is a dark continent; Africa has no history—you know these things are not true, and you instantly want to react. The way out is through intelligent argumentation. Put your point out as forcefully as possible.

When a whole continent has been so badly marginalized, its people have a lot of repair work to do. The international audience is very important. This is not said out of a certain exogenist malady. By talking to Africans we are also talking to an American audience; by talking to our fellow Africans, we are also talking to the English audience. Humanity is one. My travels around the world have shown me we are more united than politicians want us to believe. So I see literature—in a variety of languages and in translation—as a bridge.

Q. Would you talk about your dual roles as professor of literature and poet, that is, your identity as a poet of the people? Do you find this dual position difficult to negotiate at times?

A. Oh, yes! The university system here is very similar to what we have in Nigeria. The University of Ibadan, the oldest in Nigeria, was modeled after Oxford and Cambridge, but it has slowly "Americanized" its system in the past two decades. This means that the problem of cohabitation within the university curriculum for the so-called scholar and the so-called creative writer is a big one in Nigeria, as it is in America. When I was an undergraduate, I began to sense this. After my first year in the university in 1970, I went to one of my professors and I said, "Now we are reading all these books, but nothing is being done to make us creative writers."

A very stern, scholarly Scottish don with a red beard, he put down his head and said, "Yes, that's something to think about." And that was the last time he ever talked to me about it. What did we do? We then got together and formed an organization of creative writers that later became the poetry club of Ibadan University. We had to do on the side what the classroom couldn't offer us. Now at that time we had a teacher who was discriminated against by the Appointments and Promotions Committee because they said they couldn't promote somebody who was a "mere" creative writer, and this was the most prominent poet and playwright and essayist in the country. There was another case where a creative writer and a so-called scholar were put up for promotion at the same time. In its infinite wisdom, the Appointment and Promotions Committee turned down the creative writer because he was merely a poet and a dramatist, but they promoted the scholar. It turned out that the scholar got promoted over articles that he did on the works of the competing creative writer! So, these contradictions we are trying to resolve. I made up my mind to become an academic very early in my university education, and when I became a teacher at the same university where I was a student, I made it a point to teach creative writing and poetry, and the reaction and the responses have been really tremendous.

But there is a danger with creative writing programs, and that is that they tend to take the poets out from the streets and put them into seminar rooms, and when that happens there are problems. The reason people call me "poet of the people" is that I try to resist being academicized, as it were. That was why in 1985 I started a poetry column in a newspaper, and the principles were: 1) that the poems would be topical, 2) that they would also have some beauty about them so they're not just doggerel passing for poetry, and 3) that they would be accessible. The editor said let's try this for three weeks, later six weeks, then later he started getting letters from readers, response poems, etc. It went on for over five years!

Nigeria is a society that is so musical, so lyrical, that I knew I had to write poems like new songs. Some of the esoteric and academic journals that published my poems didn't reach more than 500 people at most, and you read an English poem there and nobody pays any attention, whereas poets in the indigenous languages fill up large halls. But I thought it should be possible for me to reach my people with poetry in the kind of English idiom they found accessible, and about the kind of issues which touched their lives. And it has worked.

In Nigeria, I often talk about two beauties: the beauty of form, but we also need the beauty of content. We need to adapt a middle way between the content and the container, between manner and matter. I believe that the work of art should be able to speak to people both by the beauty of what is being said and the beauty of how it is said. The what and the how!

Q. The poems in your early books—for example, *A Nib in the Pond* (1986)—are already very rich in both the "what" and the "how." They abound in aural effects and linguistic word play verging on proverb and trope. Let me read two brief examples. The first one is from the poem, "Atewolara" in *A Nib on the Pond*: "We have teemed in desert temples/ crawled in mystery mosques/ mumbling carrion of forgotten tongues" (Selected Poems 13). The second passage, from the same volume, is from the poem "Collage":

From praying ground to preying ground
from democracy to demoncrazy

...

Allies or all lies

...

When the pestle fights the mortar
It is the yam that suffers
(*Selected Poems*, 22).

Q. These stylistic elements are already important aspects of what we might say becomes your signature voice. Could you talk about how your voice developed and the relationship of these stylistic elements to the traditional Yoruba chants of subversion, the *orin ote*, which you mention in your acceptance speech for the honorary doctorate from the University of Toulouse earlier this year (1999)?

A. This question raises the problem of tropes and the consciousness behind their use. The Yoruba appreciate the word, not just because it makes community possible, but because it is also an object of art. People delight in exchanging words, exchanging proverbs, exchanging idioms. These verbal acts are part of our communal rituals of renewal—making new words out of old words, creating new meanings out of old contexts, and so forth. Most of these things remind me of the games we used to play when we were young. This type of verbal play has become an important part of my composing process. I believe that what we call clichés are very important in poetry. Of course, it depends on how they are used. But clichés come down to us through the centuries. If we look at the morphological and phonological changes, we can see how important it is to deconstruct and reconstruct words in the way poetry can.

i had the occasion to read "Atewolara" about three weeks ago in Birmingham, Alabama, where the young man to whom this poem is dedicated, Tunde Odunlade, happens to be going to school. "Atewolara" means in Yoruba "the hand is the best companion." We believe that the hand "talks" because it works, because we work with it. Your "hand" is a gift. In your hand lies your fate, but it depends what you make of it, like art.

Q. In your early work, although you use "I" often, your lyric subject seems to be more collective than personal. And then in *The Eye of the Earth* (1986), you burst into what we might call a more dialogic or performatively collective voice. The poem "Forest Echoes," for example, is very multi-voiced (and you start working seriously with drums). Could you talk a bit about the development of your poetic persona?

A. The first person pronoun "I" is one of the most common words in the English language. It is also one of the most complex, most problematic, and one of the most potent. We tend to take it for granted because we use it all the time. Each time we want to reach out, each time we want to intrude upon the world, each time we want to bring something from inside us out into the outside world, we say: "I do this; I do that."

But in Yoruba, there is a counter proverb, which says: you cannot say "I" unless there is a "we." So for me, there is always an interesting interplay between the first person pronoun "I," singular, and the first person pronoun "we," plural. In Yoruba culture, the official use of the "I" depends upon the kind of person speaking. I don't think that this is something restricted to the Yoruba. In English, when somebody says, "I now pronounce you husband and wife," and another person says, "I now declare that you be hanged by the neck until you are dead," they are pronouncing something into being, making something happen. We have to interrogate the "I" who is saying this. What kind of power lies behind the pronoun that we use? If a street person comes into the room and says, "I now declare that you be hanged until you are dead," people would burst into laughter because there's dissonance between the use of the "I" and the person that I represents.

In most of my poems, the "I" is literally singular but metaphorically plural, and this plural "I" is typical of the African writer. It is a placeholder for the "we" of the community and is most evident in *Midlife* (1993). The autobiography of the African writer is like the biography of the continent because as an African writer, there is no way you can talk about what is happening in your life without also talking about what is happening in the lives of the people on the continent. There is no way you can talk about your present life without talking about your past lives. There is no way you can talk about the personal without the ancestral. This aspect of African culture always reminds me of that line from Walt Whitman's Leaves of Grass, "I am large, I contain multitudes."

A writer in Africa is not just somebody who can hold a pen and make one or two scribblings on a blank piece of paper. The writer is a person that people look up to, in whose work people are trying to see how they relate to the social, cultural, and political problems that we are facing in Africa. People write to me and say, "I have read this or that poem by you, but what does it tell us about the price of bread or the price of yams? What does it tell us about the dictator who is messing up our lives?" In other words, people tell you your "I" is also their "I."

Q. You spoke in your acceptance speech at the University of Toulouse about the duty of the writer in the world, that writers have a duty to make the world aware of itself and that literature is an important weapon against tyranny. Is that in some sense how this collective "I" is also functioning?

A. Oh yes. Absolutely. Not for even one single moment can you think about the "death of the author" in Africa. People see the writer not just as somebody who writes, but as a warrior. Nothing can be more touching than getting a letter from a reader telling you, "Oh, you expressed what I have been seeing in my mind for the past ten years but haven't had the right words to say." That kind of statement makes you stop short and then reconsider the work, and also re-appreciate the power of the pen, the power of poetry, the power of art. Literature, as I said in the speech, matters, and it matters utterly, crucially.

We have to stress this, because we live in a world in which, in some parts at the end of twentieth century, people just think that literature doesn't matter. They have forgotten that Europe and America wouldn't have developed to the state they are now without the works of Homer, without the works of Virgil, without the works of Chaucer and Shakespeare. All those works prepared the minds of people, sharpened and refined their sensibility. I don't know whether there would be any science if there hadn't been literature. There is a tendency for people to discard literature the way people discard the ladder when they have climbed to the top of the mountain. But I think it is the writing woman, the writing man who should always remind the world where we started.

We also have to be aware of our position in the world. This means knowing where you came from, knowing where you are going, appreciating that little part of the world where you grew up, appreciating the relationship, the interconnection that little part of the world has with the rest of the world. In other words, considering the essential interdependence of all part of the globe, of all aspects of humanity. When other people tried to separate humanity, to separate strands that weave us together, I think that it is the artist who should say to the world, "Oh no! We need all these disagreements, all these dissonances." They're an essential aspect of unity, and it's a unity, which doesn't call for a deadening uniformity of humankind. There is diversity, yes, but amid this diversity there is an essential common ground, a common goal. I feel that literature is relevant, that humanity mounts the wrong horse when we forget the beauty that writes our songs and fables.

Q. In *Midlife*, you speak of many world writers, among them Soyinka, Heaney, Neruda, Whitman, Vallejo, Tagore, and Milosz. How have these writers influenced your own work, and what is their importance to you?

A. I am one who is grateful that these others lived as poets. I am a voracious reader of poetry. And I've been blessed by all these others from Asia, the U.S., Australia, Greece, Latin America, and Africa whom I have read. Hearing voices of other poets from other parts of the world has a way of affirming my own confidence in myself and in my art. They tell me, "Oh yes, it is so here as it is in other parts of the world." They reconfirm my belief in the essential commonality of humanity. The high ideals that I see in these authors have served as a kind of shield for me behind which I protect my own sanity, my sensibility. It is a shield that has been able to protect me against cynicism and negativity that I see in other parts of the world, that I see even in my own country, in Africa generally, in Europe, in America, everywhere.

But I'm not the naive kind of person who says everything is beautiful, immaculate. I think such romanticism bottoms out as sheer delusion, as a disservice to authentic memory. There are evil people in the world; history's road is littered with skeletons from their cupboard. We have to agree that evil exists before we can then do battle with it. What we have witnessed in the past decade or so in Nigeria, for instance, is nothing short of rampant evil—annulment of legitimate national elections by the military, political assassinations, detentions and incarcerations, harassments of all kinds. Of course, you remember the hanging of my fellow writer, Ken Saro-Wiwa, an act of barbarism, which shocked the entire world. The opponents of the Nigerian evil became its victims: Wole Soyinka, the Nobel laureate; Gani Fawehinmi, Femi Falana, Olisa Agbakoba, Beko Ransome-Kuti, Kunle Ajibade, Chris Anyanwu, George Mbah, and many others.

But it is to people of this caliber that we owe our victory over the Babangida/Abacha dictatorship, and it is also such people who keep the fire of hope burning, make it possible to say, after all this, let there be a new beginning. After the gruesome darkness of night, dawn has a way of announcing its triumphant arrival. So we have to make sure we don't judge the entire human race by the tiny minority who are always out to do evil. As my mother is fond of saying, "If you blind yourself after seeing a bad person, you will not be able to see the good one when s/he is passing by." We must also have a way of countering evil by making good attractive, by making virtue inevitable. Personally, I am a strong believer in the essential goodness of humanity. I have never for one moment subscribed to the notion of "original sin."

Q. Is this optimism some of what you are condensing into your title *Waiting Laughters* (1990)? You quote Zero Mostel in that collection: "The freedom of any society varies proportionally with the volume of its laughter." And as you say in *Midlife*: "My question, Africa, is a sickle seeking/ ripening laughers in your deepening sorrows" (*Midlife* 94). There's always that sense of paradox and contrast when you refer to laughter—the laughter that's ripening and waiting. Can you talk about what you mean by "laughter?" You refer to it again and again, and it seems so central to your work.

A. I don't know what humanity would have been like if there were no laughter! There is something about our souls that is released by the kind of laughter we engage in, also something about inner personality that is demonstrated by the way we laugh. I recognize people by their voices and also by their laughter. Laughter looks so easy, but it is difficult to achieve.

Laughter in Africa today is very difficult to come by. You are surrounded by tyranny, surrounded by slaughter—in Rwanda and Burundi, where people's limbs are being chopped off, or in Somalia. Look beyond Africa; look at what is happening in Kosovo. Before Kosovo, it was Bosnia and Hertsogovena. You look at the killing fields of the world and you ask, "How can human beings do this to one another?" There is a lot in the world today, which is out to make us sad, sorrowful, and lose hope. But we fall back on our reserves, and say, "In spite of this, let me have a new beginning."

It is that beginning which makes laughter possible. I believe that laughter is the music of the soul. As long as that soul is there, as long as that feeling is there, we'll be able to weather whatever storm comes our way. The worst thing that can happen to a group of people is for them to lose their laughter. The moment they lose their laughter, they are on their way to losing their sanity, to losing that which makes it possible for them to live. Yes, Africa is a paradox today. I have been asked so many times how I can continue to write about laughter when all around us are so many tears. I say: "Yes, if you have ever looked at a teardrop, you see that it is transparent." That means when we cry, we also see. When we cry, we allow our tears to wash our eyes and prepare them for better vision.

Ripening laughter in Africa gives me sorrow, yes, but the word "ripening" is very important, the i-n-g. It is ripening; it is a process, an ongoing thing. Our laughter hasn't arrived. It is still waiting, and let's remember that waiting is also problematic. In one of the poems I signified on Langston Hughes's poem "Harlem" ("What happens to a dream deferred?/ Does it dry up/ like a raisin in the sun?"):

> What happens to the song which waits too long
> In the labyrinth of the throat

What happens to the prayer which waits too long
Without an amen

What happens to the face which waits too long
Without the memory of a mask

What happens to LAUGHTER which waits too long
In the compost of anguished seasons?
(*Waiting Laughters* , 94).

We have to make sure that the waiting doesn't prolong itself into eternity.

Q. Don't you think that your emphasis on humor and laughter is associated with the notion of unity? It occurs to me that your poetry is not about conveying messages. It's about that collective "I," it's a sort of consciousness-raising enterprise. And it seems to me that humor is also a part of that function; the idea of laughter is a kind of bonding experience.

A. Oh, yes. Call humor the mother of laughter. Without it, we really cannot have laughter. The universe is composed of two different kinds of laughers. The first group consists of those who laugh without any reason; those ones are called morons or imbeciles. The second category consists of people who laugh for and with a reason. These are people who laugh because they have been provoked by really serious humor. We should be able to laugh at ourselves and in spite of ourselves. No matter how bad a situation, there is always room for relaxation; there is always room for some kind of joy of life. But even when there is a funeral, a mourning family, there is always room for some kind of celebration.

Take Shakespeare, the world's greatest tragedian. Shakespeare was such a good student of the human mind and the human soul. He knew that too much sadness makes the appetite sick and people lose interest. He knew when to interject his comic interludes, when to bring in the Fool in King Lear, the Porter in Macbeth.

When we laugh, we charge our battery; we recharge ourselves. Laughter prepares us for the task at hand. I find it difficult to trust people who don't have a sense of humor. I believe that those with a robust sense of humor are those who are capable of serious laughter—and those people are also capable of a lot of positivity.

Q. Your 1998 collection, *Horses of Memory*, is clearly an elegy for your father, but it also seems to be a lament for what has happened to Nigeria under the dictatorship. You write often in that collection of the importance of memory. "Skin Song" (3), for example, opens:

> And pale shadows descend
> Upon our noon of bronze:
>
> "You have no past," declare they
> "Your history is darkness
> Which never knew the faintest sun"
>
> "Tell us another lie,"
> Retort the griots
> (*Horses of Memory* , 50).

As the griots' words suggest, the collection tries to work against that declaration of the "pale shadows" that "You have no past." Who are they and what is the importance of the function of memory in your work?

A. I remember saying that a human being without memory is like an alphabet without its letters. In Yoruba, we say the toad lost its memory the day it lost its tail. The tail is regarded by many Yoruba people as the memory of the animal and also the beauty. Can you imagine a horse without a tail? For the tail is to the animal what memory is to the human being. How can we talk about memory without talking about history? How do we talk about today without talking about yesterday? Without talking about yesterday, there is no way you can talk about the future. As I say in "Lion Mountain,"

> The future is
> a past
> we often forget to re-
> member
> (*Horses of Memory* , 45).

I look at the world today—in my country Nigeria, in my continent Africa, the rest of the world—and I discover that there is nothing happening that is absolutely new. Our greatest atrocities: you look at them and discover that these things have happened in the past.

The question I try to explore in *Horses of Memory* is why doesn't Africa learn from history? Why do we behave like that nanny goat, which is whipped countless times for a repeated offense? Memory can empower us. And then we take memory back to its telluric origins, its primordial origin. What is there in the human brain to make it possible for it to remember what happened in the past? And what past are we talking about? Is it the remote past which stretches beyond the length of one human life, or are we talking about the immediate past, what happened five minutes ago? In other words, we should be able to talk about different kinds of memory. There is personal memory and there is communal memory. Between the two is an important interplay.

Memory is useless unless it is called into active service. And what calls memory into active service is remembrance. What happens to a people who have memory, but no remembrance? They are almost as bad as people who have no memory at all. So, call memory the capacity to remember a shared past that we have in the personal brain, or in the communal brain. It is there. It is waiting; it is dormant. It doesn't really become useful until it is called into service by remembrance. The power of remembrance is what I call the active flight of memory.

Q. In *Horses of Memory*, it seems that you are suggesting a role of remembrance as the writer's role, that the writer has a very significant role in making people remember.

A. Absolutely. Yes. Because the writer is part of the communal memory and the writer draws upon that memory. Therefore, the writer has to give something back, because of the writer's heightened sensibility. I am not making some kind of superman or superwoman out of the writer. Rather, because of the kind of job he or she has to do, a writer is more dependent upon communal memory. The writer has to give something back by making the people more aware of themselves, making them more aware of their past.

This takes me back to the second part of the question that you asked earlier about who "they" are. The "they" here are people who are doing everything possible to deny any history to Africa and its communal knowledge. People have written about the continent starting with Joseph Conrad's *Heart of Darkness*, which was published around 1904. Before then, it was Hegel, one of the most profound philosophers. He wrote that Africa had no weltgeist—that is, "world spirit"—no history and no place in the world. And then many years later, a professor of history at Oxford, Trevor Roper, echoed the same thing. As far as he was concerned, Africa's history began with the advent of the white person in

Africa. When the white person came to Africa, there wasn't anything on the continent. Well, what about the human beings? Oh well, yes, there were human beings, but these human beings were savages. They didn't create any history. So, all kinds of dangerous nonsense has been said about Africa.

I wonder, where does the intelligence of the people who write this way come from? What do they really think about Africa and Africans? And also, most important, and most poignant is the fact that the books people have read affected the way they look at Africa. These books still exist, and I think they should exist. I think people should read them. But I think it is the fortune of the writer, men and women of intelligence and sensibility, to take another look at what has been written about Africa and interrogate it. Most of the battles we are having with racism today, most of the problems with racism, I think emanate from the kind of things that have been said about Africa in the past.

In this year before the end of the century, I go to many places and people are still surprised to learn that an African can be a writer. I was in Europe a couple of weeks ago and an immigration officer asked me what I did for a living. I said I was a professor and a writer. He said, "A professor? Where?" I said, "The University of New Orleans." He said, "A writer too? Can an African be a writer?" I had to say, "Oh, well, I don't know if this is the answer you expected, but I tell you that the person standing before you is writer, and he comes from Africa." In the past, I would have been angry. Now I laugh, knowing that I am not responsible for the abysmal ignorance of people like that.

So, memory is important and remembrance is even more important. There are people in the world today who don't have memory or have the wrong kind of memory and therefore when they remember, they remember wrongly. We say, "Your history is darkness/ Which never knew the faintest sun," indicting Conrad's *Heart of Darkness*. I have read that novel many times. I never discovered any African human being in it, although it was set in Africa. I hope you do know that books like *Heart of Darkness* constituted the inspiration for Chinua Achebe's *Things Fall Apart*, because he also read *Heart of Darkness* as an undergraduate, and literally exclaimed, "This cannot be the Africa I know." When I say in *Horses of Memory*, "Tell me about this tree without roots," it is like saying, "Tell me about human beings who don't have a past. History has never given us any such people."

Q. Perhaps as a technique to retain and record the folk wisdom from the oral past of the Yoruba people, you will nest or couch some of their proverbs in your poems, as in that poem that you just quoted, "A root waiting for a tree." You quote as well your mother's proverbs, for instance in "Memory Chips":

> The wise person is angry
> > And slowly thinks about tomorrow
> The not-so-wise is angry
> > And instantly calls for an arrow
> (*Horses of Memory*, 61).

That proverb accurately captures the contrast, which you make so character-istically in your poetry between knowledge and wisdom.

A. The Yoruba people say that it doesn't take much to know. The first time you ride a horse, you might have problems. But if you are resilient and have patience, you will learn. After awhile, you will be able to hold the reins and gal-lop with grace. But developing a skill doesn't amount to wisdom. Wisdom is something much deeper, and something therefore much more personal because it is also very universal.

It is fashionable to say, "cogito ergo sum," "I think therefore I am." We have to interrogate the thinker and the essence of thinking itself. Wisdom means knowing how to remember, not just what to remember, because wisdom signi-fies on memory. It means knowing where you are in the world; it means dis-cretion and a sense of proportion. When we come to the nitty-gritty of human relationships, wisdom means empathy, not just sympathy. It means compas-sion, being wise enough to know how other people feel because you know how you would feel if you were in their position. That's why the foolish person looks for an arrow when he is angry, but the wise person thinks about tomorrow, because how we act when angry impacts the future. Writers know this. After all, if there is no future, it means our work is useless.

We all have a stake in the future. The Yoruba say, "When an adolescent trips and falls, what does he do?" He looks back, as if to say, "Oh my God, what tripped me, what did I stub my toe against?" But when an elder, a wise person falls, he looks forward. That is to say: One—"Well, I know I have fallen, but how am I going to pick myself up?' And two—"How am I going to avoid this in the future so that I don't fall again?" Wisdom actually draws from all kinds of cate-gories, but the innately practical is at its foundation in Yoruba epistemology.

Q. Could we go back to the notion of how one sees oneself as a poet in one's own nation, the fact that you identify yourself as a poet of the people in Nigeria?

What do you see as the role of the poet in other nations now, for instance in America?

A. Basically, I think the literature of the rich and powerful has to be different in certain important respects from that of the impoverished and unfree, so that the role of the writer in Africa, a developing part of the world, is different than in the developed, industrial part of the world. And the role of the African writer is related to a concept I call dissonance. Dissonance in the last analysis yields to anger, but it is anger, which is bound up with sympathy, empathy, protest, and resistance. Resistance, protest, and so on also have something to do with what I call the Literature of Indictment.

What this boils down to is that the African artist has always had a political role. For instance, once an English writer came to an African colleague and complained about the apparent irrelevance of western writers. The African then told the western artist, "Well, when we talk in Africa the government listens, but that is not the end of the story. The government listens in a different way. They put us in jail." In the West, democracy has developed so much that you need an imaginative leap to ever know there are parts of the world where you could have security people knocking at your door at two in the morning because of a poem or a column you published in a newspaper. But the trend is that the African ruler has found it impossible to ignore the African writer.

And again, not all African writers make use of that dissonance. In the U.S., it is possible for you to be a writer and write all your books and nobody bother about what is happening. In Africa, it is hardly so.

Q. Unless you photograph naked children. Then you get their attention, and the knock on the door at two in the morning to confiscate your film!

A. Oh yes, I was reading something recently about decency in art. Freedom and democracy are desirable for every society, although no society is perfect. We are talking about democracy in relative terms. But there is also something in democracy that is contradictory, paradoxical. Democracy leads to the flowering of free opinions, of public consciousness, and without this, creativity cannot really take place.

But democracy also leads to a kind of complacency, which may undermine that dissonance and eliminate that kick in the stomach that is necessary for every creative activity. When a society has reached a stage where writers are reduced to writing about flowers and moons and so on, when there are beggars in the street and the writers cannot construct idioms to reflect the reality of these beggars or the homeless in their works, then I begin to feel that something is missing. If our own literature in Africa is too political, then I think the literature of the U.S. is too apolitical. What we need to aspire to is some kind of "golden mean." This is not a condemnation; it is simply that every period produces its own kind of writers.

Q. You've been such an outspoken voice for human rights in Nigeria during Abacha's dictatorship. Now that the dictator is dead, what does that mean for your work and for other artists and writers in Nigeria?

A. Your question reminds me very much of the early 1990s, when apartheid was killed. People asked in South Africa, "What is going to happen to writers now that apartheid is gone?" Abacha's dictatorship is gone, but eternal vigilance is the price for freedom. We have to make sure that other dictators don't come in his wake. The situation in Nigeria at the moment is still very precarious. In an interview I had with Amnesty International recently, I said that my country reminds me of a land that has just been through a hurricane—like Honduras or Guatemala. The bridges are gone, the roofs of the houses have been blown off, the farmlands have been devastated, and then there are fingerprints of terrible floods everywhere. You have to ask: "Where do you begin to build?"

Nigeria has been devastated for so many years by the hurricane of despotism. We are talking of citizens forty years old who have never cast a ballot in their lives, who do not even know what democracy is like, who have lived all of their lives under one kind of military dictatorship or another. Democracy is not just a political gimmick. Democracy is an institution, a way of life. If you haven't seen it before, how do you begin to cultivate it? It's going to take a very long time.

As a writer, my job has just begun, because oppression is adept at changing its masks. It is left to the writer and other human beings of perception to be able to sniff it from a distance and warn people. We have seen soldiers hand over power to civilians before and the way it ended up. Therefore, we must not repeat our past errors, like that nanny goat, whipped countless times for a repeated offense. So I would say that in Nigeria, the job has just begun.

One advantage that we have now is that, because of the way we fought our battle for democracy, civil society has expanded in Nigeria. We may have one or two things to thank that ugly dictator for. One of them is that Abacha oppressed Nigeria so much that he raised our awareness. Another is that he persecuted the mass media so much that he forced them to develop their own survival strategies. All those strategies are still very much there, not just for the mass media, but also for writers. We started sharpening our parables and our tropes. Abacha remains a negative landmark in Nigeria's landscape. We can look back now and say, "Oh no, no, no—if we fought a battle and destroyed that dictatorship, we should be able to conquer this one as well." So, I think this dictatorship has come as a warning and also as a precedent. We have a country to build. We have a continent to build. And the job has not even begun.

ANOTHER INTERVIEW
WITH NIYI OSUNDARE

Frank Birbilsingh

Q: After our last interview (1986), Wole Soyinka was announced as winner of the Nobel Prize for literature. What effect, if any, has this prize had on African writing or on Soyinka's own writing? Soyinka is so versatile, producing plays, novels, poetry, and memoirs with equal facility, although he is also accused of being an ivory tower romantic who indulges himself in inscrutable, self-admi ring writing.

A: The prize brought Soyinka well deserved acclaim. It encouraged translation of his work all over the world. It was also an auspicious occasion for national celebration in Nigeria. People who had never read Soyinka acknowledged him as the man who had brought the big prize to us in Nigeria. Many Africans saw it not as a Nigerian but as an African prize. If you remember our history as one of negation, and of denial of anything noble or worthwhile to Africa, imagine our feelings now that we could say we had captured the greatest literary prize in the world.[1] It boosted our psyche. In Nigeria, people began to take literature more seriously, and writers thought that if such success could come to Soyinka, maybe it could come to them too: Soyinka was like what the Yoruba call Adesina, a child who opens up the way for the birth of other children. We must not forget too that one function of Soyinka's patron god Ogun[2] is that of a pathfinder.

Soyinka has been a pathfinder to us. But I must enter a caveat. In 1986, when Soyinka won the Nobel, I also won the Commonwealth Poetry Prize. I was in London at the time and virtually everybody was saying that the two prizes had put Africa on the literary map of the world, that they would bring recognition to African literature. This was said so often that it sounded like a mantra. And when the same thing was repeated, five years later, with Ben Okri's winning of the Booker prize for *The Famished Road*, it made me wonder whether Africa was waiting for a literary prize to discover itself. I mean, there was something patronizing about the initial comments...but we cannot deny that the Nobel Prize has done a lot for Africa. It has also done a lot for Wole Soyinka. He was never a hidden or silent figure. But the prize has given his voice greater public, political resonance, so that even dictators took notice of what he said. On top of all that, the prize worked as a catalyst. After Soyinka won it in 1986, Mahfouz followed two years later, then Nadine Gordimer in 1991, followed by Toni Morrison in 1993 and Derek Walcott[3] in 1995—all writers who are either black or from the Third World. In this sense too, Soyinka was truly a pathfinder. Unfortunately, the political and economic malaise, which gripped Nigeria soon after 1986, prevented Nigerian writers from fully enjoying the fruit of the Prize.

Q: Perhaps you could add something on his later works which I call memoirs, but which others regard as faction. *Aké*[4] is a masterpiece.

A: *Aké* remains Soyinka's most evocative prose work. *Aké* is to Soyinka's prose what *Death and the King's Horseman* is to his drama: it is majestically lyrical. "Faction" is a descriptive term about a work, which operates through a blend of fact and fiction; it is not evaluative. Soyinka did not invent the term. Kole Omotosho had used it before in *Just before Dawn*,[5] which is part history and part literary reconstruction of the Nigerian situation.

Q: How has the Nigerian situation—political and social—affected Nigerian writing? There has been no civilian rule in the country for about fifteen years, and we all know about the labyrinthine corruption that drains wealth out of the country. Yet, writing has flourished, for example, your own, Soyinka's, Ben Okri's. In your essay "Singers of a New Dawn: Nigerian Literature from the Second Generation on,"[6] you speak of the Nigerian writer's "vociferous engagement with the country's destiny." Can some of the success of Nigerian writing be attributed to this engagement?

A: Our rulers have not been able to get their act together; they have betrayed the trust of the people; they have seized power and ruled by ordinance and decree, by coercion rather than by persuasion. The political situation in Nigeria has been so bad that it is impossible for not only the writer, but for any other human being not to respond. Our writers generally have been very forthright in their opposition to the inhumanity of dictatorship in our country. Ken Saro-Wiwa[7] is an example. He became a martyr for the cause. He saw devastation in the oil producing areas and took up the challenge. Some people claimed that he died for his political beliefs not his literary practice, which is a clever way of justifying fascism. His stature as a writer gave him prominence; it also made him articulate. There have been many acts of intimidation against writers and many of us are familiar with them: the knock on the door at two in the morning; clean-shaven, stony-faced people dogging your footsteps, walking up and down on your lawn, barging into your office without knocking, harassing you in the car park, interrogating you at the airport, stalking you at domestic or international conferences. But the worse the acts of intimidation have been, the bolder has become the people's spirit of resistance. Nigerian journalists ran unimaginable risks, and Human Rights activists pounded the Nigerian Behemoth; Nigerian students and academics were not far from the barricades. At one stage, I started a column of poetry in *The Sunday Tribune*, a grassroots newspaper read by about two million people every Sunday. What every dictator wants is silence, but the Nigerian writer was not ready to oblige the tyrant. Reaction to political repression also produced change in the nature of Nigerian writing. Indirect satire became prominent. I used parables. You didn't call General Abacha[8] a dictator; you called him a hyena, while the suffering people of Nigeria became lambs or antelopes. Readers understood what you meant, and the dictator's hounds probably did too, but they couldn't accuse you of anything. Of course, all writers did not respond in the same way. Every tyrant has his own praise singers and court poets. But civil society in Nigeria has improved tremendously, and when such praise singers and court poets write, they are asked why they have betrayed the trust of the people. People, who say that Nigerians do not read, are not telling the whole truth. Not only do they read: they read between the lines. Some readers would reply to thank you for expressing thoughts which they had in mind, but lacked the ability to express; others would send cards or come to your office to greet you personally. The Soyinka/Achebe generation of writers was privileged because they came first. But even if they were lucky to be pioneers, we have to give them credit as able and skilled practitioners of their art. They caught the strength and vigor of the anti-colonial movement, although real ebullience did not enter Nigerian literature until after Independence [1960], when black rulers took over from white ones, and did more terrible things to their people than the white rulers they replaced. Writers who appeared in the 1970s were more political, more radical than the Soyinka/Achebe generation;

they also wrote in a more accessible style. Soyinka's later works are more accessible than his earlier ones; Achebe was always a good communicator—a good story teller; Okigbo, however, told the world that he did not write for non-poets—he aimed at a select côterie of readers, though his last poems pointed to a change in his style and message. My own generation felt that if literature could change the world it had to be intelligible, so the communicative imperative came to the forefront. This is why I took poetry to the newspapers. We also took poetry to the radio. When I was a university student in Ibadan I was taught only Shakespeare, Wordsworth, and company. No one mentioned alternative texts and visions, for example, the literature of the East, of Gogol, Chekhov, Tolstoy, Mayakovsky, and Yevtushenko. I had to re-educate myself after I left the university in order to become a more rounded person. My generation of writers was very political. The generation after us was unfortunate: they never saw Nigeria in its glory. Many of them are now in their forties and have never cast a ballot because of entrenched military rule. This has produced cynicism in some of them, but others are quite radical and fully engaged in the struggle to liberate Nigeria.

Q: By reacting against the obscurity of Soyinka and Okigbo you produce writing with clear and simple diction, uncomplicated structures and natural rhythms that communicate meaning without ambivalence or obstruction. But in the effort to move away from density and obscurity, is there not a danger of producing writing that is so accessible and popular that it is trivial? I do not think your writing is trivial, but you yourself have addressed this issue of côterie writing for the select few on one hand, and popular writing for the masses on the other. How do you strike the right balance?

A: I owe whatever success I have achieved in this regard to oral literature. I grew up in a family of farmers and entertainers. My father was a songwriter, singer, drummer, and conversationalist. I observed how he and his colleagues would compose songs and make them popular in a short time. Satire also played an important role in traditional society. When I was growing up, there were no law courts in Ikere. The greatest sanction was by word of mouth. People feared satire and ridicule. Society at that time had a sense of shame. If you committed an infraction and a composer produced a song about you without mentioning your name, everyone would know whom the song was about. The victim often had to go away, sometimes for years. The word had power. My forthcoming volume of poetry *The Word Is an Egg* (now published. 2000. Editor) is fired by memory of that kind of situation. My mother used to say: "When a problem becomes hard and complex, put away the knife, put away the machete; cut it with the human tongue." It is important to maintain a balance between the beautiful and the useful. African art has always maintained that balance. Nothing is there just for utilitarian purposes; it also pleases the eye or ear; it has a sensual dimension. My most difficult poems are the simple ones. In creative writing classes, I advise students to shun verbal fireworks and try to express ideas in a fundamentally philosophical and beautiful way. Look at proverbs: they are simple yet sophisticated, so repeatable. They are like coins, which you use and use over years, but they never rub clean. As I have said in one of my poems, the simple word is the shortest distance between two minds. Simplicity is not triviality. As a critic and linguist, I know when a poem is descending into bathos, and I know how to pick it up and make it shine. When I read Pablo Neruda, Walt Whitman, and Okot p'Bitek, I feel they communicate effectively without any obscurantist attitudinizing.

Q: I wonder if you could comment on what I call the universality of your poetry. For example, in "Human in Every Sense" in *Midlife* you write:

> I am every thing
> I am no thing
> So when you stab the wondering tree
> I am the one that bleeds (p.51).9

That has the ring of John Donne's well known "No Man is an Island entire of itself." And in an earlier section of "Human in Every Sense," you condemn dictators not only from Africa but from all over the world. There is a definite attempt in your poems to promote the sameness of human experience.

A: I see myself as a tree; my roots are in Nigeria or Africa, but my branches are all over the world. I have felt at home everywhere in the world that I have been. I am also a river. Our family name is taken from the river Osun, which is the longest river in Western Nigeria. A river knows no boundaries; it does not need a visa to cross from one country to the next. Look at the Rhine and how many European countries it passes through. Also the Amazon, the Mississippi, and Ganges traverse many regions or states. If a river is poisoned upstream, the people downstream will suffer. Humanity is a river, and to poison it at any point of its system means that others will drink the poison. So complementarity or mutual interdependence has always been important for me. The powerful countries in the world have never accepted this complementarity. That is why they have exploited and devastated so many developing countries. But now that we are suffering from environmental damage, climate malaise, the hole in the sky, etc. they are gradually realizing that if you destroy a tree in the Amazon jungle, or force a central African nation into an economic situation that makes them devastate their environment, the effects will be felt all over the world. Humanity is one. Whatever we carry over our skin is what I call, a mere pigmentational accident. But just as the world is united in my consciousness, I know that sources of evil have their own global, international logic. Hitler did not terrorize the world alone: he had allies in Italy and Japan. Nor did Abacha act alone: he had allies in Liberia and Burkina Faso. Like attracts like. Dictatorship is like a virus within the system. If you knock it out in one place and allow it to thrive in another, its infection will remain and spread. I see the world as essentially united. When you read a great book from any part of the world, and you are touched, automatically you become part of that work, and your history is linked with the consciousness of the writer.

Q: I am impressed by the stubborn optimism of your work. It is no secret that your subjects, dealing with corruption, exploitation, and victimization of one sort or another, are very troubling, and there seems little hope of resolution to these problems in Nigeria or other parts of the third world. Yet you stubbornly resist pessimism and always take an optimistic view. There is stubborn defiance in the following lines:

> I vision a world which says No
> To the dirge of coffin-makers. (*Midlife*, p. 49).

In your volume *Seize the Day*,[10] which is aimed at younger readers, the same optimism is evident, for example, in "Let us Thank the Sun" (p. 22–23). Considering the disastrous fate of people in your adult poems, it seems almost misleading to tell younger readers:

> Ours is a world
> Of making minds and caring hearts
> Of endless rainbows and deathless dreams
> ...
> Ours is a world of beautiful people. (p. 23).

A: My Noma award acceptance speech spoke of the possibility of hope. Some people may misunderstand my enthusiasm and "joie de vivre." I have often been asked, "This hope you are talking about, where is it?" Everywhere you look, we are doomed. But there is a lot about African (or Yoruba culture specifically, since it is the one I know best) that tells us about how to deal with tomorrow. For instance, there is a Yoruba proverb which goes thus: "No matter how fast the train may be, it will always find the earth ahead of it waiting" a saying I referred to in *Waiting* Laughters.[11] However bad things may be today, they may be different tomorrow. When things are bad our people have a way of looking beyond the horizon. You know the proverb, "As long as there is life there is hope." My African version of it is: "As long as there is hope, there is life." Five hundred years we have been in bondage. If we didn't have hope, we probably would have disappeared. I can imagine what African slaves went through many centuries ago, but despite the suffering of the Middle Passage, our people were able to survive and raise children. If our people went through all that and survived, who are we to despair on their behalf! They will be very angry with us wherever they are. I don't believe in original sin. I believe it is society and circumstances that make us what we are, and no matter what dangers there are we can always overcome them. When I was in Nigeria last year, who could have believed that Abacha would be dead by this year? I think there is always a bend in the road, something locked somewhere in the blind spot of the eye of humanity. I don't want to paint a romantic picture. There are bad people in the world, but there are far more good than bad ones. My most anxious moments are when things are going well, for it then seems too good to be true. It is in times of adversity that the best in humanity comes out. I believe very, very much in the future. I remember writing a poem about freedom in Zimbabwe in the 1970s, when Southern Rhodesia was still ruled by Ian Smith's white minority régime. Some people laughed at the poem, which said, "The Sun shall rise again, and the children of light shall see the sky." People said I was starry-eyed because the white minority government was too strongly entrenched. The same thing with South Africa: who would have thought that, after twenty seven years, Mandela would walk out of prison and lead a government over those who imprisoned him? I stick with those who say: "After all this, let there be a new beginning."

Q: My final question is about the term, "post-colonial literature," which is now widely used to describe literature produced in former British colonies. The justification, I believe, is that the term represents the idea of the impact, which all colonies shared from Britain. There is no doubt that the British impact consisting of the English language, institutions of law, government, and education were shared by all British colonies—but scarcely in a uniform way. Canada was self-governing in 1867, before British rule was even imposed in Nigeria, and

Australian nationalism was rampant in the 1890s, sixty years before a similar movement in the Caribbean. There is also the question of language where former settler colonies like Canada, Australia, and New Zealand retained the British language as their main means of communication, whereas India and African countries have several other languages besides English. To regard the literature coming out of all these different milieux as falling into a single category is quite inappropriate. Maybe the term "post-colonial" suits Canada, Australia, and New Zealand, former dominions, which ceased being colonies a long time ago, but it does not suit the Caribbean, for instance, which continues, thirty years after Independence, to feel very much like a dependent, colonial appendage to Britain and the US. I don't mean to ask you to repeat everything in your excellent essay "How Post-colonial is African Literature?" But what do you think of the term "post-colonial," and does it affect your writing?

A: I think the term "post-colonial" is a misnomer. To echo your opinion above, how post-colonial is the Caribbean? Or, how post-colonial is Nigeria, which is right now under the hammer of the IMF? There is nothing "post" in the coloniality of Africa. And when you say that Australian literature is "post-colonial," does that apply to aboriginal writers as well? I think "post-colonial" was invented to join the league of "post-modernism" and "post-structuralism" and other "posts." It all leads me to ask: What are we going to call the next stage of our discourse?

NOTES

1 Recorded on March 24, 1999

2 Ogun, the Yoruba god of iron, metallurgy, war and craftsmanship is central to Soyinka's writing.

3 Mahfouz, Nadine Gordimer, Toni Morrison, Derek Walcott

4 W. Soyinka, *Aké*, London, Rex Collings Ltd., 1981

5 Kole Omotosho, *Just Before Dawn,* Ibadan, Spectrum, 1988

6 N. Osundare, "Singers of a New Dawn: Nigerian Literature from the Second Generation on" in Uwe Boker and hans Sauer eds., *Proceedings of the Conference of the German Association of University Teachers of English*, Vol. 18, 1997

7 Ken Saro-Wiwa

8 Sani Abacha

9 N. Osundare, *Midlife*, Ibadan, Heinemann Nigeria, 1993

10 N. Osundare, *Seize the Day*, Ibadan, Agbo, Areo Publishers, 1995

11 N. Osundare, *Waiting Laughters*, Ibadan, Heinemann Nigeria, 1990

MAN MEANING TO MAN: A CLOSE ENCOUNTER WITH NIYI OSUNDARE'S POETRY.[1]

Pietro Deandrea

After months spent in the placid quietness of the University of Ghana, Legon, going to Nigeria and the University of Ibadan (in the summer of 1997) amounted to diving into a maelstrom of frantic activity. Enveloped in crowded campus walks and daily performances at the illustrious Arts Theatre, the foreign researcher on literature can end up feeling rather dizzy, thus setting aside the stale commonplace notion about time in Africa being slower. Niyi Osundare, Head of the Department of English and one of Africa's leading poets, is far from eschewing the volley of creative, teaching and bureaucratic tasks that constantly rain on him. Nevertheless, his gentle and serene outlook makes one wonder whether an eye of the storm has been reached, at last.

Soon, one inevitably marvels at his range of interests, which go well beyond writing poetry in English and producing critical works on written literature. One instance of this is his essay on *Ipolówó* poetry, where he analyses the aesthetic features of the market sellers' songs (Osundare, "Ipolówó"). After all, as he wrote in the first poem of his first collection, "Poetry is / the hawker's ditty / the eloquence of the gong / the lyric of the marketplace" (*SM*, 3).[2] Market life, then, is certainly another facet of Osundare's strategy to recover Yoruba oral lore,[3] and our conversation inevitably starts from this point:[4]

I am researching in-depth in Yoruba oral poetry, but I don't know whether it's just research. The research is part of it, that's what I do as a scholar; but there's more than that: I was born into it. And bred into it, as it were. I have always acknowledged the importance of orality and oral traditions in my poetry. I always say that I started writing poetry even before I knew the difference between A and B. It may sound paradoxical, but what I mean is that I grew up in a very oral—and orate—society. Songs were there, satires, drums, all kinds of music and instruments.

The oral tradition has always been a rich store of inspiration for me. Nowadays Yoruba oral poetry is still alive, but in a different kind of way. Like every other aspect of Yoruba life, Igbo life, Hausa life, traditional African life, a lot of change has happened to Yoruba oral tradition. When I was growing up, the competition was between who could recite the longest song or the longest line of a poem, who could memorize esoteric sayings, poems, incantations associated with Egungun and with so many gods that are worshipped in Yorubaland. Competition was also keen on whose voice was the best. Now competition has moved to other realms: people now compete in the classroom, and the nib has almost taken over from the tongue.

At that time there were no law courts. I was old enough to see the first law court. But people didn't go to court then, they considered it as the white man's institution. There was a saying: "You can't take your neighbor to court and come back to be friends again." And my father used to say: "No matter how heavy the matter can be, you are not going to cut it with a cutlass, but you are going to cut it with the tongue." In fact, in my forthcoming collection, which is tentatively titled The Province of the Tongue, all the poems are about the word, just remembering all these things I saw in the past.

Osundare's employment of *oriki* (praise poems) is a case in point, as in the following description of the majestic, worshipped rock of his hometown Ikere:

> *Olosunta* spoke first
> the eloquent one
> whose mouth is the talking house of ivory
> *Olosunta* spoke first

494

the lofty one whose eyes are
balls of the winking sun (*EE*, 13).

And, in his tribute to the Yoruba political leader Obafemi Awolowo:

Heart of steel, heart of steel
Elephant who chased the sun with legs of flint
Heart of steel
Lion who shook the shrub like a hundred storms
Heart of steel
You who dared the terror of scheming dragons (*SS* , 92).[5]

As happens in all oral cultures, the word also carries a sacred connotation. So much so for Osundare, who would accompany his diviner-physician paternal grandfather to "gather roots and herbs . . . incantations were needed to stir them to life." (Burness, 1996: 287).[6]

> *The word was—let me say, is "sacrosanct." It carries a lot of meaning. My grandmother always said: "The word is an egg. Be careful with it, because once it drops you can never put the pieces together again."[7] So, every word has its reason for being, and the reason for being is its meaning. Not just passive meaning, but also transitive. The word, according to Yoruba belief, converts the world from "it" to "itness".[8]*

After a while, it is evident that speaking to Niyi Osundare is like reading his poetry, where one gently encounters a series of delicate epiphanies "suddenly, so soberly suddenly," as the poet himself would describe it (*EE,* 3).

> *And I remember very well that words carried sanctions; they were sanctions in themselves. People who stole or who committed other social infractions were ridiculed, and nothing worked more effectively than that. I remember a man who stole some yams: songs were composed about him, and they were sung throughout the streets of Ikere, where I grew up. The man disappeared from town, and didn't come back until about three years later. At that time, social cohesion was strong and people had a sense of shame. And the word was strong. I can never forget this background; this is what is constantly at the back of my mind whenever I sit down to write.*

As far as writing is concerned, it was the same cultural milieu in which he grew in that pushed Osundare into the hands of written culture: "I remember what my father used to tell me: he would say 'You had one hand before, I'm sending you to the white man's school to develop your second hand. Don't let one cheat the other.'" The image of the hand is recurrent in his poetry, especially to bring to the fore societal injustices:

> With the gold let us turn hovels into havens
> paupers into people (not princes)
> so hamlets may hear
> the tidings of towns
> so the world may sprout a hand
> of equal fingers; (*EE*, 14).

> Let no one tell us again
> that fingers are not equal
> for we know
> how the thumb grew fatter
> than all the others (*VV*, 60).

Osundare's father seems to be a figure of fundamental import in the poet's formation:

> He also said: "I do want to have children who would be able to put black spots on a white surface." He was a farmer, a drummer, a community leader, and a very good song composer, member of the song composers' group. I used to accompany him to these meetings when I was young. Call it Freudian; that is how this whole thing began.
>
> It was magical, the way they got together and exchanged experiences and memories—people who couldn't write at all! My father used to lead, supplying the lines and the tune because he had a fantastic voice. Then there would be some kind of group criticism, such as: "That line is too long, why don't you make it shorter?" or "That one is too direct, we don't want them to know who we are talking about by mentioning the name." The technique of indirectness that I have tried to use in some of my poems was borrowed from that group.9

*I, of course, was a singer when I was young. When I was in
Elementary School, we had a highlife band. I was the drummer
and the lead singer. I inherited quite a lot from my old man. All
these things are still very much with me. To me, the word is not just
an abstract phenomenon. It is giving life by the human voice.*

Beside rooting his poetry in Yoruba lore,[10] Osundare is renowned as the leading figure of the second generation of Anglophone Nigerian poets, who broke away from the founding fathers. The latter's verse, in fact, was "distinguished by an undue eurocentrism, derivationism, obscurantism and private esotericism" (Aiyejina, 1988: 112). In his preface to *Songs of the Season*, Osundare states that "Written poetry has remained, for many years, an alienated and alienating enterprise in Nigeria" (*SS*, v). When asked whether it still is, he is stirred a recollection of what led to that historic poetical watershed:

*It is not as alienating now as it was when I was writing. In all
honesty, the pioneer poets of modern Nigerian writing did poetry
in that term. Not all of them: John Pepper Clark stands out, like
Gabriel Okara, from the rest. But Soyinka and Okigbo were so aesthetic, rigorously and painfully, about their work, that they became
very obscure, if not obscurantist.*

*In high school many of us showed interest in literature, and our
class specifically asked for African literature, because we were a
rebellious class. It was in 1964/'65. We said we wanted African
history—before then it was British Empire history: we got it. The
same happened with African literature. And then we discovered
that the poems that were given to us were unreadable. So many of
our classmates said, "Oh my God, if this is what it means to study
African poetry, then I'm going to drop literature," and quite a
number of them actually did. But I was too interested in it to drop
it for that reason. I didn't start understanding Soyinka well until
I was in my last year at university. With that kind of poetry, there's
no way you can win an audience for the genre. So written poetry
lost its audience. That is why people like me felt called upon to
bring the poet and his or her audience together.*

In Songs of the Marketplace, Village Voices, *and* A Nib in
the Pond, *there are always comments about poetry and poetic
imagination and the poetic process. "Poetry is for the people, is for*

> *this, is for that..."* In that time, I was also going from campus to
> campus—Nigeria was a much happier country then, safer, with
> no fuel shortage, and richer, people had enough to eat—so I went
> from here to the North, to the East, to the Middle Belt,[11] and every-
> where I saw that students were very much interested in poetry, pro-
> vided it touched their lives, and it wasn't terribly different from
> what they used to hear all around them.

The second generation—baptized as "Alter-Native" by the poet and critic Funso Aiyejina (Aiyejina, "Alter-Native" *passim*)—accepted socio-political commitment as an unavoidable reaction to the needs of their beleaguered country and continent. And Osundare was decisive in helping, in Odia Ofeimun's words, "to centralize the ethic of the political as a fitting element in literature" (Adeniji, 1997: 25). See, for instance, these lines of bitter, Orwellian irony culled from his first collection:

> We are all equal:
> Cocoacoffeetea growers pushing
> Bellies bloated by kwashiorkor
> And cocoacoffeetea drinkers
> Fighting a losing battle with overnourishment (*SM*, 38).

His disrespectful stance appears to be ever ready to pounce on whatever may hinder the way to social justice, including his much-cherished traditional culture:

> In the village
> people talk
> about the old confusing age with wit
> making grey hair excuse
> for frosted folly
> demanding a world prostrate
> like a fossilized lizard salaaming
> to the stiff orders
> of hoary tyranny (*SM*, 13–14)

In critical terms, his most famous attack on traditional power structures and the arts is represented by his essay on the Kabiyesi Syndrome, where he laments the undemocratic pervasiveness of Yoruba gods and chiefs on the Nigerian stage

(Osundare, "Beaded" *passim*).[12] Such a blunt standpoint was also carried out by the Alter-Natives through a varied adherence to Marxist theories (Adagbonyin, 1996: 78–80). Osundare declared: "Socialism can never end. I was a socialist before I ever read Karl Marx. I was a socialist before I ever knew the word 'socialism'. Growing up in Ikere-Ekiti, I never saw a beggar. I grew up in a culture which also stipulated that the best way to judge the society is to look at the way its weakest members live" (Stevens, 1997: 42). In terms of literary criticism, this implied a rejection of post-structuralist and deconstructionist doctrines with their "fetishization of the text and its theory" (Osundare, *Crisis* 1993: 10) at the expense of the personal and collective context in which literature is produced. In the case of the African context, the pressing issues of our times make it even more unsuitable for reified theories.[13]

Another aspect of the "Alter-Native" commitment was the conscious choice to publish one's collections in Nigeria, which Osundare has never modified— a courageous and consistent decision, though financially unprofitable.

Osundare describes his fellow "Alter-Natives" thus:

> *A very important work in this direction was Odia Ofeimun's* The Poet Lied—*it's a pity my tempestuous friend hasn't done anything since then. The first time I read that book, I just shook my head because I knew that Odia was talking to me and was talking with me. Before then, written Nigerian poetry had felt shy of making political statements, and had been characterized by all kinds of surrealism and obscurantism. Odia Ofeimun took poetry right to the village square, to the city square. So many of us owe to his boldness...*
>
> *Soon after that came Harry Garuba, although his poetry is more reflective and withdrawn. And also people like Tanure Ojaide, Funso Aiyejina, Obiora Udechukwu the artist—many people don't know that his poetry is as good as his drawings—and Ossie Onuora Enekwe, my friend in Nsukka. Somehow, then, people were beginning to say that poetry should come out from the closet. The first poem of my first collection literally became a credo: "Poetry / is / man / meaning / to / man." So the popularity of poetry owes a lot to the second generation of Nigerian poets because we really wanted to break the mould, with the "Alter-Native" Tradition. And we also have people like Biodun Jeyifo: a great friend, a great critic, and a fantastic human being, and a thorough-going Marxist scholar who understood what was happening.*

> *The idea of communicating accessibility, which we said was central to all art, also caught his attention. He followed our steps very closely, giving very important critical authority to our efforts.*

On the other hand, he is careful not to belittle the first generation's multifarious achievements:

> *But I'm not eulogizing our generation or saying, "Oh, we were the only ones who made things happen..." The Wole Soyinka who wrote* Idanre and other poems *and the more difficult* A Shuttle in the Crypt *also went ahead to write* Ogun Abibiman *and even the record* Unlimited Liability Company. *And the latter is beautiful poetry! It's in very beautiful lyrics in Pidgin, typical Soyinka—that record came out in 1983: within a day or two, everybody was singing it: "I love my country / I no go lie..." And I said to my friends, "Soyinka has struck it! This is precisely what we're talking about." Beautiful poetry, but not obscure. People understood what he was saying. I wasn't surprised that the record was banned.*
>
> *So Soyinka, too, wrote poetry that is quite accessible.*[14]

But when we talk about accessibility, audience consciousness, communicative consciousness as a kind of literary ideology, we have to talk more about the second generation of Nigerian poets and dramatists. Because what we were trying to do in poetry, Osofisan and Sowande were doing abundantly in drama.[15]

> *And there was a way in which Christopher Okigbo, too, was in the background to all this. We criticized him quite a lot, but we took the best from him because we couldn't be as obscure as Soyinka and Okigbo, and survive. So we are much more influenced by the later Okigbo, the Okigbo of* Path of Thunder.[16]

After his first three collections—*Songs of the Marketplace, Village Voices,* and *A Nib in the Pond*—Osundare's focus on contemporary issues was characterized, according to Don Burness, by a "political heavy-handedness. The songs of the marketplace have become a doxology of ideology" (1996: 289). The fourth collection, *The Eye of the Earth* (1986), marked a decisive turning point in his style.[17] From then on, his poetical idiom attains a fluid interweaving of lyrical density and subject matter. In particular, the poet seems to tap the natural dimension to construct his figurative language. The realm of nature acquires a definite centrality in his poetic vision, with overt influences by the place where he grew up and the kind of upbringing he was given:

> "My mother was a weaver and a cloth-dyer. I grew up with the rhythm of her hands ... Whenever she dipped her hands into the pot, I always wondered what was in the pot that turned her hands so blue... She was also a spinner, she loved to spin, and every time she did this she would invoke the earth, without which none of us can exist. And she usually did this in the morning" (Osundare, "Bayreuth").

The anthropomorphization of the environment allows him to bring to the fore human vices and injustices, as happens in his invocation to the chameleon:

> Don the earth
> with the preening prudence
> of your global eyes.
> Don the earth,
> not with the millennial leapnessness
> of millipede legs
> not with the ireful fire
> of the scorpion's tail
> nor the calculating meanness
> of the snail who carries his home
> on every journey; (EE, 9).

In his praises of Awolowo's accomplishments:

> Breaking walls, levelling mountains
> Giving lowly shrubs their dew
> In a jungle so darkly ruled
> By Cabals of towering trees (SS, 89).

And when he rekindles hope for the Nigerian future:

> Our laughter these several seasons is the simper-
> Ing sadness of the ox which adores its yoke,

> The toothless guffaw of empty thunders
> In epochs of unnatural drought
>
> The season calls for the lyric of other laughters
>
> New chicks breaking the fragile tyranny
> Of hallowed shells (*WL*, 96).

He also keeps on drawing on the peopled market to drive his message home, of course:

> And the vultures are fat
> crows call a feast at every dusk;
> markets wear their stalls like creaking ribs
> the squares are sour with the absence
> of friendly feet (*WL*, 45).

Osundare's metaphors make a lavish use of the most diverse formal devices, such as alliteration, consonance, internal rhyme, and show "a tireless, sustained obsession with 'playing' with language" (Jeyifo, 1988: 316). If comparisons are to be traced here, his fondness of stunning linguistic somersaults are reminiscent of the Ghanaian poet Atukwei Okai. His defiant attitude, therefore, is directed at societal ills and linguistic conventions alike, significantly merged in the following lines:

> Waiting
> for fists which find their aim
> and idioms which split their atoms (*WL*, 10).

To him, fracturing the atom of our words also implies creating a long series of neologisms pregnant with meaning:

> Talkathief like a waterfall
> Cocky like cockatoos (*SS*, 105).[18]

Osundare's effort, here, deals with the need to fill the gap between his two languages: on one hand Yoruba, which he defines as "a 'sounding' language," on the other hand English, "a 'meaning' language essentially" (Adagbonyin, 1996: 124). Filling the gap means fully exploiting the oral possibilities offered by his European idiom, like in this vision of beauty devoid of ferocity:

> The moon the moon is a crown without a king,
> the shoal without its sharks, the flame without
> its fang; the moon is the throaty clatter of
> breaking chains of breaking chains of breaking chains.
> (*MS*, 26).

Osundare's poetry, then, fits well into the parable traced by Robert Fraser in his seminal history of Anglophone West African verse: "the inception of written verse initially marked a sharp break with the tradition of oral verse, after which occurred a slow flirtatious reconciliation."(p. 2) On this linguistic basis, in each of the collections following *The Eye of the Earth*, Osundare has developed a different artistic project dictated by both his creative inclinations and the events characterizing his life. *Moonsongs* (1988) was written while recovering from a criminal attack which nearly killed him, "when twilight thundered in / with a calvary of howling axes" (*MS*, v). Social issues are present, but less pervasively so, often clouded in cryptic imagery. The general mood is one of violence and suffused sufferings linked with the moon and the natural environment, as in the following nightly meditation culled from the many included in the collection:

> And with its rhythm of rocks
> memory of meadows
> hieroglyph of hills
> with its ding-dong of dawn-and-dusk
> the moon lilts and laughs,
> a millennial tear standing hot
> in the amplitude of its eye
>
> The tear bursts into brook
> ripens into river
> then gallops like a liquid mare
> towards the sea (*MS*, 12).

Two considerations arise when reading this collection. The first one concerns the undeniable importance of the biographical dimension in the analysis of Osundare's and, more generally, of African poetry—a view that this essay-cum-interview heartily espouses. Secondly, *Moonsongs* inspired some negative reviews because of its lack of a direct political content: Chinyere Nwahunanya, for instance, fears that this new tendency by the poet might "result in an obscurantism that would mark the beginning of his disintegration as a poet," due to his "absolute chase after images, . . . his concern for neologisms instead of meaning"(p. 151).[19] The critic's uncompromising view of poetry surprisingly disparages *The Eye of the Earth*, too. He regrets the loss of a supposed brotherhood between Osundare's first three collections and the trojka of the Bolekaja critics (p. 144). One should turn to the critic Abiola Irele to remind oneself that Chinweizu, Jemie and Madubuike, in their *The Decolonization of African Literature*, propounded "a naive romanticism, if not indeed an untroubled primitivism," whereas traditional societies "produced difficult poetry" that "had to reflect on its universe in an elaborate imaginative form; it did its philosophy in song" (Irele, 1988 :104). As Osundare himself would declare in a later poem:

> I am the runic rithmetic of forgotten tribes
> hearthy flame of the parrot's unquenching tale (*WL*, 18).

In any case, Nwahunanya is likely to be satisfied with the project that Osundare undertook with *The Nigerian Tribune*, and which later resulted in the collection *Songs of the Season* (1990). Writing for the readers of the press implied a change in his poetical priorities, this time giving precedence also to accessibility. In his preface to the volume, the poet describes its intent thus: "to capture the significant happenings of our time in a tune that is simple, accessible, topical, relevant and artistically pleasing" (*SS*, v). During our interview, he recollected the very genesis of that enterprise:

> *The 1983 elections were rigged in a very shameful way, and the country was in a state of tension. I wrote articles and did all kinds of things. I had no gun and no power like a politician, and I wanted to tell the truth about the country as it were. So I picked up my pen and wrote a series of poems, published in* The Nigerian Tribune—*one full page! I didn't even know it got published—with a picture of the ballot box. Before 10 AM, I found about ten letters or notes (some with names, some anonymous) under my door because I came here straight away to teach. So I went to buy my copy of* The Tribune. *And that was the beginning: people were writing in from all over the country, commenting on the poems. It opened my eyes to the tremendous possibilities of the popular medium. For some time I didn't do anything about this because I was busy writing for* West Africa *and so on.*
>
> *In 1985, the idea coalesced again in my mind, as I state in the introduction to* Songs of the Season. *I used to write a poem or*

two every Sunday, and the reactions were very encouraging, so much so that these poems were being quoted in newspapers and books, and people were singing them.

In the following lines on "illegal" homes razed to the ground by state bulldozers, a fusion is attained between topicality, straightforwardness, and linguistic skills:[20]

> Armed with claws and iron laws
> Elephant legs on our huts and sheds
> Deaf, dead deaf, to wails and woes
> Their wake a grave of shrieks and shreds (*SS*, 17).

Having to touch the widest possible audience—probably the widest ever, for Nigerian written poetry in English—Osundare has recourse to Pidgin, to popular figures, like the iconoclastic musician Fela Anikulapo-Kuti, "Your song is the drizzle of dawn / sparing no roof, however tall" (*SS*, 95), to stinging satire, "If we all befriend the tap / Who will honour the creeks?" (*SS*, 10), "Country broke? who broke the country?" (*SS* 20), and to the composition of folktales in poetical form.[21]

Sometimes these poems would generate feedback appearing before him in flesh and blood:

> *One experience I will never forget is this: I was teaching down here, one afternoon, when somebody knocked on the door. I asked him: "Could you please wait until I've finished teaching, or go and come back?" He said, "No, I can't come back, I come from a long distance." I looked at him and I saw he was very scruffy, so I said, "Please, just wait one minute, I'll be with you." When I finished my lecture I joined him in the corridor, but he wanted us to speak in my office. There he said: "I've just come to thank you for saving my life." I replied: "I'm not a Messiah, a prophet on the beach, an Imam, a politician, or a soldier. What do you mean?"*
>
> *He put his hand in his coat pocket and brought out a copy of my* Tribune *poem of the Sunday before: "This saved my life," he said. I still didn't understand what he was saying, and he told me: "I have come all the way from Cross River State," about eight hours by bus, "to thank you for this." I then looked at the poem: it was "Retrenched." It was as if I knew what had happened to him.*

*He thought I wrote the poem for him, but how would I have
known?*

*What happened to him was that he had worked in a company
for twenty years, and the Structural Adjustment Policy came rec-
ommending that factories should slim down so as to increase their
profits. In other words, to destroy human beings and make money.
This man, with a clean record, just went to work one day only to
be told, "Go back." He had a wife and seven children, and said he
was actually going to commit suicide. And then somebody brought
a copy of* The Tribune, *used for wrapping groundnuts. After they
ate them, he just looked at this thing and his eyes caught the poem.
He told me that he used to love literature when he was at school;
he didn't have much education. The last stanza of the poem goes:
"The times are hard, but so my heart / I will never die on the rubbish heap / I've sowed my sweat, I deserve to reap." So he had
changed his mind and came to let me know all that.*

*So when people say, "Oh, poetry doesn't matter," I don't believe
that is true. We are touched by the things we read. That really
strengthened me, and made me realize that what I was doing had
a purpose. It didn't go without criticism, of course, coming from
the ivory tower. Many of my colleagues said "Oh, these poems are
too simple, you're going to destroy poetry for Nigeria, if you compare this with Soyinka's poetry you'll see that it is not poetry, etc."
They didn't realize that I was writing for the newspaper medium,
and that I was performing an experiment, too.*

As part of the effort to abate the distance between written poetry in English
and the Nigerian audience, Osundare has been involved in the phenomenon of
poetry recitals, restoring through live performances that dimension of oral delivery that distinguishes traditional poetry. This is yet another feature shared with
Anglophone Ghanaian poetry: since the 1970s, poets such as Atukwei Okai, Kofi
Anyidoho, and Kobena Eyi Acquah have brought poetry back to the stage
(Deandrea, "Page" *passim*). In our interview, Osundare explained the genesis
and development of his rapport with the stage:

*I was influenced by the African oral tradition, to start with.[22]
Then by a play reading that I saw when I was an undergraduate
in 1971. I think Femi Osofisan and Mrs. Ajayi were part of it, too:
"I challenge I challenge I challenge God to produce a relief map of*

*Purgatory," it went. I carried that experience to my Dramatic
Theory and Criticism class, which was taught by Dapo Adelugba,
a person to whom we all owe a lot. His class was very very useful,
that was where I came across Meredith, Aristophanes, and
Bergson on the theory of laughter.*

*I started out as an actor. I was first on stage before I started writ-
ing poetry. I majored in English and minored in Theatre Arts,
here. I was in Dapo Adelugba's production of Wale Ogunyemi's
Kiriji. It was wonderful, with Soyinka directing the School of
Drama, Adelugba and other great makers of Nigerian theatre
doing their best. In fact, I was more popular in the Drama than
in the English Department.[23]*

The shift from the page to the stage was carried out, once again, by a whole
generation, and Osundare identifies with the "Alter-Natives'" new outlook:

*Performance poetry is becoming a tradition, particularly on
Nigerian campuses. This started about the mid-80s, when some
kind of poetic revolution, or revolution in poetry, swept across all
our campuses.*

*I was one of the founding members of the Ibadan Poetry Club,
to which I owe a lot. Every Thursday—we used to be called 'The
Thursday Group'—we met here in room 32, and dramatized
poems.[24]*

*I try to tell as many of the students as possible that a poem is not
just something you write and mumble to yourself. There are closet
poems, quite right, and they are legitimate, but if you want to
share your poem you have to know how to read it because a poem
is not alive until you give it the human voice. Mediating that space
between oracy and literacy in poetry has been quite a challenge for
me and other members of my generation. I found it difficult to
think of myself as a poet without an audience. I started my art in
the village square, on the elementary school stage, surrounded by
all my mates, in a situation where if you start a proverb, the audience will complete it for you. So I discovered that that bridge was
broken, and I said, "Although there's something about writing that
distances the audience, it should be possible to create a kind of poetry that will unite the poet and the public."*

So at the Poetry Club, we had the stage, the costumes, and so

> on. There was a big attendance, and people used to come from
> Medicine, Law... and the tradition is still very much on. A week
> ago a lecturer in Medicine sent me a poem, which was part of the
> celebrations of my birthday, and asked me to comment on it. I had
> to sit down—I receive so many letters like that—although he's
> from this university I don't know him. I wrote back to him a cri-
> tique of the poem. We have people from different faculties and
> departments, even from town, coming.
>
> The Poetry Club is still on. So, in a way, this has become a tra-
> dition, particularly in our tertiary institutions. Now we've not been
> able to meet for a while, because the University has suffered a lot
> of disfunctions, and we're still trying to... things are not stable yet.
> For the past three years, the University of Ibadan has been closing
> down for a minimum of 5–6 months each year. But I can see the
> Association of Nigerian Authors' activities actually complement-
> ing some of the activities of the Poetry Club in a tremendous way.

The critic, Biodun Jeyifo, writes, "On some university campuses now, poetry readings draw almost as much enthusiastic, appreciative audience as do dramatic productions" (1988: 314). The mutual influence between the two genres has to be kept in mind, as Osundare reminds us through his biographical recollections:

> To come back to my poetry, my background, as an actor, is impor-
> tant too—I also write plays. One of my plays was on during my
> birthday ceremonies, A State Visit. I have written four of them, so
> far. I kept them to myself for a very long time. The one, which was
> produced in January and March of this year, had been written in
> 1981, and it never saw the light of day. It was one of the students
> here who pressurized me to release it, and he did a great job with
> a students' production that went on for many nights, very success-
> fully. A very political play, too. I was surprised we were allowed to
> put it on stage.[25]

Such an attitude towards the poetical genre necessarily influences the stylistic features of his creative output: apart from the already mentioned sound-play, Osundare's poems abound with refrains, that in a performance context can be picked up and echoed by the audience in a call-and-response manner. As he writes in his (already quoted) poem, "Poetry is":

Poetry is
a lifespring
which gathers timbre
the more throats it plucks
harbinger of action
the more minds it stirs (*SM*, 3).[26]

One finds also repetitions of all kinds, especially anaphoric constructions intended to create, as Don Burness aptly writes, "incantatory reverberations" (p. 293), as in the following lines reminiscent of Langston Hughes's celebrated "Montage of a Dream Deferred":

What happens to the song which waits too long
In the labyrinth of the throat

What happens to the prayer which waits too long
Without an amen

What happens to the face which waits too long
Without the memory of a mask

What happens to LAUGHTER which waits too long
In the compost of anguished seasons? (*WL*, 94).

Oral literature, too, according to Isidore Okpewho, makes use of repetition for its aesthetic and utilitarian values (pp. 70–104).

No wonder that Osundare's works, which lend themselves so well to dramatizations, have been taken to the stage by other artists too:

> I still remember that even before The Eye of the Earth was published, one of my favorite poems, "The Rock Rose to Meet Me," was dramatized here by a young man who now has become the editor of The Glendora Review, Dapo Adeniyi. It was put on stage, directed by him. Also "Olowo Debates Talaka," which is now a poem in Songs of the Season, was acted here. Remi Raji was one of those who took part in it.

Furthermore, Osundare never spares musical directions in his poems, suggesting to the potential performers of his lines what instruments should be used or what song should accompany the recitation. This is especially true of his collection *Waiting Laughters* (1990), a long poem where all parts are connected to a main thread, subtitled "a long song in many voices." The book was composed with the oral performance in mind, as the author makes clear both in its pages:

> My song is space
> beyond wails, beyond walls
> beyond insular hieroglyphs
> which crave the crest
> of printed waves. (*WL*, 25).

And in our interview, he said:

> Waiting Laughters *was conceived along that line. It is all one poem, from beginning to end. It's composed like an African orchestra, around a beginning, a middle, and an end. You pick up the tune right from the first poem ("I pluck these words from the lips of the wind"), and then from poem to poem to poem there are tonal contours throughout and there are also pauses. Just as one poem is ending, another voice takes it up—that it's what I mean when I write "medley of voices."*
>
> *I started working on* Waiting Laughters *in 1988, and the experience I had in 1971–1972 with that play reading just came back to me. The book is actually for orchestration. Only some parts of it were taken to the public at the Arts Theatre, here, in 1993. When the book was out in 1990, I thought that I would be able to get a theatrical group together—I was already working on that, actually—but unfortunately politics caught up with us. Universities were closed down, and that scattered the dream. In 1993, shortly after I came back from sabbatical, I was able to raise a team of about six people with a very good drummer: we did some of the poems, a performance for the Black History Month Celebrations sponsored by the American Cultural Center here. It was a very active place; it's a pity we lost it. We also did one for the British Council, and then another one for my publisher, Spectrum, when they were celebrating their 10th Year Anniversary. I got different voices together: men, women, young, old, and so on, with drums and other instruments.*

The recording of his recital in Bayreuth shows how an integration between words and music is sought for. Tunji Beier's percussions provide both a background to the reading and musical introductions, interludes, and conclusions to the poems. As for Osundare, he freely switches from plain to intoned reading, also singing some of his lines. Audience participation through call-and-response refrains, as mentioned above, is often required.[27]

Many of the poems performed during the Bayreuth event belong to the collection *Midlife* (1993). One composition, for instance, is dedicated to Ken Saro-Wiwa and to imprisoned African writers:

> I long for open spaces
> After the tongue's wordless wanderings
> In the cave of the mouth, and lips
> Which mourn the scar of keyless locks (*ML*, 85).

In the whole collection the pivotal creative pool is represented—as in *The Eye of the Earth*—by the natural environment, by memories of Ikere-Ekiti that lead the "I" of the poet into a pantheistic communion with the universe, in an admittedly Whitmanesque spirit:

> I am the speck of dust in the evening air
> bubbling butterfly in the estate of the flower,
> kite in a mellow sky,
> foe of the storm, friend of the wind, . . .
> if I settle near your garden
> I am loam of immeasurable promise;
> touch me with the dew of a generous dawn
> and I turn talkative clay in your moulding hands . . .
> I sing the plenitude of being. (*ML*, 34, 39).

The poet's "I" dissolves in language, too:

> I am the ubiquitous *and* in the broken
> scene-tax of a stammering discourse,
> the *but* which tempers the flame
> of volcanic clauses;
> I am the pronoun, loyal envoy of
> an ambiguously substantive past;

> I am the period, the stick's last tap
> on the countenance of the drum. (*ML*, 58–59).

Such lines confirm the poet's ease with linguistic and imagistic subtlety. The critic Stewart Brown, when pointing out the general tendency on the part of the Alter-Natives to "foreground content over form," defines Osundare "the 'high-priest' of the 'alter-native' vision" who offers "both an alternative politics and a notion of poetics which suggests a real way forward for Nigerian—indeed African—poetry in English" (pp. 62, 65). For the same reason, Biodun Jeyifo writes that Osundare's poetry "constitutes a distinct revolution within the new poetic 'revolution'"(p. 315).

In the midst of all his creative, critical, and teaching activities, Osundare also had to take up the exacting task of running the English Department:

> *This post as Head of Department has taken virtually every ounce of my energy since 1993 because I saw that there were so many things to set right, and I'm happy that the department is now very harmonious. We're trying to raise its academic standard. This place is like a mother and a baby to me at the same time: it was my old department, but now it is dilapidated, we're trying to see what can be done. A year and a half ago we lost four lecturers in one week, all very experienced, that was about three weeks to the exams. So I had to look all over the place; fortunately, my colleagues rallied round, and soon after a number of younger folks responded to my call. Most of those who are here are here because of their love for this department and their respect for me, because they were in different universities and they came round here to work. And when people are like that, you don't want to leave them in the lurch. I'm talking about young men and women who are also developing: seven of them have joined us since 1993. That's phenomenal.*
>
> *Now I'm close to the end of my Headship. Actually, I took it very reluctantly. It was first an Acting Headship (when I wasn't a Professor) then the Professorship was announced—at last!—in 1995, and the Vice-Chancellor wrote to me again giving me another three-year term. It took me quite some time to say yes because I was looking forward to the end of my two-year term.*

His inexhaustible efforts certainly testify to his well-known generous spirit—the same spirit I, amongst others, was so lucky to savor in Toulouse in February 1999, during the international conference entitled "Thresholds." When, on the same occasion, he was awarded a Honoris Causa Doctorate, many of us enjoyed the celebrations with a mixture of rejoice and pride that one might feel for a father, a brother, or a son, with an acute awareness of having been touched by his breathtaking humanity and by his arresting lyrics. In the days to come, his words are bound to resonate in our minds in the strangest of moments, for no apparent reason, "suddenly, so soberly suddenly."

NOTES

1   I wish to dedicate this essay to the students of the University of Ibadan, "squatted with ten in a room for two / Up every morning like a drugged punk" (SS 11), for their hospitality and generosity in the face of affliction. Greatest UI!

2   Henceforth Osundare's volumes of poetry will be quoted in the text in parentheses, with the following abbreviations: *Songs of the Marketplace*, SM; *Village Voices*, VV; *A Nib in the Pond*, NP; *The Eye of the Earth*, EE; *Moonsongs*, MS; *Waiting Laughters*, WL; *Songs of the Season*, SS; *Midlife*, ML; *Seize the Day*, SD, together with page numbers.

3   Osundare said to Kayode Stevens and Idowu Oladele: "I don't think any two weeks can lapse, without me going to a market. Even if I don't have anything to buy I will mix with the people and listen to them . . . energize myself to the language of our people." (Stevens & Oladele 38)

4   In this essay Osundare's answers during our interview will be written in italic types.

5   In the poetry performance included in this bibliography, Osundare read his own *oriki*, too:

> Child of the river, child of the rock
> child of the delicate boulder
> of the beginning,
> of burning quarries and flames
> of eloquent clay (*ML*, 9).

He also explained, "Often people say that there is no town without *oriki*, no community, no family, no individual without *oriki*. Whenever I did some good, my grandmother chanted my *oriki*, and if I did something bad she chanted it as well — and I regretted having done it. My *oriki* comes from two different sources, which are the two main physical features at Ikere-Ekiti: the rock and the river. Ikere is a very rocky area."

6   "I learnt to speak to trees and rivers, and get them to speak back to me", the poet said about those years (Osundare, "Bayreuth").

7   Such a belief is echoed in this invocation to the moon: "let me see your voice / so lithe, so light, like eggs of starsparrows / I will not let fall the eggs / I will not let the eggs fall / The moon is a mask dancing" (MS 5–6).

8   Or, as he said during his Bayreuth performance, the belief holds that "the world couldn't have come into being except through the operations of the word."

9　On the subject of satirical indirectness, cf. Adagbonyin 102–103.

10　Cf. on this Bamikunle 55–58.

11　Cf. his poem "A Song for My Land": "A pondering pilgrim / I have journeyed across my land, / Stubborn needle in her ample shreds..." (SS 2).

12　Parts of my interview with Osundare on the Kabiyesi Syndrome are included in Deandrea, "Gorges".

13　The extreme cases of oppression in extremely tyrannical African regimes may confirm the "sacrosanct" value of the word, as mentioned by Osundare. The Malawian poet Jack Mapanje, who spent 43 months in Banda's jails, declares that the features of orature he learnt in his childhood helped him stay alive and sane during his detention. Furthermore, "I wrote poems in my head and kept them there until the opportunity to transfer them availed itself." (Mapanje 18) It is interesting to note how the distinguished critic George Steiner, to explain the value of the remembered word, mentions the case of a Russian professor of English Literature who knew Byron's *Don Juan* by heart. Jailed in total darkness by Brezhnev's police, she translated mentally the whole work; once freed she had lost her sight, but managed to dictate her translation and have it published (Steiner 21).

14　J.O.J. Nwachukwu-Agbada considers this a general trend by first generation poets such as Clark, Soyinka and Echeruo, who "have since made a U-turn, and have had their post-war verses rendered in a more accessible language ("Post-War", 3).

15　Osundare expands on the relationship between the second generation of playwrights and Soyinka's dramaturgy in "African Literature Now — Standards, Texts, Canons" (pp. 28–29).

16　As for more specific connections between the two writers, it is worth noting that they both employ the popular image of the elephant — symbol of mindless power — trampling the grass he finds on his way (cf Okigbo 67 and SM 10, EE 10). Furthermore, Osundare pays explicit homage to the late poet by quoting his "Elegy for Slit-drum" (Okigbo 68) in MS 33: "The general is up, up, up / The general is up." The critic A.O. Dasylva rightly writes that, like Okigbo, "Osundare is a realistic visionary" (p. 33).

17　This opinion is expressed in Burness 291 and Aiyejina, "To Plough".

18　On the subject of Osundare's neologisms, cf. Adagbonyin 32–66.

19　The same view is expressed by J.O.J. Nwachukwu-Agbada ("Lore" 85).

20　According to Jare Ajayi, "because of his mastery of the art Osundare managed to escape the drabness that usually accompanies straightforward verses" ("Journalistic").

21　Cf. SS 102–103, 108–109, 115–117, 124–126, and also WL 60–61, 63–64, ML 26.

22 As for how Osundare 'rediscovered' oral literature, cf Adagbonyin 88–89.

23 Cf. also Adagbonyin 95–96.

24 Cf. also Adagbonyin 87.

25 Cf. also Adagbonyin 96–98.

26 As for instances of call-and-response, cf MS 1–4, ML 17. In ML 43 and 59, Osundare tries to imagine his audience's reactions and wishes.

27 The value of poetic performances is heightened in Osundare's collection for children, too: in *Seize the Day* (1995) his recorded readings are offered on request (p. x). Children's literature is the umpteenth province of his commitment, and another feature shared with Ghanaian poets such as Atukwei Okai and Kofi Anyidoho.

REFERENCES

Adagbonyin, Asomwan Sonnie. *Niyi Osundare*. Ibadan: Sam Bookman Educational for Humanities Research Centre, 1996.

Adeniji, Olayiwola. "Sounds of Niyi's Verse." *The Guardian* (Lagos). 8 March 1997: 25.

Aiyejina, Funso. "To Plough not to Plunder." *West Africa*. 6 October 1986.

———."Recent Nigerian Poetry in English: An Alter-Native Tradition." Ed. Y. Ogunbiyi. *Perspectives on Nigerian Literature: 1700 to the Present,* vol. 1. Lagos: Guardian Books Nigeria, 1988: 112–128.

Ajayi, Jare. "Journalistic Poems." *West Africa* 3826 December (1990).

Bamikunle, Aderemi. "Niyi Osundare's Poetry & the Yoruba Oral Artistic Tradition." *African Literature Today* 18 (1992): 49–61.

Brown, Stewart. "Daring the Beast: Contemporary Nigerian Poetry." Ed. A. Gurnah. *Essays on African Writing 2 — Contemporary Literature.* Oxford: Heinemann, 1995: 58–72.

Burness, Don. "Niyi Osundare." Ed. B. Lindfors and R. Sander. *Dictionary of Literary Biography: Twentieth Century Caribbean and Black African Writers,* vol. 157, Third Series. Detroit: Gale Research Inc., 1996: 286–295.

Dasylva, Ademola O. "Osundare — The Tribune-Poet at 50." *Honors* 2.2 April 1997: 33–35.

Deandrea, Pietro. "Between Page and Stage: Reflections on Contemporary Ghanaian Poetry through Conversations with Atukwei Okai, Efua Sutherland, Kojo Gyinaye Kyei, Kofi Agovi, Kofi Anyidoho, Kobena Eyi Acquah and Kojo Laing." Eds. C. Gorlier and I. M. Zoppi. *Cross-Cultural Voices: Investigations into the Post-Colonial.* Rome: Bulzoni, 1997: 19–58.

————. "Gorges to Be Gored, Wisdom to Be Wielded: Figures from Yoruba Myth and History in Some Anglophone Yoruba Writers." Ed. by S. Brown. *Yoruba/English: Strategies of Mediation*. Birmingham: Centre of West African Studies, Birmingham University African Studies Series, forthcoming.

Irele, Abiola. "Literary Criticism in the Nigerian Context." Ed. Y. Ogunbiyi. *Perspectives on Nigerian Literature: 1700 to the Present*, vol. 1. Lagos: Guardian Books Nigeria, 1988: 93–105.

Jeyifo, Biodun. "Niyi Osundare." Ed. Y. Ogunbiyi. *Perspectives on Nigerian Literature: 1700 to the Present*, vol. 2. Lagos: Guardian Books Nigeria, 1988: 314–320.

Mapanje, Jack. "Orality and the Memory of Justice." *Leeds African Studies Bulletin* 60 (1995): 9–21.

Nwachukwu-Agbada, J.O.J. "Post-War Nigeria and the Poetry of Anger". *Wasafiri* 12 Autumn 1990: 3–6.

————. "Lore & Other in Niyi Osundare's Poetry." *African Literature Today* 20 (1996): 73–86.

Nwahunanya, Chinyere. "Osundare's New Esotericism: The Genesis of Poetic Disintegration." Ed. A. U. Ohaegbu. *Language, Literature and Social Change*. University of Nigeria, Nsukka: Modern Language Association of Nigeria, Acts of the 7th Annual Conference, 8–11 February 1989: 141–154.

Okigbo, Christopher. *Labyrinths*. London: Heinemann, 1971.

Okpewho, Isidore. *African Oral Literature — Backgrounds, Character and Continuity*. Indianapolis: Indiana University Press, 1992.

Osundare, Niyi. "Theatre of the Beaded Curtain: Nigerian Drama and the Kabiyesi Syndrome." *Okike* 27–28 March 1988: 99–113.

————. "Poems for sale: Stylistic Features of Yoruba Ipolówó Poetry." *African Notes* (Institute of African Studies, University of Ibadan), vol. XV, n. 1 & 2 (1991): 63–72.

————. *African Literature and the Crisis of Post-Structuralist Theorising*. Ibadan: Options Book and Information Services, 1993.

————. "African Literature Today — Standards, Texts, Canons." *Glendora Review* 1, 4 (1996): 25–31.

————. *Songs of the Marketplace*. Ibadan: New Horn Press, 1983.

————. *Village Voices*. Ibadan: Evans Brothers, 1984.

————. *A Nib in the Pond*. Ife: Ife Monographs on Literature and Criticism, 4th Series, n. 6, 1986.

————. *The Eye of the Earth*. Ibadan: Heinemann Educational Books, 1986.

————. *Moonsongs*. Ibadan: Spectrum Books, 1988.

————. *Waiting Laughters.* Lagos: Malthouse Press, 1990.

————. *Songs of the Season.* Ibadan: Heinemann Educational Books, 1990.

————. *Midlife.* Ibadan: Heinemann Educational Books, 1993.

————. Seize the Day and other poems for the junior. Ibadan: Agbo Areo Publishers, 1995.

Steiner, George. "Ragazzi, qui ci vuole passione." *La Stampa* (Turin, Italy). 10 December 1997: 21.

Stevens, Kayode & Idowu, Oladele. "I'll Never Be Far from Those at the Bottom." *Honors* (Ibadan). April 1997: 37–44.

INTERVIEW WITH OSUNDARE

Recorded at the Department of English, University of Ibadan, 1st of August 1997.

AUDIO RECORDING

Niyi Osundare: poetry performance with Tunji Beier at the drums. Iwalewa Haus, Bayreuth, 4 October 1996.

THE POET AS
DRAMATIST: AN
INTERVIEW

Sola Olorunyomi and Remi Raji-Oyelade

In this interview, Niyi Osundare responds to questions on the creative dynamics of trans-generic narrative forms, his plays, and the challenges faced by a poet-dramatist.

Q: *What are the creative imperatives that confront the poet-dramatist? Do they strike you more as commonalities or as strictures?*

Osundare: Both. No doubt there are strictures, but there are also conjoining structures. I have always believed that a successful poem must have something dramatic about it. I think this is why my favorite poets are dramatic. I am an eternal lover of John Donne and some other metaphysical poets. I like the Latin American poets because of the drama in their works. These are people who composed lines which live, in a way in which, for me, drama and poetry complement each other. Every word has a life, the syllables which compose this word have a life of their own and, of course, the different phonemes which compose these syllables are only sound units waiting for animation by the human voice.

Drama is large, extremely large, but the distinction which used to exist between drama and poetry in the past is being erased gradually. I think that erasure began from about 1960s when poetry left the closet for the market place.

Examples abound: Alex Ginsberg, Amiri Baraka, Maya Angelo—all from the United States—and Yutsveni Yeptoshenko from the Soviet Union. The Soviet Union has a long history of performance poetry; even down to the step-shaped poetry of Mayakovsky, they chant their poetry.

I remember once in Iowa in 1988 where poets of different nationalities were invited to a reading, the two poets that everyone judged to be similar were Alexander Tashenko, from the Soviet Union, and I. It was amazing—more so that he read in Russia. The way he chanted his poetry reminded me very much of the kind of things we've been doing here. This is the kind of poetry that I really like. In like manner, "*Cenci*", one of the obscure plays written by Shirley during the romantic period, is a romantic poem. Then, "*Prometheus Unbound*", by Shirley too; you look at the very long line and there are certain anti-theatrical elements about them. There is a sense in which poetry and drama have reinforced each other. Now the strictures. No matter how much you wish to make your poem dramatic, there are advantages the dramatist has over you. To begin with, when the dramatist puts the word on stage it is no longer his or her own alone. Some other people have got to internalize those words and make them their own. Not only that gesture, mime, song and, in our own case, all the paraphernalia of total theatre will be added to your word. So what you have at the end is like being a mere catalyst. There is a way in which the word in the theatre is like a one very important element in the kitchen of so many condiments and, of course, the soup that you make is a composite drama itself.

There are times you can't make your poetry too dramatic. For example if it's something that really stirs you in the soul. There are times the occasion selects the word and you just find yourself either being obscure or being withdrawn in a certain kind of way. There are certain experiences that you express that way. So it is a disadvantage in dramatic terms but it is also an advantage because it means poetry provides you with that sort of psychological cocoon. You can dramatize yourself without putting yourself on the stage. As a dramatist, you have to start from the stage, in a manner of speaking.

There are words that you really cannot expand, words which choose you rather than you choosing them. Then there are different types of poems as well as poetry. *Oriki* you can chant very well but when you have to write about a personal experience, say love for instance, or a particularly curious aspects of it. There are people who write poems and put them away and don't allow any other person to see them.

And then the problems of harmonisation, of sound, structure – the syntactic pattern and so on. And there are certain words that you will use at times which will not really sound very well in the theatre. On the other hand if you as a poet write a play, problems are bound to arise. Words in the theatre are icons in flight – they are in a hurry – because there is no way you can stop an actor on stage and say, please repeat what you have said. On the other hand if you have a book of poems you can re-read it as often as you please. This is why you have to stretch yourself very hard; you have to be more audience-conscious when you write a play. You've got to hear it, you even have people respond to it. You know where laughter is and you know how to undercut laughter with some tropes of seriousness – how to balance. You take the audience up here, down there – at times you just leave them hanging in the middle as the case may be.

If you're not very careful as a poet, your work may be too concentrated. To take a non personal example, I mean non personal to me; when Soyinka wrote *A Dance of the Forests*, he was still a poet in the theatre. That is why I have not seen the play on stage; it is extremely difficult to stage. *Mad Men and Specialists* also is, except that at that time he had added the existentialist dimension to it. *The Road* is very poetic and has its own space. The best of them all is *Death and the King's Horseman*, where everything seems to be present; it is choric and dramatic.

Returning to The State Visit, *one finds your imageries somewhat disturbing; take the beggars scene, for instance, which tends to take a deeply pessimistic mood. One suspects that the overall satire may have been lost on this account.*

Osundare: Well, satire is like a surgeon's scalpel. To remove that offending lump in the flesh, you have to cut open in a way. I think good satires cut rather deep. They scarify us in a way. But when they cut, we can remove the lump, that surface back and allow it to regenerate and the body-politic can become healthier.

Remember my sympathy lies with those who suffer, those who suffer much more than I do. There is this lavish scene where the cabinet talks in terms of millions, and immediately after this you have the beggars. And of course these things happen all the time. When you look at these beggars on the street they look like disembodied entities. People you have to shove away, or whose bowls you have to throw something, so that they can just leave you alone. If you go to them each of them has a story to tell. The person who is lame has a story, either lame naturally through polio because he didn't receive the right injections at the right times, or was crushed by one thing or another.

In that scene, the presence of the piano is a trope. Piano is a cultural artefact, it is something that is supposed to be culturally elevating; which is why the master bought it for her daughter's birthday. But in taking it up there it stumbles and crushes this man who becomes lame and now begs for alms. The piano, which is supposed to give us joy and laughter, turns out in a terrible society to kill people, particularly to kill the underprivileged.

The visit does not happen, as we come to realise at the end of the play. Stylistically we find echoes of Waiting for Godot, *though not in a direct, literal sense. Is this a waiting continuum as a theme of repetition?*

Osundare: No. No. the repetition here is a syncopated repetition, the sort of repetition that you find in jazz. If you look at it closely it feels like finality without end. A kind of paradox is involved here. The visit does not take place but the narrator says in the end that Yanke will never be the same again. That is the first time the Hyena has ever had any such opposition.

The original ending was different; there was a coop, a complete take over, but I decided to change it a few weeks before the play came up.

The narrator begins the play, he is also the one who opens our eyes to the future. Through him the play becomes open ended. True, there is some waiting, but it is about a bright future. The Hyena's claws are being clipped. Remember when the state's agents unleash violence the people aren't just complacent – they also react, and resist them.

In terms of symbolic characterisation, one notices your sympathy for the poet in the play, as against representatives of other professions who end up betraying. The treatment of the poet is most charitable; he aggregates the collective soul of the underprivileged. How valid is this, it seems like poets, also, do lie.

Osundare: Ah! Yes they do as Odia Ofeimun knows. To prevent myself from being charged with some kind of self-fulfilling evangelism, I have made that character a painter rather than a poet, in the strict sense. He talks about the rainbow. Of course you are right to the extent that he represents all the creative essence in the country. Poet, painter, sculptor and like, yes such people still exist. If you have ten poets, if two of them lie it is likely that you'll have eight others that will stick strictly to the truth. There is something about our lives in this country today that in fact points very eloquently to that. Where is Soyinka today? A man very close to his mid sixties but can not be in the country owing to the rule of our dictator. What has he done? What god has he offended that he is now being hounded in exile. Where is Odia Ofeimun's passport. And the likes of Kunle Ajibade, Obi, – all these people are archetypes represented by that spirit in the play. A journalist met me after the production and said, "am very disturbed at the image of the journalist." Sure, there are good journalists but you can't put everybody on stage. That is just one. It is part of the anxieties of representation. This is not romanticizing the creative person but I still have that firm belief that there are many of us who are very angry today, and do not see eye to eye with the Hyena.

The epilogue appears to jut out, and is also rather didactic. Is there any particular dramatic consideration informing this?

Osundare: Two major influences are responsible here. One is traditional Africa itself, you don't just end your folktale until you really have drawn out the moral drive. And it is not because you think your audience is dumb. No, it is only a way of emphasizing what you already know. The second is Brechtian. Breacht wants to dialogue with you once the play is over. It is like oh, don't take this too seriously. Don't go out into the street trying to be a hero like the character, something must have to happen before you can be like this. You also have it in Shakespeare, asides and so on. Virtually every play too had those two moral entities: the prologue and in the epilogue, where you draw together the narrative and dramatic threads of the play.

Another way of looking at it is that there is a certain type of helplessness in our country today. In such a circumstance we need a narrator to say this play does not end here. When people call me didactic I am very happy; I am not an artist who runs away from that term. I have never believed in art for art sake. Didactic, yes, let it be didactic; in fact I am so anxious that the little am saying should be heard by people and society could be better.

But a good measure of Greek drama like the Aristotelian tragedy emphasize catharsis unlike Brecht's emphasis on the ability to distance?

Osundare: In fact it was one of the first things he criticized in the Aristotelian kind of tragedy, that is the emotional purgation, the powerlessness of human beings before gods and the like. No, I am only using an aspect, the dramaturgic rather than thematic aspect of classical drama and the Brechtian. And that is the use of the prologue and the epilogue in classical drama which translates into the use of the narrator in Brecht. Brecht's narrator is either physically there or is internally there. You may have a narrator – character who functions as such but without really telling you, but from what he or she says you know. It is like *The Caucasian Chalk Circle*. There is a lot of African dramaturgic systems that I find similar to this. In East and West Africa, even in the Maghreb in spite of the Arab influence there is always that voice. Of course the griot also compounds the function of the narrator. It is just one aspect.

How do you relate to the tendency in African drama criticism which suggests that the features of a total theatre are more represented in West African dramaturgic modes?

Osundare: It will be very difficult to give the reasons for this. I would say that perhaps the relative stress on song and spectacle among the people of West Africa, contrasted to the people of East Africa? I can only talk in relative terms because I have seen plays also in East Africa with all these features. Penina Mlama of Tanzania, for example, is doing for East Africa what Ola Rotimi, Femi Osofisan, Bode Sowande, Olu Obafemi and others are doing here.

Of course it is true that if you put your average character in East Africa on stage, he is likely to be less sartorially endowed than the ones in West Africa. Take the Agbada, what could be more regal than that. I think there are certain things that we use in our techniques of representation on the stage. Look at the booboo in the Senegal area!

If you are asked to re-present the play, what aspects would you like to rework.

Osundare: I am not sure I know what aspect I would like to rework. In fact if I had my way I would like to add and update the play, in the light of our burgeoning despotism.

In spite of the statements of the narrator, it still does appear like there is an apocalyptic tinge to the end, and also a suicidal and heroic attribute to the characters.

Osundare: I expect the end of the play to be problematic. I think the meaning one takes away from that end of the play depends upon one's vision. One's experience of our country and the continent. Revolutions are almost impossible to put on stage. In fact they are difficult to write about. History is the real channel of revolutionary discourse. The way I see it is that Yanke has never know that kind of action before, which is why the Head was so confident at the beginning. They thought that their role could not be challenged.

But then that challenge came. I believe that when the narrator says Yanke will never be the same again, my own reading is that it is not going to be a vicious circle. So a kind of break had been created; people have been killed and their blood has flowed, and that sacrifice is not going to be for nothing.

It is an attempt to help the helplessness that one has seen among us and the literature written about us, either in poetic form or drama.

What would you call the running trope of your forthcoming plays, namely: The Man who Walked Away, The Wedding Car, The State Visit and The Man who Refused to say Yes.

Osundare: Basically, a focus on our people and the kind of terrible injustice that we suffer at the hands of those who rule us. The way we are compromised and the way society is run. Also, the way some refuse to be compromised, how such spirits usually point the way to the future.

OSUNDARE'S
PLAYS

STYLE AND POSTCOLONIAL REPRESENTATION IN THE PLAYS OF NIYI OSUNDARE

Wumi Raji

We must smash this wall
built of the inequities
of class and crime
then shake new hands
over the ashes of severance
- Niyi Osundare, "A Reunion"

It appears I was able to touch that man, and
his coming also touched me.
- Niyi Osundare

In conceiving this volume of essays, it is almost certain that the editor never contemplated including a chapter on Osundare's plays. Though clearly aware that the subject of the book once tried his hands at dramatic writing, the editor made it clear both through his choice of a tentative title and the advertisement that went to prospective contributors that he intended the volume to be devoted solely to Osundare's poetry.[1] So "total" is his acceptance as a poet that many people do not consider it worthwhile to explore other aspects of Osundare's achievements.

Or this probably is not the case with regards to the drama. Many people simply do not know that Osundare has ever written a play. This much was admitted by many of the spectators of *The State Visit*, Osundare's play mounted during his fiftieth birthday celebration held between 11th and 13th March, 1997. They had certainly never paid complete attention – if ever they did at all – to the blurbs of *Songs of the Market Place* and *Village Voices* both of which at least acknowledged that the celebrated poet had some unpublished plays, one of which was performed to mark Twenty Years of Television in Africa in 1979.[1]

There is a tinge of irony here. Because, as contained in a hint he dropped during a private discussion with this writer, Osundare would most probably have preferred to be a playwright but for the intimidating talents of Femi Osofisan, his close friend and ideological soul mate. Though he was already writing poetry by the time he was in secondary school, what Stephen Arnold has so accurately described as Osundare's "civic consciousness"[2] would have made him to prefer the more public and more communal opportunities offered by the medium of theatre. This could be why, indeed, as soon as he returned from Toronto in 1979, he settled down to dramatic writing, completing work on two manuscripts that single year, and producing one of them even as he commenced work on the third. But by this time, Osofisan had already established himself as the foremost dramatist of the alternative tradition having produced such important plays as *The Chattering and the Song, Once Upon Four Robbers, Who Is Afraid of Solarin* and *Morontodun* among others. Osundare himself acknowledges his friend's achievement in a review of one of the plays in West Africa in 1980. [3] Probably because of this, the Ikere-born stylistician simply packed up his playscripts after completing work on *The State Visit* in 1981 returning fully to poetry, a field where he won his first prize in 1968. This chapter exhumes the three plays – *The Wedding Car, The Man Who Walked Away* and *The State Visit* – exploring their thematic engagements and their technical potentials as well as limitations and locating them within the context of Osundare's oeuvre.

"A Reunion", the poem from which the first epigraph to this chapter is excerpted is an autobiographical poem which this writer has described elsewhere as articulating the theme of Osundare's career.[4] This poem presents two characters: the persona who, having traversed the Atlantic in search of the golden fleece now finds himself as a member of the class of the bourgeoisie and the addressee whose dream has been betrayed as a consequence of poverty and who now is as "scorched as a sponge." The epigraph, which represents the closing lines of the poem, expressed the desire of the new arrival to smash the dividing wall and re-establish the original relationship. "A Reunion" is an old poem capturing an actual encounter of 1974, an encounter so moving as to bolster Osundare's ideological convictions, the formative stage of which can be traced to the poet's communal origins. 5 "A Reunion" is the poem that led to that "unbreakable pledge" by Osundare[6] to remain committed to the deprived of the earth. It is the point of this chapter that stylistically and thematically, Osundare's three playscripts represent unequivocal affirmation of this pledge.

A society wedding stands as the core action in *The Wedding Car*. A typical wedding programme in contemporary Nigeria itself represents a veritable study in post-colonial culture. The wedding price, the attire donned by the participants, the manner of entertainment presented as well as the actual rituals of wedding are all fusions of traditional heritage and "modern" practices. But perhaps more important for the playwright here is the characteristic ostentatiousness and superficiality associated with the programme. And Osundare's position is very clear regarding this. "Must I starve because my brother's son is getting married?" So retorts a member of the bridegroom's entourage when asked to make a contribution at the engagement ceremony. The man is at one with Osundare in expressing outrage and indignation against the people who "live in an ocean of wealth." Chief Chamberlains as the complete embodiment of this artificiality and vanity is the consistent target of derision and wit. His ultimate disgrace is not just as a consequence of smuggling a car into the country but because of his innumerable crimes committed against the dispossessed of the earth.

But it is very important to pass a comment on the role of Lasun in the play. Given the general atmosphere of despair, of dashed hopes and frustrations, it is understandable that certain ideologically committed intellectuals would begin to experience a slide. Deremi epitomises this in the play. His desperation to break the cycle of poverty explains why he has to cross over to seek a wife from the Chamberlains'.

Osundare insists however that to so compromise is to lose one's cherished freedom; it is to embark on a course of self-destruction. Lasun is that character in the play who takes Deremi on a journey down the memory lane. "What happened to the dreams we had," he asked Deremi. "The dreams we nursed together as students at the University?" I could remember we looked all around our society and what we saw were the monsters of greed and graft, of inefficiency, of lack of consideration for others, of the deification of money and property. We decided to be different. It was a solemn pledge to let the world know there is a healthy alternative that ours was not a society irredeemably bound to ruin. "What happened? Are those bow ties and tailcoats part of these dreams? Is this desperate bid to be son-in-law to a filthy millionaire part of that dream?" (p. 34). So many questions. But are the answers so easy? Would Lasun be able to claim as in the second epigraph that he "was able to touch that man?"

Beyond this level of rhetorics however, there is a definite point through which the second epigraph ties up with both *The Wedding Car* and *The Man Who Walked Away*, Osundare's second playscript. As one of the examples used to illustrate his argument on the relevance of Osundare's life to his poetry, Stephen Arnold has, in "A Peopled Persona: Autobiography, Post-Modernism and the Poetry of Niyi Osundare" cited an excerpt from a 1990 interview he had with the poet. In the excerpt, Osundare talks of how a man, having been fired from the job he has held for twenty years following the introduction in the mid eighties of the Structural Adjustment Programme in Nigeria, decided to commit suicide. Somehow, however, the man stumbles on Osundare's newspaper poem titled "Retrenched" and, having read it, decided to change his mind. He thought that "he shouldn't die and allow the enemy to triumph" (p. 156). The relationship between this incident and *The Wedding Car* is figurative. For somebody like Deremi to marry Chief Chamberlains' daughter will be ideologically suicidal. It is an event over which the enemies will rejoice. This is why Lasun warns him (Deremi) to "take care not to stumble", and why Tunji the best man accepts that though the pressure may be overwhelming, "victory lies in not yielding".

On its own, *The Man Who Walked Away* is a fictive anticipation of the event of the late eighties with the simple difference being that Deji, the central character in the play does not have the benefit of the insight that "Retrenched" has to offer. Read in another way, the poem which has now been included in *Songs of the Season*, the published selection from the "experimental weekly poetry column" in *The Nigerian Tribune* can be described as a re-written version of the playscript of 1979.

To be sure, the odds against Deji, are extremely enormous. The multi-national company with which he works launches the first assault by laying him off. The landlord follows suit by harassing him for not being able to pay his rents. Iya Agba the mother-in-law jeers at him for his inability to provide the basic needs of his family. At the night club, Chief Kogbade Jones, government contractor and imperialist ally announces boldly that he could not be bothered about the deprived of the earth. And, to cap it all, he is treated like a leper at the labour office. Very terrible experience, no doubt, but they seem hardly sufficient enough for somebody who has hope as his guiding philosophy7 to resolve to take his own life: somebody who is clear-headed enough to be able to distinguish between what is and what ought to be, who has an understanding wife and two extremely promising children; is it correct for such a person to die just like that? Osundare must have re-read *The Man Who Walked Away* in the eighties. He must have felt uncomfortable with the hero who simply chickens out and, as a consequence, must have decided to re-design Deji's fate. "Retrenched" ends with a four-line stanza, on a note of determination:

> My wife is wan, my kids are old
> The times are hard, but so my hear
> I will never die on the rubbish heap
> I've sowed my sweat, I deserve to reap. (p. 20).

It is important to make it clear that "The Man Who Walked Away" is not, everything taken together, a pessimistic play. As pointed out just a while ago, Deji has two extremely promising children and a highly determined wife. As light fades out slowly at the end of the play, Osundare takes time to make it clear that the three survivors will hold out firmly and strongly. Thus, as Abeke bursts out into profuse weeping following the confirmation of Deji's death on the news, she reaches out to Toyin and Sola, pressing "them close to her breast". The male child is not even bothered about the present. His face, as the stage instruction makes it clear "is dry, firm and far?" (p. 28).

The State Visit is by far the most ambitious of the three play-scripts.

It is also the most adventurous. In its adoption of the story-telling technique, Osundare betrays the influence on him of Femi Osofisan, his more accomplished playwright friend. And in its savage criticism of African dictators and the close depiction of their vices and absurdities, the script also reminds us of Wole Soyinka's *Opera Wonyosi* and *A Play of Giants*. The play, indeed, represents a consummation of the dreams conceived in the first two works, taking the reader, as it were, into the distance that Sola, the younger of Deji's two children in "The Man Who Walked Away" gazes at during the close of the play.

But unlike the two earlier works which have their actions played out in domestic environments, *The State Visit* utilises largely a public metaphor. Right from take-off, the audience is transformed into the epicenter of power. A fellow predator is being expected from a neighbouring jungle, a reason for which the lion of Yanke has summoned members of his family to a meeting. Osundare's sense of rage and indignation is very clear in the stage instruction.

The stage is set for a state cabinet meeting.[20] Downstage centre, somebody who looks like the head of state is seated on a throne-like chair with a prominent back rest and gold-plated arm rests. The head, chronically obsessed slumps in this monumental chair. His blood boils with the fire of idealism. And this is to the extent that he allows this to overwhelm him and bring down his art.

Take *The Wedding Car* as an example. The manner of ending that play represents a typical instance of deux ex machina. Chief Chamberlains', up till the last scene, has certainly been having his way. He is, as he would have put it, enjoying his hard-earned wealth. Part of this "enjoyment" is the expensive wedding ceremony that he has organized for his daughter. At the peak of this ceremony, two customs officials appear to effect the man's arrest – and for the simple offence of smuggling a car into the country!

The word "simple" has been so emphasized because the sociological environment of the play is one which permits such "highly - placed" people to get away with even greater offences. In fact, in the immediately preceding scene, we encounter three erstwhile idealists as they express their frustrations and despair. Tunji's words which end that scene talks of the difficulties of living in "a world of reactionary conformism which keeps beckoning you to come over to join in, to fall in line?" (p.37). What magical developments has then made the world to become so suddenly altered? From which planet have those two uniformed men descended that they could possess the temerity to disrupt such an important occasion?

Similar questions could also be posed regarding *The State Visit.*

Indeed, given the story-line up till the end of Act III, there is no Babalawo who, if consulted, would have risked predicting the kind of developments that the reader confronts in Act IV. This is because, up to that point, the lion of Yanke is still firmly in the saddle, he is still in absolute control. There is no information at all about the Trade Union Collective and no prior hint of an organized opposition. It is certainly salutary to propose a post-colonial alternative but it seems more important to be able to scientifically lead the readers along such direction.

It is necessary to establish an inter-section between the point made above and an even more fundamental weakness of Osundare's playscripts;

which weakness may not be unconnected with the fact of the Ikere-born author being instinctively a poet.

Like the novel, modern poetry is largely introverted, privately addressed, as it were, from the writer to the reader. Well, due to the heavy influence on him of his indigenous heritage, Osundare's own verses are presented in such a way that they could be accompanied with traditional musical instruments. Even so, most of the works still remain as poetry in the modern sense, they still remain essentially monologic, still lacking in actions and movements, the principal ingredients of drama.

The terms, "movements" and "actions," have been deliberately employed here especially against the more contextually popular word, dialogue. No doubt, dialogue is important to a play but it of itself does not constitute the drama. In fact, in the context of theatre, dialogue can become monologue especially if movements and actions do not propel it: movements and actions in the heart of an actor or actress, in-between actors and actresses and in between groups of actors and actresses.

To be sure, Osundare's playscripts possess great potentialities for actions. Clear evidences of this abound in the sharp oppositional relationships which often exist between his characters, in how he places heavy psychological burden on some of them and in the very clear contrasts he often draws between their principles and aspirations. The danger for monologism however arises in the process of sharing out the dramatic space. Deji, inspite of being the central character in *The Man Who Walked Away* exerts very little presence on stage; Lasun, Deremi and Tunji who, collectively, embody the alternative principle in *The Wedding Car* are consigned to the most peripheral position in the play while the Minister of Finance, the painter and the beggars are projected as both weak and helpless, a factor which explains their inability to achieve any real result in *The State Visit*. The problem of disproportionate representation is what leads to *deux ex machina*. Because the playwright is unable to sustain the dramatic action, he seeks recourse in easy solutions.

Be that as it may, Osundare's dramatic works are welcome addition to his poetic output. Inspite of the flaws highlighted, the scripts, taken together still hold out some promise. Thematically, they integrate with the poetry in exploring the possibilities of hope. Formally, they exploit and refine the resources of traditional heritage, fusing them with modern techniques. If only he would apply himself a little more to it, Osundare may just be on the way to recording some landmarks in the dramatic medium.

NOTES

1   The first paragraph of the advertisement for contributions to the present book reads in part: "This is introducing a book project on the poetry and life of Niyi Osundare, award wining Nigerian poet, essayist, playwright and human rights crusader. The book, tentatively titled 'The Total Poet', intends to explore Osundare's poetics"?

2   Stephen Arnold employs this description for Osundare in his article "A Peopled Persona: Autobiography, Post-modernism and the Poetry of Niyi Osundare" published in Shield, Ulla (ed) Autobiographical Genres in Airica (Mainz - Bayreuth), 1996.

3   In "Social Message of a Nigerian Playwright", Niyi Osundare declares that Femi Osofisan "is already on the way to doing for us (Africans) what Bertolt Brecht did for Europe." See *West Africa* Jan. 28, 1980: 147 – 150.

4   See Wumi Raji "A Feast of Reunion: Citation Read in Honour of Niyi Osundare at His Fiftieth Birthday Anniversary, 12 March, 1997." *ALA Bulletin: a Publication of the African Literature Association.* 24.2 Spring 1998.

5   In a 1990 interview with Stephen Arnold, Osundare, in answering a question on why he is a socialist, declares: "I think I have always had the tendency? I think I had practiced the socialism that I grew up to read about even before I was literate at all. I grew up in a communal situation. I never saw anybody starve. I never saw anybody have too much while the other person had nothing?"

6   In place of a prefatory note to Songs of the Market Place, Osundare's first collection of poetry, is the following quotation from Pablo Neruda: "I made an unbreakable pledge to myself: That the people would find their voices in my song." See Osundare, Niyi. *Songs of the Market Place.* Ibadan: New Horn, 1983: vii.

7   Part of the stage instruction at the beginning of "The Man Who Walked Away" reads "In the centre of the back wall is hung a cardboard chart on which the following is boldly printed: Motto – When Their's Life – Their's Hope. (author's emphasis). See Niyi Osundare "The Man Who Walked Away:" Unpublished manuscript.

REFERENCES

Arnold, Stephen "A Peopled Persona: Autobiography, Post-Modernism and the Poetry of Niyi Osundare." Ed. Ulla Shield. *Autobiographical Genres in Africa.* (Mainz - Africa Studien; Mainz - Bayreuth), 1996.

Osundare, Niyi "Social Message of a Nigerian Playwright" *West Africa,* Jan. 28, 1980: 147–150.

———. *Songs of the Market Place*. Ibadan: New Horn, 1983.

———. *Songs of the Season*. Ibadan: Heinemann, 1990.

———. *Village Voices*. Ibadan: Evans, 1984.

Osundare, Niyi. "The Man Who Walked Away." Unpublished manuscript.

———. "The State Visit." Unpublished manuscript.

———. "The Wedding Car." Unpublished manuscript.

Raji, Wumi "A Feast of Reunion: Citation Read in Honour of Niyi Osundare at His Fiftieth Birthday Anniversary, 12 March, 1997."*ALA Bulletin* 24.2 Spring 1998.

Soyinka, Wole. *A Play of Giant*. Ibadan: Spectrums, 1984.

L'ETAT CEST MOI? THE PREMIER PERFORMANCE OF *THE STATE VISIT*

Sola Olorunyomi

> Put my words in your left hand
> So they do not land in the stomach
> With the unwitting morsel
> Then plant them like yam seedling
> Which multiplies the original breed
>
> (Niyi Osundare, from *Village Voices*. Ibadan: Evans
> Brothers, 1984.)

Against the expectation of the audience, with eyes intent on the dimly lit stage, a trenchant and assertive voice rose from the back aisle:

> There is a land of Two Rivers, a land blessed with milk and
> honey, the softest of showers and the healthiest of sunshine.
> But a few men fouled up the milk, ...

This is the voice of the narrator (Charles Ihimodu) flagging off Niyi Osundare's *The State Visit*, premiered on January 12, 1997, at the Arts Theatre of the University of Ibadan. A students' production directed by Wale Oyinlola, the play takes on omnibus themes, detailing the reversals suffered by the people of "Yanke" – implying slaughter in Hausa language – and their quests to unfetter the strictures imposed on them by the state and a military regime. If this represents the abstracted trope, the sub-themes are played out in contexts of corruption, famine, rape and general abuse of power.

The narrator pre-empts the unfolding drama by nibbling at its essential features. The play opens with a cabinet session debating the coming visit of the Head of State of Wilama, partly because no one seems to be sure of the state of the nation's treasury. This generates deep passion among cabinet members. In view of the anticipated visit, the environment is to be tidied up, and beggars are to be cleared off the street. The visit does not take place eventually, but not until the civil society has been subjected to harassment and intimidation.

The first set of victims is indeed the lowliest of Yanke society: beggars and society's rejects; the students come in their tow, and all unsuspecting citizens too. Yanke's days of rage witness the most cynical interaction of state-civil society relationship. Evidence of this is amply demonstrated in the momentary demonic possession of state officials, and between the "Head" and Colonel Anapa, played by Adebisi Ademakinwa and Roland Ogidan respectively, the audience seemed to have acknowledged a familiar reality of the nascent African State.

Citizens of Yanke are however not cowed subjects; they contest the larger-than-life imagery of this dominance, and many are bruised in the process. In the tradition of a particularly symbolist representation, the painter becomes a self-crusading prosecutor on behalf of the people as he attempts to articulate their collective voice. He shuns an invitation to collaborate with state power by refusing to put his brush in the service of its representatives, he would not paint their pictures. Thundering against the cabinet session he says,

> There is no grace in your glitter, no wisdom in your 'ways'. To do your bidding, my brush would be coarser than the despot's moustache, its glide arrested in canvas-pit.

He continues,

> My hand stays rigid from powerback, my brush stiff, my paint congealed...My allegiance is not to those who order massacres and bath their lust in blood; not to them who eat the poor for lunch and their children for supper... My allegiance is to Truth...

Even at the instance of his arrest, his denunciation is undiminished. Says he:

> You murderer of the body, can you ever kill the spirit? You are
> a passing cloud. After you the rainbow shall come, and Earth's
> children shall see the light again. Shall see the light again.
> Shall see the light again. The children of light shall see the L-
> i-g-h-t a-g-a-i-n

And as his voice echoes and reverberates from outside and beyond the stage, the "Head", momentarily jolted by such unheard-of effrontery from a citizen, saunters across the stage in confusion.

A consistent refrain, also serving as a sub-text to the subject-matter through-out the performance, is the binary opposition of contending values, better cap-tured as the contest between dominance and marginality – with the latter also read as resistance. Massed against the citizenry (composed of social classes – including workers, students and the sub-culture of beggars) are diverse power blocks of the state instruments of coercion, both physical and psychological, together buttressing an ideology of acquiescence. These forces later emerge in the guise of police, soldiers, middlemen, the hyena himself, and religious pre-cepts.

This distinction is, however, not always manifest, as more subtle imageries from nature also power it on. These include the reference to "the Lion of Yanke," distant echoes of locusts and symbols of inanimate energies such as hills and rocks. The histrionics of costuming further buttress this distinction: the lean, forlorn look of the sub-culture contrast sharply to the obesity of state officials and their ostentatious attires. The drama of this contest is equally revealed in the dialogue of the beggars and the Ministers of the state. The latter come as a stock breed, identified only with their portfolios such as External, Agric, Finance and public morality against a more mobile, more dynamic set of beggars whom we encounter as Sule, Etim, Obi and Abeke. Whereas Cabinet officials stick to predictable registers and cliché, the beggars encounter reveals a process of healthy debate – even if they eventually arrive at some sort of consensus like the 18th century French revolutionaries. The revolutionaries had pronounced wealth as theft. They proclaim, "I tell you, they are rich because we are poor. And for them to remain rich, we must remain poor!"

Perhaps the grimmest of the imagery of distortion is Obi's narration of how he became lame on account of being crushed by a giant piano (a birthday gift to his master's ward), while attempting to carry the musical equipment upstairs!

All through *The State Visit* otherness is highlighted in diverse contexts: in reg-isters as in their delivery; in histrionics as in their display; as well as all instances of talking back to supremacist ideology. The underlining reading here is underscored by the playwright's sense of some sort of aesthetic dialectics, a formula with which he had begun the play with its anecdote of "a land of two rivers." The contrast of anthems better illustrates the point. The state's anthem reads:

> Land of plenty, land of Wealth
> Showered with blessing, the best of health
> We carry our fate in our very hand
> Backward never in Yankeland...

This pretentious opulence is responded to by the beggars.

> We are the rags by the long roadside
> Who challenge the pompous wardrobe
> For them who have a lot to hide
> We are the thorn, the forgotten probe

The contest accentuates. Students and other social groups join the crowd. The police attempts a dispersal but the population, in high spirit and determination, will not budge. The police responds by firing into the crowd, even as everyone on the stage freezes at that moment. And, in fidelity to traditional story-telling style, the narrator returns to drive home the message and reminds the audience:

> What you have just seen is a small fragment of an unfolding dream. This drama goes beyond the curtain call. This play does not end here.

NOTE

1 *The man who Walked Away* and *The Wedding Car* are due for publication by the University Press Ltd., Ibadan, Nigeria in the coming months. *The Man who Refused to say* Yes is a radio play.

OSUNDARE,
BIO-BIBLIOGRAPHY

THE AMBIGUITY OF AUTOBIOGRAPHY: ANATOMY OF NIYI OSUNDARE'S MID-LIFE

Niyi Afolabi

My masks are many; un
countable sunlights name every line
of my figured face.
- Niyi Osundare (*Horses of Memory*)

Who will cure Africa's swollen foot
Of its Atlantic ulcer?

My question, Africa, is a sickle, seeking
ripening laughters in your deepening sorrows.
- Niyi Osundare (*Midlife*)

A baby antelope
Once asked her pensive mother:
        Tell me, mother
How does one count the teeth
Of a laughing lion?
- Niyi Osundare (*Waiting Laughters*)

In assessing Osundare's *Midlife* as a piece of ambiguous autobiography, I assume the premise that this is a pioneering work in the African autobiographical genre in the sense that not many poets have written their autobiographies in the verse medium. From Camara Laye's *The African Child*, Wole Soyinka's *Aké* or *Isara*, Mark Mathabane's *Kaffir Boy*, through Tanure Ojaide's *Great Boys*, prose has been the norm of autobiography even for renowned poets, while poetry remains a deviation from the norm. Whether this is a coincidental pattern or not is a matter for research but it is a fact that with the exception of the semi autobiographical poetry emerging from the contexts of liberation struggles in Portuguese-speaking Africa and former Apartheid South Africa, *Midlife* sets a historic precedent in African Autobiography.

And yet, the life and times of Osundare cannot be limited to the volume of poetry the versatile poet has modestly titled *Midlife* (1993). "Midlife" may imply pre-life and after-life depending on the depth of analysis. Indeed, there is a sense in which the title "midlife" is mystical for who is god enough to know when one phase of a life begins and when it ends? Perhaps only the poet. Osundare's life is multiple and for those who have the privilege to "know" him, the poet has the rare ability to celebrate both the living, the dead and the unborn through the passion of words for all people of goodwill. In appreciating this embodiment of love for humanity, and hate for injustice, we have to regress before *Midlife* and progress thereafter in order to capture the totality of Osundareness. In fact, it is very Osundaresque to lead us into ambiguity and mythmaking through his poetic mastery and skillful manipulation of language and laughter that have become a way of life. And the reader or listener of *Midlife* must be forewarned: we are entering the threshold of African philosophy, mythology and divination; only the initiated can uncover the mysteries encoded on these pages.

In the African worldview, it is often out of place to define "autobiography" as the life of an individual since our lives are so interconnected, interwoven and essentially collective. Perhaps this is reflected in Osundare's epigraphic allusion from Walt Whitman: "I am large, I contain multitudes" (*Midlife*, viii). Every true artist must be large enough for the world to share yet small enough for the world to reach. In this sense, Osundare combines with his wealth of knowledge the modesty, simplicity and humility that make him an inspiration to many aspiring artists and accessible to the people and curious critics he serves.

A confession regarding the pun in my title: I had started out intending to use *Midlife* as a case-study in poetic autobiography when in the course of revisiting Osundare's poetry I encountered traces of "autobiography" in his earlier works. From a singular objective, the purpose of this study becomes tripartite: explore "autobiographical" moments in Osundare's poetry, situate *Midlife* within the entire Osundare's poetic corpus, uncover the mythological and philosophical

dimensions of this "autobiographical" text and problematize the notion of autobiography by re-inserting the text into a "polybiographical" context. In terms of
poetic artistry and trajectory, Osundare's published works to date attest to a commonality of orality, politics and the centrality of memory. While the use and
manipulation of language may vary by evolution and sophistication, social equi-
ty and justice loom large in the mytho-political order of things and this is where
and why autobiography cannot but be ambiguous and problematic in Osundare.

THE AMBIGUITY OF AUTOBIOGRAPHY

The problematic of ambiguity in Osundare's autobiographical piece stems
mainly from his populist and engaging penchant which makes every word,
statement, interview, construct and comment deserving of careful analysis,
given its collective and political grounding. An ordinary conversation with
Osundare is quickly and tactfully geared away from him as a Nigerian artist
toward a political commentary on the fate of the world. In a recent conversation,
Osundare laments the "war-happy" posture of the world be it in Congo or in
Iraq and sums up almost regretfully: "The same intelligence we have for wag-
ing war can also be used to make peace." Although Osundare is not a citizen of
Congo or Iraq, it is that feeling for humanity that comes into play in his identification with the world becoming the "We" instead of an "I" whenever humanity is threatened and ill-treated.

In "A Peopled Persona," a seminal article on Niyi Osundare and the complexity of autobiography, Stephen Arnold combines personal interviews, copious Nigerian newspaper commentaries, interviews by others, critical reception
and poetic texts to render perhaps the most authoritative essay on Osundare's
life and works from the autobiographical perspective. Sharing the same concern I have about the complexity of this project, Arnold confesses the challenge
of taking himself up on his own intuition: "Osundare is probably Africa's most
public and selfless contemporary poet. To pursue autobiography in his work
makes as much sense as going on a biology field trip to the deserts of the moon"
(*Autobiographiques*, 1997: 147). Arnold's initial skepticism is understandable for
a serious student of Osundare, given the breadth of the issues this poet tackles
and the depth of commitment, which comes before the self. Although the exploration of autobiography in Osundare is problematic, it is not impossible.

If a working definition of autobiography is anything to go by, "the story of one
own's life written or dictated by oneself," it captures the total import of the col-
lectiveness that Osundare stands for. To parody this definition, I suggest that
Osundare's autobiography is "the story of many lives dictated by others" since
he is compelled to be the voice of the voiceless villagers, the warrior against

injustices of the Earth, and the ear when all hell breaks loose in the market place. In the same vein, Osundare is the clarion call in the Ivory Tower, the guardian of history in metaphorical and local Bastille, the passionate singer of the songs of the seasons, a constant nib in the pond even during moments of reflection through *Moonsongs* and *Midlife*, a provider of solace, hope and resilience in waiting laughters and horses of memory.

In the same vein, Philippe Lejeune's definition of autobiography as "the retrospective narrative in prose that someone makes his own existence when he puts the principal accent upon his life, especially upon the story of his personality" (Folkenflik 1993: 13) becomes inadequate applied to Osundare. In the first instance, while personality and politics may run through his poetry, the essentializing notion of "retrospective narrative in prose" excludes Osundare's attempt at "retrospective poetry" since he composes in poetry and not in prose. Even the notion of putting primordial importance on his "own life" negates the very communal spirit upon which African existential belief is predicated.

One is then left with the most compelling reflection on autobiography by Osundare himself as articulated in an interview with Stephen Arnold:

> A poet of my category is problematic in terms of autobiography. Because of the kind of culture I was brought up in. I was reared in a collective culture and I was socialized into the collectiveness of the culture itself. In the kind of society we are in, the "I" of the person is also the "I" of the other person. So this configuration of "I"s is really what makes up the society. This is not saying that there was no individuality in Africa at the time I grew up. It is just that everybody believed the public fate depended upon personal commitment and personal duty. Now my own birth itself cannot be personal... This is why the "I" becomes just one angle of perceiving a major public issue; it doesn't personalize the issue all that much, although it doesn't remove the individual element. Not every poet responds the way I respond. Certainly the "I" here is fictive, ideological, political construct, and in the end the "I" is a mask... So I think it is time we began to make some kind of case for the African autobiography as unique... That means African autobiography subverts in some way the expectations we have derived from our knowledge of Western autobiographies. The African "I" is different. (p. 158)

The case for the ambiguity of autobiography in the African context is laid out here in no unmistakable terms. It is summed up by the notion of the "I" as a mask where it is possible to assume many voices and subjects in order to accomplish the people's mission through collectivized imagination. In the case of Osundare, not only is the "I" ambiguous, it is interchangeable with "We" as we see in his body of poetic works. A cursory look at selected works reveals an interconnectedness of autobiography with elements of collectivity and memory.

MEMORY, COLLECTIVITY AND AUTOBIOGRAPHY

Before the advent of *Horses of Memory* (1998), Osundare's poetry has always appropriated Yoruba verbal art into a popular consciousness which never ceases to combine individual artistic talents with collective memory. In this combination, autobiographical elements abound although usually not of a personalized nature. In a Lecture, "Stubborn Thread in the Loom of Being: The Writer as Memory of the World," Osundare reflects on the imperative of memory for any writer and the world:

> ... memory is a complex phenomenon whose degree and intensity vary from writer to writer. Very broadly we can distinguish between passive memory which is basically a reservoir of impressions, mostly residual, mostly dormant, retained by the individual or community, and active memory which is those impressions in dynamic recall. The second category shares the same borders with remembrance, the enabling correlative of memory. Both categories find transitive matrix in the act of reminding... (p. 40)

In distinguishing between active and passive memories Osundare highlights one of the essential characteristics of human nature, the capacity to choose what to remember and what to forget, what to remember actively or passively. In that process, memory becomes a weapon, be it individual or collective, of manipulating history and posterity through deliberate erasure or distortion of historical events as well as conscious amnesia. That is why Osundare is quick to note that social memory is more reliable and durable hence the need to ensure that this "communal baby is not thrown out with the bath water of oblivion" (p. 41).

In the same lecture, Osundare remembers his response to a journalist who questions him on his overall purpose as a writer:

> My answer? To make the world a smaller place: to shrink up
> the seas, level all intruding mountains, bridge all gulfs, put a
> lamp in every tunnel. To write in such a way that every human
> being irrespective of race, creed, sex, and age will stand tall
> and proud in it. Above all, to remind humanity of the tortu-
> ous, avoidable oppressive journey so far, and make sure it does
> not forget. (p. 40)

This confessional statement, like his vocational testament in "Ars Poetica," captures the political commitment of Osundare as a writer not only of his native Nigeria but also of the world. In "shrinking the seas" and "bridging the gulfs," the poet-scholar sees the world as a village where all human beings must be cog-nizant and reminded of past horrors that continue to haunt us.

In "A Reunion" (*Village Voices* [1984]), memory travels back in time as a real-ity of the present compels compassion for a former classmate who is a victim of a twist of fate that befalls many Nigerian youth: dashed hopes and dreams in the face of lacking financial and educational opportunities. This poem provides a powerful example of ambiguous autobiography as the poetic voice combines the "We" with "I" and "You" throughout the poem. Three movements are iden-tifiable in this poem: the early school days, the path of destiny and the aftermath. In the first, Osundare reminiscences on the beginnings of a reunion that start-ed out innocently: "We started school the same day /... together we parroted the ABC / till we scribbled our first broken letters / in the whiteman's tongue" (p. 27). In the second, Osundare sympathizes with this former classmate address-ing him directly: "After so many years / here you are, scorched like a sponge / granite hands and back bent / by toil and want /... stooping to "sir" me" (p. 28), adding apologetically, "So many things have stood between us / so many I can-not count all" (p. 28).

Finally, Osundare returns once again to the collective "we," identifying with the fate of his former friend and urging for the breaking of the wall of such inequalities:

> We must smash this wall
> built of the inequities
> of class and crime
> then shake new hands
> over the ashes of severance. (p. 29).

The question then is: whose "autobiography" is being told in "A Reunion"? That of the poet or of his friend? In a sense, the ambiguity is consistent with the poet's collective consciousness as it is rewarding in the enactment of two contrastive lives that are interwoven by sheer circumstance of destiny, time and place.

The political consciousness of Osundare has never been in question since most of his poetry is geared toward the plight of the common people. In *A Nib in the Pond* (1986) in which the poet dedicates a considerable number of his poems to political, artistic, and progressive social figures, "I am the Common Man" (*Selected Poems*, 24–25) may be considered a confessional poem. Adopting the Yoruba traditional praise song approach, Osundare turns the usual praise into a sarcastic song of abuse as he enumerates the predicament of the "common man": "I / am the base element," "I / am a housing problem," only to end the poem in a stoic self-dignity and renewed vigor against oppression:

> Unfellable
> Like a tree with a million roots
> I will shake the earth
> with giant fruits
> lading the four winds
> with seeds of change. (p. 25).

In other earlier poems especially from *The Eye of the Earth* (1986), the poetic "I" actually becomes the "I" of the Earth as if the poet is playing a dialogic game with the "I" and the "Eye". In addition, the poems are multivoiced in that while in some poems the persona is "I," in others it is "We," "Our" or "They". The persona in "What The Earth Said" is actually the voice of the Earth enumerating and exposing multiple injustices of its inhabitants:

> I have seen
>> native executhieves hold fort for alien wolves
> I have seen
>> labouring mouths famish like desert basins
> I have seen
>> factorylords roll in slothful excess
> I have heard
>> backs creak on heartless machines
> I have felt
>> lungs powdered with asbestos death. (p. 46).

When contextualized within the corrupt Nigerian political reality of the 80's, the coded characters self-define through mirroring images and juxtaposition such as "executhieves" and "alien wolves," who are contrasted with "labouring mouths" and "asbestos death" in order to heighten the effect of the indictment against political brutality and indifference. The persona represents the voice of the people and the memory of the times while the individuality of the poet is technically minimized and collectivity maximized. The oppressive "wolves" in sheep's clothing, the multinational companies who force "Structural Adjustment Programs" (SAP) on Nigeria resulting in the devaluation of the Nigerian currency, thus making life unbearable for many, are as guilty as their Nigerian collaborators who sell the country cheaply to fatten their own selfish pockets.

"They too are the earth" is a reminder of the collectivity echoed in "A Song for Ajegunle" where the poet points to the squalor and decadence of Ajegunle, a poor neighborhood in Lagos metropolis. The poetic voice invites the listener to identify not only with the "I" of the Earth but with the "They" of the Earth, the wretched and the downtrodden of the country, but of the world. All those who are too "poor" to have a voice, too silenced to speak or sing, and if they do sing, whose song is a subservient anthem of begging:

> They too are the earth
> the swansongs of beggars sprawled out
> in brimming gutters
> they are the earth
> under snakeskin shoes and Mercedes tyres. (p. 45).

Through ambiguous "autobiography," Osundare makes a call for compassion with the oppressed while ridiculing oppressors.

Returning to the "I" in "Farmer-Born," the poet-persona delves into autobiographical detail of his background as a son of a farmer, the attributes that accompany such an upbringing, and how as a poet, he transforms this knowledge of the earth/Earth into cutlass and cudgel of the Word:

> Farmer-born peasant bread
> I have traced the earthworm's intricate paths
> on the map of dawn
> heeded dew-call to the upland farm
> and, sun-sent, have sought iroko refuge
> at hungry noons. (p. 43).

Far from being a simple poetic osmosis between his upbringing and his art, Osundare's multivalent technique makes ample use of memory and consciousness in this rendition and questioning of the life of others as opposed to his. To be "farmer-born" is one thing, to be "bred" as a farmer is another and the poet-persona combines this duality in his poetic consciousness. The analogy between the farmer who cultivates the land and the poet who composes on and about the land is implicit and well interwoven. At the same time, such tellurian awareness makes individualism almost impossible.

if autobiography is not ambiguous in the examples discussed so far, we only need to consult with *Waiting Laughters* (1990), a "long song in many voices," in order to appreciate the optimistic vision of a poet whose autobiography is practically writing itself through his selfless works. The structural interplay between waiting and laughter allows for myriad possibilities of questioning the dilemma of Africa which he assumes as a burdened and agonized poet of the people:

> What happens to the tendril which waits too long
> In the furnace of the sun
>
> What happens to the song which waits too long
> In the labyrinth of the throat
>
> What happens to the prayer which waits too long
> Without an amen
>
> What happens to the face which waits too long
> without the memory of a mask
>
> What happens to LAUGHTER which waits too long
> In the compost of anguished seasons?
>
> What....? (p. 94).

I suggest that this long interrogation captures Osundare's subconscious ideological task in the apparently optimistic long poem. The art of waiting is challenging and painful enough to not speak the truth about Africa's predicament. Through the primary prism of Nigeria and the three-decade military nightmare which continues to disenchant us as a people, *Waiting Laughters* is that timely double-edged solace which on the one hand, preaches hope and on the other, warns of the possibility of explosion. Echoing Langston Hughes's "What happens to a dream deferred?" Waiting Laughters is a subdued anger which then makes the title either affirmative or interrogative. Artistically speaking, it takes the "memory of a mask" to recollect the imprints of past events in Nigeria in particular and Africa at large, hence Osundare becomes the "memory" and the "mask" at the same time, Osundare's theoretical and political question in this long poem is answered in the very last movement when the poet painfully confesses:

> Our laughter these several seasons is the simper-
> Ing sadness of the ox which adores its yoke. (p. 97).

Only to add with a contrastive and declarative effect:

> A boil, time-tempered,
> About to burst. (p. 97).

The plurality of "laughters" in the title and its singularity toward the poetic conclusion is noteworthy. The many voices the poet-persona employs to conceal his own voice are fused into one collective voice when laughter becomes possessively "our". Even in this betrayal of the subconscious, laughter, the positive anecdote to sadness and weeping, is a shared experience. While the poet is unable to focus on self, he seems content with his place as the voice and memory of the people, the modern griot who is both the "horse of memory" and the "memory of the horse" as captured in his 1998 volume, *Horses of Memory*.

In *Horses of Memory*, Osundare celebrates memory, history and remembrance while at the same time engaging the image of Africa as a "proverbial nanny goat" which has been subjected to many seasons of tribulations and errors. Osundare occasionally interchanges the poetic "I" with "We," reminding his audience of the role of remembrance and the collective responsibility of memory as in "We shall remember":

> We shall remember
> We shall remember
> For the hunchback cannot forget his burden. (p. 40).

The hunchback is a vivid metaphor for contemporary Africa. Given the visibility and immensity of his burden, he represents multiple symbols and implications for the society at large: the burden of Africa, the burden of the writer, and that of memory. It is this concern for Africa's burden that the poet evokes in "Africa's memory" asking why Africa's historical artifacts and memories are decorating different museums and private homes in major world cities outside the continent:

> I ask for Oluyenyetuye bronze of Ife
>> The moon says it is in Bonn
> I ask for Ogidigbonyingbonyin mask of Benin
>> The moon says it is in London
> I ask for Togongorewa bust of Zimbabwe
>> The moon says it is in New York
> I ask
> I ask
> I ask for the memory of Africa
>> The seasons say it is blowing in the wind
>
> The hunchback cannot hide his burden. (p. 43).

In an apt colloquiall tone, the poet engages the moon, his muse, while lamenting the tragedy of Africa's impoverishment and dispossession.

If the memory of Africa is, figuratively, "blowing in the wind," the poet carries the burden of arresting that wind through the power of the word suggested by the title poem, "Horses of Memory," where Osundare draws on the symbols of galloping horses and the prints left behind by their hoofthrongs. Memory is likened to the remembrance triggered by the noise of such gallops. In a binary structure, the poet lists images which trigger memory of one by the need of the other as in rain and drought, desert and sea, egg and hen, or even of the fate that awaits those who do not heed memory:

> The ram wanders without remembering
> it becomes an instant guest of the butchernife;
> the antelope jumps into an open trap,
> wondering why it left its eyes at home
>
> The nanny goat forgets its head,
> whipped countless times for repeated offenses;
> there is a simmering tale, still,
> in the hearth of a thousand seasons. (p. 130).

Although this volume has been inspired by the memory of the poet's late father, the variety of its aspirations reveals Osundare's sensibility in translating personal circumstances into artistic and ideological "Testament" as a poem of the same title confirms:

> I am a poet:
> my memory is a house
> Of many rooms. (p. 66).

Perhaps this ability to create mansions from a singular house of memory is what is perfected in the mythmaking and philosophising that are the thresholds of *Midlife*.

MIDLIFE AS POLYVALENT AUTOBIOGRAPHY

Of all the poetic works by Osundare to date, *Midlife* clearly demonstrates an autobiographical penchant, and yet, remains an ambiguous one. On a deeper structure, the volume is an in-depth examination of the golden age of Africa. *Midlife* must be understood in its multifaceted possibilities in which myth-making combines with philosophy and poetic mastery to provide a delicate theory in African tellurianism and divination. On the one level, *Midlife* is a piece of autobiography and on the other, it is a response to a claim as well as a contribution to the ranging controversies about the existence and validity of African philosophy.

The immediate reaction to *Midlife* for a reader unrooted in Yoruba cosmology is that of puzzle and awe. And this is the crux of the innovative dimension of Osundare's poetic evolution. Here, poetry is pretext, here, poetry is paratext, here, poetry is mythology. For those knowledgeable about Yoruba proverbial code, the saying that *L'owe, l'owe ni a nlu ilu agidigbo, ologbon ni njo, omoran ni imo idi e* (The beats of agidigbo drum resonate with proverbs, demanding wisdom from the dancer and perception from the interpreter) is the closest analogy to *Midlife*. The volume takes us on a long journey of mythmaking, pretending to acquaint the reader with Osun river and rocks, familiar landscapes and birthplace of the poet, but actually engaging us in a dialogue with his people, his humanity, his country, his continent and its philosophy. The movement continues in the poet's exposition of prison images where walls must be broken through many seasons of mystification and demystification, pausing to reflect about "midlife" and finally returning to the stoic image of the poet as a stubborn "caller at noon."

Structurally, the seven movements only hint at the mythological and philosophical dimension of the volume. While the structuring motif is the noon, a multivalent metaphor for mid-day, mid-life and mid-age, when the sun is still shining and one can take stock of the past while projecting the future, the long poem progresses into more mystifications with numbers, alphabets, and seasons especially in the "Diary of the Sun" and "Thread in the Loom". These two movements connect numerically to render the Yoruba divinatory number of sixteen. Seven is another significant number which implies completion as can be deduced from biblical allusion or even Yoruba notion of seven heavens and seven spirits where the power of mysticism, spirituality and "occultism" is believed to be at its catharsis. As a diviner and interpreter of seasons, the poet-persona is able to look through the eye of the sun in order to formulate his theory on the world that he sees as "bent" and also assumes the caretaker role of that same world: "I am mode and medium for its straightening" (p. x).

Confessing his ever-constant indebtedness to the Yoruba oral poetic tradition in the "Foreline," the poet sets the tone for the understanding of the multivocal drama and the riddle-laden patterning in *Midlife*:

This volume, therefore, is informed by an inescapably panoramic vision where voices are many, protean, even kaleidoscopic. In keeping with the oral poetic tradition whose inexhaustible lifespring I am for ever indebted to, poetry here is confession, declaration, reflection, play, struggle, vision... It is exchange, an unwavering engagement with the world. (p. x)

This explains the inter- and intra-variations in the seven movements from the viewpoint of structure, orality, memory and politics.

The first two movements, "Rocksong" and "What the River Said," capture familiar landscapes of the poet's place of birth, Ikere, providing the context for more daunting mythmaking. In paying homage to Osun river and rocks, the poet falls into a nostalgic mood using the metaphor of a "caller at noon" as a structuring motif. Only a caller at noon can look back in time to see how well-spent the day has been. The poet takes great interest in identifying himself as multivalent constructs: "caller at noon," "child of the rock," "child of the river," and "a running river." In the process of self-identification, he not only identifies with these images of the rock and the river, he becomes them. The enumerative patterning of "I am ..." echoes the *Oriki* tradition and the interconnectedness of place and naming. Autobiography here is double-edged and ambivalent for it weaves the story of Ikere with the poet's life. The poet-persona writes in "Rocksong":

> I am child of the river, child of the rock
> Child, of rocky hills holding hands
> Above the tallest roofs.

> Dawns are grey, dusks brown:
> Whoever craves the blue legend of Ikere skies,
> Let him turn his neck like a barber's chair,
> For here the rock is earth, the rock is sky;
> Squatters we all on the loamy mercy
> Of generous stones. (p. 11).

While the reader may be tempted to see this in a limited perspective, a further probe into this excerpt reveals an implied dialogue for when the poet says, "whoever craves the blue legend of Ikere skies, / Let him turn his neck like a barber's chair," he is actually involving the audience impersonally, though not in direct speech. This approach turns this praise of Ikere rocks and rivers into a universal phenomenon as in the lines: "Squatters we all on the loamy mercy / Of generous stones."

Continuing the celebration of his birthplace, Osundare in "What the River Said," craftily initiates his larger mythmaking agenda by introducing the "sixteen-flamed lamp" (p. 27) phenomenon where "Every flame a nail on Ifa's prodigious finger" (p. 27) thus suggesting the illuminative prowess of Ifa divination. And it is from this point on that the poet ceases to be an ordinary person for he has now invoked the powers of the night and divination in order to step into the thresholds of mysteries:

> Sixteen flames has the lamp
> Of She of the Luminous Eyes
> In one socket the Sun
> In the other the Moon
> Which mothers the grove of milky feathers. (p. 27).

The "She of the Luminous Eyes" is a metaphor for Osun river and Osun goddess whose attributes as symbol of justice and fertility echo the triumph of good over evil as well as of light over darkness. By foregrounding the divinatory number sixteen which refers to ceremonial lamps here, and seasons of the sun and of the moon later, the poet seems conscious of the overall composition of this validating treatise on African mythology.

As a response to the "subhuman" colonial representation of African personality, history and culture, the poet declares in the longest movement, "Human in Every Sense," that:

I am human in every sense
lover of life without regret
ample hips, the bouncing bosom
handsome lips alive with joy. (p. 37).

In this positive awareness of self derived from various appreciation there is an identification with nature such as water, river, fountain, sea and sky. The poet, in singing "the plenitude of being" (p. 39) and the "lavender of eternal fragrance" (p. 34), is cautious not to minimize the hardship of his people as in the "long droughts" (p. 43) and "avoidable plagues" (p. 43) but the same people seem to be tired of these negative images of life thus asking the poet, in a series of calls, to "Sing us a happy song, oh poet!" (p. 43), "Sing us sunny songs..." (p. 44), "Sing to us about bards..." (p. 45). Responding to these calls, the poet, festive, dancing, singing, and felicitous at the engaging drama, begins to prophecy in form of parables, proverbs and tales: "Every god is man / every man is god" (p. 48), "Empires rise, decline, and fall" (p. 49), "I am nothing / I am no thing (p. 54), finally urging vigilance ("see with your whole body" [pp. 51–53]) and perception in the midst of human vulnerabilities.

There is a sense in which the remaining movements combine, "Breaking walls" with "Midlife," and "Diary of the sun" with "Thread in the loom" given their respective indicting, celebratory, and mystical dimensions. The darkness of the dungeon, the silence, the murmurs, the "jagged visions" (p. 68), the "expired faiths" (p. 68) which characterize the prison scenes of "Breaking walls" in which "Mosquitoes brook the rap without a wink" (p. 66), "the sky is once upon a season" (p. 66), "the sky is a wilderness of barbed wire" (p. 66) and a Detainee's skin "comes off in scabrous ease" (p. 66), compare and contrast with "Life's elegy" (p. 92) and "anthem of Hope" that sum up the predicament of Africa's "eternal childhood" in "Midlife". Playing with synonymous variations of midlife such as "Midstream," "Midway," "Midflight," and "Midthrob," the poet evokes the past trials and tribulations of the African continent, heightening the effect of this evocation through interluding and structuring questions that are almost tragic in their cadence:

Who will cure Africa's swollen foot
Of its Atlantic ulcer?

My question, Africa, is a sickle, seeking
ripening laughters in your deepening sorrows. (p. 110).

The shift in perspective from the humanity of the poet to the predicament of his continent must be understood as operating within that same communal paradigm that makes individuality and autobiography ambiguous.

When the poet returns to mythmaking in "Diary of the sun" and "Thread in the loom," autobiography remains ambiguous if not completely anomalous. These two movements attest to Osundare's fascination with Ifá divinatory corpus, the repository of wisdom and knowledge in Yoruba thought. The reader is first struck by the use of alphabetic numbering, A through L in "Diary of the sun," and M through P in "Thread in the loom." Through mathematical curiosity, A through L adds up to twelve while M through P add up to four. On the whole, both movements add up to sixteen, forcing the question: Are these months, seasons or movements of the sun? The answer comes in bits and pieces as one deciphers the enigma in the text when the poet recognizes *Midlife* as "masks," "acts," and "stage-centre" (p. 74). Other clues range from the identification of "d" that ties with the fourth month of the year such as April in the lines, "the grasshopper's yellow corpse awaits / the green hearse of April's unsure shower" (p. 76) or "e" identified as "alphabet of the sun" (p. 77).

In the intertwined process of mystification and demystification, the poet identifies with memory as the lasting "footprints in the dust" (p. 77), through the intermediary of the sun who "knows the geo-graphy of History" (p. 81) while the "wound" of the poet is considered a "map with bleeding rivers," struggling as a "fable maker" (mythmaker) to "mould new branches towards the sun" (p. 80). Mythmaking requires depth as well as space in order to demystify myth, hence the poet's yearning for such a space where his creativity is not limited or stifled:

> I long for open spaces
> For a sun which springs from a sea of shadows
> For the eye which unbinds the sky
> In infinite visions
>
> I long for open spaces. (p. 86).

The sun is sometimes interchangeable with the "eye" or "I" of memory as the gatekeeper of History and it is in this sense that when the poet asks for open spaces, it is well within reason that he is referring in part, to limitless possibilities of the sun which reaches the entire world with its infinite and solar energy. The interconnectedness between the poet, the sun and memory is solidified and heightened in the boastful challenge against "man slaying monsters" (p. 105) when the poet makes a call for unity and courage in the face of "tears which share borders / of waiting laughters" (p. 108):

> Trees which join leaves will form a forest
> rivers which join beds will form a sea;
> if a cocky hen dares an army of roaches
> it will not go back without a wounded beak.
> I am a long, sharp knife emboldened by the sun
> I glide clean and clear through the jungle of wax. (p. 105).

The parable of the "cocky hen" and "an army of roaches" is quite enlightening. It echoes the triumph of the underdog over the oppressor as well as hints
at what befall evildoers when good people unite. In the light of Osun's complementarity principle of creation and justice, this allusion to collectivity confirms the ambiguity of autobiography, for individualism may be likened to the
"cocky hen" when faced with the metaphorical army of roaches.

The exploration of ambiguity of autobiography in Osundare's poetry will be
incomplete without a few words on his use of language, the central tool in mythmaking. The preoccupation with justice often compels Osundare to create satiric situations, through parables, proverbs and folktales and riddles in which the
masses overcome the oppression of the tyrant in a complex projective mode.
Using the "power to send words on errands" (p. 55), these situations are sometimes hyperbolized for comic effect as in "the testicle of the tyrant inflated / in
every street like yuletide balloons / of playing children" (p. 103). Perhaps these
dialectical formulations add to the complexity and ambiguity of autobiography
in Osundare for whom "the song stands in the marketplace, / breathing bread,
breathing bullets" (p. 103). The personified song here is the polyvalent voice of
the poet, producing "bread" of life and yet "bullets" for the war against evil. This
betrays the revolutionary and regenerative spirit of a poet that cannot be confined into any singular autobiography.

Continually drawing from collective memory, Osundare constantly renews
his poetic art which is now gearing toward mythic proportions even in "autobiographical" terms. His contributions to poetic innovation in Africa have earned
him many accolades, of which Ayo Banjo's is exemplary:

> I often think that by working so conscientiously at the interface
> between indigenous literature and English literature, Osundare is
> doing for Nigerian poetry of English expression what Achebe has
> done so brilliantly for the Nigerian novel of English expression.

Until Osundare writes a less ambiguous autobiography in prose, the exploration of autobiography in his works will continue to be problematic given the multiplicity of the voices he employs and the polyvalency of his Mid-Life.

BIBLIOGRAPHY

Adagbonyin, Asomwan S. *Niyi Osundare: Two Essays and an Interview.* Ibadan: Sam Bookman, 1996.

Arnold, Stephen H. "A Peopled-Persona: Autobiography, Post-Modernism and the Poetry of Niyi Osundare." Eds. Janos Riesz and Ulla Schild. *Genres Autobiographiques /Autobiographical Genres in Africa.* Berlin: Dietrich Reimer Verlag, 1996: 141–165.

Bamikunle, Aderemi. "The Development of Niyi Osundare's Poetry: A Survey of Themes and Techniques." *Research in African Literatures* 26.4 (1955): 121–137.

———. "Niyi Osundare's Poetry and the Yoruba Oral Artistic Tradition." *African Literature Today* 18 (1992): 54–59.

Ezenwa-Ohaeto. "Patterns of Orality: Niyi Osundare." *Contemporary Nigerian Poetry and the Poetics of Orality,* vol. 45. Bayreuth: Bayreuth African Studies series, 1998: 150–170.

Folkenflik, Robert, ed. *The Culture of Autobiography: Constructions of Self-Representation.* Stanford: Stanford University Press, 1993.

Ngara, Emmanuel. *Ideology and Form in African Poetry.* London: Heinemann, 1990.

Okpewho, Isidore. *African Oral Literature.* Bloomington: Indiana University Press, 1992.

Osundare, Niyi. *The Eye of The Earth.* Ibadan: Heinemann, 1986.

———. *Moonsongs.* Ibadan: Spectrum, 1988.

———. *Waiting Laughters.* Lagos: Malthouse, 1990.

———. *Selected Poems.* Oxford: Heinemann, 1992.

———. *Midlife.* Ibadan: Heinemann, 1993.

———. *Horses of Memory.* Ibadan, Heinemann, 1998.

———. "Stubborn Thread in the Loom of Being: The Writer as Memory of the World." *ALA Bulletin.* 15.4 (1989): 40–43.

Spencer-Walters, Tom, ed. *Orality, Literacy and the Fictive Imagination: African and Diasporan Literatures.* Michigan: Bedford Publishers, 1998.

———. "A Song for Ajegunle." Eds. K E. Senanu and T. Vincent. *A Selection of African Poetry.* London: Longman, 1988: 311–312.

OSUNDARE: A MAN FOR ALL SEASONS[1]

Mobolaji E. Aluko

This is a paper on a distinguished alum of our beloved Christ's School, Ado-Ekiti, written for the alumni who are honoring Osundare. It is a task that I love very dearly, so I shall proceed expeditiously. To be honored with such an award, you must have attended Christ's School and passed in the course that you entered the school to attend (there is no "emu kankan" allowed). You must have had a distinguished career long afterward. I hope that you will agree with me that those are the three basic requirements, in addition—of course—to the fact that you must have had no blemish, like imprisonment for high crimes and misdemeanors, registered against your name. Let me assure this gathering that Professor Oluwaniyi Osundare, alias "Olu Rasco, Chief Agendo," passes all of these tests.

OSUNDARE'S CHRIST'S SCHOOL CREDENTIALS
You will have to pardon me if and when I get rather personal in some of the accounts. Senior Olu Osundare entered Christ's School in January 1967—I was then in Form Two—having completed his school certificate with a Grade One Distinction at one school not too far away, the Amoye Grammar School in Ikere-Ekiti. All of us will remember that Amoye was well known for its corps of top students in the Liberal Arts. They still studied Latin then, if I remember cor-

rectly. Olu Osundare was the embodiment of such an excellent reputation. That year, I knew of at least two other students who came from Amoye with Olu Osundare: Senior Olu Omonije (alias "Efori Bale Fun Mi o! Orisa Ogun Ti D'Ode O Eh!") and Senior Ajayi (alias "Wasco, Tissue!").

Within the first week of his arrival at Christ's School, Osundare's life intersected with mine. First, we were in the same block, Block 4B of Dallimore House, and would remain so through out his stay in Christ's School. (In fact, I was one of a few Christ's School students who did not change their rooms through out their stay in Christ's School; no strings pulled.) Secondly, Osundare walked up to me one day and anointed me his College Brother. He claimed me for himself, literally.

I was shocked! First, not all Form Two students had College Brothers, so not all faced its associated indignities, like fetching a pail of water each morning for your Senior College Brother—basically, having to be at his beck and call. It was nothing more than fagging, a benign form of slavery, and I was hoping that I would be one of the lucky few to escape it in my second year. Secondly, I did not know this guy, so I was not quite sure whether he would protect me from marauding seniors. In my Form One, I had as my college brother the inimitable Tunde Njoku, an Upper Six prefect then, who had protected me like a mother hawk protects her children. I needed a lot of protection from seniors those days, for I was short in height and had a long mouth! I saw immediately in Senior Osundare a neatly dressed gentleman who walked with a rather measured gait. He spoke English with a similarly measured cadence. I felt that I could tolerate him. Anyway, I had no choice in the matter, so I became his college brother.

Three things seared into my brain about Osundare right away: his handwriting, his studiousness, and his command of English. I would sometimes look at his lecture notes and say, "Man, how can someone write so neatly?" Secondly, if there was someone who convinced me HSC was not for me, it was Senior Osundare. He was always reading and studying, but I never saw him break a sweat on the sports field. I knew that with my devotion to sports and other nonacademic matters, I wasn't going to read that hard in HSC only to get an A-B-B or so that he got in HSC, and that was in Arts subjects! Luckily, I truncated my HSC career by doing Prelims at the University of Ife in 1971. Finally, his command of English was simply scintillating.

I could never forget the day in 1968 when in the HSC Lecture Theater, Mr. Silas Ajayi, Principal of Ado Grammar School, came to give a lecture. I forget the topic of the lecture now or what question Osundare asked after Mr. Ajayi's speech. Mr. Ajayi was no English slouch himself, but Osundare's question was so esoterically constructed, and the number of 10-letter English words so profuse that after a long pause, Mr. Ajayi simply said, "Osundare, I think you must have swallowed a dictionary!" The whole lecture theater erupted, and I don't think Mr. Ajayi ever got to answer that question until today. Perhaps he did not understand it.

That very day, I resolved that at some point in my Christ's School career, I would repeat Osundare's English feat. I had my chance four years later, at a Literary and Debating Society event in the School Quadrangle. The topic was on "The Place of Women is in the Kitchen." Although I was not one of the debaters, when it came the turn of students in the audience to make a contribution, I raised my hand, cleared my throat (I had been looking for the right word in the dictionary all day), and said, "It is rather atavistic to claim that women should be confined to the kitchen...," to the wild applause of students! Mr. Oloketuyi, who was the MC then, calmed the students down and asked me to proceed. I picked up where I stopped, again to another round of "Ehhhhhhh..." from the students! Heartened, I had succeeded in my quest to emulate Osundare, but it was rather short-lived because a classmate of mine (I believe it was Titi Ogunkua) came right after me to say that I had just mouthed "a farrago of nonsense," again to wild applause.

What about Osundare's literary prowess even then? Drama? In 1968, Osundare single-handedly adapted, if not wrote, the English play that Dallimore House acted in the Inter-House Competition. I remember that I had a small part in the play, and my wife's sister Ms. Ilugbusi ("Suzanne, Suzanne") was also a major actress in it. The play came second by one or two points to Mason Houses's "Androcles and the Lion" (I think), and I can remember very clearly that Osundare wept bitterly that night for the loss.

Privately, to Osundare and myself, that year was more famous for the Yoruba competition. His friend, Oludaisi Omonije, who later became my mother's direct colleague at the University of Ife Registry, earned the moniker *Efo ribale fun mi o!*—"bow down for me o"—because in one of the plays he was the ever-present Oba of the town who insisted in song that his subjects bow down for him. It was also that same year that Wasco acted the tough guy in the Harding House play, in which he declared "Egungun eja ni, Egungun eja ni, ko jo t'ada-ba, ko jo t'orofo, egungun eja ni!" to the wild guffaws of Christ's School students who could not take their eyes off the "yam" behind his well-endowed legs and biceps. And you will remember one Senior Ojo Joseph who, it is claimed, made Bishop House lose the Yoruba competition for saying "And now, mo ti ri opa oye mi," since English words are prohibited in the Yoruba competition.

You all remember the prestigious national John F. Kennedy essay contest, which our HSC students take part in throughout Nigeria. It was a foregone conclusion that Osundare would win. He did in 1968. I do not now remember how he did in the national level of that competition, but he is free to fill us in on it.

That same year, he won the First Prize in the Western State of Nigeria Poetry Competition.

Following his HSC year in Christ's School, Osundare taught at Christ's School before proceeding to the University of Ibadan to study English. This was now 1969, and it was during that year that he assisted that left-handed Englishman par excellence, Mr. Christopher Ward, in writing the only history of Christ's School, from 1933 to 1969, ever put in print so far, which I hold in my hands now. On the acknowledgement page, Mr. Ward (who taught English, leaving an impression on me too that I would never forget) says, "Thanks must also go to Mr. O. Osundare, who, in addition to contributing material for the years 1966 to 1969, has been the Editor's right hand man at every stage of the book's development." My impression is that had Mr. Osundare not been a mere student then; his name would have been placed alongside Mr. Ward's as co-editor of this fantastic history of our great school. (I have made photocopies of the 130-page book, and can make it available to interested persons).

Oluwaniyi Osundare graduated from the University of Ibadan with a BA in English in 1972, an MA in English from Leeds University in 1974 (I guess he followed Wole Soyinka!), became an Assistant Lecturer at the University of Ibadan upon graduation , and then finally obtained a PhD in English from York University, Toronto, Canada in 1979. His Masters Project was on "Yoruba Proverbs: A Study in the Problems of Translation", and his PhD thesis was on "Bilingual and Bicultural Aspects of Nigerian Prose Fiction."

His work since returning to Nigeria after his PhD has been breath taking, fulfilling that long-held adage that a PhD is merely a measure of persistence, not of scholarship, and that scholarship really begins after the PhD. He has won at least ten major literary prizes and awards, including a major book prize and letters of commendation by the BBC in 1981; he won the Association of Nigerian Authors (ANA) Poetry Prize in 1986, in the same year that he jointly won the overall Commonwealth Poetry Prize. In 1991, he won the Noma Award (Africa's most prestigious Book Award); in 1994, he won the Cadbury/ANA Poetry Prize (Nigeria's highest poetry prize), and most recently in 1998, he won the Fonlon/Nichols Prize for Excellence in Literary Creativity. He has also made significant contributions to Human Rights in Africa.

He is an academician through and through, having taught at York University, in Canada, and winning the Fulbright-Scholar in Residence at the University of Wisconsin-Madison. He was also a professor and the chair of the English Department at the University of Ibadan. Currently, he is a professor at the University of New Orleans, a second stint for him since he was also there from 1991–1992.

He has given lectures, written guest columns for newspapers in and out of Nigeria, served on the editorial board of countless book companies and media outlets, gone on poetry promotion tours, and been a resident artist in the USA, Canada, Dakar, the UK, Japan, Germany, Kenya, and of course, in Nigeria. All these honors and distinctions were capped recently with an honorary doctorate— PhD Honors Causa—at the University de Toulouse. In February 1999, at Le Mirail, Toulouse, France, he delivered a stirring lecture titled "Thresholds and Millenial Crossings."

In that Lecture, without naming names, he referred to Christ's School (where I guess he began to learn his French under the hapless "Baba Gadi," Reverend Gardner) as a "much older, much richer school" than Amoye Grammar School—and he was damned right.

He has written more than 12 volumes of poetry (books), 25 contributions to books or chapters in books, 4 plays, 10 travelogues, 18 articles and essays, 2 monographs, 6 reviews, 7 forewords to other peoples' books, and countless other literary contributions too numerous to mention any further. And when people begin to write critical responses to your own work (with your name in the title of their work), as at least 12 writers have done, or when people start to get their Masters and Ph.D. degrees based solely on your work, as at least five students have done, when you can speak Yoruba, English, Latin, French, and other strange tongues fluently, then you know that you are a person who has truly joined the pantheon of world-class scholars.

Let me end by adding one more personal thing that I have come to respect him for, his fight for human rights in Nigeria. During the dark Abacha period, 1993–1998, when it was most dangerous to speak out, I was forever impressed that Senior Osundare was one of those who stayed behind in Nigeria, who was NEVER cowed, and continued to speak out on the pages of the newspapers about tyranny in the land. He was very active in the academic staff union ASUU, and his poems and satires of the Nigerian system, some spiced with veiled references to Christ's School "Agidimo Hills" were biting. I am sure that only him can recount what he faced from Abacha's goons during those dark years. He has since come to tell me that he followed some of our own ceaseless contributions to the pro-democracy movement abroad just as I followed his contribution at home. Therefore, we share a mutual admiration of our society.

NOTES

1 Originally given as citation at the First Distinguished Alum Award of Christ's School Ado-Ekiti Old Students' Association, in Washington, DC, 1999.

OSUNDAREANA, 1976–1996

Bernth Lindfors

Niyi Osundare has been one of the shakers and movers in modern Nigerian literature. What follows is an attempt to pin him down and render him immobile by listing virtually everything he has written about anglophone African literature and about himself, virtually everything he has said in published interviews, and virtually everything others have written or said about him in print (excluding book reviews). Virtually everything, that is, up to 1996, for that's where my ocean of Osundareana stops. I'll have to cross the Atlantic again one of these days to catch up on his activities. I'm sure he's still shaking and moving, and I'll have to try to pick up all the rest of his pieces, wherever they may have fallen in these tumultuous times, so that I can put him back together again in a more stable form, transfixing him with the heavy glue of bibliographical accretions.

CRITICISM BY OSUNDARE

"Speech Narrative in Aluko: An Evaluative Stylistic Investigation." *Journal of the Nigerian English Studies Association* 8, 1 (1976): 33–39.

"Native, Serve Your River-God: The Poetry of Tanure Ojaide." *Greenfield Review* 5, 3–4 (1976–77): 62–66.

"Bilingual and Bicultural Aspects of Nigerian Prose Fiction." *Dissertation Abstracts International* 40 (1979): 2667A. (Ph.D. dissertation, University of York, Canada)

"Social Message of a Nigerian Dramatist." *West Africa* 28 January 1980: 147–50. On Osofisan's Once Upon Four Robbers and Morountodun.

"'As Grasshoppers to Wanton Boys': The Role of the Gods in the Novels of Elechi Amadi." *African Literature Today* 11 (1980): 97–109.

"La voie vers l'indépendance du Zimbabwe." *Peuples Noirs/Peuples Africains* 15 (1980): 23–30.

"From Oral to Written: Aspects of the Socio-stylistic Repercussions of Transition." *Journal of African and Comparative Literature* 1 (1981): 1–13.

"Caliban's Curse: The English Language and Nigeria's Underdevelopment." *Ufahamu* 11, 2 (1982): 96–107.

"Words of Iron, Sentences of Thunder: Soyinka's Prose Style." *African Literature Today.* 13 (1983): 24–37.

"Parables of Hope." *West Africa* 28 October 1985: 2268. On Rotimi's *Hopes of the Living Dead.*

"A Distant Call." *West Africa* 4 November 1985: 2313–14, 2316. On literary practice and literary awareness in Nigeria.

The Writer as a Righter: The African Literary Artist and His Social Obligations. Ife Monographs on Literature and Criticism, 4th Series, No. 5. Ile-Ife: Department of Literature in English, University of Ife, 1986.

"Style and Literary Communication in African Prose Fiction in English." *Topical Issues in Communicative Arts* 1 (1987): 134–67.

"I Don't Envy the Nobel Laureate." *West Africa* 24 August 1987: 1636. Soyinka is suffering the price of fame.

"The Poem as Mytho-Linguistic Event: A Study of Soyinka's 'Abiku.'" *African Literature Today* 16 (1988): 91–102.

"Ants of the Hill." *Newswatch* 14 March 1988: 42. Poetry readings at The Anthill, University of Nigeria, Nsukka.

"The Waves This Time." *Newswatch* 2 May 1988; 8–9. International Book Fair of Radical Black and Third World Books, London.

"'See London and Die.'" *West Africa* 18 April 1988: 692. Experiences in London.

"Bard of the Tabloid Platform: a Personal Experience of Newspaper Poetry in Nigeria." *Guardian* 22 June 1988: 10, 15; rpt. Eds. Stephen H. Arnold and Andre Nitecki. *Culture and development in Africa.* Trenton, NJ: Africa World Press, 1990: 1–47. On starting a poetry column in the *Nigerian Tribune* in order to reach a mass audience.

"The Earth, My Inspiration." *Newswatch* 12 September 1988: 7.
Joe Bruchac speaks about poetry and publishing.
"The Travails of Literary Awareness in Nigeria." *Review of English and Literary Studies* 5, 2 (1988): 91–100.
"Images of America." *Newswatch* 6 March 1989: 49–53.
Account of his year as a participant in the International Writing Program at the University of Iowa.
"Theatre of the Beaded Curtain: Nigerian Drama and the Kabiyesi Syndrome." *Okike* 27–28 (1988): 99–113.
Rotimi, Soyinka, et al.
"ANA Literature Prizes: A Rejoinder." *Daily Times* 1 July 1989: 21; *Association of Nigerian Authors Review* 4, 6 (1989): 24.
Response to anonymous article in *Daily Times* 24 June 1989: 17. Complains that poetry is being ignored by organizations sponsoring prizes. See reply by Osofisan below.
"Une nouvelle dimension du poète engagé." *Notre Librarie* 98 (1989): 77–81.
Moonsongs.
"25 Years After: Text and Counter-Text in African Literature." *ALA Bulletin* 15, 3 (1989):13–17.
Keynote address to 15th African Literature Association Conference, Dakar, 20–23 March 1989.
"Playhouse of History." *West Africa* 4–10 September 1989: 1463–64; NIGERIAN STAGE, 1, 1 (1990): 30–33.
On Sowande's TORNADOES FULL OF DREAMS.
"Stubborn Thread in the Loom of Being: The Writer as Memory of the World." *ALA Bulletin* 15, 4 (1989):40–43; GUARDIAN, 19 May 1990: 18; rpt. Eds. Femi Osofisan, Nicole Medjigbodo, Sam Asein, and G.G. Darah. *Proceedings of the International Symposium on African Literatures/Compte Rendu du Colloque sur les Litteratures Africains* 2–7 MAY 1988. Lagos: Centre for Black and African Arts and Civilization, 1991: 380–85.
"Memories of Iowa." *Daily Times* 9 December 1989: 10; 16 December 1989: 10; 23 December 1989: 10; 30 December 1990: 12.
Highlights of his participation in Iowa International Writing Program.
"Faces and Figures." *West Africa* 15–21 January 1990: 57; *Association of Nigerian Authors Review* 5, 7 (1990): 5.
Inaugural meeting of the Pan-African Writers' Association.
"Okara's Error." *Newswatch* 10 September 1990: 6.
While in public office, Okara did nothing dishonest. Hence, he is poor.
"Toni Morrison in Madison." *ALA Bulletin* 17, 1 (1991): 18–19.

"Artists and Scholars." *West Africa* 10-16 June 1991: 951.

Symposium on "The Arts in Contemporary Africa" at the University of Wisconsin at Madison.

"Squaring Up to Africa's Future: A Writer's Reflections on the Predicaments of a Continent." *Daily Times* 15 June 1991: 12–13; 22 June 1991: 12; *Guardian* 20 July 1991: 15.

"Songtime at Harbourfront." *ALA Bulletin* 17, 3 (1991): 3–4.
Readings at Toronto poetry festival.

"Possibilities of Hope." *Daily Times* 7 September 1991: 13; *West Africa* 7–13 October 1991: 1686–87; *ALA Bulletin* 17, 4 (1991):51–53; rpt. in German in *Literaturnachrichten* 31 (1991): 9–10; rpt. Ed. Don Burness. *Echoes of the Sunbird: An Anthology of Contemporary African Poetry*. Athens, Ohio: Center for International Studies, Ohio University, 1993: 128–31.
Noma Award acceptance speech.

"Festival of Renewal." *Newswatch* 23 September 1991: 50–51.
African poets at Rotterdam poetry festival.

"Of Prizes and Messianism." *West Africa* 2–8 December 1991: 2007; rpt. 9–15 December 1991: 2053–54; rpt. in German in *Literaturnachrichten* 32 (1992): 1–3.
Okri, Western criticism, et al.

"Poems for Sale: Stylistic Features of Yoruba Ipolowo Poetry." *African Notes* 15, 1–2 (1991): 62–72.

"Conversation with Syl Cheney-Coker." *Daily Times* 7 December 1991: 20–21.
Interview with Cheyney-Coker.

"The Caged Bird Sings." *Newswatch* 3 February 1992: 36.
On Maya Angelou.

"Untimely Eclipse." *Newswatch* 17 February 1992: 6.
Memorial tributes to Edith Ihekweazu and Donatus Nwoga.

"A Literary Testimony." *West Africa* 30 March 1992: 547.
Tribute to *West Africa* on its 75th anniversary. Includes autobiographical reminiscences.

"Ode to the Teacher's Son (Upon Reading ÌSARÀ, Soyinka's Voyage Around Essay)." *Guardian* 19 July 1992: B9.
Poem in tribute to Soyinka.

"Soyinka Interpreted." *Daily Times* 10 April 1993: 8.
On Oluwole Adejare's *Language and Style in Soyinka*.

"A Conversation with Don Burness." *Newswatch* 9 August 1993: 32–34.
Interview with Burness.

"Out of Banda's Gulag." *Newswatch* 18 October 1993: 39–40.

Interview with Jack Mapanje.

African Literature and the Crisis of post-structuralist Theorising. Ibadan: Options Book and Information Services, 1993; revised and rpt. as "How Post-Colonial is African Literature." Matatu 12 (1994): 203–16; rpt. Eds. Marlies Glaser and Marion Pausch. *Caribbean Writers: Between Orality and Writing.* Amsterdam and Atlanta: Rodopi, 1994: 203–16.

"A Dream Unfolding." *Newswatch* 20 December 1993: 36–37.

African Heritage Research Library.

"Sweden's Many-Sided Affair." *Guardian on Sunday* 26 June 1994: B4.

"Wole Soyinka and the Àtundá Ideal: A Reading of Soyinka's Poetry." Ed. Adewale Maja-Pearce. *Wole Soyinka: A Reappraisal.* Oxford and Portsmouth, NH: Heinemann Educational Books, 1994: 81–97.

"Literature and the City." *Glendora Review* 1, 1 (1995): 2–3.

On the difficulties of being creative in Lagos.

"Of Prizes and Literary Giants." *Glendora Review* 1, 1 (1995): 54–56.

"The World Around Kensaburo Oe." *Glendora Review* 1, 2 (1995): 5–8.

"See Lagos and Die." *Newswatch* 6 March 1995: 8–10.

"Healing Art." *West Africa* 5 June 1995: 894–95.

African literature is therapeutic.

"Literature in Cultural Diplomacy." *Newswatch* 16 October 1995: 11.

"Not an Internal Affair." *Newswatch* 19 February 1996: 6.

Hanging of Saro-Wiwa disgraced Nigeria internationally.

"The Longest Day." *Newswatch* 18 November 1996: 44–45; rpt. in *ALA Bulletin* 23, 1 (1997): 7–10.

On hearing news of Ken Saro-Wiwa's execution.

"African Literature Now: Standards, Texts and Canons." *Glendora Review* 1, 4 (1996): 25–31.

"Celebrating Soyinka." *Association of Nigerian Authors Review* October-December 1996: 26.

INTERVIEWS WITH OSUNDARE

Achema, Jonah. "Chaotic." *Newswatch* 12 December 1994: 18–19.

On the crisis in education in Nigeria.

Adebayo, Lanre. "'We must not return to the twilight zone': Interview with Niyi Osundare." *Daily Times* 14 January 1995: 8, 17; 21 January 1995: 17; 28 January 1995: 8.

Adebowale, Bayo. "48 Hours at Home with Niyi Osundare." *Gists: Authentic African Experience* 1, 3 (1995): 8–13.

Adedeji, Moses. "Osundare and the Battlesongs for Change." *Prime People* 29 September 1989:23.

Comments on his poetry and on Soyinka.

[Adeniyi, Dapo]. "Images of Japan: Niyi Osundare." *Glendora Review* 1, 2 (1995): 9.

On his visit to Japan to participate in an African Writers' Forum.

Adeniyi, Dapo, Tunde Olusunle, Hakeem Bello, and Segun Ayobolu. "Interview: Niyi Osundare." *Daily Times* October 1991: 14–15; *Association of Nigerian Authors Review* 6, 8 (1991): 24.

Adeniyi, Olayiwola. "In Africa, the writer wastes, says Osundare." *Guardian* 7 October 1995: 20.

———. "Though Wanted Abroad, This Egghead Will Not Brain-drain." *Guardian* 16 March 1996: 27.

On teaching and the literary climate in Nigeria

Ajayi, Lasisi. "'Our universe has disappeared.'" *African Concord* 20 May 1996: 18–19.

On deterioration of the Nigerian university system.

———. "'Education is a huge swindle.'" *African Concord* 31 May 1993: 14–15.

On the educational crisis in Nigeria.

———. "'We can't move forward with injustice.'" *African Concord* 24 June 1996:24–27; 1 July 1996: 30–31.

Ajibade, Kunle. "Singing for Life." *African Concord* 7 May 1990: 40–41.

———. "My Visions, My Style." *African Concord* 9 September 1991: 43–45.

———. "The Rocks Are My Bones." *The News* 25 October 1993: 44–46.

Akst, Florence. "Interview with Niyi Osundare about Poems in *The Eye of the Earth*." *BBC Arts and Africa* 675 (1986): 1–4; rpt. in *ALA Bulletin* 13, 1 (1987): 26–30.

Winner of British Airways Commonwealth Poetry Prize.

Alegbe, Ohi. "Unmasking the Moon." *African Concord* 5 December 1988: 42-43.

On MOONSONGS.

Anon. "Osundare Decries Writing Culture in Nigeria." *Daily Champion* 11 November 1995.

———. "Abacha has ruined Nigeria." *Tempo* 25 January 1996: 14–15.

Aremu, Tunde. "Why we can't dream—Osundare." *Punch* 23 October 1996: 16–17.

On his writing.

Bello, Hakeem. "No Alternative to Hope." *Daily Times* 25 December 1993, pp. 8, 17; 1 January 1994, pp. 8, 17; 8 January 1994: 8, 17.

Benson, Dayo. "'Our people are too poor to read'—Niyi Osundare." *Sunday Vanguard* 22 November 1992: 9.

Birbalsingh, Frank. "Interview with Niyi Osundare." *Presence Africaine* 147 (1988): 95–104; *Review of English and Literary Studies* 5, 2 (1988).

Bryce, Jane. "Dreams and Bullets." *West Africa* 21 July 1986: 1524–25.
Fatoba and Osundare talk about poetry.

Ekpu, Census. "An Event in the Life of Niyi Osundare." *Timseweek* 15 Feburary 1993: 42–43.
On lack of educational opportunities in Nigeria.

Enekwe, Onuora Ossie. "Interview with Niyi Osundare." *Okike* 34 (1996): 1–11.

Igwe, Dimgba. "Award-winning Poet Osundare Laments 'I have no house, I have only a rickety car.'" *Weekend Concord* 7 September 1991: 12–13, 16.

Imisim, Etim. "Writer as Righter." *Classique* 14 October 1991, pp. 14–15.

Irobi, Esiaba, and Olu Oguibe. "Night of the Firefly." *Annual Anthill* 1 (1988):91–97.

Kehinde, Seye, Tokunbo Awoshakin, Duro Meseko, and Ademola Adegbamigbe. "How I Write." *The News* 26 February 1995: 26–28.

Nwajah, Osita, Yomi Adeboye, Niran Adedokun, and Henrix Oliomelebe. "The Pen Outlasts the Palace—Osundare." *A.M News* 14 January 1996: 7; 21 January 1996:7.
On writing, publishing and politics in Nigeria.

Nwakanma, Obi. "The writer must constantly ask: What is the condition of humanity—Niyi Osundare." *Sunday Vanguard* 28 May 1995: 8, 17.

Nwanne, Ben. "Niyi Osundare's Reverse Culture Shock." *Quality* 23 February 1993: 27.
On his return to Nigeria.

Odugbemi, Sina. "Osundare's Commonwealth Triumph." *Vanguar* 29 January 1987: 8–9.
On his Commonwealth Poetry Prize.

Ogundipe, Taiwo. "Without sin there can be no art—Niyi Osundare." NATIONAL CONCORD, 28 January 1993: B1, B4.

Ogunjimi, Bayo. "Niyi Osundare: the Literary Evangelist Combs the World." *Guardian* 5 June 1993, p. 19; 12 June 1993: 19.

Oguntuwase, Gboyega. "The 'Eye' that Catches the Award." *Association of Nigerian Authors Review* 3, 3 (1987): 9–10.
Includes profile of Osundare.

Olabisi, Kolawole. "Abacha's transition, a ruse—Osundare." *Sunday Punch* 25 August 1996: 10–11.
On Nigerian politics.

Olusunle, Tunde. "Art Personality: Niyi Osundare." *Daily Times* 17 February 1990: 7.

Oni, Sanya. "Osundare, Poet of the Market Place." *National Concord* 24 June 1988: 7.

Umejie, Joy Chikodili. "The Social and Political Dimensions of Femi Osofisan's Plays: A Case Study of His Plays." Master's thesis, University of Ibadan, 1982. Includes interviews with Osundare and others on Osofisan's plays.

Wallace, Milverton, et al. "The Ife Book Fair Conversation." *Okike* 20 (1981): 35–49.

Yusuf, Tajudeen. "Ordeal of Young Writers." *New Nigerian* 21 & 28 February 1987.

COMMENTARY ON OSUNDARE'S LIFE

Adebayo, Lanre. "Osundare, Ojaide Win ANA Prizes." *Sunday Times* 6 November 1994:15.

Ade-Odutola, Kole. "Osundare: Nigeria Greets Noma Award-Winner in Harare." *Guardian* 2 September 1991: 31.

Ajibade, Kunle. "Homage to Osundare." *African Concord* 9 September 1991: 42. Noma Award winner.

Akeh, Afam. "Tributes." *Daily Times* 4 April 1990: 24. Profiles of Osundare and Ofeimun.

Anon. "Commonwealth Poetry Prize 1986." *African Book Publishing Record* 12 (1986): 202. Osundare is joint winner.

Anon. "Niyi Osundare—1986 Commonwealth Poetry Award Winner." *Theatre Forum* 1 (1987): 31.

Anon. "ANA Literary Award 1986—The Judges Have Their Say." *Association of Nigerian Authors Review* 3, 3 (1987): 22.

Anon. "Niyi Osundare Wins Noma Award." *Daily Times* 29 June 1991: 12.

Anon. "Osundare Wins ANA Prize." *ALA Bulletin* 16, 1 (1990): 34.

Anon. "Nigerian Poet Wins 1991 Noma Award." *African Book Publishing Record* 17 (1991), 199–200; rev. and rpt. in *ALA Bulletin* 17, 3 (1991): 43.

Benson, Dayo. "A Day with Niyi Osundare." *Sunday Vanguard* 31 January 1993: 13.

Dare, Olatunji. "The Poet and the Necktie." *Guardian* 3 November 1987: 9; rpt. in Olatunji Dare, *Matters Arising*. Ibadan: Paperback Publishers, 1992: 117–20. Was refused admission to Chinese restaurant at the Ikoyi Club in Lagos because he was not wearing a necktie.

Ekesie-Eke, Kudo. "Who is Niyi Osundare?" *Vanguard* 30 November 1987: 7.
On his not wearing a necktie to dinner at the Ikoyi Club in Lagos.

Ette, Mercy. "Sound of Laughter." *Newswatch* 7 October 1991: 47–48.
Wins Noma Award for *Waiting Laughters*.

———, and Matthew Faji. "Newsliners." *Newswatch* 15 July 1991: 43.
Noma Award.

Huston, Joanne. "Evening of African Poetry: Evening of Awakenings." *Wisconsin African Studies News and Notes* 37 (1991): 6.
Readings at University of Wisconsin at Madison by Osundare, et al.

Igwe, Dimgba. "Niyi Osundare: Nigeria's Nobel Laureate for the Year 2000."
Weekend Concord 7 September 1991: 1, 10, 14.
Noma Award.

Ishaka, Peter. "Osundare, Fulbright Scholar." *Newswatch* 17 September 1990: 41.
At University of Wisconsin at Madison.

Morris, Patricia. "Nigerian Poet Wins Award." *African Concord* 11 December 1986.
Commonwealth Poetry Prize.

Obosi, Nduka. "The 'Return' of a Native Son." *Sunday Vanguard* 15 September 1991: 8.
After winning honors abroad.

Odugbemi, Sina. "The Poet Lives." *Vanguard* 23 April 1987: 9.
Recovers from attack by axe-wielding assailant.

Okafor, Celestine, and Rita Ese Edah. "The Poet." *African Concord* 12 August 1991: 55.
Wins Commonwealth poetry prize and Noma Award.

Omotoso, Kole. "Praising Nigerian Efforts." *West Africa* 8–14 July 1991: 1127.
Noma Award.

Tomoloju, Ben. "*Waiting Laughters* Brings Noma Award to Osundare." *Guardian* 1 July 1991: 23.

CRITICISM ON OSUNDARE'S WORK

Adagbonyin, Asomwan Sonnie. *Niyi Osundare; Two Essays and an Interview.* Ibadan: Sam Bookman for Humanities Research Centre, 1996.

Adekoya, Segun. "Poetry and Village-Square Politics: Re-reading Niyi Osundare's *Village Voices*." *Daily Times* 13 January 1993: 22.

Adesokan, Akin. "Osundare on the 'Anxious' Generation." *Post Express* 7 December 1996: 14.

On Osundare's "Singers of a New Dawn: Nigeria's Literature from the Second Generation On" delivered at the 1996 Anglistentag conference in Germany.

Adeyemi, Seyi. "'Songs of the Season': Salute to Fecundity." *Guardian* 7 April 1986: 16.

Weekly poetic column in *Sunday Tribune*.

Aiyejina, Funso. "Recent Nigerian Poetry in English: An Alter/Native Tradition." *Komparatistische Hefte* 15–16 (1987), 49–64; *Kunapipi* 9, 2 (1987), 24–36; rpt. Ed. Yemi Ogunbiyi. *Perspectives on Nigerian Literature; 1700 to the Present (A Critical Selection from the Guardian Literary Series),* vol.1 . Lagos: Guardian Books, 1988.: 112–28.

———. "Osundare, Niyi (1947–)." Eds. Eugene Benson and L.W. Conolly. *Encyclopedia of Post-Colonial Literatures in English,* vol. 2. London and New York: Routledge, 1994: 1186–87.

Ajayi, Richard Oluwasesan. "Two of a Kind? Art and Politics in the Poetry of Niyi Osundare." Master's thesis, Obafemi Awolowo University, 1986.

Ajayi, Sesan. "Niyi Osundare: Tales, Texts and Tabloids." *Guardian* 25 August 1991: B7.

Ajiboye, Femi. "The Quest for a Revolutionary Metaphor in Niyi Osundare's *The Eye of the Earth.*" *Idoto* 10 (1988–90), 59–63.

Anon. "First Interlude: Major New Voices (1)." *Opon Ifa* 1, 2 (1980): 2–12.

Arnold, Stephen. "The *Praxis* of Niyi Osundare, Popular Scholar-Poet." *World Literature Written in Englsih* 29, 1 (1989): 1–7.

———. "A Peopled Persona: Autobiography, Post-modernism and the Poetry of Niyi Osundare." Eds. János Riesz and Ulla Schild. *Genres Autobiographies en Afrique/ Aotubiographical Genres in Africa.* Berlin: Dietrich Reimer, 1996:143–65.

Bamikunle, Aderemi. "New Trends in Nigerian Poetry: The Poetry of Niyi Osundare and Chinweizu." *Literary Criterion* 23, 1–2 (1988): 69–86; rpt. Eds. C.D. Narasimhaiah and Ernest Emenyonu. *African Literature Comes of Age.* Mysore: Dhvanyaloka, 1988: 69–86.

———. "Niyi Osundare's Poetry and the Yoruba Oral Artistic Tradition." *African Literature Today* 18, (1992): 49–61.

———. "The Development of Niyi Osundare's Poetry: A Survey of Themes and Technique." *Research in African Literatures* 26, 4 (1995): 121–37.

Bello, Hakeem Babatunde. "Songs of Our Uncertain Seasons." *Guardian* 24 November 1990: 19.

Songs of the Season.

Biakolo, Emevwo. "Explorations in New Nigerian Poetry." *Guardian* 20 January 1990, p. 12; 27 January 1990: 7.

Bodunde, Charles. "Poetry in the Newspaper: The Younger Poets in Nigeria and the Search for Artistic Medium." *Okike* 34 (1996): 76–86.

Brown, Duncan. "Daring the Beast: Contemporary Nigerian Poetry." Ed. Abdulrazak Gurnah. *Essays on African Writing:2. Contemporary Literature.* Oxford: Heinemann Educational Books, 1995: 58–72.

Burness, Don. "Niyi Osundare." Eds. Bernth Lindfors and Reinhard Sander. *Twentieth Century Caribbean and Black African Writers.* Dictionary of Literary Biography, 157. Detroit and London: Brucolli Clark Layman Book, Gale Research Inc., 1996: 286–95.

Dare, Adeyeye S. "New Wine in Old Wine Skin: Dead but Quickened Expressions in Osundare's Poetry." *OYE* 2 (1989): 18–30.

———. "Rhetorical Interrogatives and Imperatives in *The Eye of the Earth.*" *GØG* 1 (1991):116–26.

Ehling, Holger G. "Niyi Osundare (Nigeria)." *Literaturnachichten* 27 (1990): 8–10.

Ejorh, Theophilus. "Disillusionment in Selected Works of Niyi Osundare." Master's thesis, University of Lagos, 1994.

Ezeliora, Osita. "Osundare's Monocle and the Eye of Our Earth." *Guardian* 12 December 1992: 27; 19 December 1992: 27.

Ezenwa-Ohaeto. "Osundare—A Tribute." *Daily Times* 17 July 1991: 20.

———. "Dimensions of Language in New Nigerian Poetry." *African Literature Today* 17 (1991): 155–64.

———. "Orality and Craft of Modern Nigerian Poetry: Osundare's *Waiting Laughters* and Udechukwu's *What the madman Said. African Languages and Cultures.* 7 (1994): 101–09.

———. "Survival Strategies and the New Life of Orality in Nigerian and Ghanaian Poetry: Osundare's *Waiting Laughters* and Anyidoho's *Earthchild.*" *Research in African Literatures* 27, 2 (1996): 70–82.

George-Iroro, Godwin. "After Noma, the Nobel." *Tell* 16 September 1991: 41.

Ikiriko, Ibiwari D. "Art and Commitment in the Poetry of Niyi Osundare." Ph.D. dissertation, University of Port Harcourt, 1991.

Izevbaye, Dan. "Endless Beginnings: Motifs of Creation and Creativity in Nigerian Literature." Eds. Ayo Bamgbose, Ayo Banjo, and Andrew Thomas. *New Englishes: A West African Perspective.* Ibadan: Mosuro, 1995: 309–24.

Jeyifo, Abiodun. "The Poetry of Niyi Osundare." *Guardian* 10 May 1986, p. 13; 17 May 1986, p. 13; rpt. Ed. Yemi Ogunbiyi. *Perspectives on Nigerian Literature; 1700 to the Present (A Critical Selection from the Guardian Literary Series),* vol. 2. Lagos: Guardian Books, 1988: 314–20.

Johnson, Rotimi. "The Use of Orature in Contemporary African Poetry." *Southeast Asian Review of English* 18 (1989), 51–68; rpt. In *Linguistics and Contemporary Literature: Essays in Honour of M.A. Adenkunle, Visiting Professor of English*. Lagos: Misdrak Promotions and Publishing Co., 1990: 75–82.

Kpa'Kong, Ko'te. "Osundare: Poetry Rains with Ideas." *Guardian* 24 March 1986: 15.

Locher, Regula. "African Literature in English: A View from Nigeria." *Geneve Afrique* 25, 2 (1987): 177–96.

Mowah, Frank Uche. "Vision of Social Injustice in the Poetry of Niyi Osundare." *Review of English and Literary Studies* 5, 2 (1988): 101–17.

————. "Seeking a Way across the Wilderness: Niyi Osundare's *Songs of the Marketplace*." *Journal of African Studies* 15 (1988):76–79.

————. "Postmodernism and the Vision of Underdevelopment: Soyinka's *Mandela s Earth* and Osundare's *Waiting Laughters*." ASE, I, I (1991): 8–20.

————. Postcolonial Uncertainty and Osundare's Generation." *Iroro* 6, 1–2 (1994–95); 1–13.

Ngara, Emmanuel. *Ideology and Form in African Poetry: Implications for Communication*. London: James Currey; Harare: Baobab Books; Nairobi: Heinemann Kenya; Portsmouth, NH: Heinemann, 1990.

Nwachukwu-Agbada, J.O.J. "Post-war Nigeria and the Poetry of Anger." *Wasafiri* 12 (1990): 3–6.

————. "Poetry and the People in Post-War Nigeria." *New Literatures Review* 27 (1994): 70–77.

————. "Lore and Other in Niyi Osundare's Poetry." *African Literature Today* 20 (1996): 73–86.

Nwahunanya, Chinyere. "Osundare's New Esotericism: The Genesis of Poetic Disintegration." Ed. A.U. Ohaegbu. *Language, Literature, and Social Change*. N.p.: Modern Languages Association of Nigeria, 1989: 141–54.

Nwakanma, Obi. "*Midlife*: Osundare's Lyrical Invocation of Growth." CLASSIQUE, 2 August 1993: 25.

Obafemi, Olu. "Revolutionary Metaphor in the Poetry of Niyi Osundare." Ed. Tayo Olafioye. *Critic as a Terrorist: Views on New Africa Writings*. San Diego, California: Advantage Book Co., 1989: 22–36.

Obi, Amanze. "The Patient Song Bird." *Guardian* 1 September 1991, p. A8. Profile.

Odugbemi, Sina. "'Poetry is for the People'—Niyi Osundare." *Sunday Vanguard* 10 February 1985: 4, 14.

————. *The Eye of the Earth* ." VANGUARD, 29 January 1987: 9.

Ogundele, Wole. "Radicalising Nigerian Poetry in English: The Poetry and Poetics of Niyi Osundare." *Review of English and Literary Studies* 5, 2 (1988): 118–44.

———. "Niyi Osundare: Dilemma of a Revolutionary Poet." *Guardian* 22 June 1988: 9–10, 15.

Ogunjimi, Bayo. "Osundare: The Poet as Political Commentator." *Nigerian Tribune* 6 April 1993: 10.

Ogunpitan, Steve. "The Poet as Ecologist: Osundare's Forest of a Million Wonders." Ed. Rotimi Johnson. *Linguistics and Contemporary Literature: Essays in Honour of M.A. Adekunle, Visiting Professor of English* Lagos: Misdrak Promotions and Publishing Co., 1990: 70–74.

———. "Social Consciousness in the Poetry of Niyi Osundare." Ed.s Agwonorobo E. Eruvbetine. *Aesthetics and utilitarianism in Languages and Literatures*. Ojo, Nigeria: Department of Languages and Linguistics, Lagos State University, 1990: 171–79.

Okafor, Ursula Ndidi. "Social Realism in Recent Nigerian Poetry: The Examples of Osundare's and Ojaide's Poetry." Master's thesis, University of Ibadan, 1992.

Okome, Onookome. "Recent Nigerian Poetry: Objectification and Distanciation." *Daily Times* 24 March 1990, p. 11; 31 March 1991, p. 11; 7 April 1990, p. 11; 14 April 1990, p. 13.

Okon, Friday Akpan. "A Review of Niyi Osundare's *Songs of the Marketplace*." *Akwaiko* 1 (1988): 18–24.

Okunoye, Oyeniyi. "The New Ibadan Poets." *Ibadan Magazine* 1, 3 (1994), 11, 29.

Olafioye, Tayo. *Response to Creativity*. San Diego: The Beacon, 1988.

Olaogun, Modupe. "Niyi Osundare: Poet of 'the Marketplace.'" *Chimo* 12 (1986), 23.
Abstract of conference paper.

Oloruntoba-Oju, Taiwo. "Satire: From Horace to Soyinka." *Guardian* 23 June 1990:26; 30 June 1990: 8.

Onoworua, Omuabor Victor. "Marxism and the Proletariat in Nigerian Literature: Osundare, Fatunde and Iyayi." Master's thesis, University of Ibadan, 1986.

Oriaku, Remigius Onyejekwe. "The Genre of Autobiography in Modern Nigerian Writing." Ph.D. dissertation, University of Ibadan, 1990.

Osoba, Gabriel. "A Stylistic Analysis of Niyi Osundare's *Songs of the Marketplace*." Master's thesis, University of Ibadan, 1985.

————. "Accessibility as a Goal of Poetic Communication: A Stylistic Study of Some Syntactic and Lexical Patterns in Niyi Osundare's 'Excursions I.'" *Oye* 3 (1990): 64–75.

————. "Graphology as a Communicative Device in Poetry: The Example of Niyi Osundare's *Songs of the Marketplace*." *GØG* , 1 (1991): 104–15.

————. "Alliteration and Assonance: Two Symbolic Sound Patterns in Niyi Osundare's *Songs of the Marketplace*." *Journal of English Studies*, 6 (1992): 117–24.

Osofisan, Femi. "'A Forge of Busy Bellows.'" *Guardian* 26 June 1988: 8.
Moonsongs.

————. "ANA Literature Prizes: A Reply to Niyi Osundare's Rejoinder." *Daily Times* 22 July 1989, PP. 16–17; *Association of Nigerian Authors Review* 4, 6 (1989): 24.
See Osundare's essay on "ANA Literature Prizes: A Rejoinder" above.

Otiono, Tony Nduka. "Songs of the Tabloid Platform." *Guardian* 24 November 1990: 19.
Verse journalism in *Songs of the Season.*

Udumuku, Onyemaechi. "Niyi Osundare's Poetry and the Marxist Theory of Art." Master's thesis, University of Port Harcourt, 1988.

POEMS FOR OSUNDARE

1. Adeola Ikuomola

THE TOTAL POET
(NIYI OSUNDARE)

I heard the moonsong of the total poet
Roaring on the dewy grass of the night
I heard it loud and clear all night long
Like the golden steps of a thunderstorm.

I heard the moonsong of the potent poet
Thundering deep like the crawling sea
I heard it all loud and clear all day long
Like the combined melodies of clappers.

I heard the moonsong of the prophetic poet
Galloping deep into the ancient mountains
I heard it loud and clear in the firmament
Like the thick applause of the golden floods.

Mark the evergreen echoes of the moonsong
On the golden platter of the travailing scrolls
Circumcising the wakeful adventurous pupils
To behold the waiting laughter of excellence.

2. Remi Raji-Oyelade

THIS GARLAND TOO LIGHT YET ON CREATION DAY

River-born, water-bred
Your garlands tell of conquests in the forest of words...

Earth-child, your hairs a compost of fertile lore
Your tongue filled with fire and fluent in forges
You sing songs to soothe and suture
this world dressed in rags and rage.
You sing and curse the drought in the morning
and the clouds rolled your voice
into boulders of rain
and the rocks bow before your windy tunes
and the rivers rose against your thirst.
   *   *   *

When the axe-men came
Arrows in their eyes, hunger in their blood
They met you fondling the kora
In a conference of drums and tenors
They wanted to bury the hatchet
in your heart of songs
You strummed the kora
You fiddled their conscience
And spelled them into harmless slumber.

You, Oluomi, seasoned in grills of ancient metaphors
Your songs bloom on the crest of sunny nights.
   *   *   *

I thought they said poetry doesn't sell...

I thought they said you don't mean a thing
when you pine to speak in verse like God.
You taught the critic to unclasp the oral tong
and words as songs burst in cowries.
I thought they said poetry doesn't sell.

You peddle proverbs in search of Truth
You carry neither tusk nor feather
in rims of titled caps
but your heart is crowned
in the richness of laughter.
I thought they said poetry doesn't sell.

This garland too light yet on creation day.

3. Catherine Loomis

THE POET IN EXILE[1]

Machete-mouthed? No, scalpel-tongued; he cuts
To heal, his voice the sword that justice holds,
A sword he borrows, wields, and then restores.
He makes a world your mouth can say, can kiss,
Can chew, can laugh at, rhythm in, plead with, cry
Out loudly to, as fearless as drum.
He knows that silence is a drum.
He knows that silence is a sharpened bit,
A razor you are forced to swallow whole
While empty air comes whistling out your throat.
He sleeps with parted lips, his words his guards
And yours. He waits to hear you say what's worth
What's words have cost him; soundless bought with
Severed tongues.
He's spent his words to ransom you from crocodiles;
Repay him: spit their lies out, pull the knot
Out of your tongue and sing the truth.

4. Misty Crittle

AFRICAN WARRIOR

(For the Poet Niyi Osundare)

O Mighty African WARRIOR.
    You sang your song for me.
My hawk-like eyes observed you in awe.
    You unlocked the doors of your inner mystery.

You resurrected my mind with one breath of your being.
    You altered my perspective, baffled my perception.
Your discerning eyes possessed me, demanded my attention.

Your vocal chords restrained me in a vocal orgy, gluttony.
    Your African tongue, a two-edged sword, will roll for all
    eternity.
    Your hypnotic tones persuaded my hand, and now my soul
    whispers, "I see."

Nigerian narrator, poetic prophet, ostracized oracle,
    Your winged-words soared high above the clouds.
They sit at the feet of God now.

Your voice haunts me, your smile kissed me, your mechanical gestures
    seduced my eyes
    I saw your crimson-feathered halo, as deep red as your
    bloodline.
You're an angel in disguise.

Your lyrical orchard bears fruit of metaphors dressed in similes.
    It's harvest time, time to reap; how do I know?

"The winds told me."

5. John Fontenelle

MY TEACHER, THE HARVESTER OF KNOWLEDGE

The chalk and voice are his instruments for
Planting his crops.
Our minds are the fields in which he labors.
Some fields are filled with large, heavy rocks,
Others are of the richest alluvial soil,
Soil farmers only dream of.
He plants optimistically though, expecting
Each seed to grow,
With beads of stinging sweat falling from his brow,
he tends to the fields of which he has sown.
Always eager to see his crop's progress, he sees
Some plants fail to prosper—the earth has not taken
the seed.
The rest of the seeds have grown deep
into the souls of his students
In these fields, thoughts and dreams are born.

6. Michael Fontenelle

THE MASTER TEACHER

You, who came from Nigeria
And brought your talents and wisdom
To motivate, encourage, and inspire,
Will always be remembered.

You, the messenger who introduced
new ideas from poems and plays
Made it all clear, interesting, and easy to read,
Did make a difference in life.

You, who inspire and motivated
To read the words of greatmen,
Such as Shakespeare, Sophocles, and Whitman
Entranced appreciation of drama and poetry.

You, Dr. Osundare, will always be revered
As the teacher who enlightened and
Stirred critical thinking skills
You are the Master teacher.

7. Niyi Afolabi

ODE TO THE OGIDIGBO* DRUMMER
[for Niyi Osundare]

(sung to the *Iya-ilu* or *Gangan*)

> *Baba ni baba nje*
> > *Baba ni baba nje*
> > > *Won ba ta kiti ki won fi ori sole*
> > > *Baba ni baba nje***

To the river that never rests
To the interpreter of market meddlings and minglings
To the ocular perceptor of village vestiges

> Once a pioneer, always a pioneer
> No matter the nagging of nay-sayers
> Once a pioneer, always a pioneer

To the ripple in dormant ponds
To the rainmaker in hope-deprived skies
To the resonant impulse of silent seasons

> Once a pioneer, always a pioneer
> No matter the nagging of nay-sayers
> Once a pioneer, always a pioneer

To the regenerative dancer in forest fiestas
To the sharp-eyed, multi-feathered, white-necked king
To the gliding and visionary gift to the world

> Once a pioneer, always a pioneer
> No matter the nagging of nay-sayers
> Once a pioneer, always a pioneer

To the deepening steps of the moon masking and dancing
To the multivocal drum of resilient laughters
To the mythmaking resonance of noonsongs

> Once a pioneer, always a pioneer
> No matter the nagging of nay-sayers
> Once a pioneer, always a pioneer

To the string of caps that fits many heads
To the ancestral memory of a million temples
To the diviner of the "She of the Luminous Eyes"

> *Baba ni baba nje*
> *Baba ni baba nje*
> *Won ba ta kiti ki won fi ori sole*
> *Baba ni baba nje*

* The Yoruba talking drum that is drummed proverbially.
** Song translated and transcribed as refrain in this poem.

New Orleans, November

6. Veronica Uzoigwe

MID AUGUST '97: CREATIVE '350: "SO LONG ..."2

Farmer born, Peasant bred
U.I. buttered, U.S. jammed
But,
Ekiti rooted.

All inspiring muse,
Odo Osun Olonda!
Then a resting elephant,
Now a crouching bull,
   Yet,
    Ekiti rooted.
    Painter,
Whose colour never runs,
Never fades,
Never dies
"Our positive Tradition will not die!"

Just as it gradually sinks in,
The FLAME flicks away
But,
Red-hot Ekiti-rooted embers,
Shall our Enkindler always remain.

7. Nelson Nwandu P.C.

HOW I HATE TO LET YOU GO

You have sharpened me
From a rustic blade
Into a flaming sword,
Nursed me from childhood to teenagehood,
In the windmills of poetry.

You have washed me with –
The rivers of knowledge,
And the moon is just –
Within my grasp.

Oh! how I hate to let you go!
And I must let you go;
But do not let me go,
Until you watch me grow –
Full blown.
Farewell ...

8. Femi Lawani

FOR OUR BARD OF KNOWLEDGE

Your world of words
Have enlightened us
     brightened us
     frightened us

Now like clothes horses
    We are heavy
        coloured
        watered

Your words have been "foregrounded"
     by the countenance
     whose heaviness
     has weighed down
     in torrents of sincerity

     unbended by society

We have heard and revered
The gird of our gloriously greying bard
Now you are leaving
But without the words

9. Segun Awolana

OMO YORUBA

Omo Yoruba ni mi n o fi se baba wa han fun gbogbo wa patapata
O da mi loju gbangba pojulowo omo ni baba wa
Osundare ni n o pe o
Oruko laa pejoye.
Mo ranti eni a mo loju beba nijosi,
Won le beba kaakiri ibi gbogbo pe o n sayeye,
Ko waa pe ko waa jinna mo mo o tan lo waa kuro n'ibadan.
Eyin eniyan, Yoruba so wi pe
baa ba lowo ba o niwa owo olowo lani,
abo ti ko niwa rere ekun nii sun nile oko.
Iwa Osundare firu eniyan to je han wayi,
baba e maa ranti omo yin gbogbo to wa nibadan.

10. Abdul-Rasheed Na'Allah

TANI MANDALA OWU![3]

Ko s'eni mandala owu!
Owu gunungun ko se bi odidere l'oko
Owu akalamago ko se bi lekeleke
Owu aparo kose bi okin oba eye!

Ow'akorin nile, ow'akorin l'oko
Ko korin tititi, k'alabiama o fijoha
Ki t'oba t'ijoye ati mekunun pata
Ki won o f'oju odàn s'epade
Ki won o jo jojo
K'aye o se kayeefi ijo won
Ki kòkòrò mefa o pade
Ni gbangba t'oba olorin ti n m'orinko.
Olorin ni'le olorin l'oko
Olorin ni koro yara
Akorin fun dudu, akorin fun funfun!

Ko s'eni mandala o wu!
Gbogbo oju l'ope
Won wa toro lowo Olohun:
"Eyi wu wa o!"
Won n wa n wipe, "A fe se bi Oba-orin t'oluwa da lare,
Afi kalamu dara, olu akowe,
Osundare Oba-orin oninu rere.
Ok'orin fun mekunu mekunu ni laari
Ok'orin f'oba Oba ro'ra se
Ok'orin wipe ki ijoba se jeje, nitori wipe mekunu loni j'oba
Ok'orin igi inu igbo, o ko t'eja inu omi
Ok'orin fun kankanyin ti n rin nile,
Oko ti pere to yoju l'orun!"

Ewaa wo oo!
Gbogbo aye lofe d'olorin.

11. Niyi Osundare

PEOPLE ARE MY CLOTHES

Cheerful drumming, with gangan (talking drum) in the lead; then the following song:

Enia laso mi
Enia laso mi
Ti mo ba boju wehin ti mo renii mi
Enia laso mi ...*

People are my clothes
People are my clothes
When I look right, when I look right
When I look back and see my folk
My head swells like a jubilant mountain
My heart leaps with infinite joy

　　　People are my clothes
　　　My raiment dwells the loom of teeming folds

I am the alligator pepper seed
With siblings too many for the numbering eye
I am a seminal drop in the bowl of the sea,
A thread in the loom of the sky

　　　People are my clothes
　　　My raiment dwells the loom of teeming folds

Let people be my robe
　As the savannah grass secures the deer

Let people be my robe
　As the plumage surrounds the bird

Not for me the porcupine
　Which peeps at the world
　From a bunker of thorns

Not for me the tortoise
  Whose carapace sharpens
  A sword around its neck

    People are my clothes
    My raiment dwells the loom of teeming folds

One morsel can never make a feast
One finger cannot retrieve a fallen needle
One leg cannot win a race
One broomstick cannot sweep the marketplace

A lone hyena will come to grief
In a flock of resolute sheep
A lone tree cannot stand the fury
Of desert storm
The masquerade who strays
Too far from his followers
Soon loses its mask in rude, unholy lanes

With many steps the foot will tame
The tyranny of the road
With all the fingers the hand
Will grab the mightiest machete
From that machete
Let twilight come to the tree of pain

    People are my clothes
    My raiment dwells the loom of teeming folds

People are my clothes
People are my clothes
My billowy brocade, my sumptuous silk
My loom is the thronging street
Busy workbenches, farmlands of fruiting trees;
Its shuttle is the care-ful word,
Which runs life's thread from coast to coast.
A song swells in my throat,
Awaiting the chorus of a waking world

> People are my clothes
> My raiment dwells the loom of teeming folds

People are my clothes
People are my clothes
When I look right, when I look right
When I look back and see my folk
My heart leaps with infinite joy
People are my clothes
I will never fear the rage of chilling storms

> People are my clothes
> My raiment dwells the loom of teeming folds

Enia laso mi
Bi mo ba boju wehin ti mo reeni mi
Enia laso mi ...

* The first stanza of the poem carries the translation of this song

NOTES

[1] Students and a colleague of Niyi Osundare respectively at the University of New Orleans, USA, wrote the next four poems for Osundare.

[2] The next four poems were selected from an Unpublished collection written by Osundare's "The '97 Creative Writing Class, '350," students of the University of Ibadan. The collection was presented to Osundare during a farewell program in his honor in August 1997 before he left for the United States on sabbatical.

[3] A translation of the first stanza of this poem into English would look like the following:

WHO WOULDN'T WANT TO BE CELEBRATED!

None wouldn't want to be celebrated!
Gunungun (vulture) wants to be an Odidere bird in the forest
Akalamago wants to act as if it were Lekeleke
It's the wishes of Aparo to behave like Okin the king of birds!

AFTERWORD

AFTERWORD[1]

Biodun Jeyifo

The word is out that recent, post-Civil War Nigerian literature in English has found its most comprehensive thematic expansion and remarkable technical innovations in poetry. Literary history of course cautions us to be wary of apparent truths and premature judgements. A decade and a half may be an important time section in the experience of a generation, but it counts for little in the life of a society and the crystallization of a cultural or literary movement. Even so, there is no denying the poetic deluge in Nigerian literature at the present time. On some university campuses now, poetry readings draw almost as much enthusiastic, appreciative audiences as do dramatic productions. And within the republic of writers, the fraternity of poets grows and bourgeons beyond those of playwrights and novelists.

This piece on Niyi Osundare then is particularly informed by this poetic deluge which some have called a poetic revolution or a renaissance and which Funso Aiyejina, one of the "new" poets, has, in an inspired, if collectively self-promoting description, called an "alter-native tradition." Osundare occupies an increasingly looming place within this tradition. His poetry constitutes a distinct revolution within the new poetic "revolution." This observation requires some clarification before we come to an appreciation of Niyi Osundare's poetry in its own right.

Within the major genres of literature, the poetic genre has perhaps been the most problematic for our writers, given the peculiar historical and cultural factors which determined the emergence and course of development of modern African literature. It seems that within the specific genre of poetry, all the problems of a literature which arose from the womb of colonial society and is still struggling to free itself from the ambiguous legacies of its origins, achieve their most concentrated form. This is not the place to go into these problems. The essential point is that for each individual writer, and incidentally for our collective literary development, the colonial legacy and its most problematic manifestation — the umbilical ties to metropolitan European traditions — must be transcended by the forging of a distinctive voice and a demonstrable rootedness in our own realities and experience.

In the genre of poetry, more than in the genres of drama and prose fiction, these obligations and demands are more daunting for its practitioners, for the reason that while poetry seems to be the easiest, the most compact genre to "exploit", it is in fact the most "exploitative", the most "tyrannical" and rigorous of the literary genres. Thus it is that while "instant" poets are easily made, while indeed literary history is replete with legions of would-be poets, the true poets belong to a disappointingly undemocratic, charmed circle of the elect of the literary firmament.

We should not, of course, mystify poetry and the process of poetic creation. What has been said of literature in general is truer of poetry in particular: it is ninety percent perspiration and ten percent inspiration. In our new dispensation of post-civil war poetry, while there are constant flashes of inspiration, the perspiration is notably scanty. And the most dramatic manifestation of this situation is the relationship of the "new" poets to language and words. For while language may be the enabling medium of *all* literature, it is the special forte for poetry, simultaneously the bulwark and love of the true poets *and* the trap, the Achilles' heel of would-be poets.

Niyi Osundare's central, looming position in the new poetry derives, first of all, from this issue of language. It has been justifiably remarked that the "new" poetry differs from the "old", pre-Civil War poetic vintage of Christopher Okigbo, Wole Soyinka, Michael Echeruo and J. P. Clark-Bekederemo, as much in the new subjects and themes of poetic expression as in the "demystification" of the language of poetry. For while the older poets generally deployed a diction and a metaphoric, highly allusive universe calculated to exclude all but a small coterie of specialists, the new poets have taken the language of poetry, the diction of figurative expression, to the market-place, to the popular daily press even. This "revolution" in the attitude to received poetic diction assumes the character of the informing *aesthetic*, the defining poetics of Osundare's writings.

Words and images delight and excite Osundare in the way that a painter in love with his calling delights in colours, and a sculptor who works in molten bronze enthuses in the plasticity of his medium. Thus, while most of the poets of the new "alter-native" tradition have adopted the diction of ordinary speech and the accents of popular idioms in place of the arcane latinates and the learned, allusive pedantry of much of the poetic diction of the pre-Civil War poets, Osundare, within this "revolution" of poetic diction, has kept his metaphoric and semantic range copiously and manifoldly wide.

The most engrossing manifestation of this quality of Osundare's poetry is his sustained meditation, in poem after poem, on the nature and obligations of poetic creation and the means and logistics of its execution. The fist poem of the first published volume of his poetry, in fact, established this *ambience* of Osundare's verses. Appropriately, the poem is titled "Poetry is." We can usefully quote from some of the short, condensed, epiphanic stanzas of this poetic "manifesto:"

> Poetry is
> a lifespring
> which gathers timbre
> the more throats it plucks
> harbinger of action
> the more minds it stirs
>
> Poetry is
> the hawker's ditty
> the eloquence of the gong
> the lyric of the marketplace
> the luminous ray
> on the grass's morning dew
>
> Poetry is
> no oracle's kernel
> for a sole philosopher's stone
>
> Poetry
> is
> man
> meaning
> to
> man.

Within the first four volumes of Osundare's poetry, the following are some of the more refreshing, illuminating variations on this sustained meditation on the process of poetic creation in particular, and the artist's vocation or calling in general: "I sing of Change," "I wake up this Morning," "A Dialogue of Drums," "A Grass in the Meadow," "I Rise Now," and most of the poems in the section titled "Inflaming Flares" in the volume *A Nib in the Pond*. In this particular volume, some poems like "Art for Ass Sake" and "Questions for a Pandering Poet" define the poetic vocation negatively, and with subtle irony, through satirical lampoons on what Osundare regards as the corruption of the true transformative, humanistic revolutionary ends of poetry. For if it is true that the muse of poetry has chosen him for her own, it is equally true that the dialects of revolution have found a habitation in his poetry.

Let us neither mince words nor lay ourselves open to the charge of overstating the case here. In all modern African poetry, *all*, I repeat, only in the poetry of Agostinho Neto and David Diop will you find the same depth and passion and lyricism in solidarity with the oppressed, the downtrodden, the dispossessed, and a corresponding faith in their aspiration and will to revolutionary change as we confront in Osundare's poetry. The dispossession of the majority of our people, and more specifically of the rural producers, may, in fact, be said to be the grand theme of Osundare's poetry.

A descriptive, paraphrasing criticism will characterize such a passionate solidarity with the dispossessed as we get in Osundare's poetry as "poetry of engagement or commitment". But this is now an outworn label in contemporary African literary criticism. We need a different order of critical discourse and a different conceptual framework to grasp this phenomenon. I propose a modified form of Hegelian dialectics: if it is true that certain writers seek to express the most basic truths of an age in their art, it is equally true that the period itself "chooses" certain writers as the vehicles for the expression of these truths. Only such a dialectical interplay of the subjective, personal choice of the poet, and the objective, relentless impingement of realities and forces which refuse to be ignored, which demand resolution for historical advance to take place, only such an interplay will explain how the poetry of Diop and Neto, and now Osundare, can so totally and passionately encompass the aspirations of Africa's dispossessed masses and their will to revolutionary change. Is it any wonder that only in the works of these three poets, in the entire corpus of modern African poetry, do we confront just as much as immersion in the realities and multifarious lineaments of Africa's underdevelopment as you find an internationalist dimension of solidarity with all the world's oppressed peoples. Listen to Osundare:

"All eyes like a sieve
we will build an enduring nest
with a straw from the diverse forsts."

You will thus read in Osundare's volumes sometimes humorous, often searing, occasionally bitter and satirical, but always vivid and metaphorically arresting evocations of episodes from our recent history and the upheavals, triumphs
and defeats of struggles in Nigeria and other lands: Bulumkutu, Bakolori, the
fertilizer importation extravaganza, the Green Revolution plunder, the lynching
of suspected petty thieves in our cities, the rash of reasons to obliterate evidence
of fraudulent looting in our bureaucracies, the impoverishment and decay of
our rural communities, Nicaragua, Soweto, Namibia, Zimbabwe, memories of
Hiroshima, the Falklands war. You will encounter celebrations of defenders of
the oppressed and the scourge and terror of the oppressors: Balarabe Musa,
Kunle Adepeju, and other fallen student martyrs in Nigeria, Winifred and
Nelson Mandela, Fidel Castro, Walter Rodney, Agostinho Neto, Paul Robeson.
Above everything else, the justification of the will to revolution in Osundare's
poetry is based on a vigorous, sustained solicitude for one of the world's oldest
producers: the peasants, those who till the soil, and their quasi-mystical ties to
the earth.

The most extensive extrapolation of this rural-agrarian ethic, this "green
desire" in Osundare's revolutionary consciousness, is to be found in the volume
appropriately titled *Village Voices*. With its variety of subjects, cadences and
moods, this volume is a sustained celebration of the rural folk and the agrarian
ethos. Pronouncing himself "farmer-born and peasant-bred," the poet celebrates
the rural communities as sturdy producers, witty raconteurs, singers, jesters,
satirists; what is more, they are presented as being undeterred by treacherous
prodigals amongst them and are undeceived by the wiles of their expropriators
in government and business. The land, the people and the natural rhythms and
cycles are given poignant but unsentimental evocation. The kind of sensibility
which informs Mao's and Neto's poetry on the land and the people comes to
mind, the difference being that Osundare would have nothing of the austere
rigor of these poets; for him it is all metaphoric exuberance.

The strain is echoed in the second part of *Songs of the Marketplace* titled
"Songs of Dawn and Seasons." Here, even in a love poem, "Unfolding Seasons,"
the poet's observant, sensitive eye on nature yields the insight that the processes of the natural world correspond to the wishes and yearnings of the heart and,
by extension, the will to change, the will to freedom. Contrastively, evocations

of seasons of natural dryness and blight on the land, in other poems, lead the poet to muse on the "unnatural" deserts and scarcities created by man. It is, however, in the volume, *The Eye of the Earth*, that these themes of the *natural* sanction for the revolutionary reconstitution of society find their most accomplished treatment.

What Osundare's poetry seems to me to demonstrate then, is the truth that the immediacy and power of revolutionary poetry, *mature* revolutionary poetry, derive from a frank, perhaps even unapologetic importunateness. The revolutionary poet, hardly ever content to adopt the tactics of impersonality or self-effacement, everywhere secrets his self, his opinions and perceptions into his poetry. The expected consequence of this is, of course, that the exemplary "self" proffered or the opinions and perceptions advanced will jolt complacent sensibilities out of their placid state, rouse the appropriate social classes and strata to awareness and action or productively agitate that dialectical space between accommodation and resistance in a given social order. Within this *constant*, there is however the important qualification that intrusive secretion of self, opinions and perceptions in the poetry, develops varied tactics and wears many masks and disguises, some more or less adequate or effective than others.

The "voices" and "songs" highlighted in Osundare's titles relate precisely to this factor finding the personae, the media and idioms to carry the burden of his idealistic, utopian projections beyond the contradictions and negations of the present Nigerian, and by extension and implication, African social order. Thus, it is a veritable losing, though enormously invigorating, battle to keep track of the myriad tactics and masks of expressing revolutionary views adopted by this poet. If the "message" of Osundare's poetry is so strongly embedded in metaphor and imagery, proverbs and aphorism, this is the more effective in the context of the accessible, lucid poetic he uses. For it is probable that in due course Osundare will attract attention or achieve recognition as much for his meticulous, consummate deftness in the craft, the technique, the logistics of poetic expression as for his radical utopian views. For me at any rate, his greatest promise now is that these two aspects of literary expression are fused in his poetry and this again marks another point of departure from much of the earlier Nigerian English-Language poetry, where style and technique are so displaced from the substance or content of poetic expression that they often draw attention to themselves as the end of literary expression. Osundare is, again, in the company of Neto here, where craft is neither superior nor subservient to substance or content. And like Neto, the range of his technical and stylistic options are quite impressive, stretching from the part transliterated, part adapted re-working of traditional formal verbal rhetoric and songs to the austere, terse, sculptural relief of poems like "The Nigerian Railway", "Mindscope", "New Creed", and the arresting poetic pictogram, "Sundown".

I do not want to give the impression of perfection, of a definitive *arrival* in the poetic trajectory of Niyi Osundare. Definitely, the "errors of rendering" (Okigbo's wry self-criticism) are all there: astonishing moments of the wrong turn of phrase, of forced coinage, of overwrought metaphors. The volume *A Nib in the Pond* is probably the most illustrative of these "slips." But I do think that Funso Aiyejina's cautionary observation that Osundare's heavy but exultantly flexible use of oral resources may "become a mere echo of a familiar form, the oral tradition," if Osundare does not "hew a distinct personal poetic style," is insupportable from the evidence of even the first two published volumes, *Village Voices* and *Songs of the Market-place* not to mention the ambitious scope and achievement of *The Eye of the Earth*. Osundare's is the most distinctive voice among our new poets; I suggest that this may be explained by the fact that in his verses we confront both poetry of revolution and revolutionary poetry, in forms and techniques.

Censorious critics may plausibly charge Osundare with technical, logistical fastidiousness. An obvious illustration of this would be the deliberate symmetry in the arrangement of the poems and sections of each of his volumes to correspond suggestively with seasonal and calendrical cycles, and in the case of *Songs of the Market-place* with sunrise and sunset. However, in spite of, or coincident with this logistical fastidiousness, Osundare's poetry breathes and pulses with life and vitality. In his poetry abstractions like poverty, exploitation, corruption and dependence assume concrete, searing vividness.

His lines reveal a lucid, witty lyricism, sharply etched imagery, and earthy, often deliberately raucous turns of phrase, and closeness to the people, to the earth, closeness to nature. A major analysis could indeed be offered of Osundare's handling of *nature* in a way that is perhaps unique in contemporary Nigerian literature, oscillating as it does, between the accustomed animist ritualism of older poets like Okigbo and Soyinka, and careful sensitive observation and description, with something of a naturalist's eye, and the moral-philosophical rubric of projecting the processes of nature as a model and a paradigm for change and renewal in society.

Like music, like religion, poetry often serves to cushion the poet and his audience against the negations of an unjust exploitative and alienating social order as things to be endured, accommodated and ultimately sublimated. Revolutionary poetry, however, problematises both these negations and the very accommodation to them which non-revolutionary poetry insinuates. The lyrical and metaphorical exuberance and vision of Osundare does exactly this in its expression of revolutionary poetry in Nigeria.

NOTES

1 This article was originally written as "Introduction" to Osundare's *Songs of the Market-place*. It is being reproduced here as "Afterword" for its historical essence and continued significance to the development of Niyi Osundare's poetry. Editor.

NOTES ON
CONTRIBUTORS

NOTES ON
CONTRIBUTORS

Kamal Abdel-Malek, professor of Arabic and Islamic Studies, teaches at the Department of Comparative Literature, Religion, and Film/Media Studies, University of Alberta, Canada. Among his books are *Muhammad in the Modern Egyptian Popular Ballad* (Leiden-New York-Koln: E.J. Brill, 1995), *A Study of The Vernacular Poetry of Ahmad Fu'ad Nigm* (Leiden: E.J. Brill, 1990), and *Israeli and Palestinian Identities in History and Literature*, forthcoming, which he coedited with David C. Jacobson.

Titi Adepitan is a Doctoral Candidate at the University of British Columbia, Vancouver, Canada. He has taught literature at Ogun State University in Nigeria.

Akinwumi Adesokan, coeditor of *The Glendora Review*, is of the Department of English, Cornell University, USA.

Omoniyi Afolabi, Ph.D., is professor of Portuguese and African Diaspora Studies at the Department of Spanish and Portuguese, Tulane University, New Orleans. His most recent book is *The Golden Cage: Regeneration in Lusophone African Literature and Culture* (AWP, 2001).

Bolaji Aluko, Chair of Chemical Engineering Department at Howard University, is a social commentator on Nigerian affairs.

Stephen Arnold, for many years editor of *ALA Bulletin: A Publication of African Literature Association*, has written important essays on Osundare. He is Professor Emeritus of Comparative Literature at the University of Alberta, Canada. Among his edited books are *African literature studies: the present state* (1985), *Culture and Development in Africa* (edited with Andre Nitecki, 1990), and *Critical Perspectives on Mungo Beti* (1998).

Frank Birbalsingh is Professor of English, York University, Canada. He became one of the earlier interviewers of Niyi Osundare, with his first interview with Osundare in *Presence Africaine* (1988). A prolific writer, he is the author of *From Pillar to Post: The Indo-Caribbean Diaspora* (1998) and *Novels and the Nation: Essays on Canadian Literature* (1998). He also edited several books *including Jahaji: An Anthology of Afro-Caribbean Fiction* (2000), *Frontiers of Caribbean Literature in English* (1996), among others.

Charles Bodunde, poet, teaches English and African Literature at the Department of Modern European Languages, University of Ilorin, Nigeria. His book, *Oral traditions and aesthetic transfer: creativity and social vision in contemporary Black poetry* (Bayreuth: Breitinger, 2001) was published in the Bayreuth African studies series, #58.

Stewart Brown, a poet, editor and critic, has published four collections of poetry, including *Elsewhere: new and selected poems* (Peepal Tree Press, 1999). He has edited or co-edited several anthologies of African and Caribbean writing, including *Caribbean Poetry Now, Voiceprint, New Wave – the contemporary Caribbean short story, The pressures of the Text: Orality, texts and the telling of tales, The Heinemann Book of Caribbean Poetry, African New Voices* and *The Oxford Book of Caribbean Short Stories*. He has also edited critical studies of the great West Indian poets Derek Walcott, Kamau Brathwaite including, *All are involved: the Art of Martin Carter* (Peepal Tree Press, 1999). He taught for two years in Jamaica in the early seventies and later lectured for three years at Bayero University, Kano, Nigeria in the early 1980s. He is Senior Lecturer in African and Caribbean literature in the Centre of West African Studies at the University of Birmingham and an Honorary Fellow of the Centre for Caribbean Studies at the University of Warwick, United Kingdom.

Jane Bryce was born and brought up in Tanzania, and lived in Italy, the UK and Nigeria, before moving to Barbados in 1992 to teach at the University of the West Indies. She worked as a teacher, a freelance editor and a journalist before becoming an academic, and still contributes to newspapers and journals. She did her doctoral research on Nigerian women's writing at Obafemi Awolowo University in Nigeria, and her current appointment is as a specialist in African literature and postcolonial cinema. She now works in the areas of feminist and postcolonial theory, popular culture, film and creative writing. Among her recent publications are, "Inside/Out: body & sexuality in Dambudzo Marechera's fiction," in *A Reader in Dambudzo Marechera*, (AWP, 1999: 221–234) and "'Young t'ing is the name of the game': sexual dynamics in a Caribbean romantic fiction series," in *Gender and Consumer Culture Reader* (New York UP: 2000: 283–298). She is Joint editor (with John Conteh-Morgan and Daniel Gover) of *The Post-Colonial Condition of African Literature* (AWP, 2000).

Donald Burness, editor of *Critical Perspectives on Lusophone African Literature*, is Professor at Franklin Pierce College.

Pietro Deandrea, Ph.D., is a Lecturer and Researcher in English Literature and Postcolonial Literatures, University of Turin, Italy. Translator into Italian of fiction by André Brink, Buchi Emecheta, Ben Okri, Judith Ortiz Cofer, Wole Soyinka. He has published essays on West African and Caribbean Literature. His first volume, *Holistic Perspectives - Metamorphoses of Genre in Anglophone West African Literature*, is being published by Rodopi, Amsterdam/Atlanta.

Olufemi Ibukun Dunmade teaches English at the University of Ilorin, Nigeria.

Nancy Easterlin is professor at the Department of English, University of New Orleans, New Orleans, USA.

Christiane Fioupou is professor of African literature at the Université de Toulouse-Le Mirail, France, and is world renown as a French translator of African literature.

Harry Garuba, one of contemporary Nigeria's notable poets, is professor of African literature at the Center for African Studies, University of Cape Town, South Africa.

Cynthia Hogue, is Director, Stadler Center for Poetry and Associate Professor of English At Bucknell University, Lewisburg, PA 17837, USA.

Abiola Irele, Editor of the distinguished journal of African literature, *Research in African Literatures*, is Professor of French and African Comparative Literatures at Ohio State University, USA, and author of several critical works, including *The Africa Experience in Literature and Ideology*. His most recent book, *The African Imagination: Literature in Africa and the Black Diaspora* (2001), was published by Oxford University Press.

Biodun Jeyifo, Professor of English at Cornell Unversity, is a renowned critic and topmost scholar of African literature. Among his recent books are *Conversations With Wole Soyinka* (Univ. Pr of Mississippi, 2001), and *Perspectives on Wole Soyinka: Freedom and Complexity* (Univ. Pr of Mississippi, 2001). His new book is *Modern African Drama* (Norton Critical Editions) (2002).

Damola Jolayemi teaches at the Department of Modern European Languages, University of Ilorin, Nigeria.

Eldred Durosimi Jones, formerly editor of *African Literature Today*, has written extensively on the works of Wole Soyinka. He is among leading scholars in the discussion of critical approaches to African Literature. Professor Durosimi Jones is professor emeritus of Fourah Bay College, Sierra Leone.

Kamau Kemayo, Poet, Ph.D., St. Louis University, teaches English at James Madison University, USA. His book, *dancsinging*, was published in 1999.

Doug Killam, Professor Emeritus of Guelph University, Canada, recently edited a prize wining African literature guide, *The Companion to African Literatures* with Ruth Rowe (James Currey & Indiana University Press, 2000)

Bernth Lindfors, prolific author and editor of books on African Literature, is Professor of English and African Literature at the University of Texas, Austin. His regularly published reference book is *Black African Literature in English: A Guide to Information Sources*. Among his other books are *Africans on State: Studies in Ethnological and Show Business* (Indiana UP, 2000), *Approaches to Teaching Things Fall Apart* (MLA, 1992), and *Early Nigerian Literature* (Africana Pub, 1983).

Kofi N. Mensah is professor at the Department of English, University of Botswana, Gaborone, Botswana.

Abdul-Rasheed Na Allah has edited *Ogoni's Agonies: Ken Saro-Wiwa and the Crisis in Nigeria* (1998), and co-authored two volumes of *Introduction to African Oral Literature* (1991, 1994). Formally of the University of Ilorin, Nigeria, and The University of Alberta, Canada, he presently teaches at Western Illinois University, USA. His latest poetry collection, *Almajiri: A New African Poetry* (2001), was published by Africa World Press.

Emma Ngumoha teaches English and African Literature at Abia State University, Nigeria.

Sunday Enessi Ododo teaches at the Department of the Performing Arts, University of Ilorin, Nigeria.

Ezenwa-Ohaeto, a poet and scholar, authored the first Achebe Biography. He is a professor at Alvan Ikoku College of Education, Owerri, Nigeria, and *Humboldt-Universitat zu Berlin*, Germany.

Tanure Ojaide, among the leading figures in the second generation of Nigerian poets, he has won several awards in Nigeria and abroad. They include a Commonwealth Poetry Prize, the Christopher Okigbo Prize, the Association of Nigerian Authors' (ANA) Poetry Award, and a BBC Arts and African Poetry Award. Among his poetry collections are *Children of Iroko* (1973), *Labyrinths of the Delta* (1986), *The Endless Song* (1989), *The Fate of Vulture and Other Poems* (1990), *The Blood of Peace* (1991), *Invoking the Warrior Spirit* (1995). His other books include *Great Boys: An African Childhood* and *Poetic Imagination in Black Africa*.

Tayo Olafioye, poet and scholar, author of *The Saga of Sego, Sorrow of a Town Crier, Arrow to my Heart, The Excellence of Silence, Politics in African Literature, Grandma's Sun*, among others, is a prolific writer; he teaches at National University, San Diego, and Southwestern College, California, USA.

Sola Olorunyomi is a Lecturer in English at the Department of English, University of Ibadan, Nigeria. His research interest is in the African oral poetics. He has written widely on Fela Anikulapo-Kuti, the late doyen of Nigerian music.

Femi Oyebode is of Centre of West African Studies at the University of Birmingham, United Kingdom.

Aderemi Raji-Oyelade, Poet, teaches English and African Literature at the Department of English, University of Ibadan, Nigeria.

Ajewumi Bili Raji, Senior Lecturer, teaches at the Department of Modern European Languages, University of Ilorin, Ilorin, Nigeria.

Adeyeye Samson Dare lectures at the Ogun State University, Ago-Iwoye, Nigeria.

Irene Sywenky, Ph.D. Candidate in Comparative Literature at the University of Alberta, is assistant Editor of *Canadian Review of Comparative Literature*. She is co-editor of, *The Systemic and Empirical Approach to Literature and Culture as Theory and Application* (1997), with Steven Totosy.

S. Louisa Wei, Ph.D., of the Institute of Gender and Women's Studies, Josai International University (Japan), will be assuming position as assistant professor at the University of Honk Kong, China. She has worked on the fifth generation filmmakers in China. Her interests include comparative poetics and popular cultural studies.

INDEX